T0184135

Lecture Notes in Artificial Intelligence 11744

Subseries of Lecture Notes in Computer Science

More information about this series at http://www.springer.com/series/1244

Haibin Yu · Jinguo Liu ·
Lianqing Liu · Zhaojie Ju ·
Yuwang Liu · Dalin Zhou (Eds.)

Intelligent Robotics and Applications

12th International Conference, ICIRA 2019
Shenyang, China, August 8–11, 2019
Proceedings, Part V

 Springer

Editors
Haibin Yu
Shenyang Institute of Automation
Shenyang, China

Jinguo Liu
Shenyang Institute of Automation
Shenyang, China

Lianqing Liu
Shenyang Institute of Automation
Shenyang, China

Zhaojie Ju
University of Portsmouth
Portsmouth, UK

Yuwang Liu
Shenyang Institute of Automation
Shenyang, China

Dalin Zhou
University of Portsmouth
Portsmouth, UK

ISSN 0302-9743   ISSN 1611-3349 (electronic)
Lecture Notes in Artificial Intelligence
ISBN 978-3-030-27540-2   ISBN 978-3-030-27541-9 (eBook)
https://doi.org/10.1007/978-3-030-27541-9

LNCS Sublibrary: SL7 – Artificial Intelligence

This Springer imprint is published by the registered company Springer Nature Switzerland AG
The registered company address is: Gewerbestrasse 11, 6330 Cham, Switzerland

Preface

On behalf of the Organizing Committee, we welcome you to the proceedings of the 12th International Conference on Intelligent Robotics and Applications (ICIRA 2019), organized by Shenyang Institute of Automation, Chinese Academy of Sciences, co-organized by Huazhong University of Science and Technology, Shanghai Jiao Tong University, and the University of Portsmouth, technically co-sponsored by the National Natural Science Foundation of China and Springer, and financially sponsored by Shenyang Association for Science and Technology. ICIRA 2019 with the theme of "Robot Era" offered a unique and constructive platform for scientists and engineers throughout the world to present and share their recent research and innovative ideas in the areas of robotics, automation, mechatronics, and applications.

ICIRA 2019 was most successful this year in attracting more than 500 submissions regarding the state-of-the-art development in robotics, automation, and mechatronics. The Program Committee undertook a rigorous review process for selecting the most deserving research for publication. Despite the high quality of most of the submissions, a total of 378 papers were selected for publication in six volumes of Springer's *Lecture Notes in Artificial Intelligence* a subseries of *Lecture Notes in Computer Science*. We sincerely hope that the published papers of ICIRA 2019 will prove to be technically beneficial and constructive to both the academic and industrial community in robotics, automation, and mechatronics. We would like to express our sincere appreciation to all the authors, participants, and the distinguished plenary and keynote speakers.

The success of the conference is also attributed to the Program Committee members and invited peer reviewers for their thorough review of all the submissions, as well as to the Organizing Committee and volunteers for their diligent work. Special thanks are extended to Alfred Hofmann, Anna Kramer, and Volha Shaparava from Springer for their consistent support.

August 2019

Haibin Yu
Jinguo Liu
Lianqing Liu
Zhaojie Ju
Yuwang Liu
Dalin Zhou

Organization

Honorary Chairs

Youlun Xiong   Huazhong University of Science and Technology, China

Nanning Zheng   Xi'an Jiaotong University, China

General Chair

Haibin Yu   Shenyang Institute of Automation, Chinese Academy of Sciences, China

General Co-chairs

Kok-Meng Lee   Georgia Institute of Technology, USA

Zhouping Yin   Huazhong University of Science and Technology, China

Xiangyang Zhu   Shanghai Jiao Tong University, China

Program Chair

Jinguo Liu   Shenyang Institute of Automation, Chinese Academy of Sciences, China

Program Co-chairs

Zhaojie Ju   The University of Portsmouth, UK

Lianqing Liu   Shenyang Institute of Automation, Chinese Academy of Sciences, China

Bram Vanderborght   Vrije Universiteit Brussel, Belgium

Advisory Committee

Jorge Angeles   McGill University, Canada

Tamio Arai   University of Tokyo, Japan

Hegao Cai   Harbin Institute of Technology, China

Tianyou Chai   Northeastern University, China

Jie Chen   Tongji University, China

Jiansheng Dai   King's College London, UK

Zongquan Deng   Harbin Institute of Technology, China

Han Ding   Huazhong University of Science and Technology, China

Xilun Ding	Beihang University, China
Baoyan Duan	Xidian University, China
Xisheng Feng	Shenyang Institute of Automation, Chinese Academy of Sciences, China
Toshio Fukuda	Nagoya University, Japan
Jianda Han	Shenyang Institute of Automation, Chinese Academy of Sciences, China
Qiang Huang	Beijing Institute of Technology, China
Oussama Khatib	Stanford University, USA
Yinan Lai	National Natural Science Foundation of China, China
Jangmyung Lee	Pusan National University, South Korea
Zhongqin Lin	Shanghai Jiao Tong University, China
Hong Liu	Harbin Institute of Technology, China
Honghai Liu	The University of Portsmouth, UK
Shugen Ma	Ritsumeikan University, Japan
Daokui Qu	SIASUN, China
Min Tan	Institute of Automation, Chinese Academy of Sciences, China
Kevin Warwick	Coventry University, UK
Guobiao Wang	National Natural Science Foundation of China, China
Tianmiao Wang	Beihang University, China
Tianran Wang	Shenyang Institute of Automation, Chinese Academy of Sciences, China
Yuechao Wang	Shenyang Institute of Automation, Chinese Academy of Sciences, China
Bogdan M. Wilamowski	Auburn University, USA
Ming Xie	Nanyang Technological University, Singapore
Yangsheng Xu	The Chinese University of Hong Kong, SAR China
Huayong Yang	Zhejiang University, China
Jie Zhao	Harbin Institute of Technology, China
Nanning Zheng	Xi'an Jiaotong University, China
Weijia Zhou	Shenyang Institute of Automation, Chinese Academy of Sciences, China
Xiangyang Zhu	Shanghai Jiao Tong University, China

Publicity Chairs

Shuo Li	Shenyang Institute of Automation, Chinese Academy of Sciences, China
Minghui Wang	Shenyang Institute of Automation, Chinese Academy of Sciences, China
Chuan Zhou	Shenyang Institute of Automation, Chinese Academy of Sciences, China

Publication Chairs

Yuwang Liu   Shenyang Institute of Automation, Chinese Academy
                        of Sciences, China
Dalin Zhou   The University of Portsmouth, UK

Award Chairs

Kaspar Althoefer   Queen Mary University of London, UK
Naoyuki Kubota   Tokyo Metropolitan University, Japan
Xingang Zhao   Shenyang Institute of Automation, Chinese Academy
                        of Sciences, China

Special Session Chairs

Guimin Chen   Xi'an Jiaotong University, China
Hak Keung Lam   King's College London, UK

Organized Session Co-chairs

Guangbo Hao   University College Cork, Ireland
Yongan Huang   Huazhong University of Science and Technology,
                        China
Qiang Li   Bielefeld University, Germany
Yuichiro Toda   Okayama University, Japan
Fei Zhao   Xi'an Jiaotong University, China

International Organizing Committee Chairs

Zhiyong Chen   The University of Newcastle, Australia
Yutaka Hata   University of Hyogo, Japan
Sabina Jesehke   RWTH Aachen University, Germany
Xuesong Mei   Xi'an Jiaotong University, China
Robert Riener   ETH Zurich, Switzerland
Chunyi Su   Concordia University, Canada
Shengquan Xie   The University of Auckland, New Zealand
Chenguang Yang   UWE Bristol, UK
Tom Ziemke   University of Skövde, Sweden
Yahya Zweiri   Kingston University, UK

Local Arrangements Chairs

Hualiang Zhang   Shenyang Institute of Automation, Chinese Academy
                        of Sciences, China
Xin Zhang   Shenyang Institute of Automation, Chinese Academy
                        of Sciences, China

Contents – Part V

Mobile Robots and Intelligent Autonomous Systems

Robotic Vision, Recognition and Reconstruction

Robot Mechanism and Design

Robot Legged Locomotion

SLIP Model-Based Foot-to-Ground Contact Sensation via Kalman Filter for Miniaturized Quadruped Robots

Junjie Yang[1(✉)], Hao Sun[1], Dongping Wu[1], Xiaodong Chen[2], and Changhong Wang[1]

[1] Space Control and Inertial Technology Research Center, Harbin Institute of Technology, Harbin 150001, People's Republic of China
jyang.hit@foxmail.com, cwang@hit.edu.cn
[2] Shanghai Electro-Mechanical Engineering Institute, Shanghai 201109, People's Republic of China

Abstract. In the condition of torque senseless, especially for miniaturized quadruped robot with simple position-velocity motors, the foot-to-ground contact detection is not easy to be implemented. In this paper, we propose a spring-loaded inverted pendulum (SLIP) model-based algorithm for contact detection without torque sensors. The algorithm combines Kalman filter and SLIP model for foot-to-ground contact detection. Under this detection scheme, the foot-to-ground contact can be detected effectively in a sensor cycle. The proposed algorithm shows the ability of error correction and high robustness in the face of the wrong data of actual sensors and the undesirable fluctuation. Even if the robot is equipped with torque sensors, considering the possibility of sensors damage, the algorithm can be used as a supplement in long-term operation. The feasibility of the proposed algorithm is verified via a simulation.

Keywords: Contact detection · Kalman filter · SLIP model · Torque senseless

1 Introduction

Owe to their enhanced adaptability facing harsh terrain, quadruped robots have been attracting more and more attention in mobile robotics research, which are of great social significance and practical value. Facing unstructured terrains, it is important for quadruped robots to judge whether their feet contact the ground or not accurately. Traditionally, force sensors or contact switches are installed on the sole of robots' feet for contact sensation. However, force sensors may increase the weight of robots and bring external disturbance to robots. On the other hand, feedback-from-contact switches takes a longer time to feedback which brings time-delay. Moreover, both traditional force sensors and contact switches are fragile.

To overcome the two drawbacks mentioned above, methods for contact sensation without external sensors are proposed. In related work, a time-variant threshold for observer residues in joint space of a manipulator for contact detection [1], and the Contact Particle Filter (CPF) algorithm [2] have been applied successfully in manipulator.

© Springer Nature Switzerland AG 2019
H. Yu et al. (Eds.): ICIRA 2019, LNAI 11744, pp. 3–14, 2019.
https://doi.org/10.1007/978-3-030-27541-9_1

Bajo et al. also implements screw theory to define a screw motion deviation (SMD) as the distance between the expected and the actual instantaneous screw axis (ISA) of motion for contact detection [3]. Disturbance observers based on the generalized momentum (GM) of the robot [4] is a frequently-used method, it can skirt the need of acceleration measurements. Contact detection research in the field of manipulators gives inspiration to the field of quadruped robots, a probabilistic contact detection strategy which considers full dynamics and differential/forward kinematics for legged robots was proposed by Hwangbo et al. [5]. (Hydraulic Quadruped) HYQ robot estimates the probability of reliable contact and detects foot impacts using internal force sensing [6]. A task space CPG-based trajectory generation proposed by Barasuol et al. shows that CPG plays an important role in robot self-balancing requirement [7]. Typically, MIT cheetah uses proprioceptive data to implement contact detection [8]. MIT cheetah3 shows high accuracy and real-time detection ability of foot-to-ground contact, using discrete-time extension of the generalized-momentum disturbance observer and probabilistic contact model [9]. Designing controllers for unstructured terrains is also an effective method. Hutter et al. designed highly compliant series elastic actuation for StarlETH [10] facing challenging terrain. Liu et al. proposed a 1-step terrain adaptation strategy for humanoid walking based on the 3D actuated Dual-SLIP model [11]. Dai et al. presented an approach for designing nominal periodic trajectories for legged robots that maximize a measure of robustness [12], this method can be extended to quadruped robots.

However, for the miniaturized quadruped robot, the torque information of the leg joint of the robot is unavailable sometimes. Therefore, it is of great interests to develop the strategy of contact detection by using the encoder data and (Inertial Measurement Unit) IMU data. What's more, in this scenario, the actuator data and IMU data suffer greater noise since the sensors should be simpler and lighter due to the mass limitation. In this paper, a novel contact detection algorithm is designed for miniaturized quadruped robot. Instead of using torque sensors and position-velocity-torque motors, this algorithm only starts from the actuator data and IMU data, which are essential information of miniaturized quadruped robots. Then, the well-known Kalman filter is used to fuse the actuator data and IMU data to accomplish the foot-to-ground contact detection. Moreover, a spring-loaded inverted pendulum (SLIP) model is applied to calculate the approximate solution of the robot dynamics for closed-loop detection in order to improve the robustness of contact detection.

The main contribution of this paper can be summarized as follows.

(1) To the best of our knowledge, it is the first time for this paper to propose a novel algorithm for miniaturized quadruped robots to take foot-to-ground contact detection with only the actuator data and IMU data are used instead of torque information and external sensors.
(2) The proposed algorithm can preserve good performance in the face of serious noise brought by the simpler and lighter sensors.
(3) In the proposed scheme, the usage of position-velocity-torque motors is avoided, which are normally expensive in practical industrial society.

The remainder of this paper is structured as follows. Section 2 introduces a leg gait planner and its components, explaining how to make gait planning in a gait period. Section 3 calculates the approximate kinematics solution of the robot based on SLIP model for closed-loop detection and Sect. 4 describes how to use Kalman filter algorithm for data fusion and discusses the feasibility of contact detection algorithm. Section 5 shows the results of simulation experiments. A concluding discussion is offered in Sect. 6.

2 Gait Planning

Quadruped robots have multiple gaits, such as trotting, pacing, bounding and galloping. By assigning four legs to different phase signals, different gait modes can be realized. For a gait period, it can be divided into flying phase and swing phase. The legs are defined as flying phase when they move in the air, and the legs are defined as swing phase when they swing with contacting the ground. The control methods and strategies of the flying phase and the swing phase are different, in order to enhancing the balance of the robot motion in various gaits. Trajectory planning is used for flying phase, which is divided in three stages:

(1) Retraction: The knee joint of the robot contracts and the hip joint swings backwards. Aiming to get the foot off the ground rapidly and prevent unexpected friction with the ground.
(2) Swing forward: The knee joint continues to contract while the hip joint swings forwards. Aiming to control the foot at expected height, preventing from colliding with undesirable obstacles.
(3) Stretch: The knee joint stretches while the hip joint swings backwards. Aiming to guarantee that the foot-to-ground contact has a desired attack angle. In this stage, contact detection system is activated.

When the foot-to-ground contact is detected, the leg enters the swing phase, the angle of the knee joint is almost kept unchanged.

Because the leg joints have certain compliance and damping, the leg of the robot can be simplified as SLIP model in the swing phase. The SLIP model can be applied to obtain the approximate dynamic solution of the leg. According to the solution, the robot can be effectively controlled to keep its balance. If a leg is scheduled in the flying phase while the foot contacts the ground, it will cause the legs to move forcibly according to the original trajectory and cause the robot body to topple. If a leg is scheduled in the swing phase and the foot is not in contact with the ground, the leg will be planned a wrong trajectory. Therefore, the accuracy and robustness of foot-to-ground contact detection are crucial.

The contact detection system is divided into three modules: sensor data management module, Kalman filter data fusion detection module and SLIP-based closed-loop detection module. The sensor data management module calculates the encoder data through the kinematics of the robot leg. The angle and angular velocity data are transformed into the position and velocity data of the foot in inertial coordinate system. At the same time, three-axis acceleration data measured by the IMU which installed in the robot foot is transformed into the acceleration data of the foot in the inertial coordinate system. Kalman filter data fusion detection module obtains the data from sensor data management module. The discrete Kalman filter algorithm is implemented to fuse the data and detect the foot-to-ground contact. SLIP-based closed-loop detection module uses the SLIP model, modeling the dynamics of the robot and calculating the approximate solution of the dynamics of the robot foot, and implements the approximate solution to detect the foot-to-ground contact. The overall technological process of the leg planner is shown in Fig. 1. This algorithm can effectively detect foot-to-ground contact in a sensor cycle with high robustness.

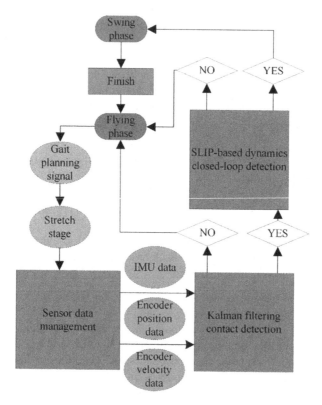

Fig. 1. Technological process of the leg planner.

3   SLIP Based Model

In this section, the SLIP-based closed-loop detection model of the robot is described, and the approximate dynamic solution of the robot is calculated by implementing simplified conditions. The solution is ultimately used in closed-loop detection to correct the foot-to-ground contact, enhancing the robustness of the contact detection.

SLIP model retains the characteristics of system mass, fuselage space movement posture, leg movement rule and leg mechanics rule to the greatest extent, and meets the motion mechanism of quadruped at high speed from the bionics point of view. So it has been widely used in legged robots. Wensing et al. have applied 3D-SLIP model in robots

[13]. And there are also active SLIP model application cases, for example, the work of Piovan et al. [14]. The presented algorithm is based on the passive SLIP model. In Sect. 4, the Kalman filter algorithm is proposed to detect foot-to-ground contact by data fusion, which also takes advantage of the characteristics of the SLIP model.

Robot legs can be simplified to SLIP model, which is shown in Fig. 2, where L1 and L2 are leg joint lengths, L0 is equivalent SLIP model length, α and β are leg joint angles, and M is equivalent body mass. L is the real-time equivalent leg length, k is the elastic coefficient of the equivalent spring and C is the damping coefficient of the equivalent spring.

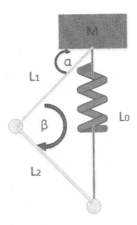

Fig. 2. Simplified SLIP model.

When the leg is in swing phase, it can be illustrated in Fig. 3, where θ is the angle between the equivalent leg and the vertical direction. Geyer et al. proposed two hypothetical conditions to simplify the dynamic equation of the SLIP model in the calculation process of approximate solution [15].

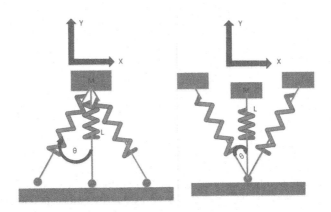

Fig. 3. Simplified SLIP model in swing phase.

(1) Assuming that the swing phase span of SLIP model is small enough, the effect of gravity is approximately linear. Then $\sin\theta \approx \theta$, $\cos\theta \approx 1$.
(2) Assuming that the relative compression of spring is very small during the swing phase of SLIP model. Then $|L - L_0| \ll L_0$.

Considering that the mass of the robot's legs accounts for a small proportion of the total mass, the mass and inertia of the legs can be neglected approximately, then the attitude angle of the robot body does not change when the robot moves steadily.

Constructing Lagrange functions:

$$\phi = T - P \tag{1}$$

where T is the kinetic energy of the system, P is the potential energy of the system. T can be described as

$$T = \frac{1}{2}M(V_L)^2 + \frac{1}{2}M(V_\theta)^2 = \frac{1}{2}M\dot{L}^2 + M(L\dot{\theta})^2 \tag{2}$$

V_L is the radial velocity of the robot body along the direction of spring, V_θ is the robot body vertical velocity of V_L along the angle of θ. According to the simplified conditions, the dynamic equation of the system is

$$\begin{cases} \frac{d}{dt}\frac{\partial\phi}{\partial L} - \frac{\partial\phi}{\partial L} = F_c \\ \frac{d}{dt}\frac{\partial\phi}{\partial\theta} - \frac{\partial\phi}{\partial\theta} = 0 \end{cases} \quad q = [L \quad \theta] \tag{3}$$

Expanding the equation to

$$\begin{cases} M\ddot{L} - ML\dot{\theta}^2 + Mg - k(L_0 - L) = -C\dot{L} \\ ML^2\ddot{\theta} + 2ML\dot{L}\dot{\theta} = 0 \end{cases} \tag{4}$$

Eventually the equation becomes a second-order linear differential equation

$$\begin{cases} \ddot{L} + 2\omega\zeta\dot{L} + \omega^2 L = H \\ \omega = \sqrt{\frac{3L^4\dot{\theta}^2}{L_0^4} + \frac{k}{M}} \\ 2\omega\zeta = \frac{C}{M} \\ H = \frac{4L^4\dot{\theta}^2}{L_0^3} + \frac{kL_0}{M} - g \end{cases} \tag{5}$$

The approximate solution can be calculated by finding the eigenvalue

$$L_t = \frac{F}{\omega^2} + e^{-\omega\zeta t}(C_1\cos(\omega t\sqrt{1-\zeta^2}) + C_2\sin(\omega t\sqrt{1-\zeta^2})) \tag{6}$$

The approximate solution can be used for closed-loop detection of foot-to-ground contact. If the foot contacts the ground as well as the leg enters the swing phase, the equivalent leg can be calculated whether it moves as expected. If it moves as expected, the swing phase will continue. If the equivalent leg does not move as expected, then we can firmly believe that the foot does not contact the ground and the control system returns to the flying phase trajectory planning. The advantage of this method is that the closed-loop detection will not affect the execution of the swing phase control, and because the legs do not contact with ground during the flying phase, the impacted flying phase will not affect the balance of the robot body.

4 Kalman Filter for Data Fusion

This section describes how to accomplish foot-to-ground contact detection by implementing Kalman filter. The important role of Kalman filter in the field of robots was explained by Chen [16]. Ma et al. have implemented extended Kalman filter algorithm in the LS3 robot [17], the system can run in the field over hours and has shown high robustness. In this section, the Kalman filter data fusion detection module was designed for data fusion.

The collision between foot and ground can be detected equivalently. When this event occurs, the system state

$$q = [L \ \theta]$$

will change in an instant. According to Hurmuzlu *et al.* [18], the impact model is

$$\begin{cases} q^+ = q^- \\ D(q)\dot{q}^+ - D(q)\dot{q}^- = J(q)^T \int F_{impact}dt \end{cases} \tag{7}$$

where $q+$ and $q-$ are the system states before and after the collision. The data updated by sensors are discrete. According to the SLIP model, in the swing phase, the relative position between the foot and the body of the robot is not rigid, which provides an application background for Kalman filter data fusion detection module. In every sensor cycle, the data obtained are encoder position data, encoder velocity data and leg IMU data. Because the basic data errors will inevitably exist, the Kalman filter algorithm can be used to fuse the data to predict the optimal estimate of the system state at the next update time. If the difference between the optimal solution and the data of the encoder at the next time exceeds the threshold, it can be considered that foot-to-ground collision has occurred. In order to enhance the robustness of the detection, we use the closed-loop method in Sect. 3.

We use the discrete Kalman filter algorithm:

$$\begin{cases} X_{n|n-1} = FX_{n-1} \\ P_{n|n-1} = FP_{n-1|n-1}F^T + Q \\ K_{gn} = \frac{P_{n|n-1}H^T}{HP_{n|n-1}H^T + R} \\ X_{n|n} = X_{n|n-1} + K_{gn}(Z_n - HX_{n|n-1}) \\ P_{n|n} = (1 - K_{gn}H)P_{n|n-1} \end{cases} \tag{8}$$

where Q is the covariance of the system process, R is the covariance of the measured data which is corresponded to sensor error V. X is the system state measured by encoder and Z is the system state calculated by sensor data measured by IMU. It can be expressed as:

$$\begin{cases} X_{n-1} = (r_{n-1}, \dot{r}_{n-1}) \\ Z_n = (\dot{r}_{n-1} + \ddot{r}_{n-1}dt) \end{cases} \quad (9)$$

where r is the position of the foot relative to the robot coordinate system, dt is a sensor cycle. According to Fig. 1, the angles of the two joints of the leg are α and β. α, β, $\dot{\alpha}$, $\dot{\beta}$ current value can be obtained from the encoders. IMU installed on the foot can be used to calculate the acceleration of the foot in the X and Y directions, m_x and m_y. Then it can be implemented by

$$\begin{cases} r_x = -L_1 \cos \alpha - L_2 \cos(\beta - \alpha) \\ r_y = -L_1 \sin \alpha - L_2 \sin(\beta - \alpha) \\ \dot{r}_x = -L_1 \dot{\alpha} \cos \alpha - L_2 \dot{\alpha} \cos(\beta - \alpha) + L_2 \dot{\beta} \cos(\beta - \alpha) \\ \dot{r}_y = -L_1 \dot{\alpha} \sin \alpha + L_2 \dot{\alpha} \sin(\beta - \alpha) - L_2 \dot{\beta} \cos(\beta - \alpha) \end{cases} \quad (10)$$

$$X = \begin{bmatrix} r_x \\ r_y \\ \dot{r}_x \\ \dot{r}_y \end{bmatrix} \quad F = \begin{bmatrix} 1 & 0 & dt & 0 \\ 0 & 1 & 0 & dt \\ 0 & 0 & 1 & 0 \\ 0 & 0 & 0 & 1 \end{bmatrix} \quad \begin{aligned} Z &= HU \begin{bmatrix} m_x \\ m_y \end{bmatrix} + \begin{bmatrix} \dot{r}_x \\ \dot{r}_y \end{bmatrix} + V \quad H = \begin{bmatrix} 1 & 0 \\ 0 & 1 \end{bmatrix} \\ U &= \begin{bmatrix} \cos(\beta - \alpha)dt & -\sin(\beta - \alpha)dt \\ -\sin(\beta - \alpha)dt & -\cos(\beta - \alpha)dt \end{bmatrix} \end{aligned}$$
$$(11)$$

By implementing Kalman filter, we can get the optimal estimation of the system state at the next update time. Compared with the system state measurements at the next update time, we can make a preliminary judgment of foot-to-ground contact, and then complete all the judgments by using the method in Sect. 3.

5 Simulation

The algorithm was verified through unite simulation environment of MATLAB and ADAMS. A simple model of quadruped robot was drawn in ADAMS. There are two joints on each leg, hip and knee joint. Using MATLAB to generate control program, the robot can generate stable trotting gait. The gait period is defined as a phase variable $S\varphi$, which can make the robot implement different gaits by changing $S\varphi$. For trotting, LF (left front leg) and RH (right hind leg) have the same $S\varphi$. LH (left hind leg) and RF (right front leg) have the same $S\varphi$ which differs 0.5.

$$S_\varphi = \frac{t - T_0}{T} \quad (12)$$

Where *t* is time the gait has been running, *T0* is starting time of gait and *T* is time of a gait period. Setting a boolean value *D*, when Kalman filter data fusion module detects contact, *D* is set from 0 to 1, then the leg enters the swing phase. When the closed-loop detection module does not detect contact, *D* is set to 0, then the leg returns to the flying phase. When the swing phase ends, *D* is reset to 0 and the leg enters the flying phase. The leg planning controller can implement the switching of flying-to-swing by identifying the value of *D*.

For miniaturized robots, the simulation parameters are given in Table 1.

The input of Kalman filter data fusion module is the calculated joint angle and velocity and the acceleration information obtained by IMU, which are shown in Figs. 4 and 5, and the output is a boolean value *D* shown in Fig. 6.

Table 1. Simulation parameters.

Parameters	Symbol	Value
Thigh length	L_1	10 cm
Lower leg length	L_2	10 cm
Mass	M	5 kg
Equivalent spring elastic	K	2000 N/m
Equivalent spring damping	C	50 Ns/m
Sensor cycle	dt	50 ms
Ground friction coefficient	μ	0.5
Encoder angle error		$\pm0.3°$
Encoder angular speed error		$\pm0.5°/s$
IMU acceleration error		±0.5 m/s^2

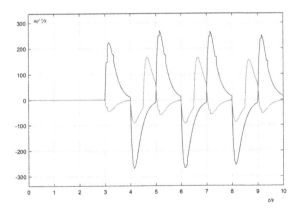

Fig. 4. Speed curves of hip and knee joints. The blue curve represents the angular velocity of the hip joint and the yellow curve represents the angular velocity of the knee joint. (Color figure online)

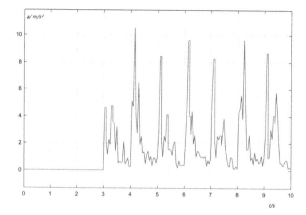

Fig. 5. Acceleration amplitude curve of foot.

In order to intuitively compare foot-to-ground contact detection results, force sensor was installed on the foot, the data of foot force sensor can intuitively express the foot-to-ground contact.

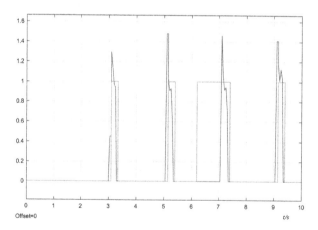

Fig. 6. Kalman filter data fusion module detection. Blue curve is the force sensor curve, which can intuitively express foot-to-ground contact. Yellow curve is the output of Kalman filter data fusion module. When the value is 1, it indicates that contact is detected. (Color figure online)

Because the actual encoder and IMU may be disturbed, the data will sometimes have large deviations, or even erroneous data. When swing-to-flying is just switched, the system will generate a greater acceleration, both will lead to the module has an error detection of contact. As can be seen from Fig. 6, contact is detected in a non-contact situation, so using this module alone is not enough to meet the actual needs. Therefore, a closed-loop detection module is added for improving the robustness of the system, comparing the actual trajectory r with the approximate solution calculated by SLIP-based model.

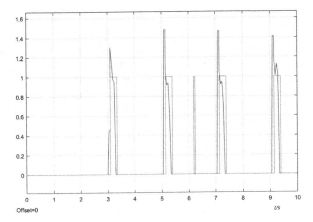

Fig. 7. Final detection results. The undesirable detection is corrected and does not affect the balance of robot body.

As can be seen in Fig. 7, an undesirable detection is quickly corrected. Although there is a short time error detection in flying phase, it does not affect the balance of the robot body. The algorithm has been validated in simulation. In a sensor cycle (50 ms), foot-to-ground contact can be effectively detected.

6 Conclusion

The algorithm presented in this paper develops an effective method to detect the foot-to-ground contact using SLIP-based model and Kalman filter algorithm in the condition of torque senseless, which is a desirable algorithm for miniaturized robots with position-velocity motors. Sensor data management module provides the effective data through the kinematics of the robot leg. Kalman filter data fusion detection module realizes a preliminary detection and SLIP-based closed-loop detection module uses the approximate solution to correct the foot-to-ground contact. In fact, in the condition of torque senseless, the algorithm has wider application areas theoretically, not implemented in quadruped robots only. For all legged robots, after conducting simple modification to the algorithm, it can also be used to detect foot-to-ground contact with torque senseless. In a sensor cycle (50 ms), the algorithm can detect accurately, but when the sensor cycle becomes shorter, the algorithm has an undesirable error rate, which limits the high-speed motion of robots. For the quadruped robots with torque sensor, torque sensors may also be damaged during long-term operation, the algorithm can still be used as a supplement.

References

1. Sotoudehnejad, V., Takhmar, A., Kermani, M.R., Polushin, I.G.: Counteracting modeling errors for sensitive observer-based manipulator collision detection. In: IEEE/RSJ International Conference on Intelligent Robots and Systems, pp. 4315–4320 (2012)
2. Manuelli, L., Tedrake, R.: Localizing external contact using proprioceptive sensors: The Contact Particle Filter. In: IEEE/RSJ International Conference on Intelligent Robots and Systems, pp. 5062–5069 (2016)
3. Bajo, A., Simaan, N.: Kinematics-based detection and localization of contacts along multisegment continuum robots. IEEE Trans. Rob. **28**(2), 291–302 (2012)
4. Luca, A.D., Albu-Schaffer, A., Haddadin, S., Hirzinger, G.: Collision detection and safe reaction with the DLR-III LIGHTWEIGHT manipulator arm. In: IEEE/RSJ International Conference on Intelligent Robots and Systems, pp. 1623–1630 (2006)
5. Hwangbo, J., Bellicoso, C.D., Fankhauser, P., Hutter, M.: Probabilistic foot contact estimation by fusing information from dynamics and differential/forward kinematics. In: IEEE/RSJ International Conference on Intelligent Robots and Systems, pp. 3872–3878 (2016)
6. Camurri, M., et al.: Probabilistic contact estimation and impact detection for state estimation of quadruped robots. IEEE Robot. Autom. Lett. **2**(2), 1023–1030 (2017)
7. Barasuol, V., Buchli, J., Semini, C., Frigerio, M., De Pieri, E.R., Caldwell, D.G.: A reactive controller framework for quadrupedal locomotion on challenging terrain. In: IEEE International Conference on Robotics and Automation, pp. 2554–2561 (2013)
8. Hyun, D.J., Seok, S., Lee, J., Kim, S.: High speed trot-running: implementation of a hierarchical controller using proprioceptive impedance control on the MIT Cheetah. Int. J. Robot. Res. **33**(11), 1417–1445 (2014)
9. Bledt, G., Wensing, P.M., Ingersoll, S., Kim, S.: Contact model fusion for event-based locomotion in unstructured terrains. In: IEEE International Conference on Robotics and Automation, pp. 1–8 (2018)
10. Hutter, M., Gehring, C., Höpflinger, M.A., Blösch, M., Siegwart, R.: Toward combining speed, efficiency, versatility, and robustness in an autonomous quadruped. IEEE Trans. Rob. **30**(6), 1427–1440 (2014)
11. Liu, Y., Wensing, P.M., Schmiedeler, J.P., Orin, D.E.: Terrain-blind humanoid walking based on a 3-D actuated dual-SLIP model. IEEE Robot. Autom. Lett. **1**(2), 1073–1080 (2016)
12. Dai, H., Tedrake, R.: Optimizing robust limit cycles for legged locomotion on unknown terrain. In: IEEE Conference on Decision and Control, pp. 1207–1213 (2015)
13. Wensing, P.M., Orin, D.E.: High-speed humanoid running through control with a 3D-SLIP model. In: IEEE/RSJ International Conference on Intelligent Robots and Systems, pp. 5134–5140 (2013)
14. Piovan, G., Byl, K.: Approximation and control of the SLIP model dynamics via partial feedback linearization and two-element leg actuation strategy. IEEE Trans. Rob. **32**(2), 399–412 (2016)
15. Geyer, H., Seyfarth, A., Blickhan, R.: Spring-mass running: simple approximate solution and application to gait stability. J. Theor. Biol. **232**(3), 315–328 (2005)
16. Chen, S.Y.: Kalman filter for robot vision: a survey. IEEE Trans. Industr. Electron. **59**(11), 4409–4420 (2012)
17. Ma, J., Bajracharya, M., Susca, S., Matthies, L., Malchano, M.: Real-time pose estimation of a dynamic quadruped in GPS-denied environments for 24-hour operation. Int. J. Robot. Res. **35**(6), 631–653 (2016)
18. Hurmuzlu, Y., Marghitu, D.B.: Rigid body collisions of planar kinematic chains with multiple contact point. Int. J. Robot. Res. **13**(1), 82–92 (1994)

Stability Analysis and Fixed Radius Turning Planning of Hexapod Robot

Dajiang Yu[✉] and Yongqin Chen

School of Electronic Mechanical Engineering, Xidian University,
Xi'an 710071, China
ydjl008@163.com, 8495472@sina.com

Abstract. In this paper, the maximum allowable rotation angle of the first rotation pair connected between the legs and the body is solved by geometric method on the premise of the hexapod robot walking steadily. Then, aiming at turning with a fixed radius, the gait of turning is planned and the calculation method of turning angle of each joint is given. Finally, considering the influence of turning radius and turning angle on stability, a critical curve which can be referred to selecting turning radius and turning angles is given. It is proved that in the process of left turning, the second group of legs are more restricted in the selection of turning radius and turning angle. Finally, the feasibility of the above method is verified by real verification and error analysis.

Keywords: Stable walking · Maximum angle · Fixed radius turning · Stability

1 Introduction

Due to its bionic characteristics, simple structure, various control modes, high traveling stability and reliability, hexapod robot has a broad application prospect. In order to adapt to a variety of complex terrain conditions, it is necessary to study the stability of hexapod robot in the process of moving. The stability analysis of the hexapod robot is mainly to calculate the stability margin of the hexapod robot and ensure the stability of the robot by limiting the minimum threshold of the stability margin [1]. On the other hand, for a hexapod robot, in the case of complex and unknown terrain, the basis for optimal path planning and obstacle avoidance walking is to be able to achieve a fixed radius turn. Different from the usual in-situ fixed-point steering mode of hexapod robot, turning with fixed radius can be carried out while moving forward and turning at the same time, which improves the moving efficiency to a certain extent and also realizes the curve trajectory walking of hexapod robot. Most of the existing researches [2–4] only give theoretical or guiding calculation methods for the correlation of stability margin, and do not study the specific hexapod structure or walking gait and mode. Most studies on hexapod robot turning with fixed radius introduce the gait planning process with illustrations or use algorithms to realize the turning planning for any gait [5–8]. Few studies comprehensively consider the turning radius and turning angle in combination with specific hexapod robot structure.

To solve the above problems, this paper takes the Dream Maker II hexapod robot as the experimental object, and analyzes the calculation method of the maximum turning

© Springer Nature Switzerland AG 2019
H. Yu et al. (Eds.): ICIRA 2019, LNAI 11744, pp. 15–25, 2019.
https://doi.org/10.1007/978-3-030-27541-9_2

angle of the first rotary pair (denoted as joint 1) connected between the leg and the body when the robot walks in triangular gait under the premise of stable walking. At the same time, the gait of turning with fixed radius is planned, the calculation method of turning angle of each joint is analyzed, the influence of turning radius and turning angle on stability is comprehensively analyzed, and the correctness of the method is verified by the real sample machine.

2   Stability Analysis of Walking Process of Hexapod Robot

2.1   Stability Margin

The stability margin refers to the shortest distance from the projection point of the center of gravity of the robot body in the horizontal plane to the boundary of the support mode (OG, OH in Fig. 1). When a hexapod robot is walking straightly in a triangular gait, the center of gravity of the body is moving forward by the swing of its legs. During the robot's walking, it must be ensured that the robot cannot roll over. That is to say, the projection of the center of gravity of the robot on the horizontal plane must always be inside the triangle in the support mode. This requires that the stability margin must be greater than zero.

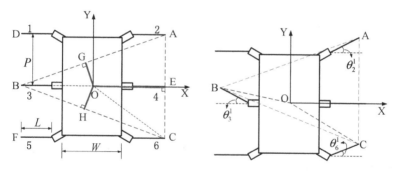

Fig. 1.   Initial state of robot   **Fig. 2.**   After leg swing state

When the hexapod robot goes straight in a triangular gait, only one group of legs are in the support mode at any time. The serial number of the legs is shown in Fig. 1. The first group of legs are leg 1, leg 4 and leg 5, and the toe points are D, E, F. The second group of legs are leg 2, leg 3 and leg 6, and the toe points are A, B, and C. At this moment, the second group of legs swing forward to the designated position, and drop the touchdown as the support legs. The horizontal swing angle of 1 joint of each leg is θ_i^1 (i = 2, 3, 6), as shown in Fig. 2. After this, the first group of legs will be lifted. It is not difficult to find that the support triangle moves forward compared to the initial state, but the position of the robot's center of gravity does not change. So, there is a maximum angle allowed by the 1 joint at this time.

2.2   Maximum Joint Angle

The mathematical condition to keep the body stable is "$|OB+OC|>|BC|$, and BC must be below O" (as shown in Fig. 2). As long as the BC side of the triangle does not cross the point O of the body's center of gravity, the body will remain stable. Firstly, the coordinate system is established with the position of the center of gravity of the body as the origin. Since the stability margin is only discussed in the horizontal plane, the z coordinates of each toe point are not written down. Then the toe coordinates of the second group of legs are,

$$
\begin{cases}
(\frac{W}{2} + L_2 \cos \theta_2^1, P + L_2 \sin \theta_2^1) \\
(-\frac{W}{2} - L_3 \cos \theta_3^1, L_3 \sin \theta_3^1) \\
(\frac{W}{2} + L_6 \cos \theta_6^1, -P + L_6 \sin \theta_6^1)
\end{cases}
\tag{1}
$$

where, W is the body width (the distance along the X-axis of the 1 joint axis of leg 1 and 2), L_i is the distance between the 1 joint axis of each leg and the toe in the horizontal plane, and P is the distance between the legs on the same side. Using the formula of distance from point to point, we can obtain,

$$
|BC| = \sqrt{(W + L_3 \cos \theta_3^1 + L_6 \cos \theta_6^1)^2 + (P + L_3 \sin \theta_3^1 - L_6 \sin \theta_6^1)^2}
\tag{2}
$$

$$
|OB+OC| = \sqrt{(\frac{W}{2} + L_3 \cos \theta_3^1)^2 + (L_3 \sin \theta_3^1)^2} + \sqrt{(\frac{W}{2} + L_6 \cos \theta_6^1)^2 + (-P + L_6 \sin \theta_6^1)^2}
\tag{3}
$$

When a hexapod robot is walking straightly, the swing amplitude of each leg must be the same. That is, the span of the toe has the same distance along the Y-axis direction. So, $L_1 = L_4 = L_5 = L$, $\theta_1^1 = \theta_4^1 = \theta_5^1 = \theta^1$. After simplifying Eqs. 2 and 3, we can get,

$$
\sqrt{\frac{W^2}{4} + LW \cos \theta + L^2} + \sqrt{\frac{W^2}{4} + LW \cos \theta - 2LP \sin \theta + L^2 + P^2} > \sqrt{(W + 2L \cos \theta)^2 + P^2}
\tag{4}
$$

In this paper, the verified robot is Dream Maker II hexapod robot, and the relevant parameters are $W = 147$ mm, $P = 100$ mm, $L = 82.7$ mm. The curves of the length of $|OB+OC|$ and $|BC|$ changing with θ are shown in Fig. 3.

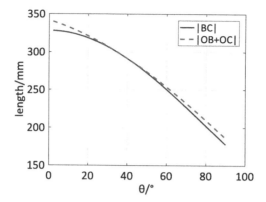

Fig. 3. The curves that the length of |OB+OC| and |BC| change with θ

As can be seen from Fig. 3, in the range of 0° to 90°, the two curves have only one tangency. That is, the B, O, and C points are collinear, and the robot is in a critical stable state. Although there is still |OB+OC|>|BC| after the tangent point, the center of gravity of the body is no longer inside the support triangle, and the robot has been unstable. Therefore, the corresponding value of the tangent to the two curves is also the maximum angle allowed by the joint. The $\theta_{max} = 37°$ is obtained by the MATLAB numerical solution method.

3   Turn Planning with Fixed Radius

3.1   The Gait Planning

There are a number of ways in which a hexapod robot can turn. The one is that the robot rotates to the desired direction around the center of gravity of the body in the horizontal plane, and then goes straight forward. The other one is realizing the mode of turning with fixed radius. This turning mode can realize turning while moving, which may save walking time. At the same time, the mode of turning with fixed radius can also be used for the trajectory planning of the robot, so that the robot can walk in accordance with the specified curve trajectory.

Triangle gait is used as the gait of turning with fixed radius for planning. Left turning is taken as an example. In the process of turning, the robot walks in a circle around O with a radius of R. A gait cycle is divided into the former half cycle and the latter half cycle,

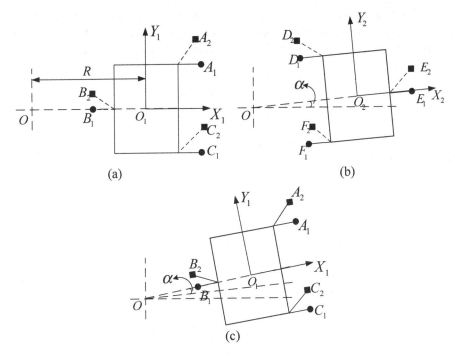

Fig. 4. Turning process (● represents the position of the toe before swinging, and ■ represents the position of the toe after swinging)

First, the second group of legs swing forward from the initial position to the designated position and dropped to the ground (as shown in Fig. 4(a)) as supporting legs. At the same time, the first group of legs are lifted, every angle of the second group of legs are restored to the initial position, the position of the center of gravity of the body moving forward, and the body turns to the left. Then, the first group of legs swing forward from the initial position to the designated position and dropped to the ground (as shown in Fig. 4(b)) as the support legs. The second group of legs are lifted, every angle of the first group of legs are restored to the initial position, and the position of the center of gravity of the body moving forward (as shown in Fig. 4(c)), and the body is turns to the left again. Therefore, in a gait cycle, the robot turns 2α in all. Thereafter, the robot repeats the above process to complete the turning action.

3.2   Joint Angle Solution

Due to the turning radius and body width, the radius difference between left and right legs of hexapod robot will make the span of legs different in the turning process of hexapod robot with fixed radius. So the swing law of each leg is different, which needs to be calculated one by one.

To solve the rotation angle of each joint of each leg in the turning process, it is necessary to know the coordinate position of the toe before and after the swing in the current robot coordinate system. The turning radius is defined as R, and the angle of rotation for each half gait cycle is α. Taking Fig. 4(a) as an example, in the coordinate system $(O_1X_1Y_1Z_1)$, the toes of the second group of legs in the first half cycle need to be moved from A_1, B_1, C_1 to A_2, B_2, C_2. The toe coordinates of the starting point are,

$$\begin{cases} (\frac{W}{2} + L_2, P, -H) \\ (-\frac{W}{2} - L_3, 0, -H) \\ (\frac{W}{2} + L_6, -P, -H) \end{cases} \tag{5}$$

The toe coordinate of the termination point in the coordinate system $(O_2X_2Y_2Z_2)$ is also the above expression. It is transformed to the coordinate system $(O_1X_1Y_1Z_1)$ through coordinate transformation, and the coordinates of A_2, B_2, C_2 in the coordinate system $(O_1X_1Y_1Z_1)$ are,

$$\begin{bmatrix} x_2 \\ y_2 \\ z_2 \end{bmatrix} = \begin{bmatrix} P\cos\alpha - R + (L_2 + R + \frac{W}{2})\cos\alpha \\ P\cos\alpha - (L_2 + R + \frac{W}{2})\sin\alpha \\ -H \end{bmatrix}$$

$$\begin{bmatrix} x_3 \\ y_3 \\ z_3 \end{bmatrix} = \begin{bmatrix} -R - (L_3 - R + \frac{W}{2})\cos\alpha \\ -(L_3 - R + \frac{W}{2})\sin\alpha \\ -H \end{bmatrix} \tag{6}$$

$$\begin{bmatrix} x_6 \\ y_6 \\ z_6 \end{bmatrix} = \begin{bmatrix} -R - (L_3 - R + \frac{W}{2})\cos\alpha \\ -(L_3 - R + \frac{W}{2})\sin\alpha \\ -H \end{bmatrix}$$

The rotation angles of the three joints can be solved by the inverse kinematics of the robot leg.

For the latter half cycle, the above method is also applied to obtain the toe coordinates of the termination point of the first group of legs in the coordinate system $(O_1X_1Y_1Z_1)$,

$$\begin{bmatrix} x_1 \\ y_1 \\ z_1 \end{bmatrix} = \begin{bmatrix} P\sin\alpha - R + (L_1 - R + \frac{W}{2})\cos\alpha \\ P\cos\alpha + (L_1 - R + \frac{W}{2})\sin\alpha \\ -H \end{bmatrix}$$

$$\begin{bmatrix} x_4 \\ y_4 \\ z_4 \end{bmatrix} = \begin{bmatrix} -R + (L_4 + R + \frac{W}{2})\cos\alpha \\ -(L_4 + R + \frac{W}{2})\sin\alpha \\ -H \end{bmatrix} \tag{7}$$

$$\begin{bmatrix} x_5 \\ y_5 \\ z_5 \end{bmatrix} = \begin{bmatrix} P\sin\alpha - R - (L_5 - R + \frac{W}{2})\cos\alpha \\ -P\cos\alpha + (L_5 - R + \frac{W}{2})\sin\alpha \\ -H \end{bmatrix}$$

Similarly, the rotation angle of each joint can be solved by inverse kinematics.

3.3   Stability Analysis

A number of factors need to be considered in the turning of hexapod robot. If the turning radius and angles of each step are too large, the swing span of the toe will become larger. It is likely to exceed the range which toe can reach. If they are too small, the number of gait cycles required in the process of turning will increase and the turning efficiency will decrease. Besides, in the turning process of the robot, both the turning radius and the angles of each step have an impact on the landing point of the toe after the leg swings. Therefore, it is necessary to analyze the stability of the turning process of the hexapod robot.

Firstly, the relationship between turning angle and turning radius R and stability is determined when the second group of legs are used as supporting legs (shown in Fig. 5). The judging method of stability is the same as above, given that $W = 147$ mm, $L_i = 60$ mm (i = 1, 2, 3, 4, 5, 6), $P = 100$ mm. We set $\alpha = 5°$, and calculate the biggest turning radius. The curves of $|O_1B_2+O_1C_2|$ and $|B_2C_2|$ with the turning radius are shown in Fig. 5.

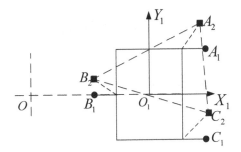

Fig. 5. Left turn second leg support mode

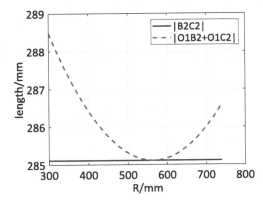

Fig. 6. The curves that the length of $|O_1B_2+O_1C_2|$ and $|B_2C_2|$ change with R ($\alpha = 5°$)

As can be seen from Fig. 6, when $R = 565$ mm, O_1, B_2 and C_2 are collinear, and the robot is in a critical stable state. R continues to increase, and line B_2C_2 crosses the center O_1 of gravity of the body, and the robot will roll over. So, when turning angle $\alpha = 5°$, turning radius should not exceed 565 mm.

We also need to determine the maximum turning radius allowed at different turning angles. So the angle is set from $0°$ to $30°$, turning radius range to 150 mm–600 mm, and MATLAB is used to map the three-dimensional scatter plot of $|O_1B_2+O_1C_2|$ and $|B_2C_2|$ with turning radius and angles (as shown in Fig. 7) (hereinafter referred to as the scatter plot). The scatter plot shows the relationship between the turning angle and turning radius and the length of $|O_1B_2+O_1C_2|$ and $|B_2C_2|$. The intersection line of two faces in the figure are the optional maximum values.

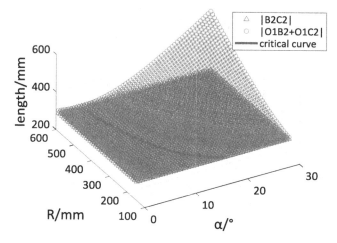

Fig. 7. The scatter plot that the length of $|O_1B_2+O_1C_2|$ and $|B_2C_2|$ change with α and R

Similarly, when the first group of legs are the supporting legs, there is also a curve like that one. The intersection lines of the two cases are drawn on the same plot (Fig. 8). These two curves are called critical curves, and each pair α and R corresponding to the region below the critical curve can ensure that the robot is in a stable state when the legs of the corresponding group are used as supporting legs.

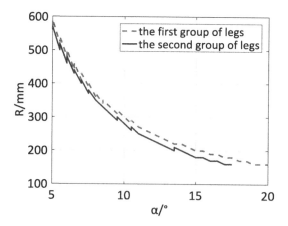

Fig. 8. The critical curve that two groups of legs serve as supporting legs

In the turning process of a hexapod robot, two groups of legs are alternately placed in the supporting mode as supporting legs. The values of angle α and turning radius R must be less than the minimum in the two cases, so as to ensure that the robot is always stable in the turning process. As can be seen from Fig. 8, when the second group of legs serve as the supporting legs, its critical curve is below that of the other group. Which indicates that in the process of left turning, the second group of legs has stricter restrictions on turning angle of each step and turning radius than the first group of legs, and the second critical curve should serve as the critical curve of the selected value of α and R.

4 Actual Product to Verify

The Dream Maker II hexapod robot is selected as the experimental machine. Select $\alpha = 5°$, $R = 350$ mm, each toe coordinates are calculated, and the angle of each joint is solved by the inverse kinematics of robotic leg. Then these angles are input into the robot. After the completion of debugging, the coordinate system is set on the ground, and the hexapod robot makes a turn to the left once from the origin. The position of the center of gravity of the body is recorded every three gait cycles, and the trajectory of the center of gravity in the horizontal plane is traced. The number of gait cycles is also recorded. The experimental process is shown in Fig. 9, and the comparison between the actual trajectory and the theoretical trajectory is shown in Fig. 10.

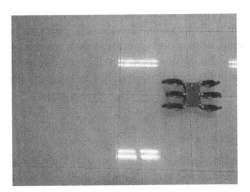

Fig. 9. The process of collecting actual trajectory

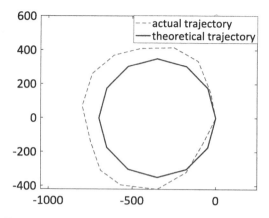

Fig. 10. The curves of actual trajectory and theoretical trajectory

The actual radius of the left turn of the robot is about 400 mm, the number of actual cycles is 39, and the number of theoretical cycles should be 36.

From Fig. 10, the source of the error of the actual trajectory and the theoretical trajectory, mainly exists in the following two aspects,

(1) The toe sliding relative to the ground. Although the rubber pad on the foot end of the robot is used to increase the friction with the ground, the toe still has relatively obvious sliding during the turning process, and the local sliding displacement can reach 30 mm, which greatly affects the point that the robot is scheduled to reach.

(2) There is an error in the installation of the servos. After the accurate joint angle is calculated and input to the robot control system, even if the servos can rotate precise angle values, the initial state is not accurate due to the installation error of the servos, and the robot cannot accurately reach the predetermined position.

5   Summary

In this paper, the geometric method is used to establish the stability constraint conditions of the hexapod robot, and the maximum allowable rotation angle of the first joint of the leg when the hexapod robot goes straight is solved. On the basis of the planned turning gait with fixed radius, the turning radius and turning angles of each step are taken into the stability analysis, and the critical curves that can be referred to selecting turning radius and turning angles are given. It is proved by the critical curves that in the process of left turning, the second group of legs have more strict restrictions on the selection of turning radius and angles. Finally, the feasibility of the above method is verified by combining with the actual product verification and error analysis.

References

1. Song, S.-M., Waldron, K.J.: Machines That Walk: The Adaptive Suspension Vehicle. MIT Press, Cambridge (1988)
2. Zhu, Y., Guo, T., Liu, Q.: A study of arbitrary gait pattern generation for turning of a bio-inspired hexapod robot. Robot. Auton. Syst. **97**, 125–135 (2017)
3. Zhang, C., Jiang, X.: Research on gait planning and static stability of hexapod robot. Group Technol. Prod. Mod. **33**(2), 40–47 (2016)
4. Mao, M., He, S.: Study on the gait of a hexapod machine beetle. Comput. Digit. Eng. **39**(5), 1–6 (2011)
5. Chen, G., Jin, B., Chen, Y.: Hexapod walking robot fixed radius turning gait. J. Zhejiang Univ. (Eng. Sci.) **48**(7), 1278–1286 (2014)
6. Su, J., Chen, X., Tian, W.: Research on omnidirectional gait of hexapod walking robot. Mach. Electron. **3**, 48–52 (2004)
7. Liu, Y., Zheng, L., Sun, H.: locomotion analysis for hexapod robot on tripod gait. J. Qingdao Univ. (E & T) **33**(3), 38–42, 46 (2018)
8. Zhuang, H., Gao, H., Deng, Z.: Gait planning research for an electrically driven large-load-ratio six-legged robot. Appl. Sci. **7**(296), 1–17 (2017)

The Mechanical Design and Torque Control for the Ankle Exoskeleton During Human Walking

Handong Xu[1(✉)], Yibing Li[1], Biwei Tang[2], and Kui Xiang[2]

[1] School of Mechanical and Electronic Engineering,
Wuhan University of Technology, Wuhan, Hubei, China
xhd472535673@163.com
[2] School of Automation, Wuhan University of Technology,
Wuhan, Hubei, China

Abstract. A mechanical design and a two-level control method for an ankle exoskeleton (AE) are represented in this paper in the case where the AE device is implemented to assist human walking. Attempting to release the burden of wearers, it remains paramount to reduce the weight of the AE. To this end, this paper implements a Boden cable to separate the motor from the exoskeleton during the mechanical design of the AE. Moreover, aiming at enhancing human locomotion ability, a two-level controller based on the iterative learning control (ILC) algorithm is represented to govern the control behavior of the AE in this paper. The feasibility and efficacy of the developed two-level controller are evaluated through experimental tests over four different subjects. The experimental results show that the muscle activity of each subject can be reduced compared to walking without the designed AE device.

Keywords: Iterative learning control · Ankle exoskeleton · Boden rope · Muscle activity

1 Introduction

The exoskeleton robotic remains a comprehensive subject, which involves various technologies, such as robotics, mechanics, bionics, kinematics, sensing technology, to name but a few [1]. Thanks to their great potential to improve human locomotion and reduce the energy expenditure, wearable robotic exoskeletons have drawn increasing attention in recent years. In order to allow exoskeletons to achieve the aforementioned potential, the mechanical design and controller development remain two key ingredients.

In an attempt to release the burden of the wearers, the weight of the exoskeleton needs to be as light as possible, which, consequently, imposes high requirements on the mechanical structure of such a device. To this end, many researchers from the community of robotics have dedicated themselves to the mechanical designs of different exoskeletons. For example, the authors in [2] have developed a light-weighted elastic unpowered exoskeleton, which acts in parallel with the user's calf muscles. Since it is easy to control the dynamics of the powered exoskeletons and widen its applications,

H. Yu et al. (Eds.): ICIRA 2019, LNAI 11744, pp. 26–37, 2019.
https://doi.org/10.1007/978-3-030-27541-9_3

the powered exoskeleton has aroused great research interests around the world [3]. However, a clumsy motor is often needed in a powered exoskeleton, so that the device is able to provide a huge assistive torque to human, which leads this kind of device to be pretty heavy [4].

Since the controlling system of the powered exoskeleton can not only apply the information acquisition module to monitor wearer's motion information, but also determines the assistive strategy that the device provides for human, the controlling system design remains a paramount question. So far, a considerable amount work has been done and numerous different control algorithms, such as the fuzzy control [5], the impedance control [6], as well as the robust control [7], have been proposed for the different powered exoskeletons in the case where such devices are applied to assist human walking. Despite having proven the feasibilities and superiorities of these aforementioned control algorithms [5–7], there still exists some issues needed to be addressed, such as the difficulty in obtaining correct gait planning due to the inter-subject differences in each subject's ankle torque curves.

Aiming at enhancing locomotion capability and reducing the energy cost during human walking, a two-level controller followed by the mechanical design of a powered ankle exoskeleton (AE) is represented in this study. In order to reduce AE's weight, a Boden rope is used to separate to the motor from the exoskeleton in terms of the mechanical design stage. Moreover, based on the analysis of kinematic and dynamic characters during human walking, a two-level controller based on the iterative learning control (ILC) algorithm and the gait period and stress information during human walking is developed to control the AE device. In the developed controller, the higher level determines the desired torque for the device according to the gait period and stress information of human. Based on the ILC algorithm, the lower level is implemented to govern the device, so that the device can provide assistance to human. The developed controller is finally evaluated via experimental tests over 4 subjects. The experimental results show that, in the case where each subject wears and device and the device is governed by the developed controller, the soleus muscle activity of each subject can be reduced compared to those of the case where each subject does not wear the device, as well as the case where each subject wears the device but without controller in the device.

The remainder of this article is organized as follows. Section 2 mainly introduces the design of ankle exoskeleton, the torque control system, as well as the method of electromyogram (EMG) signal process. Section 3 mainly presents the experimental protocol and analyzes the experimental results. The last section, that is, Sect. 4, draws conclusions of this study and shows some future work.

2   Methods

2.1   Mechanical Design of the Ankle Exoskeleton

Similar to the excellent work done in [8], as displayed in Fig. 1, a Boden rope is used as a transmission device to separate motor from the ankle exoskeleton in order to light the device and release the burden of the wearer. The exoskeleton is mainly used in the simulation of the ankle of human being. The physical drawing of the used exoskeleton is visualized in Fig. 2. Two fiberglass boards are attached at the joint location of the ankle exoskeleton, where the size of each board is similar to the length of calves. The Boden rope is fixed to the reducer, while the other end is fixed to the frame of exoskeleton. During motor operation, the Boden rope is responsible for pulling the exoskeleton, so that the toe can move downward. The designed ankle exoskeleton can provide a peak pulling force around 545.5N. The assistive forces of the ankle exoskeleton can be measured via tension sensors. Besides, a 3 mm diameter Boden rope is applied to bear the peak torque of exoskeleton motor.

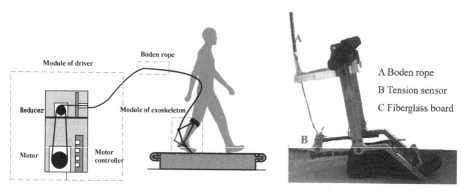

Fig. 1. The mechanical structure model of exoskeleton   **Fig. 2.** The lightweight exoskeleton

2.2 Torque Control System

As shown in Fig. 3, a two-level torque controller is designed in this paper to govern the designed ankle exoskeleton during human walking in order to enhance human locomotion and reduce the energy cost.

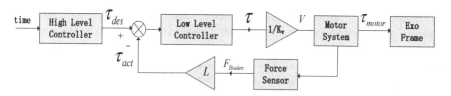

Fig. 3. The flowchart of the control system

In Fig. 3, time is the percentage of a gait cycle; t_{motor} is the output torque of the motor; K_v is the ratio of the input voltage to output torque of the motor; L is the arm of force acted on exoskeleton; F_{Boden} is the force produced by Boden rope, τ_{des} is the desired torque produced by high level controller.

The aim of the high-lever controller is to determine the desired torque trajectory for the ankle exoskeleton. During human walking, the shape of the desired torque trajectory in a gait cycle is determined by four torque control parameters [9], that is, the peak torque, the peak torque time, the rise time and the fall time, respectively. According to the four control parameters of ankle torque curve, the desired torque of ankle exoskeleton control system is determined in a gait cycle. In this study, the desired torque is measured by Moticon SCIENCE force sensor which can detect the plantar pressure distribution. 13 sensors are distributed in Moticon SCIENCE force sensor. The force sensor transfers the collected data through the wireless way. The curve of ankle torque in a gait cycle is calculated by analyzing to the data. The concrete calculating methods are as follows:

$$\tau_{ankle} = \Sigma_0^{12} F_i \times X_i \tag{1}$$

$$X_i = Y_i - Y_{ankle} \tag{2}$$

where τ_{ankle} is defined as the ankle torque. X_i is defined as the coordinate difference of every sensor's Y coordinate and ankle's Y_{ankle} coordinate. F_i is the i-th force sensor's pressure and calculated as follows:

$$F_i = P_i / S_i \tag{3}$$

where P_i refers to the i-th pressure of the pressure sensor. S_i is defined as the i-th pressure area of the pressure sensor.

The curve of ankle torque can keep stable in a gait cycle after a period of time walking. A curve of subject's ankle torque can be obtained, as shown in Fig. 4, where the grey shading indicates the standard deviation. The four parameters can be determined as [28%, 21%, 64%, 34.5 Nm], respectively.

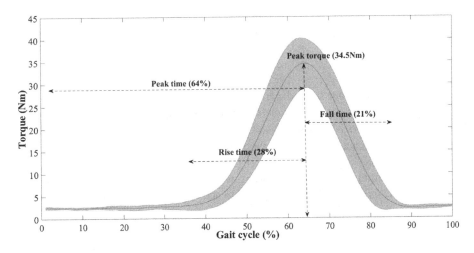

Fig. 4. The ankle torque curve

Based on ILC algorithm, the lower-level controller is used to control the ankle exoskeleton in order to guarantee that the device can provide assistance to human. Since the ILC algorithm is used in this paper, the standard ILC algorithm is first stated below.

The ILC algorithm can use the previous iteration of the input information and the output generated by error correction to modify undesirable control signal [10]. The input $u_{k+1}(t)$ in standard ILC algorithm is given as follows:

$$u_{k+1}(t) = L(u_k(t), e_k(t)) \qquad (4)$$

The updating strategy $L(u_k(t), e_k(t))$ of open-loop ILC algorithm is updated as follows:

$$u_{k+1}(t) = u_k(t) + C \times e_k(t) \qquad (5)$$

where $u_{k+1}(t)$ is a weight sum of the k-th control input $u_k(t)$ and the k-th output error $e_k(t)$. C stands for the learning factor.

In this paper, the updating strategy of ILC is represented in the developed lower-level controller as follows:

$$t_r(k+1) = t_r(k) + c_1 \times e_{t_r} \qquad (7)$$

$$t_f(k+1) = t_f(k) + c_2 \times e_{t_f} \qquad (8)$$

$$t_p(k+1) = t_r(k) + c_3 \times e_{t_p} \qquad (9)$$

$$\tau_p(k+1) = \tau_r(k) + c_4 \times e_{\tau_p} \qquad (10)$$

$$e_{t_r} = d_{t_r} - a_{t_r} \qquad (11)$$

$$e_{t_f} = d_{t_f} - a_{t_f} \qquad (12)$$

$$e_{t_p} = d_{t_p} - a_{t_p} \qquad (13)$$

$$e_{\tau_p} = d_{\tau_p} - a_{\tau_p} \qquad (14)$$

where t_r, t_f, t_p, τ_p are four control parameters of the exoskeleton input torque curve. d_{t_r}, d_{t_f}, d_{t_p}, d_{τ_p} are four control parameters of desired torque curve. a_{t_r}, a_{t_f}, a_{t_p}, a_{τ_p} are four control parameters of actual torque curve. e_{t_r}, e_{t_f}, e_{t_p}, e_{τ_p} are four errors between desired torque and actual torque. k is the number of iterations. c_1, c_2, c_3, c_4 are four iterative coefficients.

The motor outputs the torque according to the desired torque curve and pulls the Boden rope. The ankle joint turns downward to achieve the goal of assistance when the ankle exoskeleton is pulled. The actual torque of the exoskeleton's joint can be obtained by the tension sensor in series with the Boden rope as follows:

$$\tau_{exo} = F_{Boden} \times L \tag{6}$$

where τ_{exo} is the torque of the ankle. F_{Boden} is the tension of the Boden rope. L is the arm of the tension (about 110 mm in this paper).

2.3 Process of EMG Signal

The method of EMG signal process is implemented to verify the effectiveness of the two-level controller on the ankle exoskeleton in this paper. The ankle joint movement is inseparable from the muscle working. Tibialis anterior muscle is attached to the bone and controlled by the innervations. Tibialis anterior muscle contracts to move the ankle joint to produce toes move upward in the phase of dorsiflexion. Soleus muscle contracts to move the ankle joint to produce toes move downward in the phase of plantarflexion. Overall, the energy loss of ankle joint movement is related to muscle contraction. The designed ankle exoskeleton mainly focuses on the phase of dorsiflexion. Hence, the activation degree of soleus muscle is directly associated with power assistance of exoskeleton. Muscle contraction yield myoelectric signals in walking, and the signal strength is related to the energy loss in motions. Myoelectric device is firstly used to record EMG signals. Then, envelope of the soleus muscle EMG is extracted after signal is filtered, and envelope of the soleus muscle EMG is compared with actual curve of ankle torque.

In order to reduce the impact of skin impedance, the legs should be cleaned up with medical alcohol when using the myoelectric device. The electric plates are attached to the skin of soleus. The EMG signals collected are transmitted to computer via Bluetooth. The computer receives the EMG of left leg from COM1 port, receives the EMG of right leg from COM2 port. The receiving frequency of myoelectric device is 1000 Hz.

Most of the energy of EMG is between 20 to 200 Hz. The raw EMG signal has too low noise ratio to use. So that the data is needed to be pretreated. This paper mainly adopts the research methods as follows:

(1) Full Wave Rectification: The mean of all EMG from the EMG is subtracted in a period time, then the absolute value is determined, finally the commuted data is given.
(2) Envelopment Analysis: Muscle will twitch by electrical stimulation. There are studies that show the characteristics of twitch is similar to a second-order function.
(3) Normalization: Test the Maximal voluntary contraction based on muscle contracted equidistantly before the experiment. Then do the normalized process to the experimental data.

The processing results of EMG signal are shown in Fig. 5, where (A) is the raw EMG signal, (B) is the EMG rectification signal, (C) is the envelope curve of EMG signal.

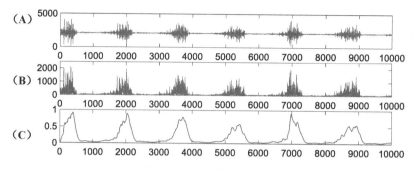

Fig. 5. The processing of EMG signal

The envelope of the soleus muscle EMG and curve of ankle torque in a gait cycle are displayed in Fig. 6. The fluctuation of the EMG is similar to the ankle torque. It can be approximately considered that muscle activation degree is positively related to muscle tone. It is supposed that the ankle angular velocity W, rotation angle θ and gait period T are constants in a gait cycle during walking. The work of the ankle torque is positively related to the RMS (root-mean-square) of the muscle activation degree. It can be considered that the RMS of the muscle activation degree can represent loss energy of shin in a period of time.

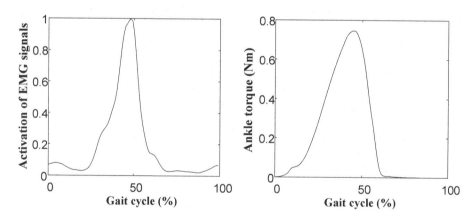

Fig. 6. The envelope of muscle activation degree curve and ankle torque curve

3   Experiment Test

3.1   Experimental Set Up

In order to verify the effectiveness of the developed controller, this paper conducts numerical simulation and experimental tests. In the executed numerical simulation, four parameters of desired torque curve and actual torque curve are firstly initialized, and then the change of actual torque curve is observed.

In the practical experiment, in order to measure desired torque curve, the microcontroller is used to collect the pressure information and get the curve of ankle torque during walking. Four healthy subjects have participated in the experiment test. The basic information of each subject is shown in Table 1.

During the experimental test, participants walk on a treadmill at 1.5 m/s under three conditions: make sure the force sensor, computer and WIFI module is properly set; raise the foot up off the ground and reset the force sensor to make the stress distributed smoothly before the experiment; walk with constant speed and walk straight. The schematic diagram of the experiment platform is displayed in Fig. 7.

For each subject, three different experiment tests are conducted after obtaining the desired torque curve. The three different tests are, respectively, walking normally without ankle exoskeleton (denoted as experiment A), walking with the ankle exoskeleton but under zero-torque condition (indicated by experiment B), as well as walking with the ankle exoskeleton and the devices being controlled by the developed two-level controller (represented by experiment C). For each subject, each experimental test lasts 15 min. During experimental test, the soleus muscle EMG of each subject is recorded from the last 3 min in each experiment test. To avoid fatigue of muscles and improve the effect of experiment, subjects will have a rest at least 10 min between each experiment and select another day to repeat the experiment. The experimental platform is displayed in Fig. 8.

Table 1. The information of experiments

Subject	Height (m)	Mass (kg)	Age (year)	Speed (m/s)
1	1.79	75	26	1.4
2	1.74	57	23	1.1
3	1.69	66	24	1.2
4	1.83	70	26	1.2

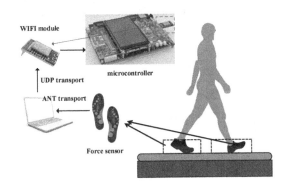

Fig. 7. The schematic diagram of torque measurement

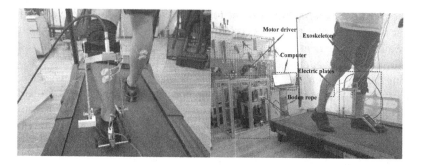

Fig. 8. The experiment platform

3.2   Experiment Results and Analysis

The numerical simulation result is display in Fig. 9, where the red and black lines, respectively, denotes the desired and actual torque of exoskeleton, n represents the number of iterations. It can be observed from Fig. 9 that the error between the actual desired torques converges after 4 iterations, which can, to some extent, reflect the feasibility of the developed controller.

In the experimental test, the soleus muscle activation degree of two feet of the first subject is shown Fig. 10. The torque tracking effect of the exoskeleton torque controller for the first subject is visualized in Fig. 11. It is notable that the soleus muscle activation degrees and the tracking effect of the exoskeleton torque controller for the rest subjects are not shown in order not to enlarge the size of this paper. The numerical experiment results for all subjects over the three experiments descried above are summarized in Table 2. The corresponding experimental data for each subject over each experiment test are illustrated in Fig. 12.

One can easily make an observation from Fig. 10 that, compared to experimental tests A and B, experimental test C can obtain the least soleus activation degree of both feet for the first subject, which indicates that the developed controller can indeed reduce

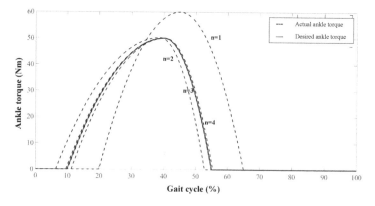

Fig. 9. The effect diagram of ILC simulation (Color figure online)

the muscle activation for this subject. Moreover, one can note from Table 2 and Fig. 12 that the developed controller can guarantee that the exoskeleton device can provide assistance for all the four subjects and consequently reduces their muscle activations, which, to a certain degree, can reflect the feasibility of the designed controller.

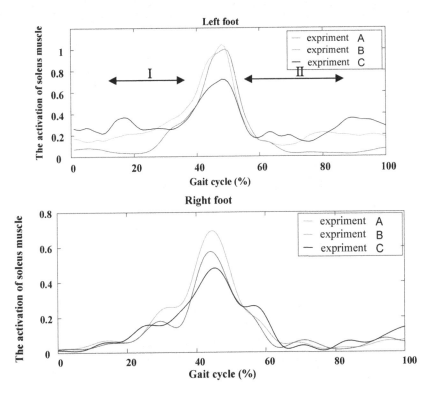

Fig. 10. The activation degree of soleus in a gait cycle for the first subject

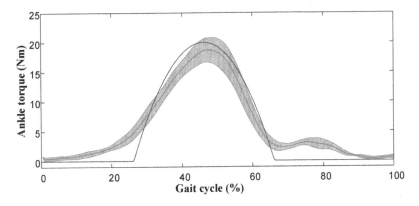

Fig. 11. The torque of exoskeleton in a gait cycle for the first subject

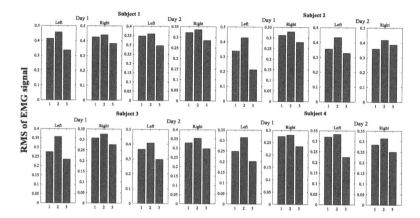

Fig. 12. The bar graph of experiment data

Table 2. The data record of different experiments

Experiment		A		B		C	
Subject	Time	Left	Right	Left	Right	Left	Right
1	Day1	0.4133	0.4254	0.4564	0.4396	0.3364	0.3829
1	Day2	0.3473	0.3216	0.3590	0.3353	0.2964	0.2852
2	Day1	0.3384	0.3119	0.4276	0.3289	0.2107	0.2794
2	Day2	0.3565	0.3586	0.4346	0.4175	0.3286	0.3869
3	Day1	0.2748	0.3586	0.4346	0.4175	0.2351	0.2753
3	Day2	0.3642	0.3275	0.4062	0.3531	0.2963	0.2967
4	Day1	0.2483	0.2742	0.3141	0.2802	0.2018	0.2342
4	Day2	0.3193	0.2841	0.3321	0.3129	0.2243	0.2503

4 Conclusion

In order to improve the locomotion capability and save energy cost during human walking, this paper first represents a mechanism design of an ankle exoskeleton, and afterwards develops a two-level controller for the designed ankle exoskeleton through leveraging ILC algorithm. The developed controller is eventually evaluated via experimental tests over different subjects. The experimental results confirm that the soleus muscle activation of each subject can be reduced under the situation where the designed ankle exoskeleton is controlled by the designed controller.

The results shown in this paper raise some valuable work which desires to be further studied. Firstly, since a lot of practice to adapt to the ankle exoskeleton probably due to the controller is designed based on the standard ILC, an improved ILC algorithm or some another advanced controlling algorithm will be developed to enhance the adaption of the device over different subjections in the forthcoming study. Secondly, the output of the exoskeleton motor is only defined according to the desired torque set beforehand and cannot adjust accordingly to changes during human walking. Thus, in order future amend the performance of the designed exoskeleton, we will develop some other methods which can drive the Boden rope of the ankle exoskeleton based on the real-time plantar pressure of human walking.

References

1. Lee, H., Kim, W., Han, J., Han, C.: The technical trend of the exoskeleton robot system for human power assistance. Int. J. Precis. Eng. Manuf. **13**(8), 1491–1497 (2012)
2. Collins, S.H., Bruce Wiggin, M., Sawicki, G.S.: Reducing the energy cost of human walking using an unpowered exoskeleton. Nature **522**(7555), 212 (2015)
3. Panzenbeck, J.T., Klute, G.K.: A powered inverting and everting prosthetic foot for balance assistance in lower limb amputees. JPO J. Prosthet. Orthot. **24**(4), 175–180 (2012)
4. Au, S.K., Dilworth, P., Herr, H.: An ankle-foot emulation system for the study of human walking biomechanics. In: Proceedings 2006 IEEE International Conference on Robotics and Automation, ICRA 2006. IEEE (2006)
5. Yin, K., Pang, M., Xiang, K., et al.: Fuzzy iterative learning control strategy for powered ankle prosthesis. Int. J. Intell. Robot. Appl. **2**(1), 122–131 (2018)
6. Vallery, H., Asseldonk, E.H.F.V., Buss, M., et al.: Reference trajectory generation for rehabilitation robots: complementary limb motion estimation. IEEE Trans. Neural Syst. Rehabil. Eng. **17**(1), 23–30 (2009)
7. Zhang, Q., Zhao, D., Wang, D.: Event-based robust control for uncertain nonlinear systems using adaptive dynamic programming. IEEE Trans. Neural Netw. Learn. Syst. **29**(1), 37–50 (2018)
8. Caputo, J.M., Collins, S.H.: A universal ankle–foot prosthesis emulator for human locomotion experiments. J. Biomech. Eng. **136**(3), 035002 (2014)
9. Zhang, J., Fiers, P., Witte, K.A., et al.: Human-in-the-loop optimization of exoskeleton assistance during walking. Science **356**, 1280–1284 (2017)
10. Jia, X.G., Yuan, Z.Y.: Adaptive iterative learning control for robot manipulators. In: IEEE International Conference on Intelligent Computing and Intelligent Systems, pp. 1195–1203 (2010)

Stable 3D Biped Walking Control with Speed Regulation Based on Generalized Virtual Constraints

Jianfei Li, Yaobing Wang, Tao Xiao$^{(\boxtimes)}$, and Dawei Zhang

Beijing Key Laboratory of Intelligent Space Robotic Systems Technology
and Applications, Beijing Institute of Spacecraft System Engineering,
Beijing, China
txiao163@126.com

Abstract. Bipedal locomotion skills are challenging due to complex dynamics. Control strategies often use the Virtual Holonomic Constraint (VHC) approach to obtain reduced dynamics and yield trackable solutions. The method has been successfully used in generating periodic gaits for planar biped. However, as for 3D walking there may not be a periodic gait with the increase of under-actuation degrees, bringing challenges for stable gait generating. This paper introduces a 3D gait generating approach based on a proposed Generalized Virtual Constraint (GVC) approach. First, by denoting the states of the legs with complex numbers and describing the GVCs with complex functions, continuous 3D bipedal gaits can be achieved as well as speed regulation. Second, virtual constraints with speed relations are enforced with feedback linearization. Finally, in full dynamics simulations considering necessary conditions including torque limits, contact dynamics, etc., 3D walking is improved by optimizing the GVC parameters with genetic algorithm, achieving a series of energetic efficient, stable as well as elegant gaits are obtained.

Keywords: Biped robot · Virtual constraints · 3D biped walking

1 Introduction

Biped robots, with better adaption abilities to environments and more attracting appearance, can be applied in a variety of tasks such as exploration, transportation and service. However, the control of bipedal walking has brought great challenges in the last several decades. The model of biped robots is hybrid, nonlinear and of high dimensions. So far, the walking performances of most existing biped robots are still far poorer than that of human beings.

A number of strategies that devoted to bipedal walking control has been proposed, among which the most prevalent is the Zero Moment Point (ZMP) based approach [1]. Passive walking is another famous approach. Neither of the two methods can achieve satisfactory performance in both efficiency and speed [2]. The virtual holonomic constraint (VHC) approach, proposed in [3, 4], has been applied to the control of under-actuated bipedal robots. Traditionally, tasks for robotic systems are specified by a desired time trajectory of the joints. The VHC approach, however, specifies the

© Springer Nature Switzerland AG 2019
H. Yu et al. (Eds.): ICIRA 2019, LNAI 11744, pp. 38–49, 2019.
https://doi.org/10.1007/978-3-030-27541-9_4

desired motions with respect to the state(s) of system rather than time, allowing one to investigate orbital stability on reduced dynamics. Robots controlled with VHC can walk very fast and are insensitive to outer interferences, which in this regard represents a promising approach in biped control. For planar biped robot, the VHC approach can generate a periodic limit cycle gait, while for 3D walking a closed gait is not guaranteed, for the dynamic model has two under-actuated DOFs (the reduced dynamics has two inner dynamics), thus some chaos phenomenon exists in gait generating. [5] worked on the 3D control of biped walking based on VHC, by optimizing walking gaits with respect to the Cost of Mechanical Transport (CMT) an efficient walking was achieved with a CMT of 0.9 at 1 m/s. While the author did not analyze the stability of the two inner dynamics. Actually, the two inner dynamics are directly related to the forward and lateral speed in 3D walking. Therefore, this paper use GVC to maintain the states of the legs within given limits, and by control the relations of the two inner dynamics walking speeds in both forward and lateral directions can be regulated. Genetic algorithm (GA) is used to optimize the GVC parameters and after optimization the CMT attains 0.057, which is quite close to that of a human.

2 Model of the Biped Walker

The biped robot DEYL is designed for 2D and 3D walking. The name DEYL comes from Do Everything You Like. DEYL consists of a pair of identical legs and a torso. Each leg has three actuated revolute joints: a pitch and a roll at the hip and a pitch at the knee. Ignoring the translation and rotation in yaw direction of the supporting foot, the system has totally 8 DOFs: two unactuated, six actuated. The weight centralizes in the torso. The torso is designed to house motors and controller so that the legs are very light, and such an arrangement is also preferred for speed modulation. Figure 2 gives the angle definition of the robot. The straight lines from each foot to the waist are called virtual legs. Some parameters are shown in Table 1 (Fig. 1).

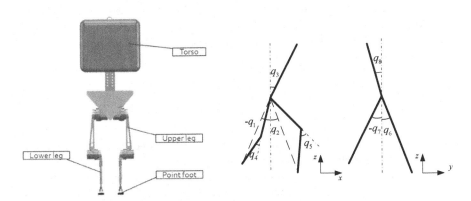

Fig. 1. The structure of DEYL

Table 1. Parameters of DEYL

Property	Lower leg	Upper leg	Torso
Length (m)	0.35	0.35	0.85
Mass (kg)	0.8	3.8	28.5

2.1 Swing Phase Model

The n-DOF biped robot is actuated with k motors. Assuming non-slippery and single support contact with the ground, the dynamics equations of the robotic system based on Euler-Lagrangian method can be expressed in gait design coordinate system as:

$$M(q)\ddot{q} + C(q,\dot{q})\dot{q} + G(q) = B\begin{bmatrix} 0 \\ \tau \end{bmatrix} = B_e \tau \tag{1}$$

where $M(q) \in \mathbb{R}^{n \times n}$ is the inertia matrix, $C(q,\dot{q}) \in \mathbb{R}^{n \times n}$ the matrix of Coriolis and centripetal force terms, $G(q) \in \mathbb{R}^n$ the vector of gravitational force terms, $\tau \in \mathbb{R}^k$ the vector of the joint torques. And B_e is the last k columns of B.

2.2 Hybrid Model

Once one foot touches the ground, the contact forces including support and friction forces are exerted to the foot. The dynamics of the robot become:

$$M(q)\ddot{q} + C(q,\dot{q})\dot{q} + G(q) = B_e \tau - J^T F_e \tag{2}$$

where J is the Jacobian matrix, $F_e = \begin{bmatrix} F_x & F_y & F_z \end{bmatrix}^T$ is the contact force at the end of the swing leg. In experiments, the contact force can be measured by force sensors while in simulations contact forces are generated with a contact model [7], which can simulate the function of the support and frictional force.

When the swing leg contacts with the ground and the vertical force at the swing leg goes beyond that of the supporting leg, the supporting leg and the swing leg undergo a role exchange, during which the controller will execute a relabeling process as:

$$\begin{aligned} q^+ &= \Delta q^- \\ \dot{q}^+ &= \Delta \dot{q}^- \\ \tau^+ &= \Delta \tau^- \end{aligned} \tag{3}$$

where the subscripts $(.)^+$ and $(.)^-$ denote the values prior and immediately after the impact event respectively, and Δ the switching function.

Equations (1) or (2) and (3) defined a hybrid model during the walk. The robot follows the dynamics (1) in swing phase and the contact model (2) while both legs are contacting to the ground. The relabeling process is inactive until the leg changing condition is satisfied.

3 Design of the Gait

3.1 Generalized Virtual Constraint

Virtual constraints regulate the relationships among the angular coordinates of the robot, thus forming a close gait system independent of time. If other variables are added into the constraints, it can be called Generalized Virtual Constraint (GVC).

Definition 1 [7]: A Generalized Virtual Constraint for system (1) of order k is a relation $h(q, x_e) = 0$, where $h : \mathbb{R}^{n+m} \to \mathbb{R}^k$ is smooth. And the set

$$\Gamma = \left\{ (q, \dot{q}) : h(q, x_e) = 0, \frac{\partial h}{\partial q} \dot{q} + \frac{\partial h}{\partial x_e} \dot{x}_e = 0 \right\} \tag{4}$$

is controlled invariant, where x_e is a vector of variables except q, such as $\dot{q}$, walking speed and time, etc. It is noted that with the absence of x_e, (4) becomes a VHC.

3.2 Gait Timing Variable

The virtual constraints are usually independent of time, but a state value (often denoted θ) of the system is always selected to denote the progress of the task. For example, in planar walking the angle between the supporting virtual leg and the vertical line (q_1) is selected. For biped control θ is called gait timing variable. Usually θ is expected to satisfy the following two conditions.

- Continuous during one step
- Strictly monotonic during on step.

In [5] θ is also assigned the angle between the supporting virtual leg and the vertical line (q_v), as is shown in Fig. 3. q_v can be calculated with (5).

$$q_v = \arctan(\tan^2 q_1 + \tan^2 q_6) \tag{5}$$

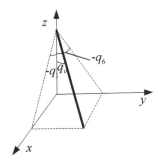

Fig. 2. The angel system of DEYL

However, q_v is not strictly monotonic during on step. It may induce a symmetric gait. In this paper, the gait timing variable is selected as:

$$\theta = (q_1 - q_{1c})\dot{q}_1 + (q_6 - q_{6c})\dot{q}_6 \tag{6}$$

where q_{1c}, q_{6c} are constants during one step. It holds that $q_1 = q_{1c}$ and $q_6 = q_{6c}$ when the center of mass of the robot is above the supporting point.

During one step, (q_1, q_6) first approach (q_{1c}, q_{6c}) and then get away from (q_{1c}, q_{6c}). θ changes from negative to positive monotonically. With this configuration, forward walking, backward walking, catwalk and marking time can all be contained into one situation.

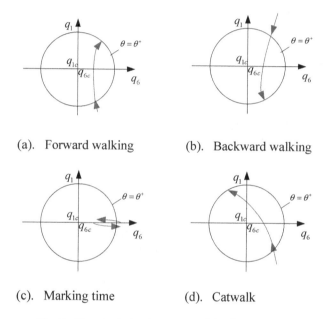

(a). Forward walking   (b). Backward walking

(c). Marking time   (d). Catwalk

Fig. 3. Four typical gaits supported by the approach

For convenience, s is derived from a normalization process of θ.

$$s = \frac{\theta - \theta^+}{\theta^- - \theta^+} \tag{7}$$

where $\theta^+ = (q_1^+ - q_{1c})\dot{q}_1^+ + (q_6^+ - q_{6c})\dot{q}_6^+$ is the initial value during a step, θ^- is the chosen maxim value of θ, which determines the step length to some extent.

3.3   Definition of the Virtual Constraints

Some GVCs are defined to regulate the joint angles with the following form.

$$q_j = \phi_j(q_1, q_6, \dot{q}_1, \dot{q}_6, x_e)$$
$$j = 2, 3, 4, 5, 7, 8 \tag{8}$$

where x_e may contain average walking speed, command and so on in some of the constraints. The GVC can also be rewritten as:

$$y = h(q_1, q_6, \dot{q}_1, \dot{q}_6, x_e) = \phi - q_l \tag{9}$$

where $q_l = [q_2 \ q_3 \ q_4 \ q_5 \ q_7 \ q_8]^T$. ϕ_j is defined with a five-order Bézier function or the combination of several Bézier functions. For continuity of the gait between two steps, it is guaranteed in gait design process that

$$\phi_j(s = 0) = q_j^+ \tag{10}$$

holds.

In this paper the angles of knees q_4 and q_5 are defined by five-order Bézier functions [8].

$$\phi_j(s) = \sum_{i=0}^{n=5} P_i C_n^i (1-s)^{n-i}(s)^i \tag{11}$$

$$j = 4, 5$$

While the angels of the swing legs are assigned as the functions of s and angles of the supporting leg, as is shown in (12), (13).

$$\tan q_2 = A(s) \tan q_1 + B(s) \tan q_6 + C_1(s) \tag{12}$$

$$\tan q_7 = A(s) \tan q_6 - B(s) \tan q_1 + C_2(s) \tag{13}$$

where $A(s)$, $B(s)$, $C_2(s)$ are all defined with 5-order Bézier functions subject to (14).

$$C_1(1) = 0$$
$$C_2(1) = 0 \tag{14}$$
$$A^2(1) + B^2(1) = 1$$

If we denote $z_1 = i \tan q_1 + \tan q_6$, $z_2 = i \tan q_2 + \tan q_7$, where i is the imaginary unit. (12), (13) can be rewritten as

$$z_2 = k_r(s)e^{i\alpha(s)}z_1 + z_0(s) \tag{15}$$

where $k_r = \sqrt{A^2 + B^2}$, $\alpha = \arctan 2(A, B)$, $z_0 = C_1 + iC_2$.

To maintain a forward speed for the robot. The α can be chosen properly so that $\alpha(1) \le 0$ (Fig. 4).

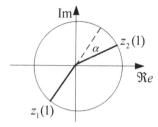

Fig. 4. The angles of the virtual legs in complex plane

3.4 Walking Speed Regulation

Walking speed of an under-actuated robot is determined by several factors including the trajectory of the knees, the inclination of the ground and the angle of the torso. [7] successfully realized planar speed tuning by controlling the angle of the torso. The speed regulation law is as follows.

$$q_3 = \arctan\left(k_{px}(\dot{x}_c - \bar{\dot{x}}) + k_{ix}\int_0^t (\dot{x}_c - \bar{\dot{x}})\mathrm{d}t\right) \tag{16}$$

where $\bar{\dot{x}}$ the average speed in forward direction, which can be calculated with the step length and time during one step. $\dot{x}_c$ is the desired forward walking speed, k_{px}, k_{ix} are positive constants.

It can be known from (16) that q_3 is kept within $\left(-\frac{\pi}{2}, \frac{\pi}{2}\right)$, which is very reasonable. The speed regulation law only samples at the beginning of one step so that the virtual constraint is invariant during the step.

The lateral speed in can be regulated at a similar manner, shown in (17).

$$q_8 = \phi_8(\theta) - \arctan\left(k_{py}(\dot{y}_c - \bar{\dot{y}}) + k_{iy}\int_0^t (\dot{y}_c - \bar{\dot{y}})\mathrm{d}t\right) \tag{17}$$

where $\bar{\dot{y}}$ is the average speed in forward direction. $\dot{y}_c$ is the desired forward walking speed, k_{py}, k_{iy} are positive constants. $\phi_8(\theta)$ defines the lateral motion of the torso during on step subject to $\phi_8(0) = \phi_8(1) = 0$.

4 Control Design

Because θ is relative to $\dot{q}_1$ and $\dot{q}_6$, the virtual constraints defined above are nonholonomic. The derivation of the GVC $y = h(q, \dot{q})$ with rank $k = n - 2$ is

$$\dot{y} = \frac{\partial h}{\partial q}\dot{q} + \frac{\partial h}{\partial \dot{q}}\ddot{q} \tag{18}$$

Assuming $rank\left(\frac{\partial h}{\partial \dot{q}}\dot{q}\right) = m$, then there exist $T \in \mathbb{R}^k$ so that

$$T\frac{\partial h}{\partial \dot{q}}\dot{q} = \begin{bmatrix} \frac{\partial h_1}{\partial \dot{q}}\dot{q} \\ 0 \end{bmatrix} \tag{19}$$

where $h_1 = \begin{bmatrix} I_m & O \end{bmatrix} Th$, then (18) can be rewritten as:

$$\dot{y}_1 = \frac{\partial h_1}{\partial q}\dot{q} + \frac{\partial h}{\partial \dot{q}}\ddot{q} \tag{20}$$

$$\dot{y}_2 = \frac{\partial h_2}{\partial q}\dot{q} \tag{21}$$

where $h_2 = \begin{bmatrix} O & I_{k-m} \end{bmatrix} Th$, subject to $\frac{\partial h_2}{\partial \dot{q}}\dot{q} = 0$. Derivative (21) with time, then

$$\ddot{y}_2 = \frac{\partial \left(\frac{\partial h_2}{\partial q}\dot{q}\right)}{\partial q}\dot{q} + \frac{\partial h_2}{\partial q}\ddot{q} \tag{22}$$

Combine of (20) and (22), substitution to (1) produces

$$\begin{bmatrix} \dot{y}_1 \\ \ddot{y}_2 \end{bmatrix} = \begin{bmatrix} \frac{\partial h_1}{\partial q}\dot{q} \\ \frac{\partial \left(\frac{\partial h_2}{\partial q}\dot{q}\right)}{\partial q}\dot{q} \end{bmatrix} + \begin{bmatrix} \frac{\partial h}{\partial \dot{q}} \\ \frac{\partial h_2}{\partial q} \end{bmatrix} M^{-1}(B\tau - C\dot{q} - G) \tag{23}$$

Denote

$$\Omega = \begin{bmatrix} \frac{\partial h_1}{\partial q}\dot{q} \\ \frac{\partial \left(\frac{\partial h_2}{\partial q}\dot{q}\right)}{\partial q}\dot{q} \end{bmatrix} \tag{24}$$

$$\Phi = \begin{bmatrix} \frac{\partial h}{\partial \dot{q}} \\ \frac{\partial h_2}{\partial q} \end{bmatrix} \tag{25}$$

Noticing that $rank(\Phi M^{-1}B) = k$, then choose the control law

$$\tau = \left(\Phi M^{-1}B\right)^{-1}\left(\begin{bmatrix} -k_1 y_1 \\ -k_{d2}\dot{y}_2 - k_{p2}y_2 \end{bmatrix} - \Omega\right) + \left(\Phi M^{-1}B\right)^{-1}\Phi M^{-1}(C\dot{q} + G) \tag{26}$$

where $k_1 \in \mathbb{R}^{m \times m} k_{p2}, k_{d2} \in \mathbb{R}^{(k-m) \times (k-m)}$ are positive definite, it holds that

$$\begin{cases} \dot{y}_1 + k_1 y_1 = 0 \\ \ddot{y}_2 + k_{d2}\dot{y}_2 + k_{p2}y_2 = 0 \end{cases} \tag{27}$$

Then $y_1 \to 0, \dot{y}_1 \to 0, y_2 \to 0, \dot{y}_2 \to 0$, as $t \to \infty$. Hence the GVCs are asymptotically enforced.

5   3D Walking Simulation

The robot is desired to walk on a plane at a commanded speed of 1 m/s with a initial speed of 0.5 m/s. Firstly the simulation is executed successively and the gait is optimized with GA to learn a steady walking performance, then with the optimized gait the robot is commanded to walk 100 s. Energy efficiency as well as walking elegance (compared with human) is concerned to evaluate the robot's waking performance (Fig. 5).

Fig. 5. 3D walking at speed 1 m/s

5.1   Optimization of the Virtual Constraints

The defined virtual constraints can roughly support a continuous 3D walking, while the performance is finally determined by the parameters of the constraints. This paper optimizes the gaits using the genetic algorithm with respect to energetic efficiency. A little to our surprise, the final gaits processes a not only efficient but elegant and natural walking manner.

The constraints to be optimized includes $\phi_4(s)$, $\phi_5(s)$, $A(s)$, $C_1(s)$, $B(s)$, $C_2(s)$, totally 24 parameters except some predefined coefficients.

The cost function is taken as the cost of mechanical transport *CMT* [6]:

$$J_{eff} = \frac{1}{gM_{tot}d} \int_0^{Ti} \sum_{i=1}^{6} \geq [p_i(t)]_+ dt \tag{28}$$

where Ti is the time duration of one step, d represents the distance traveled by the center of mass *(COM)* in one step, g denotes the gravitational constant, M_{tot} is the total mass of the robot, $pi(t)$ is actuator power, and $[p]_+ = p$ when $p \geq 0$ and equals zero otherwise.

The fitness function is selected as the average *CMT* during 5 steps. The generation number is 30 and the Crossover Fraction is 0.75.

The optimized constraint functions are shown in Figs. 7, 8 and 9. In [5], the CMT at 1 m/s reached 0.096 at best, compared with an approximate 0.05 of human beings [6]. While in this paper, the CMT attains 0.057 at 1 m/s, quite close to that of human (Fig. 6).

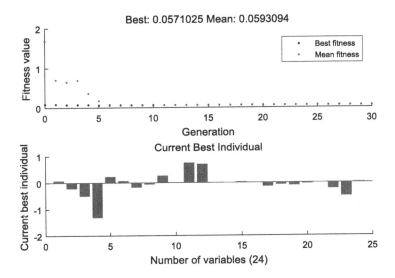

Fig. 6. CMT and parameters during the optimization process

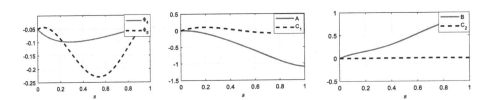

Fig. 7. Gait functions after optimization

5.2 Continuous 3D Walking

In the simulation the biped robot walks along a line on a plain for 100 s. The optimized gait is used and the speed regulation laws are enabled. It is shown from the simulation that the robot walks with a very natural gait and the CMT, which represent the energetic efficiency stay close to 0.05 (Fig. 8). After a long walking the phase trajectories of the gaits began to converge to limit cycles.

The walking speed converge to the command with a period of adjustment and then the walking gaits reach a steady and periodic state with the phase trajectories of the joints converging to limit circles (Fig. 10).

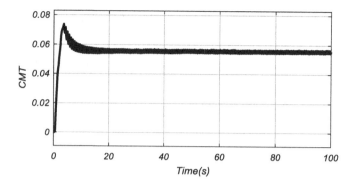

Fig. 8. CMT during the 60 s 3D walking after optimization

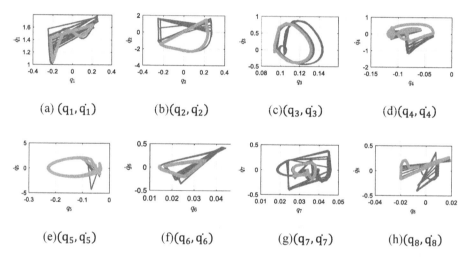

(a) $(q_1, \dot{q}_1)$ (b)$(q_2, \dot{q}_2)$ (c)$(q_3, \dot{q}_3)$ (d)$(q_4, \dot{q}_4)$

(e)$(q_5, \dot{q}_5)$ (f)$(q_6, \dot{q}_6)$ (g)$(q_7, \dot{q}_7)$ (h)$(q_8, \dot{q}_8)$

Fig. 9. Phase trajectories of the joints

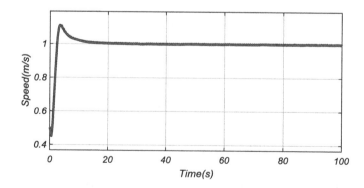

Fig. 10. Actual walking speed under a commanded speed of 1 m/s

6 Conclusion

This paper proposed a new approach for 3D walking control based on virtual constraints. A series of waling gaits are contained in one approach as well as speed tuning is achieved. In addition, the energetic efficiency, represented by the CMT, is optimized to 0.057, at the first time so close to human efficiency. In future work we'd like to combine Deep Reinforcement Learning (DRL) with GVC because it is expected that DRL has more capability in controlling biped walking than GA.

References

1. Shin, H.K., Kim, B.K.: Energy-efficient reference gait generation utilizing variable ZMP and vertical hip motion based on inverted pendulum model for biped robots. In: International Conference on Control Automation and Systems, pp. 1408–1413. IEEE (2010)
2. Gritli, H., Khraief, N., Belghith, S.: Chaos control in passive walking dynamics of a compass-gait model. Commun. Nonlinear Sci. Numer. Simul. 18(8), 2048–2065 (2013)
3. Shiriaev, A., Perram, J., Canudas-de Wit, C.: Constructive tool for orbital stabilization of underactuated nonlinear systems: virtual constraints approach. IEEE Trans. Autom. Contr. 50(8), 1164–1176 (2005)
4. Westervelt, E., Grizzle, J., Koditschek, D.: Hybrid zero dynamics of planar biped walkers. IEEE Trans. Autom. Contr. 48(1), 42–56 (2003)
5. Ramezani, A., et al.: Performance analysis and feedback control of ATRIAS, a three-dimensional bipedal robot. J. Dyn. Syst. Meas. Control 136(2), 729–736 (2014)
6. Collins, S., et al.: Efficient bipedal robots based on passive-dynamic walkers. Science 307(5712), 1082 (2005)
7. Li, J., et al.: Virtual constraint based adaptive control for biped robot with speed regulation. In: IEEE International Conference on Mechatronics and Automation, pp. 1084–1089. IEEE (2016)
8. Westervelt, E., Grizzle, J., Chevallereau, C., Choi, J., Morris, B.: Feedback Control of Dynamic Biped al Robot Locomotion. CRC Press, Taylor and Francis Group, Boca Raton (2007)

Advanced Measurement and Machine Vision System

Specular Surface Measurement with Laser Plane Constraint to Reduce Erroneous Points

Huayang Li[1], Xu Zhang[1,2(✉)], Leilei Zhuang[2], and Yilin Yang[1]

[1] School of Mechatronic Engineering and Automation, Shanghai University,
No. 99 Shangda Road, Baoshan District, Shanghai 200444, China
xuzhang@shu.edu.cn
[2] HUST-Wuxi Reasearch Institute,
No 329 YanXin Road, Huishan District, WuXi 214100, China

Abstract. For the purpose of reducing erroneous points generated by specular reflections, multiple line structured-light stripes extraction algorithm and laser plane constraint method are proposed for line structured-light scanners. At first, all laser stripes in images are extracted with multiple line structured-light stripes extraction algorithm. Then, the three dimensional (3D) points within which include the erroneous data caused by specular reflections are computed by optical-triangulation. Finally, false measurements generated by specular reflections are eliminated with the laser plane constraint method. The effectiveness of the method is verified by eliminating erroneous points in the experiment. The percentage of erroneous points before and after processing is counted to evaluate the performance of the laser plane constraint. The experimental results show that the percentage of erroneous points is 12.61% before processing and is 3.05% after processing, which indicate that the method can effectively eliminate erroneous points with good feasibility.

Keywords: Specular reflections · Removal of erroneous points · Laser plane constraint

1 Introduction

Because line structured-light scanners [1–3] has relatively high accuracy and relatively simple hardware, it has been adopted widely in 3D reconstruction [4–6], structural measurement, target detection, reverse engineering [7] and so on. The line structured-light system consists of a charge-coupled device (CCD) camera, a line laser projector and a motion control module. The laser plane scans the objects, the intersection of the laser plane and the object produces a stripe of illuminated points on the objects surface, and a sequence of images is acquired while scanning. By detecting the image coordinates of illuminated points, the 3D coordinates with respect to the world coordinate frame can be computed based on optical-triangulation [8,9].

© Springer Nature Switzerland AG 2019
H. Yu et al. (Eds.): ICIRA 2019, LNAI 11744, pp. 53–63, 2019.
https://doi.org/10.1007/978-3-030-27541-9_5

Line structured-light scanner can now construct detailed 3D models of objects, but many real-world objects have surface properties that are not ideal for it [10–12]. There are multiple laser stripes on the surface of the object due to mutual reflections and specular reflections, so there are many erroneous points on the reconstructed model surface. In order to eliminate erroneous points caused by specular reflections, many works have been developed. Some researchers have tried to do away with the problems by painting the object with removable powder to ensure that the surfaces reflect the laser in a diffuse manner [13]. Obviously, this method can do damage to objects and also cause certain measurement errors. Curless and Levoy [14] proposed a new range sensing method that is less sensitive to nonuniform light reflections by analyzing the time evolution of the light reflections. The method also improves the range data accuracy on sharp edges or discontinuous surfaces caused by sensor occlusions. However, it requires a large number of images to ensure that the laser stripe passes over every pixel in the image and, more importantly, the existence of spurious reflections is ignored. Nayar et al. [15] proposed an iterative algorithm that recovers the shape and reflectance properties of surfaces in the presence of mutual reflections. This algorithm is useful for the shape-from-intensity approach to range acquisition. This approach, however, does not produce dense and accurate range maps compared to the optical triangulation methods. Additionally, the proposed algorithm was tested only on lambertian surfaces of simple geometry. Clark et al. [16] developed a laser scanning system that uses the polarization analysis to disambiguate the primary reflections from those caused by mutual reflections. Their system was tested on shiny alminum objects with concavities, and spurious reflections were successfully discriminated. However, the system requires special equipment such as a linear polarizer, and multiple images need to be captured at each position of the laser. In their experiments, three images were acquired at three different angles of the linear polarizer. Wolff and Boult [17] showed how the surface normal are constrained to the polarimetric parameters of an unpolarized light reflected by surface. Trucco and Fisher [18] proposed a number of consistency tests for acquiring reliable range images of specular objects. Their range sensor consists of two CCD cameras observing a laser stripe from opposite sides. The consistency tests are based on the fact that the range measurements obtained from the two cameras will be consistent only if the measurements correspond to the true illuminated point. Their method was tested on a polished aluminum block with holes. However, their method does not consider the situation where more than one illuminated point is observed in the same camera scan line. The consistency tests are therefore applied only to the measurements corresponding to a single illuminated point observed per camera scan line.

Unlike most existing recent works, this paper proposes a novel method to eliminate erroneous points generated by specular reflections. The main works in this paper include: First, because there are multiple laser stripes in the acquired image and the entire image does not provides sufficient information to determine whether a laser center corresponds to a spurious reflection, multiple line structured-light stripes extraction algorithm is used to detect all laser stripes in the image. Second, according to the characteristics of line structured-light binocular 3D scanners, the true points should be on laser plane. So the laser plane constraint is used to eliminate erroneous points. The advantage of this method is that it is completely based on original images and does not depend on other information and hardware devices. The experimental results show that the proposed method can effectively eliminate the abnormal erroneous points generated by the specular reflection.

2   Principle of Novel Line Structured-Light Scanners

Traditional line structured-light scanners consists of a laser projector and a CCD camera. As shown in Fig. 1(a), point P is a central point of a laser stripe, point P_1 is the corresponding point of point P on the imaging plane. According to the principle of aperture imaging, the line between the origin of the camera coordinate frame and point P_1 passes through the Point P to be calculated. So the 3D coordinate of point P can be obtained by finding the intersection of line O_cP_1 and the laser plane. In order to perform 3D measurement with traditional line structured-light scanners, it is necessary to place the object on a conveyor belt or other moving device.

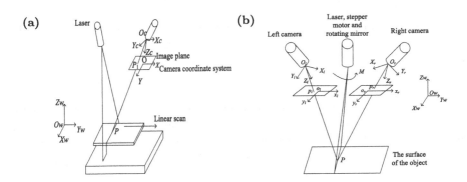

Fig. 1. (a) The traditional line structured-light scanners and $O_cX_cY_cZ_c$, $O_wX_wY_wZ_w$ and OXY represent respectively the camera coordinate frame, the world coordinate frame and the image coordinate frame. (b) The novel line structured-light scanners

Novel line structured-light scanners use stereo vision system, it consists of two CCD cameras, a line structured-light projector, a rotating mirror and a stepper motor. A stepper motor drives a rotating mirror to do the scanning of the laser plane, so the object which is scanned does not need to be placed on a conveyor belt or other moving device. A line structured-light projector projects a laser stripe over an object and two cameras take the sequence of images while the laser plane scans objects. The laser stripe is modulated due to changes in the depth of the object surface and possible gaps, the performance in the image is that the laser stripe is distorted and discontinuous. The laser centers in images are extracted by the method proposed in [19]. The 3D points are computed by the epipolar constraint and optical-triangulation.

As shown in Fig. 1(b), point P is a central point of a laser stripe, $O_l X_l Y_l Z_l$, $O_r X_r Y_r Z_r$ and $O_w X_w Y_w Z_w$ represent respectively the left camera coordinate frame, the right coordinate frame and the world coordinate frame, $o_l x_l y_l$ and $o_r x_r y_r$ represent respectively the left image coordinate frame and the right image coordinate frame, point p_l and p_r are respectively the corresponding point of the point P in the left imaging plane and the right imaging plane. The epipolar constraint is used to find the corresponding point p_l according to the point p_r, and the corresponding points are used to compute 3D points based on optical-triangulation. The advantage of the novel line structured-light scanners is its low cost and relatively high efficiency.

3   Removal of Erroneous Points Generated by Specular Reflections

As shown in Fig. 2(a), there is a single laser stripe while a single line structured-light projects onto a diffuse object. As shown in Fig. 2(b), when a single line structured-light stripe projects onto a object with specular reflections, the hypothesis that there is only one laser stripe on a laser scanning line is wrong, because the specular reflection can create lots of erroneous laser stripes. So multiple line structured-light stripes extraction algorithm and laser plane constraint are proposed, the basic idea is to detect all the laser stripes which contain spurious laser stripes and true laser stripes. Since choosing the highest intensity illuminated point does not guarantee the correctness of its corresponding 3D measurement, and the entire image does not provide sufficient information to determine whether a laser center corresponds to a spurious reflection. According to the characteristics of line structured-light binocular 3D scanners, erroneous 3D measurements generated by specular reflections are eliminated by applying the laser plane constraint test.

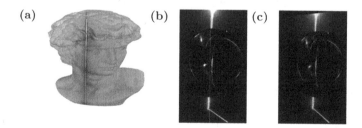

Fig. 2. (a) David model in scanning (b) Laser stripes are detected by the original algorithm [19] (c) Laser stripes are detected by the proposed multiple line structured-light stripes extraction algorithm

3.1 Extraction of Multiple Line Structured-Light Stripes

In order to extract all the line structured-light stripes in each image, the connected component analysis method is used to detect the location of laser stripes, line structured-light stripes extraction algorithm [19] is used to detect the laser centers. The connected component is a common method of region extraction in image processing field, the connected component generally refers to an image region composed of foreground pixels with the same pixel value and adjacent positions in an image, the connected component analysis refers to the identification and labeling of connected areas in an image.

The seed filling is used for connected component analysis in this paper, the seed filling originates from computer graphics and is often used to fill a graph. The idea of seeding filling is to select a foreground pixel as seed, the foreground pixels adjacent to the seed are merged into the same set of pixels according to the two basic conditions of the connected region (the same pixel value and the adjacent position), the final set of pixels are a connected region. As shown in Fig. 2(b) and (c), multiple line structured-light stripes of the image can be extracted with the proposed algorithm, but the original method cannot do it. The proposed algorithm steps are as follows.

$Step1$: An image is converted to a binary image, the image is scanned until the current pixel value $B(x,y) = 1$.

$Step2$: $B(x,y)$ is used as the seed and given a label, and then all foreground pixels adjacent to the seed are pushed onto the stack. At this time, a connected area in the image is found, and the pixel value in the area is marker as label.

$Step3$: The $Step1$ and $Step2$ are repeated until the end of the scan, and all connected area can be obtained in the image.

$Step4$: For each connected area, laser centers are extracted by line structured-light stripes extraction algorithm.

3.2 Laser Plane Constraint

After the laser stripes in images are extracted by multiple line structured-light stripes extraction algorithm, the 3D points are calculated with these laser centers based optical-triangulation, which contain lots of false points. According to the characteristics of line structured-light binocular 3D scanners, the laser plane constraint is used to eliminate erroneous points.

Left camera coordinate system $O_c X_c Y_c Z_c$ is shown in Fig. 3(a), and laser coordinate frame is constructed as follows. First, the intersection line is obtained by choosing two laser planes arbitrarily and is regarded as the Y axis of the laser coordinate frame, the angle between its direction and Y_c axis is less than $90°$. The origin of laser coordinate frame is the intersection of Y axis and $X_c Z_c$ plane. Then the cross product of X_c axis and Y axis yields Z axis, the angle between its direction and Z_c axis is less than $90°$. Finally, the cross product of Y axis and Z axis yields X axis. As shown in Fig. 3(b), the intersection of number i laser plane and the XZ plane is set to L_i, the angle α_i between L_i and X axis in right-hand coordinate frame is the rotation angle of number i laser plane.

The calculated 3D points and the calibrated parameters of laser plane are all in the left camera coordinate frame, so L_i should be changed to the intersection line of number i laser plane and the X_cZ_c plane, α_i should be changed to the angle between L_i and X_c axis in right-hand coordinate frame.

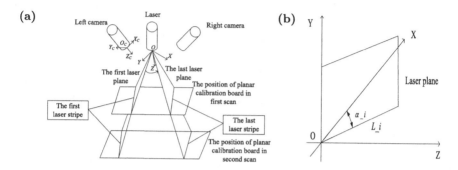

Fig. 3. (a) A sketch of laser planes (b) A schematic diagram of the projection of laser plane in the XZ plane

$Ax + By + Cz + D = 0$ is the parametric equation of the laser plane, the intersection L_i of the laser plane and X_cZ_c plane is calculated by

$$\begin{cases} Ax + By + Cz + D = 0 \\ y = 0 \end{cases} \tag{1}$$

The L_i is expressed by $ax + bz + c = 0$, cosine value of the angle α_i between L_i and X_c axis in right-hand coordinate frame is calculated by

$$cos(\alpha\_i) = \frac{|b|}{\sqrt{a^2 + b^2}} \tag{2}$$

So the laser plane constraint has been determined which can be used to eliminate erroneous points generated by specular reflections. Each 3D point is tested with the laser plane constraint, the true 3D points are just on the corresponding laser plane, the location of erroneous 3D points generated by specular reflection is uncertain and should not be near the laser plane. If a 3D point p_i is true, point p'_i is the projection point of p_i on the X_cZ_c plane, angle β_i between p'_iO_c and O_cX_c should satisfy

$$|cos(\beta_i) - cos(\alpha_i)| < \mu \tag{3}$$

where μ is a threshold.

3.3   Calibration of the Laser Plane

For our line-structured light scanner, when the scanning speed and the frame rate of cameras trigger are fixed, the laser plane of the scanner is also fixed, so the laser plane of the scanner only need to be calibrated once. A planar calibration board is used to calibrate the laser plane, the planar calibration board placed in front of the line structured-light scanner is scanned twice and two positions are shown in Fig. 3(a). The laser centers of the acquired images are extracted using multiple line structured-light stripes extraction algorithm and are converted to the camera coordinate frame using the camera parameters. Then the 3D points corresponding to number n laser centers of the first scan and the 3D points corresponding to number n laser centers of the second scan are used to fit the plane equation based on the least square method. The plane equation is given by

$$Ax + By + Cz + D = 0 \tag{4}$$

the plane equation can be rewritten as

$$z = k_0 x + k_1 y + k_2 \tag{5}$$

where $k_0 = -A/C$, $k_1 = -B/C$, $k_2 = -D/C$, $C \neq 0$. To calculated the above plane equation, a series of n points $(x_i, y_i, z_i)(i = 0, 1, \cdots, n - 1)$ are used to minimize the objective function S which is given by

$$S = \sum_{i=0}^{n-1} (k_0 x + k_1 y + k_2 - z)^2 \tag{6}$$

where the objective function should satisfy $\frac{\partial S}{\partial k_j} = 0 (j = 0, 1, 2)$. By solving k_0, k_1, k_2, the equation of laser plane can be obtained.

4 Experiments

In this section, the self-designed and manufactured line structured-light binocular 3D scanner is shown firstly. Then the calibration accuracy of the laser plane is assessed. Finally, by means of counting the proportion of false points before and after processing, the effectiveness of the laser plane constraint is verified.

4.1 Experimental System

In the paper, the self-designed and manufactured line structured-light binocular 3D scanner is shown in Fig. 4(a). The scanner consists of a laser projector, two CCD cameras (resolution 1280×1024), a stepper motor with encoder, a rotating mirror, a circuit board, two cooling fans and an industrial computer, the measurement distance is 350 mm, and the field of view of the scanner is 300×200 mm, the actual scanner is shown in Fig. 4(b).

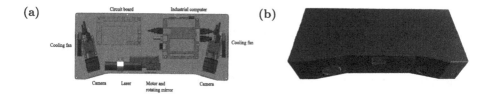

Fig. 4. (a) The 3D model of the line structured-light binocular 3D scanner (b) The actual line structured-light binocular 3D scanner

4.2 Results and Analysis

The method of Sect. 3.3 is used to calibrate each laser plane of line structured-light scanners, and the parameters of the laser plane are obtained. The David model is scanned by the scanner, the 3D points corresponding each laser stripes in scanning are calculated, point clouds of reconstructed David model are shown in Fig. 5. The distance between the 3D points corresponding the number n laser stripe and the number n calibrated laser plane is used to evaluate the calibration accuracy of the laser plane.

Fig. 5. The point clouds of the reconstructed David model by the scanner

The average and standard deviation of the distance between 3D points of laser stripes and corresponding laser plane are calculated. As illustrated in Fig. 6, the

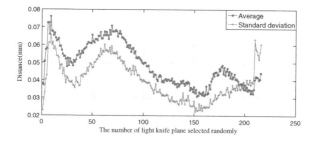

Fig. 6. The average and standard deviation of the distance between 3D points of laser stripes and corresponding laser plane

maximum of average is 0.076 mm and the maximum of standard deviation is 0.0632 mm. The experimental results indicate that the calibration accuracy of the laser plane is relatively high.

The metal board that is used in the experiment is shown in Fig. 7(a). As shown in Fig. 7(b), the reconstructed point clouds of the metal board contain lots of erroneous points generated by specular reflection and part of the point clouds in the upper left corner and upper right corner are lost. As shown in the Fig. 7(c), the point clouds contain very few erroneous points which are processed

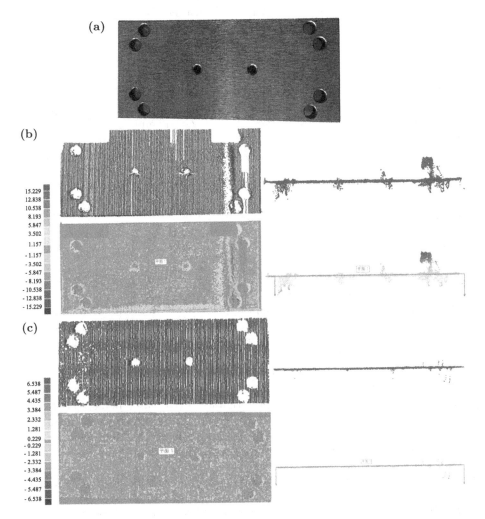

Fig. 7. (a) The metal board is used in the experiments (b) The reconstructed point clouds and pseudo-color images before processing (from the front and the side) (c) The reconstructed point clouds and pseudo-color images after processing (from the front and the side)

by the proposed multiple line structured-light stripes extraction algorithm and laser plane constraint, and the whole surface can be reconstructed. To verify the effectiveness of laser plane constraint, the number of points that do not meet the laser plane constraint is counted. The results of the statistics show that the percentage of erroneous points is 12.61% before processing and is 3.05% after processing.

In this paper, the point clouds are processed with Geomagic, all the point clouds are selected for best plane fitting. The pseudo-color images and the best fitting plane of the original measurements are shown in Fig. 7(b), we can get that average, standard deviation and maximum of distance between all points and the best fitting plane are 0.242236 mm, 1.827136 mm, and 25.17998 mm respectively (regardless of symbols). The original images are processed with multiple line structured-light stripes extraction algorithm, and 3D points which meet the laser plane constraint are retained. The pseudo-color image and the best fitting plane of the processed measurements are shown in Fig. 7(c). We can get that average, standard deviation and maximum of distance between all points and the best fitting plane are 0.005889 mm, 0.228942 mm, and 6.538318 mm respectively (regardless of symbols). After the best fitting plane is computed by Geomagic, the normal vectors and central points of the fitting plane can be obtained. The normal vector and central point of the fitting plane before processing are respectively $(0.024, -0.074, 0.997)$ and $(138.6575, 15.0549, 170.9507)$, and they are respectively $(0.006, 0.01, 1)$ and $(142.0669, -22.3584, 371.4755)$ after processing.

5   Conclusion

Aiming at erroneous points generated by specular reflections, a novel method for eliminating erroneous points is proposed. There are multiple laser stripes in the captured images due to specular reflections, multiple line structured-light stripes extraction algorithm is used to extract all laser stripes in images. The 3D points are computed based on optical-triangulation. These 3D points contain false points and true points, erroneous points are eliminated by applying the laser plane constraint test. By accounting for the proportion of erroneous points, we are able to analysis the performance of the laser plane constraint, and the experimental results show that the percentage of erroneous points is significantly reduced. The experimental results indicate that our method can effectively reduce erroneous points with good feasibility.

Acknowledgment. This research was partially supported by the key research project of Ministry of Science and Technology (Grant No. 2017YFB1301503 and No. 2018YFB1306802) and the National Nature Science Foundation of China (Grant No. 51575332).

References

1. Park, J., DeSouza, G.N.: 3-D modeling of real-world objects using range and intensity images. In: Apolloni, B., Ghosh, A., Alpaslan, F., Patnaik, S. (eds.) Machine learning and robot perception. SCI, pp. 203–264. Springer, Heidelberg (2005). https://doi.org/10.1007/11504634_6

2. Salvi, J., Pages, J., Batlle, J.: Pattern codification strategies in structured light systems. Pattern Recognit. **37**(4), 827–849 (2004)

3. Feng, H.Y., Liu, Y., Xi, F.: Analysis of digitizing errors of a laser scanning system. Precis. Eng. **25**(3), 185–191 (2001)

4. Yang, S., et al.: A dual-platform laser scanner for 3D reconstruction of dental pieces. Engineering **4**(6), 796–805 (2018)

5. Frauel, Y., et al.: Comparison of passive ranging integral imaging and active imaging digital holography for 3D object recognition. Appl. Optics **43**(2), 452–62 (2004)

6. Brenner, C.: Building reconstruction from images and laser scanning. Int. J. Appl. Earth Obs. Geoinf. **6**(3–4), 187–198 (2005)

7. Yoshioka, H., Zhu, J., Tanaka, T.: Automatic segmentation and feature identification of laser scanning point cloud data for reverse engineering. In: 2016 International Symposium on Flexible Automation (ISFA). IEEE (2016)

8. Vukašinović, N., Duhovnik, J.: Optical 3D geometry measurments based on laser triangulation. Advanced CAD Modeling. STME, pp. 191–216. Springer, Cham (2019). https://doi.org/10.1007/978-3-030-02399-7_9

9. Marques, L., Nunes, U., Almeida, A.T.D.: A new 3D optical triangulation sensor for robotics. In: International Workshop on Advanced Motion Control. IEEE (2002)

10. Park, J., Kak, A.C.: Multi-peak range imaging for accurate 3D reconstruction of specular objects. In: 6th Asian Conference on Computer Vision (2004)

11. Park, J., Kak, A.C.: Specularity elimination in range sensing for accurate 3D modeling of specular objects. In: International Symposium on 3D Data Processing (2004)

12. Park, J., Kak, A.: 3D modeling of optically challenging objects. IEEE Trans. Vis. Comput. Graph. **14**(2), 246–262 (2008)

13. Brown, G.M.: Overview of three-dimensional shape measurement using optical methods. Opt. Eng. **39**(1), 10 (2000)

14. Curless, B., et al.: Better optical triangulation through spacetime analysis. In: International Conference on Computer Vision. IEEE (1995)

15. Nayar, S.K., Ikeuchi, K., Kanade, T.: Recovering shape in the presence of interreflections. In: IEEE International Conference on Robotics Automation. IEEE (1991)

16. Clark, J., Trucco, E., Wolff, L.B.: Using light polarization in laser scanning. Image Vis. Comput. **15**(2), 107–117 (1997)

17. Wolff, L.B., Boult, T.E.: Constraining object features using a polarization reflectance model. IEEE Trans. Pattern Anal. Mach. Intell. **7**, 635–657 (1991)

18. Trucco, E., Fisher, R.B.: Acquisition of consistent range data using local calibration. In: IEEE International Conference on Robotics Automation. IEEE (2003)

19. Xu, Z., Tao, Z.: Center detection algorithm and knife plane calibration of flat top line structured light. Acta Photonica Sinica **46**(5), 512001 (2017)

Viewpoint Planning of Robot Measurement System Based on V-REP Platform

Zhonghang Ma[1,3], Xu Zhang[2(✉)], Lin Zhang[3], and Limin Zhu[1]

[1] School of Mechanical Engineering, Shanghai Jiao Tong University,
No. 800 Dongchuan Road, Minhang District, Shanghai 200240, China
[2] School of Mechatronic Engineering and Automation, Shanghai University,
No. 99 Shangda Road, Baoshan District, Shanghai 200444, China
xuzhang@shu.edu.cn
[3] HUST-Wuxi Research Institute,
No. 329 Yanxin Road, Huishan District, Wuxi 214100, China

Abstract. Automated inspection, in the form of robot measurement system, has attracted wide attention in industry. The aim of this paper is to present a new viewpoint planning method that is based on V-REP platform. As the basis of viewpoint planning, we developed a virtual simulation module for simulating scanning area. An improved grid method which is aimed to find the viewpoints on the blade surface based on curvature analysis is proposed. In order to ensure that the scanning area can cover the whole blade surface, an iteration algorithm which can recognize and eliminate the unscanned area based on the virtual simulation module is established. Compared with the existing solutions, our system considers the robot accessibility while viewpoint planning. Finally, we output pseudo-color images compared with the original CAD model based on registration of scanning point clouds. The experimental results show that we have established an effective solution for viewpoint planning of robot measurement system.

Keywords: Viewpoint planning · 3D laser scanning · Virtual simulation · Robot

1 Introduction

As a non-contact measurement technology, 3D laser scanner has attracted wide attention in industry [1]. The accessibility of the 3D laser scanner can be increased dramatically when it is mounted on industrial robots. By comparing the scanning point cloud with the CAD model, the shape detection and quality management of the manufacturing workpieces can be realized [2].

Viewpoint planning is the basis of robot measurement system. At present, some researches have been proposed on viewpoint planning. Lee and Park [3] analyzed the boolean intersections of the visibility cones at sampling points that

© Springer Nature Switzerland AG 2019
H. Yu et al. (Eds.): ICIRA 2019, LNAI 11744, pp. 64–75, 2019.
https://doi.org/10.1007/978-3-030-27541-9_6

were on the free-form shape parts to get the scanning directions and path of the laser scanner. Ding and Dai [4] proposed a planning method based on the visibility of sampling points, which was verified by simulation. Chen and Gao [5] developed a viewpoint planning method considering the self-occlusion of objects.

However, there are still some unsolved problems in the existing systems. The method proposed by Lee and Park needs a large amount of computation to search all the sampling points on the surface and do the boolean intersection, which is not suitable for medium and large workpieces. The existing systems can not simulate the actual scanning area that is generated by the laser scanner accurately, which means the scanning results of high quality can only be obtained after the actual scan.

This paper is concerned with these problems and we want to solve them in a new way by focusing on the unscanned area. In order to reduce the amount of computation, we used an improved grid method based on curvature analysis to find the potential viewpoints on the surface of the blade. With the help of virtual simulation of scanning area, we can focus on the analysis of unscanned area obtained by comparing the virtual scanning result with the CAD model. The iteration of viewpoint planning would be executed for the unscanned area until the viewpoint planning scanning area can completely cover the target workpiece. Furthermore, we consider the constraint of robot accessibility in viewpoint planning. The experimental results show that we have established an effective solution for viewpoint planning of robot measurement system.

2   Virtual Simulation of Scanning Area

Virtual simulation of scanning area is the basis of viewpoint planning method that will be introduced in Sect. 3. Virtual simulation is an important way to judge the quality of viewpoint planning before actual scan. Therefore, virtual simulation of scanning area is of great significance.

2.1   The Principle of Virtual Simulation

We propose a concise but effective method to realize the virtual simulation. First, we choose the vision sensor in perspective projection-type in V-REP (Virtual Robot Experimentation Platform) to simulate laser beam. V-REP, with comprehensive development environment, is a robot simulator developed by Coppelia Robotics GmbH. The vision sensor in V-REP can extract the coordinates of renderable entities which are in its field of view [6]. The vision sensor is mounted on a joint to simulate the rotation of the actual laser beam. According to the measurement of the actual laser scanner, we limit the rotation angle of the visual sensor, so as to ensure that the visual simulation area is in the field of view of the real laser scanner. In order to simulate the intersection of laser beam plane and workpiece surface, we set the resolution in Y-direction of the vision sensor is 1 unit, which is shown in Fig. 1.

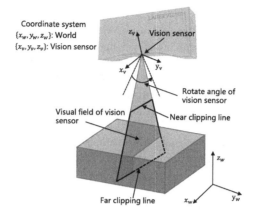

Fig. 1. Principle of the virtual simulation of scanning area.

Then we establish the vision sensor coordinate system $V = \{x_v, y_v, z_v\}$ and the world coordinate system $W = \{x_w, y_w, z_w\}$. Using the coordinates extracted from vision sensor, we add drawing items on the workpiece surface to simulate scanning area. The library function simGetObjectMatrix() in V-REP can obtain transformation matrix of specified object and simAddDrawingObjectItem() can add points at specified locations [7]. Coordinates of points detected by vision sensor are defined as $^v\mathbf{P} = \begin{bmatrix} x_v & y_v & z_v \end{bmatrix}^T$. The transformation matrix of vision sensor relative to world reference frame is defined as $^v_w\mathbf{T}$. The coordinates of added points are defined as $^w\mathbf{P} = \begin{bmatrix} x_w & y_w & z_w \end{bmatrix}^T$ and the relations among them can be introduced as Eq. (1).

$$
\begin{bmatrix} x_w \\ y_w \\ z_w \\ 1 \end{bmatrix} = \begin{bmatrix} ^w\mathbf{P} \\ 1 \end{bmatrix} = \begin{bmatrix} \mathbf{R} & \mathbf{T} \\ 0 & 1 \end{bmatrix} \begin{bmatrix} x_v \\ y_v \\ z_v \\ 1 \end{bmatrix} = {}^v_w\mathbf{T} \cdot \begin{bmatrix} ^v\mathbf{P} \\ 1 \end{bmatrix} \tag{1}
$$

where $\mathbf{R}$ is a orthogonal unit matrix and $\mathbf{T}$ is a three-dimensional translation vector. The result of virtual simulation is shown as Fig. 2. The area consisting of blue points on the turbine blade in Fig. 2 is the simulated scanning area.

2.2 Experimental Verification of Virtual Simulation

In order to compare the difference between virtual scanning results and actual scanning results, we import both the virtual scanning point clouds and the actual scanning point clouds into V-REP. First, the actual laser scanner would scan one side of the turbine blade. Then, the CAD model of turbine blade would be assigned with the actual point cloud that is transformed into V-REP. The visual comparison shows that the virtual simulation of scanning area matches with the real situation. The experimental results are shown as Fig. 3.

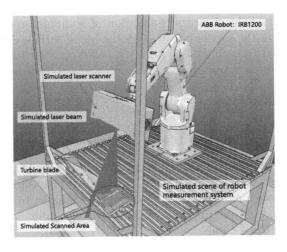

Fig. 2. Virtual simulation of scanning area on the workpiece.

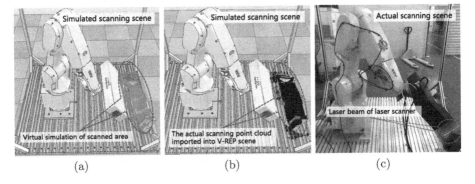

Fig. 3. The results of experimental verification. (a) The simulated point cloud. (b) The actual scanning point cloud. (c) The actual scanning situation.

3 Viewpoint Planning Based on Grid Method, Virtual Simulation and Robot Accessibility

For the problem of viewpoint planning, we divide it into three parts to solve it:

Step 1: We propose an improved grid method based on curvature analysis to find potential viewpoints on surfaces. The intersections of grid points and surface are the corresponding points of viewpoints on surface. Using grid method to find potential viewpoints can save a large amount of computation without analyzing the visibility of each point. However, the viewpoints found by grid method may not cover all of the surface and may not satisfy the accessibility of robot.

Step 2: We propose a robot path planning method to screen the viewpoints found by step 1 that satisfy the reachability of robot.

Step 3: With the help of virtual simulation of scanning area, we propose a method to recognize the unscanned area on the blade surface. Unscanned area would be recognized and scanned by iteration based on Step 1 and Step 2 until the viewpoint planning scanning area can cover the whole surface of the target workpiece.

This section will introduce the above three parts in proper order.

3.1   Improved Grid Method Based on Curvature Analysis

Curvature, as an important feature of surface, is widely used in surface feature recognition and free surface segmentation [8]. Usually, the basis of feature recognition and surface segmentation is the point cloud obtained from laser scanner [9]. We believe that considering the curvature in viewpoint planning will be helpful to improve the scanning quality.

First, we do the uniform sampling of the mesh object in STL format to generate point cloud object by PCL (Point Cloud Library). Then, we calculate the curvatures of all the points in the point cloud only by the coordinate information. The quadric surface of these fitting data points is shown as Eq. (2).

$$r(u, v) = \sum_{j=0}^{2} \sum_{i=0}^{2} Q_{ij} u^i v^j \tag{2}$$

According to the two-parameter mean cumulative chord length method and the least square principle [10], Eq. (2) can be solved. The unit normal vector of p_0 can be represented as Eq. (3).

$$\mathbf{n} = \frac{\mathbf{r}_u \times \mathbf{r}_v}{|\mathbf{r}_u \times \mathbf{r}_v|} \tag{3}$$

According to the first fundamental form and the second fundamental form of the surface, the Gaussian curvature K and the average curvature H can be solved. The principal curvatures k_1 and k_2 can be calculated from Gaussian curvature and the average curvature, which are shown as Eq. (4).

$$k_1 = H - \sqrt{H^2 - K}$$
$$k_2 = H + \sqrt{H^2 - K} \tag{4}$$

According to the definition by Chen [11], this paper use the equation below to represent the curvature information of each point in point cloud:

$$S(p_i) = \frac{1}{2} - \frac{1}{\pi} \arctan \frac{k_1(p_i) + k_2(p_i)}{k_1(p_i) - k_2(p_i)} \tag{5}$$

We classify all points in the point cloud into three categories according to the size of $S(p_i)$. The red points in Fig. 4 represent the points of which the $S(p_i)$ is 0.6–1, the yellow points represent the points of which the $S(p_i)$ is 0.3–0.6 and the blue points represent the points of which the $S(p_i)$ is 0–0.3.

Next, we establish the OBB (oriented bounding box) of the blade at the origin of the world coordinate system. Then, we build grids of different sizes based on the value of $S(p_i)$ to divide the OBB. The sizes of the grids are defined as x_{size}, y_{size} and z_{size}. The y_{size} and z_{size} are defined based on the size of FOV (field of view) of the laser scanner. In order to avoid that the number of intersection points between the grid and the blade is too small, the value of x_{size} should be as small as possible. The specific parameters of the grids are shown as Table 1. We construct the octree object and the K nearest search to find the neighbor points of the grid points in point clouds of blade. The principle of the grid method is shown as Fig. 4.

Table 1. The parameters of the grid.

Categories of point clouds	Range of $S(p_i)$	Size of the grid (m)		
		x_{size}	y_{size}	z_{size}
Point cloud A	0–0.3	0.0001	0.15	0.15
Point cloud B	0.3–0.6	0.0001	0.05	0.05
Point cloud C	0.6–1	0.0001	0.03	0.03

In this way, the computing result of the point which represents the intersection is not unique. To solve this problem, we propose an algorithm for neighbor point elimination. First, we put the points found by the grid method into another point cloud $\mathbf{P}_{original}$. Simultaneously, an array is set up to store the index of points in $\mathbf{P}_{original}$ in order. We traverse the array to analyze each point $p_i^{original}$ in $\mathbf{P}_{original}$ and delete every point within 0.5 mm radius around $p_i^{original}$. The remaining points in $\mathbf{P}_{original}$ are the required viewpoints. The algorithm of neighbor point elimination is shown as Algorithm 1.

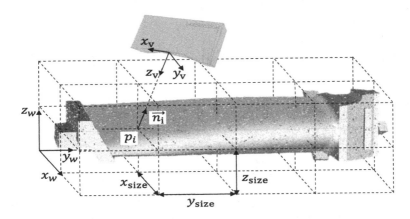

Fig. 4. The principle of improved grid method based on curvature analysis. (Color figure online)

Next, we calculate the unit normal vector $\mathbf{n}_i$ of the potential viewpoints we found according to Eq. (3). The coordinate system $V = \{x_\mathrm{v}, y_\mathrm{v}, z_\mathrm{v}\}$ which represents the pose of laser scanner is placed 700 mm offset in the normal vector direction based on the theory of visibility cone [12]. The algorithm flow chart of improved grid method is shown as Fig. 5.

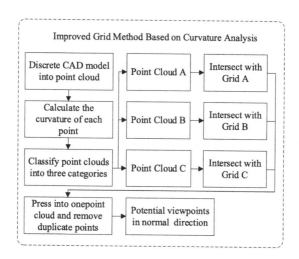

Fig. 5. The algorithm flow chart of improved grid method based on curvature analysis.

Algorithm 1. The algorithm of neighbor point elimination.

Input: The point cloud $\mathbf{P}_{original}$ constructed by grid method;
Output: The point cloud $\mathbf{P}_{viewpoints}$ which represents the viewpoints;
1: **for** each point $p_i^{original}$ in $\mathbf{P}_{original}$ **do**
2:    $Array[i] \leftarrow i$;
3: **end for**
4: **for** $i = 1; i < sizeof(\mathbf{P}_{original}); i++$; **do**
5:    **if** $Array[i] > 0$ **then**
6:       $\mathbf{P}_{viewpoints} \leftarrow p_{Array[i]}^{original}$;
7:       find all j such that $p_j^{original}$ is within $0.5mm$ around $p_i^{original}$;
8:       $Array[j] \leftarrow -1$;
9:    **end if**
10: **end for**
11: **return** $\mathbf{P}_{viewpoints}$;

3.2 Screening Viewpoints Based on Path Planning

The simulated robot control system is designed to do the path planning according to the locations and poses of potential viewpoints that are generated in Sect. 3.1.

After importing the CAD model of the entire robot measurement system in V-REP, we establish the collision pairs for path planning which are consisted of robot body and environment. After inputting the poses of viewpoints, the joint configurations which match the desired pose and does not collide would be searched firstly. After finding the suitable joint configurations, we use the rapidly-expanding random trees (RRT) to search the collision-free path between the start joint configuration and goal joint configurations. The viewpoints with collision-free path would be screened out.

3.3   Recognition and Elimination of Unscanned Area

Based on the viewpoints generated in Sect. 3.2, the scanning area would be generated with the help of virtual simulation module that is introduced in Sect. 2. We put the points that are generated by virtual scanning into point cloud $\mathbf{P}_{virtual}$. Simultaneously, we put the points that are generated by uniform sampling of the CAD model into point cloud $\mathbf{P}_{CAD}$. For each point $p_i{}^{virtual}$ in $\mathbf{P}_{virtual}$, we do Kd-tree radius search to find its neighbor point p_j^{CAD} in $\mathbf{P}_{CAD}$. For all the neighbor point p_j^{CAD}, we delete them from $\mathbf{P}_{CAD}$ to generate a new point cloud $\mathbf{P}_{unscanned}$ to represent the unscanned area on the blade surface. Then, the iterative algorithm will repeat the operations mentioned in Sects. 3.1–3.3 until the virtual scanning area completely covers the blade surface. The algorithm flow chart of recognition and elimination of unscanned area is shown as Fig. 6.

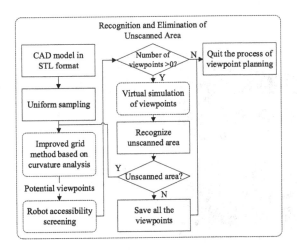

Fig. 6. The algorithm flow chart of recognition and elimination of unscanned area.

3.4   Results of Viewpoint Planning

For one side of the turbine blade, the path planning program exits the loop after 3 times of iteration in 135 s. The virtual scanning area and potential viewpoints generated by the improved grid method from each time of iteration are shown as Fig. 7. The numbers of potential viewpoints and useful viewpoints are also marked in Fig. 7. The red area in Fig. 7 is the unscanned area that is 10.61% of one side of the blade. The remaining unscanned area can not be scanned due to the constraint of robot accessibility. The results of viewpoint planning have verified the effectiveness of the iteration method in recognizing and eliminating the unscanned area.

4   Experiments

4.1   Robot Measurement System

The actual scanning test is carried out on the robot measurement system. The robot measurement system consists of binocular laser scanner, ABB IRB1200 robot and aluminum profile bracket, which is shown in Fig. 8. First, we construct the communication between C++ client and V-REP based on Remote Api of V-REP [13]. The C++ client is the control center and relay station of the robot measurement system. The collision-free path based on viewpoint planning would be solved by V-REP. The calculated paths in the form of joint rotation angles of the robot would be sent to real robot through C++ client.

4.2   Experimental Results

First, we scan one side of the blade. Then, we scan the other side of the blade. For each side of the blade, we use the results of robot hand-eye calibration to

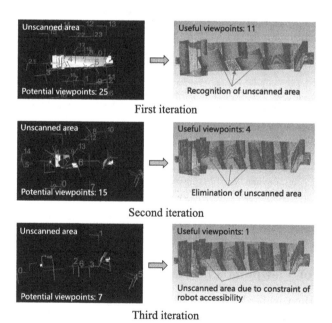

Fig. 7. The results of viewpoint planning. (Color figure online)

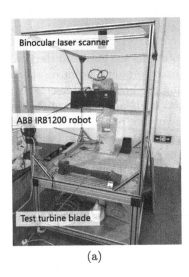
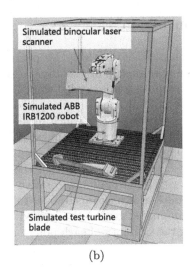

(a)   (b)

Fig. 8. The robot measurement system. (a) The actual robot measurement system. (b) The simulated robot measurement system.

do the course registration of scanning point clouds. The precise registration of point clouds could be realized by the Iterative Closest Point (ICP) method [14]. These two point clouds after precise registration that are from two sides of the turbine blade would align with the CAD model in BestFit way with the help of Polyworks. The experimental result of the registration and the pseudo-color image which represents the mismatching tolerance are shown as Fig. 9.

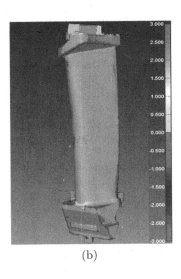

(a)   (b)

Fig. 9. (a) The scanning point clouds after registration. (b) The pseudo-color image of scanning point clouds.

5   Conclusion

At present, most of the viewpoint planning solutions are based on the analysis of positional relationship of visibility cones at each sampling point on the surface. A lot of computation is needed while analyzing the boolean intersections of visibility cones. Simultaneously, the problem of accurate simulation of the scanning area has not been solved, which means the scanning results of high quality can only be obtained after the actual scan.

This paper presents a virtual simulation module that can simulate the scanning area on the blade surface in the form of point clouds. On this basis, we develop a viewpoint planning iterative algorithm based on improved grid method and recognition of unscanned area. In order to reduce the amount of computation, the improved grid method based on curvature analysis is proposed without analyzing the visibility of each point on the blade. Furthermore, we consider the constraint of robot accessibility in viewpoint planning. The experimental results show that we have established an effective solution for viewpoint planning of robot measurement system.

Acknowledgements. This research was partially supported by the key research project of Ministry of Science and Technology (Grant No. 2017YFB1301503 and No. 2018YFB1306802) and the National Nature Science Foundation of China (Grant No. 51575332).

References

1. Phan, N.D.M., Quinsat, Y., Lavernhe, S., et al.: Scanner path planning with the control of overlap for part inspection with an industrial robot. Int. J. Adv. Manuf. Technol. **98**, 629–643 (2018)
2. Dumitrache, A., Borangiu, T., Răileanu, S.: Robotic 3D surface laser scanning for feature-based quality control in holonic manufacturing. In: Rodić, A., Borangiu, T. (eds.) RAAD 2016. AISC, vol. 540, pp. 67–79. Springer, Cham (2017). https://doi.org/10.1007/978-3-319-49058-8_8
3. Lee, K.H., Park, H.P.: Automated inspection planning of free-form shape parts by laser scanning. Robot. Comput. Integr. Manuf. **16**(4), 201–210 (2000)
4. Ding, L.J., Dai, S.G., Mu, P.A.: CAD-based path planning for 3D laser scanning of complex surface. Procedia Comput. Sci. **92**, 526–535 (2016)
5. Chen, T.F., Gao, C.H., He, B.W.: View planning in line laser measurement for self-occlusion objects. China Mech. Eng. **23**(24), 1370–1376 (2016)
6. Freese, M., Singh, S., Ozaki, F., Matsuhira, N.: Virtual robot experimentation platform V-REP: a versatile 3D robot simulator. In: Ando, N., Balakirsky, S., Hemker, T., Reggiani, M., von Stryk, O. (eds.) SIMPAR 2010. LNCS (LNAI), vol. 6472, pp. 51–62. Springer, Heidelberg (2010). https://doi.org/10.1007/978-3-642-17319-6_8
7. Coppelia Robotics GmbH.: Virtual robot experimentation platform user manual. http://www.coppeliarobotics.com/helpFiles/index.html
8. Andrade, D., Vyas, V., Shimada, K.: Automatic generation of anisotropic patterns of geometric features for industrial design. J. Mech. Des. **138**(2), 021403 (2016)

9. Dimitrov, A., Golparvar-Fard, M.: Segmentation of building point cloud models including detailed architectural/structural features and MEP systems. Autom. Constr. **51**, 32–45 (2015)
10. Wang, R.: The research on industrial robot and three dimension scanning applied technology for 3D printing. Dalian University of Technology, Dalian (2018)
11. Chen, H., Bhanu, B.: 3D free-from object recognition in range images using local surface patches. Pattern Recognit. Lett. **28**(10), 1252–1262 (2007)
12. Wu, Q., Zou, W., Xu, D.: Viewpoint planning for freeform surface inspection using plane structured light scanners. Int. J. Autom. Comput. **13**(1), 42–52 (2016)
13. Zhang, L., Zhang, X.: Scattered parts for robot bin-picking based on the universal V-REP platform. In: Wang, K., Wang, Y., Strandhagen, J.O., Yu, T. (eds.) IWAMA 2018. LNEE, vol. 484, pp. 168–175. Springer, Singapore (2019). https://doi.org/10.1007/978-981-13-2375-1_22
14. Tian, H., Yang, P., Su, C., Dong, Z.: ICP registration technology based on the coordinate system direction fit. Int. J. Secur. Appl. **9**(12), 47–56 (2015)

Research on Measurement and Deformation of Flexible Wing Flapping Parameters

Jie Yuan[1], Chao Wang[1,2], Peng Xie[1], and Chaoying Zhou[1(✉)]

[1] Harbin Institute of Technology, Shenzhen 518055, China
cyzhou@hit.edu.cn
[2] Dongguan University of Technology, Dongguan 523000, China

Abstract. In order to study the flexible deformation process of the micro flapping wing during its fluttering, the dynamic three-dimensional reconstruction of the wings is carried out by the RealSense SR300 depth camera. The wing flapping parameters is measured and the deformation of different wings flapping are analyzed. The results show that the wing deformation of the large flexible wing is irregularly adaptive during the flapping process, and it has a larger amount of arch deformation, and the asymmetry of the flexible deformation of the wings on both sides is greater than that of the small flexible wing.

Keywords: Micro flapping wing · Flexible wing · RealSense ·
Three-dimensional reconstruction

1 Introduction

The wing flexibility is an important feature of the miniature bionic flapping wing, it is represented by light, thin and dynamic flutter. A large number of numerical calculations and experimental studies show that the flexible wing has better kinematics and aerodynamic characteristics [1–4]. However, the exact correlation between the flexible deformation of the wing and the flight performance of the flapping wing is still unclear. The mechanism of the influence of the flexible wing structure, the flutter trajectory parameters and the wing deformation parameters on the aerodynamic characteristics of the flapping wing is not fully understood. In order to study the flutter parameters and flexible deformation of wings, researchers at home and abroad have done a lot of work. Wang et al. [5] used the comb-grating stripe projection method to monitor the attitude of the dragonfly in the case of forward flight and cornering flight, and measured the attitude parameters such as the flapping frequency, flapping angle, angle of attack, and wing bending deformation of the dragonfly during free flight moment, the kinematics performance of the forward flight and the turning flight was analyzed and compared. Dong et al. [6, 7] made specialized marking on wings of living dragonflies, using the three orthogonally distributed high-speed CCD cameras to monitor the free flying dragonflies. The trajectory tracking of flying dragonflies, wing kinematics parameter extraction and wing deformation measurement are realized through feature marking matching and three-dimensional reconstruction. Wang et al. [8] used the structured light projection and fringe analysis method to study the motion mechanism of bionic wing in the flapping process, analyzed the dynamic deformation of the airfoil, and

H. Yu et al. (Eds.): ICIRA 2019, LNAI 11744, pp. 76–84, 2019.
https://doi.org/10.1007/978-3-030-27541-9_7

reconstructed the wing surface during up-flapping and down-flapping process. Gao et al. [9] studied the motion characteristics of the dragonfly in climbing flight, the feature points were marked on the surface of the living dragonfly wing, and two high-speed cameras with orthogonal optical axes were used to record the airfoil features during the climbing flight. The airfoil surface was reconstructed by matching the feature points and three-dimensional reconstruction, the motion parameters of the dragonfly in climbing flight are obtained. It is found that increasing the flutter frequency, reducing the front and rear wing phase difference and increasing the flapping angle would help to achieve a higher rate of climbing. Li et al. [10] reconstructed the three-dimensional shape of the robotic bird's wing in the stable fluttering process by high-speed and high-resolution digital grating projection method, which combines the advantages of phase shifting techniques and Fourier transform method. At an acquisition speed of 5000 Hz, the high-quality topological 3D reconstruction of the flapping flight process was successfully carried out, and the wing flapping frequency was as high as 21 Hz.

At present, there are mainly two methods for monitoring the wing motion parameters. One is based on structured light projection and fringe analysis, and the other is multi-camera measurement based on feature point matching and three-dimensional reconstruction. Both methods can realize the monitoring of dynamic airfoil shape, but the multi-camera 3D reconstruction method based on feature point matching only accurately measures the coordinate values at the feature points, and other three-dimensional coordinate values of non-feature points are generated by fitting, which limits the precise analysis of the three-dimensional shape of the wings. Further research has many problems to be improved and solved, including limited field of view measurement, high-speed high-frame rate cameras and their data acquisition equipment are expensive. In this paper, the mainstream depth camera on the market is used to reconstruct the three-dimensional shape during the flapping process, and then the flapping parameters are obtained. The deformation of the wing arch is measured and the deformation process of different flexible wings is compared and analyzed.

2 RealSense SR300 Depth Camera

RealSense is a serial production of intelligent depth cameras produced by Intel. It adopts infrared structure light projection measurement principle, which can simultaneously acquire color image stream and depth image stream in the field of view. It is suitable for dynamic monitoring, 3D reconstruction, etc., RealSense SR300 depth camera shows in Fig. 1. The RealSense SR300 depth camera is mainly composed of Infra-red Laser Projector, Infra-red Camera Sensor and Color Camera Sensor. It supports up to 1920×1080 pixels, 30fps color images and 640×480 pixels, 60fps depth image, the depth measurement range is 0.2 m to 2 m.

The Librealsense open source library is an IO library for obtaining RealSense image data. The Librealsense open source library is used to obtain the depth image and color image of the RealSense camera in this paper. The data acquisition process is shown in Fig. 2.

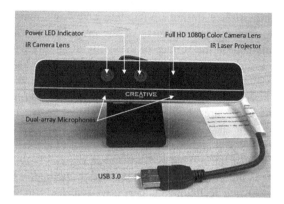

Fig. 1. RealSense SR300 depth camera.

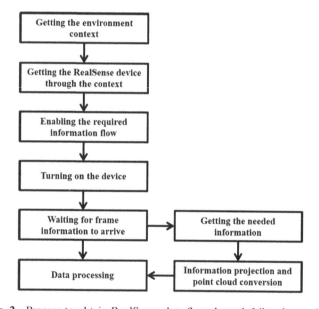

Fig. 2. Process to obtain RealSense data flow through Librealsense [11]

The Context and RealSense devices can be obtained by creating a context for managing the RealSense device. After acquiring the device, enabling the required color information flow and depth information flow, enabling the RealSense device and waiting for each frame of information to arrive. After the image frame information is ready, the corresponding stream information will be obtained, the color information and the inter-sensor information conversion function of the color sensor and the infrared sensor of the current device are used to complete the projection process of the color information and the depth information, then saving the data [11].

3 Three-Dimensional Shape Measurement and Flexible Deformation Analysis

3.1 Three-Dimensional Shape Measurement

Through the Visual Studio integrated development environment, the target program code is written in C ++, and the RealSense SR300 depth camera is used to obtain continuous color image data stream and depth image data stream of the micro flapping wings. At the flutter frequency of 3.2 Hz, the dynamic three-dimensional shape measurement of the red wing and the pink wing was reconstructed respectively. The two wing wings are identical in size, but the materials are different and the flexibility is also different. Figure 3 shows the experimental scene, and Fig. 4(a) and (b) respectively shows the acquired enhanced two-frame depth image of red wing and pink wing.

(a) Red wing   (b) Pink wing

Fig. 3. Experimental scene (color figure online)

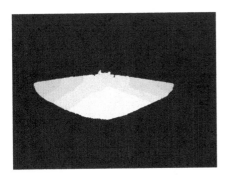
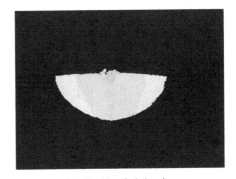

(a) Depth of red wing   (b) Depth of pink wing

Fig. 4. Depth image

3.2   Arch Deformation Analysis of Flexible Wings

Dong et al. [6] proposed the ratio of the deformation of the wing arch to the chord length to represent the deformation of the wing arch, $k = h_{max}/c_k$, as shown in Fig. 5. Where S_k is the wing section curve, k is the arch deformation coefficient of wing, h_{max} is the maximum arch deformation, c_k is the chord length, and α_k is the flapping angle.

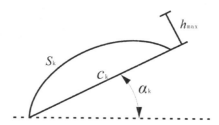

Fig. 5. Arch deformation of wing

According to the parameters defined by Dong, the deformation amount and deformation coefficient of the red wing and the pink wing were measured and shown in Fig. 6. Figure 6(a) is a reconstructed three-dimensional shape of the red wing in its up-flapping moment, Fig. 6(b) is the correspondingly span-wise section curve of the wing. The wing flap is within the lower flap angle range, flapping from bottom to top. According to the obtained section curve data, the wing arch deformation coefficient is calculated for the left and right wings. The results show the maximum arch deformation of the left wing is $h_{lmax\_red} = 5.5140$ mm, and the arch deformation coefficient is $k_{l\_red} = 0.0325$. The maximum arch deformation of the right wing is $h_{rmax\_red} = 7.7047$ mm, and the arch deformation coefficient $k_{r\_red} = 0.0515$.

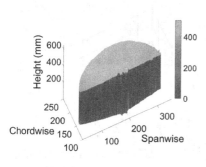

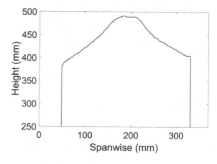

(a) Three-dimensional shape

(b) Span-wise cross-section curve

Fig. 6. Three-dimensional shape and cross-section curve of red wing (color figure online)

The measurement results show that the deformation coefficients of the left- and right-wing arches are different, and the deformation of the left wing is smaller than that of the right wing. This indicates that the wings are asymmetrical during the flapping, and the asymmetrical flutter will cause larger lateral force and lateral force moments.

Figure 7 shows the results of pink wing where the Fig. 7(a) is a reconstructed three-dimensional shape of the pink wing in its up-flapping moment, and Fig. 7(b) is the correspondingly span-wise section curve of the wing. Calculating the deformation coefficient of the wing arch of the left and right wings of the pink wings. The results show the maximum arch deformation of the left wing is $h_{lmax\_pink} = 4.3720$ mm, and the arch deformation coefficient is $k_{l\_pink} = 0.0271$. The maximum arch deformation of the right wing is $h_{rmax\_pink} = 3.8669$, and the arch deformation coefficient $k_{r\_pink} = 0.0249$.

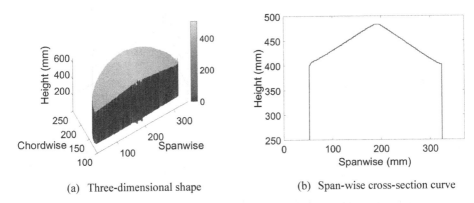

(a) Three-dimensional shape   (b) Span-wise cross-section curve

Fig. 7. Three-dimensional shape and cross-section curve of pink wing (color figure online)

The maximum arch deformation of the wings on the left and right sides of the pink wings is relatively close, which indicates that the deformation of the wings on both sides is more balanced and symmetrical during the flapping process. The pink wing has a smaller deformation coefficient than the red wing, and the pink wing is less flexible than the red wing.

3.3   Analysis of Different Span-Wise Cross-section Flapping Angles

Figure 8(a) is a reconstructed three-dimensional shape of the pink wing, and Fig. 8(b) is the front, middle and rear span-wise cross-section curves. Because of the flexible deformation of the wings, the front, middle and rear cross-section curves do not overlap. The highest points of the front, middle and rear cross-section curve are 480 mm, 483 mm and 489 mm, respectively. The wings show a generally trend of lower before and higher behind.

By fitting the span-wise cross-section curve data of one side wing, the flapping angles of the front, middle and rear positions can be obtained. After calculation, the front section flapping angle is $-30.88°$, the middle section flapping angle is $-31.08°$, and the rear section flapping angle is $-30.12°$. The data indicates that the intermediate section flapping angle is larger than the front and rear section flapping angle. This is because the fixed position of the wings are at the front and rear position of the central axis, resulting in a small deformation of the front section and the rear section wing nearing the fixed point. The middle section wing is away from the fixed point so that having a larger flexible deformation, and the absolute value of the middle section flapping angle is larger.

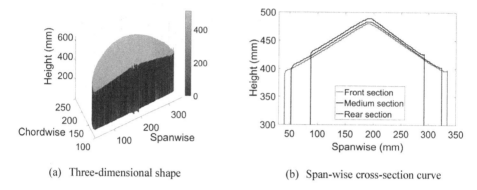

(a) Three-dimensional shape   (b) Span-wise cross-section curve

Fig. 8. Three-dimensional shape and multiple cross-section curve of pink wing (color figure online)

3.4   Comparative Analysis of Flexible Wing Flapping Process

Figure 9 is a comparison of the cycle flapping process of the red wing and the pink wing. Figure 9(a) shows the reconstructed three-dimensional shape of the five phases of the red wing in one flapping cycle, and Fig. 9(c) is a corresponding two-dimensional projection. Figure 9(b) is a reconstructed three-dimensional shape of five phases of a pink wing in a flapping cycle, Fig. 9(d) corresponds to a two-dimensional projection. Figure 9(e) and 9(f) are the span-wise middle cross-section curves of the red wing and the pink wing respectively, including 5 phases in the cycle.

Comparing Fig. 9(a) red wing with Fig. 9(b) pink wing reconstructed three-dimensional shape, it can be found that the red wing surface is not flat, the greater flexibility makes the red wing a bigger deformation than the pink wing. From Fig. 9(c) red wing and Fig. 9(d) pink wing two-dimensional projection, it can be found that the projection of the pink wing in each phase is uniform and closer to the original unde-formed wing profile, however the red wing has a significant deformation in the profile due to its greater flexibility. Comparing Fig. 9(e) red wing an Fig. 9(f) pink wing span-wise cross-section curve, it can be found that the red wing section curve is more curved, and the deformation of the wing is irregular near the upper limit flapping angle in the case of self-adaptation, the wings on the left and right sides have a certain asymmetry. The span-wise cross-section curve of the pink wing is more linear, and the wings on the left and right sides also have an asymmetry to some degree.

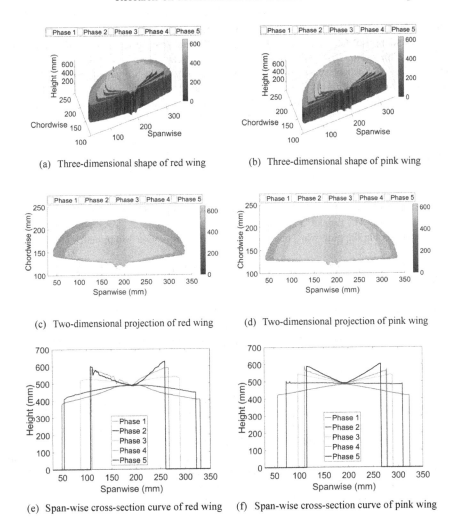

(a) Three-dimensional shape of red wing   (b) Three-dimensional shape of pink wing

(c) Two-dimensional projection of red wing   (d) Two-dimensional projection of pink wing

(e) Span-wise cross-section curve of red wing   (f) Span-wise cross-section curve of pink wing

Fig. 9. Comparison of flexible wing deformation process (color figure online)

4 Conclusion

This paper proposes a new method for measuring the three-dimensional shape of wings using the RealSense depth camera. It is suitable for studying low-frequency bionic flapping wings or insect and birds, such as butterflies, which has good application value. The degree of deformation of the wings of the miniature flapping wing aircraft is closely related to the flexibility of the wings. Experimental studies have found that there is asymmetry in the flexible deformation of the wings on both sides, and the flapping deformation of the large flexible wings exhibits an irregular self-adaptive situation. The red wing is more flexible than the pink ones, thus getting a bigger deformation, and the experimental measurements are consistent with the actual situation.

Acknowledgement. The work described in this paper was supported by the National Natural Science Foundation of China (No. U1613227), the Natural Science Foundation of Guangdong Province of China (No. 2018A030310045), the Basic Research Program of Science and Technology Project of Shenzhen (No. JCYJ20170307151117299), the China Postdoctoral Science Foundation (No. 2018M641828), the DGUT innovation center of robotics and intelligent equipment of China (No. KCYCXPT2017006) and the KEY Laboratory of Robotics and Intelligent Equipment of Guangdong Regular Institutions of Higher Education (No.2017KSYS009).

References

1. Tian, F.B., Luo, H.X., Song, J.L., Lu, X.Y.: Force production and asymmetric deformation of a flexible flapping wing in forward flight. J. Fluids Struct. **36**, 149–161 (2013)
2. Nakata, T., Liu, H., Tanaka, Y., Nishihashi, N., Wang, X., Sato, A.: Aerodynamics of a bio-inspired flexible flapping-wing micro air vehicle. Bioinspiration Biomimetics **6**(4), 045002 (2011)
3. Nguyen, Q.-V., Lee, H.: Bio-Inspired flexible flapping wings with elastic deformation. Aerospace **4**(3), 37 (2017)
4. Wang, C., Zhang, R., Xie, P., Zhou, C.: Numerical investigation on aerodynamic performance of flexible hovering wings. Chin. Soc. Mech. **9**, 1–9 (2017). (In Chinese)
5. Wang, H., Zeng, L.J., Liu, H., Yin, C.Y.: Measuring wing kinematics flight trajectory and body attitude during forward flight and turning maneuvers in dragonflies. J. Exp. Biol. **206**, 745–757 (2002)
6. Dong, H., Koehler, C., Liang, Z.X., Wan, H., Gaston, Z.: An integrated analysis of a dragonfly in free flight. In: 40th AIAA Fluid Dynamics Conference and Exhibit (2010)
7. Koehler, C., Liang, Z.X., Gaston, Z., Wan, H., Dong, H.: 3D reconstruction and analysis of wing deformation in free-flying dragonflies. J. Exp. Biol. **215**, 3018–3027 (2012)
8. Wang, X.H., Zhang, Q.C.: Three-dimensional shape and deformation measurement of flapping-wing micro air vehicle. J. Opt. **33**, 99–105 (2013). (In Chinese)
9. Gao, Q., Zheng, M.Z., Li, Z.P., Li, Q.S.: Experimental study on flight performance of dragonfly during climbing. J. Beijing Aerosp. Univ. **42**(6), 1271–1278 (2016). (In Chinese)
10. Li, B.W., Zhang, S.: Superfast high-resolution absolute 3D recovery of a stabilized flapping flight process. Opt. Express **25**(22), 27270–27282 (2017)
11. Zhang, L., Jiang, T.L.: Research on 3D object recognition based on RealSense. Inf. Technol. **10**, 78–83 (2017). (In Chinese)

Man-Machine Interactions

Robot Programming Language Based on VB Scripting for Robot Motion Control

Zheng Li[1,2(✉)], Sheng Gao[1,2], Wei Zhang[1,2], and Xiaoyuan Liu[1,2]

[1] State Key Laboratory of Robotics, Shenyang Institute of Automation,
Chinese Academy of Sciences, Shenyang 110016, China
{lizheng,gaosheng,zhangwei,liuxiaoyuan}@sia.cn
[2] Institutes for Robotics and Intelligent Manufacturing,
Chinese Academy of Sciences, Shenyang 110016, China

Abstract. The limitations such as non-universal, interactive blocking and application specificity are common in existing robot programming languages. So, a universal robot programming language based on VB(Visual Basic) scripting language is designed in this paper. The language is aim to achieve the mixed programming of robot instruction and VB scripting language by doing the constructible and interactive design for robot command functions. Finally, a robot language programming motion simulation platform was designed to verify the implementation process of the programming language. Simulation results show the designed robot programming language can realize flexible programming under the Windows platform and further realize complex robot motion control and sensing interaction function, which provides a new way for the practice and extension of robot programming language system.

Keywords: Robot programming language · VB scripting ·
Sensing interaction · Constructible interface

1 Introduction

With the continuous development of robot technology, robot language has also been developed and improved, which has become an important part of robot technology [1]. Robot Programming Language (RPL) combines robot motion and control, which is the starting point of Robot Language system research and the main way to realize the communication between human and Robot [2]. With the diversification of robot operations and the complexity of the operating environment, it is necessary to design more adaptive robot language programming to control the robots and further complete the task by collecting data of multi-purpose sensors and actuators [3]. Therefore, it is particularly important to research and develop a universal robot language system that can sense and interact with robots.

© Springer Nature Switzerland AG 2019
H. Yu et al. (Eds.): ICIRA 2019, LNAI 11744, pp. 87–98, 2019.
https://doi.org/10.1007/978-3-030-27541-9_8

Since the first industrial robot language, WAVE language, was developed by Stanford university in 1973, VAL [4] language, IML language [5] and natural language [6, 7] have been studied successively. Robot language develops in three ways, which are

(1) Produce a new language, such as natural language;
(2) Modify and add some syntax or rules to the computer common language, such as VAL language;
(3) Add a new subroutine to the original computer programming language [8, 9].

Under the guidance of the second design idea, the design of universal robot programming language is carried out in this paper. Considering the universality of VB language and its application in software development [10], we adopt VB scripting, a subset of VB language, as the general programming language for robots. On the Windows platform, the VB scripting function is extended to realize the constructible design of robot programming instructions such as robot motion control instruction and sensor interaction instruction. At the same time, the implementation process of the language is verified experimentally with the robot programming language motion simulation platform designed in this paper. The results show that the motion control, collision interference test and output kinematics data can be realized by programming and scene management.

This paper is organized as follow. Section 2 gives the analysis of Robot programming language. Then, robot programming language is designed in Sect. 3, including design of RPL instruction and constructible design of robot motion control instruction. In Sect. 4, the sensing interaction design of robot programming language is given. Furthermore, the designed robot programming language is performed in the designed platform to verify the implementation process of the language. Finally, Sect. 6 summarizes the work of this paper.

2   Analysis of Robot Programming Language

As a programmable device, the programming language of robot plays a very important role in the whole robot control system [11]. Robot programming language is a kind of programming language between human and robot to record information or exchange information. Through it, programmers can let robots perform a wide range of tasks [12]. For robot off-line programming system, robot language is also a necessary interface to connect the real robot. By combining it with computer graphics technology, we can describe, program and simulate complex motion with high accuracy. At the same time, the complex trajectory and motion parameters can also be optimized [13].

2.1   Robot Programming Language

Robot language system generally requires a robot programming environment and an editor to write robot control program. The control program, also known as program code, can be saved as a separate file or downloaded into the robot controller. Then, the robot language interpreter performs lexical analysis, grammar analysis and semantic analysis, extracts keywords and further executes program logic and instructions. The general flow of robot control by robot language system is shown in Fig. 1.

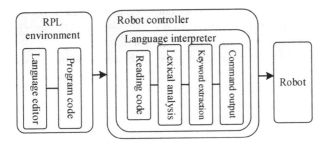

Fig. 1. Control process of robot programming language

At present, according to the level of work description, robot language is usually divided into three levels: action-level language, object-level language and task-level language. Among them the action-level language is the lowest level language that is easy for programming; In addition to the characteristics of action-level language, object-level language also has extensible functions such as sensing information processing, communication and data operation. Most robot companies have realized action-level programming language or object-level programming language, such as VAL3 for Staubli robot and RAPID for ABB robot. However, a true task-level programming language has yet to emerge.

2.2 VB Scripting Language

VB scripting language is a script language developed by Microsoft. It can invoke COM [14] through the host of Windows script, so it is a program library that can be used in the Windows system. Because it is easy to learn and easy to use, VB scripting is widely used in WEB application development and advanced application plug-in library. In the field of industrial automation, it is also widely used in configuration software logical programming technology. The goal of robot language design is to reduce the difficulty of programming while fulfilling the requirements of complex trajectory programming and control, improve the efficiency of off-line programming of the robot, and facilitate the debugging and operation of the robot. Therefore, the robot language does not adopt the idea of high-level program "edit -> compile -> run", but adopts the method of direct interpretation and execution. The advantages of VB scripting for robot language system are as follows:

(1) VB scripting language does not need to compile, so it can be directly interpreted by the interpreter and executed efficiently;
(2) VB scripting has a large number of mathematical functions, operation methods, reference objects and operators. It supports conditions, branches, loops and other common logical programming methods, so it can compile very complex programming logic;

(3) C++ language can be used to invoke its COM conveniently, and realize the interpretation and execution of the language, so it can execute the extended custom API (Application Program Interface).

In this paper, VB scripting and robot language are integrated for mixed programming, namely robot instruction API function is extended in VB scripting language. So, it can realize more extensive robot control functions.

Source programs written by programmers can be sent directly into the VB scripting interpreter engine that is responsible for analyzing syntax and lexical. The interpreter interprets and executes the source program simultaneously, and finally outputs the result. If a syntax error occurs during the interpretation and execution of the entire program, then the syntax error handler [15, 16] is executed. Finally, it executes the source program and outputs the result. The execution process of VB scripting is shown in Fig. 2.

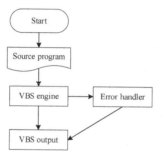

Fig. 2. VB scripting execution process

3   Design of Robot Programming Language

3.1   Design of Robot Programming Language Instruction

Robot programming is the process in which programmers or users program the desired behavior that one or more robots must perform [17]. It combines the structural features of general programming language with the special statement of industrial robots, which is the symbolic description and basis for robots to perform relevant actions. This paper takes robot programming instruction as a programming subset of VB scripting, and forms robot programming language with VB scripting. The specific design idea is shown in Fig. 3. Namely, the added robotic instructions and VB scripting language are fused together to realize mixed programming and control the motion of the robot.

Next, the MOVEL instruction is taken as an example to briefly explain the robotic instruction format customized in this paper. The specific format is shown in Fig. 4. Each robotic instruction is composed of an instruction and an operand, among which, the instruction is composed of English characters, and the operand is the parameter value of the instruction. Each instruction can have multiple operands. Table 1 shows several commonly used robot motion control instructions designed in this paper.

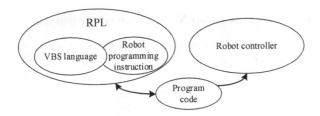

Fig. 3. VB scripting language and robot programming instruction set

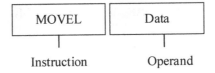

Instruction   Operand

Fig. 4. Robot instructions

Table 1. Robot language motion control instruction sets

Name	Instructions	Operand	Explanation
Motion control instruction	MOVEP	$\theta_1 \sim \theta_6$	Point-to-point movement
	MOVEL	$\theta_1 \sim \theta_6$	Rectilinear motion
	MOVEH	X, Y, Z	Rectilinear motion
	MOVER	Rx, Ry, Rz	Pose motion
	MOVEC	P1, P2	Circular motion
Sensing interactive instruction	IN	Addr	Sensor input
	OUT	Addr, Value	Sensor output

Through by the powerful mathematical and logical programming ability of VB scripting, the paper combines these custom robotic instruction functions to achieve complex control and human-computer interaction functions and so on. Table 2 lists the common control instruction sets supported by VB scripting.

Table 2. VB scripting inherent control instruction sets

Name	Instructions	Explanation
Logical control instruction	Do...Loop	Conditional loop statement
	If...Then...Else	Conditional execution statement
	For...Next	Repeat execution statement
	Select Case	Conditional branching statement
	While...Wend	Conditional loop statement
	On Error	The error handler
Interactive instruction	MsgBox	Output information through the dialog box
	InputBox	Enter information through the dialog box

3.2   Constructible Design of Robot Motion Control Instruction

VB scripting language can only recognize its inherent instructions, robotic motion control instructions and sensing interaction instructions customized in this paper cannot be recognized by VB engine. Therefore, this section further constructs and matches these custom instruction functions. Since VB engine supports custom interface extension, we encapsulate robot related algorithms and execution actions into instruction interface functions and further integrates them into VB scripting language system.

The VB script engine is a COM object that can dynamically execute script code, parse or load script statements directly, and then explicitly invokes the IDispatch interface of the script engine. Figure 5 illustrates the procedure of a host program invokes the script engine COM interface.

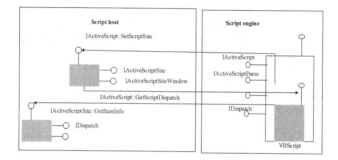

Fig. 5. VB engine and host program interface

COM interface is invoked under Windows and script host program class is written to realize the creation of script engine. The script host program interprets the code through the IActiveScriptParse interface. The designed robotic instructions are mapped to the script engine via the DISPATCH interface, then these instructions can be recognized by VB engine, see Fig. 6.

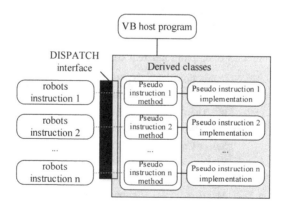

Fig. 6. The method of VB scripting extends robotic instructions

The pseudo instruction of each robot instruction is added to the VB host program that is inherited from the user program, then the specific robot instruction method is implemented in the user inheritance class. DISPATCH interface is used to match the actual robot instruction name with the corresponding pseudo instruction name. When the VB script engine executes a robot instruction defined by user, it will find the corresponding pseudo instruction from the user inheritance class through the DISPATCH interface and invoke its implementation. The robot instruction MOVEL is taken as an example to illustrate and the code is as follows.

The pseudo instruction xMOVEL method in the user class is declared as follows:

```
void xMOVEL(double pos1,double pos2,double pos3,double pos4,double pos5,double pos6);
```

Then, we match the real name of robot instruction MOVEL in its BEGIN_DIS-PATCH_MAP and the code is declared as follows:

```
BEGIN_DISPATCH_MAP(CMyHostProxy, CActiveScriptHost)
//{{AFX_DISPATCH_MAP(CMyHostProxy)
DISP_FUNCTION(CMyHostProxy,  "MOVEL",    xMOVEL,
VT_EMPTY, VTS_R8 VTS_R8 VTS_R8 VTS_R8 VTS_R8 VTS_R8)
//}}AFX_DISPATCH_MAP
END_DISPATCH_MAP()
```

where, CMyHostProxy is user inheritance class and CActiveScriptHost is VB host program class. "xMOVEL" method is the core function to realize the robotic instruction "MOVEL". In this function, the linear interpolation algorithm for robot is implemented to control the robot to make a linear motion from the current position to the target position. It can be seen that this method can be used to construct more robot programming instructions in VB scripting language.

4 Sensing Interaction Design

The robot programming language sensing interaction designed in this paper includes two aspects. One is that the robot can interact with human in the process of executing the codes and let human input information to the robot system or the robot system output information feedback to human. Another is that the robot can interact with the environment in the process of executing the code and obtain the robot sensing information and environmental information, then output it to the robot for execution according to the logic operation of the program. Figure 7 shows the interactive schematic of human, language and robot.

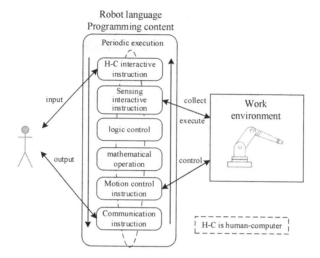

Fig. 7. Sensing interaction principle of human, robot language and robot

4.1 Sensing Interaction Between Robot Language and Environment

The robot needs constant and frequent interaction with the environment, and the change of environment will have a great impact on the behavior of the robot [18]. IN and OUT are sensing and interactive instructions designed for robot to interact with the external environment or sensors. Sensor information can be read through the IN instruction, and the internal execution state of robot language can be output to the robot actuator through the OUT instruction, which can realize the data interaction between the internal world model of robot and the external actual environment. IN and OUT instructions can be developed according to specific situations. In general, communication channels can be established through communication interfaces or drivers of external devices, which can read data of external environment sensor or output internal data to the actuators. Figure 8 shows the schematic diagram of sensing interaction between robot language and environment.

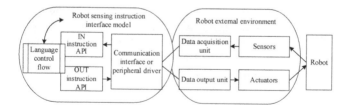

Fig. 8. Interaction interface between robot language and environment

4.2 Sensing Interaction Between Human and Robot Language

As the main body of robot control task, human not only needs to program the task for robot by using robot language, but also needs to interrupt the program, interact with robot. It's necessary to provide the interface for inputting or outputting information for human in the process of executing the program code. VB script provides human-computer interaction instructions such as input dialog box "InpuBox", output message box "MsgBox" and file operation objects, which can be used for inputting and outputting information in the process of executing program code. The constructible interface design that has been studied in Sect. 3.2 can be further used for designing and extending other human-computer interaction instructions.

5 Simulation Experiments

In order to verify the implementation process of the designed robot programming language, PUMA560 robot is taken as the experimental object to carry out the robot language programming task and motion simulation experiment.

5.1 Robot Programming Language Simulation Platform

In this paper, the simulation experiment is carried out on a self-designed robot language programming simulation platform, which is developed by VC++ language and combined with OpenGL technology to realize robot motion control simulation. The platform interface is shown in Fig. 9. On the left is the robot language program editing area for writing robot task codes, at the same time, it can also control the execution of these codes through buttons. On the right is the robot simulation area, which can illustration the execution process of robot language (these codes) in the form of robot motion simulation.

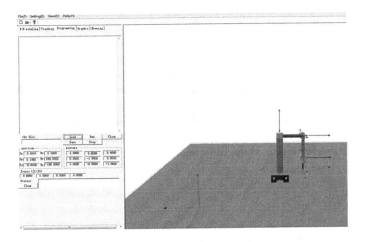

Fig. 9. Simulation platform of RPL

5.2   Motion Control Experiment

In this experiment, MOVEP, MOVEL and MOVEC instructions are input into the program editing area of the software interface respectively. Execute each instruction, and then the robot starts to simulate motion, and shows the execution process of the command through animation. The execution process of motion control instruction is shown in Fig. 10.

movep $15, -27.5, -15, 0, 42.5, 0$ corresponding figure (a);
movel $15, -27.5, -15, 0, 42.5, 0$ corresponding figure (b);
movec $0.53, 0.31, -0.47, 0.63, 0.2, -0.3$ corresponding figure (c).

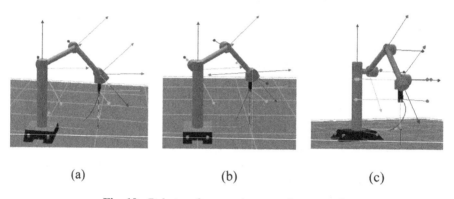

(a)   (b)   (c)

Fig. 10. Robot perform motion control commands

The simulation result shows that VB script executes the robot motion control instruction, that is, VB script engine accepts the custom extended robot control instruction, which verifies the correctness of the robot instruction designed in VB script.

5.3   Integrated Experiment

In this experiment, the designed robot programming language is used to execute human-computer interaction control tasks, which uses the human-computer interaction instruction, robot motion control instruction, VB script control instruction and mathematical operation instruction to carry out comprehensive programming. The corresponding program code is executed, and the execution effect of the code is verified by motion simulation. The following program code is used to control the interaction process of the spiral motion of the robot that is shown in Fig. 11.

```
dim tmp
tmp = inputbox("Master, starting the mission?",
"Input","1")
if tmp=1 then
movep 0,0,0,0,0,0
a=0.2
b=0.2/12.56
for i=0 to 12.56 step 0.01
x=a*cos(i)
y=a*sin(i)
z=b*i
moveh 0.5+x,0.2+y,z-0.4
next
msgbox " Master, mission accomplished!"
end if
```

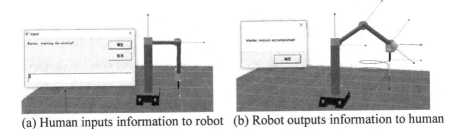

(a) Human inputs information to robot   (b) Robot outputs information to human

Fig. 11. RPL platform comprehensive experiment

It can be seen that the above experiments verify the interaction process between human and robot language. The design purpose of this paper is realized, that is, more complex robot motion control and sensing interaction tasks are realized through the instruction extension based on VB scripting.

6 Conclusions

In this paper, a robot programming language is designed based on VB scripting language, which combines the custom robot instruction and sensing interaction instruction. By means of the powerful logic control and mathematical operation functions of VB scripting, complex robot programming tasks can be performed. It opens up a new way for robot to exchange information with the outside world through robot language system. At the same time, the language can perform complex programming tasks likes

VB, so it is a new object-level robot programming language. Finally, the implementation process is verified with the robot simulation platform by experiments, and the design purpose of this paper is realized. The following research will focus on the network communication extension of the robot language.

References

1. Yang, X., Chen, F.L., Zhou, L.: Design of the industry robot language system based on Qt. Modul. Mach. Tool Autom. Manuf. Tech. **3**, 71–74 (2015)
2. Wang, F.Y., Lv, C.K.: Design and implementation of interpreter for industrial robot. Mach. Manuf. Autom. **3**, 177–180 (2018)
3. Ghazal, M., Haneefa, F., Ali, S., et al.: A framework for teaching robotic control using a novel visual programming language. In: Proceedings of IEEE International Midwest Symposium on Circuits and Systems, pp. 1–4 (2017)
4. Craig, J.J.: Introduction to Robotics Mechanics and Control, 3rd edn. China Machine Press, Beijing (2017)
5. Liu, N.: Application of industrial robot programming language and off-line programming software. Inf. Rec. Mater. **19**(08), 135–136 (2018)
6. Wang, W., Zhao, Q.F., Zhu, T.H.: Research of natural language understanding in human-service robot interaction. Microcomput. Appl. **31**(03), 45–49 (2015)
7. Zhao, Y.J., Xu, X.Z., Zhu, J.D., Zhang, Z.: A method of human-computer interaction with natural language keywords. Appl. Sci. Technol. **43**(06), 1–6 (2016)
8. Zhang, B.K., Ye, F., Zhao, C.Y., Lai, Y.Z.: Study on the lexical and syntactic analyzer for industrial robot language. Mach. Des. Manuf. **1**, 209–212 (2014)
9. Lu, T., Wang, Z., He, G.R., Wang, Y.: Design and implement of new industrial robot language and interpreter. Ind. Control. Comput. **28**(6), 33–34 (2015)
10. Ma, C.Y.: Application of VB programming language in software development. Mod. Inf. Technol. **2**(4), 26–27 (2018)
11. Liu, J.F., Ding, J.B.: Fundamentals of Robot Techniques. Higher Education Press, Beijing (2012)
12. Huang, J., Lau, T., Cakmak, M.: Design and evaluation of a rapid programming system for service robots (2016)
13. Qiu, H.N., Lin, S.G., Ou, Y.X.: Off-line programming simulation system of robotic manipulators. Mach. Tool Hydraul. **43**(21), 28–31 (2015)
14. Zhang, W., Zhang, X.M., Xue, D.J., Bian, X.F.: VB to achieve the COM component containment. Comput. Appl. **21**(10), 99–100 (2001)
15. Huang, S.L.: Script interpreter based on SCADA system. Comput. Digit. Eng. **38**(3), 188–190 (2010)
16. Wang, Z., Ma, X.D.: Design and implementation of industrial robot language interpreter. Ind. Control. Comput. **28**(3), 6–8 (2015)
17. Bravo, F.A., González, A.M., González, E.: A review of intuitive robot programming environments for educational purposes. In: Proceedings of 2017 IEEE 3rd Colombian Conference on Automatic Control (CCAC), Cartagena, pp. 1–6 (2017)
18. Yang, S., Mao, X., Ge, B., et al.: The roadmap and challenges of robot programming languages. In: Proceedings of IEEE International Conference on Systems, pp. 328–333 (2016)

The Effectiveness of EEG-Feedback on Attention in 3D Virtual Environment

Yue Wang[1], Xiaotong Shen[1], Haowen Liu[1], Tiantong Zhou[1],
Sari Merilampi[2], and Ling Zou[1(✉)]

[1] School of Information Science and Engineering,
Changzhou University, Changzhou, Jiangsu, China
zouling@cczu.edu.cn
[2] Faculty of Technology, Satakunta University of Applied Sciences,
Pori, Satakunta, Finland

Abstract. Brain-Computer Interfaces (BCIs) are communication systems capable of establishing an alternative pathway between user's brain activity and a computer system. The most common signal acquisition technology in BCI is the non-invasive electroencephalography (EEG). Virtual Reality (VR) feedback has produced positive results, offering a more compelling experience to the user through 3D environments. The fusion of VR and BCI can provide realistic scenes for biofeedback and enhance the effect of biofeedback. In this paper, the EEG signals are acquired by using self-made 16-channel EEG portable acquisition system, and EEG attention features are extracted through computing the ratio of sensorimotor rhythm and theta wave, which are combined with the virtual reality scene "undersea world". The results of the biofeedback system show this design can effectively reflect the current level of attention of the participants.

Keywords: EEG · Attention · VR · BCI · Biofeedback

1 Introduction

Attention deficit hyperactivity disorder (ADHD) is one of the most common mental illnesses in children [1]. Hyperactivity, impulsivity, and inattention are all its symptoms. Attention is defined as the ability to guide and maintain attention to objects, tasks, or events and to suppress distractions [2], it is an optional mechanism that allows the brain to prioritize relevant information in the task, even if the task has some relevance to the unrelated information [3]. A study found that, to a certain extent, the degree of concentration is related to the brain's ability to process signals and encode information, resulting in influencing learner's performance [4]. Because using self-assessment tools is difficult to measure attention, previous studies took electroencephalography (EEG) as a tool to measure changes [5–7].

Nowadays, the studies on attention involving EEG biofeedback are mainly divided into two types: "Attention Training" and "Attention Monitoring" [8]. "Attention Monitoring" monitors and measures the learner's attention state during the task, and further improves the attention through the feedback provided by the learner's performance.

H. Yu et al. (Eds.): ICIRA 2019, LNAI 11744, pp. 99–107, 2019.
https://doi.org/10.1007/978-3-030-27541-9_9

During the research, EEG equipment is used to monitor and measure attention states and provide learners with different attention feedback signals [9, 10]. The visual system is one of the factors influencing EEG activity and attention [11]. The combination of VR and BCI can not only present realistic EEG signals, but also enhance biofeedback effects.

In order to effectively reflect the current level of attention of the participants, HTC's VIVE head-mounted virtual reality helmet is adopted and "Underwater World" is designed, which is a virtual reality scene of the model, presenting attentional feature information and thus forming EEG-attention feedback system. Through experiments and comparative analysis, we found that the designed system can reflect the attention state of the current subjects, and at the same time, to a certain extent, can improve the concentration of attention of the subjects.

2   Methods

2.1   System Overview

The system design scheme is shown in Fig. 1.

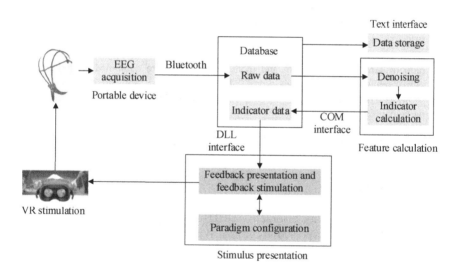

Fig. 1. Overall plan of the system.

Firstly, EEG data is obtained by EEG acquisition module, using the self-made 16-channel portable EEG acquisition device to transmit EEG data to the master computer through a high transmission rate short-range wireless transmission protocol (such as Bluetooth 4.0). The modal data acquisition software then uses the external feature calculation module to denoise and analyze the spectral components, obtain attention-related feature parameters, and create a virtual reality scene "undersea world" to feed back the attention feature parameters. When the attention value is low, the deep sea close-up scene is presented, and the details of the sea bottom scene can be observed. On the contrary, the shallow sea distant scene is presented, and more elements will be observed. Subjects control the height of the lens according to the requirements. When asked to enter the relaxation section, the observer is controlled to slowly enter the shallow sea from the deep sea. When required to be focused, the observer is gradually sinking into the seabed from the shallow sea to obtain quite a sense of silence, so through the human-computer interaction, complete the attention feedback process.

2.2 Self-made 16-Channel Brain Electrical Amplifier Design

The overall design of the system is shown in Fig. 2. The scalp EEG signal of the subject is collected through the electrode, and the original EEG signal is limited and filtered by the signal conditioning circuit. Then it is amplified and analog-digital converted by the analog front-end circuit, and the converted signal is sent to the SD card or the master computer for storage through the main control module [12].

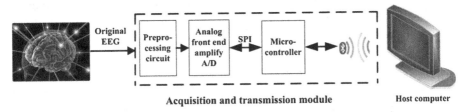

Fig. 2. Schematic diagram of the 16-channel EEG acquisition system

2.3 Participants

We found a total of ten students in college, divided into experimental group and control group. They all met the following conditions: (1) Age is between six and sixty years old and gender is unlimited, (2) Have a normal intellectual condition, (3) There is currently no mental illness and no history of mental illness, (4) I have not received EEG feedback therapy, and I do not know the purpose of this experiment, and (5) There is no abnormality in visual and auditory conditions.

The experiment was terminated when the experimenter's body had significant discomfort or they did not want to continue the experiment.

2.4 Preprocessing

EEG signals were recorded by 16 Ag/AgCl electrodes, according 10/20 systems sites. And they are filtered with a band pass of 0.5–40 Hz, at a sampling rate of 250 Hz. A new approach which combines the WD and ICA methods is approached to detect and remove artifacts. The most important of the proposed method is the introduction of an intermediate step, namely the application of WD to separate, independent components obtained through the extended Informax-ICA [13]. The above steps are compiled into a dynamic link library file (DLL) by MATLAB, imported into visual studio, and directly called by the software.

2.5 Attention Feature Parameter Estimation

This project adopts the power ratio of sensorimotor rhythm (SMR) and θ wave in time window as the characteristic of current attention. When the SMR component is higher, the subject is more nervous and more concentrated. Conversely, if the θ wave occupies the main components, it indicates that the subjects is distracted and less focused.

The SMR band has a frequency range of 12 to 15 Hz; the Theta band has a frequency range of 4 to 8 Hz. Moreover, the power ratio (R) expression of the two can be calculated as attention feedback parameter [14], shown in Eq. (1):

$$R = \frac{\sum_{i=12}^{15} Psmr(i)}{\sum_{i=4}^{8} Ptheta(i)}, i \in N^* \tag{1}$$

Psmr(i) and *Ptheta(i)* respectively represent the power of the SMR wave and the θ wave when the frequency is *i*. After the power ratio is obtained, the ratio is normalized to an integer value between 0 and 100 used in the attention feedback paradigm.

$$atn = MIN + \frac{(MAX - MIN)(R - \min)}{\max - \min} \tag{2}$$

Where $MAX = 100$, $MIN = 0$, the two are regularization upper and lower limits respectively; R is the power ratio calculated by Eq. (1); max and min are empirical constants respectively, decided by calculating a large amount of EEG data, and representing the normal interval of the power ratio. Through the formula (2), the attention is converted into a linear value between MAX and MIN to obtain the final attention index (*atn*).

2.6 EEG Feedback Training

The experimenter opened his eyes and was at rest, getting attention values. The EEG feedback system is used in the laboratory at a fixed time every day, and attention training is performed in the VR submarine scene and the experimental data is saved. The experimenter can participate in the experiment in the way he is accustomed to, each time for 5 min, and the experiment lasts for ten days.

2.7 Schulte Square Experiment

The Schulte square experiment [15] is to draw a 5 × 5 square on a square piece of paper, and then randomly fill in 1 to 25 numbers in the 25 squares. The experimenter then pointed the numbers on the grid from 1 to 25 and recorded the time the experimenter took to complete the process. The shorter time they use, the more concentrated the experimenter's attention is.

The experimental group and the control group were filled with Schulte squares before, after, and one week after the experiment, and the time they used was recorded.

3 Results

3.1 Pre-experiment Status

The average value of the Schulte square test results of the test group students was 27.5, and the average value of the Schulte square test results of the control group students was 26.9. After independent t-test of the experimental and control data, it was found that there was no significant difference between the two groups (h = 0, p = 0.481).

3.2 VR Integration Test

Figure 3 displays that the whole system integrates the EEG acquisition and VR technology, and uses the real-time algorithm to calculate the attention feature value. The virtual reality stimulus presentation part is passed by DLL, and finally the feedback is sent to participants who are tested, which constitutes the virtual realistic EEG biofeedback system. Figure 4(a) illustrates that when the level of attention is low, the deep sea close-up mode is presented, and more details, such as fish and seaweed, can be observed. On the contrary, as Fig. 4(b) shows when the level of attention of the subjects is high, the subject can enjoy the shallow sea scene. After tested, the virtual reality scene of the system can effectively reflect the current level of attention of the subjects. The entire system can work together and operate normally.

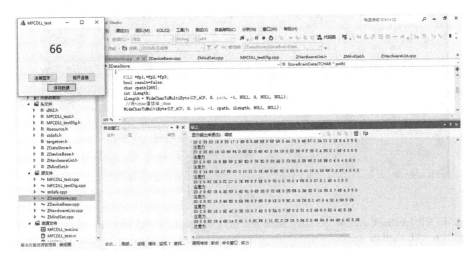

Fig. 3. Acquisition part of the integration test

3.3 Data Analysis in Experiments

After each resting state (blinking) of the experimental group and the attention value of the training state were collected, the alignment was performed, and the paired t-test was performed on the data of the first, fifth, and tenth times, respectively. When selecting data, take the average value of each half-minute data (60 data in total) before and after

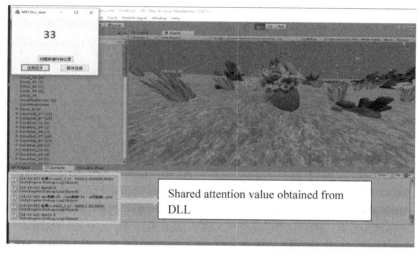

Shared attention value obtained from DLL

(a)

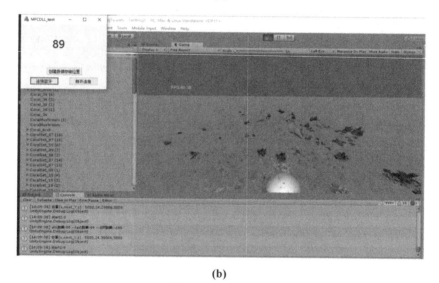

(b)

Fig. 4. VR feedback part of the integration test (a) low attention with close-up scene (b) high attention with shallow secne

the measurement data of each experimenter as the representative value of the current experimenter, and use this average value as the following paired t-test Data value.

After the paired sample t-test was performed at rest in the experimental group, the results were as follows: The fifth time compared with the first result, the mean value of attention increased by 2.0, and there was a significant difference ($h = 1$, $p = 0.016$). Comparing the results of the tenth and fifth times, it was found that the mean value of attention increased by 2.1, and there was no significant difference ($h = 0$, $p = 0.085$).

The tenth time compared with the first time, it was found that the average value of attention increased by 4.1, and there was a significant difference (h = 1, p = 0.020).

After the paired sample t-test was performed in the training state, the experimental results were as follows: The fifth time compared with the first result, the mean value of attention increased by 6.7, and there was a significant difference (h = 1, p = 0.002). Comparing the results of the tenth and fifth times, it was found that the mean value of attention increased by 7.1, and there was no significant difference (h = 0, p = 0.054). The tenth time compared with the first time, it was found that the average value of attention increased by 13.8, and there was a significant difference (h = 1, p = 0.001).

The growth of the attention value of the experimental group was fitted to a curve, and the attention data of the first measurement of the resting state was used as a standard, and the growth rate of each subsequent data with respect to the standard was calculated. Since the trend of natural logarithm is more consistent with the trend of brainwaves in EEG feedback, the function $f(x) = a\ ln(x) + b$ is used as an empirical formula for fitting (Fig. 5).

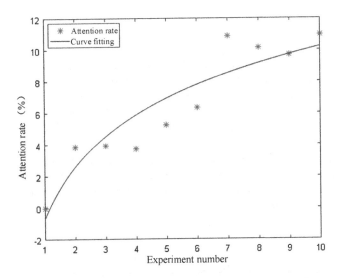

Fig. 5. Experimental group resting state attention data growth rate

3.4   Schulte Check Test Results

The Schulte square test results before, after, and one week after the experiment are shown in Fig. 6.

It can be found from the results graph that the trend of the experimental group and the control group is basically the same, but the improvement effect of the experimental group is better than that of the control group, and the progress is more. Through the variance test, the intra-group factors (between the three time periods) were significant, and the inter-group factors were not significant.

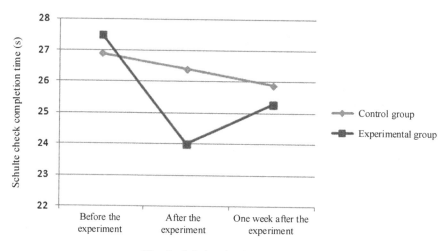

Fig. 6. Schulte check test results

4 Discussion

The system can effectively collect the EEG information of the subject, calculate the attention feature value through the real-time algorithm, and stimulate the subject to realize the biofeedback through the virtual reality rendering system.

As can be seen from Fig. 5, the level of attention of the experimenters has a steady growth trend in these ten experiments. After experimentation, the experimenter's attention increased by about 10%.

The system has the characteristics of stable operation, good reliability, simple operation, friendly interface, strong usability, good interface and strong openness. Its function basically realizes the requirements of multi-modal biofeedback therapy and the expected work objectives.

Due to the tight time, this research and development focuses on the system architecture. At the same time, the number of participants is small. There are many places in the application that have good ideas but have not been realized. The research on the disease has yet to be carried out, such as increasing the application of virtual reality biofeedback, developing the operational imagination paradigm, and applying it to the limb rehabilitation and swallowing rehabilitation of stroke patients.

Funding. This work is partially supported by the project of Jiangsu provincial science and Technology Department (To Zou L, Grant No. BE2018638), Changzhou Science and technology support program (To Zou L, Grant No. CE20175043) and the Jiangsu provincial 333 project.

References

1. Clarke, A.R., Barry, R.J., Johnstone, S.J., McCarthy, R., Selikowitz, M.: EEG development in Attention Deficit Hyperactivity Disorder: from child to adult. Clin. Neurophysiol. **130**(8), 1256–1262 (2019)

2. Barutchu, A., et al.: Multisensory perception and attention in school-age children. J. Exp. Child Psychol. **180**, 141–155 (2019)
3. Thiele, A., Bellgrove, M.A.: Neuromodulation of attention. Neuron **97**(4), 769–785 (2018)
4. Smithson, E.F., Phillips, R., Harvey, D., Morrall, M.: Response to letter that comments on published paper: the use of stimulant medication to improve neurocognitive and learning outcomes in children diagnosed with brain tumours: a systematic review. Eur. J. Cancer **50** (8), 1569–1570 (2014)
5. Patsis, G., Sahli, H., Verhelst, W., De Troyer, O.: Evaluation of Attention Levels in a Tetris Game Using a Brain Computer Interface. In: Carberry, S., Weibelzahl, S., Micarelli, A., Semeraro, G. (eds.) UMAP 2013. LNCS, vol. 7899, pp. 127–138. Springer, Heidelberg (2013). https://doi.org/10.1007/978-3-642-38844-6_11
6. Sun, J.C.Y.: Influence of polling technologies on student engagement: an analysis of student motivation, academic performance, and brainwave data. Comput. Educ. **72**, 80–89 (2014)
7. Sun, J.C.-Y., Chen, A.Y.-Z., Yeh, K.P.-C., Cheng, Y.-T., Lin, Y.-Y.: Is group polling better? An investigation of individual and group polling strategies on students' academic performance, anxiety, and attention. Educ. Technol. Soc. **21**(1), 12–24 (2017)
8. Sun, C.Y., Yeh, P.C.: The effects of attention monitoring with eeg biofeedback on university students attention and self-efficacy: the case of anti-phishing instructional materials. Comput. Educ. **106**, 73–82 (2017)
9. Chen, C.M., Huang, S.H.: Web-based reading annotation system with an attention-based self-regulated learning mechanism for promoting reading performance. Br. J. Edu. Technol. **45**(5), 959–980 (2014)
10. Lin, C.S., Lai, Y.C., Lin, J.C., et al.: A novel method for concentration evaluation of reading behaviors with electrical activity recorded on the scalp. Comput. Methods Programs Biomed. **114**(2), 164–171 (2014)
11. Gola, M., Magnuski, M., Szumska, I., Wróbel, A.: EEG beta band activity is related to attention and attentional deficits in the visual performance of elderly subjects. Int. J. Psychophysiol. Off. J. Int. Organ. Psychophysiol. **89**(3), 334–341 (2013)
12. Ye, Z., Guo, Q., Mi, C., et al.: Design and implementation of sixteen channel EEG acquisition system. Mol. Cryst. Liq. Cryst. **651**(1), 282–290 (2017)
13. Zou, L., Xu, S., Ma, Z., Lu, J., Su, W.: Automatic removal of artifacts from attention deficit hyperactivity disorder electroencephalograms based on independent component analysis. Cogn. Comput. **5**(2), 225–233 (2013)
14. Dong, D.: EEG biofeedback system and the research of its application. Doctoral dissertation (2017)
15. Xiaoya: Child attention training method: Schulte method. Chin. Tutor **9**, 36 (2011)

Continuous Estimation of Grasp Kinematics with Real-Time Surface EMG Decomposition

Chen Chen, Shihan Ma, Xinjun Sheng, and Xiangyang Zhu[✉]

State Key Laboratory of Mechanical System and Vibration,
Shanghai Jiao Tong University, 800 Dongchuan Road, Shanghai, China
mexyzhu@sjtu.edu.cn
http://bbl.sjtu.edu.cn/

Abstract. The aim of the study was to apply the real-time surface electromyography (EMG) decomposition to the continuous estimation of grasp kinematics. A real-time decomposition scheme based on the convolutional compensation kernel algorithm was proposed. High-density surface EMG signals and grasp kinematics were recorded concurrently from five able-bodied subject. The electro-mechanical delay between identified motor unit activities and grasp kinematics was characterized and utilized to optimize the multiple linear regression model for the grasp estimation. The discharge rate of each motor unit was extracted as the feature input to the regression model. On average, 36 ± 15 motor units were identified during each grasp task. The average root mean square error between estimated grasp kinematics and actual recorded signals was 0.21 ± 0.05, with the average delay of 212 ± 50 ms for the feature. The computation efficiency of the decomposition scheme and the high estimation accuracy imply the practical application for human-machine interfaces based on neural signals.

Keywords: EMG decomposition · Grasp kinematics · Motor unit · Human-machine interface

1 Introduction

Electromyography (EMG) has been widely applied for human-machine interfaces (HMI) in prosthetics, orthotics, and exoskeleton systems for decades. Several EMG-based control schemes have been proposed, such as direct control (DR) [1], pattern recognition (PR) [2,3], and simultaneous and proportion control (SPC) [4,5]. However, the control schemes of most commercial devices are still based on the simple DR, which could only realize control of 1–2 degree-of-freedoms (DoF), and lacks intuitiveness [6]. To date, it is challenging for the current schemes to realize HMI with the integration of intuitiveness, robustness, and multiple-DoF control.

© Springer Nature Switzerland AG 2019
H. Yu et al. (Eds.): ICIRA 2019, LNAI 11744, pp. 108–119, 2019.
https://doi.org/10.1007/978-3-030-27541-9_10

The development of decomposition techniques for surface EMG signals provides a new perspective for HMI based on neural signals in a non-invasive way [7–9]. Within these control schemes mentioned above, the features extracted from EMG signals only indirectly reflect the neural drive sent to the muscles from the spinal cord. Contrarily, the decomposition techniques could identify motor unit spike trains (MUST), which consist the series of discharge timings of the motor neurons locating in the spinal cord [10], and could apply the MUSTs to the neural-based HMI.

The motor unit activities have been applied to myoelectric control of wrist for able-bodied subjects and upper-limb amputees using high-density surface EMG and outperformed the classic control schemes [11–13]. The feasibility of predicting finger kinematics using decoded MUSTs has also been validated. The neural features extracted from motor unit activities has outperformed the classic EMG features with respect to the correlation, smoothness, and root mean square error (RMSE) [13,14]. However, most reports have investigated the neural interfaces under offline conditions. The real-time decomposition is of utmost importance for practical applications.

This work aimed to apply EMG decomposition to myoelectric control in real-time. For this purpose, we proposed a real-time decomposition scheme and analyzed the estimation performance of grasp kinematics using the features extracted from decomposition results.

2   Methods

2.1   Subjects

Five able-bodied subjects (three males, two females, 23–27 years old, all right-handed) participated in the experiment. All subjects had no neurological or psychiatric disorders and were recruited from Shanghai Jiao Tong University. The experiments were in compliance with the Declaration of Helsinki.

2.2   Experimental Setup

High-density surface EMG signals were recorded from the forearm muscles with three grids of 64 channels with 10 mm inter-electrode distance in both directions (ELSCH064NM3, 8×8 channels, OT Bioelettronica, Italy). The grids were mounted around the forearm as Fig. 1(a) shows, and were connected to a multichannel amplifier (EMG-USB2+, OT Bioelettronica, Italy) with a sampling rate at 2048 Hz.

Grasp kinematics were recorded concurrently with the EMG signals, using a 5DT Data Glove 14 Ultra (5DT Inc. USA). The data glove recorded angles of ten finger joints, including five metacarpophalangeal (MCP) joints and five proximal interphalangeal (PIP) joints (Fig. 1(a)). The sampling rate of angles was 50 Hz and would be up-sampled to 2048 Hz in the following analysis. The angle signals were displayed on the screen to provide a visual feedback for each participant.

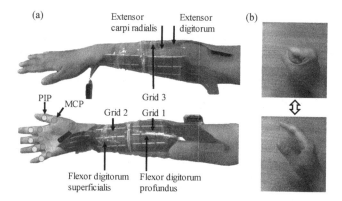

Fig. 1. Experiment setup. (a) The recording areas of surface EMG signals and finger angles. MCP: metacarpophalangeal, PIP: proximal interphalangeal. (b) The continuous grasp task.

2.3 Experimental Protocol

The experiment consisted of two sessions for each subject, training and testing. In the training session, the subjects were instructed to perform isometric contraction of grasp to follow a trapezoid trajectory of contraction level, with 5 s ascending, 10 s plain, and 5 s descending. The maximum force of the trajectory was 30% maximum volunteer contraction (MVC). A custom transducer was used to measure the grasp force. The force signals were displayed on the screen to provide real-time visual feedback. The EMG signals recorded in this session were used for the offline training module of the decomposition algorithm (Fig. 2).

In the testing session, the subjects performed continuous hand grasp circularly (Fig. 1(b)) at three speeds, corresponding to the duration of 1 s (V1), 2 s (V2), and 3 s (V3) for each cycle (rest-grasp-rest). The subjects performed two repeated trials of 20 s at each speed. There were six trials in total for each subject in this session. The EMG signals recorded in this session were used to test the online decoding module of the decomposition algorithm (Fig. 2).

All subjects were instructed to finish all tasks with the dominant hand. During the experiment, the subjects were seated in a chair with the arm fully extending and pointing toward the ground, with the palm facing inward. Before the experiment, each subject had sufficient time to familiarize with the experiment procedure and the grasp tasks.

2.4 Decomposition

The flow chart of the real-time decomposition scheme is shown in Fig. 2. The proposed algorithm consists of (1) offline training and (2) online decoding.

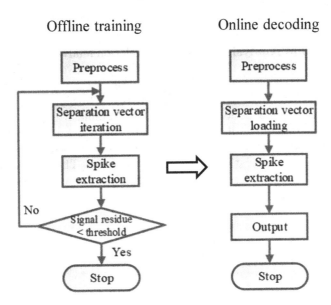

Fig. 2. The flow chart of EMG decomposition procedure.

In the offline training module, the EMG signals were decomposed into MUSTs with the offline convolutional kernel compensation (CKC)-based algorithm [14–16]. After preprocessing, the separation vector for each MUST was obtained through the iteration step of the natural gradient descent algorithm [16]. Then the discharges of the MUST were extracted. These two steps were repeatedly conducted until the residue signals were lower than the pre-set threshold. The separation matrix W containing separation vectors for all MUSTs was obtained through this training module.

In the online decoding module, the EMG signals in a sliding window of 100 ms were firstly preprocessed in the same way as the offline training module. Then the estimated spike trains were calculated by directly multiplying the separation matrix W and the processed EMG signals. The step of spike extraction was also the same as in offline training module. The computation complexity of online decoding was much lower than the offline training due to the lack of iteration procedure for separation vectors.

The decomposition procedure was applied to EMG signals recorded from each electrode grid separately. The decomposition accuracy of MUSTs was indirectly evaluated with a signal-based performance measurement called pulse-to-noise ratio (PNR) which has been validated to be highly correlated with the decomposition accuracy of CKC-based algorithms [17].

2.5 Data Analysis

Cross-Correlation Analysis. The cross-correlation analysis was used to characterize the electro-mechanical delay in time domain between grasp kinematics and motor unit activities decoded from each grid. The grasp kinematics was calculated by averaging the angle signals across ten finger joints and normalizing the averaged signal between 0 and 1. The cumulative spike train (CST) was obtained by combining all the MUSTs [18], and was smoothed with a sliding Hanning window (400 ms, zero-phase) [19]. The smoothed CST was used to calculate the cross-correlation with grasp kinematics. The maximum correlation coefficient (Pearson correlation coefficient) and the lag between the grasp kinematics and the smoothed CST were obtained.

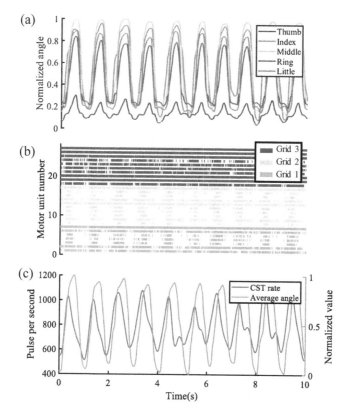

Fig. 3. Motor unit activities during the grasp task of V1 from subject 1. (a) Normalized angle signals recorded by the data glove (only angles from five MCP joints are presented for clarity). (b) Discharge timings of motor units identified by the real-time decomposition algorithm. (c) The average angle signals across ten joints and the smoothed discharge rate of the CST obtained from (b).

Kinematics Estimation. A multiple linear regression model was used to estimate the grasp kinematics. The input feature to the regression model was the number of discharges of each motor unit in an interval of 100 ms, with 90 ms overlapping between two consecutive intervals. Five-fold cross validation was performed to assess the robustness of the model. In each fold, 1/5 continuous data in each trial were used to test the model and the remaining data were used to train the model. To quantify the estimation performance, the Pearson correlation coefficient (R) and the root mean square error (RMSE) were used as the measures of goodness of estimated grasp kinematics with respect to the actual recorded signals.

Considering the electro-mechanical delay between grasp kinematics and decomposed MUSTs, the input feature was lagged ranging from 0 to 300 ms with a step of 10 ms. The estimation results of all conditions were calculated, while only the condition with the lowest RMSE was kept.

2.6 Statistics

The independent variable was the grasp speeds and the dependent variables were the R, the RMSE, and the lag under the condition with best estimation accuracy. A one-way analysis of variance (ANOVA) was used to statistically analyze the influence of the grasp speeds on the three dependent variables (Fig. 5).

Table 1. Summary of decomposition results.

		Motor unit number	PNR		Discharge rate	
			Training	Testing	Maximum	Average
Grid 1	V1	14 ± 10	21.0 ± 2.4	15.4 ± 3.0	72.1 ± 12.7	50.9 ± 16.2
	V2			16.3 ± 4.0	74.1 ± 17.7	49.9 ± 18.5
	V3			15.1 ± 3.5	74.5 ± 19.1	51.5 ± 16.6
Grid 2	V1	9 ± 9	22.0 ± 2.9	16.8 ± 3.6	69.5 ± 8.8	41.7 ± 18.1
	V2			18.4 ± 4.5	65.8 ± 15.2	39.0 ± 19.9
	V3			18.5 ± 4.7	68.9 ± 17.5	41.0 ± 21.4
Grid 3	V1	13 ± 3	24.4 ± 3.7	17.7 ± 4.5	63.9 ± 16.3	39.2 ± 20.3
	V2			18.9 ± 5.3	61.2 ± 18.2	36.3 ± 20.9
	V3			19.0 ± 5.5	61.9 ± 19.0	36.2 ± 20.3

3 Results

The average number of motor units identified by three grids during grasp tasks with three speeds and the corresponding average PNR are shown in Table 1. On average, 12 ± 7 motor units were identified from the training tasks for each grid, with the average PNR of 22.4 ± 3.3 dB. The average PNR of MUSTs identified in testing tasks was 17.4 ± 4.3 dB.

The motor unit activities during a V1 task from one representative subject are shown in Fig. 3. After identifying the motor unit activities, the cross-correlation analysis was used to characterize the electro-mechanical delay between the smoothed CST and grasp kinematics. Figure 4 illustrate the cross-correlation analysis results. For all grids except grid 3, the smoothed CSTs were always prior of the grasp kinematics.

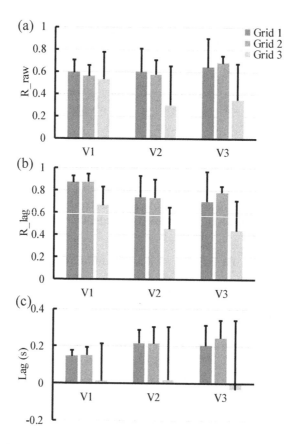

Fig. 4. The results of cross-correlation analysis. (a) The raw Pearson correlation coefficient (R_raw) between the grasp kinematics and the smoothed CST (without lag). (b) The maximum Pearson correlation coefficient (R_lag) between the grasp kinematics and the smoothed CST obtained through cross-correlation analysis. (c) The lag of the smoothed CST at which the maximum correlation coefficient was achieved. The positive lag means the smoothed CST was prior of grasp kinematics, whereas the negative lag means the smoothed CST was behind the grasp kinematics.

Figure 5 shows the estimation results of the multiple linear regression model. The regression model for V1 task performed better significantly, with higher R and lower RMSE values than the other two tasks. Moreover, the lag between features and grasp kinematics decreased significantly with the increase of the grasp speed. The estimation results from one representative subject are shown in Fig. 6.

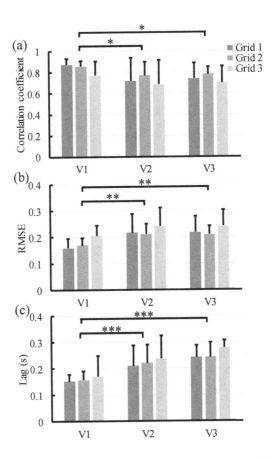

Fig. 5. The results of grasp kinematics estimation optimized with lag of features. (a) The Pearson correlation coefficient between measured and estimated kinematics. (b) The RMSE between measured and estimated kinematics. (c) The lag of the features at which the minimum RMSE was achieved. Symbols $*$, $**$, $* * *$ indicate significant differences with a level of $(0.01 < P < 0.05)$, $(0.001 \leq P \leq 0.01)$, $(P < 0.001)$, respectively.

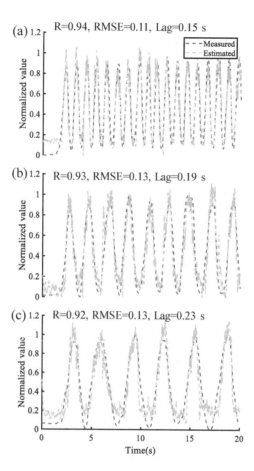

Fig. 6. An example of estimation performance for grasp kinematics with decomposition results of grid 1 from subject 5. (a)–(c) illustrate the measured and estimated grasp kinematics during the task of V1–V3, respectively.

4 Discussion

We demonstrated the feasibility of decoding motor unit activities during continuous grasp tasks in real time using high-density surface EMG signals. The electro-mechanical delay between motor unit activities and the grasp kinematics was characterized and utilized to optimize the multiple linear regression model for grasp kinematics estimation.

Real-time decomposition technique is quite important for the practical application of neural-based HMI. In this work, we proposed a real-time decomposition scheme for CKC-based algorithms. Though the average PNR value is lower than that in previous work which have investigated the decomposition accuracy under isometric contractions [8,17], the estimation results demonstrated the feasibility of applying the decoded MUSTs to grasp kinematics estimation.

The motor unit activities has been validated to be prior of finger kinematics [14], which allows for real-time prosthetic control. In this work, we characterized the electro-mechanical delay between MUSTs and grasp kinematics, and optimized the regression model depending on this lag. The smoothed CSTs extracted from all grids except grid 3 were always strongly correlated with the grasp kinematics (>0.5) with a lag ranging from 100 to 300 ms. These results can be referred for the selection of recording areas when estimating grasp kinematics.

The grasp speeds had a significant effect on the estimation performance. The RMSE between estimated grasp kinematics and the recorded signals from V1 tasks was lower than that of V2 and V3 tasks, with higher R values and shorter lags. The average RMSE across all tasks was 0.21 ± 0.05 with the average lag of 212 ± 50 ms. These matrices were comparable with the results of several reports [20,21]. The lag of the features extracted from motor unit activities decreased with the increase of the grasp speed, which corresponded to the variation regularity of the electro-mechanical delay for EMG signals [22]. This phenomenon will be taken into consideration for the estimation of more complex grasp tasks.

In this work, the feasibility of grasp kinematics estimation using the proposed real-time decomposition scheme was only validated under the offline conditions. In addition, an adaptive module in this decomposition scheme need to be investigated for the long-term application.

5   Conclusion

We proposed a real-time CKC-based decomposition scheme using high-density surface EMG signals, and estimated the grasp kinematics with the decoded motor unit activities using a multiple linear regression model. The outcomes of this work provide the prosect for real-time application of HMI based neural signals.

Acknowledgments. The authors would like to thank all the subjects for their participation in the study. This work was funded by in part the National Natural Science Foundation of China (No. 91748119, No. 51620105002), and by the Science and Technology Commission of Shanghai Municipality (No. 18JC1410400).

References

1. Paciga, J.E., Richard, P.D., Scott, R.N.: Error rate in five-state myoelectric control systems. Med. Biol. Eng. Compu. **18**(3), 287–290 (1980)
2. Salisbury, J.K., Craig, J.J.: Articulated hands: force control and kinematic issues. Int J. Robot. Res. **1**(1), 4–17 (1982)
3. Resnik, L., Huang, H., Winslow, A., Crouch, D.L., Zhang, F., Wolk, N.: Evaluation of EMG pattern recognition for upper limb prosthesis control: a case study in comparison with direct myoelectric control. J. Neuroeng. Rehabil. **15**(1), 23 (2018)

4. Jiang, N., Englehart, K.B., Parker, P.A.: Extracting simultaneous and proportional neural control information for multiple-DOF prostheses from the surface electromyographic signal. IEEE Trans. Biomed. Eng. **56**(4), 1070–1080 (2009)
5. Lin, C., Wang, B., Jiang, N., Farina, D.: Robust extraction of basis functions for simultaneous and proportional myoelectric control via sparse non-negative matrix factorization. J. Neural Eng. **15**(2), 026017 (2018)
6. Biddiss, E., Chau, T.: Upper-limb prosthetics: critical factors in device abandonment. Am. J. Phys. Med. Rehabil. **86**(12), 977–987 (2007)
7. Holobar, A., Farina, D.: Blind source identification from the multichannel surface electromyogram. Physiol. Meas. **35**(7), R143 (2014)
8. Negro, F., Muceli, S., Castronovo, A.M., Holobar, A., Farina, D.: Multi-channel intramuscular and surface EMG decomposition by convolutive blind source separation. J. Neural Eng. **13**(2), 026027 (2016)
9. Farina, D., et al.: The extraction of neural information from the surface EMG for the control of upper-limb prostheses: emerging avenues and challenges. IEEE Trans. Neural Syst. Rehabil. Eng. **22**(4), 797–809 (2014)
10. Weinberger, M., Dostrovsky, J.O.: Motor unit. Encyclopedia of Movement Disorders, pp. 204–206 (2010)
11. Farina, D., et al.: Man/machine interface based on the discharge timings of spinal motor neurons after targeted muscle reinnervation. Nat. Biomed. Eng. **1**(2), 0025 (2017)
12. Kapelner, T., Negro, F., Aszmann, O.C., Farina, D.: Decoding motor unit activity from forearm muscles: perspectives for myoelectric control. IEEE Trans. Neural Syst. Rehabil. Eng. **26**(1), 244–251 (2018)
13. Wardowski, M.D., Roy, S.H., Li, Z., Contessa, P., De Luca, G., Kline, J.C.: Motor unit drive: a neural interface for real-time upper limb prosthetic control. J. Neural Eng. **16**(1), 016012 (2019)
14. Chen, C., Guohong, C., WeiChao, G., Xinjun, S., Dario, F., Xiangyang, Z.: Prediction of finger kinematics from discharge timings of motor units: implications for intuitive control of myoelectric prostheses. J. Neural Eng. **16**(2), 026005 (2019)
15. Holobar, A., Zazula, D.: Multichannel blind source separation using convolution kernel compensation. IEEE Trans. Signal Process. **55**(9), 4487–4496 (2007)
16. Holobar, A., Zazula, D.: Gradient convolution kernel compensation applied to surface electromyograms. In: Davies, M.E., James, C.J., Abdallah, S.A., Plumbley, M.D. (eds.) ICA 2007. LNCS, vol. 4666, pp. 617–624. Springer, Heidelberg (2007). https://doi.org/10.1007/978-3-540-74494-8_77
17. Holobar, A., Minetto, M.A., Farina, D.: Accurate identification of motor unit discharge patterns from high-density surface EMG and validation with a novel signal-based performance metric. J. Neural Eng. **11**(1), 016008 (2014)
18. Savc, M., Glaser, V., Kranjec, J., Cikajlo, I., Matjacic, Z., Holobar, A.: Comparison of convolutive kernel compensation and non-negative matrix factorization of surface electromyograms. IEEE Trans. Neural Syst. Rehabil. Eng. **26**(10), 1935–1944 (2018)
19. Liu, L., Bonato, P., Clancy, E.A.: Comparison of methods for estimating motor unit firing rate time series from firing times. J. Electromyogr. Kinesiol. **31**, 22–31 (2016)

20. Ngeo, J.G., Tamei, T., Shibata, T.: Continuous and simultaneous estimation of finger kinematics using inputs from an EMG-to-muscle activation model. J. Neuroeng. Rehabil. **11**(1), 122 (2014)

21. M Hioki and H Kawasaki. Estimation of finger joint angles from sEMG using a neural network including time delay factor and recurrent structure. ISRN Rehabil. 2012 (2012)

22. van Dieen, J.H., Thissen, C.E.A.M., van de Ven, A.J.G.M., Toussaint, H.M.: The electro-mechanical delay of the erector spinae muscle: influence of rate of force development, fatigue and electrode location. Eur. J. Appl. Physiol. **63**(3), 216–222 (1991)

Intelligent Robot Arm: Vision-Based Dynamic Measurement System for Industrial Applications

Lei Chen[1(✉)], Haiwei Yang[2], and Pei Liu[2,3]

[1] Beijing Key Laboratory of Intelligent Space Robotic System Technology and Applications, Beijing Institute of Spacecraft System Engineering, Beijing, China
chenleibit@gmail.com
[2] Xi'an Jiaotong University, Xi'an, China
yanghw.2005@stu.xjtu.edu.cn, 57269529@qq.com
[3] China Academy of Aerospace Standardization and Product Assurance, Beijing, China

Abstract. Current industrial robot arms are not satisfied in flexibility and intelligence due to the lack of visual perception. The production efficiency also runs into a bottleneck because most parts must be completely fixed when assembling and welding. We propose a vision-based intelligent robot arm, which can dynamically sense the environment and perform appropriate operations. The measurement system consists of operator face authentication, gesture remote control, abnormal entry detection and moving target tracking. The capabilities of human-machine interaction and dynamic measurement meet the needs of high-performance robot arm in intelligent manufacturing, with the characteristics of intelligence, safety, efficiency and flexibility. Various functions of the intelligent robot arm are verified through a large number of experiments in laboratory.

Keywords: Robot arm · Vision-based measurement · Artificial intelligence

1 Introduction

Machine vision has been widely used in industry, including robot automation guidance, mobile robot positioning, material sorting [1, 2] and so on. With the development of intelligent manufacturing and smart factories, robot arms, combining visual perception and measurement capabilities, play more and more important role in enhancing productivity, ensuring product quality and saving labor costs, because of their reliability, intelligence and high degree of automation.

Specific to the automotive industry, so many components or parts are needed to assemble, weld and transport through robot arms, which requires the visual measurement system can identify, position and measure targets in an intelligent, accurate and fast way. In particular, it is not only necessary to measure the position of each component in 3D space, but also to determine the orientation. More seriously, due to the wide variety of automotive components, complex three-dimensional structures, large

© Springer Nature Switzerland AG 2019
H. Yu et al. (Eds.): ICIRA 2019, LNAI 11744, pp. 120–130, 2019.
https://doi.org/10.1007/978-3-030-27541-9_11

size differences and weak surface textures, these factors pose a significant challenge to the robot arm and visual measurement system.

In [3] a simulation platform of robot arm is built for manufacturing automation. The simulation platform uses a 7-DOF robot arm with dynamic obstacle avoidance and 3D positioning capabilities. A similar vision-based system is added to SCARA robot in [4], which can identify a specific target with its offset in the image coordinate system in order to guide the robot to perform the target sorting work. The added vision system enables the SCARA robot to have the capability of target positioning. However, the vision system can only determine 2D offsets instead of 3D positions. What's more, it only works for targets at rest or targets moving on the conveyor belt with a uniform speed. [5] develops a visually-guided smart robotic gripper which employs an eye-in-hand architecture. With the help of a single hand-eye camera, the robotic gripper can capture a specific target autonomously by estimating the relative position between the gripper and the target.

In this paper, we present a vision-based measurement system of intelligent robot arm, which integrates operator face authentication, gesture remote control, abnormal entry detection and moving target tracking. The system not only has good human-machine interaction, but also can estimate the position (x, y, z) and the orientation (α, β, γ) in 3D space according to the workpiece images. Therefore, the robot arm can accurately and intelligently complete a variety of tasks, such as assembling, transporting, welding and spraying. It can be widely used in automobile manufacturing, industrial automation and other fields. The measurement accuracy of 3D position and orientation is better than 1 mm and $0.1°$, with the total computing time less than 50 ms. The intelligent robot arm can operate quickly by compensating and calibrating the position and orientation of different components with the vision-based measurement system. To a large extent, this reduces the needs for alignment tools and fixtures.

2   Framework and Method

The presented intelligent robot arm, with the abilities of human-machine interaction and dynamical tracking, can improve the intelligent level of industrial production lines, through combining dynamic vision-based measurement system with traditional industrial robots. It consists of four modules, namely, operator face authentication, gesture recognition, abnormal entry detection and moving target tracking (see Fig. 1).

The operator face authentication module is responsible for identifying and authenticating the pre-authorized operators with operational qualification and authority, which can prevent the possible misoperations by unrelated personnel or inexperienced personnel to ensure the safety and reliability of the entire production process. This module collects the face images of different workers in the face authentication area to compare with the pre-stored information in the database, in order to determine whether this worker is an authorized operator or not. Only when the certification is passed, the system will open the corresponding privileges and the intelligent robot arm will respond to the operator's instruction.

The gesture recognition module is responsible for the remote control of robot arm by recognizing specific gesture commands. Different manipulations of the intelligent

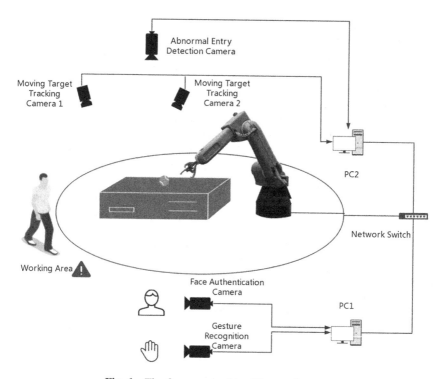

Fig. 1. The framework of intelligent robot arm.

robot arm, such as starting, accelerating, decelerating, stopping, etc., can be done remotely by the operator's gestures, which is convenient for the operator to find out problems occurred in the course of operations and to make the appropriate operation in a long distance so as to improve the production efficiency and maximize the safety of the operator.

Abnormal entry detection module is used to monitor the safety area of the whole working environment, in real time, in order to identify possible abnormal entries such as workers, vehicles, materials and so on. When abnormal entry occurs, the intelligent robot arm will decelerate first and send a warning signal at the same time. If the abnormal entry persists and moves closer to the running robot, the intelligent robot arm will continue to decelerate until it stops. If and only if the abnormal entry away or disappear, the intelligent robot arm gradually returns to normal state and continues the previous operation. The module monitors the working area with a high-resolution camera and different. The robot arm performs different operations respectively, according to the different occurrence regions of abnormal entry.

The moving target tracking module can track the target in real time, whether the target is in a stationary state, a uniform motion state or a random motion state. By dynamically measuring the position and orientation of the target, the robot arm is guided to move toward the target. Meanwhile, the relative position between the end of robot arm and the target is also calculated during the movement. Then, the position, orientation, speed and motion planning of the robot arm is constantly modified, so as to ensure all the operations, such as assembling, welding and spraying, are performed in the accurate, efficient and suitable way.

2.1   Face Authentication

Operator face authentication module includes two main parts: face detection and face recognition.

In face detection part, we use Haar-like feature [6] as the input feature descriptor to depict the brightness information of a specific rectangle area. When the Haar-like feature is calculated, the Adaboost algorithm [7] is used to classify the features and perform preliminary face recognition, which is proposed by Freund and Schapire in 1995 and is a great upgrade to the traditional boosting algorithm. It is an iterative algorithm. The core idea is to train various weak classifiers on the same training dataset, and then combine these weak classifiers to form a stronger final classifier, which is formulated as follow:

$$H_T(X) = sign\left(\sum_{i=1}^{T} \alpha_i h_i(X)\right) \tag{1}$$

where T is the number of weak classifiers and X is the input Haar-like feature. $h_i(X) \in \{-1, +1\}, i = 1, 2, \cdots, T$ is the trained weak classifiers, while α_i denotes the weight of ith weak classifier.

In the training stage, the initial weights are given respectively to the positive and negative samples, and then the weak classifier with the lowest false classification rate is selected for each feature, which results the sample weights are updated. The process is iteratively performed until the strong classifier, consisting of T weak classifiers, is obtained.

In face recognition part, we need to give identification to the detected human face. The detected face with its feature vector X is used as input, and then it is compared one-by-one with the pre-set operators' face image dataset, through computing the feature similarity:

$$w_k = D(X, Y_k), k = 1, 2, \cdots, K \tag{2}$$

where K is the number of pre-registered operators and Y_k is the feature vector for each operator face. $D(\cdot, \cdot)$ is a measure of similarity, such as Euclidean distance.

2.2   Gesture Recognition

The main steps of gesture recognition are feature extraction and feature classification.

We use invariance feature, Hu moment, for feature selection. Note that, although more complex features could be used here, we choose Hu moment since it is computationally fast. Hu proposed the invariant feature [8], which consists of a linear combination of certain second-order central moments and third-order central moments, where the $(p+q)$-order central moment μ_{pq} is defined as follows:

$$\mu_{pq} = \iint_{-\infty}^{+\infty} (x - \bar{x})^p (y - \bar{y})^q I(x,y) dx dy \tag{3}$$

where (x,y) is the pixel coordinate of the image, and $(\bar{x}, \bar{y})$ is the pixel centroid. $I(x,y)$ depicts the image value at the point (x,y).

The image moment feature is a kind of global invariant which is insensitive to noise and has good resolution for different target shapes. In this paper, we use seven Hu moments to construct a feature vector, which is used to train the feature classifier.

We use Random Forest [9] in feature classification, which is widely used machine learning algorithm in the field of artificial intelligence. The forest is an ensemble of multiple binary decision trees. Each tree has a hierarchical structure and is trained randomly and separately.

In training stage, given a set of training features $\{S\}$, the optimal split function f^* and associated threshold t^*, for each split node in each binary decision tree is determined by this objective function:

$$\{f_i^*, t_i^*\} = \arg\max_{f,t} \left\{ E(S_i) - \frac{N_i^L}{N_i} E(S_i^L) - \frac{N_i^R}{N_i} E(S_i^R) \right\} \tag{4}$$

where $\{f_i^*, t_i^*\}$ are the optimal parameters for i^{th} split node. S_i is the training features arriving at i^{th} split node with its number N_i. S_i^L and S_i^R are the training features splitting into left child and right child, with their numbers N_i^L, N_i^R, respectively. The split satisfies $S_i^L \cup S_i^R = S_i, S_i^L \cap S_i^R = \emptyset$. $E(\cdot)$ is the entropy function with:

$$E(S) = -\sum_{c \in \mathcal{L}(S)} p(c) log p(c) \tag{5}$$

where c is the class label from the label set $\mathcal{L}(S)$ with the probability $p(c)$, which is estimated based on the histogram of all labels.

For each root node, by optimizing the objective function hierarchically (see Fig. 3), a binary decision tree can be built until all training features have reached leaf nodes.

2.3 Abnormal Entry Detection

We use temporal difference to detect the abnormal entry. This method has short calculation time and fast detection output. It compares the current image with the background image and then divides the moving object directly, according to the statistical information such as grayscale, color, boundary and gradient. The basic idea is to image subtraction. If the pixel value difference is greater than a certain threshold, it is judged that this pixel belongs to the target; otherwise, this pixel is regard as background. In order to improve detection stability, we need to estimate a background model without moving objects.

Temporal difference method can detect abnormal entry by comparing the adjacent frames in the sequence image with the estimated background model. For the sake of simplicity, we can analyze the pixel values at corresponding position between adjacent frame and the background model. A threshold is used to segment the abnormal entries, which can be empirically or adaptively determined. Assumed that $f_k(x, y)$ and $f_{k+1}(x, y)$ are the kth image and $(k+1)^{th}$ image separately, the binary difference image $D(x, y)$ can be calculated:

$$D(x, y) = \begin{cases} 1 & \text{if } |f_k(x, y) - f_{k+1}(x, y)| > T \\ 0 & \text{else} \end{cases} \tag{6}$$

where T is the optimal threshold.

In the binary image, the labelled value "1" includes moving objects and the image noise. On the contrary, the labelled value "0" indicates the background with no change in these positions. Abnormal entry can be detected by analyzing the connected component with labelled value "1" in the binary image.

2.4   Moving Target Tracking

We use binocular stereo algorithm to determine the position and orientation of moving target. The two theodolites are used to calibrate the relative relationships between the robot arm and the dynamic cameras, (R_x, T_x) and (R_0, T_0). Then the robot arm can track the moving target through the vision-based measurement system.

Assuming the 3D coordinate of a arbitrary point on the target is $P = (X, Y, Z)^T$, the corresponding image coordinates in two cameras are $p_1 = (u_1, v_1)^T$ and $p_2 = (u_2, v_2)^T$. The relationship of two cameras is (R_0, T_0). According to the perspective projection model, we can get:

$$l_1 \begin{bmatrix} u_1 \\ v_1 \\ 1 \end{bmatrix} = A_1 [R \quad T] \begin{bmatrix} X \\ Y \\ Z \\ 1 \end{bmatrix}, l_2 \begin{bmatrix} u_2 \\ v_2 \\ 1 \end{bmatrix} = A_2 [R \quad T] \begin{bmatrix} R_0 & T_0 \\ 0^T & 1 \end{bmatrix} \begin{bmatrix} X \\ Y \\ Z \\ 1 \end{bmatrix} \tag{7}$$

where A_i is camera intrinsic.

By combining the above equations, we can estimate the rotation matrix R and translation vector T between the moving target and the dynamic cameras. Therefore, the relationship (R_p, T_p) between the moving target and the robot arm can be calculated, which can be used in path planning and dynamic tracking:

$$R_p = R_x R, \quad T_p = R_x T + T_x \tag{8}$$

3   Results and Applications

We set up a laboratory demonstration platform to verify each module of the intelligent robot arm, which can be applied in the automobile production.

The robot arm is Fanuc CR-35iA. The resolution of dynamic cameras is 2048 * 2048, and the others are 1024 * 1024. The environment of the platform is shown in Fig. 2.

Fig. 2. The environment and hardware components of the demonstration platform Intelligent Robot Arm: Vision-based Dynamic Measurement System for Industrial Applications.

3.1   Operator Face Authentication

In the vision-based measurement system, the operator face authentication is first performed. When someone enters the working area, the human face is marked with a green box. If the person is a registered operator, the intelligent robot arm begins to work and prepares to execute the operator's instruction (see Fig. 3).

Fig. 3. Parts of experimental results of operator face authentication.

3.2   Face Remote Control

There are 5 pre-defined gestures in the face recognition module (see Fig. 4a). The operator can issue corresponding gesture control commands according to the gesture prompts in the screen. When the gesture is correctly recognized, the intelligent robot arm will perform specific operations. For example, the intelligent robot arm will pause when the operator makes the following gesture (see Fig. 4b).

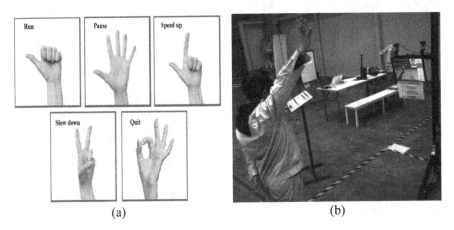

(a)   (b)

Fig. 4. The five pre-defined gestures and an example of gesture command.

3.3   Abnormal Entry Detection

The abnormal entry detection module monitors the entire working area of the intelligent robot arm with an industrial camera. If no abnormal entry, the robot arm operates at a normal speed of 750 mm/s (see Fig. 5a); the robot arm will decelerate to a speed of 400 mm/s if abnormal entry into the outer region (see Fig. 5b) and to 400 mm/s if abnormal entry into the inner region (see Fig. 5c). If someone touches the robot arm, it will stop moving for safety (see Fig. 5d). When abnormal entry disappears, the intelligent robot arm resumes normal operation (see Fig. 5a).

3.4   Moving Target Tracking

When there is a moving target (red ball in Fig. 6) in the operating area, the moving target tracking module calculates the position between the target and the robot arm in real time. Then the robot arm will track the moving target according to the calculated position. The motion planning is constantly updated depending on the current status of the intelligent robot arm, until the robot arm catches the moving target (see Fig. 6).

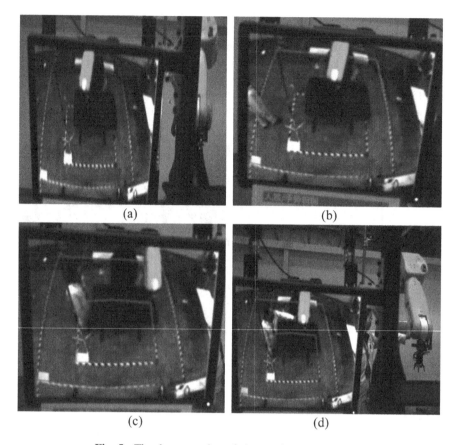

Fig. 5. The demonstration of abnormal entry detection.

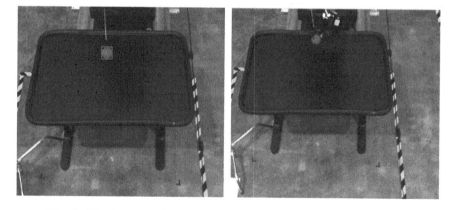

Fig. 6. The demonstration of moving target tracking. (Color figure online)

4 Conclusion and Future Work

We propose an intelligent robot arm system based on dynamic vision measurement, which is a comprehensive application of artificial intelligence in industry. Successful application of the four modules (operator face authentication, gesture remote control, abnormal entry detection and moving target tracking) makes the industrial manufacturing intelligent, safe, efficient and flexible. Operators, robot arms and production are linked up in the manufacturing processes, through the human-machine interaction and dynamic measurement, which greatly improves the personnel safety and production efficiency.

The future work is mainly focused on two aspects. The first is to improve the accuracy with the use of deep learning algorithms. In this paper, we use Haar-like feature and Hu moment as the descriptor for computational efficiency. In the future, high-level features will be introduced to enhance the adaptive capacity of the intelligent robot arm to complex background and illuminate changes. In particular, conventional neural networks (CNN) can be employed into the recognition framework for end-to-end training. On the other hand, more testing should be applied to collect the production data. Then the operating habits of different operators, the coordination between different production processes and the potential dangers during manufacturing will be mined using big data technologies. This provides targeted training for operators and fine-tuning for the intelligent robot arm to further improve the safety and efficiency.

Acknowledgment. This work was supported by the Natural Science Foundation of China (No 61603291), National Science and Technology Major Project (2018ZX01008101-004).

References

1. Kazemi, S., Kharrati, H.: Visual processing and classification of items on moving conveyor with pick and place robot using PLC. Intell. Ind. Syst. **3**(1), 15–21 (2017)
2. Mohammad, A.E.K., Hong, J., Wang, D.: Design of a force-controlled end-effector with low-inertia effect for robotic polishing using macro-mini robot approach. Robot. Comput. Integr. Manuf. **49**, 54–65 (2018)
3. Luo, R.C., Kuo, C.-W.: Intelligent seven-DoF robot with dynamic obstacle avoidance and 3-D object recognition for industrial cyber-physical systems in manufacturing automation. Proc. IEEE **104**(5), 1102–1113 (2016)
4. Hsu, H.-C., Chu, L.-M., Wang, Z.-K., Tsao, S.-C.: Position control and novel application of SCARA robot with vision system. Adv. Technol. Innov. **2**(2), 40–45 (2017)
5. Shaw, J., Cheng, K.: Object identification and 3-D position calculation using eye-in-hand single camera for robot gripper. In: IEEE International Conference on Industrial Technology, pp. 1622–1625 (2016)
6. Lienhart, R., Maydt, J.: An extended set of haar-like features for rapid object detection. In: International Conference on Image Processing, pp. 900–903 (2002)

7. Freund, Y., Schapire, R.E.: A decision-theoretic generalization of on-line learning and an application to boosting. Conf. Learn. Theory **55**(1), 119–139 (1997)
8. Hu, M.K.: Visual pattern recognition by moment invariants. IEEE Trans. Inf. Theory **8**(2), 179–187 (1962)
9. Lindner, C., Bromiley, P.A., Ionita, M.C., Cootes, T.F.: Robust and accurate shape model matching using random forest regression-voting. IEEE Trans. Pattern Anal. Mach. Intell. **37**(9), 1862–1874 (2015)

Research on Autonomous Face Recognition System for Spatial Human-Robotic Interaction Based on Deep Learning

Ming Liu[1,2], Na Dong[1], Qimeng Tan[1(✉)], Bixi Yan[2], and Jingyi Zhao[1,2]

[1] Beijing Key Laboratory of Intelligent Space Robotic Systems Technology and Applications, Beijing Institute of Spacecraft System Engineering, Beijing 100094, China
tanqimeng@foxmail.com
[2] Beijing Information Science & Technology University, Beijing 100192, China

Abstract. Face recognition which is of few advantages such as natural and non-contact to realize fluent interaction and cooperation between human and robot, has been one of important and common issues in the fields of computer vision and biometrics identification. However, the achievement of face recognition also meet few issues such as disturbances or variations in facial expression, pose, shade and environmental illumination to solve. For this reason, an autonomous face identification system based on deep learning is proposed in this article, which should be divided into 4 stages. Firstly, RGB-D images including one or more faces are captured by Kinect v2. Secondly, an algorithm of multi-view faces detection has been proposed by introducing candidate regions after filters of local binary Haar-like feature into Multi-layer perceptron (MLP) in order to obtain every candidate face area. Thirdly, typical face feature points such as left eye, right eye, nose tip, left corner of the mouth and the right corner of the mouth are located and aligned by Stacked Auto-Encoder (SAE) accurately. Finally, VIPLFaceNet has been applied to identify the similarity and difference between the image to be determined and any template in the face image database. Experimental results have shown that the proposed system not only can detect multi-faces belonging to different persons, but also could achieve well identification results with the correctness of no less than 70% regardless of few disturbance of pose, expression and illumination.

Keywords: Face recognition · Face detection · Face alignment · Face identification · Deep learning

1 Introduction

With rapid development of space robot and Artificial Intelligence (AI), the human-robot interaction has been gradually changed from the traditional pre-programmed control to a natural and non-contact mode of visual interaction. Presently, space human-robot interaction system mainly involves efficient, frequent and friendly information exchange and behavior interaction between astronauts and robots. As one

© Springer Nature Switzerland AG 2019
H. Yu et al. (Eds.): ICIRA 2019, LNAI 11744, pp. 131–141, 2019.
https://doi.org/10.1007/978-3-030-27541-9_12

of the key technologies of human-robot interaction, face recognition can automatically verify their identity information by capturing and recognizing the natural facial features of visitors.

Face recognition mainly contain face detection, feature extraction and face identification.

Face detection is mainly used to quickly and accurately detect the face area in the image or video, but it is extremely easy to be interfered by factors such as illumination, hat, bangs and black-frame glasses. In 1998, Rowley [1] took the lead in proposing a face detection algorithm based on BP neural network, which effectively broke through the technical bottleneck of traditional artificial selection in the acquisition of non-face areas in images. Zhang [2] advance a mixed face detection algorithm based on multitask cascade convolutional neural network.

Feature extraction is mainly to accurately locate, extract and characterize typical facial features such as eyebrows, glasses, nose and mouth corners. Typical facial feature point positioning algorithms include Active Shape Model algorithm [3], Active Appearance Model algorithm [4], Constrained Local Model algorithm [5], cascaded Regression algorithm [6], etc.

Face identification has gone through two stages: shallow machine learning and deep learning.

The former is to identify the shallow features of artificial design, and these features are extracted by artificial. The typical methods include geometric feature method, principal component analysis (PCA) and template matching method. Bledsoe [7] has used manually marked facial feature points to obtain a set of distance describing the face, this method is simple in principle and requires little calculation, but is sensitive to expression changes. Turk [8] first proposed the concept Eigenface and adopted multidimensional feature vector to represent face image information. On this basis, many scholars have carried out a variety of improvement studies and successively proposed features such as SIFT feature, Garbor feature, LBP feature, HOG feature and so on. In this way, face identification can be converted into feature classification problem. Pentland [9] and Bmnelli [10] respectively constructed three grayscale templates of eyes, nose and mouth as features for correlation matching. Principal component analysis (PCA) was successfully used to realize multi-angle face recognition, but this method was only applicable to static grayscale images. Lades [11] proposed a complex face dynamic recognition model based on scalable invariance, and constructed a face rectangular grid based on two-dimensional topology by using multi-scale Gabor amplitude feature descriptor. According to the similarity of each node and connection of the image to be matched, a template matching algorithm combining gray features and geometric constraints is proposed to complete face recognition. This method has strong robustness, allows elastic deformation of face image, effectively overcomes the influence of expression change on recognition, and has no strong requirement on image quantity, but still has great limitations.

In 2012, the appearance of Alexnet [12] and its wide application set off a boom in the research of deep learning in the field of computer vision, especially face recognition. Different from the traditional method of face identification, from the basic principle of deep learning, overcome the shallow machine them face recognition methods rely on artificial feature extraction technology of short board, can be represented by convolution neural network of artificial intelligence technology and big data technology effectively combine, independent training, learning, and build face models provide facial recognition results and synchronization. Deep learning face-like identification method mainly relies on many face sample image information to train accurate face recognition network, to win a high recognition rate (no less than 98%). Now, typical deep learning face recognition systems include: Facebook adopts Deepface [13] face identification method based on CNN network in 2014; DeepIDs [14] series by professor Tang Xiaoou's team at the Chinese university of Hong Kong; Baidu AI [15] of Baidu; Face++ of Megvii [16] visual technology; Cloudwalk [17] technology's dynamic face recognition system, etc. These methods or products will be face verification in the database recognition accuracy even beyond the human.

2 System Framework

Face recognition is mainly divided into three functional modules, namely face detection, face alignment and face identification. This system design uses OpenCV 3.0.0 as a tool for image processing. It first collects images of 7 people to build a small database, and then uses Kinect v2 to detect the face in the image through software processing, feature point positioning, feature extraction and comparison, the final recognition of the face, the similarity of the comparison. The process is shown in Fig. 1.

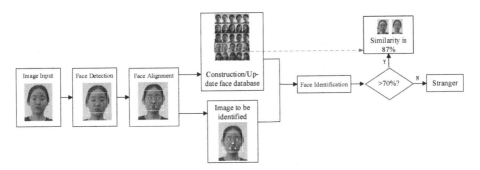

Fig. 1. System framework

3 Composition

3.1 Image Capture

The parameters and performance of different depth camera devices are different. The performance of Kinect v2 is more suitable for this research. Kinect v2 can be used to realize the recognition function of the robot face similar to human normal activities. With the development of depth camera equipment, such equipment is small in size, cheap in price, fast in acquisition speed and high in acquisition accuracy, making 3D face recognition more and more widely used in practical applications.

The Kinect v2 consists of an RGB camera, a pair of depth information cameras, and a set of microphone arrays. The RGB camera is the same as a normal camera for capturing color images; one on the two sides of the color camera is an infrared emitter, and the other is an infrared CMOS camera, which constitutes a 3D structured light depth sensor for obtaining depth data of the object space. The acquisition uses TOF (Time of Flight) technology, the principle is that the sensor emits modulated near-infrared light, and after the object is reflected, the sensor calculates the distance of the captured scene by calculating the time difference or phase difference between the light emission and reflection to generate Depth information, combined with traditional camera shooting, can present the three-dimensional contour of the object in different topographical representations of different colors.

3.2   Face Detection

This module uses a Funnel-structured cascade (FuSt) [18] to perform face detection on images. After the image is first input, a large number of non-face windows are quickly filtered out by the fast cascade classifier [19], which fusion LBP features and the processing of Haar-like features.

The features shown in Fig. 2 combine eight binary Haar-like features that are locally adjacent and share a common central rectangle. The size of the feature used in this time is 3×3, and the image is scanned centering on this feature.

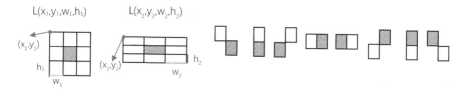

Fig. 2. Two locally binary Haar-like features and eight Binary Haar-like Features in a feature

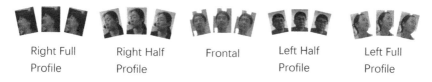

| Right Full Profile | Right Half Profile | Frontal | Left Half Profile | Left Full Profile |

Fig. 3. Face classification with multi-view

Multi-view simultaneous face detection can reduce the detection time, but locally binary Haar-like features are difficult to model the complex changes of multi-view surfaces. Therefore, the divide-and-conquer strategy is adopted. Specifically, the face is divided into five categories, which are left view, half left view, frontal view, half right view, and right view. Each class is divided into three views of $\pm 15°$, shown in Fig. 3. The face deflection angle RPY is less than $90°$, $45°$, and $45°$, respectively. c_i is the locally binary Haar-like features cascade classifier. For window x in the input image, whether the face can be determined by all locally binary Haar-like features cascade classifiers is as follows:

$$y = c_1(x)|c_2(x)| \cdots |c_v(x) \tag{1}$$

After the locally binary Haar-like features cascade phase, most of the non-facial windows are screened out, and the remaining windows are too difficult for simple locally binary Haar-like features. Thus, at a later stage, the candidate window is further verified by a more complex classifier, a multilayer perceptron (MLP) with SURF features (speed-up robust features) and multi-view feature constraints.

MLP is a neural network consisting of an input layer, an output layer and one or more hidden layers in between.

The purpose of MLP training is to minimize the mean square error between the predicted and real labels, as shown below:

$$\min_F \sum_{i=1}^n \|F(x_i) - y_i\|^2 \tag{2}$$

where x_i is the feature vector of the i-th training sample, and the corresponding label is 1 or 0, indicating whether the sample is a face. The problem in the Eq. (2) can be easily solved by using gradient descent under the backpropagation frame.

This part consists of a single layer of MLP, including an input layer, a hidden layer and an output layer. Combined with 5 SURF features in the hidden layer. Together with the SURF feature, MLP is used for window classification, which can be used to better simulate nonlinear changes in multi-view surfaces and multiple non-facial patterns using the nonlinear activation function. When multiple models are running at the same time, false detection will occur, so add a hidden layer that fusion SIFT features. Select 5 feature positions, corresponding to the left eye, right eye, nose tip, left mouth corner and right mouth corner, divided into 3 categories, namely the eye, nose tip and mouth corner. There should be at least one feature for each type. At this stage, the MLP predicts whether the two categories of labels, i.e. the candidate window, are faces. An additional shape prediction error term is added to the objective function in Eq. (2). The new optimization issues are as follows:

$$\min_F \sum_{i=1}^n \|F_c(\phi(x_i, \hat{s_i})) - y_i\|^2 + \lambda \sum_{i=1}^n \|F_s(\phi(x_i, \hat{s_i})) - s_i\|_2^2 \tag{3}$$

where F_c corresponds to the face classification output, F_s corresponds to the shape prediction output; $\phi(x_i, \hat{s_i})$ represents the shape index feature (i.e. SIFT) extracted from the i-th training sample x_i according to the average shape or predicted shape; s_i is the sample Basic shape; λ is a weighting factor that maintains a balance between the two types of errors. It can be seen from Eq. (3). MLP can be used to obtain a more accurate shape $F_s(\phi(x_i, \hat{s_i}))$ than the input $\hat{s_i}$ (Fig. 4).

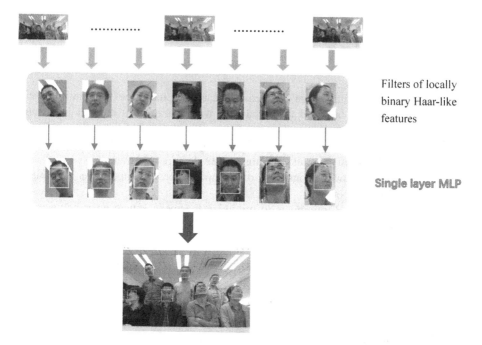

Filters of locally binary Haar-like features

Single layer MLP

Fig. 4. The process of face detection module

3.3   Face Alignment

The face alignment task automatically locates the key feature points of the face according to the input face image, such as the eyes, the tip of the nose, the corners of the mouth, the eyebrows, and the outline points of the faces of the face. Based on the face detection module, this module uses Stacked Auto-encoder (SAE) [20] to solve the problem of nonlinear mapping. In the face detection module, five feature points have been selected for training, and the five feature points are still selected at this stage. In this module, the output of the above module is used as the input image. Since the SIFT feature has been extracted around each feature point in the previous module, a stacked automatic encoder network (SAN) with three hidden layers and one linear regression layer is used in this module.

The main goal of face alignment is to solve the local feature minimum and find the optimal solution.

The number of hidden units in the three hidden layers of the stacked autoencoder used in this module is 1296, 784, 400 respectively. After initializing using Eq. (4), a general shape estimate P0 for the image is obtained. The nonlinear regression H1 is then implemented in conjunction with the known SIFT features extracted around each feature point, as follows:

$$H_1^* = arg\ min_{H_1} \left\| \Delta P_1(x) - h_k^1 \left(h_{k-1}^1 \left(...h_1^1 (\phi(P_0)) \right) \right) \right\|_2^2 + \alpha \sum_{i=1}^k \left\| W_i^1 \right\|_F^2$$

$$(4)$$

Here $H_1 = \left\{ h_{1}^{1}, h_{2}^{1}, \ldots, h_{k}^{1} \right\}$, $\sum_{i=1}^{k} \left\| W_{i}^{1} \right\|_{F}^{2}$ is the weight attenuation term. After obtaining the face shape update (ΔP_1) by the first partial SAN, an updated face shape can be obtained, which is $P_1 = P_0 + \Delta P_1$. The continuous local SAN then extracts local features around the new shape and optimizes the depth network to minimize new deviations between the current location and the ground truth. The goals of the j-th local SAN are as follows:

$$H_{j}^{*} = arg\ min_{H_j} \left\| \Delta P_j(x) - h_{k}^{j} \left(h_{k-1}^{j} \left(\ldots h_{1}^{j} \left(\phi(P_{j-1}) \right) \right) \right) \right\|_{2}^{2} + \alpha \sum_{i=1}^{k} \left\| W_{i}^{j} \right\|_{F}^{2}$$

(5)

The above weight attenuation parameter α is equal to 0.001.

3.4 Face Identification

Essentially, face identification calculates the degree of similarity between faces in the two images. One is the input phase of the registration phase (i.e. the human acquaintance process), and the other is the input of the recognition phase (i.e. the recognition process). To this end, a fully automatic face recognition system enters the third core step: face identification after completing the above steps of face detection and facial feature point extraction. This stage is also the largest breakthrough module after the deep learning is proposed. The VIPLFaceNet used in this module is directly modified from Alex Krizhevsky's 2012 design by AlexNet [12]. It implements a deep convolutional neural network (DCNN) with 7 convolutional layers and 2 fully connected layers. VIPLFaceNet splits the 5×5 convolution kernel into two 3×3 convolution kernels, increasing the network depth without increasing the amount of computation; VIPLFaceNet also reduces the number of kernels per convolutional layer and the number of nodes in the FC2 layer. At the same time, by introducing the Fast Normalization Layer (FNL), the convergence speed of VIPLFaceNet is accelerated, and the generalization ability of the model is improved to some extent.

4 Experiments

4.1 Face Detection

From the test results of the face detection part, it can be known that the face area detection can detect the face area regardless of the hair occlusion, the facial expression, whether the glasses are worn, the face or the side face. However, when the angle of the face is slightly larger, the detection error will occur.

Since the image acquired by Kinect v2 is directly detected by face detection, the detection time is approximately 3 s–5 s, and the change of image pixel size also affects the detection time. The smaller the image pixel, the shorter the detection time. The face detection time for different poses is shown in Table 3.

The system can also perform face detection for multiple people. Shown as Fig. 6, for the same multi-person image, Baidu AI can only detect up to ten people, and in the case of false detection, the module can recognize all faces in the image without false detection (Table 1).

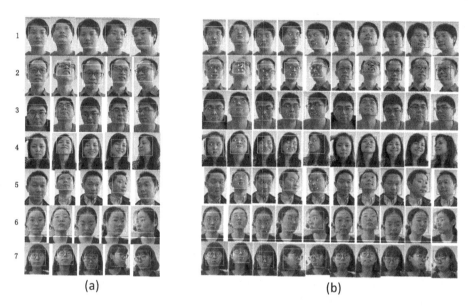

Fig. 5. Face detection result (a), Face alignment result (b)

Table 1. Time required for face detection

Sample number / Time/s	frontal	upward	down	left	right
1	3.4948	3.4712	3.4533	3.6039	3.5056
2	4.5091	5.2174	4.4904	4.6499	5.0943
3	3.7100	4.2822	4.1336	4.4652	4.3191
4	4.8244	4.2836	4.8244	4.4494	4.4330
5	4.3548	3.6887	3.6561	3.6564	3.5454
6	3.3677	3.4409	3.3602	3.3667	3.3524
7	3.7522	3.6690	3.7173	3.6439	3.7359

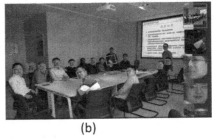

(a)   (b)

Fig. 6. Multi-person face detection (a) and Baidu AI Multi-person face detection (b)

4.2 Face Alignment

As Fig. 5(b) shows, when the feature points are located on the face, the face feature points of different face poses can be positioned to the target feature points, namely, the left eye, the right eye, the nose tip, the left mouth corner, and the right mouth corner. Although feature points can be located on some sides, the position is not accurate.

4.3 Face Identification

In the contrast of different poses of the same person, the accuracy of the downward and right contrast is the best. In the comparison of the overall results, the similarity between the face and the other poses is not good, probably because the face is In the upward posture, the positioning of the two feature points of the left eye and the right eye is not accurate enough, thus affecting the result of face recognition. From the time of running time, the face recognition time is between 25 ms and 40 ms. The correct result can be recognized when the frontal posture of the same person is not compared. The time of facial recognition is between 20 ms and 30 ms (Table 2).

Table 2. Comparison of this system and Baidu AI face identification results (Take the first set of images as an example)

Posture of ample	Similarity	Identification time/ms	Baidu AI similarity
frontal - upward	75.68%	28.16	94.52%
frontal - right	84.70%	28.28	97.66%
frontal - down	94.10%	27.04	98.86%
frontal - left	82.72%	33.68	96.48%
upward - left	74.31%	30	93.88%
upward - right	76.23%	32.02	95.74%
down - left	85.70%	26.96	96.88%
down - right	83.51%	26.7	96.60%

Table 3. Comparison of this system and Baidu AI face identification results (Take the first set of images as an example)

Contrast sample number	Similarity	Identification time/ms	Baidu AI similarity
1–2	19.39%	27.66	5.87%
1–3	17.83%	27.06	1.46%
1–4	23.42%	34.26	7.65%
1–5	13.94%	34.34	0%
1–6	33.54%	29.62	1.37%
1–7	15.96%	29.64	0%

5   Conclusion

Compared with other biometric technologies, face recognition has obvious advantages in naturalness, uniqueness, non-contact and undetected. The face pose problem is still an important factor affecting the accuracy of face recognition. This paper proposes a facial recognition system framework for different face poses, including the use of Kinect v2 for different facial pose image acquisitions, namely five poses of front, up, down, left and right; Learn to complete the three parts of face detection, facial feature point positioning and face recognition in different poses; finally get the similarity of the face. Through experimental verification, it is found that the system has realized multi-person face detection in the face detection module, and the face up posture has the lowest accuracy in recognition. Compared with Baidu AI's experimental results, there is still a gap in accuracy, but Baidu AI has missed detection when detecting gestures.

Facial recognition depends to a certain extent on the extraction of key points of face images. It is obvious from the experimental data that the extracted key points are not accurate and the recognition results are not accurate. The face data set of this experiment is small. In the follow-up work, the network lifting speed will be optimized, and the database based on more faces and different poses will be built to optimize the face recognition results of different poses.

Acknowledgement. This work is supported by 2018 Practice Training Program of Beijing Information Science and Technology University.

References

1. Henry, A.R., Shumeet, B., Takeo, K.: Neural network based face detection. IEEE Trans. Pattern Anal. Mach. Intell. **20**(1), 23–38 (1998)
2. Kaipeng, Z., Zhanpeng, Z., Zhifeng, L., Yu, Q.: Joint face detection and alignment using multitask cascaded convolutional networks. IEEE Signal Process. Lett. **23**(10), 1499–1503 (2016)
3. Cootes, T.F., Taylar, C.J.: Combining point distribution models with shape models based on finite element analysis. Image Vis. Comput. **61**(1), 38–59 (1995)
4. Cootes, T.F., Edwards, G.J., Taylor, C.J.: Active appearance models. IEEE Trans. Pattern Anal. Mach. Intell. **23**(6), 681–685 (2001)

5. Cristinacce, D., Cootes, T.F.: Feature detection and tracking with constrained local models. In: Proceedings of British Machine Vision Conference, Edinburgh, UK, pp. 929–938 (2006)
6. Jiankang, D.: Face Alignment Based on Cascade Regression Model. Nanjing University of Information Science and Technology, Nanjing (2015)
7. Beldeso, W.W.: Man-Machine Facial Recognition. Panoramic Research Inc., Palo Alto (1966)
8. Turk, M., Pentland, A: Face recognition using eigenface. In: Proceedings of international Conference on Pattern Recognition, pp. 586–591 (1991)
9. Pentlauld, A., Moghaddam, B., Stamer, T.: View-based and modular eigenspaces for face recognition. In: IEEE Conference on Computer Vision and Pattern Recognition, CVPR, pp. 1–7 (1994)
10. Brunelli, R., EalaVigan, D.: Person identification using multiple cues. IEEE Trans. PAMI **17**(10), 955–966 (1995)
11. Lades, M., Vorbruggen, J.C., Buhmann, J., et al.: Distortion invariant object recognition in the dynamic link architecture. IEEE Trans. Comput. **42**(3), 300–311 (1993)
12. Krizhevsky, A., Sutskever, I., Hinton, G.E.: ImageNet classification with deep convolutional neural networks. In: International Conference on Neural Information Processing Systems. Curran Associates Inc. pp. 1097–1105 (2012)
13. Taigman, Y., Yang, M., Ranzato, M., et al.: DeepFace: closing the gap to human-level performance in face verification. In: IEEE Conference on Computer Vision and Pattern Recognition, pp. 1701–1708. IEEE (2014)
14. Wanli, O., et al.: DeepID-Net: deformable deep convolutional neural networks for object detection. In: IEEE Conference on Computer Vision and Pattern Recognition, CVPR2015, USA, pp. 2403–2412 (2015)
15. Baidu AI Homepage. ai.baidu.com/. Accessed 2019
16. Megvii Homepage. https://www.megvii.com/. Accessed 2017
17. Cloudwalk Homepage. http://www.cloudwalk.cn/. Accessed 2019
18. Shuzhe, W., Meina, K., Zhenliang, H., Shiguang, S., Xilin, C.: Funnel-structured cascade for multi-view face detection with alignment-awareness. Neurocomputing **211**, 138–145 (2016)
19. Shengye, Y., Shiguang, S., Xilin, C., Wen, G.: Locally assembled binary (LAB) feature for fast and accurate face detection. In: IEEE Computer Society International Conference on Computer Vision and Pattern Recognition, CVPR 2008, USA (2008)
20. Shuaishi, L., Xi, C., Wenyan, G., Qi, C.: Progress report on new research in deep learning. CAAI Trans. Intell. Syst. **11**(5), 567–577 (2016)
21. arXiv.org Homepage. https://arxiv.org/abs/1811.00116v1. Accessed 31 Oct 2018

Fault Detection, Testing and Diagnosis

KPCA-Based Visual Fault Diagnosis for Nonlinear Industrial Process

Jiahui Yu[1], Hongwei Gao[1], and Zhaojie Ju[2,3(✉)]

[1] College of Automation and Electrical Engineering,
Shenyang Ligong University, Shenyang 110159, China
yujiahui77@163.com
[2] State Key Laboratory of Robotics, Shenyang Institute of Automation,
Chinese Academy of Sciences, Shenyang 110016, China
[3] University of Portsmouth, Portsmouth PO1 3HE, UK
zhaojie.ju@port.ac.uk

Abstract. With the increasingly large-scale, continuous, and complicated chemical process, it is particularly important to ensure the stability and safety of the production process. However, in past studies, the accuracy of fault diagnosis and the degree of system visualization are still insufficient. Here, in order to solve these problems, a visual fault diagnosis system based on LabVIEW and Matlab is designed. First, the system uses LabVIEW interface design, applying Matlab to compile the algorithm program, which makes the system has a powerful data calculation and processing functions, as well as a clear visual interface, the system design also optimizes the communication interface. Second, the typical chemical production process TE (Tennessee Eastman) process is the subject of systematic testing. Additionally, because most of the industrial processes are non-linear, the fault diagnosis method based on Kernel Principal Component Analysis (KPCA) is used in the system design, and the implementation process of this method is elaborated. Finally, the system achieves the functions of TE process data acquisition, data preprocessing, and fault diagnosis lamps. A large number of simulation results verify the effectiveness of the proposed method. The system has entered the stage of laboratory application and provides a good application platform for the research of fault diagnosis of complex systems such as chemical process control.

Keywords: Fault diagnosis · TE process · KPCA · Visualization system

1 Introduction

The process control method with industrial process as the main research object has the characteristics of systematic, complexity and diversity. In order to reduce accidents in the process and reduce losses to a certain extent, a set of fault diagnosis systems need to be designed to further determine what kind of faults have occurred, where and how far the faults occurred, and the causes.

Fault diagnosis is usually through the information collected by the measuring equipment in the diagnostic system to analyze and judge the status of the process, and to find the time when the fault occurred and the location and mode of the fault.

© Springer Nature Switzerland AG 2019
H. Yu et al. (Eds.): ICIRA 2019, LNAI 11744, pp. 145–154, 2019.
https://doi.org/10.1007/978-3-030-27541-9_13

Isermann clearly defines the type, location, magnitude and time of failure as the definition of fault diagnosis [1]. The United States Tennessee Eastman Chemical Co, Ltd. put forward a typical platform for research and development of process industry fault diagnosis in FORTRAN source code. Later, Bathelt et al. performed the simulation of the process on the Matlab, and continued to develop [2].

The principal component analysis (PCA) method is currently widely used in process analysis and monitoring [3]. In 1933, Hotlling proposed Principal Component Analysis (PCA), which is a multivariate statistical method that converts multiple indicators into several comprehensive indicators according to certain rules and actual needs without losing information. It is mainly used to eliminate multivariate multicollinearity to achieve dimensionality reduction [4, 5]. However, it is a linear method that does not apply to nonlinear processes. Aiming at the nonlinear characteristics of modern industrial processes, various nonlinear monitoring methods have emerged, and kernel principal component analysis is one of them [6]. It considers the nonlinear characteristics of the process, can effectively extract the nonlinear information of the data, and has no complicated nonlinear calculation in the implementation process, and has fewer adjustable parameters, so it is widely used in feature extraction, face recognition, image processing and faults diagnosis and other fields [7–9]. In the KPCA method, the correct choice of the kernel function largely determines the quality of the system's nonlinear feature extraction. Therefore, the choice of the type of kernel function and its parameters has a great impact on the results of fault detection [10].

All kernel functions can be divided into two types: global kernel function with strong generalization ability, weak learning ability, and local kernel function with strong learning ability and weak generalization ability. Using only one kernel function has certain limitations when analyzing the performance of the system. It can be known from the nature of the kernel function that a linear combination of any two kernel functions can form a new kernel function [11]. Therefore, this paper combines a Gaussian radial basis kernel function with strong learning ability and a polynomial kernel function with strong generalization ability to construct a mixed kernel function that has both advantages. The main contributions of this paper are summarized as follows.

After analyzing the characteristics of common kernel functions, this paper mixes the global kernel function with the local kernel function and improves a kernel function. The improved kernel function has powerful learning ability and generalization ability. The hybrid kernel function is applied to the KPCA method to achieve the goal of improving the traditional KPCA method. The improved KPCA fault detection method is applied to typical nonlinear processes and TE processes, and the fault diagnosis method of this KPCA is introduced. The principle and operation process of the KPCA are described in detail, and the fault detection method and the application in the normal chemical process, and the program is constructed and tested to verify the effectiveness of the improved method. The algorithm program compiles and visualizes the interface design, which makes the system have powerful data calculation and processing functions, as well as a clear visual interface. Typical nonlinear process and TE process monitoring results show that this method has higher accuracy in fault detection.

The rest of this paper is organized as follows: Sect. 2 reviews the relevant content of the TE process. The Sect. 3 introduces the process of the proposed method. The Sect. 4 gives the analysis and comparison of various experimental results. The Sect. 5 part summarizes the work of this paper.

2 TE Process

The Tennessee-Eastman Process (TEP) is a realistic industrial process and a method of fault detection and diagnosis in process control evaluation [1, 12]. It contains five operating units: reactor, condenser, recycle compressor, separator and stripper. Including eight components: A, B, C, D, E, F, G, H enter the reactor gas ACDE and inert component B, will form liquids G and H in the reactor, the various reactions of the reactor are [13, 14]:

$$A(g) + C(g) + D(g) \rightarrow G(liq)$$
$$A(g) + C(g) + E(g) \rightarrow F(liq)$$
$$A(g) + E(g) \rightarrow F(liq)$$
$$3D(g) \rightarrow 2F(liq)$$

The designed fault diagnosis system performed 22 simulations on the data in the training set, and each simulation process was different [15]. Each simulation time is 25 h. When the simulation starts, normal system operation is performed. When the simulation time reached 1 h, a fault was introduced. For each simulation, N = 500 observations were generated. Of the 500 observations, the last 480 observations were faulty. The data in the tester will be subjected to 22 different simulations. In the 22 simulations, one of them was operating in the normal state, that is, fault 0: the other could operate in a stable state, namely fault 21. The remaining 20 simulations, from fault 1 to fault 20, were run under different fault conditions, each for a duration of 48 h. When the simulation started, normal system operation was performed. When the simulation time reaches 8 h, the fault is reintroduced. For each simulation, N = 960 observations were generated. Among them, the first 160 observations are normal, and the last 800 observations are faulty.

3 Improved Fault Diagnosis Algorithm Based on KPCA

3.1 The Basic Principle of KPCA

The kernel principal component analysis method is an objective weighting method. It fully utilizes all the information of the original variables, determines the weight coefficient of the principal component according to the variance contribution rate, and can comprehensively reflect the importance degree of each variable, so that the comprehensive evaluation result More effective [16, 17].

Assume that the training sample is $x_1, x_2, \ldots, x_M$. The input space is $\{x_i\}$. The basic idea of the KPCA method is to map the input space to some high-dimensional space (often called the feature space) in some implicit way, and to implement PCA in the feature space [18]. Assuming the corresponding mapping is Φ, Its definition is as follows

$$x \longmapsto \xi = \Phi(x) \tag{1}$$

The kernel function maps implicitly implemented points to F through mapping, so that the data in the mapped feature space satisfies the concentration condition. Which is

$$\sum_{\mu=1}^{M} \Phi(x_\mu) = 0 \tag{2}$$

Then the covariance matrix in the feature space is:

$$C = \frac{1}{M} \sum_{\mu=1}^{M} \Phi(x_\mu) \Phi(x_\mu)^T \tag{3}$$

Finding the eigenvalues $\lambda \geq 0$ and eigenvectors of C

$$V \in F \backslash \{0\}, Cv = \lambda v \tag{4}$$

That is

$$(\Phi(x_v) \cdot Cv) = \lambda(\Phi(x_v) \cdot v) \tag{5}$$

Considering that all eigenvectors can be expressed as a linear expansion of, ie

$$v = \sum_{i=1}^{M} \alpha_i \Phi(x_i) \tag{6}$$

That is

$$\frac{1}{M} \sum_{\mu=1}^{M} \alpha_\mu (\sum_{w=1}^{M} (\Phi(x_v) \cdot \Phi(x_w) \Phi(x_w) \Phi(x_\mu))) = \lambda \sum_{\mu=1}^{M} (\Phi(x_v) \cdot \Phi(x_\mu)) \tag{7}$$

Among them $v = 1, 2, \ldots, M$, defining $M \times M$ dimensional matrix K

$$K_{\mu v} := (\Phi(x_\mu) \cdot \Phi(x_v)) \tag{8}$$

Then the expression (7) can be simplified as

$$M\lambda K\alpha = K^2\alpha \tag{9}$$

Obviously satisfied

$$M\lambda\alpha = K\alpha \tag{10}$$

Solving (10) can get eigenvalues and eigenvectors. The projection of the test sample in the feature vector space can be expressed as

$$(v^k \cdot \Phi(x)) = \sum_{i=1}^{M} (\alpha_i)^k (\Phi(x_i), \Phi(x)) \tag{11}$$

Replace the inner product with a kernel function.

$$(v^k \cdot \Phi(x)) = \sum_{i=1}^{M} (\alpha_i)^k K(x_i, x) \tag{12}$$

When (2) is not established, adjustments need to be made

$$\Phi(x_\mu) \rightarrow \Phi(x_\mu) - \frac{1}{M} \sum_{v=1}^{M} \Phi(x_v) \tag{13}$$

$$\mu = 1, \ldots, M$$

Then the nuclear matrix can be modified to

$$
\begin{aligned}
K_{\mu v} \rightarrow K_{\mu v} \\
- \frac{1}{M} (\sum_{w=1}^{M} K_{\mu w} + \sum_{w=1}^{M} K_{wv}) + \frac{1}{M^2} \sum_{w,\tau=1}^{M} K_{w\tau}
\end{aligned}
\tag{14}
$$

3.2   Algorithm Implementation Process

According to the principle of KPCA, the following process is obtained. Writing a batch of data of n obtained index (m samples for each index) into a (m×n) dimensional data matrix

$$A = \begin{pmatrix} a_{11} & \cdots & a_{1n} \\ \vdots & \ddots & \vdots \\ a_{m1} & \cdots & a_{mn} \end{pmatrix}.$$

Calculate the parameters in the Gaussian radial kernel function by calculating the above kernel matrix, and then calculate the kernel matrix K by Eq. (8). KL is obtained from (14) modified kernel matrix. The Jacobi iterative method is used to calculate the characteristic value $\lambda_1, \ldots, \lambda_n$ of KL, that is, the corresponding feature vectors $v_1, \ldots, v_n$. The eigenvalues are sorted in descending order (by sorting) to get feature vectors $\lambda'_1 > \ldots > \lambda'_n$, and adjusted the feature vector accordingly $v'_1, \ldots, v'_n . \alpha_1, \ldots, \alpha_n$ orthonormalized feature vectors by the Schmidt normalization method.

Calculate the cumulative contribution rate $B_1, \ldots, B_n zd$ of the eigenvalues. According to the given extraction efficiency p, if $B_t \geq p$, extract $\alpha_1, \ldots, \alpha_t$ main components.

Calculate the projection $Y = KL \cdot \alpha$ of the modified kernel matrix X on the extracted feature vector, where $\alpha = (\alpha_1, \ldots, \alpha_t)$.

The data after KPCA dimensionality reduction is projection Y.

4 System Design and Testing

4.1 System Design Process

In the process control modeling and simulation, Matlab is often used, but in order to compensate for the lack of interface development and acquisition of signals, LabVIEW software is always used [19]. In order to make the system versatile, the operating system for fault diagnosis operation is Windows 7 (64bit), and its development tools are Matlab/Simulink (2016a) and LabVIEW2012.

In this paper, our system has excellent interface display features that can perfectly display the TE process on the host computer. System design uses a combination of SIT and Simulink compiler, a good implementation of the interface display function, while solving the problem of the communication interface. The system combines Matlab with powerful data processing and LabVIEW with high-efficiency image processing. The entire system includes the functions of data acquisition, data preprocessing, and fault diagnosis of the TE process.

4.2 System Test

In the process of processing data, it is not necessary to manually input each set of data. It only needs to be imported by computer according to the address of data storage. In this way, data processing can become accurate, rapid, and reduced. The computational cost greatly improves our efficiency, enables real-time monitoring of chemical processes and facilitates the detection of failures at any time [20].

Figure 1 shows the login interface of the system. Enter the correct account password to log in to the system.

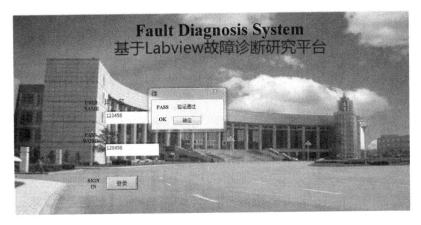

Fig. 1. Login screen

After logging in to the system, enter the system function interface, where you can choose to implement the corresponding functions of the system, as shown in Fig. 2.

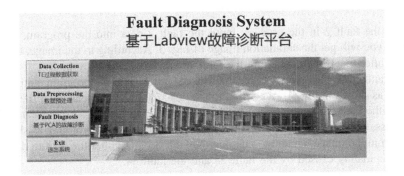

Fig. 2. Experiment platform interface

Before the simulation, the program was written for the entire process, and then the program written and able to run correctly was run on LabVIEW. Theoretically, it was clearly seen in the figure that the fault was added at the 1000th sampling point. Causes the trend of the polyline to fluctuate. This is because the man-in-the-middle joins the fault. Therefore, in the normal chemical production process, if the image above is obtained after running the program, it is not difficult to know the time when the failure occurred, so that it can be used to prevent the occurrence of failures. The following can select several representative faults to be added to the TE process and simulate them. The specific simulation results and simulation images are as follows. The T2 statistic mainly describes the change of the data in the principal element space and reflects the main operating characteristics of the industrial process. The Q statistic is built in the residual space of the monitoring model to summarize the sum of the errors caused by the modeling.

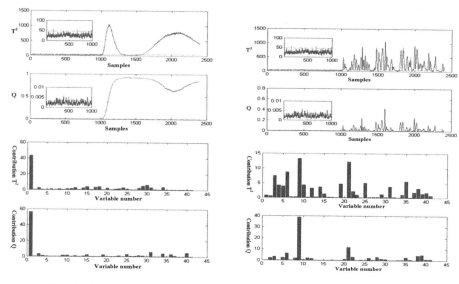

Fig. 3. Fault 2 simulation   **Fig. 4.** Fault 11 simulation

Enter the fault 2 in the process, input the fault 2 data into the program, run the program, you will get the simulation image of Fig. 3. According to the image, the fault occurred after the 1000th data, and the fault was mainly caused by fault 1.

Add fault 11 to the process, enter the data of fault 11 into the program, and run the program, as shown in Fig. 4. According to the image, the fault appears after the 1000th data, and the fault is mainly caused by the fault 9 and the fault 21. Adding fault 14 to the process, input the data of fault 14 to the program, and run the program, as shown in Fig. 5. From the image, it can be seen that the fault occurred after the 1000th data, and the fault is mainly caused by the fault 28 and the fault 34.

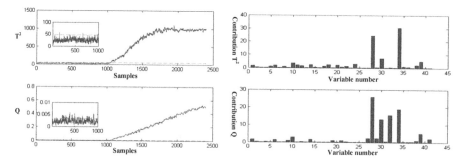

Fig. 5. Fault 14 simulation

5 Conclusion

Through the joint use of both useful platforms, fault diagnosis of the TE process is realized. The fault diagnosis system based on LabVIEW and Matlab not only has powerful data processing functions, but also has a perfect visual interface. The improved KPCA algorithm used in this system solves the problem that nonlinear engineering is difficult to reduce dimensions.

In this paper, the improved KPCA method is used to detect faults in nonlinear processes. The method uses a hybrid kernel function to perform high-dimensional mapping on data. Since the mixed kernel function has the advantages of both types of kernel functions, the mapped data has strong generalization ability. The principal element contribution rate and the fault detection rate are used as the dual indicators of the hybrid kernel function parameter optimization, so that the mixed kernel function to the optimal parameters is superior to the single kernel function in feature extraction and fault detection. The online detection of typical nonlinear processes and TE process data shows that the improved KPCA method is more effective.

The system has a clear and visible interface and has been systematically tested to verify its stability. It opens up a new way of thinking in terms of fault diagnosis and model prediction.

References

1. Downs, J.J., Vogel, E.F.: A plant-wide industrial process control problem. Comput. Chem. Eng. **17**(3), 245–255 (1993)
2. Bathelt, A., Ricker, L.N., Jelali, M.: Revision of the tennessee eastman process mode. In: International Symposium on Advanced Control of Chemical Processes, pp. 309–314. IFAC, British Columbia (2015)
3. Yan, S., Juanling, L., Dujing, S.: Research on parallel data flow based on principal component analysis. J. Nanjing Univ. Posts Telecommun. **35**(5), 100–102 (2015)
4. Yongfang, Z., Le, Y.: Research on parallel data mining algorithm based on Hadoop platform. Anhui University of Science and Technology, pp. 5–25 (2016)
5. Wang, P.L., Yan, W.J.: New monitoring method for dynamicnon-Gaussian process. Chin. J. Sci. Instrum. **30**(3), 471–476 (2009)
6. Scholkopf, B., Smola, A., Muller, K.R.: Nonlinear component analysis as a kernel eigenvalue problem. Neural Comput. **10**(5), 1299–1319 (1998)
7. Jianhua, Z.: Research on face recognition based on combined kernel function KPCA. Comput. Eng. Des. **35**(2), 631–635 (2014)
8. Jiaqiang, W., Yue, W., Liu, Y.: Improved KPCA feature extraction of classification data. Comput. Eng. Des. **31**(18), 4085–4092 (2010)
9. Chunyan, L., Chunmei, Y.: TE fault diagnosis based on improved kernel principal component analysis. Comput. Meas. Control **24**(10), 36–41 (2016)
10. Xue, L.: Research on Statistical Modeling and Monitoring Method of Intermittent Process Based on Mixed Kernel Function. Northeastern University, Shenyang (2014)
11. Yuan, Z., Shi, H.: Fault diagnosis method based on step-by-step dynamic kernel principal component analysis. Shenyang Jianzhu Univ. J. (Nat. Sci. Ed.) **29**(6), 1092–1109 (2013)

12. Li, J.C., Hu, N.Q., Qin, G.J., et al.: Optimizing method for fault diagnosis strategy based on bayesian networks. Control Decis. **18**(5), 568–572 (2003)
13. Guanxun, C.U.I., Liang, L.I., Keke, W.A.N.G., Guanglei, Z.O.U., Hang, Z.O.U.: Research and improvement of Apriori algorithm in association rule mining. J. Comput. Appl. **30**(11), 2952–2954 (2010)
14. Zhao, C.H., Wang, F.L., Lu, N.Y.: Stage-based soft-transition multiple PCA modeling and on-line monitoring strategy for batch processes. J. Process Control **17**(9), 728–741 (2007)
15. Xian-Zhen, X.U., Lei, X.I.E., Shu-Qing, W.A.N.G.: Multi-operation process monitoring based on PCA hybrid model. CIESC J. **62**(3), 743–752 (2011)
16. Shenzhen Guotaian Education Technology Co., Ltd., Shenzhen Institute of Advanced Technology, Chinese Academy of Sciences - Guotaian Financial Big Data Research Center. Big Data Analysis: R Foundation and Application. Tsinghua University Press, pp. 120–180 (2016)
17. Yu, Y., Wang, B., Zhang, L.: A fast PCA algorithm for data learning. Pattern Recognit. Artif. Intell. PR&AI **20**(4), 568–569 (2009)
18. Zhu, J.L., Ge, Z.Q., Song, Z.H.: Multimode process data modeling: a Dirichlet process mixture model based Bayesian robust factor analyzer approach. Chemom. Intell. Lab. Syst. **142**, 231–244 (2015)
19. Qiang, L., Tianyou, C., Lijie, Z.: Overview of industrial process monitoring and fault diagnosis based on data and knowledge. Control Decis. **25**(6), 801–807 (2010)
20. Duan, L., Xie, M., Bai, T., et al.: A new support vector data description method for machinery fault diagnosis with unbalanced datasets. Expert Syst. Appl. **64**, 239–246 (2016)

Data Denosing Processing of the Operating State of the Robotic Arm of Coal Sampling Robot

Rui Wang[1], Haibo Xu[1(✉)], Jun Wang[2], Xiaodong Liu[1], and Li Liu[1]

[1] Xi'an Jiaotong University, Xi'an 710049, Shanxi, China
wangruil@stu.xjtu.edu.cn, hbxu@mail.xjtu.edu.cn
[2] Xi'an Hongyu Mining Special Mobile Equipment Co,
Xi'an 710075, Shanxi, China

Abstract. The operating state information of the robot reflects the working state of the robot. Analysis of this information is an important means to understand the working state and failure of the robot. Taking the coal sampling robot as the research object, in order to extract the effective running state data of the robot under the condition of serious noise pollution. This paper focuses on the research on the denoising method of the running state data of the robot's mechanical arm. The limitations of empirical mode decomposition (EMD) based denoising method and threshold method based wavelet denoising method are analyzed and an improved threshold wavelet denoising algorithm based on EMD is proposed. Finally, the effect of denoising algorithm is measured by signal-to-noise ratio (SNR) and root mean square error (RMSE). It is verified that the denoising algorithm has adaptability to the typical signal of the robotic arm state of coal sampling robot.

Keywords: Empirical mode decomposition · Wavelet analysis · Threshold method · Adaptability

1 Introduction

As shown in Fig. 1, the coal sampling robot adopts a huge mechanical arm structure, the boom and the arm are driven by a motor, and the end effector is driven by a hydraulic cylinder. The sensor collects a large amount of data such as joint motor current, robot acceleration, end actuator hydraulics, etc.

Since the data is inevitably doped with various noise signals during the acquisition and transmission process, especially when the noise is seriously polluted by the data, these noise signals may interfere with the processing and analysis of the signal, affecting the result of the state analysis.

It can be seen that only after denoising, windowing, pre-emphasis, endpoint recognition and other processing state data can contain no other interference information and extract a useful signal segment. In this paper, the denoising method of state data is studied.

© Springer Nature Switzerland AG 2019
H. Yu et al. (Eds.): ICIRA 2019, LNAI 11744, pp. 155–164, 2019.
https://doi.org/10.1007/978-3-030-27541-9_14

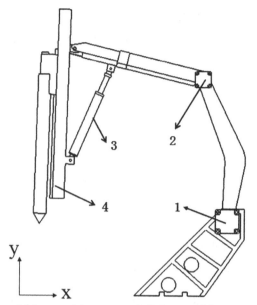

1 big arm drive motor 2 little arm drive motor
3 end effector drive hydraulic cylinder 4 end effector

Fig. 1. Structure of coal sampling robot mechanical.

2 Research on Denoising Method of Running State Data of Coal Sampling Robot

The filtering method based on empirical mode decomposition is not limited by the nonlinearity and non-stationarity of the signal and it has adaptability [1]. It is suitable for data processing of coal sampling robot, but it is found that the signal after denoising is prone to distortion when using EMD in practice.

After analysis, it is found that the intrinsic mode component (IMF) filtered by EMD contains noise. In this paper, empirical mode decomposition and wavelet theory filtering are combined to denoising the data.

2.1 Denoising Method Based on Empirical Mode Decomposition (EMD)

The x-direction acceleration on the large and small arms of the coal sampling robot and the angular velocity in the y-direction are all shock signals. The end effector is also subjected to shock vibration during the working process, so the impact signal of coal sampling robot is representative. Therefore, when studying the denoising method in this paper, the bumps impact signal is used for research. Finally, the other typical data signal types in the robotic arm of the coal sampling robot are proved.

For the bumps signal shown in Fig. 2, the signal after 10 db noise is added as the original pending signal, as shown in Fig. 3.

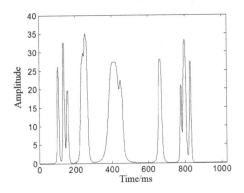

Fig. 2. Bumps original signal.

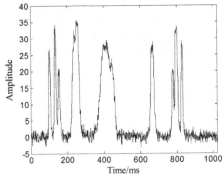

Fig. 3. Original pending signal.

The EMD denoising method is used to calculate and sets the denoising decomposition stop level to three levels. After the first two layers of IMF components are removed, the other IMF components are superimposed to obtain the denoised signal as shown in Fig. 4.

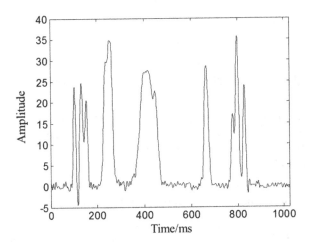

Fig. 4. EMD denoised signal.

It can be seen from the denoising diagram that the left and right detail signals are severely distorted after denoising, indicating that the first two layers of IMF components removed by EMD denoising contain valid signals. Because the wavelet threshold method has better denoising effect and has advantages for processing nonlinear signals [2], it is considered to perform threshold denoising on the first two layers of IMF components.

2.2   Wavelet Denoising Method Based on Threshold Method

Threshold denoising concentrates the energy of the signal containing noise, which is reflected in a small number of wavelet coefficients. Since the noise is still the same amplitude after the wavelet transform projection, the wavelet coefficients only need to be compared. The larger amplitude is the effective signal, the smaller amplitude and the more dispersed energy is the noise [3]. Therefore, as long as a suitable threshold value is selected and the amplitude of wavelet coefficient is distinguished, the denoising purpose can be realized.

Sym8 wavelet basis is selected and the decomposition level is 5 layers [4]. The signal is denoised by soft threshold method and hard threshold method. The results are shown in Figs. 5 and 6.

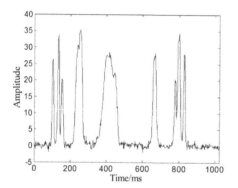

Fig. 5. Soft threshold method.   **Fig. 6.** Hard threshold method.

Comparing the denoising result graph with the original signal, it can be seen that there is distortion at the top of the soft threshold method. The denoising of the middle tip of the hard threshold method is not complete and the denoising effect of the noise signal at the bottom is poor.

2.3   Improved Threshold Wavelet Denoising Algorithm Based on EMD

Improved Threshold Wavelet Denoising Algorithm. In this paper, a hard and soft threshold function is combined by weighted average method [4] to construct a threshold function based on logarithm improvement:

$$d'_{j,k} = \begin{cases} \text{sgn}(d_{j,k})(|d_{j,k}| - \frac{t}{\exp(|d_{j,k}|-t)}) & |d_{j,k}| \geq t \\ 0 & |d_{j,k}| < t \end{cases} \tag{1}$$

In the formula: $d'_{j,k}$ is an improved wavelet coefficient.

The constructed threshold function graph is shown in Fig. 7. The sym8 wavelet base is selected and the number of decomposition layers is 5 layers [4]. The results of threshold denoising using improved threshold and threshold functions are shown in Fig. 8.

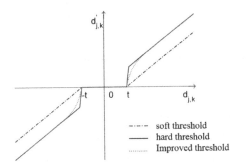

Fig. 7. Three threshold functions.

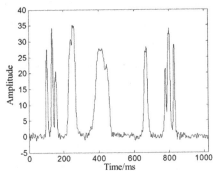

Fig. 8. Improved threshold denoising method.

It can be seen that the improved threshold method has better denoising effect than the soft threshold method in the middle protruding part, and the distortion effect is much reduced. Compared with the denoise of the hard threshold method, the denoising effect is greatly improved. However, the comparison with the original signal shows that it is still not particularly ideal.

Improved Threshold Denoising Method Based on EMD. Wavelet transform has good time-frequency analysis and multi-resolution characteristics, and can effectively distinguish the mutation part and noise in non-stationary signals. It can improve the signal-to-noise ratio and maintain a good resolution of abrupt signals. The wavelet threshold method can achieve the optimal denoising effect in the sense of minimum root mean square error [2].

In order to improve the denoising effect as much as possible, EMD decomposition is combined with threshold wavelet denoising method. The denoising steps are as follows:

Decomposition. The original signal $x(t)$ is decomposed by EMD. It is decomposed into n-layer to obtain the IMF_i component and residual $c_n(t)$ of the first n-layer.

Condition. Adopting $R_k = \left| (ET_k - ET_{k-1}) / (\frac{1}{k-1} \sum_{i=1}^{k-1} ET_i) \right|$ to determine the decomposition stop condition k, the front (k-1) layer IMF is almost entirely noise;

Choice. The appropriate wavelet basis and the number of decomposition layers were selected, and wavelet decomposition was performed on the k-th layer and all previous IMF, respectively, and the wavelet coefficient $d_{j,k}$ a was obtained;

Threshold. Utilizing $t = \frac{\sigma\sqrt{2\ln N}}{\ln(j+1)}$ to find the threshold of the k-layer and the previous layers. The wavelet coefficients of each layer are processed by using formula (1) to obtain the decomposition coefficient $d'_{j,k}$.

Instead of. Using decomposition coefficients $d'_{j,k}$ instead of wavelet coefficients $d_{j,k}$ to perform wavelet inverse transform to get the k-th layer and the previous IMF'_i;

Reconstruction. The denoised signal $x'(t)$ is reconstructed from the IMF decomposition and residual $r(t)$ after the k-th layer and the previous IMF'_i components and the k-layer after the threshold wavelet processing.

$$x'(t) = \sum_{i=1}^{k} IMF'_i + \sum_{i=k+1}^{n} IMF'_i + r_n(t) \tag{2}$$

Through the above description of the improved threshold wavelet denoising algorithm based on empirical mode decomposition, the flow of the improved algorithm can be obtained as shown in Fig. 9.

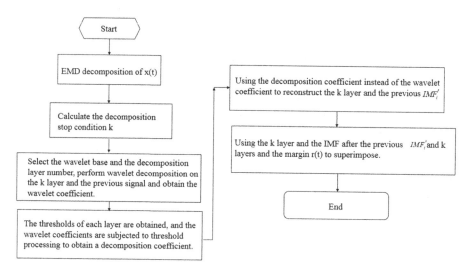

Fig. 9. Flowchart of the improved algorithm.

The improved algorithm is used to denoise the bumps signal with 10db noise. The processing result is shown in Fig. 10.

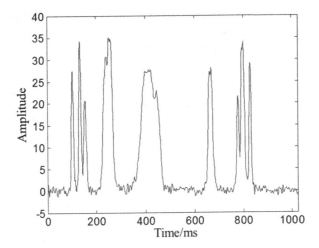

Fig. 10. Improved algorithm for denoising processed signals.

By comparing the denoising effect of the improved threshold method based on EMD with the original signal, EMD denoising, traditional soft and hard threshold method and improved threshold method, it can be seen that the improved method in this paper has no visual signal distortion and has better denoising effect than other methods.

2.4 Improved Algorithm Verification

The denoising effect needs to be quantified by the processing effect, and visually compared from the data. The measurement of the denoising effect [5] generally uses two indicators of signal-to-noise ratio (SNR) and root mean square error (RMSE). SNR refers to the ratio of the original signal energy to the noise energy. RMSE refers to the root mean square error of the denoised processed signal and the original signal without noise.

The signal to noise ratio calculation formula is:

$$SNR = 10 \lg \frac{\sum\limits_{t=1}^{N} s^2(t)}{\sum\limits_{t=1}^{N} [s'(t) - s(t)]^2} \tag{3}$$

The formula for calculating the root mean square error is:

$$RMES = \sqrt{\frac{1}{N} \sum\limits_{t=1}^{N} [s(t) - s'(t)]^2} \tag{4}$$

In the formula; $s(t)$ - the original signal without noise; $s'(t)$ - the signal after denoising; N- time series length.

In general, the smaller the RMES, the better the denoising effect of the signal when the SNR is larger.

Improved Denoising Method Compared with Other Denoising Methods. The improved method is compared with the median filtering method [6], Kalman filtering method [7], traditional soft and hard threshold method, and the SNR and RMES of various denoising methods are calculated by MATLAB. The calculation results are shown in Table 1.

Table 1. Comparison of denoising results by each method

Method	Method of this paper	Soft threshold method	Hard threshold method	Median filtering	Kalman filter
SNR	21.5338	16.9629	18.6815	18.3421	15.2741
RMES	0.1971	0.2554	0.2096	0.2179	0.3102

It can be seen from the above table that the improved denoising method in this method has higher signal-to-noise ratio than the other denoising methods in the filtering and denoising processing of the impact signal, and the root mean square error is small. Therefore, the improved denoising method is applied to the robot arm in operation. The impact signal denoising effect is better.

Applicability Verification. In order to prove that the improved method is not only suitable for the denoising filtering of the impact signal in the coal sampling robot, but also for the rectangular wave signal of the mechanical arm hydraulic cylinder, the improved method is applied for verification.

Load the rectangular signal waveform with noise in MATLAB. The figure after filtering and denoising by each method is shown in Fig. 11. Through comparison and analysis, it can be clearly seen that the improved method has the best denoising effect on rectangular signal.

The improved filtering method in this paper has a good filtering and denoising effect on the representative rectangular signal waveform and the impact signal waveform of the robotic arm of the coal sampling robot. Therefore, the improved filtering algorithm of this paper has applicability to the filtering process of the robot arm operating state data.

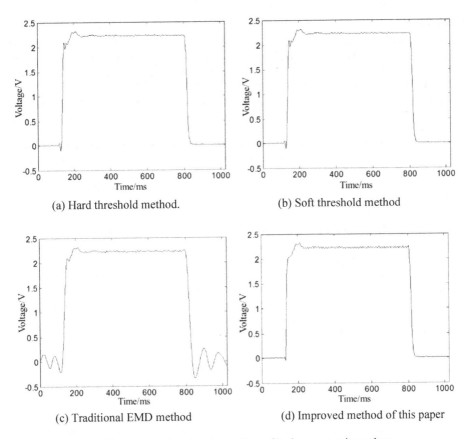

(a) Hard threshold method.   (b) Soft threshold method

(c) Traditional EMD method   (d) Improved method of this paper

Fig. 11. Rectangular signal waveform filtering comparison chart.

3 Conclusions

In this paper, the denoising method of robot manipulator running state data is analyzed. The traditional methods based on empirical mode decomposition denoising
filtering method and threshold method are analyzed. An improved threshold denoising
method based on EMD is proposed, which is different from other denosing methods.
The signal-to-noise ratio and root mean square error of this improved method are
compared and analyzed. The improved method has higher SNR and smaller RMS
error.

The modified method is compared with other methods to analyze the typical
rectangular signal and impulse signal of the coal sampling robot. The improved method
has better denoising effect than other methods. And the improved method has applicability in the denoising process in the robotic arm of coal sampling robot.

References

1. Abdelkader, R., Kaddour, A., Derouiche, Z.: Enhancement of rolling bearing fault diagnosis based on improvement of empirical mode decomposition denoising method. Int. J. Adv. Manuf. Technol. **97**(5–8), 3099–3117 (2018)
2. Alshawawreh, A.: Wavelet transform for single phase fault detection in noisy environment. In: 2014 IEEE 8th International Power Engineering and Optimization Conference (PEOCO) (2014)
3. Wang, J.-F. A wavelet denoising method based on the improved threshold function. In: 2014 International Conference on Wavelet Analysis and Pattern Recognition (ICWAPR) (2014)
4. Yang, K., Deng, C.-X., Chen, Y., Xu, L.-X.: The de-noising method of threshold function based on wavelet. In: 2014 International Conference on Wavelet Analysis and Pattern Recognition (ICWAPR) (2014)
5. Shi, C., Yu, X., Wan, W.: Research on the calculation of SNR of audio based on auditory filter. In: IET International Communication Conference on Wireless Mobile and Computing (CCWMC 2009) (2009)
6. Wierzchowski, W., Pawelczyk, M.: Median filtering approach for active control of impulsive noise. In: 2014 19th International Conference on Methods and Models in Automation and Robotics (MMAR) (2014)
7. Li, X., Chen, J., Shangguan, Y.: A method to analyse and eliminate stochastic noises of FOG based on ARMA and Kalman filtering method. In: 2014 Sixth International Conference on Intelligent Human-Machine Systems and Cybernetics (IHMSC) (2014)

A Study on Step-by-Step Calibration of Robot Based on Multi-vision Measurement

Rui Li[1(⊠)], Bingrong Wang[1], and Yang Zhao[2]

[1] Beijing Engineering Research Center of Precision Measurement Technology
and Instruments (Beijing University of Technology), Beijing, China
lirui@bjut.edu.cn
[2] China Academy of Space Technology, Beijing, China

Abstract. In this paper, an analytical method of robot error model based on multi-vision measurement system and a scheme about step-by-step calibration of robot angle and position error in the measuring space are introduced. This paper analyzes the calibration method of vision measuring system, and the transformation error model between robot coordinate system and vision coordinate system is discussed. The kinematic parameter error model of robot for each axis and the error model of the target at the end of robot caused by mechanical installation are established. According to these error models, the coordinate system transformation error, kinematic parameter error, target mechanical installation error contributing to the angle error and position error of robot are calibrated in step, and in consequence. The calibration accuracy of position and angle error for robot is improved obviously. Experiments verify that the calibration method in multi-vision measuring space that is proposed in the paper has an excellent effect on improving the robot motion control precision.

Keywords: Robot · Step-by-step calibration · Angle error compensation

1 Introduction

Currently, digital manufacturing systems based on industrial robot are widely used in senior manufacturing industry. However the common robot manufacturing method has been unable to meet the need of domestic manufacturing industry which need more and more automatic, high-precision and large-size manufacturing capacity. On one hand, robot itself is an open-loop system with limited positioning accuracy, which can not achieve close-loop precision machining level. On the other hand, when both manufacturing and measurement use the same robot servo control system to operate, they can not avoid impacting the action, which lead to adjust working path when manufacturing is broken off.

A great number of domestic and foreign experts have studied on how to improve the ability of controlling space position accuracy of industrial robot these years. Literature [1] analyzed one kind of kinematic parameter calibration method based on the distance error [1], using the coordinate measuring system to measure and calculate the kinematic parameter error for each axis of the robot; literature [2 and 3] obtained the

© Springer Nature Switzerland AG 2019
H. Yu et al. (Eds.): ICIRA 2019, LNAI 11744, pp. 165–173, 2019.
https://doi.org/10.1007/978-3-030-27541-9_15

kinematic parameter error by using axis measurements [2, 3], and verified the compensation accuracy using flexible three-coordinate measuring arm(CMA). And other papers also have proposed some different robot calibration algorithms, such as the index-based robot calibration method based on exponential product [4], the optimization algorithm based on neural network [5, 6] and the analytical algorithm based on Fourier polynomial [7] etc. With the literatures above as the representative, most of the robot kinematic parameter calibration methods currently are realized by means of independent measuring instruments such as coordinate measuring machine (CMM), optical theodolite and so on. With these high precision equipments, the systems can calibrate the 24 kinematic parameters of the robot. The calibration scheme above is mostly applied to system self-calibration purposes, which lead to the inability of tracking and closing loop compensation of robot machining system to real-time level. Without the support of independent measuring system, robot motion control still belongs to the open-loop process, which results in the uneasy to enhance the control accuracy according to the needs of the requirement. On the other hand, in contrast with position error, angle error has a smaller magnitude which actually is another key factor on robot machining accuracy. Because calibration models above for robot system can't evaluate enough influence of angel error, resulting in the low calibration accuracy when using such methods to calibrate the kinematic parameters error.

This article designs a step-by-step calibration method for both angle error and position error based on independent multi-vision measurement system. The experiments prove the novel calibration method in multi-vision measuring space has a good function in improving robot motion control precision.

2 Scheme for Measuring Position and Angel Error of Robot System

2.1 Step-by-Step Calibration Principle

Structure of real-time vision system for capturing motion is shown in Fig. 1. It uses 4 pieces of 1.3-megapixel infrared camera fixed in the space above enveloping outer enclosure of the robot spatial region. The layout of camera group is designed for the coverage of public space where target moves as much as possible at the same time. Stereo targets fixed at the end of the robot are consisted of five ball marks, which are used to establish the relationship between robot system and measurement system. Here measurement system is also called vision measurement. This method builds the parameter error model of robot in independent coordinate system. But prior to that, vision system should finish self-calibration. So Cross target is used for this purpose. L-shaped frame is here to help initiate the vision coordinate system.

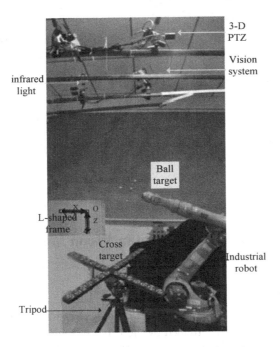

Fig. 1. Multi-vision system for robot calibration

Block diagram of calibration principle is shown in Fig. 2. Multi-vision system should pre-progress. Firstly cross target is used to accomplish self-calibration of multi-vision system to ensure high accuracy itself. Secondly, L-shaped frame is used to create initial coordinate system of cameras. After the preparations, vision system can obtain the relation of coordinates conversion through the public spherical target fixed at the end of the robot actuator. According to the kinematic parameter model, it can calculate the coordinates transformation between robot base coordinate system and vision coordinate system. The coordinate error of robot actuator is consisted of coordinates transformation error and kinematic parameter error. Moreover kinematic parameter error also is divided into angle error and position error. Despite the fact that angle error has a small magnitude, it can greatly affect the mechanical accuracy. Therefore step-by-step calibration is chosen.

The first step is to correct the error associated with the angle impact. The second step is to calibrate every error through the error model constructed based on the first step. With those steps, robot can be adjusted to more accurate situation. This is also key point differently from other robot calibration methods.

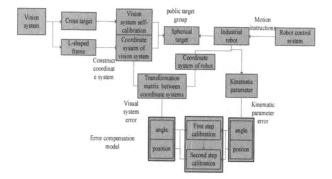

Fig. 2. Step-by-step calibration principle block program

3 Error Model Analysis of Robot in Vision Measurement System

3.1 Coordinate System Through Robot Calibration

Topological graph of robot calibration error model is simplified as Fig. 3. OpXpYpZp is vision coordinate system determined by the L-frame. OoXoYoZo is the actual base coordinate system of the robot. OrXrYrZr is the base coordinate system obtained by measurement, which can be defined as the virtual base coordinate system of robot. OaXaYaZa is the actual coordinate system of the target at the end of the robot. OcXcYcZc is the target coordinate system calculated by DH model in actual base coordinate system. The error between OaXaYaZa is caused by the kinematic parameter error. OmXmYmZm is the target coordinate system measured by vision system. Therefore, the error between it and OaXaYaZa is caused by the coordinate system conversion.

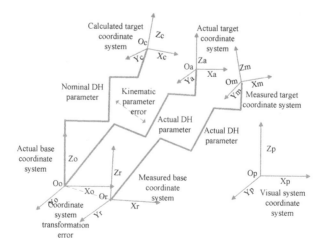

Fig. 3. Calibration error model topological graph

3.2   Error Model of Coordinate System Transformation

In order to determine target coordinates error in measuring coordinate system, it's needed to analyze the relationship between the base and vision coordinate system. The transformation error between OoXoYoZo and OrXrYrZr is so small. So the error model can be simplified as formula 1. Finally, The transformation error model consist of rotate error δ_x, δ_y, δ_z and translational error d_x, d_y, d_z.

$$T_0^r = \begin{bmatrix} 1 & -\delta_z & \delta_y & d_x \\ \delta_z & 1 & -\delta_x & d_y \\ -\delta_y & \delta_x & 1 & d_z \\ 0 & 0 & 0 & 1 \end{bmatrix} \tag{1}$$

3.3   Error Model of Robot Kinematic Parameter

The error model includes the length of the joint a_i, the displacement of the joint d_i, the angle of rotation α_i and the joint angle θ_i of each axis, totally 24 items. According to the DH model [11] of the robot, the transformation matrix of adjacent joint coordinate is described as:

$$\begin{aligned} T_{i-1}^i &= Rot(z, \theta_i) \times Trans(0, 0, d_i) \times Trans(a_i, 0, 0) \times Rot(x, a_i) \\ &= \begin{bmatrix} cos\,\theta_i & -sin\,\theta_i\,cos\,\alpha_i & sin\,\theta_i\,sin\,\alpha_i & cos\,\theta_i \\ sin\,\theta_i & cos\,\theta_i\,cos\,\alpha_i & -cos\,\theta_i & sin\,\theta_i \\ 0 & sin\,\alpha_i & cos\,\alpha_i & d_i \\ 0 & 0 & 0 & 1 \end{bmatrix} \end{aligned} \tag{2}$$

Where, $a_i, d_i, \alpha_i, \theta_i$ is respectively the length of the joint, the displacement of the joint, the angle of rotation and the joint angle.

The differential of position error between the adjacent robot axes could be expressed as:

$$dT_{i-1}^i = \frac{\partial T_{i-1}^i}{\partial \theta} \Delta\theta + \frac{\partial T_{i-1}^i}{\partial \alpha} \Delta\alpha + \frac{\partial T_{i-1}^i}{\partial a} \Delta a + \frac{\partial T_{i-1}^i}{\partial d} \Delta d \tag{3}$$

Expand the polynomial and omit the high-order polynomial, thus:

$$dT_0^n = \sum_{I=1}^{N} T_0^1 T_1^2 L T_{i-1}^i \Delta_i T_i^{i+1} \cdots T_{i-1}^i = T_0^1 T_{\theta 1} T_1^N \Delta\theta_1 + T_0^1 T_{\alpha 1} T_1^N \Delta\alpha_1 + T_0^1 T_{a1} T_1^N \Delta a_1$$

$$+ T_0^1 T_{d1} T_1^N \Delta d_1 + T_0^2 T_{\theta 2} T_2^N \Delta\theta_2 + T_0^2 T_{a2} T_2^N \Delta\alpha_2 + T_0^2 T_{a1} T_2^N \Delta a_2 + T_0^2 T_{d2} T_2^N \Delta d_2 + \cdots +$$

$$T_0^{N-1} T_{\theta N-1} \Delta\theta_{N-1} + T_0^{N-1} T_{\alpha N-1} \Delta\alpha_{N-1} + T_0^{N-1} T_{AN-1} \Delta A_{N-1} + T_{dN-1} \Delta d_{N-1} + T_0^N T_{dtx} \Delta t_x + T_0^N T_{dty} \Delta t_y$$

$$+ T_0^N T_{dtz} \Delta t_z$$

$$
= \begin{bmatrix} 0 & -\delta_{tz} & \delta_{ty} & d_{tx} \\ \delta_{tz} & 0 & -\delta_{tx} & d_{ty} \\ -\delta_{ty} & \delta t_{tx} & 0 & d_{tz} \\ 0 & 0 & 0 & 1 \end{bmatrix} \tag{4}
$$

4 Robot Error Calibration Using Vision Measuring System

4.1 Angle Error Calibration

Firstly, because magnitude of each error has large difference [12], the angle error with small magnitude will have large effect in position error at the end of robot through amplification of each axis. Secondly, usually in the machining, the attitude accuracy of tools is much more important than the position accuracy. So, this paper adopts the step-by-step calibration method. The first step is to calibrate the angle error including the angle of rotation α_i, the joint angle θ_i, and the rotation matrix error δ_x, δ_y, δ_z in the coordinates transformation matrix.

According to formula 3, the differential of angle error between the adjacent robot axes could be stated as:

$$
dT_{i-1}^i = T_{i-1}^i (T_{\theta i} \cdot \Delta\theta_i + T_{\theta i} \cdot \Delta_{\alpha i}) \tag{5}
$$

The angle items of coordinates transformation matrix can be stated as formula 2. Taking formula 5 to 4, here can obtain the transformation matrix between OaXaYaZa and OcXcYcZc.

Suppose Ta is the coordinates matrix of target in OoXoYoZo, Tc is the coordinates matrix of target calculated through the kinematic model in OoXoYoZo, Tm is the coordinates matrix of target measured in OmXmYmZm. According to the definition of coordinate system, here can get:

$$
Tm = T_0^r \times Ta = T_0^r \times Tc \times \delta T \tag{6}
$$

where

$$
\delta T = \begin{bmatrix} k_{1\theta}^x & k_{1\alpha}^x & k_{2\theta}^x & \cdots & k_{N\theta}^x \\ k_{1\theta}^y & k_{1\alpha}^y & k_{2\theta}^y & \cdots & k_{N\theta}^y \\ k_{1\theta}^z & k_{1\alpha}^z & k_{2\theta}^z & \cdots & k_{N\theta}^z \end{bmatrix} \cdot \begin{bmatrix} \Delta\theta_1 & \Delta\alpha_1 & \Delta\theta_2 & \cdots & \Delta\alpha_N \end{bmatrix} = B_i \cdot \Delta q_i
$$

The right side of formula 6 includes 15 items of angle error, and the left side is the matrix of target coordinate system measured by vision system. Taking them the formula 4 to calculate parameters.

Because the condition number of matrix Bi is extremely large, Gauss algorithm is invalid despite double precision calculation. So, the basic theory of generalized inverse matrix is used to solve the Eqs. 6 to obtain the least square solution. Setting τ the floating-point calculation precision, the item in generalized inverse matrix which is less than τ can be ignored. Owing to this method, here can get the approximate solution of Δq_i after reducing the condition number of matrix.

Using the method described in Sect. 3, here can get 60 groups of experimental measurement data which can be taken into Eq. 6. The 15 angle errors can be calibrated through the 60 data which is get through the measurement method described in Sect. 2. The result is shown in Table 1.

Table 1. Compensation result

Angle error			Translational error		
	θ	α	δ_x	δ_y	δ_z
Axis1	−0.0115	0.0032	0.0005	−0.0017	−0.0115
Axis2	0.0034	−0.0004			
Axis3	−0.0033	0.0031			
Axis4	0.0288	0.0045			
Axis5	0.0079	0.0198			
Axis6	0.0001	0.0217			

4.2 Calibration of Other 33 Errors at the Second Step

Oa is the coordinate of target center at OoXoYoZo. Oc is the coordinate of target center calculated by the kinematic model in OoXoYoZo. Om is the coordinate of target center measured in OmXmYmZm. Thus:

$$Oa = Oc + \Delta P \quad Om - Oc = T_0^r$$
$$Oa - Oc = T_0^r(Oc + \Delta P) - Oc = (T_0^r - E)Oc + \Delta P + (T_0^r - E)\Delta P \tag{7}$$

$(T_0^r - E)\Delta P$ is a quadratic higher-order term, which can be ignored. So formula 7 can be simplified as:

$$Om - Oc = (T_0^r - E)p + \Delta P \tag{8}$$

Taking them the formula 4 to calculate parameters. The left side of the formula 7 is the difference between coordinate of target in OrXrYrZr and the coordinate of target calculated by the DH model in OoXoYoZo. The right side is the 33 errors.

Here can get the 33 errors by using the basic theory of generalized inverse matrix to obtain the least square solution of formula 8. The initial angle error is compensated value in Sect. 4.1. The vision system measures 75 data which can be used to calculate the error on the basis of the least square method. The result is shown in Table 2:

Table 2. Compensation result

Kinematic parameter error

	Axis1	Axis2	Axis3	Axis4	Axis5	Axis6
θ	−0.0001	−0.0010	−0.0007	−0.0029	0.0004	0.1455
α	0.0007	0.0014	0.0002	−0.0034	−0.0097	−0.0082
a	−0.2113	0.0904	−0.0751	0.1709	−0.0006	0.2340
d	0.0019	0.0036	0.0036	−0.3133	0.0020	−0.1241

5 Error Compensation Experiment

Select 55 points to participate in calibration, and use vision system to verify the positing and angle accuracy of the target after calibration. The comparison results obtained before and after calibration are shown as Table 3. From the table, the first part show that angle error can not be corrected basically using the traditional calibration method, but can be corrected to a certain extent using the step-by- step calibration method. The second part show that both methods can reduce the position error, but the accuracy contributed by step-by-step calibration method is higher than that of the traditional method.

Table 3. Comparison results

		Before comparison			Traditional method			Step-by-step method		
1 (rad)	Angle error	δ_{tx}	δ_{ty}	δ_{tz}	δ_{tx}	δ_{ty}	δ_{tz}	δ_{tx}	δ_{ty}	δ_{tz}
	mean value	0.0412	−0.0130	−0.0065	0.0291	−0.0057	−0.0070	0.0135	0.0103	0.0008
	σ	0.1371	0.0911	0.1220	0.1238	0.0989	0.1272	0.1010	0.0536	0.0714
2 (mm)	Position error	d_{tx}	d_{ty}	d_{tz}	d_{tx}	d_{ty}	d_{tz}	d_{tx}	d_{ty}	d_{tz}
	Mean value	0.3339	−0.3247	0.6180	0.0478	0.0292	0.0077	0.0148	−0.0374	−0.0485
	σ	1.1273	0.9440	1.0362	0.3141	0.1638	0.2238	0.1582	0.1615	0.1839

6 Conclusion

According to the step-by-step calibration method based on multi-vision measurement system in the measuring space for the robot, we analyze the transformation error model between robot and vision system, the kinematic parameter error model of robot for each axis, and the installation error model of the target at the end of robot. Angle error and position error are corrected based on these error models above and accuracy related to the angle is improved after calibration. The position and angle accuracy are both improved compared to that of the traditional calibration method.

References

1. Zhang, T., Dai, X.-L.: Kinematic calibration of robot based on distance error. J. South China Univ. Technol. (Nat. Sci. Ed.) **39**(11), 98–103 (2011)
2. Xie, Z., Xin, S., Li, X.: Method of robot calibration based on monocular vision. J. Mech. Eng. **47**(5), 35–39 (2011)
3. Santolaria, J., Gine, M.: Robotics and computer-integrated manufacturing. Robot. Comput.-Integr. Manuf. **29**, 370–384 (2013)
4. Gao, W., Wang, H., Jiang, Y.: A calibration method for serial robots based on POE formula. Robot **35**(2), 156–161 (2013)
5. Zhong, X., Lewis, J., N-Nagy, F.: Inverse robot calibration using artificial neural networks. Eng. Appl. Artif. Intell. **9**(1), 83–93 (1996)
6. Shamma, J.S., Whitney, D.E.: A method for inverse robot calibration. Trans. ASME **109**(1), 36–43 (1987)
7. Alici, G., Shirinzadeh, B.: A systematic technique to estimate positioning errors for robot accuracy improvement using laser interferometry based sensing. Mech. Mach. Theor. **40**(8), 879–906 (2005)
8. Huang, G.: Study on the key technologies of digital close range industrial photogrammetry and applications. Tianjin: Tianjin University (2005)
9. Jie, X.U.: Analyzing and improving the tsai camera calibration method in machine vision. Comput. Eng. Sci. **32**(4), 45–48 (2010)
10. Li, H., Wang, J.I.: A research on camera calibration technique. Optical Instrum. **29**(4), 7–12 (2007)
11. Fang, H., Liu, X.: Parameter determination in robot kinematic model. J. Mach. Des. **28**(2), 46–49 (2011)
12. Sun, M., Ren, L., Han, H.: Series robot tracking detection system based on stereo vision. Comput. Eng. **28**(13), 240–243 (2012)

Characteristic Frequency Input Neural Network for Inertia Identification of Tumbling Space Target

Chuan Ma[1,2], Jianping Yuan[1,2(✉)], and Dejia Che[1,2]

[1] Northwestern Polytechnical University, Xi'an 710072, China
jyuan@nwpu.edu.cn
[2] National Key Laboratory of Aerospace Flight Dynamics, Xi'an 710072, China

Abstract. A novel characteristic frequency input network (CFIN) is investigated for inertia parameters identification of the tumbling space target from the quaternion measurements based on the back propagation neural network. The main innovation of the CFIN is it set the 15-dimensional characteristic frequency vector as the input of the neural network, which is extracted from the constant parameters of the target's attitude quaternion. The utilization of the characteristic frequency not only reduces the required number of nodes to less than 100, but also improves the learning rate of the neural network. The CFIN is trained using 10000 samples and tested using another 2000 data. It can work well in real-time with very little computational burden and storage space once successfully trained. Moreover, effectiveness analysis illustrates that the CFIN can provide more precise estimation of the inertia parameters than the conventional estimation method, like extend Kalman filter and unscented Kalman filter in most case.

Keywords: Inertia identification · Characteristic frequency · BP neural network · Tumbling space target

1 Introduction of the Inertia Identification Problem

In resent years, on-orbit servicing technologies have attracted extensive attention. However, the rendezvous and capture of large-size space debris, like defunct satellites and rocket boosters, is still one of the most challenging problems in on-orbit missions. The main problem is that the space debris are commonly tumbling under the effect of initial angular momentum [1,2]. In order to reduce the risk of impact, the chaser satellite must predict the target's attitude motion precisely, which requires a precise estimation of the target's inertia tensor [3–5]. What is more, the stabilization process should start immediately once the target is captured to avoid separation, which also needs a priori knowledge of the target's inertia characteristics [6–8]. Therefore, the high precise identification of the target's inertia characteristics are eagerly required for on-orbit servicing missions.

© Springer Nature Switzerland AG 2019
H. Yu et al. (Eds.): ICIRA 2019, LNAI 11744, pp. 174–187, 2019.
https://doi.org/10.1007/978-3-030-27541-9_16

The mathematical models of the inertia parameter identification problem is briefly introduce as follows. In practice, it is sufficient to model the target as a rigid body, whose attitude dynamical equation is given by

$$\begin{aligned}
\dot{q}_0 &= -\boldsymbol{\omega} \cdot \boldsymbol{q}_v \\
\dot{\boldsymbol{q}}_v &= q_0 \boldsymbol{\omega} + \boldsymbol{\omega} \times \boldsymbol{q}_v, \\
\dot{\boldsymbol{\omega}} &= \boldsymbol{J}^{-1}(\boldsymbol{J}\boldsymbol{\omega} \times \boldsymbol{\omega} + \boldsymbol{\varepsilon}),
\end{aligned} \tag{1}$$

where $\boldsymbol{q} = [q_0, \boldsymbol{q}_v]^T$ is the target's attitude quaternion, q and $\boldsymbol{q}_v = [q_1, q_2, q_3]^T$ are the scale part and vector part of it, $\boldsymbol{\omega} = [\omega_x, \omega_y, \omega_z]^T$ is the target's angular velocity, $\dot{q}_0$, $\dot{\boldsymbol{q}}_v$, and $\dot{\boldsymbol{\omega}}$ are their corresponding time derivatives, $\boldsymbol{\varepsilon}$ is the disturbing moment acts on the target, and $\boldsymbol{J}$ is the target's inertia tensor in the form of

$$\boldsymbol{J} = \begin{bmatrix} J_{xx} & & \\ & J_{yy} & \\ & & J_{zz} \end{bmatrix}, \tag{2}$$

where J_{xx}, J_{yy}, and J_{zz} are the target's principal axes moments of inertia.

Obviously, the value $\boldsymbol{J}$ can influence the $\boldsymbol{\omega}$ and $\boldsymbol{q}$, hence one can identify the target's inertia tensor by measuring its angular velocity or attitude quaternion. In practice, it is usually hard to measure the non-cooperative target's angular velocity or inertia characteristics directly, while the relative attitude could be acquired through non-contact measurement instruments, like Light Detection and Ranging (LIDAR) systems [9–11] and vision systems [12, 13]. Therefore the observation equation is given by

$$\boldsymbol{z} = \boldsymbol{h}(\boldsymbol{q}, \boldsymbol{\omega}) + \boldsymbol{w} = \boldsymbol{q} + \boldsymbol{w}, \tag{3}$$

where $\boldsymbol{w}$ denotes the measurement noise.

Consequently, the inertia parameters identification of the tumbling target boils down to the problem about how to determine the values of $\boldsymbol{J}$ from the measurements of $\boldsymbol{q}$, based on the dynamical equations (1) and the observation equation (3).

Existing literature have provided a number of methods to solve this problem, such as least squares (LS) method, extended state observer (ESO), extend Kalman filter (EKF), and particle filter (PF), etc. All these methods are based on the dynamical model Eq. (1) and the observation model (3), which leads to three main problems. First, the inertia tensor only affects the second derivative of the quaternion $\boldsymbol{q}$ and causes long-term effects on the attitude motion, hence the estimation may be trapped in local optimum after few observations when using these recursive method. Second, the attitude dynamical model has strong non-linearity, hence the algorithm with weak non-linearity assumption, like LS, ESO and EKF, may not work when the measurement frequency is too low or the target's rotating speed is too large. Finally, the nonlinear filter, like PF, usually has a very heavy computational burden, hence the algorithm cannot work on orbit in real-time.

The development of back propagation (BP) neural network provides an alternative method for inertia parameters identifications of the tumbling space target

[15, 16]. However, there are still many difficulties in applications. The main problem lies in the dimension of input of the network. As mentioned above, the effects of the inertia parameters is long-term, hence the identification of the inertia tensor needs a large number of measurements - for instance, $200-500$ inputs are necessary in most case. If the input has hundreds of dimensions, then more than one thousand nodes are necessary for the neural network and hundreds of thousands of samples are required to train these nodes. This will result in the heavy computational burden and poor stability of the neural network.

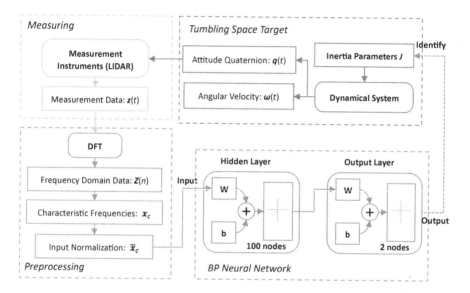

Fig. 1. The process diagram of the characteristic frequency input network (CFIN). (Color figure online)

In this paper, we apply the frequency analysis technique to extract the characteristic frequencies of the target's attitude motion, so as to reduce the input dimension to 15. Then based on the BP neural network, the characteristic frequency input network (CFIN) is designed to identify the tumbling space target's inertia tensor, as shown in Fig. 1. The CFIN is trained using 20000 simulation samples, and tested using another 2000 data. Although the CFIN has only one hidden layer and 100 nodes, it shows better performance than the conventional inertia identification methods. Moreover, the impact of input characteristics and factors on the output errors are also studied.

2   Characteristic Frequency Input Network

2.1   Discrete Fourier Transformation: A Frequency Analysis Method

As mentioned above, the affects of the inertia parameters on the attitude motion is long-term, thus a number of measurements are necessary to guarantee the accuracy of the inertia identification. On the other hand, the high dimension of input results in the heavy computational burden and instability of the neural network in training process. Therefore, the measurement data must be compressed before sent to the neural network. In this section, the discrete Fourier transformation (DFT) method is utilized to exact the characteristic frequencies of the tumbling target's attitude quaternion, so as to reduce the input dimension.

The DFT technique is widely used in signal processing and information compression [18,19]. Specifically, the DFT of the measurement data, denoted by $\boldsymbol{Z}(n)$, is given by [20,21]

$$Z_i(n) = \sum_{k=0}^{N-1} z_i(k) e^{-j\frac{2\pi}{N}nk} \quad (i = 0, 1, 2, 3), \tag{4}$$

where j is the symbol of imaginary, N is the amount of the measurement data, $z_i(k)$ is the ith component of $\boldsymbol{z}$ at the time index k, and $Z_i(n)$ is the corresponding DFT result in the frequency domain at the frequency $f = \frac{n-1}{N\Delta t}$. For a tumbling rigid body, there are three significant peaks in the frequency domain [22,24], as shown in Fig. 2 for instance. The corresponding frequencies of the three peaks are denoted by f_1, f_2, and f_3, respectively. Moreover, $p_{ij}(i = \{0, \cdots, 3\}, j = \{1, 2, 3\})$ denotes the height of peak at the frequency f_j, for the component z_i in the frequency domain.

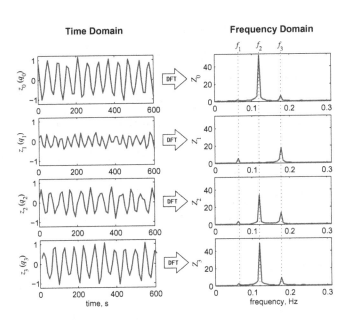

Fig. 2. The discrete Fourier Transformation (DFT) of the attitude quaternion measurements.

Then, a set of characteristic frequency parameters are exacted from the DFT results of the observation data, i.e.,

$$x_c = [f_1, f_2, f_3, p_{01}, p_{02}, \cdots, p_{33}]^T. \tag{5}$$

Namely, the information of measurement data are compressed into these 15 parameters.

The application of the characteristic frequency vector x_c results in four main advantages:

(1) The information dimension is significantly reduced. The dimension of x_c is 15, while the number of the measurements is 200−500, with 4 dimensions for each measurement. (2) Most of the measurement information is retained in the 15 parameters, because the three predominate frequency peaks contain most of the information energy. One can easily rebuild an approximation of the frequency domain from x_c, and then use inverse DFT algorithm to get an approximation of the original measurement data in time domain, with little information lost. (3) The 15 parameters are constant over time, hence the start time of the measurements will not influence their values. (4) It can filter out the measuring noise w, because the information energy of the noises are evenly distributed in the frequency domain.

2.2   Neural Network Design

The information compression of DFT make it possible to identify the inertia parameters J by using a BP neural network. Based on the characteristic frequencies and the BP neural network, in this section, a characteristic frequency input network (CFIN) is provided for inertia identification of a tumbling space target.

As shown in Fig. 1, the red box represents the dynamical system of the target, where the inertia parameters J can influence the target's attitude quaternion and the angular velocity through the dynamical models Eq. (1). The yellow box represents the measuring process, where $z(t)$ is the observation of $q(t)$ with measurement noises. In the green box is the data preprocessing. The characteristic frequencies x_c are extracted from the measurements as mentioned above, and then be normalized for inputting to the neural network. And the blue box represents the BP neural network.

For the neural network, the inertia identification problem boils down to the parameter fitting problem. Then two layers are sufficient to obtain a good result [27], including one hidden layer and one output layer. Moreover, the activation function of the hidden layer is the hyperbolic sine, while the output layer's is an identify function.

The number of nodes of the output layer should equal to the output dimension, i.e., the degree of freedom of the inertia tensor J. However, one can infer from Eq. (1) that the norm of J does not influence the derivative $\dot{\omega}$, because it is offset by the inverse J^{-1}. Therefore one can only identify the inertia ratios between components of the inertia tensor, like J_{xx}/J_{yy}, through the quaternion measurements. Without loss of generality, we assume $J_{xx} < J_{yy} < J_{zz}$, and set the output as $\boldsymbol{y} = [\frac{J_{xx}}{J_{zz}}, \frac{J_{yy}}{J_{zz}}]^T$. These two ratios are the identifiable inertia parameters, whose values are in the interval $(0, 1]$. Therefore, two nodes are needed in the output layer.

The number of nodes of the hidden layer depends on the characteristics of the input data and the internal relation between input and output. In this paper, it is set as 100 through trail and error. And the weights corresponding to these nodes are supposed to be trained using BP algorithm.

2.3   Input Preprocessing

In order to increase the learning speed of the neural network, the activation functions should work in the high-gain interval as much as possible [27,28]. It requires the input data to have a zero exception, and each component of input to have a similar variance. Therefore, the normalization of the characteristic frequencies is necessary before they are entered to the BP neural network.

In this section, the input $\tilde{\boldsymbol{x}}_c$ is normalized using the mean value and the standard deviation of N_t training samples, i.e.,

$$\tilde{\boldsymbol{x}}_c = \boldsymbol{\sigma}^{-1}(\boldsymbol{x}_c - \boldsymbol{\mu}), \tag{6}$$

where

$$\boldsymbol{\mu} = \frac{1}{N_t} \sum_{i=0}^{N_t} \boldsymbol{x}_c^{(i)} \tag{7}$$

is the mean value of inputs of the training data, N_t is the number of training samples, $\boldsymbol{x}_c^{(i)}$ is the ith training sample, and $\boldsymbol{\sigma}$ is the Cholesky decomposition of the variance matrix of the training data, i.e.,

$$\boldsymbol{\sigma}\boldsymbol{\sigma}^T = \frac{1}{N_t - 1} \sum_{i=0}^{N_t} \left(\boldsymbol{x}_c^{(i)} - \boldsymbol{\mu}\right)\left(\boldsymbol{x}_c^{(i)} - \boldsymbol{\mu}\right)^T. \tag{8}$$

Moreover, the generation of the training samples are introduced in the next subsection.

2.4   Network Training

The neural network must be trained before it can work, which needs a batch of training samples. The number of training samples N_t depends on the number of nodes of the network and the complexity of the system for fitting. Specifically, the number of samples is set to be $N_t = 10000$ for the CFIN through trail and error, which is an acceptable training scale for practical application.

It is impracticable to generate the training samples through physical experiments. Hence we get these data through simulation experiments based on the dynamical equations (1) and the observation equation (3). It is supposed that the target rigid body's mass distribution is uniformly random in the 3-dimensional space, and the target's angular rate is $0.3-0.6\,\mathrm{rad/s}$. Hence the process and parameters for generating one sample are provided as follows:

(1) Generate a random vector $\boldsymbol{m} = [m_x, m_y, m_z]^T$, where m_x, m_y, and m_z are independent identically distributed (iid.) from the uniform distribution in the interval $[-1, 1]$. Then the principal moments of inertia of this sample are calculated by

$$J_{xx} = m_y^2 + m_z^2, \ J_{yy} = m_x^2 + m_z^2, \ J_{zz} = m_x^2 + m_y^2. \tag{9}$$

For the sake of convenience in the next analysis, exchange the values of them subject to $J_{xx} < J_{yy} < J_{zz}$.

(2) Generate a random vector $\boldsymbol{\omega}_r = [\omega_{rx}, \omega_{ry}, \omega_{rz}]^T$, where ω_{rx}, ω_{ry}, and ω_{rz} are iid. from the uniform distribution in the interval $[-1, 1]$. Then the initial angular velocity is set as

$$\omega_0 = 0.5 \frac{\omega_r}{\|\omega_r\|}. \tag{10}$$

(3) Since the initial quaternion $\boldsymbol{q}_0$ does not influence the frequency parameters $\boldsymbol{x}_c$, it is set as $\boldsymbol{q}_0 = [1, 0, 0, 0]^T$ for the sake of convenience. Then one can generate the time series $\boldsymbol{q}(t)$ by utilizing the dynamical model Eq. (1).

(4) Generate 500 measurements $\{z(1), \cdots, z(500)\}$ using the observation model Eq. (3), with measuring rate of $1\,\mathrm{Hz}$, $\boldsymbol{w}$ modeled as a zero-mean Gaussian noise with variance of 0.05^2.

(5) Using DFT to the 500 measurements to get the characteristic frequency vector $\boldsymbol{x}_c^{(i)}$ and normalize it using the preprocessing technique above.

(6) Set the normalized vector $\tilde{\boldsymbol{x}}_c^{(i)}$ as the ith input, and the inertia ratios $\boldsymbol{y}^{(i)} = [\frac{J_{xx}}{J_{zz}}, \frac{J_{yy}}{J_{zz}}]^T$ as the ith output.

By repeating the 6 steps above, one can generate 10000 iid. samples. Then, the samples are divided into three parts: 8000 samples for training, 1500 for validation, and 500 for testing. The training samples are presented to the neural work during training, and the network is adjusted according to its error. The validation samples are used to measure network generalization, and to halt training when generalization stops improving. The testing samples have no effect on training and so provide an independent measure of network performance during training. Moreover, another 2000 samples are generated independently to test the CFIN performance after training.

The Levenberg-Marquardt algorithm [28] is applied for training the neural network. And the training automatically stops when generation stops improving, as indicated by an increase in the mean square error of the validation samples.

3   Effectiveness Analysis

3.1   Training Result

The training process stops after 46 epochs, while the best validation performance is 0.00380 at epoch 40, as shown in Fig. 3. Moreover, Fig. 4 shows the error histogram of the CFIN, indicating that more than 95% samples' errors lie in the interval of $-0.0925 - 0.0622$.

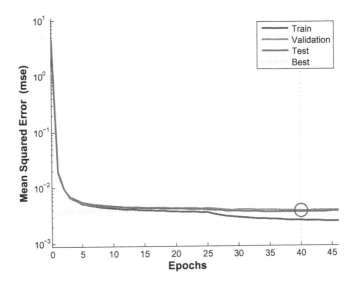

Fig. 3. Performance of the characteristic frequency input network (CFIN) in training.

In addition, Fig. 5 shows the output errors of 80 randomly selected samples in the output space, where x-axis represents $\frac{I_{xx}}{I_{zz}}$, and y-axis represents $\frac{I_{yy}}{I_{zz}}$. The blue circles denote the expected output of the samples, while the red stars denote the output of the trained CFIN. Owing to the definition of the principal moments of inertia Eq. (9), the inertia ratios are restricted to a triangle area. Moreover, the geometry meaning of the area's marginals is summarized as follows:

The red dashed line means $I_{yy} = I_{zz}$, i.e., the target has two big moments of inertia in common. This refers to the axial-symmetrical rod-like rigid body, such as the cylinder with large height.

The yellow dashed line means $I_{xx} = I_{yy}$, i.e., the target has two small moments of inertia in common. This refers to the axial-symmetrical thick-board-like rigid body, such as the cylinder with small height.

The green dashed line means $I_{xx} + I_{yy} = I_{zz}$, i.e., the target's mass is distributed in one plane. This refers to the very thin plate.

The upper right vertex means $I_{xx} = I_{yy} = I_{zz}$, i.e., the target is spherical symmetric, such as the sphere or the cube.

The upper left vertex means $I_{xx} = 0$ and $I_{yy} = I_{zz}$, i.e., the target's mass is converged in one line.

And the lower vertex means $I_{xx} = I_{yy} = \frac{1}{2}I_{zz}$, i.e., the target is a central symmetrical thin plate, such as the circular plate or the square plate.

Obviously, the longer the segment between the output and the target, the bigger the inertia identification error. One can infer from Fig. 5 that the output errors are relatively small in most case. however, when the target's mass distribution is near the green line, i.e., the target's shape is like a plate, the output error can be very big. In the next subsection, the impacts of the target's mass distribution and angular velocity will be studied in detail.

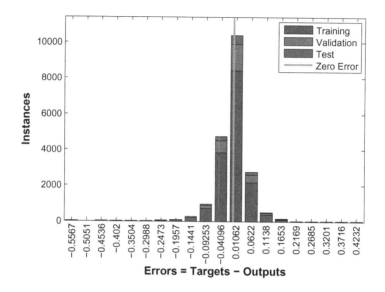

Fig. 4. Error histogram of the characteristic frequency input network (CFIN).

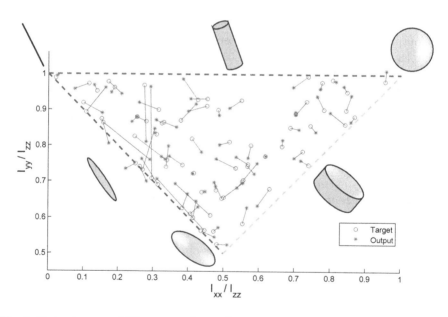

Fig. 5. Output errors of 80 test samples in the output space using CFIN. (Color figure online)

3.2   Mean Square Error Analysis

In order to analyze the impacts of the target's characteristics (include the inertia characteristics and the kinematic characteristics) on the identification accuracy of the CFIN, 2000 testing samples are entered to the CFIN, and the outputs as well as their corresponding mean square errors (MSE) are shown in Fig. 6.

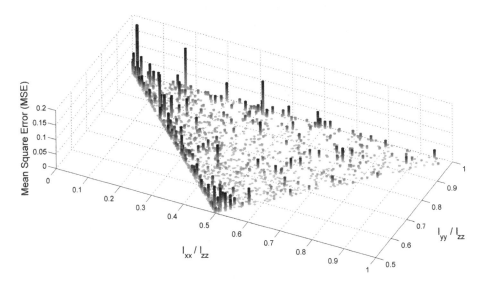

Fig. 6. MSE of 2000 test samples in the output space using CFIN.

In Fig. 6, the cylinders represent the testing samples, with the heights are the MSE, and the position represent the mass distribution parameters. This MSE map seems to indicate that the CFIN can work well in most cases, unless the sample is very near the left lower marginal ($I_{xx} + I_{yy} = I_{zz}$) or the upper marginal ($I_{yy} = I_{zz}$), corresponding to the plate-like object and rod-like object, respectively.

Based on this phenomenon, we divide the samples into two parts according to their location in the output space, and carry on the statistics analysis of their MSE. The first part contains those samples with $(I_{xx} + I_{yy})/I_{zz} < 0.1$ or $I_{yy}/I_{zz} > 0.95$, which is indicated by the shaded area in the left of Fig. 7. And the other part contains the other samples, as indicated in the right of Fig. 7. Moreover, Fig. 7 shows the distribution of the MSE of these samples with respect to the module k, where k is a indicating parameter for the direction of angular velocity with respect to the target's principal axes of inertia, defined by

$$
k = \begin{cases} \dfrac{(J_{yy} - J_{xx})(J_{zz} - I)}{J_{zz} - J_{yy}(I - J_{xx})} & (I > J_{yy}), \\[3mm] \dfrac{(J_{zz} - J_{yy})(I - J_{xx})}{(J_{yy} - J_{xx})(J_{zz} - I)} & (I \leq J_{yy}), \end{cases} \tag{11}
$$
$$
I = \frac{J_{xx}^2 \omega_x^2 + J_{yy}^2 \omega_y^2 + J_{zz}^2 \omega_z^2}{J_{xx}\omega_x^2 + J_{yy}\omega_y^2 + J_{zz}\omega_z^2}.
$$

$k = 0$ represents that the target is steadily rotating around the biggest or the smallest principal axis of inertia. Moreover, $k = 1$ represents that the target is in the unstable state of rotating around the middle principal axis of inertia. And $0 < k < 1$ represents that the target's angular velocity does not coincide with any principal axes, and is variable over time.

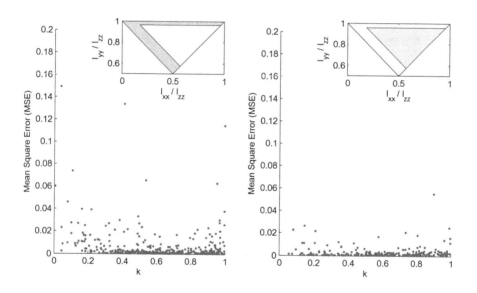

Fig. 7. Comparison of MSE between different mass distributions.

Figure 7 shows that the MSE of samples in the second part is much smaller than those in the first part. Furthermore, Fig. 8 shows the MSE of these samples in more detail. The red line is the 99% edge line, i.e., 99% samples' MSE are under the red line. And the green line means the 90% edge line. One can infer from the green line that most of the samples result in a MSE less than 0.005, which is better than the EKF [14] methods with MSE about $0.01{-}0.1$. Note that the increase of k can slightly impact to the MSE. This is mainly because that when the target's angular velocity is near the middle principal axis, i.e. $k \approx 1$, the quaternion can have more than three peaks in the frequency domain, hence the 15-dimensional characteristic frequency vector loses more information about the target's motion, so to get a worse estimation of the target's inertia parameters. On the other hand, the red line shows that the outlier values can be much bigger when k is less than 0.2. This is because that when the target is rotating around the constant axis ($k \approx 0$), the inertia parameters would have less effects on the target's attitude motion, hence the inertia identification can be rough by using the attitude quaternion measurements. Namely, the inaccuracy of the output when $k \approx 0$ is due to the deficiency of the observation data, rather than the defect of the CFIN method.

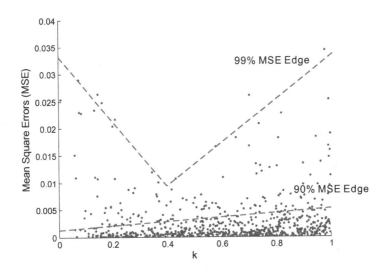

Fig. 8. MSE of the CFIN with respective to the module k. (Color figure online)

4 Conclusions

This paper investigate a novel characteristic frequency input network (CFIN) for inertia parameters identification of the tumbling space target using quaternion measurements. The main innovation of the CFIN is it set the 15-dimensional characteristic frequency vector as the input of the neural network, so as to reduce the computational burden and the storage space of the algorithm. The CFIN is trained using 10000 samples, and is tested using another 2000 inputs. The CFIN results in the mean square errors less than 0.005 for more than 90% testing samples, which is much better than the conventional EKF methods. Moreover, test results show that the mass distribution and the angular velocity's direction can influence the output errors of the CFIN. The CFIN show the best performance, when the target's mass distribution does not be like a rod or a plate, and the direction of the angular velocity is not very near to any principal axes of inertia. To sum up, one can come to the conclusion that the CFIN shows good performances in inertia parameter identification of the tumbling space target.

References

1. Shan, M., Guo, J., Gill, E.: Review and comparison of active space debris capturing and removal methods. Prog. Aerosp. Sci. **80**, 18–32 (2016)
2. Li, Q., Yuan, J., Zhang, B., Gao, C.: Model predictive control for autonomous rendezvous and docking with a tumbling target. Aerosp. Sci. Technol. **69**, 700–711 (2017)
3. Angel Flores-Abad, O., Ma, K.P., Ulrich, S.: A review of space robotics technologies for onorbit servicing. Prog. Aerosp. Sci. **68**, 1–26 (2014)
4. Flores-Abad, A., Zhang, L., Wei, Z., Ma, O.: Optimal capture of a tumbling object in orbit using a space manipulator. J. Intell. Robot. Syst. **86**(2), 199–211 (2017)
5. Luo, J., Zong, L., Wang, M., Yuan, J.: Optimal capture occasion determination and trajectory generation for space robots grasping tumbling objects. Acta Astronautica **136**, 380–386 (2017)
6. Huang, P., Wang, M., Meng, Z., Zhang, F., Liu, Z.: Attitude takeover control for postcapture of target spacecraft using space robot. Aerosp. Sci. Technol. **51**, 171–180 (2016)
7. Zhang, B., Liang, B., Wang, Z., Mi, Y., Zhang, Y., Chen, Z.: Coordinated stabilization for space robot after capturing a noncooperative target with large inertia. Acta Astronautica **134**, 75–84 (2017)
8. Wei, C., Luo, J., Dai, H., Yuan, J.: Learning-based adaptive prescribed performance control of postcapture space robot-target combination without inertia identications. Acta Astronautica **146**, 228–242 (2018)
9. Wei, C., Luo, J., Xu, C., Yuan, J.: Low-complexity stabilization control of combined spacecraft with an unknown captured object. In: Control Conference (2017)
10. Aghili, F., Su, C.Y.: Robust relative navigation by integration of ICP and adaptive Kalman filter using laser scanner and IMU. IEEE/ASME Trans. Mechatron. **21**(4), 2015–2026 (2016)
11. Lim, T.W.: Point cloud modeling using the homogeneous transformation for non-cooperative pose estimation. Acta Astronautica **111**, 61–76 (2015)
12. Obermark, J., Henshaw, C.G.: SUMO/FREND: vision system for autonomous satellite grapple. In: Proceedings of SPIE - The International Society for Optical Engineerings, vol. 6555, pp. 65550Y–65550Y-11 (2007)
13. Xiaodong, D., Liang, B., Wenfu, X., Qiu, Y.: Pose measurement of large non-cooperative satellite based on collaborative cameras. Acta Astronautica **68**(11), 2047–2065 (2011)
14. Aghili, F., Kuryllo, M., Okouneva, G., English, C.: Fault-tolerant position/attitude estimation of free-floating space objects using a laser range sensor. IEEE Sens. J. **11**(1), 176–185 (2010)
15. Augusteijn, M.F., Clemens, L.E., Shaw, K.A.: Performance evaluation of texture measures for ground cover identification in satellite images by means of a neural network classifier. IEEE Trans. Geosci. Remote. Sens. **33**(3), 616–626 (1995)
16. Zayan, M.A.: Satellite orbits guidance using state space neural network. In: IEEE Aerospace Conference Proceedings 2006. IEEE (2006)
17. Kim, S.-G., Crassidis, J.L., Cheng, Y., Fosbury, A.M., Junkins, J.L.: Kalman filtering for relative spacecraft attitude and position estimation. J. Guid. Control. Dyn. **30**(1), 133–143 (2007)
18. Harris, F.J.: On the use of windows for harmonic analysis with the discrete Fourier transform. Proc. IEEE **66**(1), 51–83 (1978)

19. Hotchkiss C, Weber E. A Fast Fourier Transform for Fractal Approximations. arXiv: Functional Analysis, pp. 315–329 (2017)
20. Oran Brigham, E.: The Fast Fourier Transform and Its Applications, vol. 1. Prentice Hall, Englewood Cliffs (1988)
21. Van Loan, C.: Computational Frameworks for the Fast Fourier Transform. SIAM, Philadelphia (1992)
22. Ma, C., Wei, C., Yuan, J., et al.: Semi-synchronizing strategy for capturing a high-speed tumbling target. J. Guid. Control. Dyn. **41**(12), 2615–2632 (2018)
23. Ma, C., Dai, H., Yuan, J.: Estimation of inertial characteristics of tumbling spacecraft using constant state lter. Adv. Space Res. **60**(3), 513–530 (2017)
24. Guyaguler, B., Horne, R.N., Rogers, L.L., et al.: Optimization of well placement in a Gulf of Mexico waterflooding project. SPE Reserv. Eval. Eng. **5**(03), 229–236 (2002)
25. ucas, R.H., Smith, P.L., McKenzie, C.H., et al.: Neural network clutter filter for large-array mosaic sensors. In: International Joint Conference on Neural Network (1989)
26. Zhang, Q.J., Gupta, K.C.: Neural Networks for RF and Microwave Design. Artech House, Norwood (2000)
27. Haykin, S.: Kalman Filtering and Neural Networks. Wiley, New York (2001)
28. Haykin, S.: Neural Network and Learning Machines. Prentice Hall, Upper Saddle River (2011)
29. Xin, M., Pan, H.: Nonlinear optimal control of spacecraft approaching a tumbling target. Aerosp. Sci. Technol. **15**(2), 79–89 (2011)
30. Crassidis, J.L., Landis Markley, F., Cheng, Y.: Survey of nonlinear attitude estimation methods. J. Guid. Control. Dyn. **30**(1), 12–28 (2007)
31. Aghili, F., Parsa, K.: Motion and parameter estimation of space objects using laser-vision data. J. Guid. Control. Dyn. **32**(2), 538 (2009)
32. Crassidis, J.L., Landis Markley, F.: Unscented filtering for spacecraft attitude estimation. J. Guid. Control. Dyn. **26**(4), 536–542 (2003)

Estimation and Identification

An FFT-based Method for Analysis, Modeling and Identification of Kinematic Error in Harmonic Drives

Xiaoli Shi, Yong Han, Jianhua Wu$^{(\boxtimes)}$, and Zhenhua Xiong

Shanghai Jiao Tong University, Shanghai 022004, China
{JXGC-shixiaoli,ramoflaple,wujh,mexiong}@sjtu.edu.cn

Abstract. Nonlinear features such as torsional compliance and kinematic error limit the transmission accuracy of harmonic drives. There is plenty of researches on modeling and torsional compliance, while the study of kinematic error still lacks. This paper presents an FFT-based analysis method for kinematic error. The measured data reveals that kinematic error is periodic with respect to the position and thus can be considered as a sum of harmonics. To obtain a spectrum of harmonic orders, the data is processed using fast Fourier transform. With the spectrum analysis, the velocity independence of kinematic error is confirmed, the linear trend observed during analysis is identified and finally, the kinematic error model is determined. Then, prominent components with analytically computed amplitudes and phases are obtained by setting a threshold of amplitude. To achieve better performance, backward motion and forward motion are addressed separately. Afterwards, the kinematic error is compensated online, referring to the position and moving directions. Experiment results illustrate that the proposed method is valid and effective.

Keywords: Harmonic drive · Kinematic error · Fast Fourier transform

1 Introduction

Harmonic drive, developed in 1955 primarily for aerospace application [6], is a compact torque transmission device with properties such as lightweight, high-ratio and zero-backlash and be capable of being directly connected to a motor and producing large torque [1]. As a reducer gear, now harmonic drive is not only implemented in the aerospace application but also accepted in a variety of applications such as precision positioning devices and play a key role with its dynamic and static characteristics [12,13]. Moreover, in recent years, some researchers try to make use of its torsional compliance in joint torque feedback (JTF) to replace high-cost torque/force sensors [5,9–11]. However, harmonic drive transmission brings about nonlinear features such as kinematic error (KE), flexibility and friction that play important roles in the overall dynamic response of the plant [4]. Though small in magnitude, KE, defined as the angular difference between

© Springer Nature Switzerland AG 2019
H. Yu et al. (Eds.): ICIRA 2019, LNAI 11744, pp. 191–202, 2019.
https://doi.org/10.1007/978-3-030-27541-9_17

flex spline input and wave generator output, is periodic in nature and unable to be removed by the harmonic drive backlash-free property [1,2]. Thus, it would produce undesirable vibrations which become dominant at higher speeds, especially at resonant frequencies [1]. Moreover, KE is also an unwanted interference item in JTF. Clearly, KE not only deteriorates control accuracy and position precision but also makes the JTF application complicated. Thus, it is of high importance to study KE.

The literature, however, still lacks a precise characterization of the mechanism responsible for KE [1]. Although as early as the 1980s, many scholars have studied various harmonic models, Seyfferth et al., for example, proposed a nonlinear harmonic drive model considering the torsional compliance together with microscopic friction [4], KE is not taken seriously and even not included in their models. With the development of harmonic drives, some scholars began to study KE. Tuttle et al. proposed a classical single tooth pair model of the harmonic drive to better understand the transmission of the harmonic drive [7]. In their work, KE is explained as a result of manufacturing together with assembly errors in the transmission and modeled as a function of the wave-generator angle relative to the flex spline in the form of a sum of three sinusoidal functions. Preissner et al. presented a new model of the harmonic drive transmission in [3] and considered the causes of KE as both manufacturing/assembly errors and the deformation of flex spline. However, their work focuses on hysteresis. Besides, their definition of KE makes the FS deformation included in KE, which would cause KE to be affected by load torques. Zou et al. proposed a harmonic drive model that considers the geometry, internal interactions and assembly error of key parts in [13] and pointed out that KE of two real harmonic drive systems may be different due to random manufacturing or assembly errors. Ghorbel et al. summarized the reasons for KE and studied the influence factors of KE [1]. However, their analysis does not separate the flexibility from KE. In JTF application, scholars paid attention to nonlinear stiffness and hysteresis of harmonic drive [5,10,11], KE is only compensated by data fitting. Except for the most adopted kinematic error causes (i.e. manufacturing and assembly errors), some scholars held the view that the kinematic error is a result of the inherent operating principle of the drive irrespective of the assembly errors [8,11]. As can be seen, there are many researches focusing on modeling and causes of KE, while analysis and compensation of KE itself are still in lack.

Under the background above, this paper presents an FFT-based method for analysis, modeling and identification of KE. The harmonic drive model is firstly introduced. Experiment data is obtained under a constant-velocity and load-free condition to eliminate the influence of deformation, since the double-encoder-obtained transmission angular error includes not only KE but also deformation-caused error. Experimental data reveals that kinematic error is periodic with respect to absolute motor position and can be considered as a sum of harmonics. As a result, a spectrum of harmonic orders is derived under the help of fast

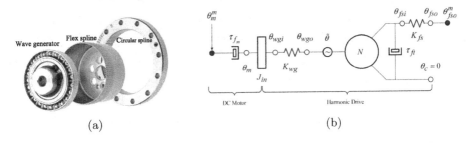

Fig. 1. Components and transmission model of harmonic drive (a) Typical harmonic drive components, (b) Model of harmonic drive transmission system [11].

Fourier transform (FFT). The assumption that KE is independent of velocity is proposed and confirmed by the analysis of harmonic order spectrum. Besides, a linear trend of the kinematic error observed during the analysis is identified. Subsequently, the model of KE is obtained. Then, a threshold is determined to obtain prominent components with analytically computed amplitudes and phases. To achieve better performance, backward and forward motion are addressed separately. Afterwards, the prominent components and the linear trend are compensated on line, referring to the position and moving directions. Experiment results illustrate that the proposed method is valid and effective.

The rest of this paper is arranged as follows. Firstly, in Sect. 2, an appropriate harmonic drive model is introduced based on [11]. Subsequently, the FFT-based analysis method together with the KE model is presented in Sect. 3. In Sect. 4, experiment setup is introduced and online compensation experiments carried out. Finally, conclusions and future work are presented in Sect. 5.

2   Preliminaries of a Harmonic Drive Transmission Model

A harmonic drive typically consists of three basic components: an elliptic wave generator (WG), a shallow-cup-shaped flex spline (FS) and a rigid circular spline (CS), as illustrated in Fig. 1a. When assembled, the WG is nested inside the flex spline, causing the FS circumference to adapt the elliptical profile of the WG and the external teeth of the FS to mesh with the internal teeth on the CS along the major axis of the WG ellipse. The angular position at harmonic drive components can be expressed as:

$$\theta_{wg} = N\theta_{fs} \tag{1}$$

where θ_{wg} denotes the WG angular position, θ_{fs} denotes the FS angular position, and N denotes the gear ratio.

However, the actual output of FS is unequal to the expected value due to the existence of KE and other nonlinear features of harmonic drive. Considering the WG/FS flexibility and KE, the harmonic drive transmission system is properly modeled, as shown in Fig. 1b where τ_{fm} is the motor friction and τ_{ft} is the

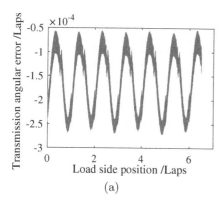
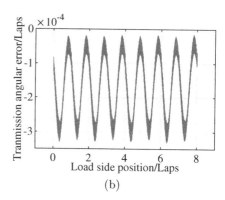

(a)   (b)

Fig. 2. Waveform of transmission angular error (a) Waveform transmission angular error for a constant velocity with loads, (b) Waveform transmission angular error for a constant velocity with no load (i.e. KE waveform).

harmonic drive lumped friction. According to Fig. 1b, the transmission angular errors of the harmonic drive components is expressed as:

$$\begin{cases} \Delta\theta_{wg} = \theta_{wgo} - \theta_{wgi} \\ \Delta\theta_{fs} = \theta_{fso} - \theta_{fsi} \\ \Delta\theta_{ke} = \theta_{fsi} - \theta_{wgo}/N \end{cases} \tag{2}$$

where $\Delta\theta_{wg}$ is the deformation of WG, $\Delta\theta_{fs}$ is the deformation of FS, and $\Delta\theta_{ke}$ is the kinematic error that is analyzed in this paper; θ_{wgi} denotes WG's input angular position that is measured by a motor-side encoder and θ_{fso} is FS's output angular position that is measured by a load-side encoder; θ_{wgo} is the unknown WG's output angular position and θ_{fsi} is the unknown FS's input angular position.

According to Eq. (2), the total angular error between the input and output of a harmonic drive can be defined as:

$$\Delta\theta_{io} = \theta_{fso} - \frac{\theta_{wgi}}{N} = \Delta\theta_{fs} + \frac{\Delta\theta_{wg}}{N} + \Delta\theta_{ke} \tag{3}$$

where $\Delta\theta_{io}$ is the total transmission error.

A waveform of the total angular error is shown in Fig. 2a. It includes, according to Eq. (3), both deformation-caused errors and KE, which are difficult to be separated. Considering that the deformation of the FS (i.e., $\Delta\theta_{fs}$) is determined by harmonic drive load torque, the effects of FS deformation on the KE waveform, therefore, can be eliminated under a load-free situation. The torsional compliance of WG (i.e., $\Delta\theta_{wg}$) is a function of motor output torque [11], namely, it is determined by the motor current. Therefore, under the constant speed and load-free condition, the current keeps constant and so does the $\Delta\theta_{wg}$. It means that though the deformation of WG still remains, it would not affect the

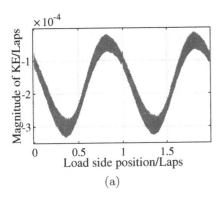
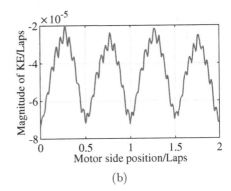

(a)   (b)

Fig. 3. Harmonic drive kinematic error waveform measured for a constant velocity of 0.0126 Laps/s (a) kinematic error with respect to two FS revolutions, (b) kinematic error with respect to two WG revolutions.

waveform of transmission angular error. Thus, the KE waveform can be obtained under load-free and constant-velocity situation, as shown in Fig. 2b.

3   Analysis and Modeling of Kinematic Error

3.1   An FFT-based Method for Analysis of Kinematic Error

With the preliminaries of a harmonic drive transmission, data used for analysis is obtained for a small constant FS velocity (0.0126Laps/s). From the typical measured KE waveform shown in Fig. 2b we can see that KE is periodic with respect to the position. However, the neighboring troughs of KE are not on the same level, making its period equals to two laps of the FS instead of one. This unusual phenomenon is also mentioned in [1], but it has not been explained. According to the KE waveform with respect to two WG revolutions shown in Fig. 3b, we can see that the KE waveform in Fig. 3b is quite similar to Fig. 3a except that the KE waveform shows two peaks with different amplitudes over one WG revolution, which may be the reason for the aforementioned unusual phenomenon. Moreover, Fig. 3 indicates that it is able to consider KE as a sum of harmonics. However, information of the prominent harmonic terms of KE is not straightforward in the position domain. Besides, whether KE is affected by the velocity remains uncovered as well in the position domain.

To solve these problems, an FFT-based method is presented for analysis of KE. It is worth mentioning that the FFT utilized in the analysis is a variant of traditional fast Fourier transform. The classic FFT is used for the time-frequency domain conversion while the FFT utilized in the present paper is able to convert the data in 'position domain' to its counterpart in 'harmonic-order domain', i.e. the angular position in the variant is analogous to the time in the classic and harmonic orders in the variant is analogous to the frequency in the classic.

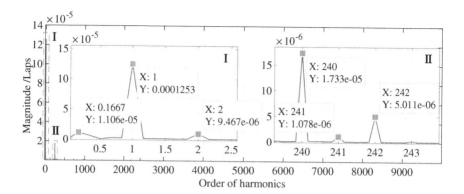

Fig. 4. Spectrum of KE for a constant speed of 0.0126 Laps/s

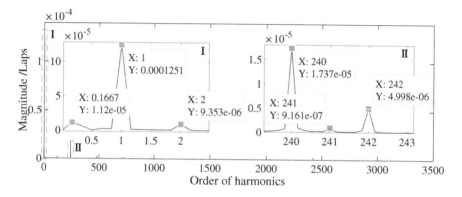

Fig. 5. Spectrum of KE for a constant speed of 0.0377 Laps/s

Therefore, the formulas for analytically computing amplitudes and phases in this variant are as follows:

$$\begin{cases} A_i = 2|\Delta\Theta_{ke}|/N_l \\ \phi_i = \angle\Delta\Theta_{ke} \\ \Delta\Theta_{ke}(k) = \sum_{j=1}^{N_l} \Delta\tilde{\theta}_{ke}(j) \cdot W_n^{(j-1)(k-1)} \quad (k \le [\frac{N_l}{2}]) \end{cases} \quad (4)$$

where N_l denotes the length of analysis data, $\Delta\tilde{\theta}_{ke}$ is the detrended version of $\Delta\theta_{ke}$, and $W_n = e^{(-2\pi i)/N_l}$ is one of N_l roots of unity. Here only the positive components are considered, hence the constraint $k \le [\frac{N_l}{2}]$.

Process the experiment data that obtained at a small constant speed (0.0126 Laps/s) by the variant FFT. According to Eq. (4), the spectrum of harmonic orders is obtained, as shown in Fig. 4. The spectrum of harmonic orders shows two major components whose harmonic orders are 1 and 240, respectively, illustrating that KE is compromised of low and high-harmonic-order components. Moreover, the amplified parts illustrate that there exist other harmonic components except these two major components. The low harmonic order components can be considered as the load-side components of KE while the high harmonic order components are motor-side components. Besides, the ratio between the major high harmonic order and the major low harmonic order is 240 instead of the gear ratio whose value is 120, exactly reflecting the phenomenon that KE shows two peaks over one WG revolution while it shows one peak over a revolution of FS.

The harmonic orders, and magnitudes and phases of the harmonic component of KE would not be influenced by the change of velocity if KE is velocity-independent. Spectrums of harmonic orders for constant velocities of 0.0126 Laps/s and 0.0377 Laps/s are shown in Figs. 4 and 5, respectively, for analyzing whether KE is unaffected by velocity. The figures illustrate that the harmonic orders of the prominent components are exactly the same despite of the change of velocity. Although the magnitudes under different testing speeds are not exactly the same, the slight difference is too small to be considered as velocity dependent since the maximum magnitude difference is less than $8e - 7$ while the maximum magnitude of harmonic components is $1253e - 7$, as shown in the figures. In a similar way, the computed phases show little difference as well under different testing speeds. Therefore, the spectrums under different testing speed can be considered the same. Namely, KE is not velocity dependent.

Since DC components would disturb spectrum analysis, it is required to be removed before applying FFT. The most common way is to subtract the DC component directly from the data. During this process, however, a linear trend is observed. For accurate identification and compensation of KE, this linear trend needs to be removed for the analysis of harmonic order spectrum while it needs to be added in the KE for the compensation. Therefore, it is required to be identified before compensation for KE. Due to the fact that the linear trend is related to the absolute position θ, the linear trend can be modeled as

$$y_{trend} = a \cdot \theta + b \qquad (5)$$

where a and b are the slop and intercept which are to be identified. The figure of the linear trend can be obtained with a MATLAB function called $detrend()$. Thus, the slop and intercept are calculated by any two points on the line.

3.2 Modeling and Identification of Kinematic Error

Based on the above analysis, KE can be modeled as a function of the absolute position in the form of a sum of harmonics plus a linear trend. i.e.

$$\Delta\theta_{ke} = \sum A_i cos(2\pi n_i\theta + \phi_i) + a \cdot \theta + b \qquad (A_i > THR) \qquad (6)$$

where THR is a threshold of amplitude for obtaining prominent harmonic components, i denotes the number of prominent components and θ denotes the link side position in laps measured by an absolute encoder.

The KE model identification procedure consists of the following steps.

$Step1$. Perform load-free motion with a low constant ·velocity. The motor-side position and load-side position are recorded by double encoders (at least one of them is able to record the absolute angular position) for obtaining the identification data of KE. The data length is denoted with N_l.

*Step*2. Compute the total error according to Eq. (3) then use MATLAB function named *detrend*() to remove the linear trend of the total error. After detrending the total error, process the data with N_l-point FFT according to Eq. (4) to obtain the spectrum of harmonic orders.

*Step*3. Set a proper value for THR to determine the prominent components and compute the parameters A_i and ϕ_i of $\Delta\theta_{ke}$ according to Eq. (4). Afterwards, the linear trend can be identified according to Eq. (5) by any two points (typically head and tail) on the line. Finally, the KE model (i.e., Eq. (6))is obtained.

4   Experimental Study

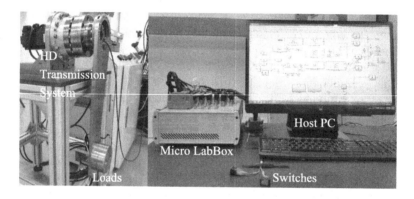

Fig. 6. Experimental setup

This section is divided into two steps, off-line identification and online compensation. Experiments are carried out under the load-free situation at different constant velocities. Moreover, to achieve better performance, backward motion and forward motion are addressed separately.

Experiments are conducted on a dSPACE MicroLabBox-based platform. Figure 6 shows the overall experimental setup. The mechanical system is comprised of a Mitsubishi servo motor with an absolute encoder whose resolution is 8192 pulses/rev, a harmonic drive with a reduction ratio of 120, an inertial load (which is disassembled during the experiments) and a load-side incremental encoder whose resolution is 1184000 pulses/rev. The control system consists of the motor driver, the MicroLabBox and a host PC. The host PC is used for running MATLAB/Simulink generates code for the MicroLabBox. After compiling, the MicroLabBox implements the code and outputs control signal to the motor driver via a digital to analog converter. Meanwhile, it receives the displacement signal from the motor driver to obtain displacement and velocity data. The sample time for the overall control system is 4 ms.

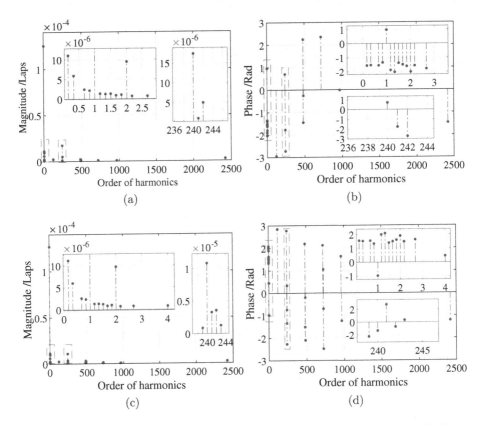

Fig. 7. Spectrums of KE model (a–b) spectrums of KE model with respect to clockwise motion and (c–d) spectrums of KE model with respect to counterclockwise motion.

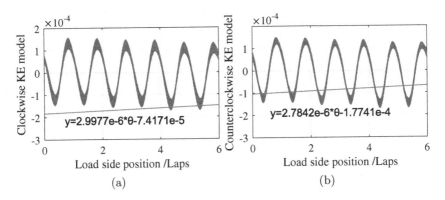

Fig. 8. Identified model of KE (a) clockwise, (b) counterclockwise.

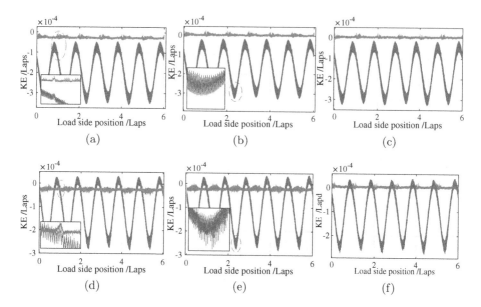

Fig. 9. Waveform of KE before and after compensation (a) clockwise KE waveform at velocity of 0.0126 Laps/s, (b) clockwise KE waveform at velocity of 0.0251 Laps/s, (c) clockwise KE waveform at velocity of 0.0377 Laps/s, (d) counterclockwise KE waveform at velocity of 0.0126 Laps/s, (e) counterclockwise KE waveform at velocity of 0.0251 Laps/s and (f) counterclockwise KE waveform at velocity of 0.0377 Laps/s.

4.1   Off Line Identification

Parameters of the KE model are identified according to the steps described in the Subsect. 3.2. First, the motor is command to move at a constant velocity of 0.0126 *Laps/s* in both clockwise and counterclockwise direction. At the same time, both the motor encoder and link encoder data are recorded. Second, the total error is computed and the spectrum of harmonic orders is obtained by applying FFT to the detrended total error. Last, the threshold is set to $8e-7$ *Laps*. Accordingly, 23 prominent components for the clockwise data and 31 prominent components for the counterclockwise are chosen. The detailed information about these components are shown in Fig. 7. The linear trend can be identified according to Eq. (5) by any two points (typically head and tail) on the line. The final identified model of KE are shown in Fig. 8.

4.2   Online Compensation

Compensation experiments at different velocities in the clockwise and counterclockwise direction and their results are shown in Fig. 9, where Fig. 9a, b and c are the clockwise-direction KE waveform at speed 0.0126, 0.0251 and 0.0377 Laps/s, respectively, and Fig. 9d, e and f are the counterclockwise-direction KE waveform at speed 0.0126, 0.0251 and 0.0377 Laps/s, respectively.

The analysis of compensation results are concluded as

(1) Due to the manufacturing of the load-side incremental encoder, there's always a peak show up at one position during one FS revolution, as demonstrated in Fig. 9a and d. However, the magnitude difference between the peak and others is rather small ($10e - 7$ or so).

(2) By comparing the waveforms before and after compensation, the KE profile error can be eliminated which verifies the effectiveness.

(3) Comparisons between Fig. 9a and d, Fig. 9b and e, Fig. 9c and f show that at the same velocity, the clockwise compensation results better than the counterclockwise compensation results. By observing the details, i.e. the amplified parts shown in Fig. 9c and f, counterclockwise KE shows obvious burr deteriorating the compensation. We consider the burr as the consequence of poor counterclockwise friction situation. Besides, the poor compensation always appears in the same location with respect to one revolution of FS due to the assembly-error-caused misalignment of drive shaft resulting in a bigger friction in some position.

(4) According to the comparisons of compensation results at different speeds in the same direction, the compensation result is relatively stable as the speed increases. Friction is unstable in the low speed zone, especially for critical areas of static friction to sliding friction, while as the speed increases, friction away from the critical section, thus, stabilizes the compensation.

In conclusion, even with a poor friction condition, the proposed method is able to reduce the kinematic error by an order of magnitude. Therefore, the effectiveness of the proposed method can be verified.

5   Conclusions

This paper presents an FFT-based method for analysis, modeling and identification of the kinematic error in harmonic drives. Kinematic error is able to be separated with other errors in harmonic drive under the load-free and constant-velocity condition. Experiment data reveals that kinematic error is periodic with respect to absolute position and can be considered as a sum of harmonics. As a result, data in "position domain" is converted to its counterpart in the "harmonic order domain" under the help of FFT for analysis. The kinematic error is proved to be velocity independent and thus modeled as a function of the position in the form of a sum of harmonics plus a linear trend. The kinematic error model then is identified from the spectrum analysis. Experiments are carried out to online compensate the kinematic error, using the identified kinematic error model. Experiment results illustrate that the proposed method is valid and effective.

Acknowledgments. This research was supported in part by the National Natural Science Foundation of China under grant number 51575355 and 91848106; and the Program of Shanghai Academic/Technology Research Leader under grant number 18XD1401700.

References

1. Ghorbel, F.H., Gandhi, P.S., Alpeter, F.: On the kinematic error in harmonic drive gears. J. Mech. Des. **123**(1), 90 (2001). https://doi.org/10.1115/1.1334379
2. Iwasaki, M., Yamamoto, M., Hirai, H., Okitsu, Y., Sasaki, K., Yajima, T.: Modeling and compensation for angular transmission error of harmonic drive gearings in high precision positioning. In: 2009 IEEE/ASME International Conference on Advanced Intelligent Mechatronics. IEEE (2009). https://doi.org/10.1109/aim.2009.5229935
3. Preissner, C., Royston, T.J., Shu, D.: A high-fidelity harmonic drive model. J. Dyn. Syst. Meas. Control **134**(1), 011,002 (2012). https://doi.org/10.1115/1.4005041
4. Seyfferth, W., Maghzal, A., Angeles, J.: Nonlinear modeling and parameter identification of harmonic drive robotic transmissions. In: Proceedings of 1995 IEEE International Conference on Robotics and Automation. IEEE (1995). https://doi.org/10.1109/robot.1995.525714
5. Shi, Z., Li, Y., Liu, G.: Adaptive torque estimation of robot joint with harmonic drive transmission. Mech. Syst. Signal Process. **96**, 1–15 (2017). https://doi.org/10.1016/j.ymssp.2017.03.041
6. Taghirad, H., Belanger, P.: Torque ripple and misalignment torque compensation for the built-in torque sensor of harmonic drive systems. IEEE Trans. Instrum. Meas. **47**(1), 309–315 (1998). https://doi.org/10.1109/19.728840
7. Tuttle, T., Seering, W.: A nonlinear model of a harmonic drive gear transmission. IEEE Trans. Robot. Autom. **12**(3), 368–374 (1996). https://doi.org/10.1109/70.499819
8. Were, M.: Analysis and control of kinematic error in harmonic gear drive mechanisms. Technical report, Dynamic Systems and Control Laboratory (1997)
9. Xia, K., Ding, L., Liu, G., Gao, H., Deng, Z.: A novel virtual torque sensor for rescue robots with harmonic drives. Eng. Lett. (2016). 10.20944/preprints201609.0084.v1
10. Yu, F., Xiao, S., Zhu, M., Wang, Z.: A novel method to improve the accuracy of torque estimation for robotic joint with harmonic drive transmission. Eng. Lett. **26**, 455–460 (2018)
11. Zhang, H., Ahmad, S., Liu, G.: Torque estimation for robotic joint with harmonic drive transmission based on position measurements. IEEE Trans. Rob. **31**(2), 322–330 (2015). https://doi.org/10.1109/tro.2015.2402511
12. Zhang, X., Jiang, G., Zou, C., Wang, S.: Modeling of compliance and hysteresis with erasure property in harmonic drive by active loading. In: 2017 IEEE International Conference on Cybernetics and Intelligent Systems (CIS) and IEEE Conference on Robotics, Automation and Mechatronics (RAM). IEEE (2017). https://doi.org/10.1109/iccis.2017.8274816
13. Zou, C., Tao, T., Jiang, G., Mei, X., Wu, J.: A harmonic drive model considering geometry and internal interaction. Proc. Inst. Mech. Eng. Part C: J. Mech. Eng. Sci. **231**(4), 728–743 (2016). https://doi.org/10.1177/0954406215621097

Real-Time Human-Posture Recognition for Human-Drone Interaction Using Monocular Vision

Chenglin Cai, Shaowu Yang[✉], Peifeng Yan, Jinkai Tian, Linlin Du,
and Xuejun Yang

State Key Laboratory of High Performance Computing (HPCL),
National University of Defense Technology, Changsha, China
`shaowu.yang@nudt.edu.cn`

Abstract. This paper presents a real-time monocular vision solution to human postures recognition for human-drone interaction. The approach achieves a more natural interaction between human and drone. Image regions and joint positions of human bodies in images from a monocular camera mounted on a micro drone are extracted by using a deep neural network. Then, feature vectors of a human body are generated by the relative distance among the joints and classified by a support vector machine (SVM) classifier. The performance of the solution is demonstrated by extensive experiments. Our method obtains an average recognition accuracy of 97.34% on the micro drone and keeps high precision even with a large distance between the human and the micro drone. Furthermore, our method consumes limited computing resources and is suitable for onboard applications of a micro drone.

Keywords: Human posture recognition · Human-drone interaction · Deep neural network

1 Introduction

Human posture recognition has been widely used in human-computer interaction, medical assistance, automotive industry, security, etc. It is currently a very active research topic. We expect machines to be able to understand human needs, to interpret human commands accurately, and to work collaboratively with human beings. To meet these requirements, in addition to correct interpretations of verbal instructions, non-verbal instructions like human postures should also be accurately understood. For direct communication between human and micro drones, non-verbal instructions can be more important. The background noise of outside can significantly limit the efficiency of verbal commands transmission, especially with a large distance between human and micro drones. Correctly understanding the information contained in human postures becomes an essential part of the understanding of robots to human beings.

© Springer Nature Switzerland AG 2019
H. Yu et al. (Eds.): ICIRA 2019, LNAI 11744, pp. 203–216, 2019.
https://doi.org/10.1007/978-3-030-27541-9_18

The recognition of the human postures have considerable challenges on micro drone platforms mainly in two aspects:

- A micro drone platform has limited payload capacity and limited computing power. Thus, a bunch of existing methods, which require heavy sensors or computing modules, can hardly be applied on such platforms.
- Most of the time, micro drones keep a long distance from people, and the background in the common image taken by micro drones is complex, which causes low-quality portraits in the image.

Human posture recognition is widely used for human-robot interaction. However, these methods are difficult to be applied on micro drone platforms. Some of these work require the use of depth cameras to get the data of human body [1,2]. However, such cameras are not accurate under harsh conditions, e.g. with long distances or poor textures. Furthermore, the weights of such cameras are normally larger than a monocular camera, and will put more pressures to the load capacity of a micro drone. Some other algorithms have high requirements for computing resources and cannot be run on the micro drone platform in real time [3].

In this paper, we propose a novel method to recognize human posture for human-drone interaction. Color or grayscale images taken from the micro drone are processed by a convolutional neural network (CNN). A set of feature maps generated by the CNN are further sent into a two-branch multi-stage CNN. Joint positions obtained by the CNNs are used to compute distances among joints. Then, the distances are normalized by a normalization regulator, resulting in a 91-dimensional vector. This vector is classified by SVM classifier, which outputs predictable human postures. Our method achieves real-time performance with high accuracy and robustness, and can accurately recognize the posture of a human body, even in blurry images when a drone keeps a large distance with the human body.

2   Related Work

The interaction between human beings and micro drones can be assumed as a particular case of human-computer interaction. The term of human-computer interaction was first used in 1975 by Card et al. [4] and popularized in their seminal 1983 book [5]. Human-computer interaction belongs to a discipline that intersects multiple research fields including computer science, behavioral sciences, robotics, and many others [6]. The latest computer technologies used in the field of human-computer interaction include face detection and recognition [7] [8], facial expression analysis [9], gesture recognition [9], human motion analysis [10], etc.

Human-drones interaction can be achieved through the graphical user interface (GUI) or natural user interfaces (NUI). The initial GUI is the command line interface (CLI) [11]. However, the CLI operators have to interact with the micro drone by typing orders with the help of command prompts and operating instructions, which make it difficult for novices to maneuver the micro drone [12]. Currently, the most widely used GUI, formerly known as WIMP (windows, icon, menu, and Pointer), uses a series of visual user interface elements as input and output to interact with micro drones. [11,13]. It is much easier for people, even novices, to use the method of identifying and selecting commands compared with remembering and typing, which is why WIMP can become the mainstream [11].

The GUI has gained significant attention in the market and research of human-machine interface (HMI) in the past few decades. However, the research trends in related fields have changed. NUI is gaining growing attention. The state-of-the-art methods of current human-drone interaction normally use inherent human features such as sound, gestures, and vision [14]. Hand gestures are rich in information and very intuitive. There are many applications in term of NUI. Hand gestures using NUI are started with glove-based devices. The work in [15] makes DataGlove get gestures to implement remote control of objects. The effectiveness of this strategy depends on the bulky sensor on the glove being worn, which will dramatically affects the user experience. The work in [16] interacts with the controlled device by recognizing gestures with the wearable devices. The effect of this method is also limited by wearable devices. The demand for more natural interaction between human and machines drives new developments. As a result, applications of gesture recognition system based on a depth camera such as Kinect develop rapidly. For example, the work in [17] controls micro drone by gesture recognition which obtains depth images using Kinect. However, depth cameras do not achieve high accuracy at long distances and can be too heavy for a micro drone.

With the rapid development of Natural Language Processing (NLP), speech command interaction is also becoming more and more popular in NUI. The work in [18] utilizes gestures and voice to control micro drones in the simulator. This work neither considers the possible noise and other interference, nor experiences on a real drone platform. We can hardly find work of NLP applied to human-drone interaction. The possible reason is that most of the micro drones are operated outdoors. Because of background noise, the accuracy of speech recognition is difficult to be guaranteed. Moreover, the distance between people and micro drones also limits the direct interaction between human and micro drones. Many methods require an extra ground station to transmit instructions to the micro drone [19,20].

The development of human posture estimation makes it possible to command micro drones by human posture. The work in [1,19] uses skeleton data and joint positions to recognize human postures. Both of these works obtain high accuracy, and the work in [1] can even achieve real-time recognition. However, they all rely on a heavy Kinect unsuitable for micro drone platform to get image data. The work in [21] uses the micro drone to collect videos, then estimates human postures from the video to detect a suspicious action. This idea can be better migrated to the commanding of micro drones, but their solution is only 71% accurate, which makes it difficult to be applied to micro drone control directly. An important reason why the results of the paper are not satisfactory is that human body recognition is less effective. There are two popular strategies to achieve human posture estimation, top-down and bottom-up [22]. Top-down approaches detect the person in the picture and then performs a single-person posture estimation for each person detected [23,24]. The runtime of these ways is directly proportional to the number of people in the picture. Bottom-up approaches detect all parts of the body in the picture and stitch these parts into individuals. The bottom-up approaches could not directly get the global contextual clues of the body part, which causes a huge price for the final stitching. The previous bottom-up methods perform poorly in real time [25,26]. The average processing time of the seminal work takes about a few hours [25]. Currently, this situation has changed dramatically. The work in [22] could realize real-time estimation.

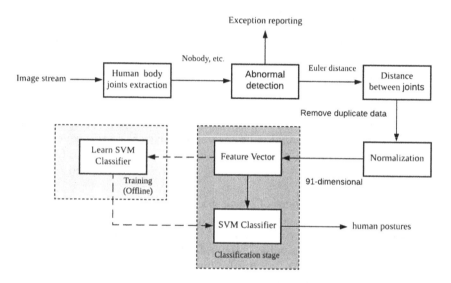

Fig. 1. System overview, showing all the essential steps, including human body joints extraction, Abnormal detection, feature generation, normalization, and classification. SVM classifier requires offline training

3   Method

Figure 1 illustrates the overall pipeline of our method. The system takes image stream, as input, and figures out, as output, the category of human postures. First, we detect the 2D joint positions for all person in each image. Then, we calculate the euclidean distance between all joints to form a feature matrix. The feature matrix will be normalized by scaling and shifting. Finally, we can get the category of human postures by the SVM classifier.

3.1   Joint Position Coordinates

We characterize human postures by extracting the joint positions of the person in the image. Considering the limited computing resources of the micro drone platform and the requirements for calculation accuracy, OpenPose [22,27,28] is utilized for this work.

OpenPose takes the image of size $w * h$ as input. A set of feature map F will be generated by analysing the raw image using a convolutional neural network, i.e., the first ten layers of VGG-19. Then, the network can be divided into multiple similar stages. In each stage, there are two branches, one for confidence maps, which obtains the joint position candidates, and the other one predicts the affinity fields (PAF), which is used to correlate the relationships between joint points to splicing into the full-body postures of an unknown number of people. The first stage takes the feature map F as input and generates a set of confidence maps S^1 and a set of part affinity fields L^1. In the rest of the stage $t(t > 1)$, the output of the previous stage, S^{t-1} and L^{t-1}, and the feature map F will be used as input of the current stage. The loss functions of both branches at stage t are

$$\begin{cases} f_S^t = \sum_{j=1}^{J} \sum_p W(p).\|S_j^t(p) - S_j^*(p)\|_2^2, \\ f_L^t = \sum_{c=1}^{C} \sum_p W(p).\|L_c^t(p) - L_c^*(p)\|_2^2, \end{cases} \tag{1}$$

where S_j^* is the groundtruth part confidence map of the jth joint point, L_j^* is the groundtruth part affinity vector field of the jth joint point, and W is a binary mask. When the annotation is missing at an image location p, $W(p) = 0$ [22]. The complete loss function is

$$f = \sum_{t=1}^{T} (f_S^t + f_L^t). \tag{2}$$

For each part, we may get more than one candidates (e.g., n elbows and m wrists). We use OpenPose to pick out joints belonging to the same person in the candidate set. OpenPose converts this issue into a set of bipartite matching sub-problems and solves it by Hungarian algorithm.

OpenPose features the mechanism of bottom-up, which obtains all part conditions before forming body posture. The increase in the number of people does not significantly affect the running time of OpenPose. Results on the MPII Multi-Person Dataset [29] and the COCO Dataset [30] show that OpenPose has high accuracy while achieving real-time performance. OpenPose also has consistent performance in our system.

3.2   Feature Generation and Normalization

The performance of the human posture classification highly depends on the feature vector used by the classifier. We take advantage of euclidean distance among skeleton points as the feature vector. When the distance between the person and

the camera changes, the distance between two skeleton points will keep changing synchronously. We traverse each point a in the set of joint candidates G and
figure out the distance from other points b to the point a. The following formula
is used to compute the euclidean distance,

$$D_{ab} = \sqrt{\sum_{i}^{N}(x_{ai} - x_{bi})^2},$$ (3)

where D_{ab} is the euclidean distance between point x_a and point x_b. x_a and point
x_b are two points in the N-dimensional euclidean space. Shown in Fig. 2, each
person has 14 joint points. Therefore, there will be 196 times of calculation for
each person. Considering $D_{ab} = D_{ba}$ and $D_{ab} = 0$ while $a = b$, we can reduce
the number of calculations to 91 times. The result of the calculation is to form a
91-dimensional vector for each person. It should be noted that when calculating
features, we require the drone to face the person to rule out the influence of the
pose of the camera.

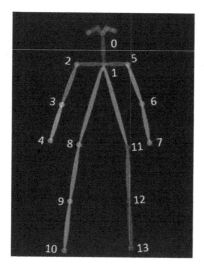

Fig. 2. Human joint diagram. Each person has 14 joint points.

The distance between the joints varies with the distance between the camera
and the target. We solve this problem by normalizing it. We normalize the data
by the following formula,

$$N_i = \frac{(S_i - S_{min}) * (\alpha - \beta)}{S_{max} - S_{min}} + \beta,$$ (4)

where S_i is the original number in the feature vector, S_{max} and S_{min} are lower
and upper bound in the vector. $\alpha = 0$ and $\beta = 200$ are the maximum number
and the minimum number we set.

3.3   Classification

The selection of the classification algorithm is directly related to the character-istics of our data. We mark unselected human postures as the negative sample, which results in a much larger number of negative samples than the number of positive samples. SVM, a supervised learning algorithm, is an efficient algorithm for this situation. SVM aims to maximize the spacing between classes and is not sensitive to positive and negative samples of varying numbers [31,32].

If the given training data set $D = \{(x_1, y_1), (x_2, y_2), ..., (x_n, y_n)\}, y \in \{-1, 1\}$ is linearly separable, there are innumerable hyperplanes in the feature space that can correctly divide the positive and negative samples. The hyperplane can be described by the following formula,

$$w^T x + b = 0, \tag{5}$$

where $w = (w_1; w_2; ...; w_d)$ is a normal vector of the hyperplane, b is the dis-placement, determining the distance between the hyperplane and the origin. If the hyperplane can correctly divide the training samples, each sample (x_i, y_i) satisfies the following constraints,

$$\begin{cases} w^T x_i + b \geq +1, & if \ y_i = +1, \\ w^T x_i + b \leq -1, & if \ y_i = -1. \end{cases} \tag{6}$$

It is not enough to satisfy the above formula. We expect that the resulting hyperplane will maximize the distance between the closest samples in the two classes. In SVM, the formula below describes this idea.

$$\begin{aligned} \max_{w,b} \quad & \frac{\gamma}{\|w\|} \\ s.t. \quad & y_i(w.x_i + b) - 1 \geq 0, \quad i = 1, 2..., N \end{aligned} \tag{7}$$

γ is the functional margin, and therefore $\frac{\gamma}{\|w\|}$ is the geometrical margin. Because the value of the function margin does not affect the solution of the problem, it is often taken as 1. It should be noted that formula 7 only applies to linearly sep-arable data. When the data is linearly inseparable, we use the following formula to solve the two-class classification problem,

$$\begin{aligned} \min_{w,b,\zeta_i} \quad & \tfrac{1}{2}(w^T)w + C\sum_i \zeta_i \\ s.t. \quad & y_i(w^T \phi(x_i) + b) \geq 1 - \zeta_i, \\ & \zeta_i \geq 0, \quad i = 1, 2, ..., m, \end{aligned} \tag{8}$$

where ζ is called slack variable, and its role is to avoid overfitting by allowing some samples dissatisfy the constraint from (6). C is regularization parameters. It adjusts the penalty for misclassification. $\phi(x_t)$ is the kernel function. Kernel function converts data to a higher dimension. When the data is linearly insepa-rable, it is difficult to find a hyperplane for dividing the two classes. If we project the data into higher dimensional space, a linear decision boundary may be achiev-able [33]. This work was implemented with the histogram intersection kernel.

The histogram intersection kernel, $K_{GHI}(\mathbf{x}, \mathbf{z}) = \sum_{i=1}^{n} \min(|x(i)|^{\beta}, |z(i)|^{\beta})$, maps the data set to a multi-resolution histogram and calculates the weighted histogram intersection [34]. The histogram intersection kernel can be used to SVMs because it is positive definite and also satisfies the Mercer's theorem [35, 36]. We also tested a variety of kernel functions, such as linear kernel, polynomial kernel, and Gaussian kernel. The histogram intersection kernel has the best performance for our task compare with the others.

Our task is a multiclass classification because we need to distinguish multiple human postures. There are two main methods, one-versus-one and one-versus-all, to complete this task. Directly using a single SVM formulation to solve multiclass classification problems usually does not achieve good results. A better approach is to use a combination of several binary SVM classifiers to achieve precise performance. One-versus-all method uses winner-takes-all strategy and one-versus-one method is implemented by max-wins voting and error-correcting codes [37, 38]. One-versus-one is used to solve this problem. We have designed a SVM classifier for any two categories in the training data. This means that if there are k selected human postures, $k(k-1)/2$ classifiers are constructed. Each classifier will classify the data points x, and the result of the classification is considered to be a vote. The data point x is assigned to the class that receives the most votes.

4   Results

4.1   Experiment Setup

Our system is implemented in the Robot Operating System (ROS). ROS is a flexible framework designed to help software developers create robotic applications. To demonstrate the performance of our system under outdoor conditions, we developed a micro drone platform for the experiment.

As shown in Fig. 3, we use DJI Matrice 210 (M210) as an experimental platform, equipped with NVIDIA Jetson TX2 (TX2) as the computing device. We use Point Grey FMVU-03MTC-CS, an industrial camera, to collect image data. TX2 has dual-core NVIDIA Denver2, quad-core ARM Cortex-A57, and integrated 256-core Pascal GPU. It can provide more than 1TFLOPS computing power. TX2 is an embedded device with a maximum power consumption of 15W. The operating system is Ubuntu 16.04 64-bit. The photo size taken by FMVU-03MTC-CS is 752×480. We used 3D printing to make a mold for fixing the camera. The camera is mounted $45°$ to the horizontal.

4.2   Recognition Accuracy

We select four human postures and label them as C1, C2, C3, C4. We mark all the other postures that appear in images as C5. As shown in Fig. 4(e), color information is not necessary for our algorithms. To analyze the performance of our method, we record image data as rosbags, and process the data offline use the same TX2 onboard of the M210.

Fig. 3. Extended M210. M210 is equipped with the NVIDIA Jetson TX2 embedded computing device and the FMVU-03MTC-CS camera. This camera is at an angle of 45° to the horizontal

Table 1. Confusion matrix of five class

	C1	C2	C3	C4	C5	AS
C1	141	0	0	0	5	1
C2	0	204	0	0	0	3
C3	0	0	120	0	0	1
C4	0	0	0	128	0	2
C5	0	0	0	0	140	8

Hint: AS refers to an abnormal situation

We collect the data from the experiment and compile it into Table 1. It shows that our method can accurately recognize four postures of C1, C2, C3, C4. When determining the C1 posture, a small number of samples are classified as C5 by mistake. There are two possible reasons. Firstly, when the person keeps standing like C1, the distance between the limbs and the torso is very close. Especially when the micro drone is far away from the person, the tiny distance of joints is heavily disturbed by the image noise, resulting in incorrect classification. Secondly, when the person walks, there are many postures very close to the standing posture, causing the class C1 and the class C5 can be very close in the feature space.

Moreover, abnormal data caused by missing joint points when we estimate the position of joints are filled in the AS field of Table 1. When the person keeps walking, it is difficult for the micro drone to catch complete postures. This is the reason for more abnormalities in C5.

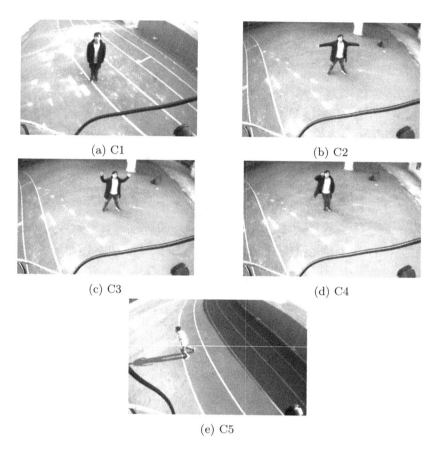

(a) C1   (b) C2

(c) C3   (d) C4

(e) C5

Fig. 4. C1, C2, C3 and C4 are the four postures we selected, and C5 is one of the other postures that appear during the shooting.

Based on statistical data, we calculate the accuracy of our method at different distances. Because the camera mounted on the micro drone is 45° to the horizontal line, the distance is calculated as $a\sqrt{2}m$, where a is the horizontal distance between the person and the micro drone. As shown in Table 2, our method can accurately classify most human postures even when the micro drone has a long distance from people. Our approach achieves high accuracy. As the distance increases, the C1 and C5 misclassification increases. This situation is also in line with our analysis above. The smaller the distance between the joints, the higher the probability of misclassification, especially when the micro drone is far away. This is also the reason why techniques such as gesture recognition and facial recognition are hard to apply on human-drone interactions. The average accuracy of our method reaches 97.34%, which is satisfactory for human-drone interaction. Table 2 shows that our system has good performance even when the micro drone is more than 7 m away from the person.

Table 2. Accuracy at different distances

	Accuracy($3\sqrt{2}m$)	Accuracy($5\sqrt{2}m$)
C1	97.14%	94.37%
C2	99.01%	98.06%
C3	100%	98.33%
C4	98.36%	98.51%
C5	95.71%	92.86%

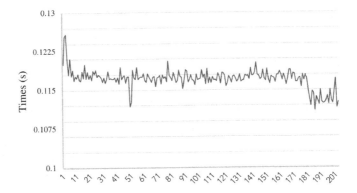

Fig. 5. The timecost for each frame. The average timecost is 0.117 s.

4.3 Runtime Analysis

We record the time cost for processing each frame to show the real-time performance of our system. As shown in Fig. 5, the time cost for each image is relatively stable, mostly between 0.115 s and 0.12 s. The average time is 0.117 s per frame.

5 Conclusion and Future Work

Human gestures recognition is an essential part of the machine understanding of human commands and has broad application prospects in the fields of natural interaction, games, security and so on. Our study focuses on the application of human gesture recognition in human-drone interaction. This paper proposes a method for human gesture recognition for the micro drone platform. Our approach first estimates human postures from images by a deep neural network. Then, feature vectors are generated by the distance between the joints. Finally, support vector machine is used to recognize the human gesture. Experiments show that our system has high accuracy, robustness, and real-time performance on a micro drone platform. We make the source code related to this work publicly available.

We will continue to study the application of human gesture recognition in human-drone interaction on autonomous drones. An interesting topic will be applying our method to an autonomously flying drone enabled by a visual simultaneous localization and mapping (SLAM) system [39].

Acknowledgements. This work was partially supported by the National Natural Science Foundation of China (grants 61803375 and 91648204), by the National Key Research and Development Program of China (grants 2017YFB1001900 and 2017YFB1301104), and by the National Science and Technology Major Project.

References

1. Zafar, Z., Venugopal, R., Berns, K.: Real-time recognition of human postures for human-robot interaction. In: Proceedings of the 11th International Conference on Advances in Computer-Human Interactions (ACHI), Rome, Italy (2018)
2. Patsadu, O., Nukoolkit, C., Watanapa, B.: Human gesture recognition using kinect camera. In: 2012 Ninth International Conference on Computer Science and Software Engineering (JCSSE), pp. 28–32. IEEE (2012)
3. Hu, C., Yu, Q., Li, Y., Ma, S.: Extraction of parametric human model for posture recognition using genetic algorithm. In: Proceedings of Fourth IEEE International Conference on Automatic Face and Gesture Recognition (Cat. No. PR00580), pp. 518–523. IEEE (2000)
4. Carlisle, J.H.: Evaluating the impact of office automation on top management communication. In: Proceedings of the National Computer Conference and Exposition, 7–10 June 1976, pp. 611–616. ACM (1976)
5. Card, S.K., Moran, T.P., Newell, A.: The keystroke-level model for user performance time with interactive systems. Commun. ACM **23**(7), 396–410 (1980)
6. Jaimes, A., Sebe, N.: Multimodal human-computer interaction: a survey. Comput. Vis. Image Underst. **108**(1–2), 116–134 (2007)
7. Hjelmås, E., Low, B.K.: Face detection: a survey. Comput. Vis. Image Underst. **83**(3), 236–274 (2001)
8. Zhao, W., Chellappa, R., Jonathon Phillips, P., Rosenfeld, A.: Face recognition: a literature survey. ACM Comput. Surv. (CSUR) **35**(4), 399–458 (2003)
9. Fasel, B., Luettin, J.: Automatic facial expression analysis: a survey. Pattern Recogn. **36**(1), 259–275 (2003)
10. Aggarwal, J.K., Cai, Q.: Human motion analysis: a review. Comput. Vis. Image Underst. **73**(3), 428–440 (1999)
11. Wigdor, D., Wixon, D.: Brave NUI World: Designing Natural User Interfaces for Touch and Gesture. Elsevier, Amsterdam (2011)
12. Nielsen, J.: Noncommand user interfaces. Commun. ACM **36**(4), 82–100 (1993)
13. Hinckley, K., Wigdor, D.: Input technologies and techniques. In: Jacko, J.A. (ed.) The Human-Computer Interaction Handbook: Fundamentals, Evolving Technologies and Emerging Applications, pp. 151–168. Lawrence Erlbaum Associates, Hillsdale (2002)
14. Suárez Fernández, R.A., Sanchez-Lopez, J.L., Sampedro, C., Bavle, H., Molina, M., Campoy, P.: Natural user interfaces for human-drone multi-modal interaction. In: 2016 International Conference on Unmanned Aircraft Systems (ICUAS), pp. 1013–1022. IEEE (2016)

15. Baudel, T., Beaudouin-Lafon, M.: Charade: Remote control of objects using free-hand gestures. Commun. ACM **36**, 28–35 (1993)
16. Rekimoto, J.: GestureWrist and GesturePad: unobtrusive wearable interaction devices. In: Proceedings Fifth International Symposium on Wearable Computers, pp. 21–27. IEEE (2001)
17. Mantecón, T., del Blanco, C.R., Jaureguizar, F., García, N.: New generation of human machine interfaces for controlling UAV through depth-based gesture recognition. In: Unmanned Systems Technology XVI, vol. 9084, p. 90840C. International Society for Optics and Photonics (2014)
18. Jones, G., Berthouze, N., Bielski, R., Julier, S.: Towards a situated, multimodal interface for multiple UAV control. In: 2010 IEEE International Conference on Robotics and Automation, pp. 1739–1744. IEEE (2010)
19. Pestana, J., Sanchez-Lopez, J., Saripalli, S., Campoy, P.: Computer vision based general object following for GPS-denied multirotor unmanned vehicles, pp. 1886–1891, June 2014
20. Dudek, G., Sattar, J., Xu, A.: A visual language for robot control and programming: a human-interface study. In Proceedings 2007 IEEE International Conference on Robotics and Automation, pp. 2507–2513, April 2007
21. Penmetsa, S., Minhuj, F., Singh, A., Omkar, S.N.: Autonomous UAV for suspicious action detection using pictorial human pose estimation and classification. ELCVIA Electron. Lett. Comput. Vis. Image Anal. **13**(1), 18–32 (2014)
22. Cao, Z., Simon, T., Wei, S.-E., Sheikh, Y.: Realtime multi-person 2D pose estimation using part affinity fields. In: Proceedings of the IEEE Conference on Computer Vision and Pattern Recognition, pp. 7291–7299 (2017)
23. Belagiannis, V., Zisserman, A.: Recurrent human pose estimation. In: 2017 12th IEEE International Conference on Automatic Face and Gesture Recognition (FG 2017), pp. 468–475. IEEE (2017)
24. Bulat, A., Tzimiropoulos, G.: Human pose estimation via convolutional part heatmap regression. In: Leibe, B., Matas, J., Sebe, N., Welling, M. (eds.) ECCV 2016. LNCS, vol. 9911, pp. 717–732. Springer, Cham (2016). https://doi.org/10.1007/978-3-319-46478-7_44
25. Pishchulin, L., Andriluka, M., Gehler, P., Schiele, B.: Poselet conditioned pictorial structures. In: Proceedings of the IEEE Conference on Computer Vision and Pattern Recognition, pp. 588–595 (2013)
26. Pishchulin, L., et al.: DeepCut: joint subset partition and labeling for multi person pose estimation. In: Proceedings of the IEEE Conference on Computer Vision and Pattern Recognition, pp. 4929–4937 (2016)
27. Simon, T., Joo, H., Matthews, I., Sheikh, Y.: Hand keypoint detection in single images using multiview bootstrapping. In: CVPR (2017)
28. Wei, S.-E., Ramakrishna, V., Kanade, T., Sheikh, Y.: Convolutional pose machines. In: CVPR (2016)
29. Andriluka, M., Pishchulin, L., Gehler, P., Schiele, B.: 2D human pose estimation: new benchmark and state of the art analysis. In: Proceedings of the IEEE Conference on computer Vision and Pattern Recognition, pp. 3686–3693 (2014)
30. Lin, T.-Y., et al.: Microsoft COCO: common objects in context. In: Fleet, D., Pajdla, T., Schiele, B., Tuytelaars, T. (eds.) ECCV 2014. LNCS, vol. 8693, pp. 740–755. Springer, Cham (2014). https://doi.org/10.1007/978-3-319-10602-1_48
31. Vapnik, V.: Support-vector networks. Mach. Learn. **20**, 273–297 (1995)
32. Cherkassky, V., Ma, Y.: Practical selection of SVM parameters and noise estimation for SVM regression. Neural Netw. **17**(1), 113–126 (2004)

33. Rasmussen, C.E.: Gaussian processes in machine learning. In: Bousquet, O., von Luxburg, U., Rätsch, G. (eds.) ML 2003. LNCS (LNAI), vol. 3176, pp. 63–71. Springer, Heidelberg (2004). https://doi.org/10.1007/978-3-540-28650-9_4

34. Grauman, K., Darrell, T.: Pyramid match kernels: discriminative classification with sets of image features (version 2) (2006)

35. Xi, H., Chang, T.: Image classification based on histogram intersection kernel. J. Comput. Commun. **3**(11), 158 (2015)

36. Barla, A., Odone, F., Verri, A.: Histogram intersection kernel for image classification. In: Proceedings 2003 International Conference on Image Processing (Cat. No. 03CH37429), vol. 3, pp. III–513. IEEE (2003)

37. Platt, J.C., Cristianini, N., Shawe-Taylor, J.: Large margin DAGs for multiclass classification. In: Advances in Neural Information Processing Systems, pp. 547–553 (2000)

38. Duan, K.-B., Keerthi, S.S.: Which is the best multiclass SVM method? An empirical study. In: Oza, N.C., Polikar, R., Kittler, J., Roli, F. (eds.) MCS 2005. LNCS, vol. 3541, pp. 278–285. Springer, Heidelberg (2005). https://doi.org/10.1007/11494683_28

39. Yang, S., Scherer, S.A., Yi, X., Zell, A.: Multi-camera visual SLAM for autonomous navigation of micro aerial vehicles. Robot. Auton. Syst. **93**, 116–134 (2017)

HSVM-Based Human Activity Recognition Using Smartphones

Santiago Grijalva[1], Gonzalo Cueva[1], David Ramírez[1],
and Wilbert G. Aguilar[1,2,3(✉)]

[1] CICTE, DEEL, Universidad de las Fuerzas Armadas ESPE,
Sangolquí, Ecuador
wgaguilar@espe.edu.ec
[2] FIS, Escuela Politécnica Nacional, Quito, Ecuador
[3] GREC, Universitat Politècnica de Catalunya, Barcelona, Spain

Abstract. Human Activity Recognition (HAR) based on smartphones has a lot of applications to our daily life. Through the years, researchers reached different goals in this topic. Different issues were presented at each approach like accuracy, computational cost, device placement, battery life and limited hardware and software resources. In this paper we developed an HSVM that is capable of classifying 5 types of human activities walking, running, jumping, standing and sitting. 5-fold cross validation was used for the offline training achieving very high accuracy, but in online validation the result was no as accurate as in offline validation. A device placement (orientation) in pocket was considered too, then we present a variety of confusion matrices with four, possible device placement, and their respective accuracy. Wavelet Transform was used to minimize noise into the feature vector.

Keywords: Human Activity Recognition · HSVM · Sensor fusion

1 Introduction

HAR emerged as an important research area over the past decade because a variety of applications rely on sensing and recognizing user activities, including health and environment monitoring applications, home and industry automation applications, and security and surveillance applications [1–4].

The history of human activity recognition can be tracked back to the late 1990s [5, 6]. As there were not devices with sensors built-in, investigators used to design systems bases on sensors placed directly on the body. Thanks to the develop of technology, microcontrollers, microprocessors made this task much easier, these devices now have a more efficient computational power and capability.

The advancement in technology in the past few years has resulted in miniature, low-cost yet highly reliable accelerometers that can be used to collect information about the physical activities of a user in a highly pervasive and invisible manner.

Human activity recognition (HAR) has a lot of applications, since medical area personal daily life, military field [7], entertainment and others. So HAR is getting more and more importance [8, 9].

© Springer Nature Switzerland AG 2019
H. Yu et al. (Eds.): ICIRA 2019, LNAI 11744, pp. 217–228, 2019.
https://doi.org/10.1007/978-3-030-27541-9_19

Smartphones are essential tech-articles in daily life of human beings. Software applications like Facebook, Twitter, YouTube, games, etc., use multiple sensors for different purposes. Sensors like accelerometer and gyroscope allow us to get advantages in the HAR research. In this way, researches can obtain data from the human daily activities.

However, the accuracy of the analyzed data is very important but difficult to get it, also the position of the sensors or smartphone, and the movement of the body are an issue [10, 11]. Different techniques about predict HAR like walk, run, sit was developed through the years. There are considerations from the performance of the different algorithms applied to HAR, some better than others. However, each algorithm was useful to the year that was proposed. In some cases, false motion recognition could happen, then the results are non-reliable data. Thus, an advanced classifier is required.

In this paper a review of different approach, algorithms and techniques are develop and their comparative is explained. We will develop SVM (Support Vector Machine) technique.

The rest of the paper is organized as follow: Sect. 2 talks about related work about HAR. Section 3 explain SVM and other techniques applied in HAR. Section 4 presents our analysis of different experiments of the authors of HAR. Finally, we conclude our work in Sect. 5.

2 Related Work

Considerations about HAR process are quite different between authors, however getting data from sensors [12] is very similar. Every single algorithm must use a classifier like ANN (Artificial Neural Network), SVM (Supported Vector Machine), Decision Tree (DT) [13, 14], etc.

Given enough data sample, a model can be trained using proper learning algorithms [15–17]. Techniques like recollect data sensor, analyze frames and correlate information are going to be discussed.

A new approach was developed with better results. Hybrid model was proposed by [18]. This work consists of DTs and artificial neural network (ANN). The input of the hybrid model classifier is the combination of three-axis output from de accelerometer and the output from proximity sensor. An excellent performance was reached.

In fact, getting excellent performance wasn't enough; computational cost is a task too. Thus, computational cost reduction with a new treatment of SVM was reached by [8]. This method adapts the standard SVM and exploits fixed-point arithmetic.

Anguita [8] introduced the concept of Hardware-Friendly SVM (HF-SVM), the method exploits the fixed-point arithmetic in the feed-forward phase of the SVM. This technique allows to get better performance when the hardware resources are limited.

The SVM algorithm was originally proposed only for binary classification, but problems like noise, position of the device, hardware and others, represents a very important issue. Thus, a complementary algorithm to SVM was necessary.

In 2014, Khan et al. [19] demonstrated that data collected by the sensors depends on the position in which the portable device is carried, therefore it is necessary to improve the discriminant power of these features. Most commonly used techniques for this purpose include principal component analysis (PCA), linear discriminant analysis (LDA), and kernel discriminant analysis (KDA). KDA was chosen as it showed the best performance with an RBF kernel function. The proposed system employs SVMs for activity classification with 99% accuracy.

Zheng et al. [20] propose a model considering two factors: power efficiency and reliable HAR. This can be approached reducing the sample rate at 1 Hz, showing that very low sample rates have just the same accuracy as systems with high sample rate. Bayat et al. [21] showed that Combining the three best classifiers in their research (MP, LogicBoost, SVM) using the average of probabilities method turned out to be the best classifier for activity recognition, outperforming all individual classifiers.

However, a new treatment of the initial information has an important repercussion in the following procedures. Jiang and Yin [5] propose to transfer al signals from accelerometer and gyroscope into an activity image. This new image contains hidden relations. The authors applied DCNN (Deep Convolutional Neural Networks) to generate a probability distribution from the image. Then Discrete Fourier Transform is applied to the signal image. Finally, an SVM classifier was trained to mitigate the uncertainly due the probability distribution. The results were unexpected, the new way of treatment was better than MC-SVM.

Smartphones was not the unique resource used to HAR. In 2011 He et al. [22] used Embedded Smart Cameras to detect persons. A Histogram of Oriented Gradients (HOG) was employed for detection. The idea of HOG is that local features can be characterized by its local intensity gradients or edge directions. An image is divide into cells then 1-D histograms are calculated. After, all histograms of each cell are normalized over cells to get the HOG. Finally, the researchers used a SVM to classify regions at images, human and no human.

Once a person is detected a rectangle is drawn around it. The processing time was 37 s, however, choosing a determinate region the it is possible to decrease the time.

Wearable accelerometers have proved to be effective sensors for human activity recognition. Some of the earliest work on wearable sensor-based activity recognition used multiple accelerometers placed on different parts of the body [10, 23, 24].

Finally, Satake et al. [25] proposed to integrate various cues such as appearance-based object detection [26], depth estimation, visual odometry [27], and ground plane detection using a graphical model for pedestrian detection. Also, in this paper, they proposed a person tracking method using stereo. A several depth templates were prepared to be use for dense depth images and detect person regions by template matching, followed by a support vector machine SVM-based verifier.

3   HSVM HAR System

In this paper, an efficient method was reached applying Mallat algorithm to filter the data collection and HSVM identify the activity in online way. The overview of our system is shown in Fig. 1. Different phases were developed since activity signal until activity inference.

Techniques like Wavelet, feature extraction and SVM were applied in this paper.

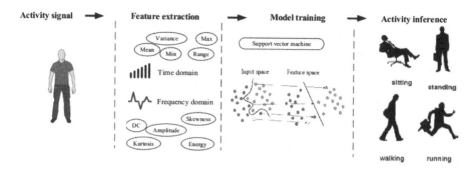

Fig. 1. Overview of our system

An iPhone 6s was used for data collection. The smartphone has built-in tri axial accelerometer, tri axial gyroscope and tri axial magnetometer that can record the participant's motion. The output of the sensors is sampled at 10 Hz. Then data generated by the sensors were transmitted to a personal computer via wireless through Matlab mobile application to Matlab R2017b.

Activities like walking, running, jumping, standing and sitting were performed.

3.1 Sensor Fusion

Considerations about HAR sensor fusion are quite different between authors. Algorithms based on wavelet, SVM, K-NN and others, was reached just by using accelerometer signal and gyroscope. However, we propose a sensor fusion with 4 different sensors: accelerometer, gyroscope, magnetometer and angular velocity sensor.

3.2 Noise Reduction

Shen et al. [11], reported that daily activities like sitting, walking, running and others, has the major energy band at 0.3–3.5 Hz. So, daily activities are highly characterized by low – frequency of signal. Then, a technique that involves discrimination or classification is required. We decompose the original signal from the 4 sensors, in other words, we calculated the three and two level's discrete wavelet using Daubechies 3 and obtain wavelet coefficients of node 2, 3 which represents the low-frequency signal. Once we obtained the expansion of wavelet transform, we reconstruct the signal from the coefficients [28], so all signals at time domain will contain just low – frequency information.

3.3 Feature Selection

Normally the data collected from the smartphone in HAR is analyzed through time domain transformation, frequency domain transformation and time-frequency domain, like as wavelet transform. We extracted several numbers of features once the signal was filtered by wavelet, applying Mallat algorithm. Features like mean, min, max, mad, iqr, rms value, correlation, std, power, frequency, were calculated from the data collection. It important to mention that we worked with 120 features, generated by 4 sensors.

3.4   Support Vector Machine

Support Vector Machine (SVM) is a supervised machine learning algorithm which can be used for classification or regression. This technique allows us to plot data in n-dimensional space. Then, by finding the hyper-plane that separate the two classes, the classification is done. Formally, it tries to optimize the following problem:

$$\text{Min } \gamma, w, b \frac{1}{2} \left\| w^2 \right\| + C \sum_{i=1}^{m} \xi_i \tag{1}$$

$$s.t. y^{(i)} \left(w^T x^{(i)} + b \right) \geq 1 - \xi_i, i = 1, \ldots, m \tag{2}$$

$$\xi_i \geq 0, i = 1, \ldots, m \tag{3}$$

By introducing the term $C \sum_{i=1}^{m} \xi_i$ term, we allow an example to have margin less than 1, but at a cost of increasing the objective by $C\xi_i$. C controls the balance between our two goals of making $\|w\|^2$ small and of ensuring that examples have margin less than 1 [29].

3.5   Hierarchical SVMs

A Hierarchical Support Vector Machine (HSVM) for multi-class classification is a decision tree with an SVM at each node.

At the root node of the decision tree, all classes are available for prediction. The number of classes available for prediction keeps decreasing as we descend the tree.

Before learning the SVM classifier at a node, the classes available at that node are partitioned into two using a max-cut unsupervised decomposition. The classification model to distinguish between the two class partitions is then learnt using the bipartite decomposition as two-class input to train the SVM at that node.

During classification, one traverses the decision tree from the root and keeps applying the SVM classifier at each visited node until one reaches a leaf node indicating the output class.

The training algorithm in summarized in Algorithm 1.

Algorithm 1: Training algorithm

1: Construct feature set (*{f1, f2,...,fn}*). The feature set is composed with 120 features, generated by 4 sensors.
2: Once we load the feature matrix (120 features at each sensor); select just two activities to classify.
3: Separate 80 percent of the set to train and the rest to test.
4: Train a binary classifier SVM.
5: The resulting classifier is one-node SVM classifier, as an N-Class classification needs an N-1 node classifier.

The algorithm described at Algorithm 1, was applied between different activities: dynamics activities vs statics activities, Standing vs. Sitting, Jumping vs Walking-Running and finally Walking vs Running. We will explain this approach at Fig. 3.

4   Experiments and Results

The experiment consists of four parts, (1) data collection, (2) Design of the HSVM Model for multiclass classification, (3) Offline recognition via 5-fold cross validation and (4) Online Validation of the obtained model.

4.1   Data Collection

For data collection, a smartphone (iPhone 6s, Apple Inc.) was placed in the right-front pocket of the pants, as showed in Fig. 2. The sensors used in the experiments were accelerometer, gyroscope, magnetometer and angular velocity sensor. In Table 1 we show the different samples taken from the study participants.

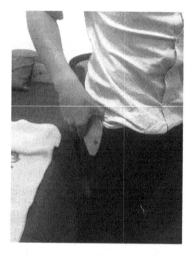

Fig. 2. iPhone 6s placement on the right-front pocket

Table 1. Volunteers' description for the experiment

Volunteer description	Sampling rate	Time Window	Overlap Time
1 (male, 23 years old)	10 Hz	10 s	0 s
1 (male, 27 years old)	10 Hz	10 s	0 s
1 (male, 23 years old)	10 Hz	10 s	0 s
1 (male, 43 years old)	10 Hz	10 s	0 s
1 (male, 36 years old)	10 Hz	10 s	0 s
1 (female, 22 years old)	10 Hz	10 s	0 s
1 (female, 25 years old)	10 Hz	10 s	0 s
1 (female, 26 years old)	10 Hz	10 s	0 s
1 (female, 45 years old)	10 Hz	10 s	0 s
1 (female, 50 years old)	10 Hz	10 s	0 s

The volunteers were asked to perform 5 different activities in the specified order: walking, running, jumping, standing and sitting. Sampling was performed with the following description: (1) walking for 10 s, wait 5 s, (2) running for 10 s, wait 5 s, (3) jumping for 10 s, wait 5 s, (4) standing for 10 s, wait 5 s and (5) sitting for 10 s, wait 10 s; this last waiting time it is given by the change between volunteers, we did not wanted to get tired and get misunderstood data for the training and testing set. Performing these set of instructions, we recollected a total of 50 samples of each activity giving a total of 250 samples for the training and testing data.

4.2 HSVM Model

We propose the model showed in Fig. 3, we based our selection, by the criterion of Dynamics vs Static Activities in Node 1 (SVM1), and then if the prediction corresponds to a Static or Idle Activity SVM2 classifier comes to act at node 2 and predicts whether it is Standing or Sitting posture.

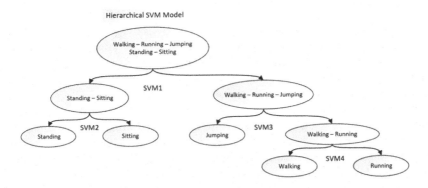

Fig. 3. Proposed HSVM Model

On the other hand, if it is a Dynamic Movement, e.g. Walking, Running or Jumping, SVM3 at node 3 predicts if it is an activity that produces a horizontal translation in space or not, if not then jumping is the correct prediction, but if it corresponds to a Horizontal Translation Activity SVM4 at node 4 predicts if it is whether walking or running based mainly on accelerometer data.

4.3 Offline Recognition via 5-Fold Cross Validation

The purpose of this experiment was evaluating the performance of the Kernel Discriminant Analysis, for the RBF function, with this Sequential Feature Selection was evaluated too.

First, we divide randomly the training set from the testing set for the offline validation, we choose to take 80% for the training data and 20% for the testing data, e.g. 200 training samples and 50 testing samples.

For this experiment, the training data were divided into 5 subsets. Of these, the data from one subset was retained as the validation data, whereas the data from the remaining four subsets were used as the training data. The while process was repeated 5 times, each time picking a different subset as the validation subset.

With the obtained model from 4.2, we tested each node SVM, and got the following accuracies for the testing data validation (Table 2).

Table 2. Classification accuracy at each node for the testing data

Node	Dividing set	Accuracy (%)
1	Static vs Dynamic Activities	100
2	Sitting vs Standing	100
3	Jumping vs Displacement	100
4	Walking vs Running	95

4.4   Online Recognition

For this validation, ten participants performed each activity five times. The time between activities recognition was about 2.3 s. It is necessary to mention that Wavelet Transform was not applied on Sitting and Standing data, because it is stationary and if one performs this on these types of signal, the Transform will filter the most significant picks (few in statics activities) in the signal.

Only walking, running and jumping data was filtered by Wavelet Transform. The results obtained in the live validation are close enough to the offline recognition, this is cause mainly by the time between activities, it happens frequently when someone is attempting to stand up from the sitting position, and a walking is miss predicted, the same happens between jumping and running activities.

The online recognition was developed with two device placements. In Fig. 4, the related positions are presented. Just first and second position was adopted by energy efficiency and battery life considerations.

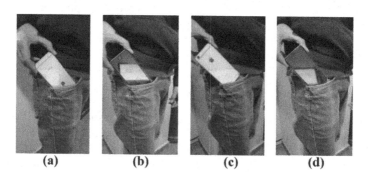

Fig. 4. (a) First Position, (b) Second Position, (c) Third Position, (d) Fourth Position

The confusion matrices present below are calculated from all results of the participants.

In Table 3, confusion matrix for smartphone first position into the pocket is shown, the screen was facing the body and the charge jack was facing upwards. Just one misprediction was committed, it may be produced due to the change between activities, on the other hand, other activities did not present misclassifications.

Table 3. Confusion matrix for Online Validation with Smartphone on Position 1

	Walking	Running	Jumping	Standing	Sitting	
Walking	10	0	0	0	0	
	20.00%	0.00%	0.00%	0.00%	0.00%	
Running	0	9	0	0	0	
	0.00%	18.00%	0.00%	0.00%	0.00%	
Jumping	0	1	10	0	0	
	0.00%	2.00%	20.0%	0.00%	0.00%	
Standing	0	0	0	10	0	
	0.00%	0.00%	0.00%	20.0%	0.00%	
Sitting	0	0	0	0	10	
	0.00%	0.00%	0.00%	0.00%	20.0%	
Individual Precision	100%	90.0%	100%	100%	100%	98.00%
	0.00%	10.0%	0.0%	0.0%	0.0%	2.00%
	Walking	**Running**	**Jumping**	**Standing**	**Sitting**	**Total Precision**

In Table 4, confusion matrix for smartphone second position into the pocket is shown, the screen was not facing the body and the charge jack was facing upwards. Mispredictions between Running and Jumping were committed, it may happen due to the excess of speed in Running activity, as this may produces wrong readings from sensors.

Video results are provided on https://www.youtube.com/watch?v=9veDFQD3PcM.

Table 4. Confusion matrix for Online Validation with Smartphone on Position 2

	Walking	Running	Jumping	Standing	Sitting	Total Precision
Walking	10 20.00%	0 0.00%	0 0.00%	0 0.00%	0 0.00%	
Running	0 0.00%	8 16.00%	0 0.00%	0 0.00%	0 0.00%	
Jumping	0 0.00%	2 4.00%	10 20.0%	0 0.00%	0 0.00%	
Standing	0 0.00%	0 0.00%	0 0.00%	10 20.0%	0 0.00%	
Sitting	0 0.00%	0 0.00%	0 0.00%	0 0.00%	10 20.0%	
Individual Precision	100% 0.00%	90.0% 10.0%	100% 0.0%	100% 0.0%	100% 0.0%	96.00% 4.00%

5 Conclusion and Future Work

This paper presents Human Activity Recognition system that applies iPhone 6s sensors like accelerometer, gyroscope, magnetometer and angular velocity sensor. An excellent accuracy and low computational cost were reached.

Techniques like Mallat algorithm, decimation's wavelet was important to filter all signal without lose information and allow us to get low-frequency information.

Thus, future work will be a combination of energy efficiency, classification directly in our smartphone and compare our system with other classifiers.

Due to the energy efficiency and the respective battery life of the smartphone, the device placement three and four (Fig. 4) was omitted because many smartphone enterprises suggest avoiding placement in which the charge port stablish contact with the pocket bottom, this approach will prevent the entry of dust and others harmful particles.

In future versions, a study of how to establish which are the best combinations for the HSVM, will be performed, such that, it will be possible for us to give a better perspective of how to classify activities, because it is not necessarily the best option to start classifying them between Static and Dynamic activities.

References

1. Aguilar, W.G., Angulo, C.: Real-time model-based video stabilization for microaerial vehicles. Neural Process. Lett. **43**(2), 459–477 (2016)
2. Aguilar, W.G., Angulo, C.: Real-time video stabilization without phantom movements for micro aerial vehicles. EURASIP J. Image Video Process. **1**, 1–13 (2014)

3. Aguilar, W.G., et al.: Real-time detection and simulation of abnormal crowd behavior. In: De Paolis, L.T., Bourdot, P., Mongelli, A. (eds.) AVR 2017. LNCS, vol. 10325, pp. 420–428. Springer, Cham (2017). https://doi.org/10.1007/978-3-319-60928-7_36

4. Aguilar, W.G., et al.: Statistical abnormal crowd behavior detection and simulation for real-time applications. In: Huang, Y., Wu, H., Liu, H., Yin, Z. (eds.) ICIRA 2017. LNCS (LNAI), vol. 10463, pp. 671–682. Springer, Cham (2017). https://doi.org/10.1007/978-3-319-65292-4_58

5. Jiang, W., Yin, Z.: Human activity recognition using wearable sensors by deep convolutional neural networks. In: Proceedings of the 23rd ACM International Conference on Multimedia - MM 2015, pp. 1307–1310 (2015)

6. Pei, L., et al.: Human behavior cognition using smartphone sensors. Sensors (Switzerland) 13(2), 1402–1424 (2013)

7. Aguilar, W.G., Cobeña, B., Rodriguez, G., Salcedo, V.S., Collaguazo, B.: SVM and RGB-D sensor based gesture recognition for UAV control. In: International Conference on Augmented Reality, Virtual Reality and Computer Graphics (2018)

8. Anguita, D., Ghio, A., Oneto, L., Parra, X., Reyes-Ortiz, J.L.: Human activity recognition on smartphones using a multiclass hardware-friendly support vector machine. In: Bravo, J., Hervás, R., Rodríguez, M. (eds.) IWAAL 2012. LNCS, vol. 7657, pp. 216–223. Springer, Heidelberg (2012). https://doi.org/10.1007/978-3-642-35395-6_30

9. Larrey Ruiz, J., Morales Sánchez, J., Sancho Gómez, J.L., Verdú Monedero, R., García Laencina, P.J.: Algoritmo KNN basado en información mutua para clasificación de patrones con valores perdidos (2008)

10. Mimouna, A., Khalifa, A.B., Khalifa, A.B.: Human action recognition using triaxial accelerometer data: Selective approach. In: 15th International Multi-Conference on Systems, Signals and Devices, SSD 2018, pp. 491–496 (2018)

11. Shen, C., Chen, Y., Yang, G.: On motion-sensor behavior analysis for human-activity recognition via smartphones. In: ISBA 2016 - IEEE International Conference on Identity, Security and Behavior Analysis (2016)

12. Aguilar, W.G., Morales, S.: 3D environment mapping using the kinect V2 and path planning based on RRT algorithms. Electronics 5(4), 70 (2016)

13. Khandnor, P., Kumar, N.: A survey of activity recognition process using inertial sensors and smartphone sensors, pp. 607–612 (2017)

14. Sousa, W., Souto, E., Rodrigres, J., Sadarc, P., Jalali, R., El-Khatib, K.: A comparative analysis of the impact of features on human activity recognition with smartphone sensors, pp. 397–404 (2017)

15. Su, X., Tong, H., Ji, P.: Activity recognition with smartphone sensors. Tsinghua Sci. Technol. 19(3), 235–249 (2014)

16. Aguilar, W.G., et al.: Pedestrian detection for UAVs using cascade classifiers and saliency maps. In: Rojas, I., Joya, G., Catala, A. (eds.) IWANN 2017. LNCS, vol. 10306, pp. 563–574. Springer, Cham (2017). https://doi.org/10.1007/978-3-319-59147-6_48

17. Aguilar, W.G., Luna, M., Moya, J., Abad, V., Parra, H., Ruiz, H.: Pedestrian detection for UAVs using cascade classifiers with meanshift. In: IEEE 11th International Conference on Semantic Computing (ICSC), San Diego (2017)

18. Shin, B., Kim, C., Kim, J.H., Lee, S., Kee, C., Lee, T.: Hybrid model-based motion recognition for smartphone users. ETRI J. 36(6), 1016–1022 (2014)

19. Khan, A.M., Tufail, A., Khattak, A.M., Laine, T.H.: Activity recognition on smartphones via sensor-fusion and KDA-based SVMs. Int. J. Distrib. Sens. Networks 10(5), 503291 (2014)

20. Zheng, L., et al.: A novel energy-efficient approach for human activity recognition. Sensors 17(9), 2064 (2017)

21. Bayat, A., Pomplun, M., Tran, D.A.: A study on human activity recognition using accelerometer data from smartphones. Procedia Comput. Sci. **34**(C), 450–457 (2014)
22. He, L., Wang, Y., Velipasalar, S., Gursoy, M.C.: Human detection using mobile embedded smart cameras. In: 2011 Fifth ACM/IEEE International Conference on Distributed Smart Cameras, pp. 1–6 (2011)
23. Dernbach, S., Das, B., Krishnan, N.C., Thomas, B.L., Cook, D.J.: Simple and complex activity recognition through smart phones. In: 2012 Eighth International Conference on Intelligent Environments, pp. 214–221 (2012)
24. Tapu, R., Mocanu, B., Bursuc, A., Zaharia, T.: A smartphone-based obstacle detection and classification system for assisting visually impaired people. In: 2013 IEEE International Conference on Computer Vision Workshops, pp. 444–451 (2013)
25. Satake, J., Miura, J.: Robust stereo-based person detection and tracking for a person following robot. In: People Detection and Tracking, Proceedings of the IEEE ICRA 2009, pp. 1–10 (2009)
26. Aguilar, W.G., Casaliglla, V.P., Pólit, J.L.: Obstacle avoidance based-visual navigation for micro aerial vehicles. Electronics **6**(1), 10 (2017)
27. Aguilar, W.G., Salcedo, V.S., Sandoval, D.S., Cobeña, B.: Developing of a video-based model for UAV autonomous navigation. In: Barone, D.A.C., Teles, E.O., Brackmann, C. P. (eds.) LAWCN 2017. CCIS, vol. 720, pp. 94–105. Springer, Cham (2017). https://doi.org/10.1007/978-3-319-71011-2_8
28. Tian, Y., Chen, W.: MEMS-based human activity recognition using smartphone. In: Chinese Control Conference, CCC, pp. 3984–3989 (2016)
29. Ma, Y., Li, Z., Jiang, Y.: Human Activity Recognition: Accelerometers Unveil Your Actions

Mobile Robots and Intelligent Autonomous Systems

Human-AGV Interaction: Real-Time Gesture Detection Using Deep Learning

Jiliang Zhang[1,2], Li Peng[1(✉)], Wei Feng[1], Zhaojie Ju[2],
and Honghai Liu[2]

[1] Jiangnan University, Wuxi 214122, China
`penglimail2002@163.com`
[2] University of Portsmouth, Portsmouth PO1 3HE, UK

Abstract. In this paper, we present a real-time human body gesture recognition for controlling Automated Guided Vehicle (AGV) in facility. Exploiting the breakthrough of deep convolutional networks in computers, we have developed a system that can detect the human gestures and give corresponding commands to the AGV according to different gestures. For avoiding interference of multiple operational targets in an image, we proposed a method to filter out the non-operator. In addition, we propose a human gesture interpreter with clear semantic information and build a new human gesture dataset with 8 gestures to train or fine-tune the deep neural networks for human gesture detection. In order to balance accuracy and response speed, we choose MobileNet-SSD as the detection network.

Keywords: Human gesture · AGV · MobileNet-SSD · Deep learning

1 Introduction

Goods production flow in manufacturing plants has been largely and deeply automated in the last decades. To increase efficiency and reduce the cost of manual operators in manufacturing and distributing logistics, companies and organizations use robots as an effective tool. The Automated Guided Vehicle (AGV) is type of effeminate mobile vehicle that is primarily used to move materials from one place to another. AGVs are commonly used in manufacturing plants, warehouses, distribution centers and terminals. For navigation, an AGV system usually uses lane paths, signal paths or signal beacons. Various main sensors are also used in AGV, such as optical sensors, laser sensors, magnetic sensors and cameras.

AGV system has a strict requirement on environment. AGVs cannot work at the place where has no lane or signal. In this way, we hope that we can propose a new control method to break this limitation so that it can be applied to a wide range of scenarios, such as rural areas, urban outside, etc. The Natural User Interface (NUI) has been proposed recently instead of the physical remote. Visual human gesture is one of the most appealing methods to build an AGV system. We present a fast and accurate detector that finds the hands, faces and bodies of multiple people in RGB images at the frame-rate, which can be used directly as an input to an AGV system.

© Springer Nature Switzerland AG 2019
H. Yu et al. (Eds.): ICIRA 2019, LNAI 11744, pp. 231–242, 2019.
https://doi.org/10.1007/978-3-030-27541-9_20

The contributions of this paper are: (i) We create a new way to control AGV with deep learning. This method can enable AGVs to get rid of environmental constraints and apply them in a wider range of fields. (ii) We propose a filtering algorithm based on high level features, which is effective and low time cost, to filter out visual disturbances from non-operators in the image and implement them in our software program. The software uses a scalable CNN model that can be resized for speed/accuracy trade-off based on MobileNet-SSD; (iii) We propose a novel, simple but effective and semantically clear static gesture detection method for transmitting instruction commands based on the angle of the hand relative to the face; and establish a dataset based on the representation method which contains 8 human gestures.

The rest of the paper is structured as follows:

Section 2 reviews the development of object detection and the related research status of AGV system and human-robot interaction.

Section 3 presents the overall architecture of our system.

Section 4 introduces the network structure we choose and compares it with the current frequently-used object detection network model.

Section 5 describes the proposed method of human gestures and introduces the establishment of the matched dataset.

Section 6 explains the filtering algorithm of the AGV system and the process of filtering out the interference from non-operators.

Section 7 is the experimental results of the actual test of the system.

2   Background

2.1   Object Detection

The purpose of object detection is to identify objects from different backgrounds of complexity and separate the background to complete follow-up tasks such as tracking and recognition. Therefore, object detection is the basic task of high-level understanding and application, and its performance will affects the performance of mid- and high-level tasks directly such as subsequent target tracking, motion recognition, and behavioral understanding.

Object detection is important in the field of computer vision and image processing because of its wide range of applications for video surveillance, intelligent transportation, medical diagnostics and vision guidance. Therefore, it's important to have a robust and fast object detection algorithm. There are two branches particularly compelling in many CNN-based algorithms. The first uses two steps to solve the problem such as R-CNN [1], SPPnet [2], Fast R-CNN [3], and Faster R-CNN [4]. In this series, the first step is to find possible candidate regions, and then predict the corresponding categories and perform a box regression of the boundary candidate regions. Second is single stage series, including You Only Look Once (YOLO) [5], YOLOv2 [6], Single Shot MultiBox Detector (SSD) [7], which aim to remove the region proposal stage and then predict confidence and offset for every default box. The SSD network provides a new neural network model for deep learning. In this architecture mode, some researchers replaced the front network VGG-16 [8] with other types of networks such as Residual-101 [9] and inception [10], which are much deeper and more powerful to achieve a higher accuracy. The deepening of the network structure means more calculation parameters, which will bring the loss of calculation speed. So we hope to use a network to balance calculation speed and accuracy. Recently MobileNet [11] has been proposed to establish a real-time-capable object locator, providing the possibility of implementing neural networks on mobile devices.

2.2 The Development of AGV

The world's first automated guided vehicle was developed by Basrrett Electronics in the United States in 1953. It was converted from a towed tractor with a car hopper. It worked based on the routine of the wire set in the air. In the late 1950s and early 1960s, there were many types of towed AGVs used in factories and warehouses. Recently, there are about 20,000 AGVs in the world running in thousands of large and small warehouses.

Starting from the electromagnetic induction guidance technology of underground embedding in the United Kingdom in 1954, the early AGVs were driven along the signals on the ground. The sensors on the AGV are selected the electromagnetic signals of a certain frequency to provide guidance for the AGV according to the strength of the signal. With the rapid development of electronic technology and microprocessor technology, AGV's intelligent technology has been generally developed. In the late 1980s, wireless guidance technology was introduced into the AGV system, such as laser and inertia guidance, greatly improving the flexibility and accuracy of the AGV system. The introduction of computer technology allows AGV to handle almost all manually controlled material handling processes. Figure 1 shows an example of an AGV from the internet.

Fig. 1. An AGV in the factory.

2.3 Human-Robot Interaction

Using gestures to achieve human-computer interaction has recently become popular. Many researchers have done relevant research. In [12–14], authors use Microsoft

Kinect to capture images of operators which contain RGB and depth data. With this data, local machine can derive the skeletal model of the operator and match the corresponding vocabulary based on the skeletal features. But RGB-D sensors have frustrating problems, involving the Kinect with its driver and API library makes the system costlier and has a noticeable latency. Motion-based detection is one of the ways of implementation such as waving [15]. These recognition methods work slowly and are vulnerable to frame loss in the video stream, so they are hard to apply in real-time detection. Some researchers use more obvious objects, such as arm gestures [16] and colored gloves [17], to avoid the effects of the environment.

3   System Architecture Overview

Figure 2 shows high level architecture of the system. Images are captured by on-board camera, then forward through pretrained neural network model. The outputs of the model are boxes including face, hands and body. According to the position of these boxes, local machine can interpret the gesture operator want to express, and then send matched command to the AGV. After receiving the command, the AGV will send feedback message to the local machine. The entire system works in a Wi-Fi environment.

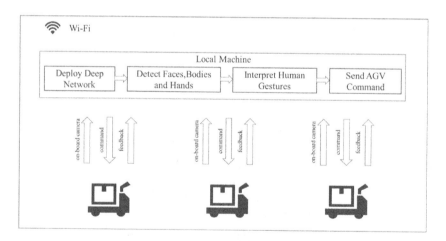

Fig. 2. High level architecture.

4   CNN Model

The network model we choose is MobileNet-SSD, which is an improvement of standard SSD model. Single Shot MultiBox Detector (SSD) is one of the fastest algorithms in the current object detection field, which uses fully convolutional neural network to detect all scaled objects in an image. This method discretizes the output space of bounding boxes into a set of default boxes over different aspect ratios and scales per feature map location. The network outputs a predicted score for each object category in each default box and adjusts the output box to better match the shape of the object. In addition, the network extracts features from feature layers with different resolutions and combines prediction results of multiple feature maps together to identify natural objects in different sizes.

The architecture of the network presents in Fig. 3. The front layers of standard SSD is VGG-16 while the network we chose is MobileNet. According to [11], the author has made the comparison of MobileNet to other popular models. The result shows in Table 1. We can see, the parameters of the MobileNet are greatly reduced, and the accuracy is reduced a little. We can conclude that MobileNet loses a small amount of accuracy to achieve a higher speed increase, which is the key of real-time detection. The system works based on three objects - hands, faces and bodies. In order to cater for the requirement, we changed the number of filters in the last convolutional layer of the model.

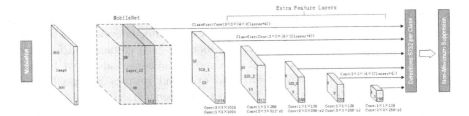

Fig. 3. Architectures of MobileNet-SSD

Table 1. MobileNet comparison to popular models

Model	ImageNet accuracy	Million mult-adds	Million parameters
MobileNet	70.6%	569	4.2
GoogleNet	69.8%	1550	6.8
VGG 16	71.5%	15300	138

5 Human Gestures

5.1 Gesture Interpreter

Many researchers have proposed multiple ways of gesture representation. In [18–20], researchers have presented different sets of gestural vocabularies. Due to little semantic information and real-time problems, they are not suitable for an AGV system. Some researchers defined some motion-based gestures such as waving-based gestures [15], based on sequence of different postures for frames. However, these detection methods are too slow to widely meet the requirements for real-time detection under the conditions of existing hardware devices in industrial environment. Relying on skin detection enabled detection of a user's arms and to generate richer commands [16], but skin detection lacks robustness and is not always feasible. The gestures we need are those stable enough to be uninterrupted by environmental factors, they should contain clear semantic information, so that users do not need calibration or training. And they should be easy to be understood by AGV system. In this way, we use static (posture) not dynamic gesture recognition in our proposal, make the system identify the command expressed by each frame and regard every four frames as a sequence. If the four commands contained in the sequence are all same, the command will take effect, which can avoid the unexpected effect caused by the loss or misidentification of certain frame to the current AGV state.

5.2   Gesture Design

Our static gesture detection works based on the angle of each hand box's center to that of face's box. Different angles represent different gestures. We define $\angle\alpha_1$ as the angle between the line from the center point of the right-hand box to the center point of the face box and the line in the center of the face box. While $\angle\alpha_2$ is defined as the left one (Fig. 4). These two angles can present 8 human gestures with the different ranges of each one. We believe that gestures should have clear semantic information in practical applications, so we divide the gesture set into four one-hand gestures and four two-hand gestures. One-hand gestures present AGV movement commands (move forward, move backward, move left, move right), and two-hand gestures indicate function commands (lift up, lift down, turn CW 180°, focus on operator) as illustrated in Fig. 5. We divide the 360° two-dimensional area into eight areas in each 45°, which represent the one-hand gesture area and the two-hand gesture area alternately, aiming to overcome the wrong interpretation of the instruction in the process of gesture formation caused by a high degree similarity of the same type gestures. Table 2 summarizes the correspondence between postures and AGV controlling commands. 'Stop' is a default command when the operator gesture does not satisfy any threshold mentioned in Table 2.

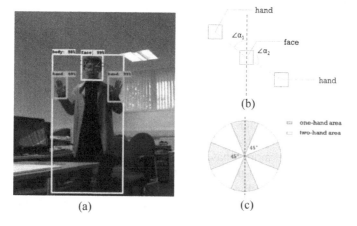

Fig. 4. (a) (b) Demonstrates of how the angles $\angle\alpha_1$ and $\angle\alpha_2$ are determined from the bounding boxes. (c) Areas of controlling commands.

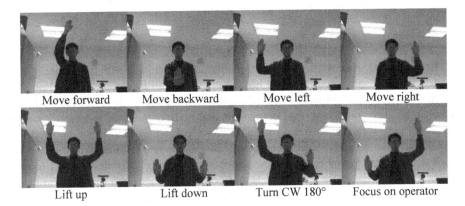

Fig. 5. Different gestures are designed to control the AGV.

Table 2. The correspondence between postures and the AGV controlling commands.

$\angle\alpha_1$	$\angle\alpha_2$	Corresponding command
One-hand gestrues (Movement commands)		
0°:22.5°	Or 0°:22.5°	Move forward
67.5°:112.5°	–	Move left
157.5°:180°	Or 157.5°:180°	Move backward
–	67.5°:112.5°	Move right
Two-hand gestures (Function commands)		
22.5°:67.5°	22.5°:67.5°	Lift up
22.5°:67.5°	112.5°:157.5°	Turn CW 180°
112.5°:157.5°	22.5°:67.5°	Focus on operator
112.5°:157.5°	112.5°:157.5°	Lift down

6 Classification Filtering

Considering the actual working environment of AGV, the video frames captured by the on-board camera may contain more than one person, which can be recognized as misleading commands. We use high level features to filter the output classification to solve this problem. The main idea of classification filtering is to match the results of the model and filter out the output boxes that have not been matched. A complete gesture consists of three parts: hands, face and body. If the output box cannot be part of the three parts then it will be filtered out. We use two parameters A_{hb}, A_{fb} to indicate how well the hand and face match the body. The parameters are defined as shown:

$$A_{hb} = \frac{S_{hand \cap body}}{S_{hand}}$$

$$A_{fb} = \frac{S_{face \cap body}}{S_{face}}$$

The agreement score A_{hb} for the functionality hb is calculated with the square of the common part of hand output box and body output box and the square of hand output box. In this way, the agreement score A_{fb} for the functionality fb is calculated with the square of the common part of face output box and body output box and the square of face output box. If the value of A_{hb} (or A_{fb}) is close to 1, we can think that the hand (or face) output box is in the body output box, so that these two output boxes can be regarded matched. Figure 6 shows the process of filtering. MobileNet-SSD model outputs predicted boxes for faces, hands and bodies. The first loop matches the faces and bodies. The second loop matches the hands and bodies. Finally check if each matched body box contains face and hand, if not remove them all.

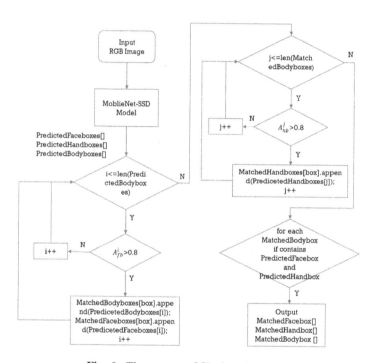

Fig. 6. The process of filtering algorithm.

7   Experiments

7.1   Training

Our training dataset includes 4287 images focusing on human's hands, faces and bodies captured by the on-board camera. The camera resolution is of 640×480 pixels, 30 fps. We obtained one frame from videos every 5 frames, and all the images would be resized into 300 × 300 pixels before being fed to the network model. In order to enable the network to adapt to different distance to the operator, all these images were taken in the range from 0.5 m to 5 m. We used MobileNet-SSD model pretrained on COCO 90-class dataset, and got applied model after 200000 steps of iteration. The ground station is a desktop PC (with an Intel Core i7-3820 @ 3.60 GHz × 8 and equipped with NVIDIA GPU GeForce GTX 690), which performs not so good in calculation but closes to industrial computers.

7.2   Experiments on Human-AGV Interaction

We create a test dataset with the same distribution as the training dataset for evaluation, which contains all eight gestures. There are 200 images for each gesture. The test frames in this section all contain single operator without background interference from non-operators. Table 3 presents the accuracy of MobileNet-SSD and some popular object detection models working based on our proposed gesture method. From Table 3 obviously, MobileNet-SSD achieves the real-time requirement for gesture detection beside preserving the detection accuracy in terms of gesture interaction. InceptionV2-SSD are also fast enough with 14.23 fps to be applied in practice, but MobileNet-SSD can work at a higher speed, which means it can be applied to a wider scope of environments and have less requirement for hardware devices.

Table 3. The accuracy of MobileNet-SSD compared with popular models

Network model	Move forward	Move backward	Move left	Move right	Lift up	Lift down	Turn CW 180°	Focus on operator	Total	fps_mean
MobileNet-SSD	88%	92%	**95.5%**	95.5%	75.5%	95%	82.5%	86.5%	88.81%	**27.74**
InceptionV2-SSD	93%	**100%**	87.5%	90.5%	85.5%	97%	91%	89%	91.69%	14.23
Faster-rcnn-InceptionV2	96.5%	95.5%	91%	**100%**	94%	**100%**	99.5%	98.5%	**96.88%**	1.17
Faster-rcnn-resnet50	**97%**	76.5%	94.5%	92.5%	**97.5%**	**100%**	99.5%	**99.5%**	94.63%	0.29

7.3   Experiments on Classification Filtering

We have established a dataset specifically for evaluating the filtering effect, which has 2000 images. Each gesture has 250 images, of which 20% have interferences from non-operators. Table 4 lists the comparison results of the filtering algorithm applied in MobileNet-SSD model. It can be clearly seen that our proposed algorithm can effectively eliminate interference from non-operators, because the algorithm utilizes high level features without involving too many calculations, so it has less impact on real-time performance. There are comparisons of two frames in Fig. 7.

Table 4. The results of the filtering algorithm

	Move forward	Move backward	Move left	Move right	Lift up	Lift down	Turn CW 180°	Focus on operator	Total	fps_mean
Unfiltered	75.6%	82%	78.8%	80.4%	64%	82.4%	72.4%	73.6%	76.15%	27.76
Filtered	88%	90%	92%	91.2%	72%	97.6%	81.2%	83.6%	86.95%	27.44

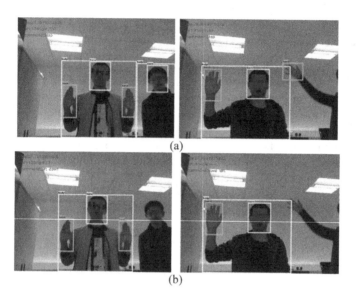

(a)

(b)

Fig. 7. (a) The output frame without being filtered. (b) The output frame after being filtered.

8   Conclusion

In this paper, we introduce a system to control AGV through a series of human gestures successfully, which can work at a high accuracy and fast speed even if the hardware devices are not so powerful. With our new collected dataset built for human gestures, we design an interpreter mapping each gesture to a controlling command. In addition, the gesture method and classification filtering algorithm we designed get better results in the experiment, which can achieve real-time and preserve high gesture detection accuracy.

Acknowledgements. This research was supported by the 111 Project (B12018) and Jiangsu Planned Projects for Postdoctoral Research Funds (1601085C). We thank our colleagues from Portsmouth University, England and Jiangnan University, China, who provided insight and expertise that greatly assisted the research.

References

1. Girshick, R., Donahue, J., Darrell, T., Malik, J.: Rich feature hierarchies for accurate object detection and semantic segmentation. In: The IEEE Conference on Computer Vision and Pattern Recognition, CVPR 2014, pp. 580–587 (2014)
2. He, K., Zhang, X., Ren, S., Sun, J.: Spatial pyramid pooling in deep convolutional networks for visual recognition. In: Fleet, D., Pajdla, T., Schiele, B., Tuytelaars, T. (eds.) ECCV 2014. LNCS, vol. 8691, pp. 346–361. Springer, Cham (2014). https://doi.org/10.1007/978-3-319-10578-9_23
3. Girshick, R.: Fast R-CNN. In: The IEEE International Conference on Computer Vision, ICCV 2015, pp. 1440–1448 (2015)
4. Ren, S., He, K., Girshick, R., Sun, J.: Faster R-CNN: towards real-time object detection with region proposal networks. IEEE Trans. Pattern Anal. Mach. Intell. **39**, 1137–1149 (2017)
5. Redmon, J., Divvala, S., Girshick, R., Farhadi, A.: You only look once: unified, real-time object detection. In: The IEEE Conference on Computer Vision and Pattern Recognition, CVPR 2016, pp. 779–788 (2016)
6. Redmon, J., Farhadi, A.: YOLO9000: better, faster, stronger. arXiv preprint arXiv:1612.08242 (2016)
7. Liu, W., et al.: SSD: Single Shot MultiBox Detector. In: Leibe, B., Matas, J., Sebe, N., Welling, M. (eds.) ECCV 2016. LNCS, vol. 9905, pp. 21–37. Springer, Cham (2016). https://doi.org/10.1007/978-3-319-46448-0_2
8. Karen, S., Zisserman, A.: Very deep convolutional networks for large-scale image recognition. arXiv preprint arXiv:1409.1556 (2014)
9. He, K., Zhang, X., Ren, S., Sun, J.: Deep residual learning for image recognition. In: The IEEE Conference on Computer Vision and Pattern Recognition, CVPR 2016, pp. 770–778 (2016)
10. Szegedy, C., et al.: Going deeper with convolutions. In: The IEEE Conference on Computer Vision and Pattern Recognition, CVPR 2015, pp. 1–9 (2015)
11. Howard, A.G., et al.: MobileNets: efficient convolutional neural networks for mobile vision applications. arXiv preprint arXiv:1704.04861 (2017)
12. Lichtenstern, M., Frassl, M., Perun, B., Angermann, M.: A prototyping environment for interaction between a human and a robotic multi-agent system. In: 7th Annual ACM/IEEE International Conference on Human-Robot Interaction (HRI), Ser. HRI 2012, pp. 185–186. ACM, New York (2012)
13. Sanna, A., Lamberti, F., Paravati, G., Manuri, F.: A kinect-based natural interface for quadrotor control. Entertain. Comput. **4**(3), 179–186 (2013)
14. Naseer, T., Sturm, J., Cremers, D.: FollowMe: person following and gesture recognition with a quadrocopter. In: IEEE/RSJ International Conference on Intelligent Robots and Systems (IROS), pp. 624–630 (2013)
15. Monajjemi, M., Mohaimenianpour, S., Vaughan, R.: UAV, come to me: end-to-end, multi-scale situated HRI with an uninstrumented human and a distant UAV. In: IEEE/RSJ International Conference on Intelligent Robots and Systems, IROS 2016, pp. 4410–4417 (2016)
16. Sun, T., Nie, S., Yeung, D.Y., Shen, S.: Gesture-based piloting of an aerial robot using monocular vision. In: IEEE International Conference on Robotics and Automation, ICRA 2017, pp. 5913–5920 (2017)
17. Nagi, J., Ngo, H., Gambardella, L.M., Caro, G.A.D.: Wisdom of the swarm for cooperative decision-making in human-swarm interaction. In: IEEE International Conference on Robotics and Automation, ICRA 2015, pp. 1802–1808 (2015)

18. Ng, W.S., Sharlin, E.: Collocated interaction with flying robots. In: 20th IEEE International Symposium on Robot and Human Interactive Communication (RO-MAN), pp. 143–149 (2011)
19. Taralle, F., Paljic, A., Manitsaris, S., Grenier, J., Guettier, C.: A consensual and non-ambiguous set of gestures to interact with UAV in infantrymen. In: 33rd Annual ACM Conference Extended Abstracts on Human Factors in Computing Systems, Ser. CHI EA 2015, pp. 797–803. ACM, New York (2015)
20. Cauchard, J.R., Zhai, K.Y., Landay, J.A.: Drone & me: an exploration into natural human-drone interaction. In: ACM International Joint Conference on Pervasive and Ubiquitous Computing, Ser. UbiComp 2015, pp. 361–365. ACM, New York (2015)

Coverage Path Planning for Complex Structures Inspection Using Unmanned Aerial Vehicle (UAV)

Randa Almadhoun[1(✉)], Tarek Taha[2], Jorge Dias[1], Lakmal Seneviratne[1], and Yahya Zweiri[1,3]

[1] Khalifa University of Science and Technology, Abu Dhabi, UAE
{randa.almadhoun,jorge.dias,lakmal.seneviratne}@ku.ac.ae
[2] Algorythma's Autonomous Aerial Lab, Abu Dhabi, UAE
tarek.taha@algorythma.com
[3] Faculty of Science, Engineering and Computing, Kingston University London, London SW15 3DW, UK
y.zweiri@kingston.ac.uk

Abstract. The most critical process in the inspection is the structure coverage which is a time and resource intensive task. In this paper, Search Space Coverage Path Planning (SSCPP) algorithm for inspecting complex structure using a vehicular system consisting of Unmanned Aerial Vehicle (UAV) is proposed. The proposed algorithm exploits our knowledge of the structure model, and the UAV's onboard sensors to generate coverage paths that maximizes coverage and accuracy. The algorithm supports the integration of multiple sensors to increase the coverage at each viewpoint and reduce the mission time. A weighted heuristic reward function is developed in the algorithm to target coverage, accuracy, travelled distance and turning angle at each viewpoint. The iterative processes of the proposed algorithm were accelerated exploiting the parallel architecture of the Graphics Processing Unit (GPU). A set of experiments using models of different shapes were conducted in simulated and real environments. The simulation and experimental results show the validity and effectiveness of the proposed algorithm.

Keywords: Autonomous exploration · Coverage planning · Aerial robots · View planning · 3D reconstruction

1 Introduction

A wide variety of robotic applications is integrating different kinds of vehicular systems particularly UAVs. The field of infrastructure inspection could be revolutionized using aerial robots which ensure safety, improve efficiency, and are considered a cost saving assets. Using UAVs facilitates capturing visual data of the occluded regions of the structure which simplifies the reconstruction process utilized in inspection. The performance and serviceability of large complex

© Springer Nature Switzerland AG 2019
H. Yu et al. (Eds.): ICIRA 2019, LNAI 11744, pp. 243–266, 2019.
https://doi.org/10.1007/978-3-030-27541-9_21

structures such as aircrafts are maintained by performing inspection for different applications including: model digitizing, defects detection and fault traceability.

Various robotic capabilities are required for the application of structures inspection such as: localization, path planning and navigation (computing achievable routes), and sensing and perception (information gathering). Therefore, the robot must be equipped with intelligent sensing capabilities, that enhance the quality of the gathered information along the generated route, in order to provide accurate 3D reconstructed models.

Various challenges and contributions in the field of structure inspection have been documented in the literature. These challenges and contributions have been addressed depending on the environment, the shape of the structure, and the level of the required details. Coverage Path Planning (CPP) is the main challenging topic related to infrastructure inspection. It is defined as the process of generating a feasible coverage path that encapsulates of a set of viewpoints from which the robot can completely scan the structure of interest. CPP is categorized in literature into model based and non-model based categories [35,36]. The proposed algorithm follows a model based CPP approach which generates a set of waypoints based on an existing reference model of the structure of interest. The non-model based approach provides a set of waypoints that facilitates exploring the structure area so that every region of that structure is visible.

Our work presented in [4,5] proposed a CPP algorithm that targets coverage, distance and accuracy using a single sensor, and it was tested in simulation using one model. Due to the size, geometric complexity, and the application significance (inspection) of various complex structures, a Search Space Coverage Path Planning (SSCPP) algorithm that explicitly targets the coverage, and accuracy requirements is proposed here. SSCPP consists of three main components: viewpoints generation, coverage path planning, and coverage evaluation. The iterative processes in the main components of the algorithm are accelerated using GPU architecture to enhance the speed of the algorithm. The new contributions in this paper includes:

- Multiple sensors integration is proposed to cover occluded areas in complex structures to decrease coverage mission time.
- A weighted heuristic reward function is proposed to perform viewpoints selection based on the travelled distance, turning angle, accuracy and the covered volume.
- Achieved coverage percentage and produced model resolution are evaluated using different models in simulation and real experiments to illustrate the effectiveness and applicability of the approach.

An overview of the related work is presented in Sect. 2. An overall description of our proposed algorithm is presented in Sect. 3. The details of each algorithm component are presented as follows: viewpoints generation in Sect. 3.1, coverage path planning in Sect. 3.2, and coverage evaluation in Sect. 3.3. The simulated and real experiments used to verify the proposed algorithm are presented in Sect. 4. Finally, our conclusions and proposed future work are presented in Sect. 5.

2   Related Work

Various number of structure CPP algorithms are applied on different robotics systems, and have been documented in the literature addressing the challenges of this field and the contributions made towards these challenges. CPP is a process during which a coverage path consisting of selected viewpoints from which the robot must collect data about a workspace, whether it was a structure or an environment of interest, avoiding all possible obstacles. An extensive review is provided by Galceran and Carreras [16] about the most successful CPP methods discussing their application domains and functionalities. CPP algorithms are classified in literature into model based exploration, and non model based exploration. Some of the current presented work follows a model based approach by which partial information is required to be known a priori about the environment in order to be utilized to plan the coverage path [29]. Model-based methods generate a set of viewpoints that ensures covering every area of a structure or an environment [35]. The main properties considered by these methods include: material properties and object shapes, specifications of sensors (Field Of View (FOV), shadow and frustum effects), and image overlapping [35,36].

In [13,23], a CPP approach is proposed to provide full coverage of a ship hull utilizing its polygonal mesh. The waypoints are formed as a redundant roadmaps which are generated by solving a Set Cover Problem (SCP). The path was generated by solving a Travelling Salesman Problem (TSP) using the generated roadmaps and applying lazy collision checking performed using Christofides approximation [10] and chained Lin-Kernighan heuristic (LKH) [19]. In order to reduce the generated path length, an improvement step was performed using a modified Rapidly Exploring Random Tree algorithm (RRT*) [25]. Additionally, the planar parts of the ship hull were covered applying feature based navigation [23]. The work in [11] proposed various search based algorithms including SCP with TSP and greedy variants algorithms to provide full coverage utilizing a known map. This work showed that TSP with SCP provides the best set of waypoints in terms of path cost and computation time [11]. Another computational geometry model based method was proposed in [7] in which a set of waypoints is generated utilizing a triangular mesh model for solving an Art Gallery Problem (AGP). The path is then generated by solving a TSP using LKH which includes a modified LKH heuristic rules in order to direct the search. This work is extended in [8] to support multiple sensors and operate on meshes and occupancy map environment representations. Additionally, Alexis et al. [3] proposed a Uniform Coverage of 3D Structures Inspection Path Planner (UC3D-IPP) that generates inspection paths by computing viewpoints and solving a TSP. An iterative strategy is used to improve the generated inspection path utilizing different remeshing techniques.

Moreover, a set of triangular meshes of objects of interest were used in [24] in order to generate coverage spaces and motion planning roadmap, and find the inspection path using self-organizing neural network. A coverage and exploration algorithm is presented in [20] which explores unknown environments by choosing viewpoints that maximizes coverage and information gain in real-time using a UAV. A sub-modular orienteering problem approximated to a modular problem was used to generate the path. The generated path in this work provides the maximum coverage since it includes a variety of yaw angles but it is not the shortest path. The work presented in [17] proposed a hybrid path planning approach to construct a ground map, utilizing a genetic algorithm for global path planning and local rolling optimization to enhance the results of the genetic algorithm. In addition to this, Hailong et al. [33] proposed a two-layered exploration strategy for unknown environments consisting of a coarse exploration layer and a fine mapping layer. An optimized next view planning framework is proposed for exploration and volumetric navigation.

Additional literature work following model based approach and performing continuous coverage is presented in [6,9,39]. A grid based method was used in [39], in which a cell decomposition was performed on a prior known map to be fully covered by a UAV. This approach generates a path minimizing: coverage completion time, turning angle, and the number of turns in order to insure the continuity of the path. A continuous smooth coverage path is generated by solving a grid graph to perform continuous sensing of the environment easily. Three approaches are used in [39] to solve the grid graph including heuristic based search using wavefront planner and backtracking method, tree based search, and the pedestrian pocket algorithm. An automatic body painting planning method was proposed in [6] and it performs segmentation and simplification for the complex 3D models in order to plan continuous coverage paths that fully covers these segments in a contour following form. Similarly, the work in [9] proposed CPP approach that generates planar looping trajectories to cover urban buildings by simplifying the models. Using simplification, the problem is converted to non-planar surfaces coverage instead of complex structures. The trajectories are generated to consider the dynamics of the UAV and to minimize the coverage time.

Furthermore, several work have been documented in literature which involves reconstruction uncertainty in the coverage path computation, such as the work presented in [18,38]. The main focus of [18] is accuracy optimization based on reducing the reconstruction uncertainty performing Next Best View (NBV) planning. In order to achieve their focus, they modeled the reconstruction uncertainty using a statistical E-criterion in addition to combining the NBV, reconstruction, and feature tracking. They assessed the accuracy by comparing the distances between the reconstructed model points and a ground truth of the model. The other work presented in [38] is extending the work presented in [13] by proposing uncertainty driven view planning approach in which uncertainty is modeled as a non-parametric Bayesian regression in an active inspection scenario of a ship hull. The uncertainty modeling is performed in the viewpoints generation step by which views that provide maximum variance reduction are selected. This step is computationally costly to be calculated at all the views so an exponential drop-off is used to approximate the uncertainty. As described in the work, following the uncertainty based approach will lead to variance reduction on the expense of sacrificing some surface coverage.

Overall, several approaches were presented in literature in order to perform inspection including: random sampling [7,13,23], model segmentation [6,35] and simplification [9], contour following [6,36], and back and forth sweeping [23,27]. Each of these approaches improves critical aspects on the expense of others. For example, random sampling perform fast path planning and guarantees coverage but it is not resolution complete. Simplification, segmentation guarantees coverage but it masks the details of the structure or the critical inspected defects. Both contour following, and back and forth sweeping guarantee accurate coverage but they are time and energy consuming approaches.

Assessing any CPP algorithm requires addressing issues related to coverage completeness, path feasibility, and generated model accuracy. In the surveyed literature, the work presented in [14,31,37,40] provides guarantees of completeness and convergence to an optimal path that provides full coverage. Various proposed work in literature was optimized for path distance [7,13,14], number and quality of viewpoints [7,40] or computation duration [6,7,11,12,14]. Additionally reconstruction uncertainty was reduced in [38] on the expense of coverage while in [18], it was applied using exploratory based approach on small structures.

In this paper, a volumetric CPP algorithm is proposed with a weighted heuristic reward function that evaluates the expected model accuracy (as derived from the sensors' noise model), distance, turning angle and covered volume. This guarantees a predefined coverage percentage, and generates accurate 3D reconstructed models. The proposed algorithm is resolution complete which means as the discretization resolution decreases, the generated path becomes closer to the optimal path. The generated viewpoints define a traveling path that the UAV has to follow in order to perform 3D reconstruction of the structure with the predicted resolution. Furthermore, the algorithm computation is accelerated using the parallelized architecture of the GPU in order to make viewpoints generation and path computation fast for large structures.

3   Proposed System

The proposed SSCPP was developed as a model based CPP approach that utilizes an existing mesh model of the desired complex structure and the sensors mounted on the UAV. The three main components of the proposed algorithm include: viewpoints generation, coverage path planning, and coverage evaluations. An overview of the proposed SSCPP procedure is presented in Algorithm 1.

3.1   Viewpoints Generation

The viewpoints generation process generates a set of viewpoints from which the structure of interest is visible. Our proposed viewpoints generation starts by discretizing the structure's workspace using a grid resolution adjusted based on the structure model of interest. Next, a set of yaw angles are sampled at each waypoint position by performing an orientation based discretization step to allow

---

Algorithm 1. Coverage Planning Overview

Input   : 3D structure model, grid resolution, angular resolution, sensors FOV
and range limitations

Output: waypoint trajectory, 3D reconstructed model, coverage percentage,
model accuracy

1 Discretize workspace into a cubic grid with input grid resolution.
2 Discretize orientations at each grid with input angular resolution.
3 **foreach** *sensor in sensors* **do**
4   Preform transformation to generate the sensor viewpoints at each waypoints
     sample (position and angle)
5   Filter out the grid samples according to the sensor range limitations.
6 **end**
7 Perform path planning using the filtered set of viewpoints.
8 Navigate through the waypoints, and perform 3D reconstruction
9 Compute completeness: constructed vs reference model

---

the UAV perform inspection from. The generated waypoints are represented by
(x, y, z) coordinates and ψ yaw angle. Then based on the number of used sensors,
a transformation that defines the sensor location with respect to the UAV body
frame is performed to generate each sensor viewpoint. The generation of the
waypoints and the corresponding viewpoints is shown in Fig. 1 illustrating an
example of performing orientation based discretization of $\pi/4$. The Figure shows
two sensors mounted on the UAV, one sensor is mounted under the UAV with
a rotation of 20° around the y axis and a translation of -6 cm, while the other
sensor is placed on top of the UAV with a rotation of -20° and a translation of
6 cm.

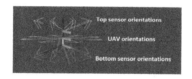

Fig. 1. Yaw orientation samples for the UAV body frame is shown as blue arrows, and
the corresponding top sensor orientation is shown as yellow arrows, while the bottom
sensor orientations are shown as orange arrows. The UAV and sensor frames are shown
with x in red, y in green and z in blue. (Color figure online)

Filtering these samples is then performed applying three levels of filtering
including collision, distance and coverage based filtering approach to reduce the
number of effective samples. Collision based filtering eliminates the sample viewpoints that collides with the model. The distance based filtering is performed
in order to keep viewpoints that are within the defined distance range from the
model. This defined distance is determined based on the sensors' maximum and

minimum effective ranges. Coverage based filtering eliminates viewpoints that does not provide coverage by extracting visible surface at each sensor viewpoint by performing frustum culling and occlusion culling. The frustum culling process starts by extracting the part of the structure that lies inside the sensor FOV, then the visible surface from the FOV frustum is extracted using the occlusion culling process. The occlusion culling starts by creating a 3D voxel grid over the point cloud data available in the FOV frustum. Then, it performs raytracing by creating a set of rays that start at the sensor origin and ends at the center of each corresponding voxel. Each of these rays are used to check if their corresponding voxel is occluded by another one in order to provide the visible surface finally. Extracting the visible surface is essential to quantify the viewpoints coverage and filter out the viewpoints that provide no coverage. The detailed occlusion culling algorithm is presented in Algorithm 2 and Fig. 2 shows an illustration of this process and the final filtered viewpoints.

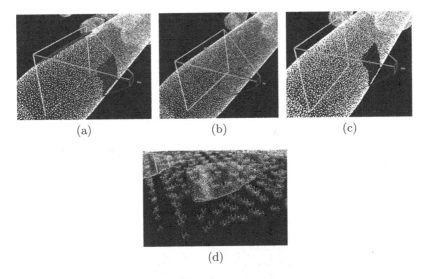

Fig. 2. (a) The frustum cull (purple) of an aircraft model (white) from one sensor viewpoint. (b) The blue target voxel is occluded by the red voxel across the red ray. (c) The visualization of the visible surface (blue) of an aircraft model (white) and the FOV planes from one viewpoint. (d) a set of filtered waypoints in red and the corresponding sensors' viewpoints in yellow (top sensor) and purple (bottom sensor). (Color figure online)

3.2   Coverage Path Planning

The next significant component of the proposed SSCPP is the coverage path planning. At this stage, a discretized sample space is produced at the viewpoint generation step, which consists of a set of filtered sample waypoints W, and the corresponding sets of sensor viewpoints V. The search space is generated using

---

Algorithm 2. Occlusion Culling

Input   : sensor FOV, sensor origin o, leaf size l
Output: visible surface point cloud
1 Identify the point cloud inside FOV frustum
2 Filter the point cloud into a voxel grid of l resolution
3 **foreach** *voxel in the voxel Grid* **do**
4 | Estimate the direction d of a ray to the target voxel
5 | Estimate the entry point of the target voxel
6 | initialize the step size using l, d and o
7 | initialize *rayVoxel* to start at o
8 | **while** *rayVoxel is not the target voxel* **do**
9 | | if *rayVoxel is occupied* **then**
10 | | | the target voxel is occluded
11 | | | break and continue to another target voxel
12 | | **end**
13 | | *rayVoxel = rayVoxel* + step size
14 | **end**
15 | Store the occluded free voxel point cloud
16 **end**

---

the discretized sample space by connecting the generated samples graphically with their neighbors based on a defined connection radius r as shown in Fig. 3. The developed SSCPP, with a heuristic reward function, is then used to search the generated search space for an optimized path that achieves the target coverage percentage. SSCPP is resolution complete graph search heuristic algorithm which increases the possibility of getting an optimal path as the discretization resolution increase.

Fig. 3. The generated connections applying a specified connection radius (3 m) using the search space samples.

The proposed heuristic reward function R minimizes turning angle δa and travel distance δd, and maximizes the coverage C computed at each step and the accuracy. The coverage C represents the model volume. It is computed by performing several steps at each viewpoint being evaluated including: extracting the visible surface point cloud, creating a 3D voxel grid over the point cloud data, and finally calculating the extra covered volume by finding the extra voxels.

Quantifying the coverage based on the volume provides more efficient results than evaluating the coverage of the model points since the structure is usually not uniformly dense. Using the voxel grids facilitate down-sampling the points into a set of voxels using a suitable grid resolution, where all the points in each voxel will be represented by one point which is their centroid.

The main target of the reward function is to select waypoints that minimize the turning angle δa and travelled distance δd, and maximize volumetric coverage C and the average accuracy $\bar{\sigma}_z$ of the visible point cloud encapsulated in the FOVs at the sensors' viewpoint. The reward function is presented in Eq. (1), the first part of the equation is inversely proportional to the distance travelled, the longer the distance and the lower average accuracy, the lower the ratio of the coverage C contribution to the reward. The second part of the reward function is proportional to δa when the next waypoint involves only a rotation. Both parts of the reward function is also proportional to the average accuracy $\bar{\sigma}_z$ of the visible point cloud at the viewpoint. The average accuracy $\bar{\sigma}_z$ is computed as the average of the calculated standard deviation of error in depth of each point in the visible point cloud.

A set of weights are given to each part of the reward function including α to the distance, β to the turning angle, and γ to the average accuracy, in order to prioritize them according to the desired aim. The main target of the heuristic function is to prioritize the selection of the viewpoints that provide high accuracy, shorter travelled distance and shorter turning angles, where the highest priority is given to the accuracy and the lowest to the turning angle. Generating an accurate 3D model is of great significance especially for inspection applications of large structures. The distance is the next significant component since the UAVs have limited flight time. The turning angle has the lowest contribution in the heuristic since only yawing motions are considered and the roll and pitch are assumed zero.

The proposed CPP algorithm is presented in Algorithm 3 which takes as inputs the target coverage percentage and tolerance, the connection radius r and the set of waypoints and viewpoints, and outputs the path that will provide the specified target coverage. Algorithm 3 is graph based search algorithm of a time complexity of $O(n \, log(n))$ where n is the number of nodes. The algorithm time complexity will be affected by the heuristic complexity since a proposed heuristic function is used in the proposed approach.

$$R = \begin{cases} (\alpha \, (1 - \frac{\delta d}{r}) + \beta \, (1 - \frac{\delta a}{2\pi}) \\ \quad\quad + \gamma \, (1 - \frac{\bar{\sigma}_z}{\max \sigma_z})) \times C, & \text{if } \delta d > 0 \\ (\beta \, (1 - \frac{\delta a}{2\pi}) + \gamma \, (1 - \frac{\bar{\sigma}_z}{\max \sigma_z})) \times C, & \text{if } \delta d = 0 \end{cases} \quad (1)$$

The proposed CPP include two time consuming and computationally intensive processes which are frustum and occlusion culling. These two processes are used to process a computationally expensive type of data which is 3D point cloud. In addition to this, they are used iteratively in the proposed approach in order to find the extra coverage at each sensor viewpoint. In order to accelerate these processes, an algorithmic parallelization utilizing Compute Unified Device Architecture (CUDA) framework [21] was performed. This is performed by dividing the intensive tasks into small tasks that can run in parallel on the available GPU resources instead of executing them sequentially on a CPU. In order to exploit the GPU computing power, a large number of calls to the same function should be performed using different data taking into consideration that these calls are independent of each other and do not require synchronization. This function represents checking points inside FOV in the frustum culling process and raytracing in the occlusion culling process. A detailed diagram of the GPU implementation of both processes is shown in Fig. 4.

Algorithm 3: Search Space Coverage Path Planner

Input : set of waypoints W and viewpoints V,
    connection radius r, starting pose $start$, target
    coverage percentage and coverage tolerance t.
Output: coverage path $C.P(s|S)$, coverage percentage

1 $W, V \subset \mathbb{R}^3$
2 Generate the search space nodes $S \leftarrow W, V$
3 Generate graph network by connecting S nodes based on radius r
4 Find the closest search space node to $start$
5 Initialize Open List O and Closed List C
6 Add the start node to O
7 **while** $s \in S$ & *target coverage not achieved* **do**
8   Pick s_{best} from O such that $f(s_{best}) \geq f(s), \forall s \in O$
9   Remove s_{best} from O and add to C
10   Expand s_{best}: for all $n \in Star(s_{best})$ & $n \notin C$
11   **foreach** n in $Star(s_{best})$ **do**
12   compute the extra coverage at n_v
13   compute the distance between s_w & n_w
14   compute the angle difference between s_w & n_w
15   compute the average accuracy at n_v
16   compute $R(n)$
17   **if** $n \in O$ **then**
18     $p \leftarrow n$
19   **if** $R(p) > R(n)$ **then**
20   remove n from O
21   **end**
22   **else**
23   remove p from O
24   **end**
25   **end**
26   **else**
27   add n to O
28   **end**
29   **end**
30   $C.P(s|S) \leftarrow s$
31 **end**

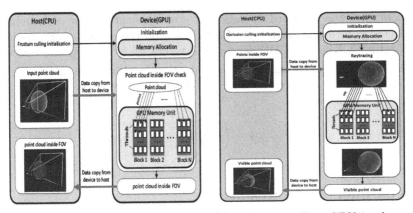

(a) frustum culling GPU implementation (b) occlusion culling GPU implementation

Fig. 4. Data flow diagram for GPU implementation of frustum culling and occlusion culling

3.3   Coverage Evaluation

In order to asses the accuracy of the CPP algorithm, a comparison between the predicted volume and covered volume is performed. The predicted volume is constructed by performing occlusion culling at the generated path waypoints and accumulating the volume along the path. However, the covered volume is considered the actual structure volume which is constructed by gathering data while following the generated path in real or simulated experiments. A grid of voxels is used to represent each of the volumes of the structure. Figure 5 illustrates the voxels of the covered volume for a target coverage of 20%. The coverage percentage is then evaluated using these voxel grids as described in Eq. (2).

$$Coverage\ \% = \frac{Covered\ Volume_{Voxel\ Grid}}{Predicted\ Volume_{Voxel\ Grid}} \times 100 \tag{2}$$

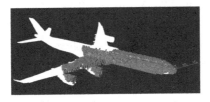

Fig. 5. The voxels representing the covered volume of 20% represented in green (Color figure online)

Furthermore, the accuracy of the generated model is evaluated based on the used RGBD sensor model. This is performed following Eq. (3) presented in [26] which computes the standard deviation of error in depth Z for each point in the collected point cloud during the CPP. Based on the results of [26] achieved by calibrating a Kinect RGBD sensor, the values of $\frac{m}{f_b}$ and σ_d were used as 2.85×10^{-5} and $\frac{1}{2}$. Performing accuracy evaluation facilitates identifying regions of the model with the lowest accuracy in order to improve them and provide accurate 3D reconstruction.

$$\sigma_z = \left(\frac{m}{f_b}\right) Z^2 \sigma_d \tag{3}$$

4 Experiments and Results

In order to evaluate the proposed algorithm, a set of experiments were performed in a realistic robot simulator Gazebo [2] and in a real indoor environment using three mesh models including: a A340 aircraft, Hoa Hakananaia Statue, and a representative model for the indoor experiment. These models represent environments with different volumes, geometric complexities, and textures. A real experiment was conducted in an indoor environment to validate the applicability and effectiveness of proposed approach.

The experiments were designed to check the predicted coverage percentage (as defined in the SSCPP's target coverage percentage) and compare it with the real coverage achieved after executing the coverage path, and assess the resolution accuracy of the constructed models. The parameters used in each scenario are summarized in Table 2. Different voxel resolutions are used for each model based on the density, the volume and the complexity of the mesh model. In order to determine the best discretization resolution, different discretization levels were used to generate different sets of viewpoints. The best grid resolution is selected based on the calculated maximum theoretical coverage % for each viewpoints set by going through all the samples in the viewpoints set. Table 1 presents three different levels of discretization and the corresponding maximum theoretical coverage % when applied on two of the selected models, taking into consideration the effective sensor range of 1–4 m from the model. Due to the volume and geometric complexity difference of each of the models, the same

Table 1. Maximum theoretical coverage % of three discretization levels applied on the selected models taking into consideration 1–4 m sensor effective range, an angular resolution of 45° and two mounted sensors

Discretization resolution	Maximum theoritical coverage %	
	Aircraft	Hoa Hakananai'a statue
4.5 m	81.9%	78.3%
3.0 m	90.7%	89.9%
1.5 m	99.1%	98.9%

discretization resolution produces different theoretical coverage percentages as illustrated in Table 1. For example, some models are small compared to the sensor FOV so they could be covered using less number of viewpoints compared to large models. The table shows that our proposed algorithm is resolution complete as stated previously, the finer the resolution, the more coverage could be achieved and the closer the solution is to the optimal one.

Table 2. SSCPP parameters used in the three scenarios

Parameter	Scenario 1	Scenario 2	Scenario 3
Model dimension (L,W,H)	(35,30,10)m	(7,4,18)m	(0.4,0.5,1.5)m
Model faces	31952	126446	72287
Grid resolution	1.5m	1.5m	1.0m
Sensor FOV	[58H, 45V]°	[58H, 45V]°	[96H, 54V]°
Effective sensor range	1-4m	1-4m	1-4m
Voxel resolution	0.25m	0.05m	0.05m
Connection radius	2.5m	2.5m	1.5m
Coverage tolerance	1%	1%	1%
Number of sensors	2	2	1
Sensor tilt angle (pitch°)	(20°,-20°)	(20°,-20°)	10°
Distance Weight α	0.5	-	-
Turning Angle Weight β	0.1	-	-
Average accuracy Weight γ	0.8	-	-

The proposed SSCPP was evaluated based on metrics that include: the path distance, duration of path generation, the number of selected viewpoints, the average extra volume coverage % per viewpoint and the target coverage percentage and the end coverage percentage. Additionally, the accuracy based evaluation

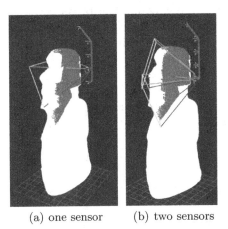

(a) one sensor   (b) two sensors

Fig. 6. Sample path (red) generated to produce 10% coverage of Hoa Hakananai'a statue model consisting of a set of waypoints (yellow) and their corresponding viewpoints (cyan). (a) shows the coverage using one sensor and (b) shows the coverage using two sensors. (Color figure online)

of these paths were computed using the RGBD sensor noise model described previously in order to determine areas with low and high accuracies. Figure 6 illustrates the sensor FOV along some sampled viewpoints along a generated coverage path applied on the Hoa Hakananai'a statue.

Our proposed SSCPP algorithm was compared against three state-of-the-art approaches including: Structural Inspection Planner [7], LKH based TSP using Euclidean heuristic [19], and LKH based TSP using RRT for collision avoidance [19]. TSP is used in these approaches to generate a coverage path that connects the sampled viewpoints. In the Structural Inspection Planner [7], a set of viewpoints is generated by solving an AGP. In order to evaluate LKH based TSP approaches presented in [19] (with distance heuristic with RRT local planner, and euclidean distance heuristics), our viewpoints sampled using our approach presented in Sect. 3.1 were used.

A set of parameters are required to be defined for the approach presented in [7] including: the minimum and maximum distance from the model, the sensor FOV, incidence angle, sensor pitch mounting angle, and the number of iterations. These parameters were set as follows: minimum viewpoint distance of 4 m, maximum viewpoint distance of 10 m, sensor FOV = $[120H, 120V]°$, incidence angle of $30°$, camera sensor mounting angle of $25°$, and 50 optimization iterations.

4.1 Simulation Setup

A Software-In-The-Loop (SITL) experiments were conducted in the first two scenarios using RotorS simulation environment [15] with an Iris quadrotor platform. The quadrotor has two RGBD sensors of a maximum depth range of 7 m with a FOV of $[58H, 45V]°$. The first sensor is mounted under the quadrotor at $20°$ and the other one is mounted on top of the quadrotor at $-20°$. The same experiment was repeated applying different target coverage percentages on each model. The generated path that achieves the maximum target coverage (within specified tolerance) was evaluated in simulation using Gazebo SITL.

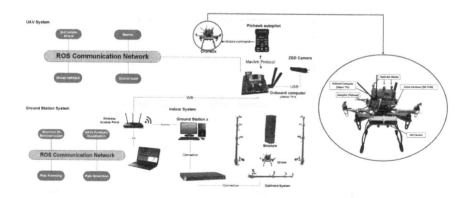

Fig. 7. Indoor system architecture

A simulated PX4 firmware similar to that used on a real UAV is executed in SITL. A ROS plugin (Mavros) was used to communicate between the PX4 firmware of the autopilot system, and the onboard computer through the mavlink protocol. Two methods were used in order to 3D reconstruct the selected models using the gathered data including Octomap [22] and Real Time Appearance Based Mapping (RTAB) [28].

4.2 Real Experiment Setup

The third scenario was performed in a real indoor environment using a real UAV platform. A DJI F550 Hexrotor based frame is used for the UAV platform, with Pixhawk autopilot system running PX4 firmware for low level control. The onboard computer of the UAV (Jetson TX1) is connected to the autopilot system via mavlink. A ZED camera was mounted on the UAV at $-17\,cm$ in the z direction with tilt angle of $15°$.

A system architecture of indoor experiments is shown in Fig. 7. The architecture consists of three systems including the ground station system, UAV System and the indoor system. All of these systems are connected over a local network using a wireless access point. The UAV in this system is given a unique IP address. The ground station system runs the mapping, path generation, and most importantly the path following node which reads the set of waypoints and send them to the drone control node.

The UAV system uses the Pixhawk autopilot which runs the PX4 autopilot firmware [32]. The onboard computer, a Jetson TX1 board, runs a series of Robot Operating System (ROS) [34] nodes implementing the various algorithmic components. The developed algorithms issue navigation commands (e.g., waypoints) and receive updated information (e.g., UAV pose data) by communicating over a physical serial connection with the autopilot system. In the indoor system architecture shown in Fig. 7, An Optitrack motion capture system [30] is used to determine the position of the UAV.

4.3 Experimental Results

Aircraft Model: An aircraft model is used in this experiment in order to be 3D reconstructed by following the path generated by our proposed approach SSCPP. A maximum coverage of 98% was achieved by our approach. The collected images during the path following were used to generate a volumetric and dense point cloud maps.

The experimental results obtained by our method compared to the state-of-the-art methods are shown in Table 3. The coverage and the path generated are shown in Fig. 8 illustrating the maximum achieved theoretical coverage for the aircraft model. This Figure illustrates the selected waypoints in yellow and their corresponding viewpoints in cyan, the final generated coverage path in red, and the covered part in purple. The plots shown in Fig. 9 illustrates the

Table 3. Scenario 1 SSCPP experimental results

Model	Aircraft					
Algorithm	Search duration	Path length	# of viewpoints	Max accuracy	Min accuracy	Avg. extra coverage per viewpoint
SSCPP	4156.56 s	270.57 m	149	0.23 cm	11 cm	0.57%
Structural Inspection Planner [7]	812.544 s	2729.1 m	3989	0.14 cm	40 cm	0.09%
LKH with RRT [19]	93.3 s	2966.2 m	6039 (Our Samples)	0.15 cm	19 cm	0.18%
LKH with Euclidean heuristic [19]	150 s	2381.5 m	6039 (Our Samples)	0.15 cm	19 cm	0.12%

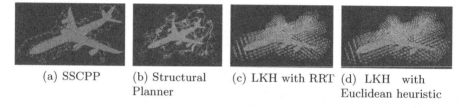

(a) SSCPP   (b) Structural Planner   (c) LKH with RRT   (d) LKH with Euclidean heuristic

Fig. 8. The generated path achieving maximum coverage of the aircraft model using our proposed approach and other state-of-the-art approaches presented in (b) [7] and (c)(d) [19]

differences between our proposed approach compared to the other state-of-the-art approaches in terms of path length average extra coverage and accuracy (sensor noise) per viewpoint, and number of selected viewpoints.

As shown in the Figs. 8 and 9, an effective coverage path was generated by our proposed SSCPP approach for the aircraft model compared to the other state-of-the-art approaches, as illustrated in Table 3 by the average extra coverage per viewpoint, number of selected viewpoints, path length, and average accuracy per viewpoint.

The path generated for the aircraft model using the approach in [7] consists of 3993 viewpoints. This approach generates a comprehensive set of viewpoints since it targets the faces' visibility of the mesh model. It is shown that significantly larger set of viewpoints was generated even with the simplification performed on the model. This makes it hard to follow this complex path to generate 3D reconstruction for large complex geometrical structures. Furthermore, a much longer path than that computed by visiting the set of viewpoints generated by our proposed approach (270 m) is computed with a length of 2729 m. Generating a shorter inspection path is highly desirable due to the fact that UAVs have limited flight time.

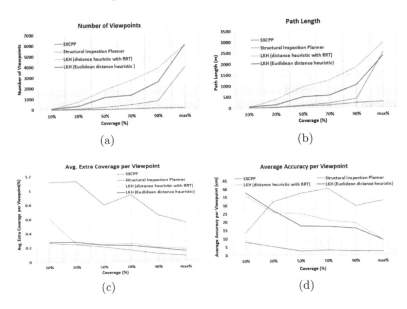

Fig. 9. The results plots of evaluating different aspects applying our approach and the other state-of-the-art approaches on the aircraft model

Figure 8 illustrates that the other approaches generate paths which constantly change in rotation (yaw angle) and translational movements. This could result in more complex trajectories. The plots shown in Fig. 9 show the high average extra coverage achieved at each viewpoint compared to other approaches.

The models 3D reconstruction shown in Fig. 10 was generated by executing the path generated by SSCPP in simulation. It's worth mentioning that the maximum achievable coverage percentage is 99.3% for the aircraft particular setup (considering all the samples in the search space) due to the proximity of some of the models to the ground, sensors mounting position, and the fact that only stable horizontal hovering of the UAV was considered. Additionally, the proposed algorithm is applied on the complete model surface, but not all parts of a model's surface are actually visible due to occlusions, for example the bottom side of the model where it faces the ground.

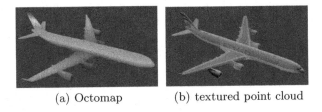

(a) Octomap   (b) textured point cloud

Fig. 10. The final model 3D reconstruction using the collected images following the generated path that achieves 98% for aircraft model using our proposed approach

Hoa Hakanaia Model: A simulated environment using Hoa Hakananaia Statue model is used to validate the proposed approach in this experiment. This simulated environment consists of a denser model (Hoa Hakananaia Statue) than aircraft with 126446 and 63225 vertices.

The experimental results are shown in Table 4 illustrating the maximum coverage achieved using our proposed approach against the other state-of-the-art approaches. The coverage and the path generated are shown in Fig. 11 showing the maximum theoretical coverage for the statue model achieved by the generated path. The plots shown in Fig. 12 illustrates the differences between our proposed SSCPP and the other approaches results.

Table 4. Scenario 2 experimental results

Model	Hoa Hakananai'a Statue					
Algorithm	Search duration	Path length	# of viewpoints	Max accuracy	Min accuracy	Avg. extra coverage per viewpoint
SSCPP	7932.48 s	232.279 m	125	0.15 cm	11.3 cm	0.82%
Structural Inspection Planner [7]	43.42 s	195.13 m	244	0.85 cm	51 cm	0.42%
LKH with RRT [19]	17.3 s	1147.5 m	1858 (Our samples)	0.21 cm	10.3 cm	0.31%
LKH with Euclidean heuristic [19]	70 s	1137.6 m	1858 (Our samples)	0.21 cm	10.3 cm	0.42%

Similarly, a feasible path for the Hoa Hakananai'a statue model is generated by our proposed SSCPP approach as shown in the Fig. 11. The maximum coverage percentage of structure is achieved covering all the critical regions using less number of viewpoints, and achieving low average accuracy (low sensor noise) and higher average extra coverage per viewpoint.

Furthermore, Table 4 demonstrates that our SSCPP approach was able to generate the shortest path compared to the other approaches. Our approach generated a path achieving higher extra coverage per viewpoint and consisting of fewer number of viewpoints than the other approaches. Figures 11(c), (d) and the plots in Fig. 12 illustrates that even solving the TSP problem using the same set of viewpoints generated coverage paths that are long and of low average coverage per viewpoint.

The models 3D reconstruction shown in Fig. 13 was generated by executing the coverage path generated by SSCPP in simulation. Considering all the search space samples, the maximum achievable coverage percentage of this model is 98.9% since some of the faces of the mesh model are not visible including the faces at the bottom of the statue.

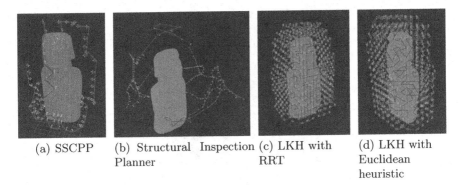

(a) SSCPP   (b) Structural Inspection (c) LKH with   (d) LKH with
                 Planner   RRT   Euclidean
                                                   heuristic

Fig. 11. The generated path achieving maximum coverage of the Hoa Hakananai'a statue model using our proposed approach and other state-of-the-art approaches presented in (b) [7] and (c)(d) [19]

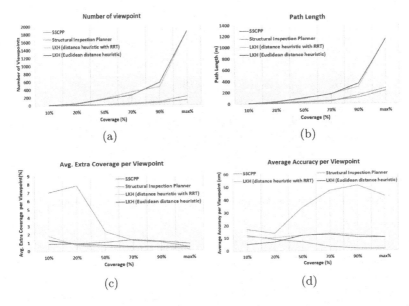

Fig. 12. The results plots of evaluating different aspects applying our approach and the other state-of-the-art approaches on the Hoa Hakananai'a statue model

Indoor Experiment: The experiment aims at showing the reliability of performing structural coverage for a representative model in an indoor lab environment. Initially, SSCPP was performed to generate the path that provides full coverage of the representative structure. The generated path was then executed using previously shown UAV platform. The path consists of 15 waypoints, with a path length of 16.19 m achieving 100% coverage. Figure 14 shows the expected path (red) and the followed path (purple) using the real system.

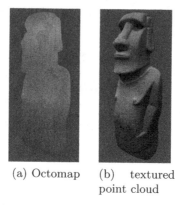

(a) Octomap   (b)   textured
point cloud

Fig. 13. The final model 3D reconstruction using the collected images following the generated path that achieves 99% for Hoa Hakananai'a statue model using our proposed approach

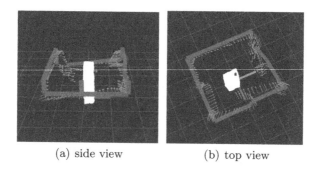

(a) side view   (b) top view

Fig. 14. The expected path vs the followed path in real experimentation (Color figure online)

The collected images during the path execution and their corresponding locations were used to perform offline 3D reconstruction of the lab representative structure as shown in Fig. 15. The path followed online was 21.2 m in length, and it took 170.9 s to follow and achieve a coverage of 100%. Table 5 shows the details of the real experiment results. A video of the indoor lab experiment is shown at https://youtu.be/6fgRQHVLtVg.

As evident by the achieved results, a feasible coverage path is generated by our proposed SSCPP method for the indoor representative model. The followed coverage path is generated by the proposed algorithm as a set of waypoints sent to the UAV system. A path trajectory optimized for the vehicle velocity or acceleration could be generated as a further enhancement.

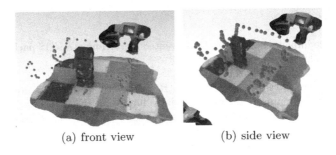

(a) front view   (b) side view

Fig. 15. The final model 3D reconstruction using the collected images during coverage path execution. The positions of the gathered images are shown in green. (Color figure online)

Table 5. Real experiment results

Experiment	Time	Distance	Achieved coverage
Box in real Lab	170.9 s	21.2 m	100%

5 Conclusion

In this paper, a search space coverage path planning algorithm with viewpoint sampling method is proposed to construct accurate 3D models of large complex structures using UAV for the purpose of inspection. The proposed work supports multiple sensors to cover large occluded areas to reduce consumed time. The search space is generated using our sampling method that takes into consideration the number of used sensors, and targets areas with no coverage to generate a reduced set of viewpoints. A heuristic reward function is proposed and it targets the turning angle, travelled distance, the average accuracy and the additional volume coverage at each viewpoint. Additionally, the proposed SSCPP algorithm is accelerated utilizing the GPU parallel architecture implementation for both the frustum and occlusion culling processes using Nvidia CUDA framework. The overall proposed approach was verified in simulation where a quadrotor follows the generated coverage path using a realistic robot simulator and generates a 3D reconstructed model. The generated coverage path was also verified in a real indoor experiment. Experimental results show that our approach outperforms the state-of-the-art approaches, especially improves average extra coverage, number of viewpoints, path length, and accuracy. An open source ROS package of the presented algorithm is accessible in [1]. In future, the work will focus on extending the proposed method to multi-robot systems and using deep learning for identifying occluded regions.

Acknowledgements. This publication is based upon work supported by the Khalifa University of Science and Technology under Award No. RC1-2018-KUCARS.

References

1. Open source implementation of the presented algorithm as a ROS package. https://github.com/kucars/sspp
2. Gazebo (2015). http://gazebosim.org/
3. Alexis, K., Papachristos, C., Siegwart, R., Tzes, A.: Uniform coverage structural inspection path-planning for micro aerial vehicles. In: IEEE International Symposium on Intelligent Control - Proceedings, October 2015, pp. 59–64 (2015). https://doi.org/10.1109/ISIC.2015.7307280
4. Almadhoun, R., Taha, T., Seneviratne, L., Dias, J., Cai, G.: Aircraft inspection using unmanned aerial vehicles. In: International Micro Air Vehicle Competition and Conference, pp. 43–49 (2016). http://www.imavs.org/papers/2016/43_IMAV2016_Proceedings.pdf
5. Almadhoun, R., Taha, T., Seneviratne, L., Dias, J., Cai, G.: GPU accelerated coverage path planning optimized for accuracy in robotic inspection applications. In: 2016 IEEE 59th International Midwest Symposium on Circuits and Systems (MWSCAS), pp. 1–4 (2016). https://doi.org/10.1109/MWSCAS.2016.7869968
6. Atkar, P.N., Conner, D.C., Greenfield, A., Choset, H.: Hierarchical segmentation of surfaces embedded in R3 for auto-body painting. Algorithmic Found. Robot. VI **1**, 27–42 (2005)
7. Bircher, A., et al.: Structural inspection path planning via iterative viewpoint resampling with application to aerial robotics, pp. 6423–6430 (2015)
8. Bircher, A., et al.: Three-dimensional coverage path planning via viewpoint resampling and tour optimization for aerial robots. Auton. Robots (2015). https://doi.org/10.1007/s10514-015-9517-1
9. Cheng, P., Keller, J., Kumar, V.: Time-optimal UAV trajectory planning for 3D urban structure coverage. In: 2008 IEEE/RSJ International Conference on Intelligent Robots and Systems, IROS, pp. 2750–2757 (2008). https://doi.org/10.1109/IROS.2008.4650988
10. Christofides, N.: Worst-Case Analysis of a New Heuristic Prepared for the Travelling Salesman Problem, February 1976
11. Dornhege, C., Kleiner, A., Kolling, A.: Coverage search in 3D. In: 2013 IEEE International Symposium on Safety, Security, and Rescue Robotics, SSRR 2013 (2013). https://doi.org/10.1109/SSRR.2013.6719340
12. Englot, B., Hover, F.: Inspection planning for sensor coverage of 3D marine structures. In: IEEE/RSJ 2010 International Conference on Intelligent Robots and Systems, IROS 2010 - Conference Proceedings, pp. 4412–4417 (2010). https://doi.org/10.1109/IROS.2010.5648908
13. Englot, B., Hover, F.: Sampling-based coverage path planning for inspection of complex structures. In: ICAPS, pp. 29–37 (2012)
14. Englot, B., Hover, F.S.: Sampling-based sweep planning to exploit local planarity in the inspection of complex 3D structures. In: IEEE International Conference on Intelligent Robots and Systems, pp. 4456–4463 (2012). https://doi.org/10.1109/IROS.2012.6386126
15. Furrer, F., Burri, M., Achtelik, M., Siegwart, R.: RotorS—a modular Gazebo MAV simulator framework. In: Koubaa, A. (ed.) Robot Operating System (ROS): The Complete Reference (Volume 1). SCI, vol. 625, pp. 595–625. Springer, Cham (2016). https://doi.org/10.1007/978-3-319-26054-9_23
16. Galceran, E., Carreras, M.: A survey on coverage path planning for robotics. Robot. Auton. Syst. **61**(12), 1258–1276 (2013). https://doi.org/10.1016/j.robot.2013.09.004

17. Ground, A., Uav, V.: A hybrid path planning method in unmanned. IEEE Trans. Veh. Technol. **65**(12), 9585–9596 (2016). https://doi.org/10.1109/TVT. 2016.2623666
18. Haner, S., Heyden, A.: Discrete Optimal View Path Planning (2011)
19. Helsgaun, K.: Effective implementation of the Lin-Kernighan traveling salesman heuristic. Eur. J. Oper. Res. **126**(1), 106–130 (2000). https://doi.org/10.1016/ S0377-2217(99)00284-2
20. Heng, L., Gotovos, A., Krause, A., Pollefeys, M.: Efficient visual exploration and coverage with a micro aerial vehicle in unknown environments. In: IEEE International Conference on Robotics and Automation (2015)
21. Hong, S.: Accelerating CUDA graph algorithms at maximum warp. ACM SIGPLAN Not. **46**, 267–276 (2011)
22. Hornung, A., Wurm, K.M., Bennewitz, M., Stachniss, C., Burgard, W.: OctoMap: an efficient probabilistic 3D mapping framework based on octrees. Auton. Robots **34**(3), 189–206 (2013). https://doi.org/10.1007/s10514-012-9321-0
23. Hover, F.S., et al.: Advanced perception, navigation and planning for autonomous in-water ship hull inspection. Int. J. Robot. Res. **31**(12), 1445–1464 (2012). https:// doi.org/10.1177/0278364912461059
24. Janousek, P., Faigl, J.: Speeding up coverage queries in 3D multi-goal path planning. In: Proceedings - IEEE International Conference on Robotics and Automation, vol. 1, pp. 5082–5087 (2013). https://doi.org/10.1109/ICRA.2013.6631303
25. Karaman, S., Frazzoli, E.: Sampling-based algorithms for optimal motion planning. Int. J. Robot. Res. **30**(7), 846–894 (2011). https://doi.org/10.1177/ 0278364911406761
26. Khoshelham, K., Elberink, S.O.: Accuracy and resolution of kinect depth data for indoor mapping applications. Sensors **12**(12), 1437–1454 (2012). https://doi.org/ 10.3390/s120201437
27. Krainin, M., Curless, B., Fox, D.: Autonomous generation of complete 3D object models using next best view manipulation planning. In: Proceedings - IEEE International Conference on Robotics and Automation, pp. 5031–5037 (2011). https:// doi.org/10.1109/ICRA.2011.5980429
28. Labbe, M., Michaud, F.: Online global loop closure detection for large-scale multi-session graph-based SLAM. In: Proceedings of the IEEE/RSJ International Conference on Intelligent Robots and Systems, pp. 2661–2666 (2014)
29. Luo, C., Mcclean, S.I., Parr, G., Teacy, L., Nardi, R.D.: UAV position estimation and collision avoidance using the extended Kalman filter. IEEE Trans. Veh. Technol. **62**(6), 2749–2762 (2013). https://doi.org/10.1109/TVT.2013.2243480
30. Optitrack, 25 March 2017. http://www.optitrack.com/
31. Papadopoulos, G., Kurniawati, H., Patrikalakis, N.M.: Asymptotically optimal inspection planning using systems with differential constraints, pp. 4111–4118 (2013)
32. PX4, 16 July 2015. http://px4.io/
33. Qin, H., et al.: Autonomous exploration and mapping system using heterogeneous UAVs and UGVs in GPS-denied environments. IEEE Trans. Veh. Technol. **PP**(c), 1 (2018). https://doi.org/10.1109/TVT.2018.2890416
34. ROS, 16 July 2015. http://www.ros.org/
35. Scott, W.R.: Model-based view planning. Mach. Vis. Appl. **20**(1), 47–69 (2009). https://doi.org/10.1007/s00138-007-0110-2
36. Scott, W.R., Roth, G., Rivest, J.F.: View planning for automated three-dimensional object reconstruction and inspection. ACM Comput. Surv. **35**(1), 64–96 (2003). https://doi.org/10.1145/641865.641868

37. Sehestedt, S., Paul, G., Rushton-smith, D., Liu, D.: Prior-knowledge assisted fast 3D map building of structured environments for steel bridge maintenance, pp. 1040–1046 (2013)
38. Trummer, M., Munkelt, C., Denzler, J.: Online next-best-view planning for accuracy optimization using an extended E-criterion. In: Proceedings - International Conference on Pattern Recognition, pp. 1642–1645 (2010). https://doi.org/10.1109/ICPR.2010.406
39. Valente, J., Barrientos, A., Cerro, J.D.: Coverage path planning to survey large outdoor areas with aerial robots: a comprehensive analysis. In: Introduction to Modern Robotics (2011)
40. Wallar, A., Plaku, E., Sofge, D.A.: A planner for autonomous risk-sensitive coverage (PARC OV) by a team of unmanned aerial vehicles. In: IEEE Symposium on Swarm Intelligence (SIS) (2014). https://doi.org/10.1109/SIS.2014.7011807

Development of Four Rotor Fire Extinguishing System for Synchronized Monitoring of Air and Ground for Fire Fighting

Shihan Liu[✉] and Lifu Hu

Shenyang Aerospace University, Shenyang, Liaoning, China
1251849466@qq.com

Abstract. In view of the increased fire hazards, the fires in the places of high-rise buildings and crowded have caused work burdens on firefighters due to various factors, resulting in failure to rescue in time in recent years, this paper studies the four-rotor fire-extinguishing system for fire-fighting air-ground synchronous monitoring. The system is divided into two parts: the air-ground communication positioning navigation system based on STM32 core processor and the fire detection and fire-extinguishing system based on STC89C51 core processor, the two parts realize the functions of four-rotor obstacle avoidance navigation, information positioning, ZigBee wireless communication, fire detection, and fire extinguishing device startup. The design of this system makes the fire hazard greatly reduced, achieves real-time communication and positioning navigation more smooth, it's applicable to urban community high-rise building security, large-scale shopping mall fire, forest orchard fire and other natural disaster fire facilities.

Keywords: Four-rotor · Synchronous monitoring ·
Obstacle avoidance navigation · Fire fighting · Information location

1 Introduction

With the advancement of society and the wide application of materials, fire hazards around people are improving, so more efficient fire fighting has become an increasingly concerned topic to society. We always hear the phenomenon of fires expanding after the fires in high-rise buildings and large shopping malls are not timely due to lack of timely rescue, or some large forests have failed to be discovered in time due to natural disasters, resulting in a large number of tree plant coking deaths in our daily life. Therefore, appropriate measures for fire protection should be taken, and reasonable fire fighting equipment should also be developed. In recent years, the development and application of some new fire protection technologies in China have appropriately improved the efficiency of fire fighting. ZHU Ying et al. used the top coaxial double rotor to provide main lift, and quad rotor as a travel and attitude adjustment system to optimize the ducted fan of high-rise building fire-fighting flying robot. CHENG Lina et al. designed a robot with 51 single-chip microcomputer as the core, and the relay motor is controlled by a relay achieved intelligent inspection of fire sources and

© Springer Nature Switzerland AG 2019
H. Yu et al. (Eds.): ICIRA 2019, LNAI 11744, pp. 267–278, 2019.
https://doi.org/10.1007/978-3-030-27541-9_22

extinguishing. These theories and development have solved some of the hidden dangers in the fire from different aspects. However, there are very few references to fire-fighting four-rotor firefighting.

Fire-fighting technology based on four rotors is still a technology that must be faced in the breakthrough and development of fire-fighting. Smoke concentration detection, infrared flame detection and temperature and humidity detection can be performed on the surrounding environment without external factors. Realizing autonomous navigation obstacle avoidance flight, monitor fire safety always and sending locations of fires to the control center via wireless communication in order to ground treatment of fire conditions. This paper proposes fire protection system based on four rotors, and the system can achieve environmental information collection of each sensor, autonomous navigation obstacle avoidance, image positioning and control of fire extinguishing devices and other functions at the aircraft terminal, and transfer the collected information to the control center terminal through wireless communication, take specific emergency measures after the control center detects the situation. Facing the increasingly serious problem of fire hazards, the development of fire and fire protection systems is an important prerequisite, it's important for people's daily life and personal safety.

2   Overall System Structure

Fire protection system based on four rotors includes quad rotor end and ground control end. The overall structure of fire extinguishing system is shown in Fig. 1.

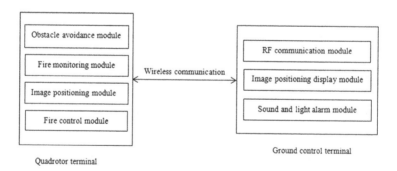

Fig. 1. The overall structure of the fire extinguishing system.

Quad rotor terminal contains obstacle avoidance module, fire monitoring module, image positioning module and fire control module. Obstacle avoidance module and image positioning module use STM32 as the control core, use ultrasonic transmission and reception time intervals to judge obstacles during flight, the collected images are stitched by triangulation and other algorithms to establish positioning coordinates. Fire monitoring module and fire control module use STC89C51 as the control core, use a variety of flame detection sensors monitor the environmental safety, and motorized fire suppression system for short-term fire suppression.

Ground monitoring terminal integrates RF communication module, image positioning display module and sound and light alarm module, mainly to achieve man-made view of the state of the drone and take control measures for the fire situation. The radio frequency communication module receives the quad rotor end signal of the ZigBee wireless communication, so that the ground control center can obtain the position information of the four rotors in real time. The image positioning display module displays the received image and alarms through the sound and light alarm module.

3   Hardware Design of the System

The system can be divided into two parts: positioning navigation system and fire detection fire extinguishing system, mainly complete the monitoring of environmental information, the acquisition of image positioning coordinates, the start of the fire extinguishing device and the information transmission of wireless communication. Through hardware modularization of the entire system, the environmental information monitoring system is mainly composed of infrared flame sensor, smoke concentration sensor and DHT21 temperature and humidity sensor, which can realize real-time monitoring of outdoor environment conditions. The fire extinguishing system is mainly composed of a relay-controlled pump motor drive and relay, which has the function of short-term fire extinguishing treatment for fire source, and the processing core is STC89C51 single chip microcomputer. Image acquisition coordinates are mainly composed of acquisition camera, obstacle avoidance system and positioning system. The wireless communication part transmits the information to the ground control center through ZigBee communication whose processing core is the STM32 single chip microcomputer. The overall design hardware schematic of the system is shown in Fig. 2.

Where, the STM32 core processor and the serial port connection of the STC89C51 core processor are extremely important. In this design, the UART asynchronous serial port is used to connect two core processors to realize data reception, allows 2 independent controllers to process information simultaneously. The SPI synchronous serial port is connected with the ZigBee wireless communication module to realize wireless communication with the ground control terminal.

3.1   Sensor Module

Infrared flame sensor: Infrared flame sensor used is based on the principle of infrared detection to directly detect the infrared spectrum of 4.20–4.50 μm in the flame, it's composed of infrared sensor and amplifier circuit. Due to the voltage effect stability of this type of sensor is not high, in this design, this module is used as temperature and humidity sensors and smoke concentration sensors. Three sensors work simultaneously, when two of them detect that the value in the environment exceeds the threshold it can start the fire extinguishing device and transmit it via wireless communication.

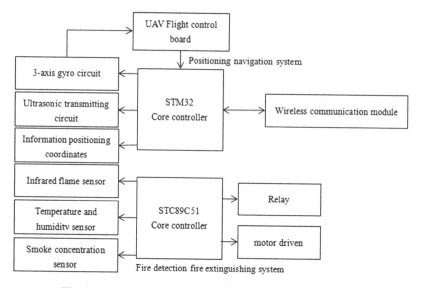

Fig. 2. The overall design hardware schematic of the system.

Smoke concentration sensor: The circuit connection of the smoke sensor and the STC89C51 core processor in this design is shown in Fig. 3. The resistor R2 of the circuit is used to limit the current of the circuit, R3 = R4 = 10K, dividing voltage of the circuit, R2 = 10K, R1 = 150 Ω, C1 = 220 uF. Transistor Q1 can increase the drive capability of pin 3, the P1^2 pin of the core processor is used as the output pin of the PWM pulse, providing input signals to the sensor and detecting smoke concentrations in the environment.

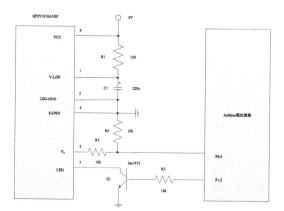

Fig. 3. Smoke sensor circuit connection diagram.

3.2 Ultrasonic Transmitting/Receiving Circuit

Ultrasonic transmitting circuit is based on multiple ultrasonic distance detection. This design optimizes the ultrasonic distance detection of common robotic obstacle avoidance systems, in this system ultrasonic distance is detected by 5 ultrasonic sensors, which are set in the front, left, right, back, and top five directions of the four rotors to measure the distance of obstacles in five directions and to avoid obstacles in time. The ultrasonic ranging sensor used in the obstacle avoidance process is ranging from 20 to 600 cm, meets the obstacle avoidance requirements of the four-rotor UAV during autonomous flight. The half-duplex serial communication of the serial port is realized by five ultrasonic sensors through the circuit, so in the design process, the sensors of 5 different addresses are set in the same serial port, and send the ranging data to the STM32 core processor for pre-judgment sequentially.

3.3 Positioning Coordinate Image Acquisition Module

Ground Control Center receives OpenMV data in real time, by receiving GPS positioning information provided by UAV. The system uses Real-time monitoring with obstacle avoidance systems and OpenMV to monitor coordinate point position by wireless communication, achieving effective detection of targets. After finding the fire point, the ground control terminal turns on the rescue mode to extinguish the target point.

In the design, the full-featured machine vision module OpenMV is used as the acquisition camera for system position information image acquisition. Image acquisition part works by OV7725 camera chip with STM32 as the core processor, implement visual algorithms through C language efficiently. Python programming interface in STM32 core processor is provided. The visual environment on the OpenMV vision module can be used to perceive the surrounding environment, providing a visual inspection function for UAV's autonomous flight. UART, I2C, SPI, PWM, ADC, DAC and GPIO et al. interfaces are provided from the STM32 core processor to OpenMV for easy to expand during the circuit construction process. The SD card slot has a read/write speed of 100 Mbs, which allows the OpenMV camera to record video and extract machine vision material from the SD card. It also has a SPI bus with speeds up to 54 Mbs allows image data to be passed to the LCD expansion board, WiFi expansion board, or other controller. The connection diagram of the OpenMV machine vision target positioning module is shown in Fig. 4.

3.4 Fire Control Module

JRC-21F relay is used in fire extinguishing device, which has two contacts to control on and off and uses a normally open contact to connect to an external solenoid valve. When the core controller detects the smoke concentration and the temperature and humidity concentration exceeds the threshold, its pin will output a high level signal, and the transistor is turned on, the coil of the relay is turned on and its normally open contact is closed. Therefore, the solenoid valve is opened, and the water pump drive motor is controlled. The circuit diagram of the pump driven fire extinguishing module is shown in Fig. 5.

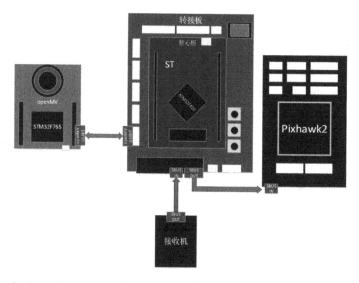

Fig. 4. OpenMV machine vision target positioning module connection diagram.

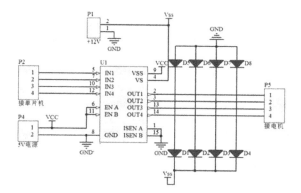

Fig. 5. Fire extinguishing control module hardware circuit diagram.

4 System Software Design

The mainly function of system software design part is controlling the four-rotor navigation flight system, which achieves self-starting fire extinguishing device while monitoring fire conditions in real time, and transmits the image coordinates of the fire place to the ground control terminal through the STM32 core processor using wireless communication technology. The overall design flow chart of the software part system is shown in Fig. 6.

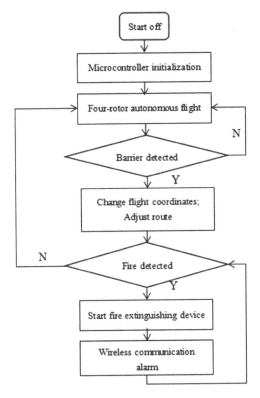

Fig. 6. Overall system software design flow chart.

4.1 Start Fire Extinguishing Device

The fire extinguisher drive module is mainly controlled by a relay to control the drive of the air pump motor. When the three environmental detection sensors above detect smoke concentration, temperature and humidity exceed the standard, the single chip microcomputer controls the relay to drive the motor and activates the fire extinguishing device. Fire extinguishing devices can be loaded with different fire extinguishing components depending on the environment in which they are used: for the larger probability area of Class A fires (Solid material fire, wood, coal, cotton, wool, etc.), water should be put into the fire extinguishing device to extinguish the fire, the gas cylinder should be driven to pressurize; for the larger probability area of Class B fires (Liquid fires and metal solid matter fires), dry powder fire extinguishing material should be stored in the fire extinguishing device, and dry powder contains substances such as ammonium phosphate, it can effectively save fires caused by petroleum and its products, flammable gases and electrical equipment. The flow chart of starting the fire extinguishing device is shown in Fig. 7.

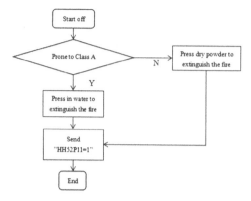

Fig. 7. Start fire extinguishing device flow chart.

4.2 Ultrasonic Obstacle Avoidance

In the design, the ultrasonic avoidance adapts an embedded program. In the program, the distance data measured by the ultrasonic sensor is collected from different addresses in the form of a software serial port, when the measured distance exceeds the threshold set STM32 core processor corrects AHRS information in time to avoid obstacles. After the obstacle avoidance, it will continue to fly autonomously according to the route. The flow chart of the four-rotor autonomous obstacle avoidance software based on multiple ultrasonic distance detection is shown in Fig. 8.

When the obstacle avoidance system is working, the ultrasonic pin output pulse is set to 45 kHz and connected to the ultrasonic transmitting end through an amplifying circuit. Special temperature and humidity sensor are considered in consideration of the influence of temperature fluctuation, and the feedback sound wave is connected to the input terminal through an amplifying circuit. Ultrasonic obstacle avoidance combined with temperature and humidity sensor monitoring data transfer internal timer to calculate time. The counter stops timing when the last pulse arrives, time calculation at the moment is "t", the distance between the UAV launch point and the obstacle is

$$S = vt/2 \tag{1}$$

Temperature T measured by temperature and humidity sensor and ultrasonic measurement distance should be satisfied

$$v = 331.5 + 0.607T \tag{2}$$

$$S = (331.5 + 0.607T)t/2 \tag{3}$$

The autonomous obstacle avoidance system consisting of 5 ultrasonic waves in the quad rotor is simple in structure, which greatly reduces the risk of uncontrolled flight due to fire, and simple algorithm design for sequential ranging reduces the load on the embedded processor at the same time.

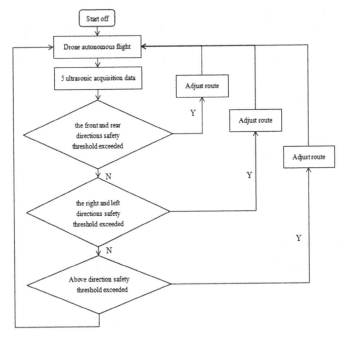

Fig. 8. Four-rotor autonomous obstacle avoidance software flow chart for multiple ultrasonic distance detection.

4.3 Positioning Coordinate Acquisition

During the acquisition of the positioning coordinates of the four-rotor fire alarm, firstly the observed images are spliced through UAV remote sensing technology to achieve image fusion, and then the fused image is embedded using the GDAL data conversion library, finally the process is simplified to improve the stitching efficiency of the image. Calculating the mean and mean square error of the positioning information by triangulation based on the geographical coordinate, controlling and checking information.

5   Test and Performance Analysis

The fire-fighting air-ground synchronous monitoring four-rotor fire-extinguishing system includes two parts: the fire-monitoring alarm fire-extinguishing system and the positioning and navigation system.

5.1   UAV Simulation Obstacle Avoidance Flight Testing

The positioning navigation system consists of an image acquisition and processing system and a UAV autonomous flight control system. Capture images and geographic information are got through OpenMV machine vision modules and GPS modules, and the field information is fed back to the ground receiving station in real time through the data transmission and image transmission technology. UAV autonomous flight control system is mainly composed of flight control board and STM32 control board. In the actual environmental test, the SBUS protocol analog remote control method is used to realize the autonomous cruise of the drone. When the UAV detects a fire occurrence point, it will immediately alert the staff to remind the staff to carry out the subsequent fire fighting operation. Simulation result of UAV obstacle avoidance flight test is shown in Fig. 9.

Fig. 9. UAV simulation obstacle avoidance flight test result map.

5.2   UAV Autonomous Flight Modeling Simulation Testing

During the design process, the system for autonomous flight pitch balance adjustment of UAV is corrected by MATLAB modeling and simulation. UAV uses ailerons, elevators, and rudders to ensure that flights in a three-dimensional space follow a fixed route. In practical applications, ultrasonic obstacle avoidance ranging data in five directions are fitted and analyzed during UAV flight, the fit of 6 directions data are set. The flight data fitting report is shown in Fig. 10.

In the simulation, the transfer function during the UAV flight is set to

$$G(s) = \frac{18(s + 0.015)(s + 0.45)}{(s^2 + 1.2s + 12)(s^2 + 0.01s + 0.0025)} \tag{4}$$

Setting the controller to

$$Gc(s) = K(s + 2) \tag{5}$$

The root locus of the system under this condition is drawn, and the appropriate K value is selected from the root locus. UAV autonomous flight correction modeling simulation diagram is shown in Fig. 11. After multiple points, it is determined that K = 0.5908, when the natural oscillation frequency $\omega n > 2$, the damping ratio $\zeta > 0.8$.

Equation: UNTITLED Workfile: UNTITLED::Untitled\

View | Proc | Object | Print | Name | Freeze | Estimate | Forecast | Stats | Resids

Dependent Variable: Y
Method: Least Squares (Gauss-Newton / Marquardt steps)
Date: 05/07/17 Time: 00:29
Sample: 2001 2015
Included observations: 15
Y=C(1)*X^8+C(2)*X^7+C(3)*X^6+C(4)*X^5+C(5)*X^4+C(6)

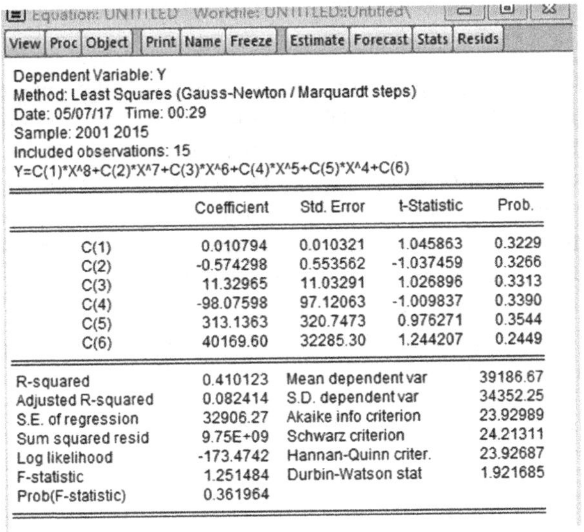

	Coefficient	Std. Error	t-Statistic	Prob.
C(1)	0.010794	0.010321	1.045863	0.3229
C(2)	-0.574298	0.553562	-1.037459	0.3266
C(3)	11.32965	11.03291	1.026896	0.3313
C(4)	-98.07598	97.12063	-1.009837	0.3390
C(5)	313.1363	320.7473	0.976271	0.3544
C(6)	40169.60	32285.30	1.244207	0.2449

R-squared	0.410123	Mean dependent var	39186.67
Adjusted R-squared	0.082414	S.D. dependent var	34352.25
S.E. of regression	32906.27	Akaike info criterion	23.92989
Sum squared resid	9.75E+09	Schwarz criterion	24.21311
Log likelihood	-173.4742	Hannan-Quinn criter.	23.92687
F-statistic	1.251484	Durbin-Watson stat	1.921685
Prob(F-statistic)	0.361964		

Fig. 10. UAV obstacle avoidance flight data fitting report.

The unit step response curve tends to be smooth in accordance with the pitch balance of the autonomous flight.

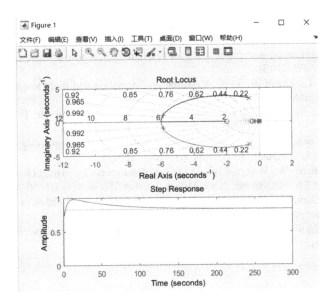

Fig. 11. Simulation diagram of UAV autonomous flight correction.

6 Conclusion

The fire-fighting fire-extinguishing system based on four rotors integrates four-rotor obstacle-avoidance flight, environmental monitoring, data analysis, fire-fighting devices, and communication alarms. It can be judged based on the actual situation of the environment, and the control center can know the environmental status of the area where the four rotors are located in time when a fire occurs. The control center can make the four-rotor perform cruise fire in the area according to the positioning indication and obstacle avoidance indication by simple operation. The quad rotor fire extinguishing system can achieve real-time monitoring of ambient air characteristics, storage of data, hazard warning and so on. The system realizes complete intelligent automatic basically, it's easy to operate and suitable for large shopping malls, residential high-rise building fires, forest orchards, etc. It has certain reference value in fire safety.

References

1. Wu, T., Bai, R., Zhu, L., et al.: Design of AHRS based on Kalman filter. Chin. J. Sens. Actuators **29**(4), 531–535 (2016)
2. Wang, H.: Geographic Information location technology based on UAV mapping. Mod. Electron. Technol. **22**(032), 130–132+13 (2018)
3. Hu, H., Wang, G., Lai, Z., et al.: Design and implementation of autonomous obstacle avoidance system for quadrotor UAV. Mod. Electron. Technol. **22**(033), 133–137 (2018)
4. Yang, L.: Application research of UAV in fire fighting and rescue. Fire Prot. Technol. Prod. Inf. **10**, 44–45+76 (2017)
5. Kang, K.: Application research of UAV in fire fighting and rescue work. J. Armed Police Coll. (10), 27–29 (2013)
6. Lv, S., Yan, L., Zhang, B., et al.: Research on integration and flight test of UAV remote sensing system. Surv. Sci. (01), 84–86+163 (2007)
7. Liu, Y., Xue, M.: Application of drone in fire rescue. Technol. Exch. **19**(064), 131–132 (2017)
8. Cheng, L., Chen, Y.: Design and research of intelligent fire extinguishing robot based on C51 single chip computer. Tech. Appl. **03**, 38–41 (2012)
9. Wang, Y., Huang, W., Wang, X., et al.: Design of automatic fire extinguishing device based on traditional fire extinguisher. Sens. Detect. Internet Things Syst. **07**, 90–91 (2015)
10. Zhang, Q., Zhang, Y.: Research on Monte Carlo localization algorithm in wireless sensor networks. Comput. Sci. **12**, 77–80+116 (2018)
11. Shi, F.: Design of flame sensor based on purple infrared detection principle. Electron. World. **6**, 36–39 (2015)

A Small Envelope Gait Control Algorithm Based on FTL Method for Snake-Like Pipe Robot

Wenjuan Du, Jian Wang$^{(\boxtimes)}$, Guigang Zhang, and Manxian Liu

Institute of Automation, Chinese Academy of Sciences, Beijing, China
jian.wang@ia.ac.cn

Abstract. Benefit from the characters of multi-DOFs and slender body, the snake-like robot is flexible and suitable for detecting the unstructured, narrow, tough ancient pipes with rectangular cross section. However, the motion envelopes of the existing gaits of the snake robot are quite large. It may cause collision between the robot and the pipes or obstacles and lead to motion failure. Aiming to solve the problem mentioned above, a small envelope gait (SEG) based on the follow-the-leader (FTL) method is proposed to reduce the envelope of the path for avoiding the collision between the robot and the pipe walls or the obstacles. The SEG is realized on our existing prototype, a novel active-passive (AP) type snake-like pipe robot which has both active and passive modules. Firstly, the kinematics model of the AP type snake robot is build. Secondly, the SEG control algorithm is proposed for controlling the snake body to follow the path of head. Lastly, experiments are taken both in the laboratory and ancient pipes to verify the effectiveness of the SEG control algorithm.

Keywords: Small envelope gait · AP type snake pipe robot · Follow-the-leader

1 Introduction

Due to the long history of China, many ancient buildings are remained. The ancient pipes are usually made of bricks, and most of them are underneath the ground, or worse, underneath the buildings. For protecting the ancient buildings, we cannot detect the pipes by removing the buildings. Therefore, there is few efficient ways to detect the pipes underneath the buildings. The existing researches aim at the pipes underneath the ground by digging the road up. However, most of the pipes are underneath the buildings and haven't been detected yet.

Many types of pipe robots have been designed by researchers. However, they are designed for the city pipes which has round cross section and the inside walls are much smoother than the ancient pipes. Therefore, these pipe robots cannot

© Springer Nature Switzerland AG 2019
H. Yu et al. (Eds.): ICIRA 2019, LNAI 11744, pp. 279–288, 2019.
https://doi.org/10.1007/978-3-030-27541-9_23

be applied on the detection mission of the ancient pipes. The snake robot has multi-module, multi-DOF and high length-diameter ratio, and can adapt to the inner environment of the ancient pipes better than the pipe robots. The multi-module keeps the robot from falling down a ditch. The multi-DOF and the high length-diameter ratio make the robot flexible and can pass through narrow pipes easily.

However, the existing snake like robot has the following shortcomings in terms of mechanical design and control algorithms.

According to the mechanical design, the existing snake robots can be divided into two types, the passive type and the active type. Many passive type snake robots are made by researchers like Choset [1–4], Liljeback [5], and Shugen Ma [6,7], and they have small volume and light weight that can be applied on tasks in narrow space. However, the driving force of the passive type, generated by deformation of the body, is quite small, and the robot may knock against the inside walls when it moves in pipes. Therefore, the passive type is not suitable for moving on rough terrains. The active type, like the KR-II [8], omni-tread [9] and kohga [10,11], consists of active modules and active or passive joints and can pass through the rough terrain easily. But it is less flexible, has larger volume and bigger weight compared to the passive type. Hence, it's not suitable for moving in narrow space.

The existing control algorithms for the snake like robots are mostly based on gait control. The envelope of the gaits generated by cyclic deformation, like the serpentine gait, the concertina gait, the lateral serpentine gait and the helical rolling gait, are quite big can may collide the inside walls of the pipes during the motion.

A light-weight, small-sized active-and-passive (AP) type snake robot was designed in our previous work. It consists of active head and tail modules and passive body modules, and connected them with active joints. The active head and tail make it pass through the rough terrains much easier, and the passive body modules make the miniaturization possible by decreasing the ratio of weight to volume.

In this paper, a small envelope gait based on the FTL method is proposed, aiming to decrease the motion envelope for the snake robot to adapt to the ancient pipes. This paper is organized as follows. Section 2 simply introduces the mechanical construction of the AP type snake robot. Sections 3 proposes the small envelope gait control algorithm. Experiments in both lab and real ancient pipes are taken to test the validity of the control algorithm in Sect. 4. Finally, the conclusion and future work are mentioned in Sect. 5.

2   AP Type Snake Robot

The AP type snake robot designed in our previous work is shown in Fig. 1. It contains 2 active modules and 6 passive modules. The modules are connected with each other by 7 active joints, of which three are pitch joint and four are yaw joint.

2.1   Mechanism Construction

The active modules are designed as differential track mechanisms, which can provide enough driving force for moving in rough terrains and small turning radius for passing through narrow space. The passive modules are designed quite simple, but they are necessary as they increase the length-diameter ratio to avoid the collision between two active modules when the robot is turning, thus increase the maximum turning angle for the robot.

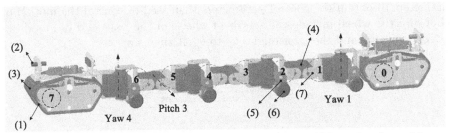

(1) Track, (2) Camera, (3) Speed servo motor, (4) Angle servo motor, (5) Base of passive module,
(6) Passive wheel, (7) Frame of passive module

Fig. 1. The mechanism of the AP type snake robot

The modules are numbered from tail to head as module 0 to 7. A passive module consists of a frame (7) for fixing two angle servo motors (4) perpendicular to each other and a base (5) for connecting two passive wheels (6). An active module consists of two track wheels (1) that are driven by a speed controllable servo motor (3). The active modules are differential mechanisms as the speeds of the track wheels can be adjusted independently. The size of active modules is 125 mm × 90 mm × 75 mm, and the weight is 400 g. The size of passive modules is 40 mm × 40 mm × 20 mm, and the weight is 60 g.

2.2   Tele-Operation System

As the inner environment of the ancient pipe system is unknown, it's not suitable for robot to move by itself without the guidance of a professional archaeologist, hence, the control system of the AP type snake robot is designed as a tele-operation system that consists of a host and a client.

The host provides the real-time images inside of the pipe system to the operator, and code the order received from the operator who decides the next move of the robot according to the images, after that, the coded order will be transmitted to the client through RS-485 communication protocol. The client will decode the order in its main controller and then recode it as two parts, one is the coded joint angles that will be transmitted to the angle servo motors to control the angles of the 7 active joints, the other is head and tail's motor speeds that will be passed to the 4 speed servo motors.

3   Small Envelope Gait Control Algorithm

In the section, a SEG control algorithm is proposed to reduce the envelope of path for avoiding unexpected collision between the robot and pipe walls or obstacles. A simple but efficient way for reducing the envelope is to control the rest modules to follow the motion of the head module. As the robot is designed as a tele-operation system, at each time step k, the input operation parameters have been given by the operator, including the moving speed v_{k-1}^h and the turning radius r_{k-1}^h of the head module. Then the robot analyzes the input operation parameters to obtain the control parameters that used to control the motion of robot directly, which include the speeds of wheels of the head and tail modules $\boldsymbol{v}_k^{hl}$, $\boldsymbol{v}_k^{hr}$, $\boldsymbol{v}_k^{tl}$, $\boldsymbol{v}_k^{tr}$ and the joint angles θ_k^0 to θ_k^3 at time step k.

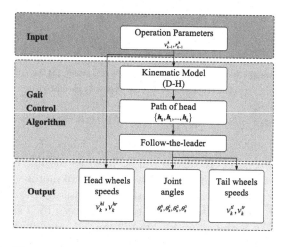

Fig. 2. The process of the small envelope gait control algorithm.

The process of the SEG control algorithm is shown in Fig. 2. Firstly, the head module's wheel speeds can be computed from the operation parameters directly. Then, a kinematic model of the AP type snake robot is built by the Denavit-Hartenberg method to obtain the path of the head. After obtaining the path of the head, the joint angles and tail module's wheel speeds can be computed by FTL method.

Hence, the aim of the algorithm is to transform the input operation parameters given by the operator into the output control parameters that used to control the AP type snake robot directly. Namely, in the narrow and terrain pipe, the operator can drive the snake robot as a car, the moving speed and the turning radius of the head module are the only things the one should concern about, the rest control will be done by the SEG control algorithm.

Limited by the length of this paper, the pitch joints will be ignored, as they can be inherited from the discussion of the yaw joints easily.

The path of head can be indicated as a set of discrete points, which indicate the position of the head module's mass center at each time step. Let (1) indicate the path of head in step k, where $^w h_i, i = 0, 1, 2, ...$ indicates the position of the head module's mass center in the world coordinate system at time step i.

$$Path_k = \{^w h_0, ^w h_1, ^w h_2, ..., ^w h_k\} \tag{1}$$

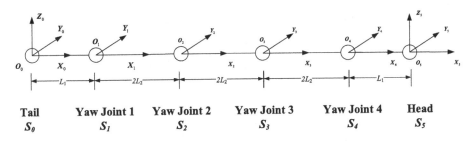

Tail	Yaw Joint 1	Yaw Joint 2	Yaw Joint 3	Yaw Joint 4	Head
S_0	S_1	S_2	S_3	S_4	S_5

Fig. 3. The body coordinate systems of the AP type snake robot

The initial position of the head $^w h_0 = [L, 0, 0, 1]^T$, where $L = L_1 + 7L_2$ as the original point of the world coordinate system is located at the center point of the head.

3.1 Wheel Speeds of Head Module

At time step k, the head module's moving velocity v_{k-1} and the turning radius r_{k-1} are given by the operator, then a new path point $^w h_k$ is generated and be added to the end of the set to update the path of the head, as shown in Fig. 4(a).

Let the velocity v_{k-1} always along the X-axis of S_{k-1}^5, namely, $^{k-1} v_{k-1} = [v_{k-1}, 0, 0]^T$. If the robot is turning left, r_{k-1} is positive, otherwise, it will be negative.

The speeds of the left/right wheels of the head module at time step $k-1$ can be computed by (2), where l is the width of the head module. Furthermore, if r_{k-1} is equal to zero, then $v_{k-1}^{hr} = -v_{k-1}^{hl}$, and the they can be set up as any value, but this situation won't happen in our experiments limited by the mechanism design.

$$\begin{aligned}
v_{k-1}^{hr} &= v_{k-1} + \frac{v_{k-1}l}{2r_{k-1}} \\
v_{k-1}^{hl} &= v_{k-1} - \frac{v_{k-1}l}{2r_{k-1}}
\end{aligned} \tag{2}$$

3.2 Kinematic Model

After time step k, a new path point h_k will be produced and added to the end of the set to update the path. To obtain h_k, a kinematic model of the AP type snake robot is built by Denavit-Hartenberg method.

Firstly, the world coordinate system and the body coordinate systems are established as shown in Fig. 3. The world coordinate system S^w coincides with the body coordinate system of the tail module S^0 at the beginning.

Then, the D-H table is obtained, as shown in Table 1, where $L_1 = 125\,\text{mm}$ is the length of an active module, and $L_2 = 40\,\text{mm}$ is the distance between two adjacent active joints, namely, the length of a passive module. Let $_i^{i-1}T$ indicate the translate matrix from S^{i-1} to S^i, as shown in (3), and the translate matrix from S^0 to S^5 can be obtained by (4). Let $^i p$ indicates a vector $p \in \mathbb{R}^3$ with respect to the coordinate system S^i, and it can be obtained by (5).

$$_i^{i-1}T = \begin{bmatrix} \cos\theta^i & -\sin\theta^i & 0 & a^{i-1} \\ \sin\theta^i \cos\alpha^{i-1} & \cos\theta^i \cos\alpha^{i-1} & -\sin\alpha^{i-1} & -\sin\alpha^{i-1}d^i \\ \sin\theta^i \sin\alpha^{i-1} & \cos\theta^i \sin\alpha^{i-1} & \cos\alpha^{i-1} & \cos\alpha^{i-1}d^i \\ 0 & 0 & 0 & 1 \end{bmatrix} \quad (3)$$

$$_5^0T = {}_1^0T\,{}_2^1T\,{}_3^2T\,{}_4^3T\,{}_5^4T \quad (4)$$

$$^i p = {}_j^i T^j p, i, j \in \{0, 1, ..., 5\} \quad (5)$$

Table 1. The compare of the active and passive modules

i	α^{i-1}	a^{i-1}	d^i	θ^i
1	0	$\frac{L_1}{2}$	0	θ^0
2	0	$2L_2$	0	θ^1
3	0	$2L_2$	0	θ^2
4	0	$2L_2$	0	θ^3
5	0	$\frac{L_1}{2}$	0	0

3.3   Path of Head

With the kinematic model built above, the new position of the head $^w h_k$ can be obtained by (6), after each time step, adding the new head point to the path set to update the path of head $Path_k$.

In (6), $_5^0T_0$ indicates the transformation matrix at the initial state from the coordinate system S_0^0 to S_0^5, and $_k^0A = {}_1^0A\,{}_2^1A...{}_k^{k-1}A$ indicates the transform matrix from head coordinate system at time step 0 to it at k, and $^k h_k = [0, 0, 0, 1]^T$ indicates the center of the head module in the head coordinate system at time step k. The above S_j^i indicates the body coordinate system S^i at time step j. The transform matrix of the head coordinate system from time step $i - 1$ to $i, i = 1, 2, ..., k$ is shown in (7). In (7), $\phi_{i-1} = (v_{i-1}^{hr} - v_{i-1}^{hl})dt/l$ is the angle that the head module rotates along the Z_{i-1}^5 axis after dt seconds, dt is the step size.

$$^w h_k = {}_5^0T_0\,{}_k^0A\,{}^k h_k \quad (6)$$

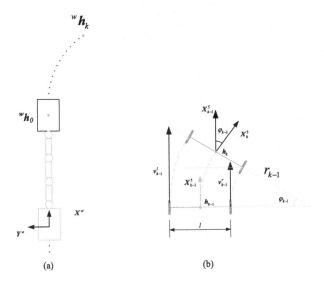

(a)   (b)

Fig. 4. The path of the head module (a) and one step control of the head module (b)

$$
{}_i^{i-1}\boldsymbol{A} =
\begin{bmatrix}
\cos(\phi_{i-1}) & -\sin(\phi_{i-1}) & 0 & r\phi_{i-1}\cos(\phi_{i-1}) \\
\sin(\phi_{i-1}) & \cos(\phi_{i-1}) & 0 & r\phi_{i-1}\sin(\phi_{i-1}) \\
0 & 0 & 1 & 0 \\
0 & 0 & 0 & 1
\end{bmatrix}
\tag{7}
$$

3.4 Follow-The-Leader Method

After obtaining the path of head, a FTL method for the AP type snake robot to obtain the control parameters of the passive modules and the tail module, namely, the yaw joints θ^0 to θ^3, and the wheel speeds of the tail module v^{tl} and v^{tr}, is proposed.

As shown in Fig. 5, firstly, putting each joints and the tail on the path of head, and computing the position of them in the world coordinate system. Let $\boldsymbol{p}_k^{yi}$ indicates the i-th yaw joint's position at time step k, and $\boldsymbol{t}_k$ indicates the position of the tail module's mass center.

As the yaw joint 3 is fixed with the head module, the position of it in the head coordinate system will always be the same, namely, ${}^k\boldsymbol{p}_k^{y3} = [L_1/2, 0, 0, 1]^T$. Then its position in the world coordinate system can be obtained by (9). We notice that the yaw joint 3 is not always on the path.

Then the yaw joint 2 is put on the path, and its position $\boldsymbol{p}_k^{y2}$ is the intersection of the path and the circle (a sphere in 3 dimensions) with the central point $\boldsymbol{p}_k^{y3}$ and radius $2L_2$, and can be computed by the following steps.

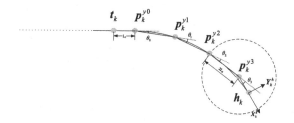

Fig. 5. Follow-the-leader method for AP type snake robot.

(1) From $i = 0$ to k, computing the distance between h_i and p_k^{y3} and finding out the i that satisfied the condition (8).

$$||h_{i-1} - p_k^{y3}|| \geq 2L_2$$
$$||h_i - p_k^{y3}|| \leq 2L_2 \tag{8}$$

(2) Finding out an $\alpha \in [0, 1]$ that makes $||h_{i-1} + \alpha(h_i - h_{i-1}) - p_k^{y3}|| = 2L_2$.
(3) Obtaining the position of yaw joint 2 by $p_k^{y2} = h_{i-1} + \alpha(h_i - h_{i-1})$.

The position of the yaw joint 0 and 1 and tail module can be obtained by similar procedure. Mention that the distance between the yaw joint 0 and tail's mass center is L_1.

$$^{w}p_k^{y3} = {}_5^0 T_{0k}^{0} A^k p_k^{y3} \tag{9}$$

Secondly, computing the joint angles θ^i. Taking θ^3 as an example, θ^3 is the angle between vector $p^{23} = p^{y3} - p^{y2}$ and $p^{3h} = h_k - p^{y3}$, hence, θ^3 can be obtained by (10). The sign will be decided by direction of $p^{23} \times p^{3h}$, if it's along the same direction of the Z^4, θ^3 will be positive, otherwise, θ^3 will be negative. The rest angles can be computed by similar procedure.

$$\theta^3 = \arccos(\frac{p^{23}p^{3h}}{||p^{23}||||p^{3h}||}) \tag{10}$$

Lastly, computing the wheel speeds of the tail module. Assuming the tail center is located on the line segment $\overline{h_{i-1}h_i}$, then we can obtain the moving velocity v_{i-1} and the turning radius r_{i-1} at time step $i-1$, then we can compute the wheel speeds of the tail module by (2) by simply replacing the operation parameters at time step $k - 1$ to $i - 1$.

By the above three steps, the control parameters θ^i, v^{tl} and v^{tr} are obtained. Combining with the v^{hl} and v^{hr}, the AP type snake robot's SEG is generated.

4   Experiments

Experiments are taken in laboratory to test the validity of the SEG control algorithm, and the result is shown in Fig. 6(a). In the experiment, we control the

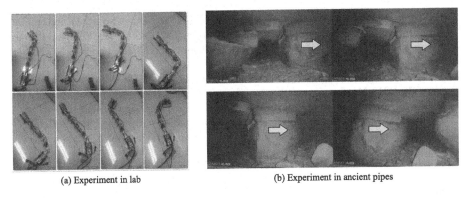

(a) Experiment in lab   (b) Experiment in ancient pipes

Fig. 6. Experiments in lab (a) and ancient pipes (b).

robot to generate a L-shape path, and we can see that the robot is following the path strictly.

Experiments are take in an ancient pipe as well, and the images of the head camera are shown in Fig. 6(b), we can see that the robot is turning right. The robot move through a 110 mm width pipe full of dirt and small stones, and feedback the images inside the pipe.

5   Conclusion and Future Work

In this paper, a small envelope gait control algorithm is proposed for the AP type snake robot. It helps the AP type snake robot to reduce the envelope of path for avoiding unexpected collision that may cause motion failure when the robot moves in the narrow rough terrain pipes. The algorithm is verified by experiments in both lab and an ancient pipe.

During the experiments in the ancient pipe, it turns out that the torque of the angel motor is not enough to lift the head module, and as the terrain inside of the pipe is rough, the robot cannot follow the path as strictly as in the lab. Hence, in our future work, the motor's torque-weight ratio should be improved and sensors will be added on the robot to increase the precision of the SEG control algorithm.

Acknowledgements. This work is supported by The National Natural Science Foundation of China (61872443).

References

1. Rollinson, D., Alwala, K.V., Zevallos, N., Choset, H.: Torque control strategies for snake robots. In: 2014 IEEE/RSJ International Conference on Intelligent Robots and Systems, pp. 1093–1099, September 2014

2. Ferworn, A., Wright, C., Tran, J., Li, C., Choset, H.: Dog and snake marsupial cooperation for urban search and rescue deployment. In: 2012 IEEE International Symposium on Safety, Security, and Rescue Robotics (SSRR), pp. 1–5, November 2012

3. Whitman, J., Zevallos, N., Travers, M., Choset, H.: Snake robot urban search after the 2017 Mexico city earthquake. In: 2018 IEEE International Symposium on Safety, Security, and Rescue Robotics (SSRR), pp. 1–6, August 2018

4. Rollinson, D., Choset, H.: Virtual chassis for snake robots. In: 2011 IEEE/RSJ International Conference on Intelligent Robots and Systems, pp. 221–226, September 2011

5. Liljeback, P., Haugstuen, I.U., Pettersen, K.Y.: Path following control of planar snake robots using a cascaded approach. IEEE Trans. Control. Syst. Technol. **20**(1), 111–126 (2012)

6. Lu, Z., Ma, S., Li, B., Wang, Y.: 3D locomotion of a snake-like robot controlled by cyclic inhibitory CPG model. In: 2006 IEEE/RSJ International Conference on Intelligent Robots and Systems, pp. 3897–3902, October 2006

7. Ma, S., Ohmameuda, Y., Inoue, K., Li, B.: Control of a 3-dimensional snake-like robot. In: 2003 IEEE International Conference on Robotics and Automation (Cat. No.03CH37422), vol. 2, pp. 2067–2072, September 2003

8. Hirose, S., Morishima, A., Tukagosi, S., Tsumaki, T., Monobe, H.: Design of practical snake vehicle: articulated body mobile robot KR-II. In: Fifth International Conference on Advanced Robotics' Robots in Unstructured Environments, vol. 1, pp. 833–838, June 1991

9. Oh, S.J., Kwon, H.J., Lee, J., Choi, H.: Mathematical modeling for omni-tread type snake robot. In: 2007 International Conference on Control, Automation and Systems, pp. 1445–1449, October 2007

10. Kamegawa, T., Yarnasaki, T., Igarashi, H., Matsuno, F.: Development of the snake-like rescue robot "KOHGA". In: IEEE International Conference on Robotics and Automation, 2004. Proceedings, ICRA 2004, vol. 5, pp. 5081–5086, April 2004

11. Kamegawa, T., Yamasaki, T., Matsuno, F.: Evaluation of snake-like rescue robot "KOHGA" for usability of remote control. In: IEEE International Safety, Security and Rescue Rototics, Workshop, 2005, pp. 25–30 (2005)

Trajectory Tracking Control of Wheeled Mobile Robots Using Backstepping

Sunxin Wang[1(✉)] ⑩, Xuefeng Bao[2] ⑩, Shaohua Zhang[2] ⑩,
and Gaopan Shen[2] ⑩

[1] School of Mechanical and Precision Instrument Engineering,
Xi'an University of Technology, Xi'an 710048, China
wsx8280@xaut.edu.cn
[2] School of Mechanical Engineering, Northwestern Polytechnical University,
Xi'an 710072, China

Abstract. This paper proposes a trajectory tracking control method for wheeled mobile robots with nonholonomic constraints using the combination of the backstepping and direct Lyapunov method. Firstly, we establish the robot's kinematic model and analyze the trajectory tracking problem. Then, the Sigmoid function is introduced to the backstepping method to improve the convergence rate and global asymptotic stability of the trajectory tracking controller. In addition, the Barbalat Lemma is employed to prove the asymptotic stability of the controller tracking errors. Finally, the co-simulation using V-REP and MATLAB software are presented to validate the performance of our trajectory tracking controller.

Keywords: Trajectory tracking · Wheeled mobile robot · Backstepping · Sigmoid function · Co-simulation

1 Introduction

The multi-mobile robots formation control has received considerable attention over the past decade, since the general practical applications [1] such as the cooperative rescue, group stalking and exploration, and transportation of large objects. As one of the several formation control of multi-mobile robots approaches, the leader-follower approach is the most popular one due to its simplicity and modularity [2]. In this approach, one robot of the formation (designated as the leader robot) moves along the predefined trajectory, meanwhile the others are assigned as follower robots to autonomously keep the track of the leader robot and maintain the desired distance and bearing angles [3]. Therefore, the key issue of the leader-follower approach is how to design the follower controller to autonomously tracking the reference trajectory so as to complete the given task.

The procedure of design the trajectory tracking controller contains two aspects: design the controller law and prove its global asymptotic stability. There are many methods to design the trajectory tracking controller, such as the sliding mode control [4], the Neural Network Controller [5], the direct Lyapunov method [6], the backstepping method [7], and the adaptive tracking control [8]. The drawback of the sliding

© Springer Nature Switzerland AG 2019
H. Yu et al. (Eds.): ICIRA 2019, LNAI 11744, pp. 289–300, 2019.
https://doi.org/10.1007/978-3-030-27541-9_24

mode control and neural network controller is complexity. And the direct Lyapunov method lack of constructivity, which can be overcame by the backstepping method. In addition, the backstepping method is a typical nonlinear control approach that can be used to design a controller recursively and effectively. Therefore, the tracking controller based on the combination of the backstepping and the direct Lyapunov method is designed to achieve the trajectory tracking in this paper. Besides, in order to validate the performance of the controller, the simulations were carried out based on the MATLAB in paper [9–11].

In the above design process of the tracking controller by the backstepping, the hypothesized control quantity is set to be constant, so that not only the convergence rate and global asymptotic stability are not adjustable, but also multiple control parameters need to be adjusted repeatedly for different trajectories (circular trajectory, straight trajectory). Therefore, in order to solve the problem, we introduce the Sigmoid function [12] with the bounded, differentiable, and uniform convergence in the setting process of the hypothesized control quantity. we can effectively adjust the convergence rate and asymptotic stability of the controller by adjusting one parameter of the function, and meanwhile the adaptability of the controller to different types of trajectories has been improved.

In terms of controller algorithm simulation verification, most existing literatures simplify the nonholonomic mobile robots into a particle in MATLAB environment. This is not only lack of intuition, but more importantly, it is impossible to determine whether the robot breaks through the nonholonomic constraints [13] in the simulation process. Based on this issue, we adopt a form of the co-simulation [14] using V-REP and MATLAB software, which can monitor whether the wheeled mobile robot breaks through the nonholonomic constraint in real time while demonstrating the intuition of the simulation.

The paper is organized as follows, in Sect. 2, the kinematic model of the nonholonomic wheeled mobile robot is established and the trajectory tracking problem are described. The controller based on the combination of the backstepping and the direct Lyapunov method is designed and the asymptotic stability of tracking errors has been proved in Sect. 3. The co-simulation using V-REP and MATLAB software and discussions are presented in Sect. 4. Finally, conclusions and future research of this work are given in Sect. 5.

2 Kinematic Model and Trajectory Tracking Problem Statement

2.1 Kinematic Model of Wheeled Mobile Robot

In a group of nonholonomic mobile robots, the kinematic model (see Fig. 1) is established for each three-wheeled mobile robot. The two rear wheels of the mobile robot are actuated wheels, and the front wheel is passive wheel. The distance between the center of two actuated wheels is L and the radius of actuated wheel is r. And d is the distance from the center of mass M of the mobile robot to the middle point C between the right and left actuated wheels.

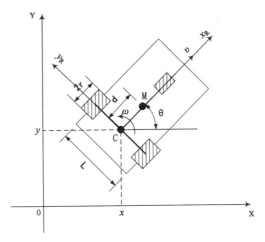

Fig. 1. Kinematics model of wheeled mobile robot.

The (C, x_R, y_R) is local coordinate system, it take robot's movement as reference standard. $P = (x, y, q)^T$ is robot's current pose, where (x, y) is the cartesian position of point C, θ is the angle between the heading direction and the X axis. The robot's velocity vectors are represented by $(v, w)^T$ (v is the linear velocity, w is the angular velocity). The equation for converting the robot's velocity vectors to the angular velocity of motors is as follows:

$$\begin{cases} w_L = (2v - Lw)/2r \\ w_R = (2v + Lw)/2r \end{cases} \tag{1}$$

where w_L is angular velocity of the left motor, w_R is angular velocity of the right motor. Then the nonholonomic constraint equation of wheeled mobile robot can be written as follows:

$$\dot{x}\sin\theta - \dot{y}\cos\theta = [\sin\theta \quad -\cos\theta \quad 0] \begin{bmatrix} \dot{x} \\ \dot{y} \\ \dot{\theta} \end{bmatrix} = 0 \tag{2}$$

So the kinematic equation of the robot can be expressed by the following equation:

$$\dot{P} = \begin{bmatrix} \dot{x} \\ \dot{y} \\ \dot{\theta} \end{bmatrix} = \begin{bmatrix} \cos\theta & 0 \\ \sin\theta & 0 \\ 0 & 1 \end{bmatrix} \begin{bmatrix} v \\ w \end{bmatrix} = JP \tag{3}$$

J is Jacobian matrix.

2.2   Controllability Analysis of the Trajectory Tracking Problem

The model (see Fig. 2) of the robots trajectory tracking error as follows, $P_g = \left(x_g, y_g, \theta_g\right)^T$ is the desired pose and the $q_g = \left(v_g, w_g\right)^T$ is the robot's desired velocity. The current pose is $p = (x, y, \theta)^T$ and the current velocity is $q = (v, w)^T$ Therefore, in the local coordinate system (C, x_R, y_R), the actual tracking error of the robot is $P_e = P_g - P = \left(x_e, y_e, \theta_e\right)^T$.

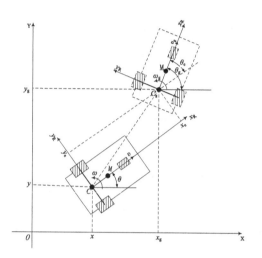

Fig. 2. The model of the trajectory tracking error.

After the coordinate transformation, the tracking error of robot can be expressed as follows:

$$P_e = \begin{bmatrix} x_e \\ y_e \\ \theta_e \end{bmatrix} = \begin{bmatrix} cos\theta & sin\theta & 0 \\ -sin\theta & cos\theta & 0 \\ 0 & 0 & 1 \end{bmatrix} \begin{bmatrix} x_g - x \\ y_g - y \\ \theta_g - \theta \end{bmatrix} = R_e\left(P_g - P\right) \tag{4}$$

R_e is the orthogonal revolving matrix. (x_e, y_e) is the vector coordinate of $\overrightarrow{C\,C'}$ in the local coordinate system. Then, the dynamic error differential equation of robot is obtained:

$$\dot{P}_e = \begin{bmatrix} \dot{x}_e \\ \dot{y}_e \\ \dot{\theta}_e \end{bmatrix} = \begin{bmatrix} y_e w - v + v_g cos\theta_e \\ -x_e w + v_g sin\theta_e \\ w_g - w \end{bmatrix} \tag{5}$$

According to the above error differential equation of the trajectory tracking process, the duty of controller design is to find the appropriate control law $q = (v, w)$, where

$w = w(x_e, y_e, \theta_e, v_g, w_g)$ and $v = v(x_e, y_e, \theta_e, v_g, w_g)$ to make the $\lim_{t \to \infty} \| (x_e, y_e, \theta_e)^T \| = 0$ satisfied.

3 Trajectory Tracking Controller Design

The structure diagram (see Fig. 3) of the closed-loop trajectory tracking control system of the wheeled mobile robot as shown in follows. The inputs of the control system is the desired pose $p_g = (x_g, y_g, \theta_g)^T$ and the desired velocity $q_g = (v_g, w_g)^T$, and the output is the actual pose $p = (x, y, \theta)^T$ of the robot. The inputs of the central controller of the system is the tracking error $p_e = (x_e, y_e, \theta_e)^T$ and the desired velocities $q_g = (v_g, w_g)^T$, output is the control law $q = (v, w)^T$. After the kinematic constraints and integrator operation will produce the actual pose $p = (x, y, \theta)^T$, meanwhile the $p = (x, y, \theta)^T$ is used as the feedback. Finally, the system will achieve the global stability and implements $\lim_{t \to 0} p_e = 0$ after such repeated adjustments.

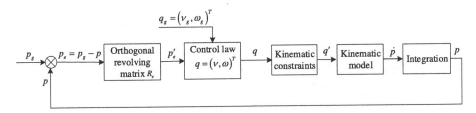

Fig. 3. The closed-loop structure diagram for trajectory tracking control system.

In this paper, the Sigmoid function is introduced to design the trajectory tracking control law based on [9, 11]. According to the kinematics model of the nonholonomic mobile robot, the erroneous component x_e in $p_e = (x_e, y_e, \theta_e)^T$ is selected as the hypothesized control quantity and a new hypothesized feedback variable is constructed as follows:

$$\bar{x}_e = x_e - k_1 S(w) y_e \tag{6}$$

The $S(w) = \frac{2}{1 + e^{-aw}} - 1$ is the Sigmoid function [12] and its convergence rate figure (see Fig. 4) as shown in follows. It's a mathematical function having a characteristic sigmoid curve. Introducing this function can make the hypothesized feedback variable $k_1 S(w) y_1$ uniform convergence between $[-1, 1]$. k_1 is a positive constant, and a is the parameter of the function convergence rate. The convergence rate of the hypothesized feedback variable $\bar{x}_e$ is controlled by adjusting the parameter a.

The detailed of the controller principle analysis and the Lyapunov scalar function construction process could reference to [11]. Finally, the Lyapunov scalar function and its derivative about time t can be obtained as following:

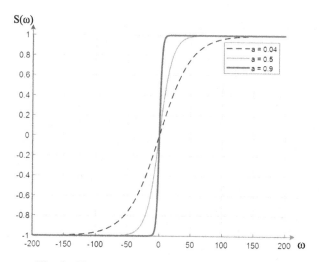

Fig. 4. The convergence rate of sigmoid function.

$$V = \frac{1}{2}\bar{x}_e^2 + \frac{1}{2}y_e^2 + \frac{2}{k_3}\left(1 - \cos\frac{\theta_e}{2}\right) \tag{7}$$

The k_3 is a positive constant, and define $\theta_e \in [0, 2\pi]$, obviously $V \geq 0$ is satisfied and the equal sign can be obtained when $(\bar{x}_e, y_e, \theta_e)^T = 0$.

$$
\begin{aligned}
\dot{V} =& \bar{x}_e\dot{\bar{x}}_e + y_e\dot{y}_e + \frac{\dot{\theta}_e}{k_3}\sin\frac{\theta_e}{2} \\
=& \bar{x}_e\left[-v + v_g\cos\theta_e - ak_1y_e\dot{w}(1 + S(w))\left(1 - \frac{1 + S(w)}{2}\right) - k_1S(w)\left(-wx_e + v_g\sin\theta_e\right)\right] \\
& - k_1wS(w)y_e^2 + \frac{1}{k_3}\sin\frac{\theta_e}{2}\left(w_g - w + 2k_3y_ev_g\cos\frac{\theta_e}{2}\right)
\end{aligned}
\tag{8}
$$

For $\forall t \in [0, +\infty)$, $v_g, w_g, \dot{v}_g, \dot{w}_g$ is bounded and v_g, w_g does not converge to 0 at the same time. Therefore, the following control law can be obtained:

$$
\begin{cases}
w = w_g + 2k_3y_ev_g\cos\frac{\theta_e}{2} + k_t\sin\frac{\theta_e}{2} \\
v = v_g\cos\theta_e - ak_1y_e\dot{w}(1 + S(w))\left(1 - \frac{1 + S(w)}{2}\right) - k_lS(w)\left(-wx_e + v_g\sin\theta_e\right) + k_2[x_e - k_1S(w)y_e]
\end{cases}
\tag{9}
$$

Where:

$$\dot{w} = \dot{w}_g + \left[\frac{k_4}{2} \left(w_g - w \right) + 2k_3 \left(v_g^2 \sin \theta_e - v_g w x_e + \dot{v}_g y_e \right) \right] \cos \frac{\theta_e}{2} - k_3 v_g y_e \sin \frac{\theta_e}{2} \quad (10)$$

In the above formula (10), for a straight trajectory:

$$v_g = c, w_g = 0, \dot{v}_g = 0, \dot{w}_g = 0 \quad (11)$$

for a circular trajectory:

$$v_g = c_1, w_g = c_2, \dot{v}_g = 0, \dot{w}_g = 0 \quad (12)$$

Where, the c, c_1, c_2 are constants and bring the control law (9) into (8):

$$\dot{V} = -k_2 \bar{x}_e^2 - k_1 w S(w) y_e^2 - \frac{k_4}{k_3} \sin^2 \left(\frac{\theta_e}{2} \right) \quad (13)$$

For $\forall t \in [0, +\infty)$, $v_g, w_g, \dot{v}_g, \dot{w}_g$ is bounded, so $\forall t \in [0, +\infty)$, x_e, y_e, θ_e is bounded. As we can see from Eq. (13), $\dot{V} \leq 0$. And V is positive definite, continuous, differentiable and bounded, so according to the Barbalat Theorem [15], $\lim\limits_{t \to \infty} \dot{V} = 0$. Then the following equation can be obtained:

$$\lim\limits_{t \to \infty} \sin^2 \left(\frac{\theta_e}{2} \right) = 0, \quad \lim\limits_{t \to \infty} w S(w) y_e^2 = 0, \quad \lim\limits_{t \to \infty} \bar{x}_e^2 = 0 \quad (14)$$

Because v_g, w_g can't be zero at the same time and according to the control law (9), w is not constant to 0. Therefore, according to formula (14), the following equation can be obtained:

$$\lim\limits_{t \to \infty} \theta_e = 0$$
$$\lim\limits_{t \to \infty} y_e = 0 \quad (15)$$

Because $\lim\limits_{t \to \infty} \bar{x}^2 = 0$, so $\lim\limits_{t \to \infty} x_e = k_1 y_e S(w)$. Then the following equation can be obtained:

$$\lim\limits_{t \to \infty} x_e = 0 \quad (16)$$

According to the above analysis and the stability criterion of Lyapunov [16], the pose error of the closed-loop system $p_e = (x_e, y_e, \theta_e)^T$ is globally bounded and satisfied the following formula:

$$\lim\limits_{t \to \infty} \left\| (x_e, y_e, \theta_e)^T \right\| = 0 \quad (17)$$

4 Results and Discussions of the Simulations

In order to validate the proposed control law (9) in this paper, we shown the co-simulation results of the wheeled mobile robots tracking trajectory using V-REP and MATLAB software. Therefore (see Fig. 5), the simulation model is established in V-REP's visual simulation environment could execute the control algorithm instructions from the remote client (MATLAB client) and display the motion information in real time as an image.

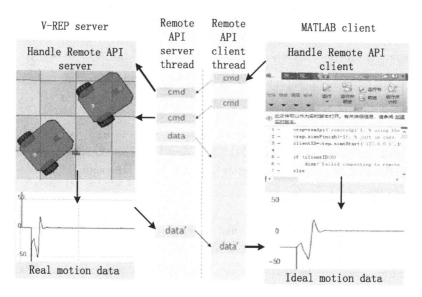

Fig. 5. Co-simulation Using V-REP and MATLAB.

At the same time, the MATLAB could also collect and analyze the robot's ideal motion data while sending the algorithm instructions to it. Through the comparative analysis of the real data in V-REP and ideal data in MATLAB, the problems in the closed-loop trajectory tracking control system could be clearly reflected.

The parameter a in sigmoid function and the parameters k_1, k_2, k_3, k_4 in control law (10) are both positive constants, and they decide the system movement's vibration and the rate of error convergence. The performance of the controller is validated by taking a circular trajectory.

Set $a = 0.5, k_1 = k_2 = 1.5, k_3 = 25, k_4 = 5.2$, $q_g = \left(v_g, w_g\right)^T = \left(0.4m/s, 0.1\,rad/s\right)^T$. And the circle line's initial desired and actual pose are $p_g = \left(x_g, y_g, \theta_g\right)^T = (0.99m, -0.18m, 90°)^T$, $p = (x, y, \theta)^T = \left(1.70m, -0.82m, 120°\right)^T$. So the initial tracking error $p_e = \left(x_e, y_e, \theta_e\right)^T = \left(-0.71m, 0.64m, -30°\right)^T$. The final circular trajectory tracking result as shown in Figs. 6, 7, 8, 9 and 10, and the every figure's (a) is the ideal motion data recorded by MATLAB, and the (b) is the actual executed data recorded by V-REP. The co-simulation experiment video of the circular trajectory tracking can be found at Supplementary Materials https://youtu.be/OEmnNlDJ_YY.

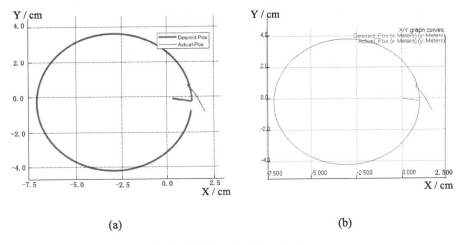

(a)   (b)

Fig. 6. Tracking circular trajectory.

The proposed trajectory tracking control algorithms makes the nonholonomic wheeled mobile robots achieve good performance when tracking the circular trajectory. We can see from the Fig. 6, the actual tracking trajectory is almost identical to the desired trajectory and the rate of convergence is faster than [11]. And we can see from the Figs. 7 and 8, the time of the pose error and angular error in the global coordinate system convergences to zero less than 2.5 s and no singularities [17] appear during the tracking of a cycle time. Finally, Figs. 9 and 10 show that the mobile robot's linear velocity and angular velocity converge to the desired value in less than 3 s and could maintain the global stability.

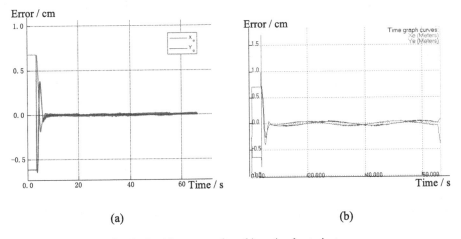

(a)   (b)

Fig. 7. Position error of tracking circular trajectory.

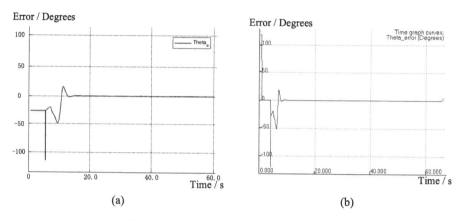

Fig. 8. Angular error of tracking circular trajectory.

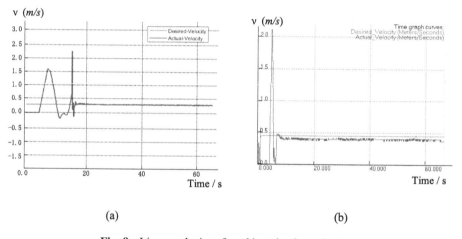

Fig. 9. Linear velocity of tracking circular trajectory.

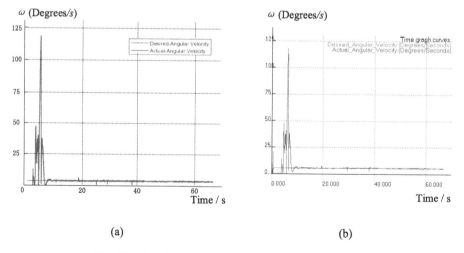

Fig. 10. Angular velocity of tracking circular trajectory.

5 Conclusion

In this paper, the trajectory tracking controller for nonholonomic wheeled mobile robots has been proposed by using the combination of the backstepping and direct Lyapunov method. In the process of design the controller, the Sigmoid function is introduced to improve its convergence rate and adaptability. In addition, the convergence of the tracking error has been proved by using the Barbalat Lemma. Finally, the performance of the trajectory tracking controller is verified by the co-simulation using V-REP and MATLAB software. Improving the adaptability of the controller in tracking more complex trajectories (such as elliptic trajectory, sinusoidal trajectory and even arbitrary curve trajectory) is the work that we need to accomplished in the future.

Supplementary Materials:
The co-simulation experiment video of the circular trajectory tracking can be found at Supplementary Materials https://youtu.be/OEmnNlDJ_YY.

Acknowledgments. This research has been supported by the Scientific Research Program Funded by Shaanxi Provincial Education Department (No:118-431018002), and the Starting Doctoral Research Program Funded by Xi'an University of Technology.

References

1. Eoh, G., Jeon, J.D., Choi, J.S., Lee, B.H.: Multi-robot cooperative formation for overweight object transportation. In: 2011 IEEE/SICE International Symposium on System Integration, pp. 726–731. (2011)
2. Yasuda, Y., Kubota, N., Toda, Y.: Adaptive formation behaviors of multi-robot for cooperative exploration. In: 2012 IEEE International Conference on Fuzzy Systems, pp. 1–6. (2012)
3. Alonso-Mora, J., Baker, S., Rus, D.: Multi-robot formation control and object transport in dynamic environments via constrained optimization. Int. J. Robot. Res. **36**(9), 1000–1021 (2017)
4. Solea, R., Filipescu, A., Nunes, U.: Sliding-mode control for trajectory-tracking of a wheeled mobile robot in presence of uncertainties. In: 2009 Asian Control Conference, pp. 1701–1706 (2009)
5. Peng, Z., Wang, D., Li, T., et al.: Leaderless and leader-follower cooperative control of multiple marine surface vehicles with unknown dynamics. Nonlinear Dyn. **74**(1–2), 95–106 (2013)
6. Sadowska, A., Huijberts, H.: Formation control design for car-like nonholonomic robots using the backstepping approach. In: 2013 Control Conference, pp. 1274–1279 (2013)
7. Shao, J., Xie, G., Yu, J., et al.: Leader-following formation control of multiple mobile robots. In: 2005 IEEE International Symposium on, Mediterrean Conference on Intelligent Control, pp. 808–813 (2005)
8. Fukao, T., Nakagawa, H., Adachi, N.: Adaptive tracking control of a nonholonomic mobile robot. In: 2000 IEEE/RSJ International Conference on Intelligent Robots & Systems, 16(5), pp. 609–615 (2000)
9. Jiangdagger, Z.P., Nijmeijer, H.: Tracking control of mobile robots: a case study in backstepping. Automatica **33**(7), 1393–1399 (1997)

10. Cao, C., et al.: Trajectory tracking control of nonholonomic mobile robots by backstepping. In: 2011 International Conference on Modelling, pp. 134–139 (2011)
11. Chuan, W., Huaiyu, W., Fen, W., et al.: Trajectory tracking control of mobile robots based on backstepping. Mod. Electron. Tech. **24**(287), 113–115 (2008)
12. Han, J., Moraga, C.: The influence of the sigmoid function parameters on the speed of backpropagation learning. In: Mira, J., Sandoval, F. (eds.) IWANN 1995. LNCS, vol. 930, pp. 195–201. Springer, Heidelberg (1995). https://doi.org/10.1007/3-540-59497-3_175
13. Xiang, X., Lapierre, L., Jouvencel, B., et al.: Coordinated path following control of multiple nonholonomic vehicles. In: OCEANS 2009-EUROPE, pp. 1–7 (2009)
14. Schloegl, F., Rohjans, S., Lehnhoff, S., et al.: Towards a classification scheme for co-simulation approaches in energy systems. In: 2015 International Symposium on Smart Electric Distribution Systems and Technologies (EDST), pp. 516–521. (2015)
15. Ploplys, N.J., Kawka, P.A., Alleyne, A.G.: Closed-loop control over wireless networks. Control Syst. IEEE **24**(3), 58–71 (2015)
16. Lyapunov, A.M.: The general problem of the stability of motion. Int. J. Control **55**(3), 531–534 (1992)
17. Pérez-Cruz, J.H., de Jesús Rubio, J., Encinas, R., et al.: Singularity-free neural control for the exponential trajectory tracking in multiple-input uncertain systems with unknown deadzone nonlinearities. Sci. World J. **2014**(1), 1–10 (2014)

The Design of Inspection Robot Navigation Systems Based on Distributed Vision

Lei Wang[1,2], Hua Zhu[1,2(✉)], Peng Li[1,2], Change Chen[1,2], Shao-ze You[1,2], Meng-gang Li[1,2], and Zheng Zhang[1,2]

[1] School of Mechanical and Electrical Engineering,
China University of Mining and Technology, Xuzhou 221116, China
Zhuhua83591917@163.com
[2] Jiangsu Collaborative Innovation Center of Intelligent Mining Equipment,
China University of Mining and Technology, Xuzhou 221008, China

Abstract. This paper focuses on inspection robot navigation systems based on distributed vision in order to solve the navigation problem for indoor inspection robots in an unknown environment. Firstly, the robot platform of the navigation system is designed, the system is built, and the software of the host computer interface and driver of the bottom driver are designed. Secondly, the key technologies of path planning and image processing in visual navigation are studied theoretically and experimentally. Finally, the performance of the navigation system is tested. Experimental results demonstrate that the inspection robot navigation system based on distributed vision can undertake autonomous localization and navigation tasks in unknown environments.

Keywords: Inspection robot · Navigation systems · Distributed vision

1 Introduction

Visual navigation [1] plays an important role in the intelligent research of mobile robots [2], and experimentation within this field has flourished in recent years. Regular and uninterrupted inspection is indispensable to ensure the normal operation of working equipment in dangerous working conditions such as spray painting workshops, chemical waste treatment centers, and flour manufacturing facilities. At present, manual inspection is the main inspection method of production lines in dangerous environments. Manual inspection is not only inefficient, but also carries a high likelihood of bodily harm for those working in the high-risk environment for a long time. Therefore, there is an urgent need to develop an indoor inspection robot [3] to work in dangerous operation environments to assist or replace manual inspection tasks.

Autonomous walking is a prerequisite for indoor inspection robots to complete inspection tasks. The research and development of navigation systems [4] are of great significance to improve the intelligence level of indoor inspection robots and the efficiency of inspection.

Vision is an important perception method of mobile robot navigation technology. In early research, due to the expensive hardware and unrealistic computing speed required, magnetic navigation [5], inertial navigation [6], infrared navigation [7], laser

© Springer Nature Switzerland AG 2019
H. Yu et al. (Eds.): ICIRA 2019, LNAI 11744, pp. 301–313, 2019.
https://doi.org/10.1007/978-3-030-27541-9_25

navigation [8], ultrasonic navigation [9] and LiDAR navigation [10] were generally used instead. In recent years, due to the development of large-scale integrated circuits, as well as the increase of computing speed and the reduction in cost of visual sensors, the use of visual navigation [11] is a development trend in robot navigation technology.

The main contribution of this paper is to study the navigation system based on distributed vision [12]. This is undertaken by designing a software and hardware platform of visual navigation using image acquisition and processing technology [13] to obtain a grid map [14] of the robot path planning [15] and image in the visual navigation. The key technologies, such as processing, are analyzed theoretically and experimentally, and the ant colony algorithm is selected as the best algorithm for path planning. Finally, a performance test of the inspection robot navigation system is conducted, and the autonomous positioning and navigation task based on distributed vision is carried out.

2   Platform Design

2.1   Hardware Design

In this paper, the visual navigation platform is made up of a PC, router, serial port transfer module, bottom controller, motor driver, motor, infrared obstacle avoidance sensor, switch, global surveillance camera, inspection camera, and a 24 V lithium battery. The host computer selects the notebook computer to display and process various types of information acquired by the sensor, and uses image processing and path planning technology to carry out the planning and motion trajectory monitoring of the inspection robot motion route. The host computer performs wireless communication with the bottom controller through a router. The core control chip of the bottom controller is STM32F407ZGT6, which uses IO port to control the motor driver. The final robot hardware system architecture is presented in Fig. 1.

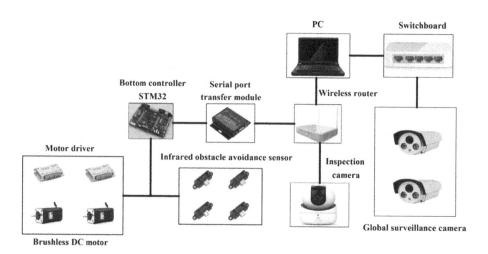

Fig. 1. Robot hardware system architecture

2.2 Software Design

The software framework design of the robot mainly includes the upper computer interface software and bottom controller driver. The host computer interface is illustrated in Fig. 2. The framework of the host computer interface software is as shown in Fig. 3, and includes a sensor information acquisition and display system, image splicing system, path planning system, decision system, target tracking system, manual remote control operating system, and communication system. According to the control requirements of the robot, the design of the bottom driver program is then completed and precise control of the robot is carried out.

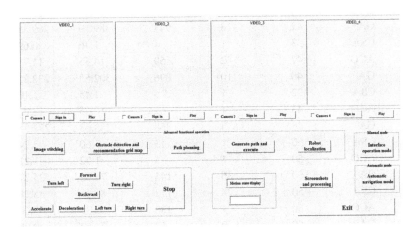

Fig. 2. Upper computer interface

3 Research on Path Planning Algorithm

Path planning is the key technology of mobile robot navigation, and refers to planning a collision free and direct path from the starting point to the end point in an environment with obstacles [16]. At present, an increasing amount of bionic intelligent algorithms are applied in robot path planning including Holland's proposed genetic algorithm (GA) [17], Dorigo's ant colony optimization (ACO) [18], and Burnet's clonal selection algorithm (CSA) [19]. These algorithms can quickly and accurately find the optimal path for the robot in a complex environment. The performance of GA, ACO and CSA are tested separately using classical test functions including Shubert, Hansen, Bohachevsky, Ackley, Shekel's foxholes, and the Sphere model.

The function test results of the three algorithms are presented in Table 1. The number of optimal solutions obtained by the algorithm is one of the most important indicators to measure its performance. As seen from the optimal number of solutions of the six groups of functions in Table 1, ACO displays the strongest search ability. From the three groups of tests of minimum convergence algebra, maximum convergence algebra, and average convergence algebra, it is demonstrated that ACO can quickly converge. The results of the three groups of test data show that ACO is the smallest, indicating that ACO has the best convergence performance. From the test results of algebraic standard deviation, the performance of ACO is relatively stable.

Table 1. Function test results of GA, CSA and ACO

Number of cities	Algorithm name	Optimal number of times	The shortest distance	The longest distance	The average distance	Distance standard deviation
f1	GA	20	6	867	111.65	243.79
	CSA	50	5	289	64.68	64.57
	ACO	50	1	87	27.08	22.44
f2	GA	42	13	941	389.19	289.35
	CSA	33	1	4	1.36	0.69
	ACO	47	2	59	14.55	11.71
f3	GA	40	10	896	302.55	232.25
	CSA	22	1	6	1.45	1.10
	ACO	43	1	65	16.65	13.22
f4	GA	48	3	868	283.68	272.55
	CSA	50	1	13	3.60	3.24
	ACO	50	1	5	1.72	1.22
f5	GA	50	36	143	76.52	25.27
	CSA	50	28	172	81.18	35.18
	ACO	50	4	138	32.38	33.60
f6	GA	50	9	53	24.52	9.08
	CSA	50	8	46	18.90	7.79
	ACO	50	1	39	10.90	8.91

Taking the Hansen function f3 as an example, Figs. 3 and 4 show the distribution of the initial position and final position of the ant colony when the ACO performs 50 independent function optimization tests. As 50 independent functional test experiments were conducted in this paper, and the initial number of ant colonies was 40, a total of 2000 ants participated in the optimization. As illustrated in Fig. 3, in the initial state, 2000 ants are discretely distributed in the two-dimensional space of $xy(y \in [-10, 10], \ x \in [-10, 10])$. Ant colony algorithm has high parallelism and positive feedback, global optimization, and strong robustness. After continuous iterative optimization, individual ants gradually move closer to the optimal value. As shown in Fig. 4, a large number of ant colonies are concentrated in the location of the minimum function, fully reflecting the superior optimization performance of the ant colony algorithm.

Through the function test, ACO demonstrates strong performance in solving the problem of multi-dimensional function optimization which can be globally optimized. The algorithm also displays fast convergence speed and superior performance.

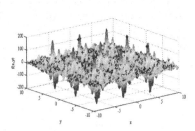

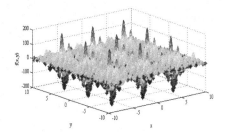

Fig. 3. Initial position distribution   **Fig. 4.** Final position distribution

In order to further verify the performance of the three algorithms, the TSP [20] problem is tested using Matlab software. Considering the randomness of the algorithm, six different cities are selected and tested separately for this study. The parameters of the GA, CSA, and ASO algorithms are the same as those of the function test and the test environment is Windows 7, 64-bit operating system, Intel Core i5-4570, 4G RAM, MATLAB R2014a.

The number and specific azimuth distribution of the six cities in this test are provided in Fig. 5, specifically including 16, 29, 31, 101, 130 and 225 cities. The number of cities is set from least to most. As the number of cities increases, the test environment of the TSP problem becomes increasingly complex, and the algorithm performance is required to be higher.

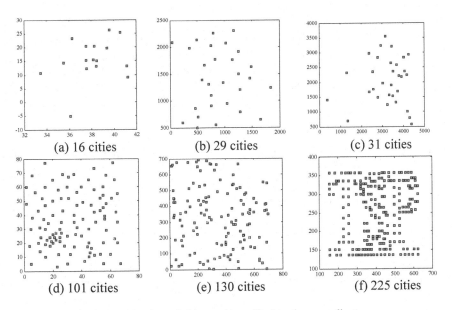

Fig. 5. Number of cities and specific location coordinates

The results of the three algorithms for TSP testing are illustrated in Table 2. It can be seen from the shortest distance, the longest distance, and the average distance that the three sets of data obtained by ACO are the smallest, indicating that ACO has the strongest search ability. Meanwhile, the standard deviation of the distance for ACO is the smallest, indicating that the ant colony algorithm displays the highest stability and the overall performance of this algorithm is the best.

Table 2. Test results in TSP questions of GA, CSA and ACO

Number of cities	Algorithm name	Optimal number of times	The shortest distance	The longest distance	The average distance
16	GA	74.71	113.91	75.32	3.72
	CSA	74.61	122.31	75.76	5.23
	ACO	74.11	76.02	74.21	0.26
29	GA	9331.25	22830.68	9985.03	1737.91
	CSA	9280.95	23444.30	10019.26	2220.64
	ACO	9251.95	10628.51	9282.18	84.60
31	GA	17370.82	38418.35	18198.33	2743.89
	CSA	16673.01	41690.50	18218.29	4030.16
	ACO	16383.27	17364.15	16390.76	82.93
101	GA	841.13	3116.30	1241.27	449.07
	CSA	763.28	3147.58	1236.29	516.32
	ACO	675.78	890.46	684.33	17.56
130	GA	9832.37	42003.51	16915.99	7113.83
	CSA	7900.49	41023.86	14364.62	7292.58
	ACO	6388.27	8153.59	6412.01	138.38
225	GA	8841.97	37043.22	14844.54	5995.27
	CSA	7946.71	37958.74	15302.38	7300.67
	ACO	4284.15	5538.41	4326.09	82.62

In this test, taking the number of cities at 101 as an example, the optimal paths corresponding to the three algorithms of GA, CSA and ACO are respectively (a), (b) and (c) in Fig. 6. The optimal path obtained by ACO is a simple path with few cross paths, so the distance is relatively short, indicating that ACO shows superior path planning performance in complex environments.

The convergence curve of GA, CSA and ACO for optimizing the TSP problem in 101 cities is presented in Fig. 7. In this situation, ACO shows a high degree of parallelism and positive feedback. The initial route obtained is relatively better than GA and CSA, and the convergence speed is the fastest, showing a convergence trend at 20–30 generation.

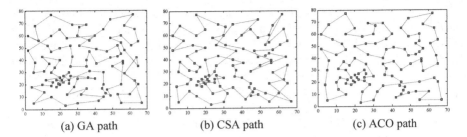

(a) GA path   (b) CSA path   (c) ACO path

Fig. 6. 101 cities TSP path planning map

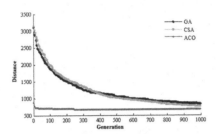

Fig. 7. 101 cities TSP optimal convergence curve

4   Research on Multi-image Stitching Technology

Multi-image stitching technology [21] is a key technology based on the distributed vision navigation systems. The image information of the motion space of the robot is acquired by multiple cameras, image information obtained by each camera is independent, and the acquired graphics are stitched. In this way, the entire robotic motion environment space is finally obtained (Table 3).

Table 3. Three algorithms of image matching test data

Image name	Resolution	Algorithm name	Matching feature points	Time
Image 1	800 × 600	SIFT	100	3.316
		SURF	70	0.8108
		ORB	31	0.696
Image 2	1280 × 960	SIFT	120	11.551
		SURF	97	2.795
		ORB	12	2.264
Image 3	1600 × 1200	SIFT	275	14.107
		SURF	123	2.414
		ORB	166	2.361

The extraction and matching of image feature points is the key technology of image stitching. At present, well known feature detection operators are mainly SIFT [22], SURF [23], and ORB algorithms [24]. In order to verify the performance of the three algorithms, multiple sets of image sequences are used for testing. The nearest neighbor thresholds of all three algorithms are 0.6, and the test environment is Windows 7, 64-bit operating system, Intel Core i5-4570, 4G RAM, Visual Studio 2013, OpenCV 3.0.

Figures 8, 9 and 10 illustrate the matching results of feature points of the image 1, 2 and 3 respectively. Experimental results show that the three algorithms can obtain a large number of feature matching points, which can meet the needs of subsequent work. The ORB algorithm displays the highest efficiency and the shortest time consumption through experimental comparison of three sets of outdoor images. Thus, the ORB algorithm has better performance and higher efficiency in image feature point matching.

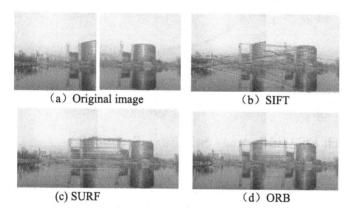

(a) Original image   (b) SIFT

(c) SURF   (d) ORB

Fig. 8. Matching result of image 1

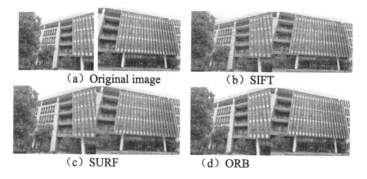

(a) Original image   (b) SIFT

(c) SURF   (d) ORB

Fig. 9. Matching result of image 2

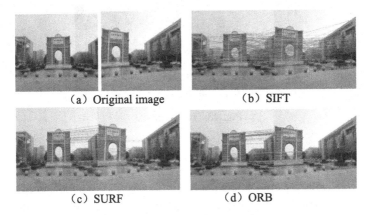

(a) Original image   (b) SIFT

(c) SURF   (d) ORB

Fig. 10. Matching result of image 3

Through the comparison of three feature matching experiments, it is determined that the splicing of graphics should be performed using the ORB algorithm. The exterior Image 3 is taken as an example to complete the stitching. To splice the right image to the left image, a perspective transformation on the right image is required.

The perspective image is provided in Fig. 11. This perspective image is then copied to the left image, and the result is provided in Fig. 12. The splicing of the two images is not coordinated, and the transition between the two images at the junction of the splicing graphs is very poor due to the different illumination colors of the two images. In this paper, the weighted fusion method is used to synthesize a new image by adding the pixel values of the overlapped areas of the image according to certain weights. The mosaic image after fusion is shown in Fig. 13.

Fig. 11. Perspective image   **Fig. 12.** Image after copying

In the navigation system, multiple cameras are used to acquire the motion space image information of the robot. Image mosaic technology is used to splice multiple images together to obtain the complete motion environment space of the robot, and prepare for the path planning and navigation of the robot.

Fig. 13. Fused image

5 Experimental Analysis

According to the above software and hardware design, the navigation system is tested based on a distributed visual inspection robot. The system can acquire real-time accurate image information of the ground through the monitoring cameras, and use OpenCV to complete image mosaic, obstacle detection, and grid map building. It can utilize the ant colony algorithm to carry out path planning and other operations and, according to the acquired path which is converted into a corresponding motion instruction, the autonomous walking of the robot is realized.

The bottom control of the navigation system is first tested, as well as the motion performance of the inspection robot. This includes the deviation analysis of straight line driving deviation, driving speed, turning radius, and local turning. The analysis results are taken into account in the navigation system test process. Following this, a test environment is set up in which the ground is irregularly distributed with different sized and shaped obstacles, according to the size of the environment space. A number of global cameras are also installed on the ceiling. This test environment is illustrated in Fig. 14. By processing the acquired image, as seen in Fig. 15, the edge of the obstacle image is detected by Canny algorithm, then the entire contour image is drawn by OpenCV, and the image is expanded. Finally, the contour is filled with black and white, and the grid map is obtained.

Fig. 14. Experimental environment

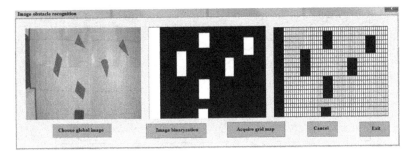

Fig. 15. Image processing

Using the grid map, the parameters of the ant colony algorithm are obtained through multiple experiments using the bacterial foraging algorithm [25]:

$\alpha = 10.075$, $\beta = 18.893$, $\rho = 0.019$, $Q = 132.631$. Under the group parameters, the ant colony algorithm is used to plan the path of the grid map, and the upper computer realizes the effect as shown in Fig. 16.

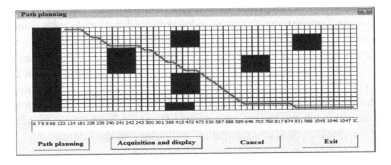

Fig. 16. Upper computer path planning

A comparison of the two routes is provided in Fig. 17. The red curve represents the theoretical path of the robot obtained by the ant colony algorithm, and the black curve represents the actual path of the robot obtained by template matching and positioning. The motion performance error of the robot is due to slippery test ground, and an inexpensive camera used in the experiment which experienced severe distortion. There is also an error in the matching positioning. Therefore, a certain deviation exists between the actual path of the obtained robot and the theoretical path. However, the general trend of the path is the same, which can truly reflect the movement trajectory of the robot.

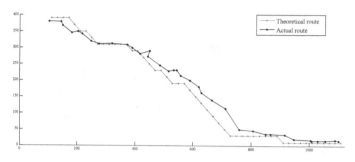

Fig. 17. Path contrast diagram (Color figure online)

6 Conclusions

Inspection robots are widely used in fields such as military reconnaissance and disaster relief, and the study of vision-based navigation systems for use in dangerous work environments has become a popular topic. In this paper, existing research of autonomous navigation systems for inspection robots based on distributed vision was discussed. Research and development of software and hardware for indoor inspection robots and navigation systems was then undertaken, and the key to path planning and image processing in visual navigation was investigated. The theory was then analyzed and experimentally studied, and the ant colony algorithm was chosen as the best algorithm for path planning. Test results demonstrated that performance of the navigation system software is stable, the host computer interactive interface software can accomplish the various operation instructions well, and the indoor inspection robot can undertake autonomous navigation inspection. These findings lay a foundation for improving the research of visual navigation technology in the future.

Acknowledgments. This work has been supported by grant of the National Key Research and Development Program of China (No. 2018YFC0808000) and the Priority Academic Program Development of Jiangsu Higher Education Institutions (PAPD), China.

References

1. Huang, H., Gartner, G.: A survey of mobile indoor navigation systems. In: Gartner, G., Ortag, F. (eds.) Cartography in Central and Eastern Europe. Lecture Notes in Geoinformation and Cartography, pp. 305–319. Springer, Heidelberg (2009). https://doi.org/10.1007/978-3-642-03294-3_20
2. Lambrinos, D., Möller, R., Labhart, T.: A mobile robot employing insect strategies for navigation. Robot. Auton. Syst. **30**(1), 39–64 (2000)
3. Kawaguchi, Y., Yoshida, I., Kurumatani, H.: Internal pipe inspection robot. Proc. IEEE **1**, 857–862 (1995)
4. Baus, J., Wahlster, W.: A resource-adaptive mobile navigation system. In: DBLP, pp. 15–22 (2002)
5. Phillips, J.B.: Magnetic navigation. J. Theor. Biol. **180**(4), 309–319 (1996)

6. Barshan, B., Durrant-Whyte, H.F.: An inertial navigation system for a mobile robot. In: IEEE/RSJ International Conference on Intelligent Robots and Systems, vol. 3, pp. 2243–2248 (1993)
7. Gui, Y., Guo, P., Zhang, H.: Airborne vision-based navigation method for UAV accuracy landing using infrared lamps. J. Intell. Rob. Syst. **72**(2), 197–218 (2013)
8. Pagnottelli, S., Taraglio, S., Valigi, P.: Visual and laser sensory data fusion for outdoor robot localisation and navigation. In: Proceedings of the IEEE, pp. 171–177 (2005)
9. Kurz, A.: Constructing maps for mobile robot navigation based on ultrasonic range data. IEEE Trans. Syst. Man Cybern. Part B Cybern. Publ. IEEE Syst. Man Cybern. Soc. **26**(2), 233–242 (1996)
10. Gao, Y., Liu, S., Atia, M.M.: INS/GPS/LiDAR integrated navigation system for urban and indoor environments using hybrid scan matching algorithm. Sensors **15**(9), 23286–23302 (2015)
11. Liu, W., Zhang, S., Fan, S.A.: visual navigation method of substation inspection robot. In: International Conference on Progress in Informatics and Computing. IEEE (2017)
12. Indelman, V., Gurfil, P., Rivlin, E.: Distributed vision-aided cooperative localization and navigation based on three-view geometry. In: Aerospace Conference, pp. 1–20. IEEE (2011)
13. Nishimura, H., Nonami, T.: Image processing device and image processing method in image processing device. J. Oral Rehabil. **8**(3), 203–208 (2018)
14. Yong, D.: Navigation for mobile robot based on uncertainty grid-map. Control Theory Appl. **23**(6), 1009–1013 (2006)
15. Guruji, A.K., Agarwal, H., Parsediya, D.K.: Time-efficient A* algorithm for robot path planning. Proc. Technol. **23**, 144–149 (2016)
16. Stentz, A.: Optimal and efficient path planning for partially-known environments. In: Hebert, M.H., Thorpe, C., Stentz, A. (eds.) Intelligent Unmanned Ground Vehicles, vol. 388, pp. 203–222. Springer, Boston (1997). https://doi.org/10.1007/978-1-4615-6325-9_11
17. Tu, J., Yang, S.X.: Genetic algorithm based path planning for a mobile robot. In: IEEE International Conference on Robotics and Automation, vol. 1, pp. 1221–1226 (2003)
18. Gutjahr, W.J.: Aco algorithms with guaranteed convergence to the optimal solution. Inf. Process. Lett. **82**(3), 145–153 (2002)
19. Shang, R., Jiao, L., Gong, M., Lu, B.: Clonal selection algorithm for dynamic multiobjective optimization. In: Hao, Y., et al. (eds.) CIS 2005. LNCS (LNAI), vol. 3801, pp. 846–851. Springer, Heidelberg (2005). https://doi.org/10.1007/11596448_125
20. Rais, H.M., Othman, Z.A., Hamdan, A.R.: Improved Dynamic Ant Colony System (DACS) on symmetric Traveling Salesman Problem (TSP). In: International Conference on Intelligent and Advanced Systems, pp. 43–48. IEEE (2008)
21. Brown, M., Lowe, D.G.: Automatic panoramic image stitching using invariant features. Int. J. Comput. Vision **74**(1), 59–73 (2007)
22. Lowe, D.G.: Distinctive image features from scale-invariant keypoints. Int. J. Comput. Vision **60**(2), 91–110 (2004)
23. Bay, H., Ess, A., Tuytelaars, T.: Speeded-Up Robust Features (SURF). Comput. Vis. Image Underst. **110**(3), 346–359 (2008)
24. Rublee, E., Rabaud, V., Konolige, K.: ORB: an efficient alternative to SIFT or SURF. In: International Conference on Computer Vision, pp. 2564–2571. IEEE (2012)
25. Li, P., Zhu, H.: Parameter selection for ant colony algorithm based on bacterial foraging algorithm. Math. Probl. Eng. **3**, 1–12 (2016)

Mobile Robot Autonomous Navigation and Dynamic Environmental Adaptation in Large-Scale Outdoor Scenes

Qifeng Yang[1,2,3,4(✉)], Daokui Qu[1,2,4], and Fang Xu[1,2,4]

[1] State Key Laboratory of Robotics, Shenyang Institute of Automation,
Chinese Academy of Sciences, Shenyang 110016, China
[2] Institutes for Robotics and Intelligent Manufacturing,
Chinese Academy of Sciences, Shenyang 110016, China
[3] University of Chinese Academy of Sciences, Beijing 100049, China
[4] Shenyang SIASUN Robot & Automation Co., Ltd., Shenyang 110168, China
yangqifeng@siasun.com

Abstract. In this paper, the problem of dynamic obstacle recognition and dynamic obstacle avoidance path planning for mobile robots in outdoor environment is studied. Based on the odometer data and the online matching algorithm of 3D laser scanning point clouds, the topological map and the global path planning are realized in this paper firstly. Based on the analysis of the geometric characteristics of obstacles, a novel approach of dynamic obstacle recognition method is presented. At the same time, a dynamic obstacle avoidance method based on the obstacle motion prediction is adopted to solve the reliable obstacle avoidance path planning problem of outdoor mobile robot. A series of experiments are conducted with a self-designed mobile robot platform in large-scale outdoor environments, and the experimental results show the validity and effectiveness of the proposed approach.

Keywords: Outdoor mobile robot · 3D map · Dynamic obstacle avoidance · Path planning

1 Introduction

Nowadays, robotics are very important for the development of science and technology. Driven by the demands of market and the developments of technology, mobile robot has become a hot research topic in the field of robotics. Due to the structural operating environments of the indoor mobile robots, there are many mature techniques on the indoor mobile robots, such as map construction, navigation and localization and path planning. Compared with the indoor mobile robots, the outdoor mobile robots encounter more complicated environments and have many challenging problems to be solved [1]. Among these challenges, the autonomous navigation and localization of the outdoor mobile robots are most outstanding [2].

There are several commonly used techniques for the local path planning of outdoor mobile robots, e.g. the path planning technique based on template matching, the path planning technique based on artificial potential field, the path planning technique based

© Springer Nature Switzerland AG 2019
H. Yu et al. (Eds.): ICIRA 2019, LNAI 11744, pp. 314–325, 2019.
https://doi.org/10.1007/978-3-030-27541-9_26

on map construction, and the AI-based path planning technique [3, 4]. Sezer and Gokasan proposed an improved artificial potential field algorithm to deal with the local minimum problem of the local path planning based on artificial potential field. However, the algorithm cannot pass narrow paths [5]. Based on artificial moment of force and the model of robot, Xu and Zhao proposed a method to drive the robot towards the potential field to avoid the obstacle. However, the method does not consider the global optimality of path planning [6]. Bayili and Polat proposed an improved A* algorithm. However, the algorithm is not optimal in the environments having many dynamic obstacles [7]. To increase the efficiency of path planning, Zhang, Ma, and Liu proposed a path planning algorithm combining framed-quadtree representation with hybrid-simulated annealing (SA) and ant colony optimization (ACO) algorithm called SAACO [8]. Andrey proposed an autonomous road extraction and navigation method by computing relative 3D position and orientation solution based on parameters of planar surfaces that are extracted from scan images [9]. Nevertheless, the method cannot effectively identify the fast moving dynamic obstacles.

This paper studies path planning for outdoor mobile robots to avoid the dynamic obstacles in the non-structural outdoor environments. Topological map construction and global optimal path planning are realized based on the data from the odometer and the 3D point cloud maps. An dynamic obstacle identification method is proposed based on geometrical feature analysis of the obstacles. Meanwhile, we present a dynamic obstacle avoidance method based on the obstacle motion prediction. The proposed methods can achieve autonomous navigation and dynamic obstacle avoidance for a high-speed mobile robot.

2 Large-Scale Outdoor 3D Environment Perception and Modelling Based on Laser Scanning

2.1 3D Point Cloud Data Acquisition

Laser sensors have been widely applied to mobile robots due to their precise measurement of distances and strong anti-interference ability. In outdoor environment, multi-line lasers are widely used to obtain the point cloud of the environment. However, the vertical resolution of multi-line lasers is limited due to the number limitation of laser beams. When the robot is moving at a low speed or at rest, multi-line lasers are unable to efficiently obtain the 3D data of the environment.

In this paper, the 3D point cloud information of the environment is obtained by a two-dimensional laser with rotating axis. The proposed method is characterized by dense point cloud data, and even when the robot is stationary, it can completely obtain 3D point cloud data of the environment. The process of obtaining 3D point cloud information by this method is as follows. First, the 2D laser sensors obtain the distance data from the same plane with it, thereby we can establish 2D contour point cloud. Second, as shown in Fig. 1, we add a rotation axis parallel to the scanning plane. The laser sensor rotates along the axis during the scanning process so as to obtain 3D point cloud data of the environment.

Fig. 1. 3D point cloud acquisition schematic

2.2   Construction of 3D Point Cloud Map

In this paper, we combine the 3D point cloud date obtained by the laser with the encoder odometer. This paper adopts the improved 3D-NDT [10] point cloud matching method and obtains the 3D high-precision map of outdoor scene after the close-loop processing. By matching two point clouds with intersecting regions, the relative position of the point cloud is calculated. And together with wheel odometer, a priori map is established. It is used as the basis of global path and local dynamic path planning. The steps of constructing the priori map are as follows.

1. Manipulate the robot to run in the experimental environment. As the robot moves, the 3D point cloud data obtained by the laser sensor and the wheel odometer are stored.
2. In a short time, the wheel odometer data is used as the relative position of point cloud data for point cloud storage.
3. After the robot has moved a certain distance, the current point cloud is matched with the stored point cloud for position so as to correct the deviation of the odometer.
4. With the operation of the robot, the environment point cloud with relative position scanned by the robot during the whole operation is obtained.
5. The closed-loop crossings in the environment is used as the adjustment nodes to correct the point cloud map.
6. The corrected point map is used as the priori map.

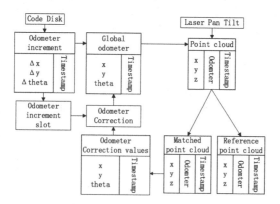

Fig. 2. The process of 3D point cloud adjustment

The correction process of the 3D point cloud map is shown in Fig. 2. The point cloud map generated by the above method is shown in Fig. 3. After being processed, it can be used as a basic reference for path planning in robot operation.

Fig. 3. The 3D laser points map

3   Mobile Robot Autonomous Navigation and Dynamic Environment Adaptation

3.1   Large-Scale Outdoor Topological Map Construction and Global Path Planning

Due to the large amount of the 3-D point cloud data, before the global path planning, the map shall be firstly processed by dimension reduction, that is, converted from 3-D to 2-D map. For all the 3-D point cloud data on the same horizontal coordinates, it is believed that there are obstacles that cannot be passed by the robot on this coordinate if point cloud exists between the height of the threshold H_L and H_H. Then we display the corresponding laser point at the corresponding coordinate on the 2-D map. Otherwise, it will be processed as empty area. H_L is determined by the highest obstacles on the ground allowed by the robot platform, while H_H is related to the height of the robot, which reflect the interference of the obstacles in the air. By further abstracting the 2-D map, we can obtain the robot walkable path map corresponding to the global environment, as shown in Fig. 4. The blue solid lines are the feasible global paths, the black points are the key nodes in the feasible paths, the green node is the current position, and the red node is the target position.

For navigation, a number of key nodes in the feasible region of the robot are selected as topology nodes of the map, and each topology node contains information such as the pose of the robot, the scanned point cloud, and the distance and orientation of its adjacent nodes, etc.

This paper considers two autonomous operation modes, one is to traverse topology nodes according to the task order, and the other is to carry out global path planning based on the strategy of shortest path evaluation between starting and target position according to the specific task. When the robot encounters obstacles that unable to be bypassed, the robot will search other feasible paths in the global path to move to the next target node and complete the task according to the shortest distance strategy.

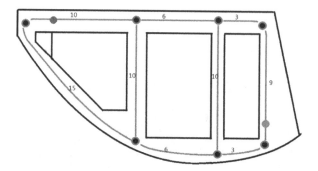

Fig. 4. Abstract representation of 2D Topological map (Color figure online)

3.2   Three-Dimensional Point Cloud Obstacle Identification

Before autonomous navigation the robot needs to distinguish "obstacle area" and "feasible area" in the surrounding environment. This can be done by analysing the point cloud data obtained from the 3D laser sensor in the robot systems. Note that directly analysing the laser data are inconvenient since the amount of these data are huge. To cope with this difficulty, we map these data to a two-dimensional grid located on the ground, then proceed identification based on the absolute height or relative height of the laser spot in the grid. If the height value of a grid is greater than a predefined threshold, we think that this grid is occupied by obstacles. For clarification, we depict the process in Fig. 5.

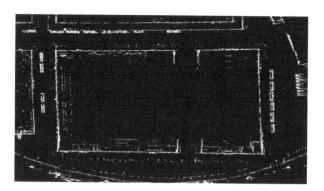

Fig. 5. An illustration of obstacle recognition with 3D laser

3.3   Dynamic Obstacle Recognition and Motion Trend Prediction

In factory area, the most typical dynamic obstacle is pedestrian. Thus, this paper investigates the dynamic pedestrian recognition based on obstacle clustering and closest leg matching. As we can see from Fig. 6, the robot successfully recognizes the multiple pedestrians walking side by side in front of the robot.

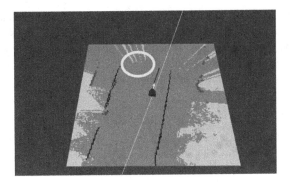

Fig. 6. Pedestrian identification

In the judgment of dynamic obstacle, the hollow object and the object whose cross section is a concave polygon are easily misjudged as dynamic. More specifically, the points of the obstacle scanned by the robot are different during the movement and because of the blind zone, the interference to the dynamic pedestrian detection is inevitable. Therefore, it is necessary to further process the determined dynamic grid according to the characteristics of the human leg. Figure 7 shows the leg features of 3 pedestrians in different states.

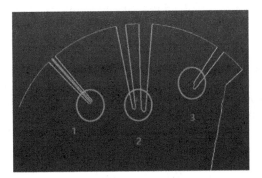

Fig. 7. An illustration of the leg feature

As shown in Fig. 7, there are three pedestrians from left to right. Note that the legs of pedestrians 1 and 2 are separated, while the legs of pedestrian 3 are overlapped. Therefore, to distinguish the legs are separate or overlapped, abstraction of the legs situation is necessary. Figure 8(a) depicts the abstraction of the overlap of the legs. Herein, the black dots denote the points scanned by laser. We first find point O which is closest to the laser. Then, with point O as origin, the laser incident point to point O as X-axis, the O-point perpendicular to this ray as Y-axis, a rectangular plane coordinate system is established. Based on this system, we need to construct a triangle ABC by traversing the laser points, then calculate $\angle CAB$ using cosine theorem. Finally, the case of overlapped legs can be indicated if only one point satisfies the maximum projection value of point A on X axis, and $\angle CAB$ is greater than the angle threshold; Otherwise, the separated legs are indicated. Under the case of separated legs, the shape in Fig. 8(b) can be obtained by dividing the legs. Whether the obstacles are legs or disturbances can be judged by performing Parabolic fitting ($Y = a*X^2 + bX$) on the coordinate points. If a satisfies the threshold interval, it is a human leg.

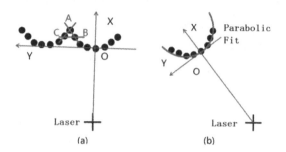

Fig. 8. Clustering analysis of the leg feature

To proceed, we need to match the identified legs with the nearest ones and cluster them into a specific pedestrian. Before this, the cluster center coordinates of the single-leg obstacles need to be calculated. In other words, the nearest leg matching problem is converted into the nearest plane point problem. In this paper, we find the closest plane point pair using the "divide and conquer" method. More specifically, if an independent pedestrian is indicated, the corresponding two points are deleted. Then, we re-find the nearest point pair in the remaining points. This process is repeated until the nearest point pair found does not satisfy the distance requirement.

It can be seen that the trajectory of pedestrian in a short time (1 s) is approximately straight and the number of received laser spots does not change much. Based on these observations, an evaluation function $F(i)$ of pedestrian matching is constructed. The evaluation function is as follows and can be used to evaluate the possibility of the same pedestrian.

$$F(i) = P(i) * G(i) \tag{1}$$

$$P(i) = \alpha/\pi \tag{2}$$

$$G(i) = (n_1 + n_3)/2n_2 \tag{3}$$

where a is the angle formed by the position of the obstacles in the three-frame raster image. if three positions are approximately connected as a straight line, then $P(i) = 1$; n represents the number of laser points in which the obstacles are hit in the three-frame image. The closer the evaluation function is to 1, the closer the obstacle point is to the same moving pedestrian, and then the speed and direction of the pedestrian can be determined.

3.4   Obstacle Avoidance Path Planning Based on Behavioral Intention

During the walking process, if there are obstacles e.g. pedestrians and cars, human will first analyze their movement intentions based on the historical trajectory and the current state. Then plan the next route according to the obtained movement intention of the obstacles. In this paper, we proposes a dynamic path planning method based on the movement intention of obstacles. As shown in Fig. 9, in the process of moving obstacles avoidance, the reliability and safety are improved by imitating the walking habits of people and analyzing the intention of moving obstacles. In the process of local path planning, the grid method is used to plan the local obstacle avoidance path. The moving intention of the dynamic obstacle reflects the occupation of the grid by the dynamic obstacle. As the basis for the local path planning of the obstacle, the robot carries out the shortest path planning in the grid map according to the current position and the target position on the basis of the local environment gridding. After obtaining the shortest path, a feasible path cluster is generated according to a certain distance in the feasible area between the obstacle and the roadbed.

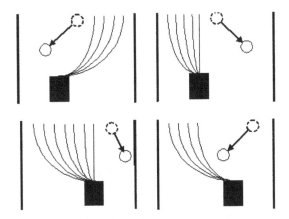

Fig. 9. Dynamic obstacle avoidance path planning

By analyzing the historical states of obstacles, the robot can estimate the speed of the obstacles and the direction and distance of the obstacles during the obstacle avoidance. Then, we do path planning considering the possible trajectory of dynamic obstacles. More specifically, by determining the path with the highest priority using energy-optimized strategy and judging the real-time state of moving obstacles, the robot operation is adjusted. In the case that no feasible path can be found because of obstacles, the robot changes to waiting mode or re-plans the global path. The details of local dynamic obstacle avoidance algorithm are as follows:

(1) Obtained 3D point cloud data in real time;
(2) Map 3D point cloud to 2D plane with height information, obtain all obstacles distributions, get all feasible areas, cluster analysis of 2D laser data and identify motion obstacles;

(3) Predict the behavior of obstacles, infer their directions and speed of motion, and give the interference area by the obstacles during the obstacle avoidance operation;

(4) Based on the behavior prediction of the dynamic obstacles, find all feasible trajectories and select the optimal one according to the energy-optimal strategy.

4   Experiments

4.1   Experimental Platform and Site

As shown in Fig. 10, the main body of the hardware platform adopts a rear-drive front-steering body, and the rear wheel is equipped with a photoelectric encoder, wheel odometer is to roughly estimate the position and posture of the robot. The top of the robot is equipped with a self-designed three-dimensional laser scanning platform, which is composed of a servo motor control system and two-dimensional laser sensor SICK LMS 511. The detection distance can reach 80 m. The laser scanning platform is used for dynamic obstacle identification and self-accurate positioning in navigation process. In addition, the robot is equipped with an industrial computer to collect sensor data, analyze environmental data and control the movement of the robot.

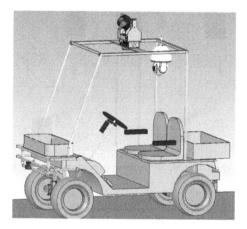

Fig. 10. The hardware platform of the mobile robot

In the hardware platform of the system, the three-dimensional laser scanning platform is the environment sensing sensor of the mobile robot, which is installed on the top of the robot. The laser scanning platform is the core module of the whole system, which is responsible for acquiring the three-dimensional point cloud data of outdoor large-scale environment. The laser platform will drive laser to swing back 250° from the lowest position by motor and collect the three-dimensional environment point cloud data. The collected point cloud data will be used to construct a three-dimensional

Fig. 11. Experimental environment

high-precision map of the robot's operating environment. In the process of robot operation, the collected data can also be used to determine the precise location of robot and collect information about static and dynamic obstacles. The speed of the robot platform can reach more than 3 m/s.

To verify the effectiveness of the proposed method, a series of forward and backward tests are carried out in the experimental site shown in Fig. 11. The experimental environment is a typical factory area with static obstacles such as vehicles and green areas, and dynamic obstacles such as pedestrians and vehicles. The area of the experimental area is more than 45,000 m².

4.2 Autonomous Environment Adaptation Experiment Results

In this paper, the continuous closed-loop autonomous navigation test is carried out in the experimental site shown in Fig. 12. The experimental content includes static obstacle avoidance test and dynamic pedestrian obstacle avoidance test. In the experiment, the designed robot is able to run autonomously at the highest speed of 3 m/s and can accurately identify pedestrians for automatic obstacle avoidance. The obstacle avoidance processes are presented in the figure below.

During the continuous 8-shape autonomous navigation test in the park, the robot can monitor the static and dynamic obstacles in real time and run autonomously along the given topological map in the prior map. As shown in Fig. 13, The blue points is the trajectory of the robot when building a priori map, and the red line is the actual trajectory collected by the robot during the 8-shape test. The actual trajectory of the robot is obtained by extracting static and dynamic obstacles in the environment through self-made three-dimensional laser platform according to the topological map, and making dynamic obstacle avoidance path planning.

Fig. 12. Dynamic obstacle avoidance experiment

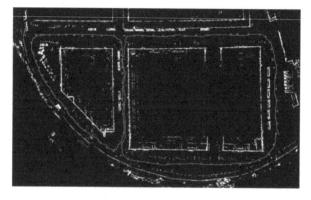

Fig. 13. Dynamic obstacle avoidance path planning trajectory (Color figure online)

5   Conclusion

This paper proposes a path planning strategy for mobile robots based on the analysis of geometric characteristics of the environment and pedestrian dynamic identification and dynamic obstacle movement prediction. The actual outdoor environment autonomous navigation experiment with a continuous 8-shape was carried out by using the mobile robot platform developed by ourselves. In the process of autonomous navigation test, the robot accurately identified the static and dynamic obstacles in the environment. And the local path planning of dynamic obstacle avoidance was carried out in real time by referring to the prior topological map. This test verifies the effectiveness and reliability of the navigation obstacle avoidance algorithm of the robot path planning method proposed in this paper.

References

1. Kümmerle, R., Ruhnke, M., Steder, B., et al.: Autonomous robot navigation in highly populated pedestrian zones. J. Field Robot. **32**(4), 565–589 (2015)
2. Mur-Artal, R., Montiel, J.M.M., Tardos, J.D.: ORB-SLAM: a versatile and accurate monocular SLAM system. IEEE Trans. Rob. **31**(5), 1147–1163 (2015)
3. Guernane, R., Achour, N.: Generating optimized paths for motion planning. Robot. Auton. Syst. **59**(10), 789–800 (2011)
4. Dakulović, M., Petrović, I.: Two-way D* algorithm for path planning and replanning. Robot. Auton. Syst. **59**(5), 329–342 (2011)
5. Sezer, V., Gokasan, M.: A novel obstacle avoidance algorithm: "follow the gap method". Robot. Auton. Syst. **60**, 1123–1134 (2012)
6. Xu, W.B., Zhao, J., Chen, X.B., et al.: Artificial moment method using attractive points for the local path planning of a single robot in complicated dynamic environments. Robotica **31**(8), 1263–1274 (2013)
7. Bayili, S., Polat, F.: Limited-damage A*: a path search algorithm that considers damage as a feasibility criterion. Knowl. Based Syst. **24**(5), 501–512 (2011)
8. Zhang, Q., Ma, J.C., Liu, Q.: Path planning based quadtree representation for mobile robot using hybrid-simulated annealing and ant colony optimization algorithm. In: Proceedings of the World Congress on Intelligent Control and Automation (WCICA), pp. 2537–2542. IEEE Press, Beijing (2012)
9. Andrey, S., Maarten Uijt, D.H.: Three-dimensional navigation with scanning ladars: concept & initial verification. IEEE Trans. Aerosp. Electron. Syst. **46**(1), 14–31 (2010)
10. Magnusson, M.: The three-dimensional normal-distributions transform — an efficient representation for registration, surface analysis, and loop detection. Renew. Energy **28**(4), 655–663 (2012)

Movement Analysis of Rotating-Finger Cable Inspection Robot

Changlong Ye[1(✉)], Jingpeng Li[1], Suyang Yu[1], and Guanglin Ding[2]

[1] Shenyang Aerospace University, Shenyang 110136, China
changlye@163.com
[2] Shenyang Equipment Manufacturing Engineering School,
Shenyang 110026, China

Abstract. The robot detection and maintenance routine of high-voltage cables are of great significance to the normal operation of electrical power system. Aiming at the problems of poor obstacle-crossing capability and insufficient drive capability to the inspection robot at present, a three-module rotating-finger cable inspection robot is developed, which can move over a long distance on the cable. The robot is composed of three standard rotating-finger modules in series, each of which can cross obstacles via staggered rapid movement of the rotating-finger. According to the structure and movement characteristics of the modular robot, the static model of the robot under various obstacle-crossing attitudes is established, and the detailed static analysis of the movement process is carried out to obtain two relationships: the relationship among drive force, friction force, and permissible gradient, the relationship between robot configuration and obstacle-crossing attitude. The obstacle-crossing movement is optimized to realize the high-efficiency obstacle crossing. The correctness of the above analysis is verified by experiments and motion simulation.

Keywords: Inspection robot · Rotating-finger · Obstacle crossing

1 Introduction

In daily life, the stable operation of high-voltage cables is of vital importance, which directly affects people's life. Under the influence of environmental conditions, human factors and aging equipments, the damage of high voltage cables have caused great inconvenience to people's lives, such as damage to cables and leakage of electricity. It is necessary to inspect the cables regularly to ensure the safe and stable operation of high-voltage cables. Numerous scholars at home and abroad have carried out extensive research in the field of inspection robot. Sawada et al. from Tepco in Japan developed the first high-voltage cable inspection robot in the world [1]. TRC in USA developed the cantilever wire inspection robot [2]. Nakamura et al. from Tokyo Hosei University in Japan developed a snake-like inspection robot [3]. Institut de recherche d'Hydro-Qukbec in Canada developed the LineScout robot [4–10]. Kansai Electric Power and Hibot jointly developed the Expliner inspection robot [11], et al. Meantime, there are some inspection robots with relatively mature technology in China. Professor Wu Gongping from Wuhan University of Hydraulic and Electrical Engineering developed

© Springer Nature Switzerland AG 2019
H. Yu et al. (Eds.): ICIRA 2019, LNAI 11744, pp. 326–337, 2019.
https://doi.org/10.1007/978-3-030-27541-9_27

the aerial wire inspection robot [12, 13]. Shenyang Institute of Automation developed a 500 kV ground wire inspection robot [14], et al. All of the above robots adopt 2 or 3-mechanical arm suspended structure to achieve dislocation movement and rotation, realizing crossing the obstacle. But the movement of these robots has some short-comings. The TRC robot and the LineScout robot are too limited in their ability to cross general obstacles on the cable. The Expliner robot and the 500 kV ground wire inspection robot are not stable enough in the process of obstacle crossing.

Aiming at the above problems such as poor obstacle-crossing capability and insufficient drive capability, the movement performance of the three-module rotating-finger robot was analyzed based on the developed model, and the optimized mechanism was verified by simulation and experiments to make its movement stable and efficient.

2 Robot Mechanism

2.1 Working Environment

High voltage cables are usually equipped with electric power fittings such as suspension strings, suspension clamps and pdz etc. to ensure transmission security and reliability. In the process of robot inspection, the electric power fittings become obstacles for inspection, as shown in Fig. 1. According to the characteristics of robot working environment, a rotating-finger cable inspection robot is developed [15].

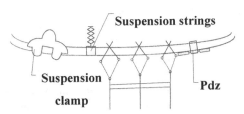

Fig. 1. Route diagram of cable inspection

2.2 Robot Mechanism

Based on Bionics Principles, the rotating-finger cable inspection robot is designed and developed to simulate the climbing action of firefighters hanging ropes upside down, as shown in Fig. 2. The robot is composed of three same rotating-finger climbing modules in series, as shown in Fig. 3.

Fig. 2. Fireman's rope climbing upside down to rescue

Fig. 3. Overall configuration of the robot

The rotating-finger climbing module of the robot consists of a moving part and an obstacle-crossing part. The moving part consists of a drive motor (motor 1), a transmission shaft, synchronous belts, a set of bevel gears and rotating-finger rollers. The rotation of the transmission shaft is driven by motor 1, which drives the bevel gears to rotate through the synchronous belt, and finally drives rollers to roll along the cable forward or backward. The obstacle-crossing part is composed of a drive motor (motor 2), a coupling, nut screw pair, connecting rods and rollers. Motor 2 drives the lead-screw nut through the coupling to move up or down, driving the connecting rod 1 and connecting rod 2 to form a crank slider mechanism. Rollers and connecting rod 1 rotate around a fixed axis, so that the open-close action is operated by the rotating-finger which realizes the robot's obstacle crossing. Polyurethane rollers with good abrasion resistance are used in the contact part between the roller and the cable to improve the robot's moving performance on the cable.

However, the opening and closing of the rotating-finger during the movement of the robot will make the robot oscillate greatly, resulting in poor motion stability. In order to make the robot stable in motion, the mechanism was optimized by adding the structure of passive roller into the overall mechanism of the robot, so that the rotating-finger and the passive roller could keep three-point contact with the cable during the motion of the robot, which enhanced the motion stability and safety performance of the robot without the risk of tipping over.

3 Analysis of Climbing Performance of Robot

After the optimization of the mechanism, motor 2 is controlled to drive the rotating-fingers holding the cable. The rotating-finger is subjected to greater static friction force to overcome the component of the gravity, enabling the robot to climb the cable with greater inclination.

When motor 2 drives the rotating-finger to exert the stress F_c on the cable, in the process of climbing, the equations of the static can be got as follows.

$$\mu(3mg + F_c)\cos\theta \geq 3mg\sin\theta$$
$$\theta \leq \arctan\left(\mu + \frac{\mu F_c}{3mg}\right) \tag{1}$$

It can be seen that the climbing performance of the robot depends on the value of F_c and the friction coefficient μ when the rotating-finger is in the closed state. By the controlling variable method, the friction coefficient μ is chosen as constant to analyze the holding force F_C of single-module rotating-finger on the cable from the static point of view.

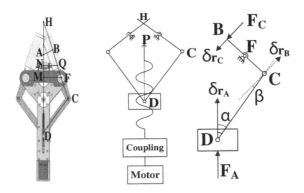

Fig. 4. Force analysis diagram of single module mechanism

As shown in Fig. 4, $a = \overrightarrow{FC}, b = \overrightarrow{CD}, c = \overrightarrow{BF}$. It can be deduced from the virtual work principle:

$$F_A \cdot \delta_{r_A} = F_C \cdot \delta_{r_C} \tag{2}$$

$$\begin{cases} \delta_{r_A} \cdot \cos \alpha = \delta_{r_B} \cdot \cos \beta \\ \dfrac{\delta_{r_B}}{\delta_{r_C}} = \dfrac{\overrightarrow{FC}}{\overrightarrow{FB}} \end{cases} \tag{3}$$

$$F_A = P = \frac{2\pi \eta T}{L}$$

Among them, P is the thrust in the direction of screw drive. L is the lead of the screw. δ is the screw transmission efficiency. T is the torque of the motor.

By solving the above simultaneous equations,

$$\frac{\delta_{r_A}}{\delta_{r_C}} = \frac{\cos \beta}{\cos \alpha} \cdot \frac{a}{\overrightarrow{FB}} \tag{4}$$

$$F_C = \frac{\cos \beta}{\cos \alpha} \cdot \frac{a}{\overrightarrow{FB}} \cdot \frac{2\pi \eta T}{L} \tag{5}$$

From the Eq. (5), it can be known that the value of F_C is related to the value of α, β and $\overrightarrow{FB}$. The relationship between $\alpha, \beta, \overrightarrow{FB}$ and F_C is derived.

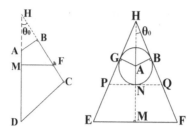

Fig. 5. Structure parameter diagram of single module mechanism

As shown in Fig. 5, $\overrightarrow{EF} = 2\overrightarrow{MF} = 2h$, $d = \overrightarrow{NM}$. It can be obtained by geometric principle:

$$\angle D = \alpha = \arcsin \frac{h + a \cdot \sin \theta_0}{b} \tag{6}$$

$$\beta = \frac{\pi}{2} - \theta_0 - \arcsin \frac{h + a \sin \theta_0}{b} \tag{7}$$

$$c = \frac{h - r \cos \theta_0}{\sin \theta_0} \tag{8}$$

$$\theta_0 = \arctan \frac{h^2 - r^2}{\sqrt{h^2 + 2dr + d^2} + h^2(r + d)} \tag{9}$$

Combining (5), (6), (7) and (8), the relations of F_C, a, b, h and θ_0 can be got as

$$F_C = \frac{\sin\left(\theta_0 + \arcsin \frac{h + a \sin \theta_0}{b}\right)}{\cos\left(\arcsin \frac{h + a \sin \theta_0}{b}\right)} \cdot \frac{a \sin \theta_0}{h - r \cos \theta_0} \cdot \frac{2\pi\eta T}{L} \tag{10}$$

After the simultaneous Eqs. (1), (9) and (10), it can be seen that the limit value of permissible gradient θ is related to the radius r of cable. The Origin software is used to conduct a simulation study on the limit value of permissible gradient θ and the diameter D of the cable for viewing convenience. The diagram of the relationship between them is drawn, as shown in Fig. 6.

It can be seen from Fig. 6 that the relationship between the limit value of permissible gradient and cable diameter is non-linear. As the cable diameter increases, the limit value decreases first, and then increases. When D is 13.6 mm, there is the minimum limit value, which is 58.47°.

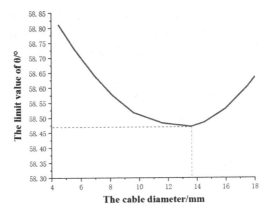

Fig. 6. Diagram of the relationship between the cable diameter D and the limit value of θ

4   Analysis of Robot's Performance of Crossing Obstacles

The process of obstacle crossing can be divided into three stages: first, middle and last. The static analysis model of robot system is implemented, as shown in Fig. 7.

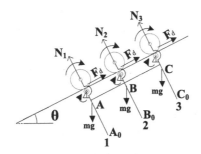

Fig. 7. Mechanical basic model of robot's obstacle crossing

The equations of the static can be got as follows.

$$\begin{cases} F_{d1,2} \geq 3mg \, \sin(\theta - \delta) \\ F_{d1,2} - \mu(N_1 + N_2 + N_3) = 0 \\ F_{d3} \geq \mu(N_1 + N_2 + N_3) - 3mg \sin(\theta - \delta) \\ N_1 - G_1 \cdot \cos(\theta - \delta) - 2F_c \cdot \cos\theta_0 = 0 \\ N_2 - G_2 \cdot \cos(\theta - \delta) - 2F_c \cdot \cos\theta_0 = 0 \\ N_3 - G_3 \cdot \cos(\theta - \delta) - 2F_c \cdot \cos\theta_0 = 0 \\ G_1 + G_2 + G_3 - 3mg = 0 \\ N_2 \cdot L - mg \cdot (l_A + l_B + l_C) = 0 \end{cases} \qquad (11)$$

Among them, $F_{d1,2}$ is the driving force of the robot in the first or middle stage. F_{d3} is the driving force of the robot in the last stage. N1, N2, N3 is the stress which roller 1,

2, 3 subjected to. δ is the included angle between the robot and the cable. l_A, l_B, l_C is the distance from the center of rotation of the robot to the point A, B, C. G1, G2, G3 is the weight assigned to each module by the robot. F_c is the force exerted by the rotating-finger. θ is the angle between the cable and the horizontal plane. θ_0 is the included angle between the rotating-finger and the vertical plane.

In the Eq. (11), the constraint, $F_{d1,2} \geq 3mg \sin(\theta - \delta)$, ensures that the robot has enough power to climb up along the cable. Other equations are the basic conditions for static equilibrium.

4.1   Static Analysis of Performance of Crossing Obstacles

In the First Stage
When the sensor detects an obstacle in front, the robot performs collision detection firstly, and then roller 3 releases the cable, with roller 1 and 2 driving. Roller 1 is in the closed state and roller 2 is in the half-closed state which adjusts the angle conveniently. N3 = 0, G3 = 0, as shown in Fig. 8.

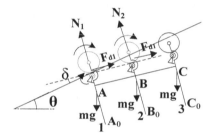

Fig. 8. The 1st obstacle-crossing stage

The equations of the static can be got as follows.

$$\begin{cases} F_{d1} = \mu[3mg \cos(\theta - \delta) + 4F_C \cdot \cos\theta_0] \\ N_1 = 3mg \cos(\theta - \delta) - \frac{mg \cdot (l_A + l_B + l_C)}{L} + 4F_C \cdot \cos\theta_0 \\ N_2 = \frac{mg \cdot (l_A + l_B + l_C)}{L} \\ N_3 = 0 \end{cases}$$

Under the constraint condition, the robot can climb up and complete the pre-obstacle preparation.

In the Middle Stage
Roller 1 and 3 are the driving wheels which do not subject to F_C. N2 = 0, G2 = 0, δ = 0, as shown in Fig. 9.

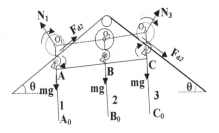

Fig. 9. The middle obstacle-crossing stage

The equations of the static can be got as follows.

$$\begin{cases} F_{d2} = \mu(3mg \cos\theta + 4F_C \cdot \cos\theta_0) \\ N_1 = N_3 = \frac{3mg}{2\cos\theta} \\ N_2 = 0 \end{cases}$$

In the Last Stage
Roller 1 releases the cable, with roller 2 and 3 driving. Roller 3 is in the closed state and roller 2 is in the half-closed state which adjusts the angle conveniently. N1 = 0, G1 = 0, as shown in Fig. 10.

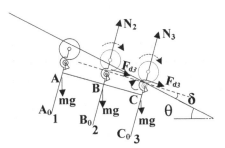

Fig. 10. The last obstacle-crossing stage

The equations of the static can be got as follows.

$$\begin{cases} F_{d3} \geq \mu[3mg \cos(\theta - \delta) + 4F_C \cdot \cos\theta_0] - 3mg \sin(\theta - \delta) \\ N_1 = 0 \\ N_2 = \frac{mg \cdot (l_A + l_B + l_C)}{L} \\ N_3 = 3mg \cos(\theta - \delta) - \frac{mg \cdot (l_A + l_B + l_C)}{L} + 4F_C \cdot \cos\theta_0 \end{cases}$$

Under the constraint condition, the robot can move and complete the post-obstacle preparation.

4.2   Analysis of Obstacle-Crossing Distance

When the mechanism is in the 1st obstacle-crossing stage, the relationship between the obstacle-crossing distance and δ is studied to analyze the capability of crossing obstacles of the robot, as shown in Fig. 11.

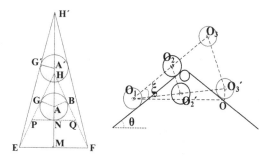

Fig. 11. Diagram of the limit value of the obstacle-crossing distance

Among them, $l = \overrightarrow{H'N}$, $l_0 = \overrightarrow{H'E} = \overrightarrow{H'F}$, $2L_0 = \overrightarrow{O_1O_3} = \overrightarrow{O_1O'_3}$. It can be obtained by geometric principle:

$$L_C = \overrightarrow{O_1O} = 2L_0 \cdot \cos(\theta - \delta) = 2L_0 \cdot \cos\left(\theta - 2\arcsin\left(\frac{l - r - \frac{r \cdot l_0}{h}}{2L_0}\right)\right)$$

The limit value of obstacle-crossing distance L_C is related to θ and r. According to the above analysis, the Origin software is used to conduct a simulation study on the limit value of obstacle-crossing distance of the robot. The diagram of the relationship between them is drawn, as shown in Fig. 12.

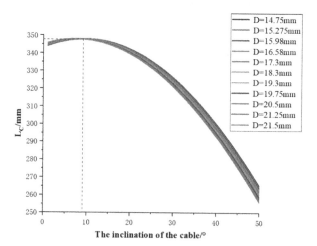

Fig. 12. Diagram of relationship between L_C and the inclination of the cable

It can be seen from Fig. 12 that the relationship between the limit value of obstacle-crossing distance and the inclination of the cable is non-linear. As the inclination increases, the limit value decreases first, and then increases. When the inclination approaches 10°, there is the maximum limit value, which is approximately equal to the whole length of the robot. The limit value of obstacle-crossing distance is 348 mm.

5 Experiments

Aluminium cable steel reinforced LGJ-50/8, the cable diameter of which is 9.6 mm, used as high-voltage cables is adopted in the experimental environment. The suspension insulator string is used as obstacles of cable.

Figure 13(a) shows the pre-obstacle-crossing stage of the robot. In the process of climbing, when the sensor detects an obstacle in front, the robot performs collision detection firstly, and then roller 1 releases the cable, with roller 2 and 3 driving. Roller 3 is in the closed state and roller 2 is in the half-closed state. The robot maintains a stable state under the combined action of the passive roller and the rotating-finger hanging on the cable. In this state, the robot moves along the cable to the position shown in Fig. 13(b). At this time, roller 2 is in front of the obstacle.

Figure 13(c) shows the middle obstacle-crossing stage of the robot. The rotating-finger 1 is driven to be closed first. When roller 1 successfully crosses the obstacle and grabs the cable on the other side, roller 2 releases the cable, with roller 1 and 3 driving.

Figure 13(d) shows the post-obstacle-crossing stage of the robot. The robot moves along the cable. When roller 2 successfully crosses the obstacle and grabs the cable on the other side, roller 3 releases the cable, with roller 1 and 2 driving. Roller 1 is in the closed state and roller 2 is in the half-closed state. The robot maintains a stable state under the combined action of the passive roller and the rotating-finger hangs on the cable.

Fig. 13. Diagram of the experiment

6 Conclusions

Based on the bionics principle, an optimized rotating-finger cable inspection robot is developed. Through the force analysis and simulation experiment carried out on the climbing stage and several main obstacle-crossing stages of the optimized mechanism, the relationship between the driving force and the inclination of the cable, the relationship between the friction force and the radius of cable, the relationship between the robot configurations and the obstacle-crossing distance are all obtained. The simulation results show that the relationship between the limit value of permissible gradient and cable diameter is non-linear. When D is 13.6 mm, there is the minimum limit value of permissible gradient is 58.47°. The relationship between the limit value of obstacle-crossing distance and the inclination of the cable is non-linear. When θ is 10°, the limit value of obstacle-crossing distance is 348 mm. The experimental results show that the robot can cross obstacles such as insulator strings, et al.

Future work will be focused on optimizing the mechanism to improve the environmental adaptability of the robot and conduct in-depth kinematic analysis to study the movement characteristics of the robot.

Acknowledgment. This paper is supported by Natural Science Foundation of Liaoning Province, China. (No. 20170540704 and No. 20180520033).

References

1. Sawada, J., Kusumoto, K., Maikawa, Y., et al.: A mobile robot for inspection of power transmission lines. IEEE Trans. Power Deliv. **6**(1), 309–315 (1991)
2. Robots repair and examine live lines in severe conditions. Electrical World, (United States) **203**(5) (1989)
3. Kobayashi, H, Nakamura, H, Shimada, T.: An inspection robot for feeder cables–basic structure and control. In: Proceedings of the 1991 International Conference on Industrial Electronics, Control and Instrumentation - IECON 1991, 28 October 1991–1 November 1991, pp. 992–995 (1991)
4. Montambault, S, Pouliot, N.: The HQ LineROVer: contributing to innovation in transmission line maintenance. In: ESMO 2003 Proceedings; The Power is in Your Hands, 6 April 2003–10 April 2003, pp. 33–41 (2003)
5. Montambault, S., Pouliot, N.: LineScout technology: development of an inspection robot capable of clearing obstacles while operating on a live line. In: ESMO 2006 - IEEE PES 11th International Conference on Transmission and Distribution Construction, Operation and Live-Line Maintenance, 15 January 2006–19 October 2006 (2006)
6. Montambault, S, Pouliot, N.: Hydro-Québec's power line robotics program: 15 years of development, implementation and partnerships. In: International Conference on Applied Robotics for the Power Industry, pp. 1–6 (2015)
7. Montambault, S., Pouliot, N., Lepage, M.: On the latest field deployments of LineScout technology on live transmission networks. In: International Conference on Applied Robotics for the Power Industry, pp. 126–127 (2013)
8. Pouliot, N., Montambault, S.: Field-oriented developments for LineScout technology and its deployment on large water crossing transmission lines. J. Field Robot. **29**(1), 25–46 (2012)

9. Pouliot, N., Richard, P.L., Montambault, S.: LineScout technology opens the way to robotic inspection and maintenance of high-voltage power lines. IEEE Power Energy Technol. Syst. J. **2**(1), 1–11 (2015)
10. Richard, P.L., Pouliot, N., Montambault, S.: Introduction of a LIDAR-based obstacle detection system on the LineScout power line robot. In: IEEE/ASME International Conference on Advanced Intelligent Mechatronics, pp. 1734–1740 (2014)
11. Debenest, P., Guarnieri, M., Takita, K., et al.: Expliner - robot for inspection of transmission lines. In: 2008 IEEE International Conference on Robotics and Automation, ICRA 2008, 19 May 2008–23 May 2008, pp. 3978–3984 (2008)
12. Wu, G., Cao, H., Xu, X., et al.: Design and application of inspection system in a self-governing mobile robot system for high voltage transmission line inspection. In: 2009 Asia-Pacific Power and Energy Engineering Conference, APPEEC 2009, 27 March 2009–31 March 2009. Chinese Society for Electrical Engineering; IEEE Power and Energy Society; Scientific Research Publishing; Wuhan University (2009)
13. Wu, G., Dai, J., Guo, Y., et al.: Small running vehicle with automatic surmount obstacles on high voltage transmission line. Water Conserv. Electr. Power Mach. (01), 46–49+54 (1999)
14. Sun, C., Wang, H., Wang, L., et al.: An improved obstacle navigation method for ultra-high voltage power line inspection robot. Robot **04**, 379–384 (2006)
15. Ye, C., Yan, F., Jiang, C., et al.: A modular high-voltage inspection robot with the finger-wheeled mechanism. J. Shenyang Aerosp. Univ. **35**(02), 28–34+40 (2018)

Autonomous Indoor Mobile Robot Exploration Based on Wavefront Algorithm

Chunhua Tang, Rongchuan Sun[✉], Shumei Yu, Liang Chen,
and Jianying Zheng

School of Mechanical and Electric Engineering, Soochow University,
Suzhou 215006, China
sunrongchuan@suda.edu.cn

Abstract. Autonomous' exploration is an important part of mobile robots. In an unknown environment, if a mobile robot wants to complete a task, the robot must be able to explore the environment. This paper proposes a new exploration strategy based on the wavefront algorithm. The wavefront algorithm is used to find the closest frontier point in very short time for the mobile robot. After determining the next frontier point, the mobile robot moves to the frontier point according to the path planned by the wavefront algorithm, which is the shortest. The exploration task is completed when there are no frontier points in the map. Finally, the exploration strategy is tested using the Robot Operating System (ROS). Simulation experiments show that the exploration based on the wavefront algorithm can find the frontier points rapidly and ensure the integrity of the exploration environment.

Keywords: Exploration · Wavefront algorithm · Frontier points ·
Path planning

1 Introduction

Autonomous robot exploration is an important part of the intelligent mobile robot function. When the mobile robot performs a task in an unknown environment, it is necessary to model surrounding environment. After the mobile robot gets a map of the surrounding environment, the robot can complete some specific tasks quickly and accurately. In order to explore the entire environment, the mobile robot needs to be constantly guided to the junction of the known and unknown areas of the map. The points at the junctions are called the frontier points.

In order to direct the mobile robot to an unknown area, all exploration algorithms are looking for frontier points. When many frontier points are found, the optimal point is selected as the frontier point of the next exploration according to the judgment condition. There are usually two ways to find frontier points. The first way is to find the frontier points by means of image processing. This method requires traversing the whole map. If the map is large, finding frontier points will cost a lot of computation and time. Yamauchi [1] was the first to propose the frontier-based exploration method. The algorithm navigates the mobile robot to the unknown area as much as possible to collect environmental information. Finding the frontier points in the algorithm is the

© Springer Nature Switzerland AG 2019
H. Yu et al. (Eds.): ICIRA 2019, LNAI 11744, pp. 338–348, 2019.
https://doi.org/10.1007/978-3-030-27541-9_28

core idea of the current exploration strategy and is widely used. But this way of finding frontier points needs to traverse the entire map. Therefore, the amount of computation is large. Latombe et al. [2] proposed the Next Best View (NBV) method. The frontier points found by this method balance the size of the unknown area and the distance of the current robot position to the frontier point. These two standards determine the best frontier point. Vallvé et al. [3] considered the reduction of robot pose entropy and map entropy to improve the accuracy of mapping. The pose and map interact with each other. This is why it is difficult to build accurate maps. Bai et al. [4] proposed a new method for predicting mutual information using Bayesian optimization. After several iterations, Bayesian optimization gives the optimal candidate perceptual action.

The second method is a random search exploration strategy. For example, Umari et al. [5] proposed a new exploration strategy based on Rapidly-exploring Random Trees (RRT) [6, 7]. The frontier points in the environment can be detected by the RRT algorithm. To speed up the detecting of the frontier points, the algorithm uses both local trees and global trees to detect frontier points. The growth of RRT trees is random. The advantage of random exploration strategy is to speed up the discovery of the frontier points. However, if the map has many corners and the width of the border is small, the growth of the RRT tree is limited, which leads to inefficiency in finding the frontier points, and even RRT tree cannot converge. Randomness may also result in ignoring near frontier points.

In general, the first step in both exploration algorithms is to find the frontier points in the map. Then, the optimal frontier point is selected according to the requirements. However, in complex environments, the efficiency of existing methods for finding frontier points is not too high. In addition, in order to move the robot to the frontier point, an additional path from the current position of the mobile robot to the frontier point is required. This step increases the amount of computation and exploration time.

This paper presents a new strategy based on wavefront algorithm [8] for detecting frontier points. The wavefront algorithm is a path planning algorithm. This algorithm is used to plan the path from the starting point to the target point. The wavefront algorithm spreads layer by layer from the target point to the starting point. The wavefront algorithm has two processes. The first process is to reach the starting point. The second process is the planning path. When the wavefront algorithm is used for exploration, the first process of the wavefront algorithm is used to find the frontier points, and the second process of the wavefront algorithm is used to plan a path to the frontier points. In the process of searching for the frontier points, the frontier points can be found rapidly. The path is also the shortest.

The implementation of exploration strategy is based on ROS framework. There are three steps in the whole exploration process. In the first step, a two-dimensional grid map is obtained by Gmapping algorithm [9, 10]. Gmapping algorithm is Simultaneous Localization and Mapping (SLAM) [11] algorithm. There are occupied areas, free areas and unknown areas on the map. In the second step, the first process of the wavefront algorithm is used to find the frontier point according to the map. In the third step, the mobile robot is guided to the frontier point by the path planned by the second process of the wavefront algorithm. After the whole map is traversed and no frontier points are found, the task of exploring the map is completed.

This paper is organized as follows. Section 2 introduces the structure of exploration based on wavefront algorithm. Section 3 describes the whole exploration process in detail. The simulation and practical experiments are given in Sect. 4. Finally, the conclusion of this paper is in Sect. 5.

2 Exploration Framework

The autonomous robot exploration consists of three parts: mapping, frontier point finding and path planning. In order to ensure the accuracy of the map, it is necessary to use the technology of SLAM. By selecting the Gmapping algorithm, a two-dimensional (2D) grid containing occupied, free, and unknown information can be obtained. When there is map information, the wavefront algorithm quickly finds the closest frontier point to the robot based on the information of the two-dimensional grid map. Finally, the mobile robot continues to collect environmental information by reaching the frontier point according to the path planned by the wavefront algorithm.

Figure 1 shows the framework of our exploration strategy. The whole exploration process has three modules, namely SLAM module, frontier point finding module and path planning module. The SLAM module implements localization and mapping functions, and provides map information for frontier point finding module and the path planning module. The frontier point finding module is used to find the frontier point of the next exploration and provides a series of grid Cartesian coordinates for the path planning module. The path planning module implements the fixed point navigation function and guides the mobile robot to the frontier points one by one.

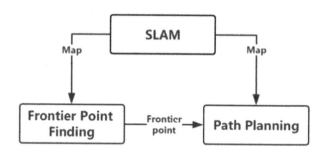

Fig. 1. Exploration framework

The SLAM module is implemented using the ROS 'gmapping' package [12]. The module that finds the frontier points is a ROS node written in C++. The path planning module uses the ROS 'move_base' package [13]. The path is not planned by 'move_base' package. The 'move_base' package is used to move between the two grids.

The definitions related to the exploration algorithm are listed as follows (The noun at the beginning of a lowercase letter is a variable, and the noun at the beginning of a capital letter is a function).

mapArray: This is a two-dimensional array that holds grid map data. The array consists of −1 (unknown), 0 (free) and 100 (occupied). The number of rows and columns of an array is the same as the number of rows and columns of a grid map.

x, y: The x is the number of rows in a two-dimensional array. The y is the number of columns in a two-dimensional array.

stopExploration: This is the sign to judge the end of the exploration.

costMap: A two-dimensional array generated by the wavefront algorithm. The number of rows and columns of an array is the same as the number of rows and columns of a grid map. The information stored in the array is the value of each grid after exploring with the wavefront algorithm.

pathCoord: This is an array that holds the world coordinates of a series of grids. These grids are the moving paths of the robot.

InflatMap: This is a function to inflate the map.

CheckGrid: This is a function that implements the judgment of the grid value.

Path: This is a function that implements path planning. The return value of the function is the world coordinates of a series of grids.

Algorithm 1 lists the outline of the whole exploration process. In 1st line, the Gmapping algorithm gives the map information. In 2nd line, the obstacles in the map are inflated. In 4th to 13th lines, one exploration is completed. In 14th to 15th lines, if there are no frontier points in the map, the exploration process ends. In 17th line, the path to the frontier point is planned. In 18th line, the mobile robot moves to the frontier point.

Algorithm 1. Exploration Process

```
1.   mapArray ← Gmapping algorithm gets map;
2.   mapArray ← InflatMap(mapArray);
3.   while there are frontier points in the map
4.      while not find frontier points
5.         if (CheckGrid(mapArray,x,y))=100;
6.            continue;
7.         else if CheckGrid(mapArray,x,y)=-1;
8.            break;
9.         else if costMap!=0;
10.           continue;
11.        end if
12.     create wavefront and assign values to a grid
13.     end while
14.     if stopExploration=1;
15.        break;
16.     end if
17.     pathCoord ← Path(costMap);
18.     The mobile robot moves to frontier point;
19.  End while
```

3 Exploration Process Description

3.1 Gmapping Algorithm

Gmapping is a particle filtering algorithm based on Rao-Blackwellized. Gmapping can be used to build indoor map in real time. In a small scale environment, the amount of computation required is small and the map accuracy is high.

Gmapping algorithm outputs a two-dimensional grid map. The probability of each grid is represented by a number from 0 to 1. Then, the occupancy probability value is converted to −1, 0, 100. As shown in Fig. 2(a), the value of each grid represents occupancy information: −1 for unknown (gray), 0 for free (white), and 100 for occupied (black). With the map information, the task of finding the frontier points can be realized.

When the mobile robot moves in the environment, the size of the robot cannot be ignored. The mobile robot should avoid collision with obstacles. Therefore, the robot should keep a distance from the obstacles. Inflating map is an effective solution. The exploration process is performed on a two-dimensional grid. The Gmapping algorithm outputs the occupation information of each grid. The coordinates of the points in the Cartesian coordinate system need to correspond to the corresponding grid number. In the actual conversion process, due to the numerical rounding problem, the grid number of the coordinate point may have an error with the actual calculated serial number. In addition, the frontier points found with the wavefront algorithm tend to be at the corners. The situation is shown in Fig. 2(b). When the mobile robot plans a path based on the wavefront algorithm, the robot moves along the wall to the frontier points. This way of movement has risk. Therefore, in order to solve the above problem, the obstacle grid is usually inflated outward by several grids. The number of inflated grids α is

$$\alpha = d/r + c \tag{1}$$

Here d is the diameter of the robot and r is the resolution of the map. The c is an optional parameter. If the value of c is greater, the mobile robot will be farther away from obstacles. However, if the value of c is too large, the robot will ignore the smaller channel space. These places will not be explored. Therefore, the value of c is determined by the specific environmental structure.

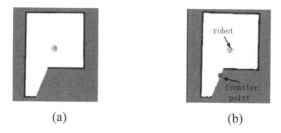

(a)   (b)

Fig. 2. (a) Grid map. (b) Location of frontier point

3.2   Wavefront Algorithm

The wavefront algorithm is a path planning algorithm for breadth-first search. The initial map is shown in Fig. 3(a). Firstly, the occupied grid (black grid) value is set to 1. Next, the value of the target point grid is set to 2. The waveform is created starting from the target point grid. All adjacent grid values with grid value 2 are set to 3. The value of the occupied grid does not change. The value of the adjacent grid with a grid value of 3 is set to 4. The waveform is diffused all the time, and the value of each layer of the grid increments until the grid of the starting point is encountered. Finally, starting from the starting point, the path is planned in descending order of grid values. The result is shown in Fig. 3(b).

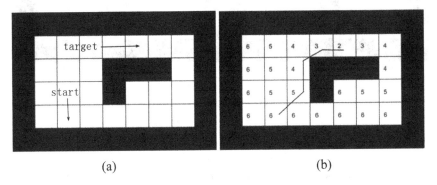

(a)   (b)

Fig. 3.   (a) Finding frontier. (b) Planning path

3.3   Finding Frontier Points by Wavefront Algorithm

The starting point of the wavefront algorithm is the position of the current robot. The target point is the nearest frontier point. However, the frontier point is unknown at first. The wavefront algorithm explores all around by layer-by-layer diffusion. The wavefront algorithm stops when the encountered grid is unknown. The frontier point is the target point. The speed at which the frontier point is found is very fast. Because wavefront algorithm does not traverse the whole map. In addition, the speed at which the wavefront algorithm finds the frontier points is independent of the complexity of the map. No matter how complex the map is, the time to find the frontier point is basically the same. Sometimes the first encountered grid is not taken as the frontier point of the next exploration. But a threshold is set. For example, the unknown grid encountered on the 15th is considered a frontier point. The advantage of doing this is to avoid frontier points at the corners. The results of the exploration are shown in Fig. 4(a).

3.4   Path Planning

Path planning refers to planning a path from the starting point to the target point. When the mobile robot moves to the frontier point, one exploration is completed. A very mature path planning algorithm package 'move_base' has been integrated into the

ROS. But planning the path with the 'move_base' package requires extra time and increased computation. The advantage of using the wavefront algorithm for exploration is that you can directly plan a shortest and safe path. Starting from the found frontier point grid, a path is planned in the order in which the grid number is descended. The planned path is as shown in Fig. 4(b).

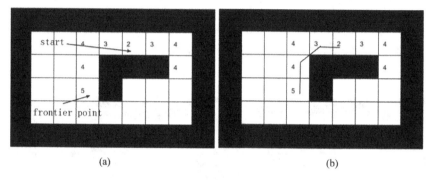

(a)   (b)

Fig. 4. (a) Finding frontier point. (b) Path

4   Simulation and Experiment

The exploration method based on wavefront algorithm is compared with the exploration method based on RRT algorithm. In the same simulation environment, two exploration algorithms were implemented respectively. The time at which the frontier points are found and the exploration time of the entire map are the objects of comparison. Simulation experiments were carried out in two environments. In practical experiment, with the exploration based on wavefront algorithm, mobile robots can perform exploration tasks.

4.1   Environments Used in Simulation

The simulation was performed using a Gazebo simulator [14]. The simulator can simulate the real environment rapidly and realistically and facilitate the verification of various algorithms.

Experiment results were compared in two simulation environments. The first environment, shown in Fig. 5(a), has a length of approximately 10.15 m, a width of approximately 7.77 m, and an area of approximately 78.86 m^2. The mobile robot has a radius of 0.178 m. The resolution of the map is 0.05. The laser has a scan range of 20 m. The second environment, shown in Fig. 5(b), has a length of about 9.72 m, a width of about 9.70 m, and an area of about 94.28 m^2. Figure 5(c) and (d) show the resulting two-dimensional occupied grid map.

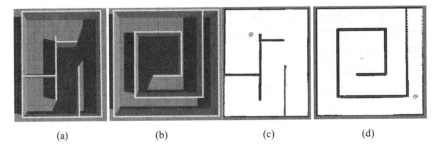

Fig. 5. Simulation environments and grid map

Each simulation environment is explored using a wavefront algorithm and an RRT algorithm respectively. The time to find the frontier point and the time to explore the entire environment are recorded.

The experiment process of the second environment is shown in Fig. 6. Figure 6(a) is the initial position of the mobile robot and the current map information. Figure 6(b) is the result of the first exploration. The red small squares in the figure are the found frontier points. This result also verifies that the frontier points generally appear at the corners. Figure 6(c) shows the mobile robot reaching the frontier point and finding the second frontier point. Figures 6(d), (e), (f) and (g) are the results of the next exploration. Figure 6(h) is the final exploration map.

The experiment results of the simulation are shown in Fig. 7. The first line is the method of exploration. The last line is the total time of exploration. The middle lines are the time to find the frontier point. The unit of time is second. Figure 7(a) is the experiment result of the first environment. Figure 7(b) is the experiment result for the second environment.

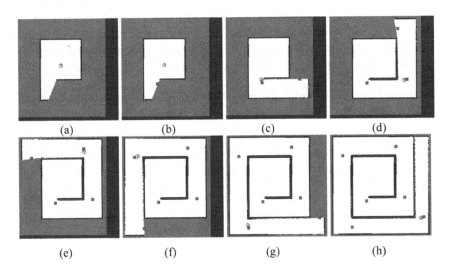

Fig. 6. The exploration process of second environment (Color figure online)

	Wavefront	RRT
Point 2	0.7	4
Point 3	1.0	3
Point 4	1.2	5
Point 5	0.5	6
Total Time	132	147

(a)

	Wavefront	RRT
Point 2	1.5	9
Point 3	1.6	20
Point 4	1.9	2
Point 5	1.0	13
Point 6	2.1	18
Total Time	275	332

(b)

Fig. 7. Experimental results

4.2 Simulation Results

The first environment is a simple environment with several rooms. The second environment is a spiral environment with many corners in the environment.

In Fig. 7, the first line of the table shows the method of exploration. The middle lines of the table shows the time it takes to find the nth frontier point. The last line of the table shows the time it takes to explore the whole environment.

The simulation results show that the speed of searching for the frontiers point based on wavefront algorithm is fast. The exploration of the base RRT takes more time to find the frontier points. Sometimes, the efficiency is even low. In the second simulation environment, the exploration based on the wavefront algorithm takes less time to explore the whole map.

4.3 Experiment in True Environment

The platform we used to validate the method, shown in Fig. 8(a), is TurtleBot 2. TurtleBot 2 is currently the most popular low cost, open source educational and research robot. The laser is RPLIDAR A1. The RPLIDAR A2 is a low cost sensor and is suitable for indoor robot SLAM applications. The scanning angle of the RPLIDAR A2 is 360° and the effective distance of the laser is 8 m. The real environment of the experiment is shown in Fig. 8(b), (c) and (d). The grid map obtained after the exploration is shown in Fig. 8(e).

From the experiment results, the proposed method can complete the exploration task. The mobile robot constantly looks for frontier points in the map until the whole environment is explored.

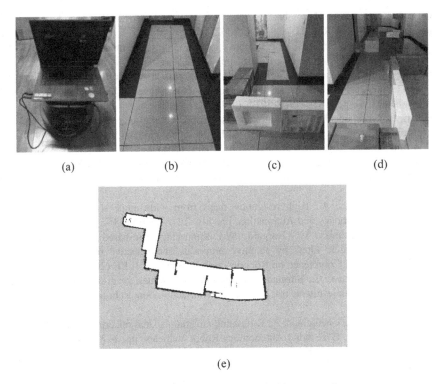

(a)   (b)   (c)   (d)

(e)

Fig. 8. True environment and experiment result

5   Conclusion

This paper presents a new exploration strategy using wavefront algorithm. Wavefront algorithm is used to find frontier points. The method of finding the frontier points does not need to traverse the entire map, and can find the next frontier point rapidly. This is more efficient than finding a frontier based on the RRT algorithm. At the same time, wavefront algorithm is a path planning algorithm. A path is created after the frontier point is found. However, this grid-by-grid movement is less efficient. Sometimes it will take longer than the RRT-based exploration to complete the entire exploration task based on the wavefront algorithm. In addition, since the frontier points are mostly at the corners, the path planned based on the wavefront algorithm is close to the wall. Therefore, future work can be considered in path optimization to achieve a smoother movement of the robot and a safer path.

References

1. Yamauchi, B.: A frontier-based approach for autonomous exploration. In: 1997 IEEE International Symposium on Computational Intelligence in Robotics and Automation, pp. 146–151, IEEE (1997)

2. Gonzalez-Banos, H.H., Latombe, J.C.: Navigation strategies for exploring indoor environments. Int. J. Robot. Res. **21**, 829–848 (2002)
3. Vallve, J., Andrade-Cetto, J.: Mobile robot exploration with potential information fields. In: European Conference on Mobile Robots, pp. 222–227 (2013)
4. Bai, S., Wang, J., Chen, F., Englot, B.: Information-theoretic exploration with Bayesian optimization. In: 2016 IEEE/RSJ International Conference on Intelligent Robots and Systems (IROS), pp. 1816–1822. IEEE (2016)
5. Umari, H., Mukhopadhyay, S.: Autonomous robotic exploration based on multiple rapidly-exploring randomized trees. In: 2017 IEEE/RSJ International Conference on Intelligent Robots and Systems (IROS), pp. 1396–1402. IEEE (2017)
6. Lavalle, S.M.: Rapidly-exploring random trees: a new tool for path planning (1999)
7. LaValle, S.M., Kuffner, J.J.: Randomized kinodynamic planning. Int. J. Robot. Res. **20**, 378–400 (2016)
8. Moravec, H., Elfes, A.: High resolution maps from wide angle sonar. In: 1985 IEEE Conference on Robotics and Automation, pp. 116–121. IEEE (1985)
9. Grisetti, G., Stachniss, C., Burgard, W.: Improving grid-based SLAM with Rao-Blackwellized particle filters by adaptive proposals and selective resampling. In: 2005 IEEE International Conference on Robotics and Automation. IEEE (2005)
10. Grisetti, G., Stachniss, C., Burgard, W.: Improved techniques for grid mapping with Rao-Blackwellized particle filters. In: 2007 IEEE Transactions on Robotics, pp. 34–46. IEEE (2007)
11. Smith, R., Self, M., Cheeseman, P.: Estimating uncertain spatial relationships in robotics. In: Cox, I.J., Wilfong, G.T. (eds.) Autonomous Robot Vehicles, pp. 167–193. Springer, New York (1990). https://doi.org/10.1007/978-1-4613-8997-2_14
12. Gmapping ROS package.Internet. http://wiki.ros.org/gmapping
13. Move_base ROS package.Internet. http://wiki.ros.org/move_base
14. Gazebo simulator.Internet. http://gazebosim.org/. http://wiki.ros.org/move_base14. Gazebosimulator.Internet

Multi-robot Path Planning for Complete Coverage with Genetic Algorithms

Rongchuan Sun[1], Chunhua Tang[1], Jianying Zheng[2], Yongzheng Zhou[1], and Shumei Yu[1(✉)]

[1] School of Mechanical and Electric Engineering, Soochow University, Suzhou, China
yushumei@suda.edu.cn
[2] School of Rail Transportation, Soochow University, Suzhou, China

Abstract. Complete coverage path planning (CPP) generates a path following which a robot can cover all free spaces in an environment. Compared with single robot CPP, multi-robot CPP gains both efficiency and challenges. In large scale environments, one robot is not competent to the coverage task, such as doing cleaning work in airports, supermarkets, shopping malls, etc. The proposed approach firstly creates a global map with a simultaneous localization and mapping (SLAM) method, and partitions the map into a set of small sub-regions according to the environment's topological structure. Then the multi-robot CPP formed a multiple traveling salesman (mTSP) problem, where a genetic algorithm (GA) allocates the sub-regions to each robot and gives the robots their visiting orders to the sub-regions. This paper mainly focuses on how to model the multi-robot CPP problem with mTSP and how to solve the task allocation problem with an improved GA algorithm offline. Two SLAM-based environmental experiments validated the proposed method's feasibility and efficiency in terms of time consumption.

Keywords: Cleaning robots · Complete coverage path planning · Multi-robot system · Task allocation · Genetic algorithm

1 Introduction

Complete coverage path planning (CPP) generates a path following which a robot can cover all of the free spaces in the environments, while traditional path planning methods generates the path between the starting and ending points. The CPP has a wide range of utilization in robotic domains, such as cleaning robots, lawn mowers, among others. At present, CPP methods for single robot have been studied by researchers, such as boustrophedon cellular decomposition [1], Morse-based cellular decomposition [2], wavefront algorithm [3], spanning tree coverage (STC) algorithm [4], neural network-based coverage algorithm [5], viewpoint-resampling and tour optimization algorithm [6], and so on. With both the increasing complexity of traditional tasks and the extension of new application scenes, a single robot can hardly meet some complicated situations in large-scale environments, such as superstores, shopping malls, the departure room

© Springer Nature Switzerland AG 2019
H. Yu et al. (Eds.): ICIRA 2019, LNAI 11744, pp. 349–361, 2019.
https://doi.org/10.1007/978-3-030-27541-9_29

of airports, etc. Consequently, the CPP technology of multi-robot has received more and more focus. Combining the advantages of a multi-robot system and the CPP technology, using multiple robots can not only decrease the time to finish the tasks, but also increase the whole system's robustness and the flexibility of executing tasks.

There have been numerous multi-robot CPP methods proposed in the literature. Most of them are developed as extensions of traditional single-robot CPP methods. Janchiv et al. proposed a CPP method that can be used for multiple cleaning robots by combining the exact cellular decomposition method, the template based method, and the heuristic algorithm [7]. Their method takes consideration of region segmentation results, based on which templates are used to decrease shifts when robots execute the coverage tasks. However, their method does not study the task allocation method and all of the robots execute tasks without planning in advance. Rekleitis et al. proposed a CPP method for multiple robots on the basis of the boustrophedon cellar decomposition [8]. In their method, robots are divided into two groups: exploration robots and coverage robots. The formers are used to achieve the boundary of the environment, while the lattes perform a raster scanning to cover the target space. Their main concern about the multi-robot is how to use a robot formation to minimize repeat coverage. Hazon et al. proposed the multi-robot spanning tree coverage (MSTC) out of a single-robot STC algorithm to solve the multi-robot CPP problem [9,10]. In their method, the standard single-robot STC is firstly to build a coverage path of the whole environment. Based on the generated path, all the robots are distributed to different positions to cover the environment simultaneously. However, the method is inefficient because of the lack of task allocation mechanism. Based on the single-robot BA* algorithm [11], Viet et al. proposed the BOB approach in which the robots can coordinately cover local regions by boustrophedon motions [12]. This method uses local interactions to coordinate all the robots' movements. When a robot falls into a "deadlock" (a situation in which a robot is surrounded by obstacles or covered cells), an intelligent backtracking mechanism is used to help the robots find the next positions to be covered.

Although the above methods can ensure that the robots completely cover a target region with planned paths, the lack of effective task allocation mechanisms leads to inefficiency because that they do not make full use of the advantages of a multi-robot system. The task allocation problem raised in multi-robot CPP asks the questions that how to allocate sub-regions to robots and how to plan a route for each robot that can do coverage work one sub-region after another, and finally return back to the starting positions in shortest time.

In this paper, an efficient task allocation approach was proposed for a multi-robot CPP problem to enable all of the robots do coverage work as soon as possible. The algorithm proposed in this paper divides the whole coverage work into three steps. Firstly, the map of the target workspace was divided into several sub-regions according to the environment's topological structure. Then, the task allocation algorithm is used to distribute these sub-regions to the robots. Finally, each robot covers their allocated regions, respectively. The proposed method is an off-line method using a priori environmental map. This is reasonable in many scenarios where the robots need to do coverage work daily in a mostly invariant environment, i.e. doing cleaning works in shopping malls.

The rest of this paper is organized as follows: Sect. 2 describes the mathematical model of multi-robot CPP problem. Section 3 presents the proposed method on how to allocate coverage tasks to robots. Section 4 presents experimental results, and Sect. 5 concludes the paper.

2   Problem Definition

2.1   Problem Description

The multi-robot task allocation (MRTA) for multi-robot CPP is how to assign a set of coverage tasks to several robots. In this paper, the whole workspace are denoted by an environmental model $\mathbb{M}$, which will be divided into several sub-regions $M_i\{i = 1, 2, ..., n\}$ and covered by a group of mobile robots $\mathbb{R} = \{R_j, j = 1, 2, ..., m\}$. Each robot R_j can cover one or more sub-regions, which are considered as the tasks assigned to them. Suppose the robot R_j needs to cover n_j sub-regions. Then its task is denoted by $T_j = \{M_{i_k}, k = 1, \cdots, n_j\} \subseteq \mathbb{M}$. Here, T_j is a sorted list, meaning that a robot will start from its origin to cover all of the sub-regions in T_j in order, and return back to the starting position after it has covered the last sub-region M_{n_j}. For all of the robots, the whole task allocation scheme is denoted as $T = \{T_1, T_2, \cdots, T_m\}$.

2.2   Mathematical Model

There have been many methods proposed to model the MRTA problem, such as the fair division problem [18], the optimal assignment problem [19], the multi-objective optimization problem [20], the multiple traveling salesman problem (mTSP) [21–24], etc. In this section, mTSP models a multi-robot CPP problem that how to minimize the total cost for all of the salesmen to visit their assigned cities, given as follows:

$$\check{T} = \operatorname*{arg\,min}_{\forall T}\ C^{TSP}(T) \tag{1}$$

where,

$$C^{TSP}(T) = \sum_{j=1}^{m} TSP(T_j) \tag{2}$$

Here, T_j is a task assignment scheme for the jth salesman, while T is the whole task assignment scheme for all of the salesmen. $TSP(T_j)$ is an evaluation function giving the cost of jth salesman to visit all of its assigned cities T_j, and $C^{TSP}(T)$ is the whole cost for all of the salesmen.

We develop a genetic algorithm (GA) to solve the mTSP problem with a cost function (2) as the basis and prerequisite for the genetic operators. The population in GA makes an evolution by selecting the chromosomes with high fitness, i.e. low cost.

Compared with mTSP, in addition, to consider the cost of traveling among each sub-regions, the multi-robot CPP problem needs to consider the cost of covering each sub-regions in extra. In this paper, we make the following definition:

Definition 1. The cost of completing the coverage tasks for the robots is consist of both the cost of traveling among each sub-regions and the cost of covering these sub-regions.

Therefor, the cost of completing the tasks for single robot can be regarded as C_j:

$$C_j(T_j) = TSP(T_j) + \sum_{M_{i_k} \in T_j} Cover(M_{i_k}) \tag{3}$$

Here, $Cover(\bullet)$ means the cost for a robot to cover the free spaces in its assigned sub-regions. Then the whole cost for all of the robots to cover the environment is given by:

$$C^{CPP}(T) = \sum_{j=1}^{m} C_j(T_j) \tag{4}$$

Although the multi-robot CPP problem can be solved to achieve an optimal solution that having a shortest total distance in the manner of mTSP described in formulas (1)–(2), it is likely that one of the routes is too long, while the others are too short. According to the buckets effect, the coverage efficiency of a multi-robot system depends on the most inefficient robot which consumes the most time. So a natural choice of the cost function is the maximum time consumed by all of the robots:

$$J(T) = \max\{C_1, C_2, \cdots, C_m\} \tag{5}$$

By minimizing the target function (5), a solution of multi-robot CPP problem is achieved. This is a classical *min-max* problem. Furthermore, the solution potentially balances the robots' workload. The differences among the robots' workload will be as small as the maximum one is small.

The optimal task allocation scheme $\check{T}$ can be solved by:

$$\check{T} = \arg\min_{T} \ J(T) \tag{6}$$

s. t.

$$\bigcup_{j=1}^{m} T_j = \mathbb{M} \tag{7}$$

$$T_i \cap T_j = \emptyset, \quad \forall i, j \in \{1, 2, \cdots, m\}, i \neq j \tag{8}$$

Similar to the mTSP problem, the multi-robot CPP problem can be considered as NP-hard as well. Compared with the traditional mTSP problem, the cost to be minimized in the multi-robot CPP problem is related to not only the length of path following which the robots visit all the sub-regions, but also the length of path following which the robots doing coverage works in each sub-region.

3   GA Based Task Allocation for Multi-robot CPP

The genetic algorithm (GA) [25] is adopted to solve the task allocation problem in multi-robot CPP. The selection and mutation operators are used in this paper, while the crossover operator is not used because that it will produce ill-state chromosomes which do not satisfy the constraints.

3.1   Coding

The natural number coding method is used to represent the feasible solutions of task assignment. If the global map are divided into n sub-regions, then the chromosomes are coded in the form of $\langle k_1, k_2, \cdots, k_n \rangle$ $(k_i \in \{1, 2, \cdots, n\})$, which is a permutation of the natural numbers ranging from 1 to n. To distinguish the sub-routes for m robots embedded in a chromosome, $m-1$ separators are used to segment a chromosome into m parts, which are corresponding to the m robots, respectively.

For example, assuming that the global environment is divided into 10 sub-regions and 3 robots will be used to carry out the complete coverage task on these sub-regions. Then these sub-regions will be coded with natural numbers ranging from 1 to 10, respectively. And 2 separators will be used to segment a chromosome into 3 parts for these robots. In this paper, these separators' position that denoting the last sub-region for a robot are saved in a vector. The separator of the last robot is not saved in the vector as it is considered as n in default. For example, a chromosome $\langle 1, 6, 2, 4, 9, 3, 5, 10, 7, 8 \rangle$ together with a separator vector $[3, 7]$ will represent the coverage order for these 3 robots, namely: Robot 1 $\langle 0 \to M_1 \to M_6 \to M_2 \to 0 \rangle$, Robot 2 $\langle 0 \to M_4 \to M_9 \to M_3 \to M_5 \to 0 \rangle$, and Robot 3 $\langle 0 \to M_{10} \to M_7 \to M_8 \to 0 \rangle$. Here, 0 denotes the starting position for all of the robots.

3.2   Fitness Function

A natural choice of fitness function is using a variant of the cost function (5), e.g. its reciprocal:

$$fitness(T) = \frac{1}{J(T)} \tag{9}$$

Because the robot's starting position and ending position in each sub-region is unpredictable, the cost functions $TSP(\bullet)$ and $Cover(\bullet)$ cannot be calculated accurately. According to the characteristics of multi-robot CPP, we tender the following assumptions.

Assumption 1. All robots are homogeneous with equal capabilities, e.g. speed, size of the shape, etc. Furthermore, they complete their tasks independently without mutual interferences.

Assumption 2. The cost of visiting a set of sub-regions (the function $TSP(\bullet)$) is approximately proportional to the length of the path that is planned between the centers of the sub-regions. The cost of executing coverage work (the function $Cover(\bullet)$) is approximately proportional to the area of free spaces in the sub-region. Both of the two cost functions are with the same metric.

Given the above two assumptions, Fig. 1 illustrates the calculation of the two cost functions. The cost of the robot R_j visiting the subregions $T_j = \{M_1, M_5, M_n\}$, namely $TSP(T_j)$, is proportional to the actual distance needed to travel all these sub-regions, as the green curves in Fig. 1. The cost of the robot covering the sub-regions T_j, namely $Cover(M_1) + Cover(M_5) + Cover(M_n)$, is proportional to the area of free spaces in these sub-regions.

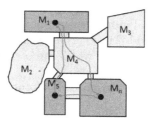

Fig. 1. An example of cost functions $TSP(\bullet)$ and $Cover(\bullet)$.

3.3   Selection Operator

The selection operator keeps a small number of chromosomes in the current generations from the parent generations. One of the implementations is the commonly known roulette-wheel method. In order to prevent the optimal solutions from being destroyed in the process of evolution, the optimal maintenance strategy is used to maintain the effectivity of genetic evolution. A small number of superior chromosomes including the best one in each generation are copied to the next generation.

3.4   Mutation Operators

To avoid precocious convergence in a sub-optimal solution, three genetic mutation operators are used on the parent chromosomes to produce the children chromosomes.

(1) Inversion operator

The inversion operator reorders one or more gens in a chromosome. The positions and number of the gens to be inversed are selected randomly. For example, as shown in Fig. 2(a), the chromosome $\langle 1, 6, 3, 8, 9, 4, 5, 10, 7, 2 \rangle$ represents a coverage order of a set of sub-regions. Now, the sub-regions from the 3rd to the 7th is reversed to produce a new chromosome $\langle 1, 6, 5, 4, 9, 8, 3, 10, 7, 2 \rangle$.

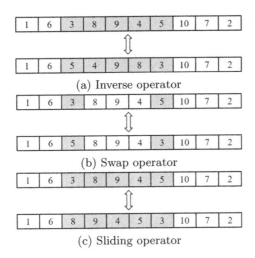

Fig. 2. Examples of three genetic mutation operators.

(2) Swap operator

The swap operator exchanges a pair of gens' position in a chromosome. The positions of the gens to be exchanged are selected randomly. For example, as shown in Fig. 2(b), the chromosome ⟨1, 6, 3, 8, 9, 4, 5, 10, 7, 2⟩ represents a coverage order of a set of sub-regions. After the swap operator, the 3rd sub-region is swapped with the 7th sub-region to produce a new chromosome ⟨1, 6, 5, 8, 9, 4, 3, 10, 7, 2⟩.

(3) Sliding operator

The sliding operator moves gens locating in a sliding window in circulation, namely the later gens move forward while the genes that are moved out the sliding window are compensated to the rear. Both the window's size and the sliding length are generated randomly. For example, as shown in Fig. 2(c), the chromosome ⟨1, 6, 3, 8, 9, 4, 5, 10, 7, 2⟩ represents a coverage order of a set of sub-regions. Now, the sub-regions from the 3rd to the 7th is moved circularly to produce a new chromosome ⟨1, 6, 8, 9, 4, 5, 3, 10, 7, 2⟩.

3.5 Separator Operator

By using the above three mutation operators, one chromosome from the parent generation will produce four ones in current generation including itself. These four chromosomes are generated by using the separator vector inherited from their parent chromosome.

The separator operator will randomly generate a new separator vector of size $1 \times (m - 1)$. Its elements are different integers and ranging from 1 to $n - 1$. By applying the new separator to the chromosomes produced after mutation operation, another four new chromosomes will be generated.

4 Experiments

4.1 Experiment 1

Figure 3 shows the first experimental environment and its grid map. The free areas, the occupied areas, and the unknown areas are drawn in white, black, and gray, respectively.

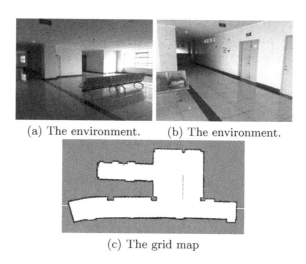

(a) The environment.   (b) The environment.

(c) The grid map

Fig. 3. The first experimental environment (a–b) and its grid map (c).

In the single robot CPP experiment, the robot started from the bottom right corner of the grid map and performed the boustrophedon motions to cover the environment. The coverage result is shown in Fig. 4, in which the red lines denote the coverage paths. When all of the free areas in the grid map has been covered, the robot returned to the starting position (the black square in Fig. 4).

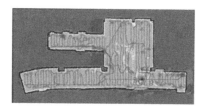

Fig. 4. The coverage trajectories of single robot in the first experiment.

In the multi-robot CPP experiment, the grid map was divided into 7 sub-regions, as shown in Fig. 5(a). Then according to the task assignment method proposed in this paper, the 7 sub-regions were divided into 3 groups. As shown in Fig. 5(b), there are three kinds of colors. Each robot is corresponding to a color tone and they cover these sub-regions in order from the lighter color to the darker one. When all robots have completed the coverage task, they returned back to the starting position. The process of coverage was finished after the last robot has returned back. As shown in Fig. 5(c)–(e), the red lines, the green lines and the blue lines denote the coverage trajectory of Robot R_1, Robot R_2 and Robot R_3, respectively.

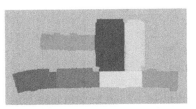
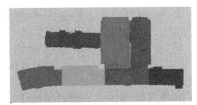

(a) The result of map segmentation   (b) The result of task assignment

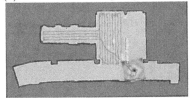
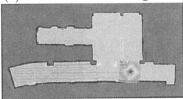

(c) The coverage trajectory of robot R_1 (d) The coverage trajectory of robot R_2

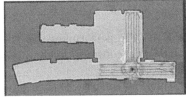

(e) The coverage trajectory of robot R_3

Fig. 5. The coverage trajectories of multi-robot in the first experiment. (Color figure online)

4.2 Experiment 2

Figure 6 shows the second environment and its grid map. As same as the first experiment, at first, the coverage experiment of single-robot was carried out. The Turtlebot2 performed the boustrophedon motions to cover the entire workspace (Fig. 7). In the experiment of multi-robot (Fig. 8), the global grid map was divided into 8 sub-regions. Then, these sub-regions were divided into 3 groups. After that, three robots performed the boustrophedon motions to cover these sub-regions respectively. Finally, when all of the robots have completed their assigned tasks, they returned back to the starting position.

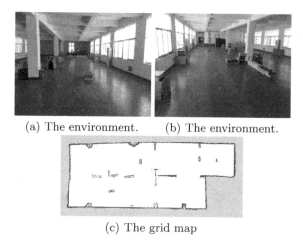

(a) The environment. (b) The environment.

(c) The grid map

Fig. 6. The second experimental environment (a–b) and its grid map (c).

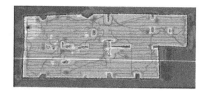

Fig. 7. The coverage trajectories of single robot in the second experiment.

This section compares the CPP performance of the multi-robot with the single-robot. Table 1 shows the time consumption and path length for each robot to cover the environment.

In the first experiment, the time consumed by the single robot is three times of the maximum one in the multi-robot system, while the path length of the single robot is a little less than three times of the maximum one in the multi-robot system. It can conclude that the proposed method greatly reduces the time consumption for the CPP problem. Although the time is not reduced with the robot number linearly, it shows that the proposed multi-robot CPP method can allocate the CPP workload in balance to all of the robots with a consideration that the environment cannot be divided evenly due to its inherits topological structure. Furthermore, when taking consideration that the target function to be minimized is the maximum cost rather than a balanced degree in formula (5), the proposed method's merit is validated once more that the time consumption and path lengths of each robot in the multi-robot system are without too much discrepancy.

In the second experiment, the efficiency of the multi-robot system is a little lower than the first experiment. The maximum time consumption in the multi-robot system is more than a half of the one consumed by a single robot, while

(a) The result of map segmentation   (b) The result of task assignment

(c) The coverage trajectory of robot R_1 (d) The coverage trajectory of robot R_2

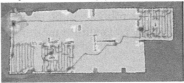

(e) The coverage trajectory of robot R_3

Fig. 8. The coverage trajectories of multi-robot in the second experiment.

Table 1. Completion time and the length of path of two methods in two environments

			Task areas (m^2)	Time (min)	Path length (m)
Exp. 1	Multi-robot	Robot 1	84.98	12.3	187.16
		Robot 2	57.08	8.87	130.95
		Robot 3	80.36	10.61	164.68
	Single robot		222.42	38.55	463.58
Exp. 2	Multi-robot	Robot 1	105.56	23.38	218.02
		Robot 2	88.26	22.58	212.74
		Robot 3	88.95	27.95	236.26
	Single robot		282.77	52.83	600.48

the maximum path length is about a third of the single robot. As in the first experiment, it can still conclude that the proposed method improves the multi-robot system's efficiency in terms of time consumption and path length.

5 Conclusion and Future Work

This study introduced a GA based task-allocation method for a multi-robot CPP problem in large-scale environments. It has a broad application prospect in the aspect of cleaning works in large scale SLAM-based environments, such as departure room of airports, supermarkets, shopping malls, etc. The main contributions of this paper are modeling the multi-robot CPP problem with a mTSP model and solving the task allocation problem with an improved GA algorithm. Compared with single robot CPP methods, the proposed method enables using a team of robots to cover a large scale environment quickly. Two SLAM-based experiments have validated the proposed method's feasibility and efficiency.

Currently, the maximal detectable range of the sensor Rplidar A1 used in the experiments is about 4 meters. This limits the experimental environment's scale. In future work, more powerful sensors, such as SICK LMS series of laser rangefinders, will be adopted to enable the robots to work in larger environments. Furthermore, the proposed approach assumed that all of the robots are homogeneous that they have the same size of the shape, similar motion abilities, etc. In future work, heterogeneous robots will be researched to completely cover a large SLAM-based environment to facilitate more real working scenarios.

References

1. Choset, H.: Coverage of known spaces: the boustrophedon cellular decomposition. Auton. Robot. **9**(3), 247–253 (2000)
2. Acar, E.U., Choset, H.: Sensor-based coverage of unknown environments: incremental construction of morse decompositions. Int. J. Robot. Res. **21**(4), 345–366 (2002)
3. Zelinsky, A., Jarvis, R.A., Byrne, J.C.: Planning paths of complete coverage of an unstructured environment by a mobile robot. In: Proceedings of International Conference on Advanced Robotics, pp. 533–538 (1993)
4. Gabriely, Y., Rimon, E.: Spiral-STC: an on-line coverage algorithm of grid environments by a mobile robot. In: Proceedings of IEEE International Conference on Robotics and Automation, pp. 954–960 (2002)
5. Luo, C., Yang, S.X.: A bioinspired neural network for real-time concurrent map building and complete coverage robot navigation in unknown environments. IEEE Trans. Neural Netw. **19**(7), 1279–1298 (2008)
6. Bircher, A., et al.: Three-dimensional coverage path planning via viewpoint resampling and tour optimization for aerial robots. Auton. Robot. **40**(6), 1059–1078 (2016)
7. Janchiv, A., Batsaikhan, D., Kim, G.H., et al.: Complete coverage path planning for multi-robots based on. In: Proceedings of International Conference on Control, Automation and Systems pp. 824–827 (2011)
8. Rekleitis, I., Ai, P.N., Rankin, E.S., et al.: Efficient boustrophedon multi-robot coverage: an algorithmic approach. Ann. Math. Artif. Intell. **52**(2–4), 109–142 (2008)
9. Hazon, N., Kaminka, G.A.: Redundancy, efficiency and robustness in multi-robot coverage. In: Proceedings of IEEE International Conference on Robotics and Automation, pp. 735–741 (2005)
10. Hazon, N., Kaminka, G.A.: On redundancy, efficiency, and robustness in coverage for multiple robots. Robot. Auton. Syst. **56**(12), 1102–1114 (2008)
11. Viet, H.H., Dang, V.H., Laskar, M.N.U., et al.: BA*: an online complete coverage algorithm for cleaning robots. Appl. Intell. **39**(2), 217–235 (2013)

12. Viet, H.H., Dang, V.H., Choi, S.Y., et al.: BoB: an online coverage approach for multi-robot systems. Appl. Intell. **42**(2), 157–173 (2015)

13. Grisetti, G., Stachniss, C., Burgard, W.: Improved techniques for grid mapping with rao-blackwellized particle filters. IEEE Trans. Robot. **23**, 34–46 (2007)

14. Kohlbrecher, S., Stryk, O.V., Meyer, J., Klingauf, U.: A flexible and scalable SLAM system with Full 3D motion estimation. In: Proceedings of IEEE International Symposium on Safety, Security and Rescue Robotics, pp. 155–160 (2011)

15. Koch, P., et al.: Multi-robot localization and mapping based on signed distance functions. J. Intell. Robot. Syst. **82**(3–4), 409–428 (2016)

16. Hess, W., Kohler, D., Rapp, H., Andor, D.: Real-time loop closure in 2D LIDAR SLAM. In: Proceedings of IEEE International Conference on Robotics and Automation, pp. 1271–1278 (2016)

17. Zhou, Y., Yu, S., Sun, R., et al.: Topological segmentation for indoor environments from grid maps using an improved NJW algorithm. In: Proceedings of IEEE International Conference on Information and Automation, pp. 142–147 (2017)

18. Longueville, M.D.: A Course in Topological Combinatorics. Springer, New York (2012). https://doi.org/10.1007/978-1-4419-7910-0

19. Kuhn, H.W.: The Hungarian method for the assignment problem. Nav. Res. Logist. **52**(1), 7–21 (2005)

20. Lattarulo, V., Parks, G.T.: A preliminary study of a new multi-objective optimization algorithm. In: IEEE Congress on Evolutionary Computation, pp. 1–8 (2012)

21. Xu, Z., Wen, Q.: Approximation hardness of min-max tree covers. Oper. Res. Lett. **38**(3), 169–173 (2010)

22. Sarin, S.C., Sherali, H.D., Bhootra, A.: New tighter polynomial length formulations for the asymmetric traveling salesman problem with and without precedence constraints. Oper. Res. Lett. **33**(1), 62–70 (2005)

23. Bektas, T.: The multiple traveling salesman problem: an overview of formulations and solution procedures. Omega **34**(3), 209–219 (2009)

24. Koubaa, A., et al.: Move and improve: a market-based mechanism for the multiple depot multiple travelling salesmen problem. J. Intell. Robot. Syst. **85**(2), 307–330 (2017)

25. Reeves, C.R., Rowe, J.E.: Genetic Algorithms-Principles and Perspectives: A Guide to GA Theory. Kluwer Academic Publishers, Dordrecht (2002)

26. Croes, G.A.: A method for solving traveling salesman problems. Oper. Res. **6**(6), 791–812 (1958)

Design and Magnetic Force Analysis of Patrol Robot for Deep Shaft Rigid Cage Guide

Tang Hongwei, Tang Chaoquan[⊠], Zhou Gongbo, Shu Xin,
and Gao Qiao

Jiangsu Key Laboratory of Mine Mechanical and Electrical Equipment,
School of Mechatronic Engineering, China University of Mining
and Technology, Xuzhou 221116, Jiangsu, China
tangchaoquan@cumt.edu.cn

Abstract. Rigid cage guide is an important part of coal mine hoisting system, and its fault detection is an indispensable work of mine daily maintenance. In this paper, a patrol robot for detecting the fault of rigid cage guide in coal mine hoisting system is proposed, which will change the low efficiency of manpower maintenance during the maintenance of the hoisting system. Firstly, the three-dimensional model of the robot is built and the static analysis of the robot is carried out. In addition, the influence of the design parameters of the magnetic wheel on the magnetic force of the magnetic wheel is studied, and the magnetic wheel is optimized accordingly. Also, to obtain greater magnetic force under the same mass, it is proposed that the two magnetic wheels on the same axis should be arranged in a mutually exclusive mode. Compared with the mutually attracting arrangement, the former has a maximum magnetic force of 1.73 times that of the latter while the cost of magnetic wheel arrangement proposed in this paper is only one third of that of Halbach arrangement. Finally, a prototype of the robot is made and tested. The robot can detect potential faults and defects in the ultra-deep vertical shaft hoisting system as early as possible, and realize real-time monitoring of wellbore health status.

Keywords: Wall-climbing robot · Fault detecting ·
Permanent magnet adsorption · Magnetic wheel arrangement

1 Introduction

Now in the process of coal mine production, the hoisting system will stop for two hours every day to test the hoisting system, and its main content is the hoisting system can channel fault detection. However, the detection of hoisting system is still based on manual observation. Due to the characteristics of the mine itself, the inspection environment is harsh and there are certain risks. With the mining of deep coal mines, the increase of the tank passage length, the low efficiency and poor reliability of manual detection, it will not be able to meet the requirements of coal mine safety production. Therefore, it is a wise choice to use the wall-climbing robot to perform fault detection [1].

© Springer Nature Switzerland AG 2019
H. Yu et al. (Eds.): ICIRA 2019, LNAI 11744, pp. 362–374, 2019.
https://doi.org/10.1007/978-3-030-27541-9_30

Some experts and scholars at home and abroad have done some research on wall-climbing robots. Tang *et al.* [2] proposed a new inspection robot to detect the faults in the rail of coal mine hoisting system. Also, corresponding detection method is proposed to detect the faults and magnetic wheels are arranged by the halbach array to improve the adsorption capacity. The robot system will replace the manual inspection work in the mine, and will greatly improve the efficiency of inspection Song *et al.* [3] proposed a water-jetting wall-climbing robot, which could produce a large adhesive force with a small mass. At the same time, the coupling relationship between the magnetic attachment system and the pneumatic tire is determined to give the initial air gap and inflation pressure, which is very important for the normal operation of the attachment motion system of the robot. Huang *et al.* [4] designed a wall-climbing robot combining magnetic caterpillars and magnets, which can climb ferromagnetic and uneven surfaces. The robot is equipped with a special probe clamping device, which can perform ship inspection tasks in unfriendly and inaccessible environments by utilizing magnetic properties, thus reducing the cost. Cai *et al.* [5] proposed a new type of magnetic wheeled wall-climbing robot while the toroidal ring permanent magnet is divided into two pieces. Ishihara [6] proposed a wall-climbing robot, consisting of two driving wheels and 4 passive wheels with magnetic tire. The introduction of passive wheels enables the robot to cross a 10 mm step or clearance and the casters also achieve a smooth change in direction. Hu *et al.* [7] designed a magnetic adsorption wall-climbing robot. The crawler-type may give the reliability of adsorption, strong load capacity and strong adaptability to wall because magnets directly contact with the wall. Similarly, more research had been carried out. Wu *et al.* [8] designed a permanent magnetic climbing robot. By adjusting the distance between permanent magnet and steel plate, an adjustable bonding mechanism is designed to improve the maneuverability. When multiple magnets alternately distribute N and S and ferromagnetic plates are installed at the bottom of the magnet, the adsorption force is larger. Liu *et al.* [9] proposed a permanent magnetic wall-climbing robot. The way of adding two universal permanent magnet wheel can greatly improve the adsorption. Yan *et al.* [10] proposed a multidirectional magnetized adsorption device for wall-climbing robots. The novel device can significantly increase the adsorption force under the same mass. Li *et al.* [11] developed a novel Mecanum omnidirectional climbing robot for the inspection of large equipment such as storage and spherical tank. The adjustable magnetic adsorption mechanism installed on the wheel can change the position and magnetic size of the magnet in three degrees of freedom, provide stable and reliable robot adsorption force, and adapt to different curvature of tank wall. Because of the special working position, the robot is equipped with gyroscope sensors, which can automatically adjust the position and direction to ensure smooth movement. In order to meet the requirements of ship wall climbing robot for adsorbing and flexible moving hull surface, Mao *et al.* [12] also proposed a new tracked permanent magnet adsorbing device for wall-climbing robot and the parameters of magnet were optimized.

In the field of coal mine, robot research mainly focuses on monitoring and rescue, and is mostly used in underground roadways and working faces. However, in the ultra-deep shaft hoisting system, complex geological conditions, time-varying operating environment and other factors may lead to vertical, circumferential and radial deformation of the shaft. Therefore, the application of patrol robot in the hoisting shaft can find out the potential faults and defects in the super-deep shaft hoisting system as early as possible and change the low efficiency of manpower maintenance during the maintenance period of the hoisting system, and finally realize the real-time monitoring of the wellbore health status, which is particularly important and urgent for improving the safety and reliability of the mine hoisting system and ensuring the safety of life and property. At the same time, in order to obtain greater magnetic force under the same mass, it is suggested that the two magnetic wheels on the same axis should be arranged in a mutually exclusive mode. Compared with the mutual attraction arrangement, the former has a maximum magnetic force of 1.73 times that of the latter. Also, the cost of magnetic wheel arrangement proposed in this paper is only one third of that of Halbach arrangement.

The structure of this paper is as follows. The second part introduces the structure design of the inspection robot body. In the third part, the statics of inspection robot is analyzed. The fourth part studies the influence of various design parameters of the magnetic wheel on the magnetic force. In the fifth part, a prototype of the robot is made and tested. The last is the conclusion.

2 Structural Design of the Climbing Robot

Compared with the ground, the working stability of the robot in the vertical wall surface is relatively complex. At this time, there are different levels of requirements for the structure of wall-climbing robot:

(1) Firstly, because of the need for efficient patrol inspection, the robot should be able to move quickly, flexible and easy to control;
(2) Secondly, robot should be able to walk in safe and reliable paths to prevent derailment accidents. Considering the special working condition of the target, the robot should be able to adjust the direction of small angle;
(3) Finally, due to the need for inspection work on vertical wall, it requires reliable adsorption, small size and light weight to ensure the efficient operation of inspection work.

According to the above requirements, we designed the robot model with 3D software and made the robot prototype. The robot is driven by two electric motors, and four magnetic wheels are responsible for walking and providing enough adsorption force. Power is output from the motor. It drives the magnetic wheel through the reducer and a pair of bevel gears. In order to prevent the robot from going off track, a mechanism must be designed to prevent this situation from happening. Therefore, we proposed an anti-deflection mechanism to correct the direction of the robot. The flexible contact in the lateral direction of the robot and the automatic assistant orientation adjustment are realized by using the spring preload and the pressure of the guide wheel. The model and physical prototype of the climbing robot is shown in Figs. 1 and 2.

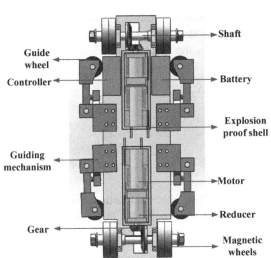

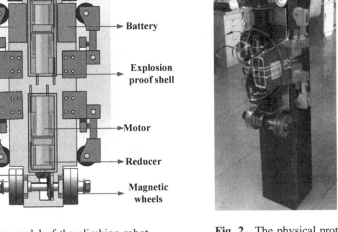

Fig. 1. The model of the climbing robot

Fig. 2. The physical prototype of the climbing robot

3   Stability Analysis of the Robot

Due to the particularity of the work surface, the forces and stability of the robot must be calculated accurately to ensure the reliability of the robot. Three dangerous situations may occur for wall-climbing robots: insufficient friction causes the robot to slip off the wall, insufficient adsorption overturns the robot and insufficient adhesion causes the magnetic wheel to skid. The force analysis of robot is shown in Fig. 3.

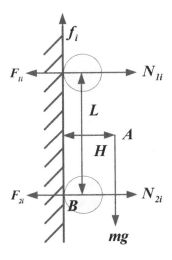

Fig. 3. Static analysis of robot

3.1   The Detaching from Wall of the Robot

The wall-climbing robot carries detection equipment to move up and down on the surface of the target under test. How to ensure that the magnetic wheel is reliably adsorbed on the surface of the target under test is the focus of our design.

$$
\begin{cases}
\sum_{i=1}^{2} F_{1i} + \sum_{i=1}^{2} F_{2i} = \sum_{i=1}^{2} N_{1i} + \sum_{i=1}^{2} N_{2i} \\
\sum_{i=1}^{4} f_i = \mu \left(\sum_{i=1}^{2} N_{1i} + \sum_{i=1}^{2} N_{2i} \right) \\
\sum_{i=1}^{4} f_i = kmg
\end{cases}
\tag{1}
$$

Where F_{1i} is the adsorption force provided by two upper magnetic wheels; F_{2i} is the adsorption force provided by two lower magnetic wheels; N_{1i} is the support force provided by two upper magnetic wheels; N_{2i} is the support force provided by two lower magnetic wheels; $\sum_{i=1}^{4} f_i$ is the total friction provided by four magnetic wheels; μ is the friction coefficient between magnetic wheel and wall; k is the safety factor; mg is the robot mass.

3.2   The Overturn of the Robot

When the adsorption is inadequate, then the robot may be overturned. As shown in Fig. 3, the robot may flip around the point B. Therefore, the adsorption force provided by two upper magnetic wheels should meet:

$$
\sum_{i=1}^{2} F_{1i} L \geq mgH
\tag{2}
$$

Where L is the length between the upper wheels and lower wheels, and H is the height of the wall and the center of robot.

3.3   The Wheel-Slippage of the Robot

While ensuring that the magnetic wheel does not break away from the wall, the robot may have the phenomenon of magnetic wheel skidding. Similar to the vehicle driving on the road, the ground has a limit value of the tangential reaction force on the tire, which is called the adhesion force. The tangential reaction force on the ground caused by the driving moment should not be greater than the adhesion force, otherwise the tire skidding will occur. Therefore, the force should meet the equation:

$$\frac{\sum\limits_{i=1}^{4} f_i}{\sum\limits_{i=1}^{2} N_{1i} + \sum\limits_{i=1}^{2} N_{2i}} < \varphi \tag{3}$$

Where $\sum\limits_{i=1}^{4} f_i$ is the tangential reaction force on the wall surface of the magnetic wheels, and it is equal to the friction force between the wall and the magnetic wheels; $\sum\limits_{i=1}^{2} N_{1i} + \sum\limits_{i=1}^{2} N_{2i}$ is normal reaction force between the wall and the magnetic wheels; φ is adhesion coefficient between the wall and the magnetic wheels.

4 The Influence of Magnetic Wheel Design Parameters on Magnetic Force

4.1 The Effect of Air Gap on Magnetic Force

In this study, the experimental platform is a square steel with 200 mm side length and 10 mm thickness. Therefore, we use finite element analysis COMSOL to study the relationship between the magnetic force and the air gap between the center and the edge of the experimental platform.

From the Figs. 4 and 5, we can easily know that the force at the center is higher than at the edge. This also gives us an enlightenment: put the magnetic wheel as far as possible in the center.

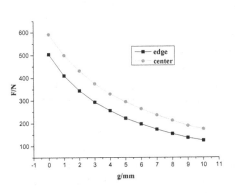

Fig. 4. The effect of air gap on magnetic force

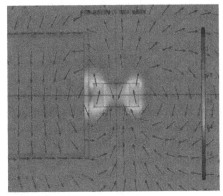

Fig. 5. Distribution of magnetic induction lines

4.2 The Effect of Wheel Size on Magnetic Force

In order to improve the magnetic wheel's adsorptive capacity, save cost and reduce the difficulty of processing and assembling, a ring magnet based on axial magnetization is adopted. The magnetic wheel has three parameters: the d is the internal diameter of magnetic wheel, the D is the external diameter of magnetic wheel and the h is the thickness of magnetic wheel. Obviously, the three parameters will affect the magnitude of the magnetic force of the magnetic wheel. Therefore, we explored how these three parameters affect the magnitude of magnetic force, and simulated them by finite element software.

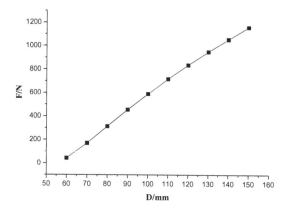

Fig. 6. The effect of the external diameter of magnetic wheel on magnetic force

The influence of the external diameter of magnetic wheel on magnetic force is studied, where the external diameter of magnetic wheel D is controlled as a single variable, and the g = 0 mm, d = 54 mm and h = 38 mm are set. The relationship curve between the single variable D and the magnetic adsorption force through finite element software is obtained, as shown in Fig. 6.

The influence of the internal diameter of magnetic wheel on magnetic force is studied, where the internal diameter of magnetic wheel d is controlled as a single variable, and the g = 0 mm, D = 100 mm and h = 38 mm are set. The relationship curve between the single variable d and the magnetic adsorption force through finite element software is obtained, as shown in Fig. 7.

The influence of the thickness of magnetic wheel on magnetic force is studied, where the thickness of magnetic wheel h is controlled as a single variable, and the g = 0 mm, D = 100 mm and d = 54 mm are set. The relationship curve between the single variable h and the magnetic adsorption force through finite element software is obtained, as shown in Fig. 8.

From the Figs. 6, 7 and 8, we could easily know that there is a linear relationship between the size of the magnetic wheel in the height direction and the magnitude of the magnetic force, while the size increases first in the width direction and then tends to be stable.

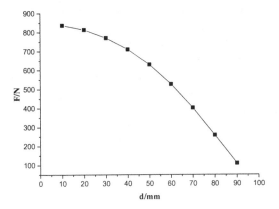

Fig. 7. The effect of the internal diameter of magnetic wheel on magnetic force

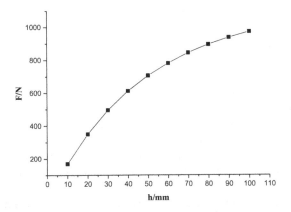

Fig. 8. The effect of the thickness of magnetic wheel on magnetic force

4.3 Optimization of Dimension Parameters of Magnetic Wheels

It can be seen that according to Figs. 6, 7 and 8, the internal and external diameter of magnetic wheel are approximately directly proportional to the magnetic adsorption force. But the magnitude of the magnetic adsorption force tends to be stable when the thickness of the permanent magnet increases to a certain value. The increases of dimension parameters of the magnetic wheel will cause the increases of the weight and force of the magnetic wheel. In order to study the effect of size parameters on the magnitude of magnetic force, we define a parameter to characterize the influence of various size parameters on the magnetic adsorption force (Fig. 9). So the λ is defined as the magnitude of the magnetic force added per unit weight.

$$\lambda = \frac{F}{G} \tag{4}$$

Where F is the magnetic adsorption force; G is the weight of the magnetic wheel.

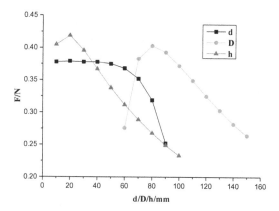

Fig. 9. The effect of the thickness of magnetic wheel on magnetic force

From the Fig. 9, it could be easily known that when D = 80 mm, h = 20 and d is between 0 and 60 mm, the λ can get the maximum value. Therefore, the size of the magnetic wheel should be as close as possible to the above datas when designing the magnetic wheel.

4.4   Optimization of Magnetic Wheel Arrangement

As shown in Fig. 10, due to the axially magnetized magnetic wheel there are two magnetic wheel arrangement: mutual exclusive and mutual absorbing. In the finite element simulation software, we arranged the two magnetic wheels on a transmission shaft according to the above arrangements and calculated the magnitude of their magnetic force.

We study the relationship between the distance between two magnetic wheels and the magnitude of magnetic force in two different arrangements. From the Fig. 11, We can easily see that the magnetic force of the magnetic wheels in the exclusive arrangement decreases with the increase of the distance. However, the magnetic force of the magnetic wheels in the absorbing arrangement increases with the increase of the distance at the beginning, and decreases with the increase of the distance only when the distance is greater than a certain value. When the distances of repellent magnetic wheels are closer, more magnetic induction lines pass through the wall due to the aggregation of magnetic induction lines, which makes the magnetic force larger. With the increase of distance, the aggregation of magnetic induction lines gradually weakens and the magnetic force decreases. Because most of the magnetic induction lines will pass through the magnet wheels at close distances, the magnetic induction lines passing through the wall are less, so the magnetic force is smaller. With the increase of distance, more and more magnetic induction lines will pass through the wall, making the magnetic force gradually larger. But because the wall is a square steel, the closer the magnetic wheel is to the edge of the wall, the less the magnetic induction lines across the wall will be, and the magnetic force will be attenuated accordingly.

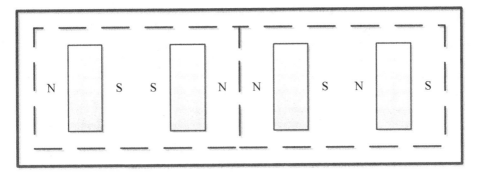

Fig. 10. Arrangement of mutual exclusive and mutual absorbing

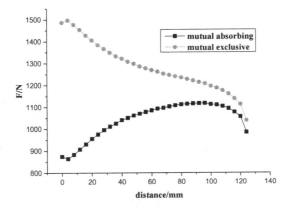

Fig. 11. The relation between distance and magnetic force in two arrangements

5 Prototype Manufacture and Experiment

Through the static analysis of the robot and the finite element simulation analysis and optimization of the magnetic wheel, we can easily get the magnitude of the magnetic force required by the robot as well as the parameters of the robot (Table 1).

Then we made a prototype of the robot based on the above parameters and carried out experiments, as shown in Figs. 12, 13 and 14. The parameters of the robot are shown in the following figure.

Table 1. The parameters of the robot

Parameter	Value
Robot Length	700 mm
Robot Width	200 mm
Robot Height	150 mm
Robot weight	20 kg
Load capacity	20 kg
Mileage	1500 m
Inspection speed	≥0.25 m/s
External diameter of magnetic wheel(D)	100 mm
Internal diameter of magnetic wheel(d)	54 mm
Width of magnetic wheel(h)	38 mm

Fig. 12. The indoor climbing test

Fig. 13. The deviation correction test

Fig. 14. The outdoor climbing test

6 Conclusion

In this study, to solve the problem of the detection of rigid cage guide in coal mine hoisting system, we proposed a patrol robot based on magnetic wheels adsorption. The main work and conclusions are as follows.

(1) Three-dimensional modeling and static analysis of the robot are carried out. The robot is provided with adsorbing force by magnetic wheels and has high reliability. Also, the three dangerous conditions that the robot does not break away from the wall, does not overturn and does not slip are analyzed. To solve the possible deviation of the robot, an anti-deviation mechanism was designed. Through calculation and analysis, it can be known that the robot needs a adsorption force of 2000 N and a driving moment of 30 Nm;

(2) The influence of the design parameters and the arrangement of the magnetic wheel on the magnetic force of the magnetic wheel is studied. From the simulation results, it can be seen that the diameter parameters of the magnetic wheel have a greater impact on the magnitude of the magnetic force than the height parameters of the magnetic wheel. Moreover, the magnetic wheels on the same axis can obtain greater magnetic force (about 1.73 times) in the way of mutual exclusion arrangement than in the way of mutual attraction arrangement. Also, compared with Halbach arrangement, the cost of magnetic wheel arrangement proposed in this paper is only one third of that of former arrangement;

(3) A prototype of the robot was made and tested. The indoor wall climbing test, anti-deviation test and outdoor wall climbing test were carried out respectively. The weight of the robot is 20 kg, and the additional load can be up to 20 kg. In the outdoor experiment, the maximum patrol speed of the robot is 0.25 m/s and its patrol mileage is 1500 m. Experiments show that the robot can meet the requirements of inspection.

The next step we need to do is to equip the robot with detection equipment in order to achieve fault detection.

Acknowledgement. This research is financially supported by National key research and development program (2016YFC0600905), National Nature Science Foundation of China (61603394 & 51575513) and a project funded by the Priority Academic Program Development of Jiangsu Higher Education Institutions (PAPD).

References

1. Zhou, G., Wang, P., Zhu, Z., Wang, H., Li, W.: Topology control strategy for movable sensor networks in ultradeep shafts. IEEE Trans. Ind. Inform. **14**(5), 2251–2260 (2018)
2. Tang, C., Zhou, G., Gao, Z., Shu, X., Chen, P.: A novel rail inspection robot and fault detection method for the coal mine hoisting system. IEEE Intell. Transp. Syst. Mag. **11**, 110–121 (2019)
3. Song, W., Jiang, H., Wang, T., Ji, D., Zhu, S.: Design of permanent magnetic wheel-type adhesion-locomotion system for water-jetting wall-climbing robot. Adv. Mech. Eng. **10**(7), 1687814018787378 (2018)
4. Huang, H., Li, D., Xue, Z., Chen, X., Liu, S., Leng, J., Wei, Y.: Design and performance analysis of a tracked wall-climbing robot for ship inspection in shipbuilding. Ocean Eng. **131**, 224–230 (2017)
5. Cai, J., He, K., Fang, H., Chen, H., Hu, S., Zhou, W.: The design of permanent-magnetic wheeled wall-climbing robot. In: 2017 IEEE International Conference on Information and Automation (ICIA), pp. 604–608. IEEE (2017)
6. Ishihara, H.: Basic study on wall climbing root with magnetic passive wheels. In: 2017 IEEE International Conference on Mechatronics and Automation (ICMA), pp. 1964–1969. IEEE (2017)
7. Hu, S., Peng, R., He, K., Li, J., Cai, J., Zhou, W.: Structural design and magnetic force analysis of a new crawler-type permanent magnetic adsorption wall—climbing. In: 2017 IEEE International Conference on Information and Automation (ICIA), pp. 598–603. IEEE (2017)
8. Wu, S., Zheng, G., Liu, T., Wang, B.: A magnetic wall climbing robot with non-contactable and adjustable adhesion mechanism. In: 2017 IEEE International Conference on Real-time Computing and Robotics (RCAR), pp. 427–430. IEEE (2017)
9. Liu, J., Hu, F., Wang, H., Chen, J.: Calculation and analysis of the safety of pressure vessel wall climbing robot. In: 2016 International Conference on Computational Science and Engineering (ICCSE 2016). Atlantis Press (2016)
10. Yan, C., Sun, Z., Zhang, W., Chen, Q.: Design of novel multidirectional magnetized permanent magnetic adsorption device for wall-climbing robots. Int. J. Precis. Eng. Manuf. **17**(7), 871–878 (2016)
11. Li, J., Wang, X.S.: Novel omnidirectional climbing robot with adjustable magnetic adsorption mechanism. In: 2016 23rd International Conference on Mechatronics and Machine Vision in Practice (M2VIP), pp. 1–5. IEEE (2016)
12. Mao, J., He, K., Li, J., Sun, X.: Simulation and experimental verification of permanent magnet adsorption unit for wall-climbing robot. In: 2016 IEEE International Conference on Information and Automation (ICIA), pp. 1189–1194. IEEE (2016)

Improved Driving Stability with Series Elastic Actuator and Velocity Controller

Jin-uk Bang, Ha-neul Yoon, Ji-hyeon Kim, and Jang-myung Lee[⊠]

Department of Electrical and Computer Engineering, Pusan National University, Busan 49241, Korea
{jinuk1696, jmlee}@pusan.ac.kr

Abstract. In this study, we propose a suspension system that can be attached to Segway and a velocity controller to control the slip generated during driving. Segway has undergone many years of development and research, but it still lacks research on safety devices and controllers. In order to solve these problems, the suspension device used in the automobile is attached to improve the stability of the user. Four suspension are attached to the Segway to suppress the shaking and impact that occur during driving. In order to design the speed controller for precise control during turning, the appropriate slip ratio is derived using Magic Formula. The actual slip ratio value at the time of turning is calculated and the velocity is controlled by comparing with the target slip ratio. By using such an algorithm, it is possible to turn to a desired target path by suppressing slippage occurring of turning.

Keywords: Segway · Series Elastic Actuator · Magic Formula · Velocity controller · Suspension

1 Introduction

Recently, various transportation means such as an electric car or an electric kickboard have been developed. And the demand for it is also increasing. Electricity-driven products are also attracting attention due to environmental pollution and resource depletion. Among them, personal mobility, which is a transportation means for one person, is widely used. Personal mobility refers to personal moving means such as electric wheels, electric kick boards, and Segway. Among other things, Segway uses two transverse wheels unlike other products. And it is driven by the center of gravity of the user and the steering angle of the steering wheel. The body uses a sensor to measure the degree of tilt and balance itself. This kind of unfamiliarity has attracted a lot of attention and users are increasing. There are a lot of developments in distance and speed, but at present there is a lack of development for safety devices [1]. As a result, accidents are increasing every year. Among the causes of the accident, slip caused by slip during turning operation is one of them.

In this study, to improve the running stability of Segway, a suspension system is attached and a speed control algorithm is applied to prevent slip. As the suspension, a Series Elastic Actuator (SEA) is used. The series elastic actuator connects the motor and the load in series, and connects the spring to the connection part to compensate the

© Springer Nature Switzerland AG 2019
H. Yu et al. (Eds.): ICIRA 2019, LNAI 11744, pp. 375–385, 2019.
https://doi.org/10.1007/978-3-030-27541-9_31

external force. By attaching four series elastic actuators to the footrest, the following functions are implemented. The first function is to mitigate the shock caused by the elastic force of the spring, the second function is to reduce the inertia of the occupant by raising or lowering the footrest when driving. In addition, the slip rate for the system is obtained through tire modeling using the "Magic Formula" method [2]. Slip-rate error and yaw rate are used to design a velocity controller to improve the turning stability.

2 Modeling of Series Elastic Actuator

2.1 Series Elastic Actuator

The Series Elastic Actuator (SEA) were first developed at MIT in the United States. It is used as a structure in which a spring is connected in series between the motor and the load of the actuator. Springs are used to measure external forces and to mitigate shocks. It basically provides high impedance through force control or position control [3, 4, 7].

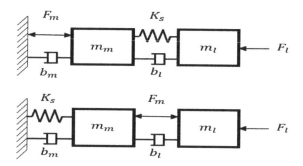

Fig. 1. FSEA model (top), RFSEA model (bottom).

The SEA is divided into two types. One is Force-sensing Series Elastic Actuator (FSEA) and the other is Reaction Force-sensing Series Elastic Actuator (RFSEA). Two models differ the position of the spring [4]. As shown in Fig. 1, the FSEA is located between the load and the motor, and the spring and motor rotors are mechanically connected. However, RFSEA is located between the ground and the motor, and the spring and motor rotors have different dynamic relationships, they are used separately [5]. In this study, SEA is used for measuring external force, so it is used as an FSEA structure which is easy to measure external force.

We analyze the dynamic model of FSEA to obtain the spring constant suitable for the system. The motor part includes ball-screws and pulleys and belts associated with motor drive. The rod part corresponds to all the parts moving by external force. The system is divided into a total of three parts including spring, and the expression relation for each part is (1)–(3).

$$m_x \ddot{x}_m + b_m \dot{x}_m = F_m + F_l \tag{1}$$

$$K_s x_s = F_i \tag{2}$$

$$m_l \ddot{x}_l + b_l \dot{x}_l = F_l - F_{ext} \tag{3}$$

In the equation, x means the length of movement of each part, F means the external force and the compensating force, b means the damping coefficient, and K means the spring constant.

Equations (1)–(3) is Laplace transformed, it can be expressed as (4)–(6). The spring constant can be derived through simulation by summarizing the Laplace transformed equations.

$$P_m(s) = \frac{1}{m_m s^2 + b_m s} \tag{4}$$

$$P_s(s) = \frac{1}{K_s} \tag{5}$$

$$P_l(s) = \frac{1}{m_l s^2 + b_l s} \tag{6}$$

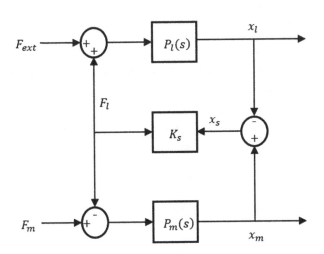

Fig. 2. Block diagram of FSEA.

Figure 2 shows the diagram for (4)–(6). And outputs the compressed length (x_l) and the compensated length (x_m) through each system by inputting the external force (F_{ext}) and the compensation (F_m) for the external force. In this system, the spring constant can be derived through the response speed and the compensation rate.

2.2   Series Elsatic Actuator Design

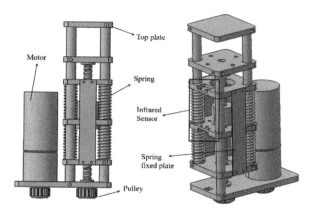

Fig. 3. Designed SEA.

The design of the SEA using the CATIA program is shown in Fig. 3. The motor and load sections were connected in series using a pulley and a belt. It is used to measure external force by using infrared sensor on both ends of spring. Use four springs with two on the top and two on the bottom. When the external force is applied, the spring at the top is compressed and the spring at the bottom is tensioned. The length of the compressed spring is measured by an infrared sensor, and the external force is calculated through the Hooke's law ($F = K \times \Delta x$). The force corresponding to the calculated external force is compensated through the motor, so that the SEA always maintains the same height.

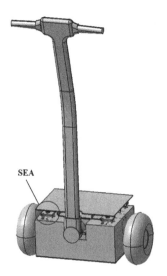

Fig. 4. Segway and SEA placement.

Figure 4 shows the attachment of four SEAs to the footrest. Four SEAs are individually controlled to maintain balance of the footrest.

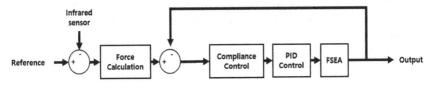

Fig. 5. Control algorithm of SEA.

Figure 5 shows the algorithm applied to control SEA. The PID controller is basically used and the experiment is carried out by applying the compliance controller using the spring stiffness. If the force control is generally performed without a controller, there is a possibility that an error occurs in the position, and when only the position control is performed, an error may occur using a force exceeding the usable range. Therefore, more flexible control is possible by controlling the force and position within the allowable range through the compliance controller. The PID controller provides more accurate compensation and shortens the response time.

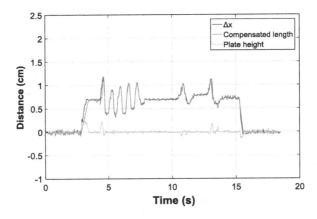

Fig. 6. Compensation experiment of SEA.

Figure 6 is an experimental graph for checking the compensation force of the motor for external force. If a certain external force is applied, compensation is carried out through the motor. The graph compares the compressed spring length (Δx) through the infrared sensor and the compensated length of the motor to see how much the top plate maintains balance.

3 Magic Formula

Tire modeling is performed to derive the force on the wheel for the slip-ratio. Using the Magic Formula method, it was proposed by Professor H. B. Pacejka of the Netherlands. With the Magic Formula, only one set of formulas can perfectly represent the mechanical properties of the tire in pure working conditions. The expression of tire force characteristics is accurate, concise and used in cars under various working conditions.

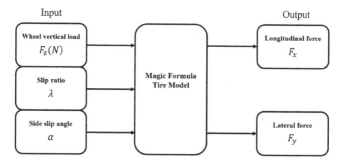

Fig. 7. Block diagram of Magic Formula.

Figure 7 shows the diagram for the Magic Formula. Basically, it can output longitudinal force and lateral force by inputting values of wheel vertical load, slip ratio, and side slip angle. Camber angles are present in cars, but it can omitting them, because there is no value for instruments with wheels on the abscissa, such as Segway.

The basic form of the Magic Formula is as follows.

$$Y = D\sin\{Cartan[Bx - E(Bx - artanBx)]\} + S_v \tag{7}$$

Y means F_x(lateral force) or F_y (lateral force) depending on the situation, and x means slip angle or side slip angle depending on the situation. A and B, C, D, and E are fitting constants, and values for general road conditions are used. S_h is the horizontal drift of the curve, and S_v is the vertical drift of the curve.

3.1 Longitudinal Force

The relationship between the tire longitudinal force and λ and F_z under single braking conditions can be expressed as:

$$F_{x0} = D_1\sin\{C_1 artan[B_1\lambda - artanB_1\lambda]\} \tag{8}$$

3.2   Lateral Force

The relationship between the tire lateral force and α and F_z under single braking conditions can be expressed as:

$$F_{y0} = D_2 \sin\{C_2 artan[B_2 x - E_2(B_2 x - artan B_2 x)]\} + S_v \tag{9}$$

$$x = \alpha + S_h \tag{10}$$

3.3   Longitudinal and Lateral Forces in Combined Braking and Steering Conditions

The relation between the longitudinal force and the lateral force of the tire using the side yaw angle, slip ratio, and F_z can be expressed as:

$$F_x = \frac{\sigma_x}{\sigma} F_{x0} \tag{11}$$

$$F_y = \frac{\sigma_y}{\sigma} F_{y0} \tag{12}$$

Figure 8 shows the response of the longitudinal force of the tire under single braking conditions. When the slip ratio is 10%, the longitudinal force reaches the peak value, and when the slip rate exceeds 10%, the longitudinal force gradually decreases. It can be seen from the graph that the longitudinal force has maximum efficiency at 10%. Figure 9 shows the response of the lateral force of the tire under single braking conditions. Side slip angle increases linearly from 0 to 5, and nonlinearly from 5 to more.

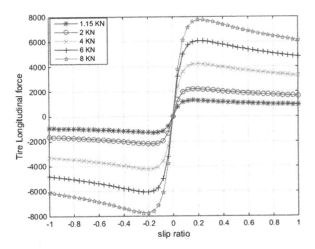

Fig. 8. Simulation of longitudinal force-slip rate.

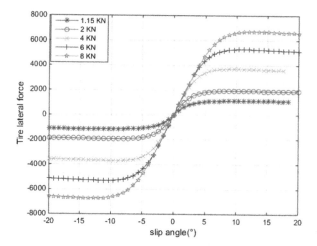

Fig. 9. Simulation of lateral force-slip rate.

4 Control Algorithm

We propose a slip control algorithm for precise control during Segway driving. By applying the velocity control algorithm using the slip ratio and the yaw angle, the user can travel on a desired route.

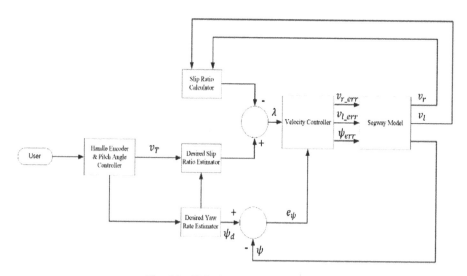

Fig. 10. Velocity control algorithm.

Figure 10 shows the velocity control algorithm applied to Segway. The user manipulates the segment handle to control the yaw rate or the tilt to control the target velocity. Using these two values, the appropriate slip ratio is determined and the velocity is controlled by the error value with the actual slip ratio.

5 Experiment

Four SEAs are attached to the footrests and are used to maintain the balance of the footrests. Initially, we run straight at a speed of about 10 km/h from uneven terrain to see if the equilibrium maintenance using SEA is controlled. At this time, we measure the tilt of the footrest to check the test results. In order to confirm the slip control, a circular motion with a turning radius of 3 m was performed on the asphalt. Two experiments were conducted with and without the controller.

Figure 11 shows the experimental results for foot control in uneven terrain. When the SEA is not attached, it can be confirmed that the angle of the footrest is shaken by about −4° to 6°, and when the SEA is attached, it can be confirmed that the control is relatively stable from about −1° to 1°.

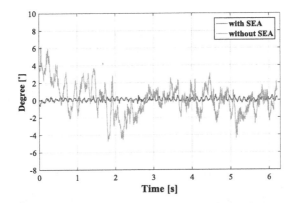

Fig. 11. Experiment on balancing maintenance of footrest.

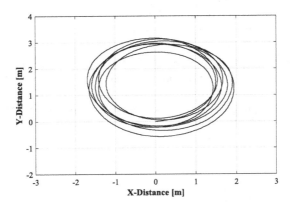

Fig. 12. Turning experiment without velocity controller.

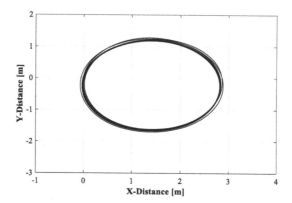

Fig. 13. Turning experiment with velocity controller.

Figure 12 shows the travel path when the velocity controller is not applied when the turning driving with a certain radius is repeated on the asphalt. In the moving path, the center of the circle is not constant and the radius is not constant. Figure 13 shows the travel path using the velocity controller designed in the previous chapter. It can be seen that the graph turns more stable than the graph without the velocity controller.

6 Conclusion

In this paper, SEA and velocity controller are applied to improve the stability and safety of Segway. The FSEA model was used to design SEA that can be attached to the Segway, and the stability of the user is improved by keeping the angle of the footrest at equilibrium while driving. In addition, slip ratios suitable for the system were derived through tire modeling, and the velocity controller was controlled by comparing the slip ratios generated during the turning.

Although the performance of the SEA and the velocity controller proposed in this paper has been sufficiently proved, it has not been able to provide stable control of driving at high speeds or running on low-friction roads. In the future, we will carry out researches so that the torque control based on the current sensing based on the velocity control of the Segway can be carried out stably even on a road with low friction.

Acknowledgment. This material is based upon work supported by the Ministry of Trade, Industry & Energy (MOTIE, Korea) under Industrial Technology Innovation Program. No. G01201605010048 '40 km/h of balancing robot with active suspension'.

References

1. Chen, Y., Wang, Z.L., Qiu, J., Huang, H.Z.: Hybrid fuzzy skyhook surface control using multi-objective microgenetic algorithm for semi-active vehicle suspension system ride comfort stability analysis. J. Dyn. Syst. Meas. Control **134**, 1–14 (2012)

2. Burhaumudin, M.S., Samin, P.M., Jamaluddin, H., Rahman, R.A.B.D., Sulaiman, S.: Modeling and validation of magic formula tire model. In: ICAMME 2012, Penang, 19–20 May 2012
3. Arumugom, S., Muthuraman, S., Ponselvan, V.: Modeling and application of series elastic actuators for force control multi legged robots. J. Comput. **1**(1), 26–33 (2009)
4. Paine, N., Oh, S., Sentis, L.: Design and control considerations for high-performance series elastic actuators. IEEE/ASME Trans. Mechatron. **19**(3), 1080–1091 (2014)
5. Lee, C., Kwak, S., Kwak, J., Sehoon, O.: Generalization of series elastic actuator configurations and dynamic behavior comparison. Actuators **6**(3), 1–26 (2017)
6. Ruziskas, A., Sivilevicius, H.: Magic formula tyre model application for a tyre-ice interaction. Procedia Eng. **187**, 335–341 (2017)
7. Park, Y., Paine, N., Oh, S.: Development of force observer in series elastic actuator for dynamic control. IEEE Trans. Ind. Electron. **65**(3), 2398–2407 (2018)

Monocular Vision-Based Dynamic Moving Obstacles Detection and Avoidance

Wilbert G. Aguilar[1,2,3(✉)], Leandro Álvarez[4], Santiago Grijalva[1], and Israel Rojas[1]

[1] CICTE, DEEL, Universidad de las Fuerzas Armadas ESPE, Sangolquí, Ecuador
wgaguilar@espe.edu.ec
[2] FIS, Escuela Politécnica Nacional, Quito, Ecuador
[3] GREC, Universitat Politècnica de Catalunya, Barcelona, Spain
[4] IDPayer, Quito, Ecuador

Abstract. In this paper, we proposed an UAV system for obstacle avoidance depending of a ground station processing based on monocular vision. To accomplish detection, tracking, proximity estimation and dynamic obstacles avoidance that are approaching the UAV, a series of methods and techniques are implemented. To detect movement, frame differentiation was applied to consecutive frames, once the moving object is detected, we detect Shi-Tomasi feature points to track the object using optical flow method Lucas-Kanade. To make possible proximity estimation, a linear regression method based on the area covered by the object was used. A fuzzy logic controller was designed to avoid the moving object, we considered the approach rate and the area of the object to control UAV's position in relation to the object as fuzzy inputs.

Keywords: Obstacle avoidance · Proximity estimation · UAV-control

1 Introduction

UAVs (Unmanned Aerial Vehicles) [1, 2] cover a wide range of civil [3, 4] and military applications [5, 6] due to their ability to perform both outdoor and indoor [7] missions in challenging environments [8–10], often they equip various sensors and cameras to perform intelligence, surveillance [11, 12] and reconnaissance mission [13, 14]. Other applications comprehend search and rescue missions, environmental protection, mailing and delivery, mission to oceans or other planets and other diverse applications [15].

Nowadays, UAVs usage has had a remarkable growth in both research and commercial applications, for example, in precision agriculture a UAV can be useful for control and monitoring of crops. Exploration and rescue in places of difficult access such as caves, cliffs, surveillance, reconnaissance navigation, among others [16–18].

This paper is organized as follows: Sect. 2 presents a quick review of the literature about autonomous UAVs and different approaches to provide full autonomous navigation to UAVs. Section 3 presents our approach to give the UAV the capability to avoid dynamic moving obstacles that can compromise the integrity and stability of the

© Springer Nature Switzerland AG 2019
H. Yu et al. (Eds.): ICRA 2019, LNAI 11744, pp. 386–398, 2019.
https://doi.org/10.1007/978-3-030-27541-9_32

UAV, in addition, results with different objects, distances and approaching rates are presented in Sect. 4. Conclusions and future work are presented in the last section.

2 Related Works

Design of autonomous UAVs requires an appropriate navigation system [19] for obstacle detection [20, 21], pose estimation [22–24] an environment perception [25, 26]. In [27, 28] the Inertial Measurement Unit (IMU) is described as a conventional navigation sensor, LIDAR in [29] is described as a suitable device for cartography and obstacle detection, since it measures environment range directly through a laser beam. Cameras stand out as a popular method for environment recognition [30, 31], since they are portable, passive and a compact sensor, providing extensive information about the movement of the vehicle and its relative pose.

Yilmaz et al. [32] describe several methods for detecting and tracking objects in the environment, object can be represented as geometric shapes, points, contours, in the case of person as an articulated model [33] of density probabilities, taking into consideration tracking characteristics such as color, texture, optical flow or edges.

Optical flow is a method often used to avoid collisions not based on stereoscopic vision. It can be understood as a visual phenomenon with daily experience when observing an object that moves at a speed different from that of the observer [34, 35]. The movement of the observed obstacle depends on the distance between the observer and the obstacle and its relative speed [36].

The detection algorithms based on feature points, such as SIFT [37] or SURF [38] detector being the most robust and resistant to image deformations but not the most efficient are commonly used for object tracking. Image segmentation algorithms are used to divide the image into perceptually similar regions as the exclusive method for real-time tracking Mean Shift [14].

Tendency of several research groups is navigation over known environments [39], that is, the place is previously explored, since the main problem is obstacle avoidance. Ritcher showed aggressive maneuvers for quadcopters flying in clogged indoor environments [40] path planning algorithm used was RRT*, but it was not implemented in real time. The planning phase was carried out offline, with an a priori map of obstacles, producing reference points that are at the minimum distance, not necessarily the minimum time to the final objective.

There are multiple solutions for obstacle avoidance, traditionally using active detection such as sonar, infrared LIDAR mentioned in Gageik et al. work [29], these sensors can be expensive, both in terms of real cost and payload, without neglecting power consumption. The common passive detection is stereo vision that is in charge of obtaining 3D information from 2 points of view (2 monocular cameras) [41] having as a limit the field of view of the cameras. Currently there is a navigation and obstacle avoidance system called S.L.A.M dunk on market that allows the development of autonomous UAVs.

3 Our Approach

When movement has been detected on the scene, it is possible to discriminate the object that is in movement. It should be mentioned that a defined template is not necessary to locate the object; the template will be defined automatically, once the movement of the object has occurred. That is, the object is not defined, it can be any that meets the minimum characteristics for detection.

3.1 Object Detection and Encapsulation

Let $I_{(x,y)}(t)$ be the actual frame that UAV sends to the ground station and $I_{(x,y)}(t-1)$ be the previous frame. Absolute difference between the actual and previous frame is defined as follows:

$$D_{(x,t)}(t) = |I_t - I_{t-1}|$$

Where $D_{(x,t)}(t)$ is a matrix which values are between 0 and 255, describing which pixels as different from the previous frame as a consequence of movement. Then a binary matrix is obtained from $D_{(x,t)}(t)$ as follows:

$$M_{(x,y)}(t) \begin{cases} 1, & D_{(x,y)}(t) \geq U(t) \\ 0, & D_{(x,y)}(t) < U(t) \end{cases}$$

Where:

$$U(t) = \overline{D}(t) + \sigma(t)$$

$U(t)$ is the threshold that a pixel must pass to be considered as an interest value. $\overline{D}(t)$ is the mean value of differences of all pixels in $D_{(x,t)}(t)$ and $\sigma(t)$ is the standard deviation. All this values are obtained in real time.

Once a binary image is ready, we consider that adjacent pixels that forms the images has similar colors, therefore these pixels can be excluded and divide the object in small parts. Canny border detection [42] was used to extract borders from the binary image, previous to that an opening morphological transformation was performed to handle noise present in the binary image (Fig. 1).

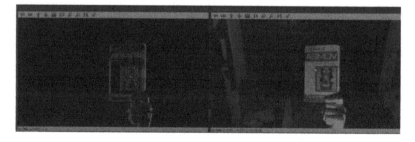

Fig. 1. Consecutive frames absolute difference

Border filtering is done discriminating area of quadrilaterals that are very large in comparison to movement objects. These areas appear due to UAVs positions is elevated and presents small variations when it is hovering, therefore, these areas should not be considered when encapsulating the object in a single geometric shape (Fig. 2).

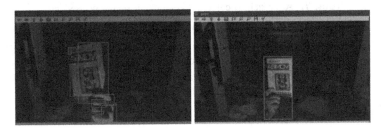

Fig. 2. Border detection on raw image from UAV's camera (left) – Moving object capture (right)

The moving object consists of several edges, which are represented by quadrilaterals of different sizes, it is necessary to integrate all these edges so that the object is represented by a single geometric shape. To achieve this, we considered the closest point to the upper left corner and closest to the lower right corner.

3.2 Object Tracking

It is important to know the approaching rate of the object to the UAV, Shi-Tomasi method was used to extract local characteristics giving good result when the feature points moves at fast velocities.

Optical flow allows us to estimate a vector field that describes the movement of each feature point, Lucas-Kanade method estimates this vector assuming that movement of the nearest neighbor pixels will have similar movement (Fig. 3).

Fig. 3. Tracking of Shi-Tomasi feature points

3.3 Approaching Rate

Approaching rate is the relation between distance and time; it describes the distance traveled by an object in a time unit. Taking this concept is possible to calculate velocity of each feature point in relation to the pixel's distance traveled in consecutive frames obtained from UAV's camera, this calculus depends on the shutter speed of the camera. In our case is 30 FPS. Table 1, describes how to calculate the distance by means of pixels per second.

Table 1. Approach to calculate velocity in pixels per second

Parameter	Formula	Description	Unit
Distance	$p1-p0$	Distance in pixels traveled by each point between consecutive frames	[*pixels*]
Time	1 Frame = 0.03 [s]	Distance can relate to the shutter speed by means of FPS, 30 Hz	[*second*]
Velocity	$\frac{p1-p0}{0.03}$	Pixels traveled in one frame at 30 FPS	$\left[\frac{pixels}{second}\right]$

The tracker loses feature points often. To solve that we assume that all points belonging to an object must move at the same speed.

Let

$$\overline{V}_p = \frac{1}{N}\sum_{i=0}^{N} V_p(i)$$

Be the mean velocity of every feature point and $V_p(i)$ velocity of each feature point. We can discard if a point loses track if the velocity of a feature point does not pass the threshold value, in this case the mean velocity. Threshold values are calculated as follows:

$$pv(t) = \begin{cases} V_p(i), & V_p(i) \geq \overline{V}_p - \sigma_p \\ V_p(i), & V_p(i) \leq \overline{V}_p + \sigma_p \\ 0, & out\ of\ threshold \end{cases}$$

Finally, kmeans method is used to ensure that a feature point does belong to the object; it is based on Euclidean distance for a set of points with correlated covariance and different variance in their axes.

3.4 Approaching of the Moving Object

To determine if the object is approaching to the UAV or moving away from it, area growth rate is calculated from a linear regression by means of the area present at the last 15 frames.

Let

$$Y = mX + b,$$

be the equation resulting of a linear regression, where Y is the area and X represents time, m suggest whether the object is approaching or moving away. If m grows the object is approaching and if *m* decreases the object is moving away. Figure 4 represents the linear regression obtained when an object is approaching the UAV. In Fig. 5 we show an example of an object approaching and moving away with speed, area and estimated position.

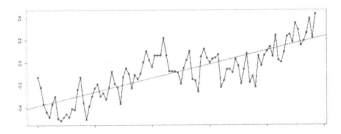

Fig. 4. Example of an approaching object

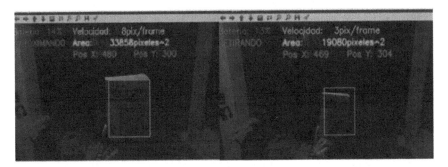

Fig. 5. Approaching (left) and withdrawal (right) of an object

3.5 Fuzzy Logic Controller

Fuzzy controller for moving object avoidance has two fuzzy inputs: (1) area of the moving object and (2) approaching rate. Its output corresponds to linear speed in x-axis showed in Fig. 6.

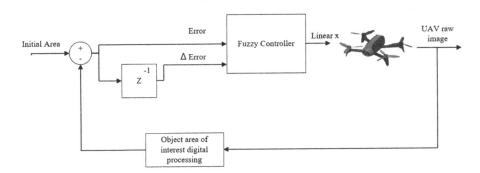

Fig. 6. Fuzzy control scheme for moving object avoidance

3.5.1   Membership Functions

Membership function for area input was determined so that we met the criterion of maintaining the moving object far from the UAV. Linguistic values are (Table 2, Fig. 7):

Table 2. Description of area membership function

Linguistic value	Value in universe of discourse	Description
Z: zero	[0, 0, 3]	There's no error
PC: little close	[2, 3, 5]	Object is not close
C: close	[3, 5, 7.5]	Object is close
MC: very close	[5, 7.5, 10]	Object is considerably close
SC: super close	[7.5, 10, 10]	Object is too close

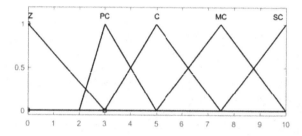

Fig. 7. Area membership function

Membership function for approaching rate was designed having in consideration to avoid a possible collision with the moving object. Linguistic values are (Table 3, Fig. 8):

Table 3. Description of approaching rate membership function

Linguistic value	Value in universe of discourse	Description
Z: zero	[0, 0, 2]	Object is not moving
PR: little fast	[1.5, 2, 3]	Object is approaching slowly
R: fast	[2, 3, 4]	Object is approaching
MR: very fast	[3, 4, 5]	Object is approaching considerably
SR: super fast	[4, 6, 6]	Object is approaching too fast

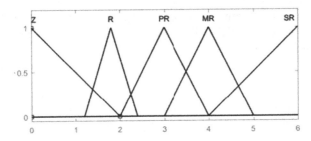

Fig. 8. Membership function for approaching rate

3.5.2   Fuzzy Output

The reaction speed that UAV must have directly depends on the approaching rate of the moving object. If the object approaches too fast UAV action must be as fast as possible, but if the object is too close and its approaching rate is not too fast, UAV must take a soft reaction to avoid the moving obstacle. Figure shows membership function for linear speed in x-axis (Fig. 9).

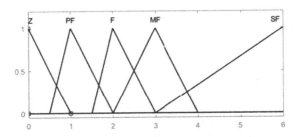

Fig. 9. Membership function for UAV linear speed in x-axis

3.5.3   Fuzzy Rules

In order to associate fuzzy sets of area and approaching rate it is necessary to establish fuzzy rules. Each fuzzy set is composed by 5 linguistic values therefore 25 rules are obtained in Table 4.

Table 4. Fuzzy rules

	Speed	Area				
		Z	PC	C	MC	SC
Approaching rate	Z	Z	Z	F	MF	MF
	PR	Z	F	F	MF	MF
	R	Z	F	MF	SF	SF
	MR	Z	MF	MF	SF	SF
	SR	Z	MF	SF	SF	SF

Output from the fuzzy controller when the object is approaching too fast is strong, but if its approaches moderately the UAV performs a soft evasion. This is shown in the fuzzy control surface in Fig. 10.

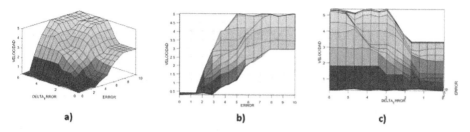

Fig. 10. Fuzzy control surfaces for UAV linear speed in x-axis (a) 3D view (b) Area-Speed view (c) Approaching rate-Speed

4   Results and Discussion

To measure the performance of our algorithms, we tested them under four evaluation criteria (Table 5).

Table 5. Evaluation criteria

Criteria	Description
Detection distance	Distance between the object and UAV's camera lens when it detects the moving object
Number of characteristics	Number of features point extracted with Shi-Tomasi method
Response time	Time in which UAV reacts to an event
Speed	Estimated approaching rate of the moving object

Objects used to test our approach were, 1 – Ballon, 2 – Book, 3 – Carton Box, 4 – hand.

4.1   Scenario: Maximum Detection Distance and Number of Characteristics

All the objects described above where placed and moved at different distances until UAV detects them, then the number of feature points was captured (Table 6).

Table 6. Number of feature points at different distances

Number of feature points	Distance 0.5 [m]	Distance 1 [m]	Distance 1.5 [m]	Distance 2 [m]
Object 1	74 ± 8	43 ± 13	35 ± 5	7 ± 4
Object 2	53 ± 7	45 ± 8	22 ± 7	2 ± 2
Object 3	38 ± 10	29 ± 5	15 ± 8	3 ± 4
Object 4	39 ± 15	28 ± 14	21 ± 11	8 ± 5

5 Conclusions and Future Work

There are several techniques and algorithms for feature point detection, to mention the most relevant SIFT, SURF, ORB and Shi-Tomasi. ORB algorithm detects considerable a larger set of feature points, but its response time exceeds and influence on transmission rate of UAV raw images.

Several trackers were tested in this project such as KCF, MOSSE and TLD, they all presented track loss due to change in luminosity caused by the moving object, optical flow approach lost feature points but did not lose track of the moving object.

Fuzzy controller is the one that fits the best to this approach, due to its instinctive nature it is possible to use imprecise expressions or events, for example, in the case that the object is approaching super-fast but is not near to the UAV, the avoidance reaction should be low in preparation for extreme avoidance. The parameters of the controller are adjusted to this type of eventualities.

References

1. Orbea, D., Moposita, J., Aguilar, W.G., Paredes, M., Reyes, R.P., Montoya, L.: Vertical take off and landing with fixed rotor. In: Chilean Conference on Electrical, Electronics Engineering, Information and Communication Technologies (CHILECON), Pucón, Chile (2017)
2. Orbea, D., Moposita, J., Aguilar, W.G., Paredes, M., León, G., Jara-Olmedo, A.: Math model of UAV multi rotor prototype with fixed wing aerodynamic structure for a flight simulator. In: De Paolis, L.T., Bourdot, P., Mongelli, A. (eds.) AVR 2017. LNCS, vol. 10324, pp. 199–211. Springer, Cham (2017). https://doi.org/10.1007/978-3-319-60922-5_15
3. Andrea, C.C., Byron, J.Q., Jorge, P.I., Inti, T.C.H., Aguilar, W.G.: Geolocation and counting of people with aerial thermal imaging for rescue purposes. In: De Paolis, L.T., Bourdot, P. (eds.) AVR 2018. LNCS, vol. 10850, pp. 171–182. Springer, Cham (2018). https://doi.org/10.1007/978-3-319-95270-3_12
4. Pardo, J.A., Aguilar, W.G., Toulkeridis, T.: Wireless communication system for the transmission of thermal images from a UAV. In: Chilean Conference on Electrical, Electronics Engineering, Information and Communication Technologies (CHILECON), Pucón, Chile (2017)
5. Jara-Olmedo, A., Medina-Pazmiño, W., Mesías, R., Araujo-Villaroel, B., Aguilar, W.G., Pardo, J.A.: Interface of optimal electro-optical/infrared for unmanned aerial vehicles. In: Rocha, Á., Guarda, T. (eds.) MICRADS 2018. SIST, vol. 94, pp. 372–380. Springer, Cham (2018). https://doi.org/10.1007/978-3-319-78605-6_32

6. Jara-Olmedo, A., Medina-Pazmiño, W., Tozer, T., Aguilar, W.G., Pardo, J.A.: E-services from emergency communication network: aerial platform evaluation. In: International Conference on eDemocracy & eGovernment (ICEDEG) (2018)

7. Aguilar, W.G., Manosalvas, J.F., Guillén, J.A., Collaguazo, B.: Robust motion estimation based on multiple monocular camera for indoor autonomous navigation of micro aerial vehicle. In: De Paolis, L.T., Bourdot, P. (eds.) AVR 2018. LNCS, vol. 10851, pp. 547–561. Springer, Cham (2018). https://doi.org/10.1007/978-3-319-95282-6_39

8. Chen, J.: UAV-guided navigation for ground robot tele-operation in a military reconnaissance environment. Ergonomics **53**(8), 940–950 (2010)

9. Zhang, C., Kovacs, J.M.: The application of small unmanned aerial systems for precision agriculture: a review. Precis. Agric. **13**(6), 693–712 (2012)

10. Zhang, J., Liu, W., Wu, Y.: Novel technique for vision-based UAV navigation. IEEE Trans. Aerosp. Electron. Syst. **47**(4), 2731–2741 (2011)

11. Aguilar, W.G., et al.: Real-time detection and simulation of abnormal crowd behavior. In: De Paolis, L.T., Bourdot, P., Mongelli, A. (eds.) AVR 2017. LNCS, vol. 10325, pp. 420–428. Springer, Cham (2017). https://doi.org/10.1007/978-3-319-60928-7_36

12. Aguilar, W.G., et al.: Statistical abnormal crowd behavior detection and simulation for real-time applications. In: Huang, Y., Wu, H., Liu, H., Yin, Z. (eds.) ICIRA 2017. LNCS (LNAI), vol. 10463, pp. 671–682. Springer, Cham (2017). https://doi.org/10.1007/978-3-319-65292-4_58

13. Aguilar, W.G., et al.: Pedestrian detection for UAVs using cascade classifiers and saliency maps. In: Rojas, I., Joya, G., Catala, A. (eds.) IWANN 2017. LNCS, vol. 10306, pp. 563–574. Springer, Cham (2017). https://doi.org/10.1007/978-3-319-59147-6_48

14. Aguilar, W.G., Luna, M., Moya, J., Abad, V., Parra, H., Ruiz, H.: Pedestrian detection for UAVs using cascade classifiers with meanshift. In: IEEE 11th International Conference on Semantic Computing (ICSC), San Diego (2017)

15. Liu, Z., Zhang, Y., Yu, X., Yuan, C.: Unmanned surface vehicles: an overview of developments and challenges. Annu. Rev. Control **41**, 71–93 (2016)

16. Martínez-Carranza, J., Valentín, L., Márquez-Aquino, F., Gonzáles-Islas, J.C., Loewen, N.: Detección de obstáculos durante vuelo autónomo de drones utilizando SLAM monocular. Res. Comput. Sci. **114**, 111–124 (2016)

17. Aleotti, J., et al.: Detection of nuclear sources by UAV teleoperation using a visuo-haptic augmented reality interface. Sensors **17**(10), 1–22 (2017)

18. Odelga, M., Stegagno, P., Bulthoff, H.H.: Obstacle detection, tracking and avoidance for a teleoperated UAV. In: Proceedings - IEEE International Conference on Robotics and Automation, pp. 2984–2990 (2016)

19. Aguilar, W.G., Angulo, C., Costa-Castello, R.: Autonomous navigation control for quadrotors in trajectories tracking. In: Huang, Y., Wu, H., Liu, H., Yin, Z. (eds.) ICIRA 2017. LNCS (LNAI), vol. 10464, pp. 287–297. Springer, Cham (2017). https://doi.org/10.1007/978-3-319-65298-6_27

20. Aguilar, W.G., Casaliglla, V.P., Pólit, J.L.: Obstacle avoidance based-visual navigation for micro aerial vehicles. Electronics **6**(1), 10 (2017)

21. Aguilar, W.G., Quisaguano, F.J., Rodríguez, G.A., Alvarez, L.G., Limaico, A., Sandoval, D.S.: Convolutional neuronal networks based monocular object detection and depth perception for micro UAVs. In: Peng, Y., Yu, K., Lu, J., Jiang, X. (eds.) IScIDE 2018. LNCS, vol. 11266, pp. 401–410. Springer, Cham (2018). https://doi.org/10.1007/978-3-030-02698-1_35

22. Aguilar, W.G., Salcedo, V.S., Sandoval, D.S., Cobeña, B.: Developing of a video-based model for UAV autonomous navigation. In: Barone, D.A.C., Teles, E.O., Brackmann, C. P. (eds.) LAWCN 2017. CCIS, vol. 720, pp. 94–105. Springer, Cham (2017). https://doi.org/10.1007/978-3-319-71011-2_8

23. Salcedo, V.S., Aguilar, W.G., Cobeña, B., Pardo, J.A., Proaño, Z.: On-board target virtualization using image features for UAV autonomous tracking. In: Boudriga, N., Alouini, M.-S., Rekhis, S., Sabir, E., Pollin, S. (eds.) UNet 2018. LNCS, vol. 11277, pp. 384–391. Springer, Cham (2018). https://doi.org/10.1007/978-3-030-02849-7_34

24. Galarza, J., Pérez, E., Serrano, E., Tapia, A., Aguilar, W.G.: Pose estimation based on monocular visual odometry and lane detection for intelligent vehicles. In: De Paolis, L.T., Bourdot, P. (eds.) AVR 2018. LNCS, vol. 10851, pp. 562–566. Springer, Cham (2018). https://doi.org/10.1007/978-3-319-95282-6_40

25. Basantes, J., et al.: Capture and processing of geospatial data with laser scanner system for 3D modeling and virtual reality of Amazonian Caves. In: IEEE Ecuador Technical Chapters Meeting (ETCM), Samborondón, Ecuador (2018)

26. Aguilar, W.G., Rodríguez, G.A., Álvarez, L., Sandoval, S., Quisaguano, F., Limaico, A.: Visual SLAM with a RGB-D camera on a quadrotor UAV using on-board processing. In: Rojas, I., Joya, G., Catala, A. (eds.) IWANN 2017. LNCS, vol. 10306, pp. 596–606. Springer, Cham (2017). https://doi.org/10.1007/978-3-319-59147-6_51

27. Hassaballah, M., Abdelmgeid, A.A., Alshazly, H.A.: Image features detection, description and matching. In: Awad, A.I., Hassaballah, M. (eds.) Image Feature Detectors and Descriptors. SCI, vol. 630, pp. 11–45. Springer, Cham (2016). https://doi.org/10.1007/978-3-319-28854-3_2

28. Yi, J., Zhang, J.: IMU-based localization and slip estimation for skid-steered mobile robots. In: 2007 IEEE/RSJ International Conference on Intelligent Robots and Systems (2007)

29. Gageik, N., Benz, P., Sergio, M.: Obstacle detection and collision avoidance for a UAV with complementary low-cost sensors. IEEE Access 3, 599–609 (2015)

30. Aguilar, W.G., Rodríguez, G.A., Álvarez, L., Sandoval, S., Quisaguano, F., Limaico, A.: Real-time 3D modeling with a RGB-D camera and on-board processing. In: De Paolis, L.T., Bourdot, P., Mongelli, A. (eds.) AVR 2017. LNCS, vol. 10325, pp. 410–419. Springer, Cham (2017). https://doi.org/10.1007/978-3-319-60928-7_35

31. Aguilar, W.G., Rodríguez, G.A., Álvarez, L., Sandoval, S., Quisaguano, F., Limaico, A.: On-board visual SLAM on a UGV using a RGB-D camera. In: Huang, Y., Wu, H., Liu, H., Yin, Z. (eds.) ICIRA 2017. LNCS (LNAI), vol. 10464, pp. 298–308. Springer, Cham (2017). https://doi.org/10.1007/978-3-319-65298-6_28

32. Yilmaz, A., Javed, O., Shah, M.: Object tracking: a survey. ACM Comput. Surv. 38(4) (2006)

33. Aguilar, W.G., Cobeña, B., Rodriguez, G., Salcedo, V.S., Collaguazo, B.: SVM and RGB-D sensor based gesture recognition for UAV control. In: De Paolis, L.T., Bourdot, P. (eds.) AVR 2018. LNCS, vol. 10851, pp. 713–719. Springer, Cham (2018). https://doi.org/10.1007/978-3-319-95282-6_50

34. Aguilar, W.G., Angulo, C.: Real-time model-based video stabilization for microaerial vehicles. Neural Process. Lett. 43(2), 459–477 (2016)

35. Aguilar, W.G., Angulo, C.: Real-time video stabilization without phantom movements for micro aerial vehicles. EURASIP J. Image Video Process. 1, 1–13 (2014)

36. Zingg, S., Scaramuzza, D., Weiss, S., Siegwart, R.: MAV navigation through indoor corridors using optical flow. In: 2010 IEEE International Conference on Robotics and Automation, pp. 3361–3368 (2010)

37. Vedaldi, A.: An implementation of SIFT detector and descriptor (2006)

38. Amaguaña, F., Collaguazo, B., Tituaña, J., Aguilar, W.G.: Simulation system based on augmented reality for optimization of training tactics on military operations. In: De Paolis, L. T., Bourdot, P. (eds.) AVR 2018. LNCS, vol. 10850, pp. 394–403. Springer, Cham (2018). https://doi.org/10.1007/978-3-319-95270-3_33
39. Aguilar, W.G., Morales, S.: 3D environment mapping using the kinect V2 and path planning based on RRT algorithms. Electronics 5(4), 70 (2016)
40. Ritcher, C., Bry, A., Roy, N.: Polynomial trajectory planning for aggressive quadrotor flight in dense indoor environments. Robot. Res. 114, 649–666 (2016)
41. Marr, D., Poggio, T.: A computational theory of human stereo vision. Proc. R. Soc. B Biol. Sci. 204(1156), 301–328 (1979)
42. Canny, J.: A computational approach to edge detection. In: Reading in Computer Vision, pp. 184–203 (1987)

Path Planning Based Navigation Using LIDAR for an Ackerman Unmanned Ground Vehicle

Wilbert G. Aguilar[1,2,3(✉)], Sebastián Sandoval[1], Alex Limaico[1],
Martin Villegas-Pico[1], and Israel Asimbaya[1]

[1] CICTE, DEEL, Universidad de las Fuerzas Armadas ESPE,
Sangolquí, Ecuador
wgaguilar@espe.edu.ec
[2] FIS, Escuela Politécnica Nacional, Quito, Ecuador
[3] GREC, Universitat Politècnica de Catalunya, Barcelona, Spain

Abstract. Path planning techniques for UGVs has been studied to reach valuable results of performance in avoiding obstacles and recognizing the best path to displace when it is trying to approach from the point A to the B. The path is estimated by computer algorithms that take data from the environment of the UGV in terms of space and depth in function of its actual position. But one problem that must be affronted is to recognize the orientation of the UGV on a specific time. This can be solved by a correctly mathematic modeling of the UGV's cinematic. In this paper we expose a path planning algorithm for an UGV of Ackermann displacement geometry to avoid nearby obstacles using a LIDAR sensor, considering limitations of movement of the UGV cause of its mechanism. The work proposed is to develop a path planning algorithm and simulate it based on the mathematical model of cinematic displacement and considering mechanical constraints of an existing UGV.

Keywords: Path planning · Ackerman · Mechanical constraints

1 Introduction

UGVs research has made important advances on navigation and exploration, requiring better equipment to analyze information from different sensors such as DARPA project [1], in addition to processing images [2, 3] captured by cameras [4] to detect obstacles near the vehicle [5, 6] or construct and 3D scene [7], texture sensors are also used to determine the conditions of the surface where the vehicle is moving in addition to considering the time of operation of the vehicle to determine the speed of displacement, as mentioned [8] in the summer the vehicle traveled at a speed of 32 km/h in the day, and 16 km/h at night. A robust technique to generate a robust path planning is to use information from a UAV [9, 10] or MAV (micro-air vehicles) [11] that overcome limitations from the UGV sensors in order to improve the performance in obstacle detection [12], also is common using complex devices, as MMWR (millimeter wave radar), to detect boundaries [13] of roads data to recognize obstacle [14, 15] and off-road sections [16, 17], but these sensors can present false positive detections due to

© Springer Nature Switzerland AG 2019
H. Yu et al. (Eds.): ICIRA 2019, LNAI 11744, pp. 399–410, 2019.
https://doi.org/10.1007/978-3-030-27541-9_33

limited sensed data. LiDAR is used for its efficient obstacle detection [18] and its disposition in the vehicle improves acquisition of data, and later, construction of 3D environments.

Nevertheless, this article proposes to create a path planning system [7, 19, 20] of an unknown environment using just a LIDAR sensor, that is fundamental for developing a robust point-to-point approach to reach a desired location, also using both devices will complement weaknesses of each other. After choosing the devices is required a mathematical model of cinematic displacement considering constraints of movement [21]. To accomplish this goal, our first task is to model the movement cinematic of an existing UGV with Ackermann displacement geometry to develop a simulation of how this path planning will function. Using techniques of computer vision [22–24] and depth sensors we are capable of receive a feedback of the environment that the robot is displacing in, but the latent problem is determining pose estimation [25], and localization [26] on a certain time.

2   Mathematical Model of an Ackermann UGV

The mechanical displacement geometry is a trapezoid conformed by bars and arms that are connected to the wheels and make possible the turn of the vehicle by changing the angles of the wheels, been the two angles different. The center of the rotation is outside the vehicle and displacement has constraints for its construction. Figure 1 provides a scheme of the vehicle used to develop this paper.

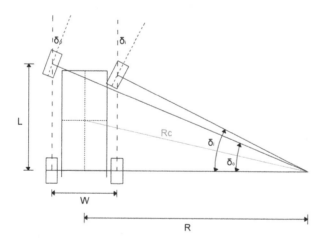

Fig. 1. Scheme of an UGV with Ackermann displacement geometry

Also, can be expressed as

$$\cot \delta_o - \cot \delta_i = \frac{W}{L} \tag{1}$$

Which is obtained by a trigonometric relation from the center of rotation and the mechanical components [27]. Using the approach of the two angles we obtain the Ackermann angle to simulate approach movements, also, we consider that all the movements are circles based on the radius of rotation and a velocity vector, considering x as the direction as show in Fig. 2.

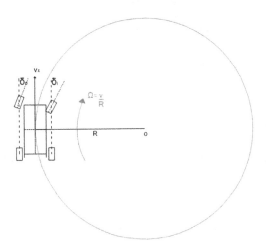

Fig. 2. Circular movement

Where the Ackermann angle is

$$\cot \delta = \frac{\cot \delta_i + \cot \delta_o}{2} \tag{2}$$

And can be expressed as

$$R = \frac{L}{\delta_{ACK}} \tag{3}$$

where

$$\delta_i + \delta_o = \delta = \delta_{ACK} \tag{4}$$

Therefore, we can express the movement of the vehicle using the radius of rotation and angular velocity. However, this displacement implies a rotation of the coordinate system as show in Fig. 3 and defining this rotation as Ψ.

In addition, we can express the velocity of rotation with

$$\dot{\Psi} = \frac{v_X}{R} \tag{5}$$

And with Eq. (3) we can express (5) as

$$\dot{\Psi} = \frac{v_X}{L} \delta_{ACK} \tag{6}$$

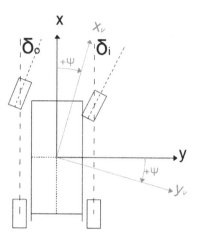

Fig. 3. Rotation of coordinate system

The coordinate system can be expressed as a vector that includes the principal coordinates (X, Y) and the coordinates of the vehicle (x, y) while it in displacement show in Eq. (7).

$$\begin{bmatrix} \hat{I} \\ \hat{J} \end{bmatrix} = \underbrace{\begin{bmatrix} c\Psi & -s\Psi \\ s\Psi & c\Psi \end{bmatrix}}_{[T^t]_{xy}^{XY}} \begin{bmatrix} \hat{i} \\ \hat{j} \end{bmatrix} \tag{7}$$

Therefore, the velocity vector of the vehicle can be related with the coordinated system of the vehicle as

$$\overrightarrow{v_{veh}}^{XY} = [T^t]\overrightarrow{v_{veh}}^{cy} \tag{8}$$

$$\begin{bmatrix} v_x \\ v_y \end{bmatrix} = \underbrace{\begin{bmatrix} c\Psi & -s\Psi \\ s\Psi & c\Psi \end{bmatrix}}_{[T^t]} \begin{bmatrix} v_x \\ 0 \end{bmatrix} \tag{9}$$

$$v_{veh}^x = (c\Psi \cdot V_x)\hat{I} \tag{10}$$

$$v_{veh}^y = (c\Psi \cdot V_x)\hat{J} \tag{11}$$

Finally, to define the pose of the vehicle we integrate the vehicle's velocity on its own coordinates and then integrate the angle of rotation

$$X_{veh} = \int v_{veh}^x dt \tag{12}$$

$$Y_{veh} = \int v_{veh}^y dt \tag{13}$$

$$\Psi = \int \dot{\Psi} dt \tag{14}$$

3   Simulation of the Mathematic Model

The cinematic model in space 2D of the vehicle can be expressed by the Eqs. (15) and (16) that includes width and longitude of the physic model

$$v_x = \left[v_x \cdot \cos(\Psi) - \left(\frac{L}{2} \right) \cdot \omega \cdot \sin(\Psi) \right] \tag{15}$$

$$v_y = \left[v_x \cdot \sin(\Psi) + \left(\frac{L}{2} \right) \cdot \omega \cdot \cos(\Psi) \right] \tag{16}$$

The block scheme for the cinematic model Fig. 4 define a simulation of movement of the vehicle, also define its pose as show in Fig. 6.

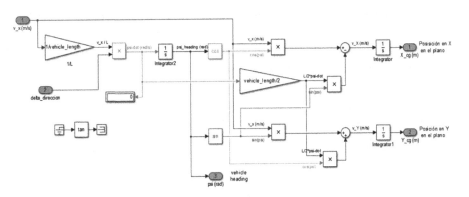

Fig. 4. Block scheme of cinematic model

The result of the simulation is show in Fig. 5.

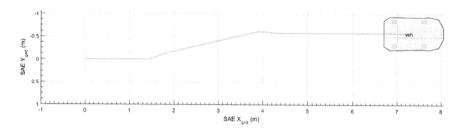

Fig. 5. Simulation of cinematic model

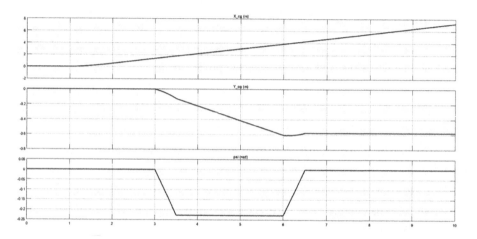

Fig. 6. Response of (a) position x, (b) position y (c) orientation Ψ

In Fig. 7 is show the block diagram of the vehicle that also includes directions parameters, engine speed and cinematic model.

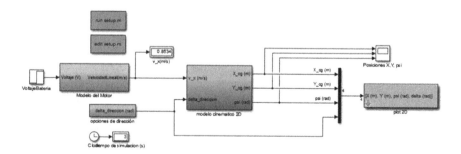

Fig. 7. Block diagram of vehicle simulation

4   Location and Mapping

Location and pose estimation are established with the environment perception obtained with the LiDAR sensor which establish a 2D mapping. Then Core SLAM algorithm is used to define a known space map using initial parameters.

We can observe the resulting map generated in Fig. 8 considering a depth perception.

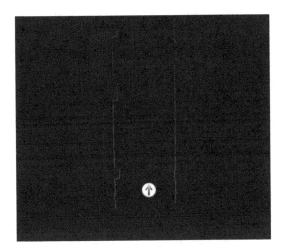

Fig. 8. Depth profile for initial state

After obtained the 2D map we use Profile lecture 2D to establish an Ethernet connection and stock the data acquired by the sensors. Using a simplified Montecarlo algorithm we achieve join profiles in a 2D map integrated. Visual odometry is used just to establish an initial point and map resolution is of one pixel per cm. The result is show in Fig. 9.

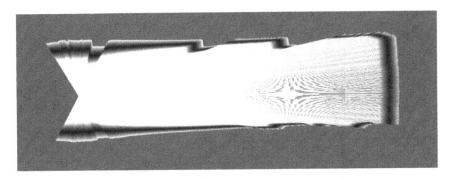

Fig. 9. 2D map PGM of the mapped environment

5 Path Planning

We assume that the vehicle will trace a circular path, indeed, we use initial parameters: travel angle defines by time, start angle, start point of trace, point on 2D space, center of turn radio that is defined by Ackermann angle, to trace the path. The radio of the circle path is defined in Eq. (17) and different paths are traced by changing values of time, velocity and angle.

$$R = \lim_{\delta_{ack} \to 0} \frac{1}{\tan \delta_{ack}} = \lim_{\alpha \to 0} \frac{1}{\tan \alpha} = 0 \tag{17}$$

Possible paths are show in Fig. 10 where we change all the parameters.

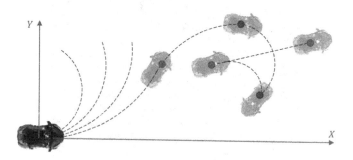

Fig. 10. Possible paths of vehicle

Simulation results path of vehicle, as show in Fig. 11, trace its position in 2D environment and its viable estimate movement in real environment.

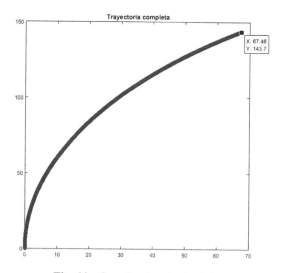

Fig. 11. Completed path simulation

To build a global planner we use Risk-RRT algorithm base to modify it for working in known environments and it has the task of perceptions of fixed and mobile obstacles in order to avoid collisions, also it will plan a safe path. Is required a mathematic function to identify risk of the final position, this can be expressed in a covariance function as show in Eq. (20).

$$f(x) \sim G(m(x), k(x, x'))$$ (18)

$$m(x) = E[f(x)]$$ (19)

$$k(x, x') = E[(f(x) - m(x))(f(x') - m(x'))]$$ (20)

Where $G(\mu, \Sigma)$ is the Gaussian process with average μ and covariance Σ functions of a known space E. Algorithm to avoid obstacles has initial aspects as initiation, search, path follow and environment identification.

It is necessary to choose the correct nodes while the trajectory is growing. The heuristic is defined by (21).

$$\overline{w}(q_N) = \frac{\sqrt[n]{L_\pi(q_N)}}{dist(q_0, q_N, P)}$$ (21)

$$w(q_N) = \frac{\overline{w}(q_N)}{\Sigma_q \overline{w}_q}$$ (22)

The result is show in Fig. 12 where the grow of the trajectory search for the final point for a period of time until the tree restarts and a new trajectory is beginning [28].

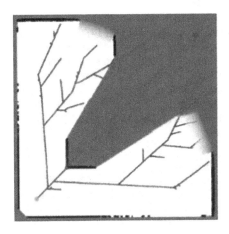 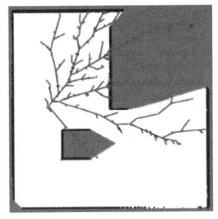

Fig. 12. Trajectory growth in function of the environment explored

An NHR-RRT algorithm does not find the propose goal at the beginning, but it allows to be adaptable and dynamic at the map and find a path that brings closer the vehicle to the goal.

6   Conclusions and Future Work

This paper showed a propose for a path planning using sensor LIDAR in order to create a 2D map without the aid of external factors. Path planning is built by an algorithm NHR-RRT to search for the best path that is closer to the final goal, reaching this with the interactions of ramifications of the tree and choosing the best nodes according to the parameters mentioned previously.

Results show that in a certain time the ramifications will reach the final point by extending ramifications and choosing nodes, also its pose is established supposing the vehicle as a rectangle and considering previous values of turn radius and angular velocity.

Acknowledgment. This work is part of the projects VisualNavDrone 2016-PIC-024 and MultiNavCar 2016-PIC-025, from the Universidad de las Fuerzas Armadas ESPE, directed by Dr. Wilbert G. Aguilar.

References

1. Douglas, W.: Defence Technical Information Center, junio 1995. https://apps.dtic.mil/docs/citations/ADA422845. Accessed 28 febrero 2019
2. Aguilar, W.G., Angulo, C.: Real-time model-based video stabilization for microaerial vehicles. Neural Process. Lett. **43**(2), 459–477 (2016)
3. Aguilar, W.G., Angulo, C.: Real-time video stabilization without phantom movements for micro aerial vehicles. EURASIP J. Image Video Process. **1**, 1–13 (2014)
4. Basantes, J., et al.: Capture and processing of geospatial data with laser scanner system for 3D modeling and virtual reality of Amazonian Caves. In: IEEE Ecuador Technical Chapters Meeting (ETCM), Samborondón, Ecuador (2018)
5. Matthies, L., et al.: IEEE Xplore Digital Library, septiembre 1998. https://ieeexplore.ieee.org/abstract/document/713790. Accessed 28 febrero 2019
6. Aguilar, W.G., Casaliglla, V.P., Pólit, J.L.: Obstacle avoidance based-visual navigation for micro aerial vehicles. Electronics **6**(1), 10 (2017)
7. Aguilar, W.G., Morales, S.: 3D environment mapping using the kinect V2 and path planning based on RRT algorithms. Electronics **5**(4), 70 (2016)
8. Shoemaker, C.M., Bornstein, J.A.: IEEE Xplore Digital Library, septiembre 1998. https://ieeexplore.ieee.org/abstract/document/713784. Accessed 28 febrero 2019
9. Orbea, D., Moposita, J., Aguilar, W.G., Paredes, M., Reyes, R.P., Montoya, L.: Vertical take off and landing with fixed rotor. In: Chilean Conference on Electrical, Electronics Engineering, Information and Communication Technologies (CHILECON), Pucón, Chile (2017)

10. Orbea, D., Moposita, J., Aguilar, W.G., Paredes, M., León, G., Jara-Olmedo, A.: Math model of UAV multi rotor prototype with fixed wing aerodynamic structure for a flight simulator. In: De Paolis, L.T., Bourdot, P., Mongelli, A. (eds.) AVR 2017. LNCS, vol. 10324, pp. 199–211. Springer, Cham (2017). https://doi.org/10.1007/978-3-319-60922-5_15

11. Dewan, A., Mahendran, A., Soni, N., Krishna, K.M.: IEEE Xplore Digital Library, 7 Nov 2013. https://ieeexplore.ieee.org/abstract/document/6697188. Accessed 23 Apr 2019

12. Kim, J.H., Kwon, J.-W., Seo, J.: IET Digital Library, 25 septiembre 2014. https://digital-library.theiet.org/content/journals/10.1049/el.2014.2227. Accessed 28 febrero 2019

13. Galarza, J., Pérez, E., Serrano, E., Tapia, A., Aguilar, W.G.: Pose estimation based on monocular visual odometry and lane detection for intelligent vehicles. In: De Paolis, L.T., Bourdot, P. (eds.) AVR 2018. LNCS, vol. 10851, pp. 562–566. Springer, Cham (2018). https://doi.org/10.1007/978-3-319-95282-6_40

14. Aguilar, W.G., et al.: Real-time detection and simulation of abnormal crowd behavior. In: De Paolis, L.T., Bourdot, P., Mongelli, A. (eds.) AVR 2017. LNCS, vol. 10325, pp. 420–428. Springer, Cham (2017). https://doi.org/10.1007/978-3-319-60928-7_36

15. Aguilar, W.G., et al.: Statistical abnormal crowd behavior detection and simulation for real-time applications. In: Huang, Y., Wu, H., Liu, H., Yin, Z. (eds.) ICIRA 2017. LNCS (LNAI), vol. 10463, pp. 671–682. Springer, Cham (2017). https://doi.org/10.1007/978-3-319-65292-4_58

16. Zhang, Y., Wang, J., Wang, X., Li, C., Wang, L.: IEEE Explore Digital Library, 23 Sept 2015. https://ieeexplore.ieee.org/abstract/document/7320746. Accessed 23 Apr 2019

17. Zhang, Y., Wang, J., Wang, X., Li, C., Wang, L.: IEEE Explore Digital Library, 18 Sept 2015. https://ieeexplore.ieee.org/abstract/document/7313180. Accessed 25 Apr 2019

18. Shang, E., An, X., Li, J., He, H.: IEEE Explore Digital Library, 11 Oct 2014. https://ieeexplore.ieee.org/abstract/document/6957888. Accessed 23 Apr 2019

19. Cabras, P., Rosell, J., Pérez, A., Aguilar, W.G., Rosell, A.: Haptic-based navigation for the virtual bronchoscopy. In: 18th IFAC World Congress, Milano, Italy (2011)

20. Aguilar, W.G., Abad, V., Ruiz, H., Aguilar, J., Aguilar-Castillo, F.: RRT-based path planning for virtual bronchoscopy simulator. In: De Paolis, L.T., Bourdot, P., Mongelli, A. (eds.) AVR 2017. LNCS, vol. 10325, pp. 155–165. Springer, Cham (2017). https://doi.org/10.1007/978-3-319-60928-7_13

21. Moga, G.L., Girbacia, T.M.: SpringerLink, 24 May 2018. https://sci-hub.tw/https://link.springer.com/chapter/10.1007/978-3-319-79111-1_30. Accessed 25 Apr 2019

22. Aguilar, W.G., Salcedo, V.S., Sandoval, D.S., Cobeña, B.: Developing of a video-based model for UAV autonomous navigation. In: Barone, D.A.C., Teles, E.O., Brackmann, C. P. (eds.) LAWCN 2017. CCIS, vol. 720, pp. 94–105. Springer, Cham (2017). https://doi.org/10.1007/978-3-319-71011-2_8

23. Amaguaña, F., Collaguazo, B., Tituaña, J., Aguilar, W.G.: Simulation system based on augmented reality for optimization of training tactics on military operations. In: De Paolis, L. T., Bourdot, P. (eds.) AVR 2018. LNCS, vol. 10850, pp. 394–403. Springer, Cham (2018). https://doi.org/10.1007/978-3-319-95270-3_33

24. Salcedo, V.S., Aguilar, W.G., Cobeña, B., Pardo, J.A., Proaño, Z.: On-board target virtualization using image features for UAV autonomous tracking. In: Boudriga, N., Alouini, M.-S., Rekhis, S., Sabir, E., Pollin, S. (eds.) UNet 2018. LNCS, vol. 11277, pp. 384–391. Springer, Cham (2018). https://doi.org/10.1007/978-3-030-02849-7_34

25. Mezouar, Y., Chaumette, F.: IEEEXplore Digital Library, agosto 2002. https://ieeexplore.ieee.org/abstract/document/1044366. Accessed 28 febrero 2019

26. Andrea, C.C., Byron, J.Q., Jorge, P.I., Inti, T.C.H., Aguilar, W.G.: Geolocation and counting of people with aerial thermal imaging for rescue purposes. In: De Paolis, L.T., Bourdot, P. (eds.) AVR 2018. LNCS, vol. 10850, pp. 171–182. Springer, Cham (2018). https://doi.org/10.1007/978-3-319-95270-3_12

27. Zhao, J.-S., Liu, X., Feng, Z.-J., Dai, J.S.: ResearchGate, 7 enero 2013. https://www.researchgate.net/publication/265755401_Design_of_an_Ackermann_Type_Steering_Mechanism. Accessed 11 marzo 2019

28. Fulgenzi, C., Spalanzani, A., Laugier, C., Tay, C.: HAL-Inria, 19 Oct 2010. https://hal.inria.fr/inria-00526601/. Accessed 25 Apr 2019

Robotic Vision, Recognition and Reconstruction

Improved Simple Linear Iterative Clustering Algorithm Using HSL Color Space

Fan Su[1], Hui Xu[1], Guodong Chen[1(✉)], Zhenhua Wang[1], Lining Sun[1], and Zheng Wang[2(✉)]

[1] School of Mechanical and Electric Engineering, Jiangsu Provincial Key Laboratory of Advanced Robotics, Collaborative Innovation Center of Suzhou Nano Science and Technology, Soochow University, Suzhou 215123, China
guodongxyz@163.com
[2] Shanghai No. 6 People's Hospital, Shanghai 200233, China
wangzheng6th@163.com

Abstract. Image processing is a very important technical support in robotic vision. As a preprocessing step for image processing, superpixel segmentation is one of the significant branches of image segmentation. Simple linear iterative clustering (SLIC) algorithm, as a widely used superpixel segmentation algorithm, can help to deal with boundary adherence and reduce computational cost for image segmentation. However, the segmentation result of the original SLIC algorithm fails to adhere well to boundary of object, causing undersegmentation sometimes. Therefore, the work proposed an improved method based on SLIC to address the problem of undersegmentation. First, HSL color space was introduced to have a better recognition and processing of color instead of CIELAB color space. In addition, adding flexible combinations of weight coefficient for HSL can achieve different results. Finally, an edge detection strategy was used to enhance the accuracy of superpixel segmentation. The quantification effect of the proposed method was verified using the dataset BSDS500. The experimental results show that the improved algorithm has better accuracy and efficiency.

Keywords: Robotic vision · SLIC · HSL color space · Sobel operator · Superpixel

1 Introduction

Image segmentation is a process of dividing image space into a certain number of regions according to the characteristics of gray level, spectrum and texture, which is an important part of robotic vision. The traditional segmentation method takes pixels as the basic processing unit. However, with the development of technology, the size of image is getting larger and larger, which fails to meet the application requirements of the direct pixel-based segmentation method when facing large images. Compared with pixels, superpixels are more conducive to extracting local features and expressing structural information, and can greatly reduce the computational complexity of post processing. Therefore, Superpixels can provide better and more useful images for robotic vision applications.

© Springer Nature Switzerland AG 2019
H. Yu et al. (Eds.): ICIRA 2019, LNAI 11744, pp. 413–425, 2019.
https://doi.org/10.1007/978-3-030-27541-9_34

Currently, algorithms for generating superpixels can be broadly divided into two categories: graph-based or gradient-ascent-based algorithms. Graph-based algorithms consider the each pixel as a node in an image. The edge weight between two nodes is proportional to the similarity between neighboring pixels. Final superpixels are obtained by minimizing a cost function defined over the image [1]. The normalized cuts method, proposed by Jianbo Shi, globally minimize the cost function using contour and texture characteristics. This algorithm has a bad boundary adherence and computational efficiency [2]. Moore et al. proposed superpixel lattice to generate superpixels. This method preserves the information of topological structure of the image, but its performance depends heavily on the pre-extracted edges of the image [3]. Entropy rate superpixel was proposed by Mingyu Liu. In this method, an objective function including random walk entropy and balance term is proposed. The segmentation is achieved by maximizing the objective function, generating regular and uniform superpixels [4].

Gradient-ascent-based algorithms adopt the idea of image segmentation and pixel clustering based on gradient. Mean shift, proposed by Comaniciu et al., is an iterative mode-seeking process. It can generate regular shape of the superpixels but fails to control the number and compactness of superpixels [5]. Another mode-seeking algorithm named quick shift proposed by Vedaldi and Soatto. Estimating the density of each pixel, the algorithm assigns each pixel to a pattern in accordance with the gradient of density, which represents the final segmentation result [6]. SLIC, presented by Achanta et al., is used to generate superpixels based on similarity of color and distance. Because of the simple theory and perfect result, this method has become a widely used superpixel segmentation algorithm [7].

This research proposes some new improvements based on SLIC. First, we convert RGB color space to HSL color space for processing when measuring the color distance. Second, adding flexible combinations of weight coefficient for HSL can achieve different results. Finally, we introduce the sobel operator to replace the edge detection algorithm of original algorithm. To sum up, there are two main advantages: On the one hand, the proposed algorithm has better boundary adherence. On the other hand, the proposed algorithm has better computational efficiency.

Fig. 1. Image segmented using SLIC algorithm into superpixels of (approximate) size 64, 256, and 1024 pixels. The superpixels are compact, uniform in size, and adhere well to region boundaries.

2 SLIC Algorithm

Simple linear iterative clustering, proposed by Achanta et al. in 2010, is simple to use and understand. The method adopted k-means clustering algorithm to generate superpixels of regular size. Each superpixel consists of a cluster center and multiple pixels. The algorithm can obtains superpixels by clustering color and distance characteristics of pixels. Figure 1 shows the result of segmentation by this algorithm.

The first step is initialization of cluster centers. Assuming the number of total pixels in an image is N, we desire to segment into K superpixels of the same size. Then, the size of each superpixel is N/K, and the step between adjacent cluster centers is roughly equal to $s = \sqrt{N/K}$. Transforming the image from RGB color space to CIELAB color space, the cluster center can be represented as a five-dimensional feature vector $C_i = [l_i, a_i, b_i, x_i, y_i]^T, i = 1, 2 \ldots K$, which consists of color values in CIELAB color space and coordinates of each pixel. The centers are moved to locations where the gradient is the lowest in a 3×3 neighborhood. Gradient is defined as follows:

$$G(x, y) = \|I(x+1, y) - I(x-1, y)\|^2 + \|I(x, y+1) - I(x, y-1)\|^2 \qquad (1)$$

where $I(x, y)$ is the lab vector corresponding to the pixel at position (x, y); $\|.\|$ is the L_2 norm. Equation (1) considers both color and position information of pixels.

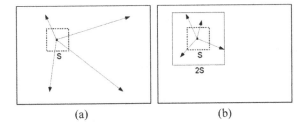

(a)   (b)

Fig. 2. Reducing the superpixel search regions. (a) Standard k-means searches the whole image; (b) SLIC searches within a limited region.

The second step is assignment. Each pixel is assigned a label by searching region around a cluster center. Unlike the standard k-means algorithm searching in the whole image, the search range of SLIC is limited to $2S \times 2S$, which can accelerate the convergence of the algorithm (See Fig. 2). Each pixel is represented as $[l_i, a_i, b_i]^T$ in CIELAB color space, and the position of the pixel can be represented as $[x_i, y_i]^T$. These two have different meanings, so it is not appropriate to directly calculate the five-dimensional Euclidean distance here. In order to integrate the two distances into a unified measurement, the author proposed the calculation between pixel and cluster center as follows:

$$d_{lab} = \sqrt{(l_k - l_i)^2 + (a_k - a_i)^2 + (b_k - b_i)^2}$$
$$d_{xy} = \sqrt{(x_k - x_i)^2 + (y_k - y_i)^2} \tag{2}$$
$$D_s = d_{lab} + \tfrac{m}{s} d_{xy}$$

where d_{lab} is the color proximity between pixels; d_{xy} is the spatial proximity between pixels; D_s is the similarity between pixels. Obviously, the lower the value D_s, the higher the similarity is. s is the step between adjacent cluster center; m controls the compactness of superpixels, adjusting the proportion of spatial distance and color distance. The larger the value m, the more compact and regular each superpixel is. In general, the range of value m is $[1, 40]$.

The last step is iterative optimization. The label of the pixel i is initialized to $l(i)$, and the distance between the pixel and cluster center is initialized to $d(i) = \infty$. Do the following calculation:

$$d(i) = \begin{cases} D_s, & \text{if } D_s < d(i) \\ d(i), & \text{if } D_s \geq d(i) \end{cases} \tag{3}$$

$$l(i) = \begin{cases} K, & \text{if } D_s < d(i) \\ l(i), & \text{if } D_s \geq d(i) \end{cases} \tag{4}$$

where K is the number of superpixels. If the value D_s is less than $d(i)$, the label of cluster center will be assigned to this pixel i. When all the pixels are attached to the nearest cluster center, the average of all the pixels in each superpixel is calculated as the new cluster center θ_j:

$$\theta_j = \frac{1}{N_j} \sum_{x_k \in G_j} C_k \tag{5}$$

where G_j is clustering region; N_j is the number of pixels in G_j; C_k is the five-dimensional feature vector of pixel x_k in G_j [8]. The step can be repeat iteratively until the error computed by new cluster center locations and previous cluster center locations converges. Experiments show that 10 iterations is appropriate for most images. At last, some isolated pixels are assigned to the nearest cluster center using the adjacent merging strategy for the better connectivity.

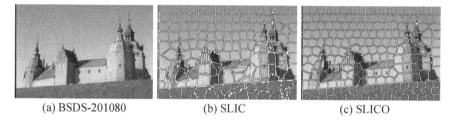

(a) BSDS-201080   (b) SLIC   (c) SLICO

Fig. 3. Comparison between SLICO and SLIC with 200 superpixels. We can see that SLICO algorithm better deals with textured and non-textured regions in the image.

This is the main procedure of SLIC algorithm above. Later, the author improved the original algorithm and proposed a zero-parameter version of SLIC, namely SLICO. Figure 3 shows the comparison between results of SLICO and SLIC algorithm. The basic steps of the two algorithms are similar. However, SLICO does away with this problem of setting parameters completely. The user no longer has to set the compactness parameter or try different values of it. SLICO adaptively chooses the compactness parameter for each superpixel differently. This generates superpixels of regular shape in both textured and non-textured regions alike. The improvement comes with hardly any compromise on the computational efficiency – SLICO continues to be as fast as SLIC. Of course SLICO has the same problem of undersegmentation. As shown in Fig. 4(b), the algorithm cannot handle the branches in the image well, causing bad boundary adherence. Therefore, our work will improve the SLICO algorithm for obtaining the better result.

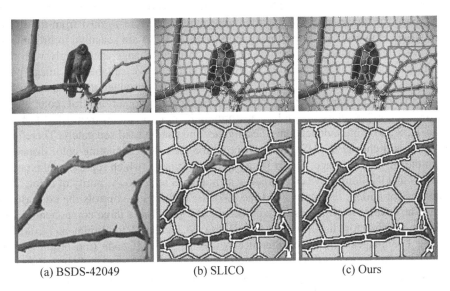

(a) BSDS-42049   (b) SLICO   (c) Ours

Fig. 4. Comparison between SLICO and our proposed approach with 200 superpixels. From the local enlarged image, we can obviously see that our proposed approach is better than the original in dealing with the boundary of branches, and the resulting superpixels adhere to region boundary very well.

3   The Proposed Approach

In this section, we describe some new improvements which contain two parts. The key point is the application of HSL color space, which largely affects the computational efficiency and segmenting accuracy. The technical details are discussed below.

3.1   Color Proximity

Since superpixels normally serve as a preprocessing task for image segmentation, how to generate superpixels with good boundary and high computational efficiency is a crucial problem [9]. For the SLICO algorithm, distance measure, the core part of the algorithm, greatly determines the final segmentation results. Edge detection algorithm affects the position of cluster center, which is a prerequisite for distance measure. Based on this, we proposed some improvements on the basis of the original algorithm. Figure 4 shows the comparison between results of SLICO and our proposed approach. From the local enlarged image, we can obviously see that our proposed approach is better than the original in dealing with the boundary of branches, and the resulting superpixels adhere to region boundary very well.

Whether the segmentation result of SLICO algorithm adheres to boundary well depends largely on the color difference of pixel. The color information collected by the existing image device is RGB value, so the RGB is the most basic and commonly used color space for image processing. Other color models are transformed from the RGB color space. However, since the three components of RGB are sensitive to brightness and have a close connection, the three components can change accordingly with the brightness changing. Therefore the RGB color space is not suitable for image processing. Human visual sensitivity to brightness is much stronger than sensitivity to shade of color. In order to facilitate color processing and recognition, HSL color space is introduced to computer vision by transforming pixel information from RGB to HSL mode. H, S and L are independent of each other and can be used separately. Therefore, our work will choose the HSL color space as the basis for calculating color distance.

In the HSL color space, hue H is an attribute of vision, which represents the range of colors that the human eye can perceive; saturation S refers to the purity of color. The larger the saturation, the more vivid the color is; lightness L controls the contrast of color. The smaller the lightness, the darker the color is. These three components have different weights for distance measure. H can be increased for bright and colorful images. For images with little difference between light and shade (too bright or too dark), the L can be reduced, whereas for those with obvious changes in light and shade, the L component should be increased. Generally speaking, the weight of S is not need to be changed too much [8]. Figure 7 shows an example of setting weights for different types of images. Assuming each pixel can be represented as $[h_i, s_i, l_i]^T$ in HSL color space, color proximity is calculated as follows.

$$d_{hsl} = \sqrt{\alpha(h_k - h_i)^2 + \beta(s_k - s_i)^2 + \gamma(l_k - l_i)^2} \tag{6}$$

where d_{hsl} is the color proximity between pixels; h_k, s_k and l_k are components of cluster center; h_i, s_i and l_i are components of certain pixel in cluster region. Weight coefficients α, β and γ are used to adjust the proportion of three components in order to adapt to different types of images. Generally, weight coefficients are denoted as 3, 1 and 5. The square root in Eq. (6) is unnecessary, because the formula only compares the distance between pixels without requiring to calculate the specific distance, which can greatly reduce the computational complexity and improve the operating efficiency of the algorithm. Based on the improvements above, the complete distance measure changes as follows.

$$d'_{hsl} = \alpha(h_k - h_i)^2 + \beta(s_k - s_i)^2 + \gamma(l_k - l_i)^2$$
$$d'_{xy} = (x_k - x_i)^2 + (y_k - y_i)^2 \tag{7}$$
$$D = \frac{d'_{hsl}}{m^2} + \frac{d'_{xy}}{s^2}$$

where d'_{hsl} is the color proximity between pixels; d'_{xy} is the spatial proximity between pixels; D is the similarity between pixels. Obviously, the lower the value D, the higher the similarity between the pixels is. s is the step between adjacent cluster center; m controls the compactness of superpixels, changing adaptively from 10 by default.

3.2 Edge Detection Strategy

The original algorithm makes a relocation for cluster centers so as to avoid them falling into boundary or noise point. Different from the calculation of gradient proposed by the original algorithm, our work proposes sobel operator to replace it. Compared with the original algorithm considering 4-connected regions, sobel operator considers the 8-connections of the cluster center and combines the differential operation with the local weighted average to extract the edge. This method strengthens the weights in the four directions of the center pixel and weakens the noise meanwhile. The gradient is defined as follows:

$$\begin{aligned}
Gx &= [f(x+1, y-1) + 2*f(x+1, y) + f(x+1, y+1)] \\
&\quad - [f(x-1, y-1) + 2*f(x-1, y) + f(x-1, y+1)] \\
Gy &= [f(x-1, y-1) + 2*f(x, y-1) + f(x+1, y-1)] \\
&\quad - [f(x-1, y+1) + 2*f(x, y+1) + f(x+1, y+1)] \\
G &= |Gx| + |Gy|
\end{aligned} \tag{8}$$

where $f(x, y)$ is the HSL vector of the corresponding pixel (x, y); an approximation G without square root is used to improve the efficiency. Figure 8 shows a comparison of the segmentation before and after using the sobel operator.

4 Experimental Result and Analysis

Our method is implemented in C++ and runs on a PC with Intel Core i7-7500 CPU with 2.70 GHz, 8G RAM, and 64bit operation system. We compare our proposed method with SLICO algorithm on the Berkeley Segmentation Data Set and Benchmarks 500 (BSDS500) [10], using the evaluation methods proposed in Ref. [11, 12] and [13]. 200 images of resolution 481 × 321 from BSDS500 are selected randomly for evaluate the two algorithms.

4.1   Benchmark

The benchmark aims to score the requirements for the SLICO and our proposed algorithms, including Boundary Recall (*BR*), Undersegmentation Error (*UE*), Explained Variation (*EV*) and Runtime (*RT*). *BR*, *UE* and *EV* are the metrics to evaluate boundary adherence. *RT* is the metric to evaluate computational efficiency. Let $S = \{S_j\}_{j=1}^{K}$ and $G = \{G_i\}$ be partitions of the same image $I : x_n \mapsto I(x_n), 1 \leq n \leq N$, where S and G represent a superpixel segmentation and a ground truth segmentation, respectively [14].

Boundary Recall (*BR*) [15] reflects agreement of the boundary between superpixel segmentation and ground truth segmentation. It is calculated as Eq. (9).

$$BR(G, S) = \frac{TP(G, S)}{TP(G, S) + FN(G, S)} \tag{9}$$

where $TP(G, S)$ and $FN(G, S)$ are the number of true positive and false negative boundary pixels in S with respect to G. High *BR* represents better boundary adherence. Figure 5(a) shows the comparison between SLICO and our proposed algorithm. It is obvious that the proposed algorithm has higher boundary recall.

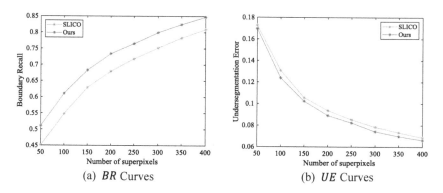

(a) *BR* Curves   (b) *UE* Curves

Fig. 5. *BR* curves and *UE* curves

Undersegmentation Error (*UE*) [16] reflect the degree that superpixels do not precisely overlap the ground truth segmentation, which also implicitly measures boundary adherence. It is defined as

$$UE(G, S) = \frac{1}{N} \sum_{G_i} \sum_{S_j \cap G_i \neq \emptyset} min\{|S_j \cap G_i|, |S_j - G_i|\} \tag{10}$$

where N is the total number of pixels in an image; Lower *UE* means more overlapped superpixels and that the result is close to the ground truth. As shown in Fig. 5(b), the performance of the two algorithms is almost similar, and our proposed algorithm is slightly better than the original algorithm.

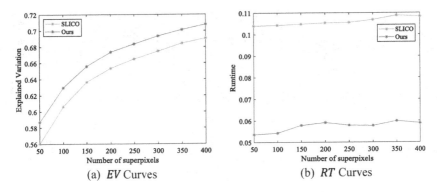

(a) *EV* Curves (b) *RT* Curves

Fig. 6. *EV* curves and *RT* curves

Explained Variation (*EV*) [17] quantifies the quality of a superpixel segmentation without considering a ground truth. The information of local and global image can be combined to evaluate adherence to the boundary. EV is calculated as follows.

$$EV(S) = \frac{\sum_{S_j} |S_j| (\mu(S_j) - \mu(I))^2}{\sum_{x_n} (I(x_n) - \mu(I))^2} \tag{11}$$

where $\mu(S_j)$ and $\mu(I)$ are the mean color of superpixel S_j and the image I, respectively. *EV* quantifies changes of image that can be interpreted by superpixels. Higher is better. Figure 6(a) shows the comparison results between the original algorithm and the proposed algorithm under this standard. The proposed algorithm presents better performance.

Runtime (*RT*) reflects the average time to process a picture by the algorithm. Therefore, the lower the time, the higher the computational efficiency of the algorithm is. From Fig. 6(b), we can clearly see that the computational efficiency of our proposed algorithm is much better than that of SLICO algorithm, and nearly twice faster.

4.2 Analysis

Setting of the Weight Coefficient. The superiority of the HSL color space is that the three components can be processed independently. For different types of images, the proportion of the three components can be adjusted to obtain a better segmentation result. As shown in Fig. 7, it can be seen that these are two different types of images. The top image is richer and brighter. We can increase the proportion of H slightly, and the desired effect can be obtained. The image below is dim and contrasted. Obviously, we can increase the proportion of L, and can get a good segmentation. Therefore, the introduction of HSL color space has played a certain role in improving the boundary adherence of superpixel segmentation. As shown in Figs. 5 and 6(a), our proposed algorithm has a better performance with respect to boundary adherence.

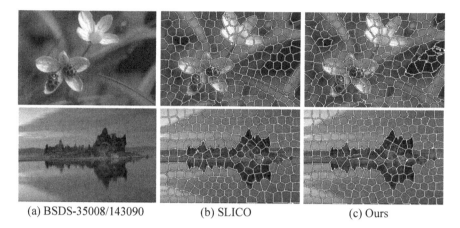

(a) BSDS-35008/143090   (b) SLICO   (c) Ours

Fig. 7. Setting of the weight coefficient for different types of images. The weight coefficients of the top image are 2, 1, 1, and the bottom are 1, 1 and 4, respectively. This flexible method can obtain the better boundary adherence.

Impact of Edge Detection Algorithms. The purpose of introducing the edge detection algorithm is mainly to prevent the initial cluster center from falling into the edge or noise point. In fact, the impact of this step on the results is not very large, but it still affects the final segmentation. As shown in Fig. 8, under the conditions of introducing the HSL color space, we want to compare the effect on the result using edge detection algorithm of SLICO and sobel operator. As can be seen from the comparison for the top images, the adherence to the boundary is quite good for both algorithm, but the superpixels with a slightly regular shape can be obtained by using sobel operator. The comparison below clearly illustrates that using sobel operator can effectively improve the boundary adherence. Therefore, experiments have shown that the introduction of sobel operator to replace the original edge detection algorithm is helpful for the segmentation result.

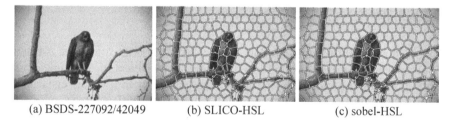

(a) BSDS-227092/42049   (b) SLICO-HSL   (c) sobel-HSL

Fig. 8. Impact of edge detection algorithms under the condition of introducing the HSL color space. For the top images, the superpixels with a slightly regular shape can be obtained by using sobel operator. For the bottom images, using sobel operator can effectively improve the boundary adherence.

Number of Superpixels. The number of superpixels has a great influence on the boundary adherence of the segmentation result. If the number is too small, it is hard to obtain the desired result. As the number of superpixels increases, the segmentation result will get better and better. As shown in Fig. 9, it can be clearly seen that from left to right, the segmentation effect becomes better and better with the number enlarging gradually, and the proposed algorithm is better than the original in treatment of details corresponding to superpixels. This result also corresponds exactly to the curves of Figs. 5 and 6(a).

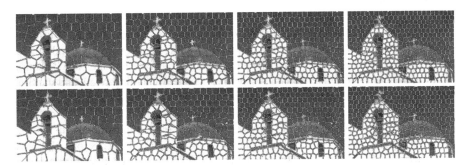

Fig. 9. The results of segmentation with different number of superpixels (BSDS-118035): 100, 200, 300 and 400 from left to right. The top and the bottom are the results of SLICO and the proposed algorithm, respectively. Our proposed algorithm is better than the original in treatment of details corresponding to superpixels.

Computational Efficiency. Like the original algorithm, the proposed algorithm also achieves an $O(N)$ time complexity. For a good superpixels method, it must have lower computational cost as the preprocessing algorithm for image. We can clearly see from Fig. 6(b) that the computational efficiency by using our proposed algorithm is much better than the original, and the speed is nearly twice faster as before. In order to verify which improvement make a difference, we can make an experiment. Under the condition of introducing the HSL color space, we measure the runtime by using edge detection algorithm of SLICO and sobel operator with different number of superpixels: 100, 200, 300 and 400. As shown in Table 1, there is not much change in the runtime (in ms) corresponding to the number of superpixels. Therefore, in combination with the *RT* curves of Fig. 6(b), it can be concluded that the introduction of the HSL color space greatly improves the computational efficiency of the algorithm. As for why there is such a big improvement, it is mainly because the RGB color space cannot be directly converted to CIELAB color space in original algorithm. By using XYZ color space as intermediary, you can convert RGB color space to XYZ color space, and then convert XYZ color space to CIELAB color space. However, the RGB color space to the HSL color space can be directly converted.

Table 1. Runtime (ms) by using edge detection algorithm of SLICO and sobel operator

Edge detection	100	200	300	400
Original[a]	53.77	59.01	57.74	59.14
Sobel[b]	54.25	59.14	57.75	58.89

[a]Original denotes the edge detection algorithm of SLICO.
[b]Sobel denotes the sobel operator.

5 Conclusion

In this work, we present an improved method based on simple linear iterative clustering algorithm, which is able to address the problem of undersegmentation and helpful for further image segmentation. By improving the distance measure and the edge detection algorithm, the boundary adherence of superpixels is effectively improved, and the time cost of superpixel segmentation is greatly reduced. The proposed method utilizes the superiority of the HSL color space to provide good segmentation result for different types of images. Compared with the original algorithm, the computational efficiency is greatly improved, and the processing speed is almost twice faster as before. We have used various evaluation metrics on the BSDS500 to demonstrate that our proposed algorithm is superior to the original algorithm in both performance and efficiency.

References

1. Radhakrishna, A., Appu, S., Kevin, S., Aurelien, L., Pascal, F., Sabine, S.: SLIC superpixels compared to state-of-the-art superpixel methods. IEEE Trans. Pattern Anal. Mach. Intell. **34**(11), 2274–2282 (2012)
2. Shi, J., Malik, J.: Normalized cuts and image segmentation. IEEE Trans. Pattern Anal. Mach. Intell. **22**(8), 888–905 (2000)
3. Moore, A.P., Prince, S.J.D., Warrell, J., Mohammed, U., Jones, G.: Superpixel lattices. In: IEEE Computer Vision and Pattern Recognition, pp. 1–8 (2008)
4. Liu, M.Y., Tuzel, O., Ramalingam, S., Chellappa, R.: Entropy rate superpixel segmentation. In: IEEE Computer Vision and Pattern Recognition, pp. 2097–2104 (2011)
5. Comaniciu, D., Meer, P.: Mean shift: a robust approach toward feature space analysis. IEEE Trans. Pattern Anal. Mach. Intell. **24**(5), 603–619 (2002)
6. Vedaldi, A., Soatto, S.: Quick shift and kernel methods for mode seeking. In: Forsyth, D., Torr, P., Zisserman, A. (eds.) ECCV 2008. LNCS, vol. 5305, pp. 705–718. Springer, Heidelberg (2008). https://doi.org/10.1007/978-3-540-88693-8_52
7. Achanta, R., Shaji, A., Smith, K., Lucchi, A., Fua, P., Süsstrunk, S.: Slic superpixels. Ecole Polytechnique Fédéral de Lausssanne (EPFL), 149300, pp. 155–162 (2010)
8. Han, C.Y.: Improved slic imagine segmentation algorithm based on k-means. Clust. Comput. **20**(2), 1017–1023 (2017)
9. Zhao, J., Bo, R., Hou, Q., Cheng, M.M., Rosin, P.: FLIC: fast linear iterative clustering with active search. Comput. Vis. Media **4**(4), 333–348 (2018)

10. Martin, D., Fowlkes, C., Tal, D., Malik, J.: A database of human segmented natural images and its application to evaluating segmentation algorithms and measuring ecological statistics. In: Proceedings Eighth IEEE International Conference on Computer Vision, pp. 416–423 (2001)
11. Stutz, D.: Superpixel segmentation: an evaluation. In: Gall, J., Gehler, P., Leibe, B. (eds.) GCPR 2015. LNCS, vol. 9358, pp. 555–562. Springer, Cham (2015). https://doi.org/10. 1007/978-3-319-24947-6_46
12. Stutz, D., Hermans, A., Leibe, B.: Superpixel Segmentation Using Depth Information. RWTH Aachen University, Aachen (2014)
13. Pablo, A., Michael, M., Charless, F., Jitendra, M.: Contour detection and hierarchical image segmentation. IEEE Trans. Pattern Anal. Mach. Intell. **33**(5), 898–916 (2011)
14. Stutz, D., Hermans, A., Leibe, B.: Superpixels: an evaluation of the state-of-the-art. Comput. Vis. Image Underst. **166**, 1–27 (2018)
15. Neubert, P., Protzel, P.: Superpixel benchmark and comparison. In: Proceedings of Forum Bildverarbeitung, Heidelberger (2012)
16. Martin, D.R., Fowlkes, C.C., Jitendra, M.: Learning to detect natural image boundaries using local brightness, color, and texture cues. IEEE Trans. Pattern Anal. Mach. Intell. **26**(5), 530–549 (2004)
17. Dai, T., Fu, H., Cao, X.: Topology preserved regular superpixel. In: IEEE International Conference on Multimedia and Expo, pp. 765–768 (2012)

Active Affordance Exploration
for Robot Grasping

Huaping Liu[1(✉)], Yuan Yuan[2], Yuhong Deng[1], Xiaofeng Guo[1], Yixuan Wei[1],
Kai Lu[1], Bin Fang[1], Di Guo[1], and Fuchun Sun[1]

[1] Department of Computer Science and Technology,
Tsinghua University, Beijing, China
hpliu@tsinghua.edu.cn
[2] School of Astronautics, Northwestern Polytechnical University, Xi'an, China

Abstract. Robotic grasp in complicated un-structured warehouse environments is still a challenging task and attracts lots of attentions from robot vision and machine learning communities. A popular strategy is to directly detect the graspable region for specific end-effector such as suction cup, two-fingered gripper or multi-fingered hand. However, those work usually depends on the accurate object detection and precise pose estimation. Very recently, affordance map which describes the action possibilities that an environment can offer, begins to be used for grasp tasks. But it often fails in cluttered environments and degrades the efficiency of warehouse automation. In this paper, we establish an active exploration framework for robot grasp and design a deep reinforcement learning method. To verify the effectiveness, we develop a new composite hand which combines the suction cup and fingers and the experimental validations on robotic grasp tasks show the advantages of the active exploration method. This novel method significantly improves the grasp efficiency of the warehouse manipulators.

Keywords: Active exploration · Affordance map · Robotic grasp

1 Introduction

With the rapid development of e-commerce, an increasing demand has been put on using autonomous robots in logistics. While there are already lots of mobile robots working at real warehouses for product transportation, it is still a great challenge for the robot to pick and sort products in real scenarios automatically and this kind of work is highly dependent on human workers nowadays, which is not economically and efficient.

Though the robot grasping is extremely important in practical scenarios, most of existing systems work under the structured environments, which call for simple grasp strategy only. In fact, most industrial manipulators working in the factory belong to this category. For complicated un-structured environments, the grasp point detection problem recently attracts lots of attentions from robot

© Springer Nature Switzerland AG 2019
H. Yu et al. (Eds.): ICIRA 2019, LNAI 11744, pp. 426–438, 2019.
https://doi.org/10.1007/978-3-030-27541-9_35

vision and machine learning community. A popular strategy is to directly detect the graspable region for specific end-effector such as suction cup, two-fingered gripper or multi-fingered hand. However, those work usually depends on the accurate object detection and precise pose estimation [1].

On the other hand, the affordance, which describes the action possibilities that an environment can offer, can be used for grasp the action possibilities afforded by physical objects without needing to either create a detailed three-dimensional mental model of the world or perform logical reasoning about rules-based behaviour [2], Therefore, it becomes a very promising method for grasping under clutter. In [3], the authors established an object-agnostic grasping framework to map from visual observations to actions and infer dense pixel-wise probability maps of the affordance for four different grasping primitive actions. The affordance map is a graph which includes the confidence rate of each point for grasping. This work shows powerful capability in Amazon Robotics Challenge. However, since the environment is usually complex and un-structured (e.g. a cluttered scenario), the one-shot single affordance map may not enough for the robot to perform successful grasp. In many scenarios, even though the affordance map can be calculated, the grasp strategy is still difficult to perform.

In cluttered scenes, the affordance map usually fails in two situations. The first one occurs when objects of similar height or color are in close proximity to each other, and those objects are mixed as one single object by affordance map. In this situation, the junction between these two objects will be identified as suitable picking point, and therefore the calculated grasp point is wrong. The other situation occurs when the adjacent objects are partially overlapped or over-tilted. In this case, the picking point indicated by the affordance map may not suitable for realistic operation, especially when objects' surface is not smooth enough. In Fig. 1 we show some representative examples for the affordance map cannot work well.

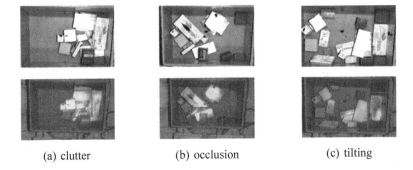

(a) clutter   (b) occlusion   (c) tilting

Fig. 1. Typical failure scenes for the grasp affordance: In the cases of clutter, occlusion or tilting, the affordance map may provide wrong picking suggestions (see the red boxes). (Color figure online)

On the other hand, the active exploration has been introduced to the area of robotics for many years but has not been fully exploited for grasp [4,5]. In [6], the robot can delicately interact with the environment and change the position of the object until it is suitable for the robot to grasp. In addition, the robot may rearrange objects by pushing to improve recognition accuracy. However, the active exploration technology has never been used for improve grasp affordance.

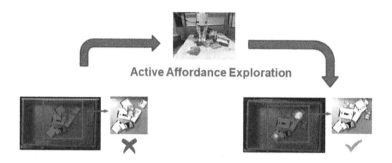

Fig. 2. Active affordance exploration: The manipulator is used to perform active affordance exploration to achieve better grasp conditions.

In this work, we leverage the advantages of affordance map and the active exploration by establishing an active affordance exploration framework for robot grasp (see Fig. 2). This new method imitates the human's behavior: When a person wants to grasp one specific object, he may push the other objects which occlude the target object and then grasp it. The developed active affordance exploration strategy helps the robot to obtain more easy grasp condition and could significantly improve the success rate. The main technical contributions of this work are summarized as follows

1. We establish an active affordance exploration framework for robot grasp in cluttered environments.
2. We design a deep reinforcement learning method to realize the active affordance exploration strategy.
3. We develop a new composite hand which combines the suction cup and fingers to validate the effectiveness of the active affordance exploration method.
4. We leverage virtual environments to conveniently simulate active exploration, saving the expensive human labeling or real-world trial-and-error.

The rest of this paper is organized as follows: The active affordance exploration framework is introduced in Sect. 2. Section 3 presents the detailed reinforcement learning algorithm. In Sect. 4 we introduce the developed novel manipulation hand. Section 5 provides the experimental setup and results.

2   Framework

The affordance map is a graph which indicates the confidence of each point in the input images for grasping [3]. In this work, we utilize the affordance map to provide pixel-wise picking candidate points for the suction cup. This effectively solves the *recognition before grasping* problem in traditional grasping strategy. However, in mace scenarios it is hard to distinguish good grasping points from the obtained affordance map, especially when the scenario is complicated. In order to solve this problem, the active exploration is introduced into the proposed system. Different from using only one static affordance map, the robot will actively explore and change the environment until a satisfactory affordance map is obtained.

The pipeline of the proposed robotic grasping system is illustrated in Fig. 1. The RGB image and depth image of the scene are obtained firstly and the affordance ConvNet proposed in [3] is used to calculate the affordance map. If it is evaluated to be not suitable for grasping, the obtained RGB image and depth image are fed into the Deep Q-Network (DQN), which guides the robotic hand to change the environment by pushing objects [7]. This process will be iterated until all the objects in the environment are successfully picked. The reinforcement learning is employed to train the DQN which indicates intelligent movements given the affordance map for the current scene (Fig. 3).

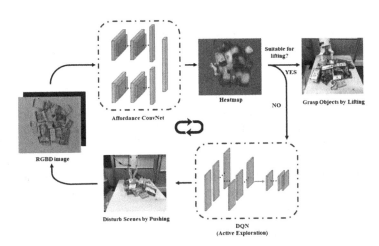

Fig. 3. System Pipeline. The system first obtains RGB-D image of the scene, then inputs the image into the affordance ConvNet, which can calculate the affordance map, the system will judge the reliability of the suction position obtained from the affordance map. If the reliability is low, the system will input current RGBD image of the scene into DQN, which can output an appropriate operation. If the reliability is high, the composite robotic hand will complete the suction operation.

3   Learning for Active Exploration

As mentioned in last section, the solution of active affordance exploration is an optimal action policy which helps the robotic hand to get a satisfactory

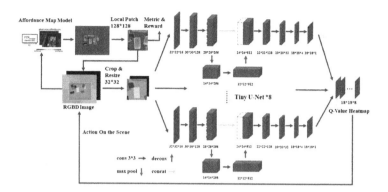

Fig. 4. Deep Q-Network Structure. For current RGB-D frame, we utilize the affordance map to output a primitive operation guidance and crop and resize input frame around the pixel with maximum confidence. We input this local patch into 8 paralleled tiny U-Net and output 8 diverse action directions on subpixel-wised locations. And reward for this network is according to the metric on affordance map around maximum value.

affordance map for reliable picking. To this end, we establish a Deep Q-Network (DQN), shown in Fig. 2, to deal with this problem.

We denote the state as s_t and the action as a_t for time instant t. During the active exploration, the robot receives a reward $r_t = r(s_{t-1}, a_t)$ at each time instant t and the accumulated reward is defined as $R_t = \sum_{i=t}^{\infty} \gamma^{i-t} r_i$, where γ is the forgetting factor. The action-value function under action policy π is then defined as $Q^\pi(s_{t-1}) = \mathbb{E}[R_t | s_{t-1}, \pi]$, and the optimal policy is determined by estimating the action-value function Q^π. The estimation can be obtained by Bellman equation recursively.

The DQN utilizes deep neural network as an nonlinear approximation to the optimal action-value function $Q(\theta) \to Q^*$. All parameters of the network are denoted as θ, and the parameters are estimated iteratively by minimizing temporal difference error:

$$\hat{\theta} = \arg\min_{\theta} \mathbb{E}\left[(r_t + \gamma \max_{a_{t+1}} Q(s_t, a_{t+1}; \theta) - Q(s_{t-1}, a_t; \theta))^2\right] \quad (1)$$

The optimization is converted into a regression problem in DQN by regarding temporal difference error as loss.

$$\mathcal{L}(\theta) = [r_t + \gamma \max_{a_{t+1}} Q(s_t, a_{t+1}; \theta) - Q(s_{t-1}, a_t; \theta)]^2 \quad (2)$$

3.1   State Representation

To obtain the state representation s_t, we use the Affordance ConvNet developed in [3], which takes RGB-D image as input and outputs the affordance map. The affordance map is a dense pixel-wise image with values ranging from 0 to 1. Values that are closer to 1 imply more preferable picking locations. The original

Affordance ConvNet has been offline trained using human annotated images. The detail can be found in [3].

Since our goal is to change the scene according to the current affordance map, we do not need to consider the whole scene at each time. Instead, we propose a local-patch U-Net structure in the network, which can obtain better scene with less steps and also minimize the model size for faster computation. Concretely speaking, assuming that in current state, the most promising picking point is the one with highest confidence score in the affordance map. We crop the input RGBD image around the corresponding pixel with a size of 128×128 and downsample it to size of 32×32 before feeding to our U-Net based network in our experiment. The state representation s_t is therefore obtained as a 1024-dimensional vector. This strategy greatly reduces the model size.

3.2 Action Representation

We define 8 specific actions to enable the robot to push the object from 8 directions with a fixed distance. The action network structure (Fig. 2) is based on the U-Net [8], which outputs the pixel-wised movement. U-Net is a powerful and lightweight network structure proposed recently for image segmentation, including times of down- and up-sampling. It reaches high performance in output pixel-wised semantic information. To minimize size of the network for speed, we adjust this structure to a more tiny one, with once down- and up-sampling and resize RGB-D image input to quarter resolution. For each action, the U-Net [8] is able to give a movement confidence score on each location. We use $O_i = i * 45°(i = 0, \ldots, 7)$ to denote the directions and the push distance is half the size of the local patch. So the whole network contains 8 U-Net modules with same structure and we have $a_t \in \{O_i | i = 0, 1, \cdots, 7\}$.

3.3 Reward Function

The reward function $r(s_{t-1}, a_t)$ are used to encourage effective actions, and the general formation of reward function is defined as below:

$$r(s_{t-1}, a_t) = \begin{cases} 1 & \text{success} \\ -1 & \text{failure} \end{cases} \tag{3}$$

4 Design of the Composite Hand

To validate the proposed active exploration method, we design and develop a new type of composite hand, which is composed of two parallel pinching fingers and a suction cup, see Fig. 4. The two fingers are symmetrically distributed on the base. We design a motor-driven parallelogram mechanism for each finger, which ensures that the surfaces of the two fingers are parallel when the finger is gripping the object.

The suction cup system consists of a suction cup, a push rod, a cylinder, two air pumps, a miniature motor and a solenoid valve. The suction cup is placed in the middle of the two fingers. Two air pumps are respectively equipped inside and outside of the composite robotic hand. The inside one and miniature motor are used for controlling the suction cup, while the outside one with solenoid valve drives the push rod with a range of 75 mm.

The motivation to use suction cup is that the it is usually with simple structure and robust to many different objects. For example, a kind of self-sealing suction cup arrays is proposed to greatly expand robotic applications in uncertain environments [9]. To increase the adhesion force of the suction cup, a stretchable suction cup with electroadhesion is designed [10]. Some suction cups are inspired by some biomimetic designs [11–15]. However, due to the working mechanism of the suction cup, there are many restrictions on the surface and postures of the object. In addition, the inconsistency between the moving direction of the suction cup and the direction of the force makes the grasping unstable [16] and causes the life of the suction cup to be short. Therefore, it is important for the robotic hand to find proper grasping points in real environment when using the suction cup.

During the process of object grasping, the two fingers are in an open state, and the suction cup is held in the initial stage. When the grasping point is found and determined, the suction cup is popped out to contact with the surface of the object to be grasped. Then the air pump generates the negative pressure in the suction cup so that the object is picked. After that, the push rod retracts to bring the object between the two fingers and the fingers close to grasp the object to improve the grasp stability (Fig. 5).

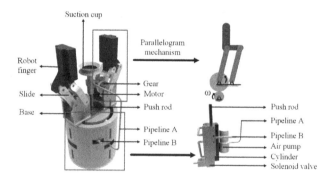

Fig. 5. Structure of the Composite Robotic Hand. The composite robotic hand is composed of two parallel pinching fingers and a suction cup system.

As illustrated in Fig. 4, the proposed composite robotic hand uses the two fingers to hold the object after the suction cup lifts the object, which increases the stability of the grasp. Especially, when the robotic is moving, the force applied by the fingers and suction cup can coordinate together to guarantee the object is stably grasped (Fig. 6).

Fig. 6. Prototype and Grasp Experiment. The prototype of the developed composite robotic hand (left) and some typical grasp demos (right).

5   Experimental Results

In this section, we perform the experimental validations in simulation environment and real-world environment. Concretely speaking, we perform the reinforcement learning training in the simulation environment and validate the grasp performance using physical experiments (Fig. 8).

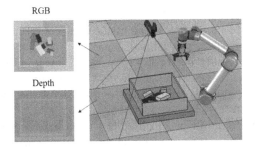

Fig. 7. Simulation environment

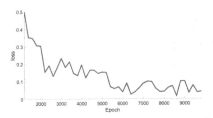

Fig. 8. The loss versus the epoch.

5.1   Training in Simulation Environment

We choose V-REP [17] as the simulation environment. In our scene (Fig. 7), a UR5 manipulator as well as a robotic hand are added to implement the process of the active exploration and a Kinect camera is utilized to obtain the visual data. To simulate a cluttered environment, 11 blocks are added into the scene as the operation objects and we manually design several challenging scenes for evaluation.

We train our U-Net based DQN model by RMSPropOtimizer, using learning rates decaying from 10^{-3} to 2.5×10^{-4} and setting the momentum equal to 0.9. The forgetting factor γ is set to 0.6 for more attention on current epoch. To give allowance for more attempt on new pushing strategies, we adopt the ϵ-greedy strategy to discover new actions and the parameter is set as $\epsilon = 0.2$. After the training period, the learned model is transferred to the true physical environment for validation.

5.2 Robotic Experiments

The practical experimental setup is shown in Fig. 9. We select 40 different objects to build different scenes for our robotic hand to grasp.

If the conventional passive affordance map is used, when the object of maximum affordance value is unable to be lifted, the robot will repeat this failure operation because the environment and affordance map are not changed. Therefore, we define a test as failure if the lift fails at the same object for three times, while a test is defined as a success if the first 10 objects within a scene are lifted successfully. Based on that, we defined 3 metrics: (1) the average number of objects grasped successfully per test, (2) suction success rate, which is defined as number of objects grasped successfully divided by number of lift operations, (3) test success rate, which is defined as the number of successful tests divided by the number of tests.

We test our robotic hand in 20 different scenes with static affordance map and with affordance map optimized by active exploration. All of the 20 scenes

Fig. 9. Grasping System. Our grasping system consists of a composite robotic hand for grasping, a UR5 manipulator for reaching the operation point, and a Kinect camera as a vision sensor. We introduce the strategy of active exploration applied on the environment for more promising grasping.

can be divided into three categories. In Fig. 10 we show three typical scenes corresponding to those categories. For the first category, which contains 11 scenes, the objects are closely packed and relatively concentrated. The proposed active exploration method works rather well. It increases the success rate of grasping from 44% to 68%. The average number of pushing operation is 8.3. More importantly, our system can increase the probability of successfully grasping more than 10 items from 10% to 63%. For the second category, which contains 4 scenes, the objects are not so closely packed. In this case, our system can increase the success rate of grasping from 49% to 71% and increase the probability of grasping more than 10 items from 0% to 75%. The mean number of pushing operation decrease to 4.5 times. For the third category, which contains 5 scenes, the object more scatters and we may find more isolated objects. In this case, the original affordance can be used to achieve 58% success rate, and the proposed active exploration method increases it to 77%. The mean number of pushing operation is reduced to 4.2, and the probability of grasping more than 10 items is increased from 60% to 80%. The results shows that for the more difficult cases such as the first category, the proposed active exploration method show better performance. This is rather reasonable since in this case the pausing operations are needed to changing the environment.

The whole result of all of the 20 scenes are recorded and summarized in Table 1. Experiments show that after active exploration optimization, the system performs better in suction success rate and test success rate. Compared with lifting only with static affordance map, the addition of active exploration reduces the possibility of repeating failure lifts, making it stronger adaptability to the scene. When the system only relies on the static affordance map to get the

Fig. 10. Three typical scenes. From Left to Right: The first, second and third category.

Fig. 11. Stage 1: Left: The manipulator determines to pick the box (marked with red eclipse), which is occluded by another box. Middle: The manipulators moves towards the occluding box (marked with blue eclipse). Right: The manipulator touches the occluding box. (Color figure online)

Fig. 12. Stage 2: From Left to Right: The manipulator pushes the occluding box away from the target box.

Fig. 13. Stage 3: Left: The manipulator emits the suction cup to pick the target box. Middle: The fingers are used to grasp the target objects and then the suction cup is withdrawned. Right: The manipulator grasps the target object to move.

Fig. 14. Stage 4: From Left to Right: The manipulator takes the target box towards to prescribed location.

decision of lifting, it is easy to make failure in cluttered scene. When the system relies on the affordance map optimized by active exploration to get the decision of lift, the system will make sure that the scene near the position for lifting is sparse. Therefore, the system can get more reliable decisions. For detailed demonstration, we show the consecutive frames of the manipulation in Figs. 11, 12, 13 and 14.

Table 1. Experimental results

Method	♯Grasped objects	Suction success rate	Test success rate
Affordance	5.35	50.5%	20%
Active affordance	8.80	70.7%	70.0%

6   Conclusions

In this work, we establish an active affordance exploration framework for robot grasp and design a deep reinforcement learning method to realize the active affordance exploration strategy. To verify the effectiveness, we develop a new composite hand which combines the suction cup and fingers and the experimental validations on robotic grasp tasks show the promising effects of the active affordance exploration method.

To the best of our knowledge, it is the first work that integrates the active exploration with a composite robotic hand for robotic grasping in a cluttered environment. The suction cup and the gripper are seamlessly coordinated to actively explore the environment. For the future work, it will be interesting and promising to develop some more complex grasping strategies for various complex environments with the proposed robotic hand. Besides the pushing policies, it is also possible for the agent to take some other action or a sequence of actions to actively explore the environment.

Acknowledgements. This work was supported in part by the National Natural Science Foundation of China under Grant U1613212.

References

1. Lenz, I., Lee, H., Saxena, A.: Deep learning for detecting robotic grasps. Int. J. Robot. Res. **34**(4–5), 705–724 (2015)
2. Hsu, J.: Machines on mission possible. Nat. Mach. Intell. **1**(3), 124–127 (2019)
3. Zeng, A., et al.: Robotic pick-and-place of novel objects in clutter with multi-affordance grasping and cross-domain image matching. In: 2018 IEEE International Conference on Robotics and Automation (ICRA), pp. 1–8. IEEE (2018)
4. Bajcsy, R., Campos, M.: Active and exploratory perception. CVGIP Image Underst. **56**(1), 31–40 (1992)
5. Chen, S., Li, Y., Kwok, N.: Active vision in robotic systems: a survey of recent developments. Int. J. Robot. Res. **30**(11), 1343–1377 (2011)
6. Zeng, A., Song, S., Welker, S., Lee, J., Rodriguez, A., Funkhouser, T.: Learning synergies between pushing and grasping with self-supervised deep reinforcement learning. In: 2018 IEEE/RSJ International Conference on Intelligent Robots and Systems (IROS), pp. 4238–4245. IEEE (2018)
7. Liu, H., Sun, F., Zhang, X.: Robotic material perception using active multi-modal fusion. IEEE Trans. Ind. Electron. (2018)
8. Navab, N., Hornegger, J., Wells, W.M., Frangi, A.F. (eds.): Medical Image Computing and Computer-Assisted Intervention — MICCAI 2015. LNCS, vol. 9351. Springer, Cham (2015). https://doi.org/10.1007/978-3-319-24574-4
9. Kessens, C.C., Desai, J.P.: Design, fabrication, and implementation of self-sealing suction cup arrays for grasping. In: 2010 IEEE International Conference on Robotics and Automation, pp. 765–770. IEEE (2010)
10. Okuno, Y., Shigemune, H., Kuwajima, Y., Maeda, S.: Stretchable suction cup with electroadhesion. Adv. Mater. Technol. **4**(1), 1800304 (2019)

11. Grasso, F.W., Setlur, P.: Inspiration, simulation and design for smart robot manipulators from the sucker actuation mechanism of cephalopods. Bioinspiration Biomim. **2**(4), S170 (2007)
12. Grasso, F.: Octopus sucker-arm coordination in grasping and manipulation. Am. Malacol. Bull. **24**(2), 13–23 (2008)
13. Sadeghi, A., Beccai, L., Mazzolai, B.: Design and development of innovative adhesive suckers inspired by the tube feet of sea urchins. In: 2012 4th IEEE RAS & EMBS International Conference on Biomedical Robotics and Biomechatronics (BioRob), pp. 617–622. IEEE (2012)
14. Tomokazu, T., Kikuchi, S., Suzuki, M., Aoyagi, S.: Vacuum gripper imitated octopus sucker-effect of liquid membrane for absorption. In: 2015 IEEE/RSJ International Conference on Intelligent Robots and Systems (IROS), pp. 2929–2936. IEEE (2015)
15. Kuwajima, Y., Shigemune, H., Cacucciolo, V., Cianchetti, M., Laschi, C., Maeda, S.: Active suction cup actuated by electrohydrodynamics phenomenon. In: 2017 IEEE/RSJ International Conference on Intelligent Robots and Systems (IROS), pp. 470–475. IEEE (2017)
16. Mantriota, G., Messina, A.: Theoretical and experimental study of the performance of flat suction cups in the presence of tangential loads. Mech. Mach. Theory **46**(5), 607–617 (2011)
17. Rohmer, E., Singh, S.P.N., Freese, M.: V-REP: a versatile and scalable robot simulation framework. In: Proceedings of The International Conference on Intelligent Robots and Systems (IROS) (2013)

Multi-vehicle Detection and Tracking Based on Kalman Filter and Data Association

Lie Guo[1] , Pingshu Ge[2(✉)] , Danni He[1], and Dongxing Wang[1]

[1] School of Automotive Engineering, Dalian University of Technology,
Dalian 116024, China
[2] College of Mechanical and Electronic Engineering, Dalian Minzu University,
Dalian 116600, China
gps@dlnu.edu.cn

Abstract. Environment perception is an important issue for autonomous driving applications. Vehicle detection and tracking is one of the most serious challenges and plays a crucial role for environment perception. Considering that the convolutional neural network (CNN) can provide high recognition rate for object detection, the vehicles are detected by utilizing Yolo v3 algorithm trained on ImageNet and KITTI datasets. Then, the detected multiple vehicles are tracked based on the combination of Kalman filter and data association strategy. Experiments on the publicly available KITTI object tracking datasets are conducted to test and verify the proposed algorithm. Results indicate that the proposed algorithm can achieve stable tracking under normal conditions even when the object is temporarily occluded.

Keywords: Vehicle detection · Data association · Kalman filter · Convolutional neural network

1 Introduction

Autonomous vehicle is an interdisciplinary product of mechanical engineering, information engineering, computer science, control engineering and other disciplines. It is a comprehensive system, which includes environment perception, dynamic decision planning, intelligent control and execution. The autonomous vehicle uses the on-board sensor to perceive the surrounding environment, and controls the steering and traveling speed of the vehicle based on the lane, vehicle and other obstacle information. In this way, the vehicle can travel safely and reliably on the road.

Environment perception technology is an important subject in the research of autonomous vehicles [1]. The quality and accuracy of environment perception can enhance its intelligence level to a certain extent. The improvement of environment perception performance will promote the development of vehicle intelligent technology. This paper focuses on the detection and tracking of multiple vehicles in the driving scenarios. Especially, the main purpose is to predict the position of the detected vehicle when it is occluded.

Multi-object detection and tracking is one of the most serious challenges in the field of computer vision research. Compared with single-object tracking, multi-object

© Springer Nature Switzerland AG 2019
H. Yu et al. (Eds.): ICIRA 2019, LNAI 11744, pp. 439–449, 2019.
https://doi.org/10.1007/978-3-030-27541-9_36

tracking is a more complicated problem that needs to be studied and solved. The challenges mainly lie in the color similarity, background complexity, object size change, occlusion and adhesion between objects. Traditionally, multi-object tracking has been achieved through multiple hypothesis tracking [2] and joint probability data association algorithm [3, 4]. The drawback of these methods is that the processing time is long and cannot fully meet the requirements of vehicular real-time systems. Moreover, it is not suitable for online tracking.

With the development of artificial intelligence, some theoretical methods based on deep learning have achieved good results in the field of multi-object tracking. For example, recurrent neural network (RNN) is applied to multi-object tracking [5]. The basic approach is to decompose the multiple-object tracking problem into two steps. The first step is the prediction and update of the single-object state. The second step is the association with other targets. The time-series RNN model is used to learn the time-series dynamic model of the target. In turn, it is able to determine the appearance and disappearance of the target. This paper applies RNN in real-time multiple-object tracking and realizes an end-to-end multiple-object tracking system.

As the convolutional neural network (CNN) succeeds in the major competitions in the field of object recognition, the tracking-by-detection method has become a mainstream for multi-object tracking method. For example, Bewley et al. [6] make full use of the CNN processing ability of images and decompose the multiple-object tracking task into three parts: object detection, pose estimation and data association. Object detection is implemented by using CNN. Each target motion is regarded as a linear model, and the position of the next frame is predicted by Kalman filter. Finally, the data association is realized by the Hungarian algorithm. In addition to using CNN to predict the position of the object in the image, it also predicts the distance of the target from the vehicle. The Poisson multi-Bernoulli mixture (PMBM) filtering can be used to achieve 3D tracking under a monocular camera [7].

The paper is organized as follows. Section 2 describes the multi-vehicle tracking method based on Kalman filter and data association. Section 3 tests the proposed method on the KITTI object tracking datasets. Section 4 concludes the paper.

2 Methodology

The proposed multi-vehicle detection and tracking method is shown in the Fig. 1. It mainly consists of the following three parts, object detection, object tracking and data association.

The object detection uses CNN to train a classifier to gain the parameters of the vehicle bounding box. The object tracking uses Kalman filter to predict the position of the bounding box in the next frame and to update its state in the current frame. The data association uses a combination of nearest neighbor algorithm and the intersection-over-union (IOU) of the bounding box. The vehicle may disappear from the scenario or emerge into the current scenario.

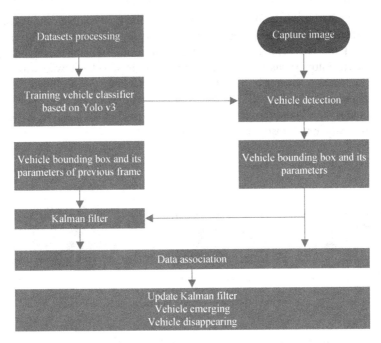

Fig. 1. Multi-vehicle detection and tracking method

2.1 Object Detection

CNN excels in target detection tasks and even exceeds human recognition levels in major challenges. The CNN used for object detection mainly includes two types. One is the two-step detection algorithm represented by R-CNN [8, 9]. The other is the one-step detection algorithm represented by YOLO [10], SSD [11]. The main idea of the two-step detection algorithm is to divide the object detection task into object location and object classification. The one-step detection algorithm directly regards the object detection task as a regression task.

The paper utilizes the Yolo v3 algorithm to detect all the vehicle targets in the image. The backbone convolutional network of Yolo v3 is pre-trained on ImageNet, and then trained on the KITTI 2D object detection datasets. Since the research focuses on the vehicle, so we only use data with the category "Car" to train the classifier. For each detected vehicle object, it is represented by four parameters:

$$F_i = [cx_i, cy_i, w_i, h_i] \tag{1}$$

where cx_i and cy_i stands for the horizontal and vertical pixel location of the ith target bounding box respectively, w_i and h_i stands for the width and the height of the ith target bounding box respectively.

2.2 Estimated Model

Consider the typical scenario that the vehicle is occluded, as shown in Fig. 2. When the blue detected vehicle overtakes the host vehicle from behind, it will block the red detected vehicle. Once this kind of occlusion occurs, the host vehicle cannot know that there is a red vehicle behind the blue vehicle simply by analyzing the current image information. If the red vehicle changes at this time, this will be a very dangerous behavior. In an autonomous driving scenario, if the host vehicle wants to make an overtaking maneuver, then it is necessary to keep tracking the occluded vehicle for overtaking safely. Occlusion will cover the original features of the target vehicle, such as color, contour, etc. Therefore, it is only possible to predict the position at the time of occlusion by its original position information.

Fig. 2. Typical scenarios that one vehicle is occluded (Color figure online)

This paper approximates the position displacement of each object between each frame with a linear model. This displacement is independent of the other objects and camera motion. The system state vector for each target is as follows:

$$X = [cx_i, cy_i, w_i, h_i, cx_i', cy_i', w_i', h_i', cx_i'', cy_i'', w_i'', h_i'']^T \tag{2}$$

where the meaning of prime and double-prime symbols of cx_i, cy_i, w_i, h_i stands for the change rate of each parameter, respectively.

The system observation vector is $Z = [cx_i, cy_i, w_i, h_i]^T$.

When the prediction result is successfully correlated with the detection result, the parameter of the detected vehicle bounding box is used to update the state equation of the object, wherein the velocity and acceleration parameters are further optimized by Kalman filter. If the object is occluded, this filter is used to predict its possible position in the next frame directly.

2.3 Data Association

When the object in the current frame is associated with the object of the previous frame, the bounding box geometry is estimated by predicting the position of the object in the previous frame. Firstly, the nearest neighbor algorithm is used to select the possible matching tracking object for each detected object, then the IOUs of these possible association pairs are calculated, and the largest IOU for the tracking object is selected as the matching object of the previous detected object. Further, if the IOU of matching pairs is less than the minimum value of the IOU, it is determined that this pair matching fails.

The detailed data association algorithm can be explained as follows:

Step 1: Calculate the distance between the center of each detected vehicle and each tracked result.

$$dist[i][j] = \sqrt{(O_{x_i} - P_{x_j})^2 + (O_{y_i} - P_{y_j})^2} \tag{3}$$

where O_{xi} and O_{yi} stands for the center horizontal and vertical pixel position of the ith detected object respectively, P_{xj} and P_{yj} stands for center horizontal and vertical pixel position of the jth tracked object respectively.

Step 2: Nearest neighbor screening. Keep matching pairs that are less than the width of the bounding box. If $dist[i][j] < O_{i\_w}$, keep $IOU[i][j]$; else $IOU[i][j] = 0$. Here, O_{i_w} is the threshold of the distance.

Step 3: Calculate the IOU. Calculate the intersection over union of each matched pairs which screened by nearest neighbors.

$$IOU[i][j] = \frac{S_{O_i} \cap S_{P_j}}{S_{O_i} \cup S_{P_j}} \tag{4}$$

where $IOU[i][j]$ is the IOU value between the ith detected object and the jth tracked object, S_{Oi} and S_{Pj} is the bounding box of the ith detected object and the jth tracked object respectively.

The remaining matching pairs that have not been filtered by the nearest neighbor are automatically set to 0 in the IOU matrix.

Step 4: Filter the IOU. Set the IOU whose value less than a certain threshold to 0. According to the previous tests and researches, the threshold can be set to an empirical value with 0.3.

Step 5: Get the result. For each detected object, the tracking object corresponding to the maximum IOU value is taken as the matching result. In addition to the data pairs that match successfully, the remaining detected results and tracking results are determined as unsuccessful matching detected and tracking results respectively.

In this way, the detected object and tracked object are divided into three parts: the successful matching data pairs, the failed matching detected data, and the failed matching tracking data. For the successfully matching data pair, the target detected data is used to update the state parameter of the corresponding Kalman filter. For the failed matching detected data, it is determined that a new target appears, and a new filter is assigned. And for the failed matching tracked data, it is taken as an occluded target, and continue tracking with this same filter.

2.4   Emergence and Disappearance of Object

When the object enters and leaves the image, its corresponding ID needs to be created and destroyed. For the failed matching object, it is determined as a new object, and a new tracker is created. Initialize the tracker with the parameters of the bounding box whose speed and acceleration is set to zero. Since the velocity and acceleration cannot be observed at this time, the covariance of the velocity and acceleration is initialized with a larger value to reflect this uncertainty.

When the target object leaves the field of view, the data predicted by the tracker will overflow the image size range. In the process of moving away from the vehicle, the bounding box parameter returned by the object detection will be abrupt. At this time, the values predicted by the filter should be artificially corrected for its width and height to make it more correlated to the detection result accurately. Moreover, the disappearance of the target is judged through an additional variable, which means the probability of the target's existence at a certain moment, and the target will be deemed to disappear when the value is less than a certain value.

3   Experiment

The experiment selected the No. 8 vehicle, No. 13 vehicle, No. 1 vehicle and No. 26 vehicle in the 2D Tracking0008 training sequence of KITTI datasets. These four cases simulate the scenarios that the object emerges ahead for a long time, the object is blocked temporarily, the object leaves the field of view and the object enters the field of view. In this case, the state parameters cx, cy, w and h are considered as independent variables, the prediction results of above four variables are observed separately.

Figures 3, 4, 5, 6 display the corresponding results for the above four scenarios. The blue lines are the actual parameters of the bounding box, using "true" as the label.

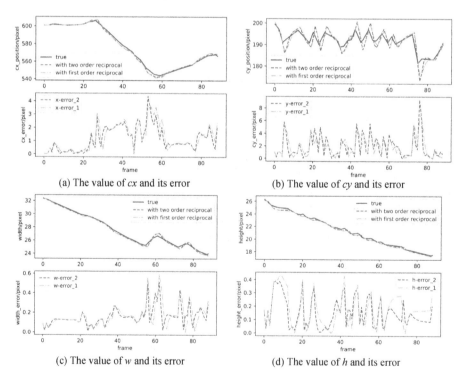

(a) The value of cx and its error

(b) The value of cy and its error

(c) The value of w and its error

(d) The value of h and its error

Fig. 3. The object vehicle emerges ahead of the host vehicle for a long time (Color figure online)

The yellow lines are the predicting results when taking the parameters and their velocities as the state vector, using "with first order reciprocal" and "error_1" as the label. The red line are the predicting results when taking the parameters, their velocities and accelerations as the state vector, using "with two order reciprocal" and "error_2" as the label.

Figure 3 shows that the prediction results of the two prediction methods are equivalent when the object vehicle emerges ahead of the host vehicle for a long time. The reason is that when the object is in front of the vehicle, its position hardly changes too much. From the figure, it can be seen that the errors of w and h variables are all within 1 pixel, the error of x component is kept within 5 pixels, the error of the y component is up to 7 pixels when fitted with first order reciprocal, and close to 10 pixels when fitting with second order reciprocal.

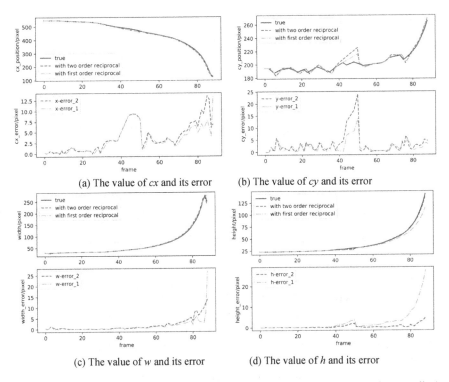

(a) The value of cx and its error   (b) The value of cy and its error

(c) The value of w and its error   (d) The value of h and its error

Fig. 4. The object vehicle is blocked for frame between 40 and 50 (Color figure online)

For the fitting of the x component, the maximum error of the first order reciprocal and the second order reciprocal is close to 13 pixels, which is within an acceptable range. For the y component, the fitting error of the second order reciprocal in the occlusion period is about twice as the fitting error of the first order reciprocal, where the maximum error is close to 25 pixels. From the h component fitting results, it can be seen that when the target reappears, it can't be quickly adapted with the first order reciprocal fitting, which leads to the final error becoming larger and larger. At the maximum error, the result of the second order reciprocal fitting is only 5 pixels, while the result of the first order reciprocal fitting has nearly 30 pixels.

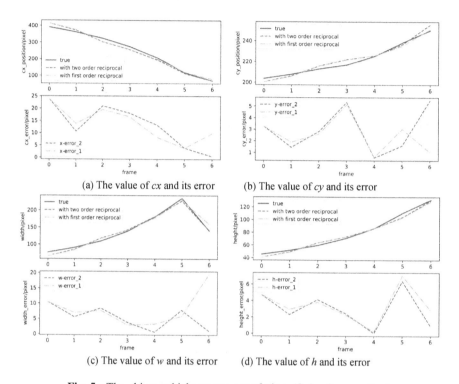

(a) The value of *cx* and its error   (b) The value of *cy* and its error

(c) The value of *w* and its error   (d) The value of *h* and its error

Fig. 5. The object vehicle moves out of view (Color figure online)

When the object moves out of view, the bounding box enlarges first as the object approaches and suddenly reduces as it leaves the field of view. From the error result of the *w* component, it can be seen that before the object leaves the field of view, the fitting result of the first order reciprocal fitting is equivalent to the second order reciprocal fitting, but when the target leaves the critical point. At the same time, the error is getting larger and larger, and finally reaches nearly 20 pixels, while the error of the second order reciprocal fitting is only 1 pixel.

When the object enters the field of view, the fitting results of the four components *x*, *y*, *w*, and *h* are equivalent and are within acceptable limits. Considering the fitting results under these four situations, the variation range of the *y* component is small, and the effect of fitting with the first order reciprocal fitting is better, and the second order reciprocal fitting is better when occlusion occurs. For the three variables *x*, *w*, *h*, its corresponding range is large, especially when the object leaves or enters the field of

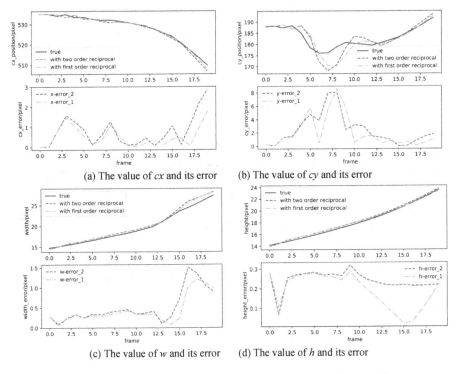

(a) The value of *cx* and its error   (b) The value of *cy* and its error

(c) The value of *w* and its error   (d) The value of *h* and its error

Fig. 6. The object vehicle enters the field of view (Color figure online)

view, so the second order reciprocal fitting can achieve better results. Finally, the state variable of the Kalman filter is determined as:

$$X = [cx_i, cy_i, w_i, h_i, cx_i', cy_i', w_i', h_i', cx_i'', w_i'', h_i'']^T \tag{5}$$

In this paper, the 0008, 0002 and 0010 video sequences of the object tracking classification of KITTI datasets are evaluated to test the proposed algorithm. The evaluation indicators are: the number of successful tracking objects (MT), the number of unsuccessful tracking objects (ML) and the ID switching times (IDsw).

The 0002 video has a total of 8 objects, the results are MT = 8, ML = 2, IDsw = 3. For the 0008 video, there is a total of 19 objects in the sequence, the results are MT = 17, ML = 2 and IDsw = 1 respectively. For 0010 sequence with 12 objects, the results are MT = 12, ML = 0, IDsw = 0, as shown in Table 1. Experiments show that the algorithm can achieve stable tracking under normal conditions even when the target is temporarily occluded. Figure 7 shows some of the experimental results.

Table 1. MOT evaluation results

Sequence no	MT	ML	ID switch times
KITTI-0002	8	2	3
KITTI-0008	17	2	1
KITTI-0010	12	0	0

Fig. 7. Partial experimental results

4 Conclusion

In this paper, an online multi-object vehicle detection and tracking method is proposed, which combines the Kalman filtering and data association strategy to solve the problem of object localization in occlusion situations. In this paper, the "Car" class in the KITTI tracking dataset is selected as the experimental data to train the vehicle detection classifier, focusing on the position prediction accuracy of the occluded object when occlusion occurs. The experimental results show that the proposed algorithm can accurately predict the position information of the occluded object in the automatic driving scenario. However, this article does not consider the fine-grained features of the object, that is, if the target object appears again after leaving the field for a long time, it will be assigned a new ID for processing. Although this paper proposes a new way to conduct data association, we also have to compare with the existing multi-target tracking methods to reflect the research significance of this paper.

Acknowledgement. This work was supported by the National Natural Science Foundation of China under grant 51575079, the Doctoral Scientific Research Foundation of Liaoning Province under grant 20170520194 and the China Postdoctoral Science Foundation under Grant 2018M641688.

References

1. Zhu, H., Yuen, K.-V., Mihaylova, L., Leung, H.: Overview of environment perception for intelligent vehicles. IEEE Trans. Intell. Transp. Syst. **18**(10), 2584–2601 (2017)
2. Reid, D.: An algorithm for tracking multiple targets. Autom. Control **24**, 843–854 (1979)
3. Bar-Shalom, Y., Fortmann, T.E.: Tracking and Data Association. Academic Press, San Diego (1988)
4. Rezatofighi, S.H., Milan, A., Zhang, Z., Dick, A., Shi, Q., Reid, I.: Joint probabilistic data association revisited. In: 2015 IEEE International Conference on Computer Vision (ICCV), pp. 3047–3055. IEEE Computer Society, Washington, DC (2015)
5. Milan, A., Rezatofighi, S.H., Dick, A.R., Reid, I.D., Schindler, K.: Online multi-target tracking using recurrent neural networks. arXiv:1604.03635v2 (2016)
6. Bewley, A., Ge, Z., Ott, L., Ramos, F., Upcroft, B.: Simple online and real time tracking. In: 2016 IEEE International Conference on Image Processing (ICIP), pp. 3464–3468. IEEE Computer Society, Washington, DC (2016)
7. Scheidegger, S., Benjaminsson, J., Rosenberg, E., Krishnan, A., Granström, K.: Mono-camera 3D multi-object tracking using deep learning detections and PMBM filtering. In: 2018 IEEE Intelligent Vehicles Symposium, pp. 433–440. IEEE Computer Society, Washington, DC (2018)
8. Girshick, R., Donahue, J., Darrell, T., Malik, J.: Rich feature hierarchies for accurate object detection and semantic segmentation. In: 2014 IEEE Conference on Computer Vision and Pattern Recognition (CVPR), pp. 580–587. IEEE Computer Society, Washington, DC (2014)
9. Ren, S., He, K., Girshick, R., Sun, J.: Faster R-CNN: towards real-time object detection with region proposal networks. IEEE Trans. Pattern Anal. Mach. Intell. **39**(6), 1137–1149 (2016)
10. Redmon, J., Divvala, S., Girshick, R., Farhadi, A.: You only look once: unified, real-time object detection. In: 2015 IEEE Conference on Computer Vision and Pattern Recognition (CVPR), pp. 779–788. IEEE Computer Society, Washington, DC (2015)
11. Liu, W., et al.: SSD: Single Shot MultiBox Detector. In: Leibe, B., Matas, J., Sebe, N., Welling, M. (eds.) ECCV 2016. LNCS, vol. 9905, pp. 21–37. Springer, Cham (2016). https://doi.org/10.1007/978-3-319-46448-0_2

Multi-scale Feature Fusion Single Shot Object Detector Based on DenseNet

Minghao Zhai[1,3], Junchen Liu[1,3], Wei Zhang[1,3], Chen Liu[1,3], Wei Li[2], and Yi Cao[1,3(✉)]

[1] School of Mechanical Engineering, Jiangnan University,
Wuxi 214122, Jiangsu, China
caoyi@jiangnan.edu.cn
[2] Suzhou Vocational Institute of Industrial Technology,
Suzhou 215104, Jiangsu, China
[3] Jiangsu Key Laboratory of Advanced Food Manufacturing Equipment
and Technology, Wuxi 214122, Jiangsu, China

Abstract. SSD (Single Shot Multibox Detector) is one of advanced object detection methods and apparently can detect objects with high accuracy and fast speed. However, detecting small objects accurately remains a problem full of challenges for SSD. To handle this troublesome problem, our paper introduce a multi-scale feature fusion single shot object detector based on DenseNet (MFSOD), which combine the dense convolutional network (DenseNet) with SSD framework. Firstly, we add additional convolutional layers after backbone network to realize multi-scale feature detection. In addition, the feature fusion module is designed to fuse the multi-scale features from different layers, introducing the contextual information in object detection. Finally, we evaluate the proposed method on PASCAL VOC2007 and MS COCO benchmark datasets. The results indicate that our proposed method achieves 78.9% mAP on PASCAL VOC2007 test and 27.1% mAP on MS COCO test-dev2015 at the speed of 23 FPS. MFSOD algorithm outperforms the conventional SSD in aspects of accuracy, especially for small objects, and satisfies the demand of real-time application.

Keywords: Deep learning · Feature fusion · Object detection · Small objects

1 Introduction

Object detection is a significant task in the fields of computer vision, which applicable to numerous areas such as home-service, environmental monitoring, traffic security and so on [1]. It can identify and locate objects in images and videos accurately, so that the computer can understand the surrounding environment and achieve a good human-computer interaction [2].

In the past, a majority of traditional object detectors follow the pipeline including feature extraction, object classification, refinement. However, these detectors extracted hand crafted features [3] and utilized classifier like neural networks [4], support vector machines (SVMs) [5] for recognition, resulting in heavy time consumption of the

© Springer Nature Switzerland AG 2019
H. Yu et al. (Eds.): ICIRA 2019, LNAI 11744, pp. 450–460, 2019.
https://doi.org/10.1007/978-3-030-27541-9_37

model. In the past few years, convolutional neural networks (CNNs) [6] has made breakthrough in image classification [7] and object detection [8]. A series of detectors using features extracted by CNNs has already improved accuracy in object detection task.

Object detection algorithms based on CNNs could be divided into two main categories: the region-based algorithms and the one-stage algorithms. The region-based algorithms including R-CNN [9], Fast R-CNN [10], ION [11], Faster R-CNN [12], and so on. In this kind of detectors, a series of high quality candidate regions are firstly generated by region proposal generation network, and then these regions are predicted and adjusted by an outstanding subnetwork. The region proposal generation network can suppress negative candidate regions, and thus the accuracy of object detection is greatly improved. However, region proposal process brings a lot of consumption in time and resource. The one-stage methods including YOLO [13], YOLOv2 [14], SSD [15], and so on. These methods regress bounding box coordinates and predict object classes directly on the feature map extracted by convolutional networks. This series of method is high efficiency due to the single shot strategy. Among all the above detectors, SSD is one of the excellent detectors that can get satisfactory balance between accuracy and speed. Therefore, our paper chooses SSD as fundamental framework.

SSD make use of pyramidal feature maps to predict objects with various sizes and aspect ratios boxes. Base on the backbone network (VGG16), SSD added additional convolutional layers to generate pyramid feature maps, improving the performance of object detection greatly. Nevertheless, detecting small objects accurately is also a problem full of challenges for SSD. There are two main reasons for this problem: (a) shallow-level feature maps have small receptive field without strong semantic information, and deep-level semantic feature maps have lower resolution, which may loss many information of small objects. (b) The small objects have limited resolution and information. Although SSD try to exploit the information of small instances, detecting small objects is the remaining challenges.

In order to handle these problems mentioned above, our paper introduce a multi-scale feature fusion single shot object detector based on DenseNet (MFSOD) by combining the dense convolutional network (DenseNet) [16] with SSD framework. Firstly, we choose DenseNet as the backbone network, instead of VGG16 used in conventional SSD. The reason is that DenseNet is one of state-of-the-art classifier which can densely connect all the layers to generate more powerful features. In addition, to realize Multi-scale representations, we add additional convolutional layers after the backbone network DenseNet, constructed pyramidal feature maps by utilizing the feature maps from bottom to top. Previous researches have shown that contextual information is effectively important for object detection, especially for small objects. Therefore, the paper designed feature fusion module to introduce the additional contextual information in object detection framework. Feature fusion module can fuse the shallow-level detail features and deep-level semantic features via deconvolution and Batch Normalization. Finally, we applied feature fusion module to generate new powerful pyramidal feature maps, which are fed to multibox detectors to detect objects of various scales.

The main contributions of our paper are as follows:

- We propose MFSOD, an excellent object detector based on SSD framework. Under the framework, additional convolutional layers are added follow the backbone network (DenseNet) to detect multi-scale objects.
- We design feature fusion module, a novel way of introducing contextual information by combining the deep-level features and the shallow-level features.
- Experimental results on PASCAL VOC2007 [17] and MS COCO [18] benchmark datasets confirm that MDSOD achieve significant improvement on the detection accuracy, especially for small objects, and satisfies the demand of real-time.

2   Related Work

There are variety of ways to improve the accuracy of small objects detection.

Better Backbone Network. Backbone networks play a core role in object detection. SSD chose VGG-16 as the backbone network. DSSD [19] applied ResNet-101 and deconvolution modules, which makes the accuracy for small objects higher. DSOD [20] proposed a framework based on Dense-Net, which can train object detector from scratch. STDN [21] integrated DenseNet-169 with Scale-transfer module to obtains significant improvements on accuracy. Faster R-CNN [12] showed that the same backbone network as SSD, proposing regions by Region Proposal Network (RPN). Kim et al. proposed PVANet [22] to improve Faster R-CNN, select Inception as backbone network. Huang et al. [23] explored various combination of backbone networks and object detector, and Faster R-CNN based on Inception-ResNet-v2 can get the best performance. In this paper, we also consider better backbone networks to improve the accuracy of object detection.

Multi-scale Representation. Multi-scale representation is extremely useful for many detection methods. In order to utilize integrated information from different layer features, many previous detection methods applied multi-scale representation, such as SSD [15], MS-CNN [24], DSOD [20] and so on. SSD predict objects on six feature maps with different sizes extracted from network. MS-CNN is a modified framework based on Faster R-CNN, exploiting multi-scale feature maps from the proposal sub-network to enhance the performance for small objects. These approaches conducted predictions and regressions on multi-scale features, handling objects of various sizes.

Feature Fusion. There are a lot of object detection approaches which attempt to fuse features extracted from CNNs. The main goal of feature fusion is introducing contextual information and enriching the feature maps. Feature fusion method can make comprehensive use of multiple image features, and obtain more robust and accurate recognition results. HyperNet [25] and FCN [26] use skip connections to concatenate multi-level feature maps from CNNs, which mainly improve the detection accuracy for small objects. FSSD [27] adopt feature fusion module that concatenate features from different layers with different scales to generate new feature pyramid. FPN [28] construct the corresponding top-down network to connect different features, and the performance of small object detection is greatly improved without increasing the calculation amount of the original model.

3   MFSOD

Due to the shortcomings of conventional SSD algorithm in the detection of small objects, a multi-scale feature fusion single shot detector (MFSOD) based on DenseNet is proposed. This section introduces the general architecture of MFSOD and the detail of components.

3.1   General Architecture

The architecture of the MFSOD is shown in Fig. 1. The DenseNet-121 is used as the backbone network. After the backbone network, following three sets of additional convolutional layers. Every set of convolutional layers contains a 1×1 convolutional layer and a 3×3 convolutional layers. The size of convolutional layers is gradually reduced, and feature maps of different scales are obtained to realize multi-scale representation. In order to utilize contextual information, our MFSOD realizes the skip connections between the deep-level layers and the shallow-level layers through the feature fusion modules. The feature fusion module enhances the contextual information of objects, and expands the receptive field of the feature maps. Then a new powerful pyramid feature maps are generated, which consist of two fused feature maps (Feature Fusion Module 1, Feature Fusion Module 2) and four original feature maps (Dense block 4, Conv1, Conv2, Conv3). The corresponding feature size is 37×37, 18×18, 9×9, 5×5, 3×3 and 1×1. Finally, a series of multibox detectors is produced on pyramid feature maps to predict objects of sundry scales. The function of non-maximum suppression (NMS) is filter out extra bounding boxes during inference.

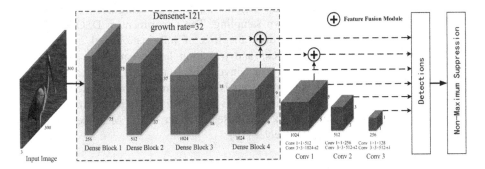

Fig. 1. The architecture of MFSOD.

3.2   Backbone Network

In this section, we first introduce the backbone network which extract features from origin images. We choose DenseNet as Backbone network. Compared with previous convolution neural network, DenseNet is a deep supervision network, which alleviate the vanishing gradient problem through the dense connection. In every dense block of DenseNet, the dense connection connects every layer with all the succeeding layers as shown in Fig. 2. Hence, DenseNet is appropriate for object detection because every layer is association of deep-level features and shallow-level features.

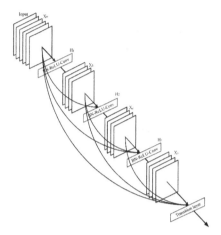

Fig. 2. The architecture of Dense Block.

Our Backbone network is an adjusted structure based on DenseNet-121, which is made up of a stem block, four dense blocks and three transition layers. Stem block is designed to take the place of the original input layers, which also mentioned in DSOD [20] and STDN [21]. the original input layers have one 7×7 convolution layers and one 3×3 max pooling layer. Stem block composed of three 3×3 convolution layers and one 2×2 mean pooling layer. the original input layers bring about information loss because of two consecutive down sampling. The experiment in DSOD and our study prove that stem block can reduce the loss of information and increase the robustness of the model. Dense blocks and transition layers connected alternately. Transition layers composed of one 1×1 convolutional layer and one 2×2 average pooling layer. The function of transition layers is down-sampling. In order to normalize the feature Weights, batch normalization layer is added after every convolutional layer. The growth rate of each dense block of DenseNet is set to 32. More details about DenseNet-121 can be found in DenseNet [16].

3.3   Feature Fusion Module

In order to fuse the different level feature maps, we introduce a feature fusion module. the architecture of feature fusion module as shown in Fig. 3. Feature maps must have the same size and channels before the fusion operation. Therefore, our paper conduct two deconvolution layers after deep-level feature map to achieve upsampling, then generate output maps with the same size of shallow-level feature map. The kernel size of deconvolution layer is 2×2. The deconvolution layers are followed by one 3×3

convolution layer, one batch normalization layers (BN), and one activate function layer (Rectified Linear Unit, ReLU). The low-level feature map is followed by one 3×3 convolution layer, batch normalization layers (BN), and activate function layer (Rectified Linear Unit, ReLU). Then, we fuse two output feature maps. Specifically, it is necessary to add a 1×1 convolution layer after fusion to achieve the dimensionality reduction of the feature map, which can reduce the interference of background noise. There are mainly two fusion methods: concatenation (Concat) and element-wise summation (Elts Sum). According to the experimental result in Sect. 4.4, element-wise summation achieves better performance than concatenation. So this paper applies element-wise summation to fuse these feature maps.

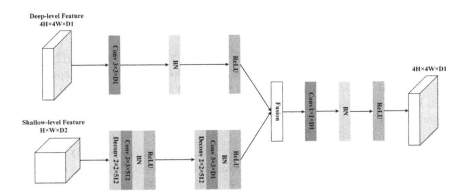

Fig. 3. The architecture of feature fusion module

3.4 Training

This paper applies training strategies which refer to SSD algorithm. In order to deal with different sizes of objects corresponding to different images, it is necessary to set different scales and different proportions of default boxes for different feature maps. The calculation method of default box refers to the SSD. The scale of lowest layer is set to 0.1, and the scale of highest layer is set to 0.9. Adding different aspect ratios to the default box on the same feature maps. Following DSSD [19] and STDN [21], aspect ratios also applies [1.6; 2.0; 3.0] for each prediction layer. The threshold in this network is set to 0.5. After the matching step, a large number of negative samples will be generated, resulting in significant imbalance between the positive and negative samples. In order to better optimize the network and train stably, hard negative mining is applied to keep the ratio of positive and negative samples around 1:3. This paper also utilize the data augmentation strategies. The training objective is the weighted sum between localization loss (Smooth L1) and confidence loss (Softmax). More details can be found in SSD [15].

4   Experimental

4.1   Experiment Setup

MFSOD is evaluated and compared on PASCAL VOC2007 and MS COCO bench-mark datasets. All the experiments are implemented in Keras on the machine with single Titan X GPU. The pre-trained DenseNet-121 model is used for MFSOD training, and then fine-tuning model on training datasets. We compare the results with other outstanding object detector about the accuracy and inference speed. For the VOC2007, the accuracy is evaluated by mean average precision (mAP), and the inference speed is evaluated by frame per second (FPS). For MS COCO, the model is evaluated by the evaluation server.

4.2   PASCAL VOC2007

Our method conduct training on the combination of 2007 trainval and 2012 trainval (VOC 07+12), and evaluate the model on PASCAL VOC2007 test. The input image size is set to 300×300. Batch size is set to 32. We set the learning rate to 10^{-3} for the first 50 k iterations, then decay it to 10^{-4} for training another 30 k iterations, and 10^{-5} for another 30 k iterations. We training model using SGD with 0.9 momentum and weight decay is set to 0.0005.

Table 1 shows results on VOC2007 test. We compared our MFSOD with other advanced object detector. MFSOD outperforms conventional SSD with the same input size, and it increase the mAP from 77.5% to 78.9%. SSD adds additional layers following VGG16 and use these feature maps for prediction. DSSD use Resnet-101 as backbone network, apply deconvolution module to introduce additional context. Our method chooses DenseNet-121 as backbone network, which is much deeper than VGG16 and Residual-101. MFSOD exceeds the DSSD321 by 0.3 points. MFSOD is higher than DSOD which also use DenseNet as backbone network, but DSOD can train object detector from scratch. However, MFSOD require a model which is pre-trained on magnanimous data. These results demonstrate that better backbone network could improve the performance of detector in a way. MFSOD can benefit from DenseNet-121, which can get deeper information by connecting different layers. Compared with other popular two stage methods, our MFSOD outperforms Faster R-CNN based on VGG16, but there is still plenty of room for improvement from R-FCN.

Table 1. Results on PASCAL VOC2007 test

Method	Backbone	GPU	Input size	Speed(fps)	mAP
Faster R-CNN [12]	VGG16	Titan X	$\approx 1000 \times 600$	7	73.2
R-FCN [29]	Resnet-101	Titan X	$\approx 1000 \times 600$	9	80.5
YOLOv2 [14]	Darknet-19	Titan X	352×352	81	73.7
SSD300 [15]	VGG16	Titan X	300×300	46	77.5
DSSD321 [19]	ResNet-101	Titan X	321×321	9.5	78.6
DSOD300 [20]	DS/64-192-48-1	Titan X	300×300	17.4	77.7
MFSOD300	DenseNet-121	Titan X	300×300	23	78.9

4.3   Inference Speed

In this paper, a single Titan X GPU was used to test the inference speed of MFSOD, and the batch size is set to 1. The comparison results are shown in Table 1. Due to the extremely deep backbone network and low efficiency of feature fusion, the inference speed of the object detector is greatly affected. Our MFSOD runs at 23 FPS with 300×300 input. Although the speed is a little lower than SSD (46 FPS), Our method is faster than the region-based methods with a large margin, and outperforms other one-stage methods except YOLOv2. MFSOD can satisfy the demand of real-time.

4.4   Ablation Study on VOC2007

This paper implement ablation experiments to investigate the effectiveness of components. All the experiments are conducted on PASCAL VOC2007. The input size set to 300×300. The results are summarized in Table 2.

Table 2. Ablation study on PASCAL VOC2007 test

Method	Pre-train	Stem block	Fusion	Fusion layer	Concat	Sum	mAP
MFSOD	✗	✗	✗	✗	✗	✗	69.7
MFSOD	✓	✗	✗	✗	✗	✗	73.2
MFSOD	✓	✓	✗	✗	✗	✗	75.6
MFSOD	✓	✓	✓	DB2-DB4	✓	✗	77.1
MFSOD	✓	✓	✓	DB2-DB4	✗	✓	77.3
MFSOD	✓	✓	✓	DB3-Conv1	✓	✗	77.9
MFSOD	✓	✓	✓	DB3-Conv1	✗	✓	76.8
MFSOD	✓	✓	✓	DB2-DB4, DB3-Conv1	✓	✗	78.2
MFSOD	✓	✓	✓	DB2-DB4, DB3-Conv1	✗	✓	78.9

Pre-train

The first row of Table 2 show that the evaluation result which trained model from scratch. the mAP on VOC2007 test is 69.7%. The second rows of Table 2 show that the evaluation result which adopted to pre-trained DenseNet-121 for initialization. the mAP is increased to 73.2%. Using the pre-trained model can bring us about 3.5% improvement.

Stem Block

As show in Table 2 (row 2 and 3), MFSOD use the original input layers can get 73.2% mAP, while stem block could increase the accuracy to 75.6%. DSOD [20] and STDN [21] speculate that the original design has certain defects. This result also prove that this assumption is correct and stem block can reduce information loss from the original input images.

Feature Fusion Module

In Table 2, this paper exploit effect factors of feature fusion modules. Firstly, we explore the appropriate layers to be fused. When we choose Dense Block 4 and conv1 to be fused with Dense Block 2 and Dense Block 3 respectively through feature fusion module, the mAP on VOC2007 test is highest. Furthermore, we select the suitable feature fuse method. As show in the eighth and ninth row of Table 2, when the detector applies concatenation to fuse features, the method can achieve 78.2% mAP. If we use the element-wise summation, the accuracy increased to 78.9%. The results show that element-wise summation is better than concatenation with a small margin.

4.5   MS COCO

In order to verify the effectiveness of the object detector, we train and evaluate our MFSOD on MS COCO. Our method conduct training on the trainval35 k and test on test-dev2015. we use the pre-trained MFSOD model to initialize our model. The input image size is set to 300×300. Batch size is set to 32. We set the learning rate to 10^{-3} for the first 250 k iterations, then decay it to 10^{-4} for training another 50 k iterations, and 10^{-5} for another 50 k iterations.

The results on MS COCO test-dev are summarized in Table 3. 'AP$_s$', 'AP$_m$', 'AP$_l$' stand for average precision of small objects (area $< 32^2$), medium objects ($32^2 <$ area $< 96^2$) and large objects (area $> 96^2$) respectively. 'AR$_s$', 'AR$_m$', 'AR$_l$' stand for average recall of small objects, medium objects and large objects respectively. MFSOD achieves 27.1% mAP while IOU set to 0.5:0.95. Compared with conventional SSD, our MFSOD can achieve tremendous improvement on all the metrics. Although the sixth and seventh rows of Table 3 show that the accuracy of MFSOD is lower than DSSD, the average precision of small objects is comparable. We also can observe that MFSOD outperforms other region-based detectors, for instance, Fast R-CNN (20.5%), ION (23.6%), and Fast R-CNN (21.9%). Furthermore, we explore the performance of small objects detection. As is shown in the fourth and tenth columns of Table 3, MFSOD achieve 7.8% AP for small objects and 12.5% AR for small objects. It exceeds SSD 1.2 points on average precision of small objects. MFSOD also outperforms other competitors except DSSD. These results indicate that MFSOD performs much better on detection of small objects.

Table 3. Results on MS COCO test-dev

Method	Data	mAP	AP$_s$	AP$_m$	AP$_l$	AR$_1$	AR$_{10}$	AR$_{100}$	AR$_s$	AR$_m$	AR$_l$
Fast [10]	train	20.5	4.1	20.0	35.8	21.3	29.5	30.1	7.3	32.1	52.0
Faster [12]	trainval	21.9	-	-	-	-	-	-	-	-	-
ION [11]	train	23.6	6.4	24.1	38.3	23.2	32.7	33.5	10.1	37.7	53.6
YOLOv2 [14]	trainval35 k	21.6	5.0	22.4	35.5	20.7	31.6	33.3	9.8	36.5	54.4
SSD [15]	trainval35 k	25.1	6.6	25.9	41.4	23.7	35.1	37.2	11.2	40.4	58.4
DSSD [19]	trainval35 k	28.0	7.4	28.1	47.6	25.5	37.1	39.4	12.7	42.0	62.6
MFSOD	trainval35 k	27.1	7.8	27.3	47.3	25.2	37.9	40.1	12.5	41.6	61.9

5 Conclusion

In order to handle the problem of small object detection accuracy of traditional SSD method, this paper proposes a novel object detector MFSOD based on multi-scale feature fusion. The method is compared and verified on some common standard datasets. Combined with the objective evaluation index, MFSOD is more accurate than the existing algorithms, and more forceful on detection of small objects under the premise of guaranteeing speed. In the future work, we will continue to research and modify the network. We can try to apply the method with better backbone networks, and adjust the corresponding structure to further enhance the performance.

Acknowledgement. This work reported here was supported by the National Natural Science Foundation of China (Grant No. 51375209), 111 Project (Grant No. B18027), the Six Talent Peaks Project in Jiangsu Province (Grant No. ZBZZ-012), and the Postgraduate Research & Practice Innovation Program of Jiangsu Province (Grant No. SJCX18-0630, KYCX18-1846). Finally, the authors would like to thanks for the support of PASCAL VOC datasets.

References

1. Ren, S., He, K.: Object detection networks on convolutional feature maps. IEEE Trans. Pattern Anal. Mach. Intell. **39**(7), 1476–1481 (2015)
2. Agarwal, S., Terrail, J.: Recent advances in object detection in the age of deep convolutional neural networks. arXiv preprint arXiv:1809.03193 (2018)
3. Uijlings, J., van de Sande, K.: Selective search for object recognition. Int. J. Comput. Vision **104**(2), 154–171 (2013)
4. Erhan, D., Szegedy, C., Toshev, A.: Scalable object detection using deep neural networks. In: Proceedings of the 2014 IEEE Conference on Computer Vision and Pattern Recognition (CVPR), pp. 2155–2162. IEEE, Columbus (2014)
5. Dalal, N., Triggs, B.: Histograms of oriented gradients for human detection. In: Proceedings of the 2005 IEEE Computer Society Conference on Computer Vision and Pattern Recognition (CVPR), pp. 886–893. IEEE, San Diego (2005)
6. LeCun, Y., Bengio, Y.: Convolutional networks for images, speech, and time series. In: The Handbook of Brain Theory and Neural Networks, vol. 3361, no. (10) (1995)
7. Krizhevsky, A., Sutskever, I., Hinton, G.: ImageNet classification with deep convolutional neural networks. In: Proceedings of the 25th International Conference on Neural Information Processing Systems, pp. 1097–1105. MIT Press, Lake Tahoe (2012)
8. He, K., Zhang, X., Ren, S., Sun, J.: Spatial pyramid pooling in deep convolutional networks for visual recognition. In: Fleet, D., Pajdla, T., Schiele, B., Tuytelaars, T. (eds.) ECCV 2014. LNCS, vol. 8691, pp. 346–361. Springer, Cham (2014). https://doi.org/10.1007/978-3-319-10578-9_23
9. Girshick, R., Donahue, J., Darrell, T.: Rich feature hierarchies for accurate object detection and semantic segmentation. In: Proceedings of the 2014 IEEE Conference on Computer Vision and Pattern Recognition (CVPR), pp. 580–587. IEEE, Columbus (2014)
10. Girshick, R.: Fast R-CNN. In: Proceedings of the 2015 IEEE International Conference on Computer Vision (ICCV), pp. 1440–1448. IEEE, Santiago, Chile (2015)
11. Bell, S., Zitnick, C., Bala, K.: Inside-outside net: detecting objects in context with skip pooling and recurrent neural networks. In: Proceedings of the 2016 IEEE Conference on Computer Vision and Pattern Recognition (CVPR), pp. 2874–2883. IEEE, Las Vegas (2016)

12. Ren, S., He, K., Girshick, R.: Faster R-CNN: towards real-time object detection with region proposal networks. In: International Conference on Neural Information Processing Systems, pp. 91–99. MIT Press, Montreal (2015)

13. Redmon, J., Divvala, S., Girshick, R.: You only look once: unified, real-time object detection. In: Proceedings of the 2016 IEEE Conference on Computer Vision and Pattern Recognition (CVPR), pp. 779–788. IEEE, Las Vegas (2016)

14. Redmon, J., Farhadi, A.: YOLO9000: better, faster, stronger. In: Proceedings of the 2017 IEEE Conference on Computer Vision and Pattern Recognition (CVPR), pp. 6517–6525. IEEE, Honolulu (2017)

15. Liu, W., et al.: SSD: single shot MultiBox detector. In: Leibe, B., Matas, J., Sebe, N., Welling, M. (eds.) ECCV 2016. LNCS, vol. 9905, pp. 21–37. Springer, Cham (2016). https://doi.org/10.1007/978-3-319-46448-0_2

16. Huang, G., Liu, Z., van der Maaten, L.: Densely connected convolutional networks. In: Proceedings of the 2017 IEEE Conference on Computer Vision and Pattern Recognition (CVPR), pp. 2261–2269. IEEE, Honolulu (2017)

17. Everingham, M., Eslami, S., Van Gool, L.: The pascal visual object classes challenge: a retrospective. Int. J. Comput. Vision 111(1), 98–136 (2015)

18. Lin, T.-Y., et al.: Microsoft COCO: common objects in context. In: Fleet, D., Pajdla, T., Schiele, B., Tuytelaars, T. (eds.) ECCV 2014. LNCS, vol. 8693, pp. 740–755. Springer, Cham (2014). https://doi.org/10.1007/978-3-319-10602-1_48

19. Fu, C., Liu, W., Ranga, A.: DSSD: deconvolutional single shot detector. arXiv preprint arXiv:1701.06659 (2017)

20. Shen, Z., Liu, Z., Li J.: DSOD: learning deeply supervised object detectors from scratch. In: Proceedings of the 2017 IEEE International Conference on Computer Vision (ICCV), pp. 1937–1945. IEEE, Venice (2017)

21. Zhou, P., Ni, B., Geng, C.: Scale-transferrable object detection. In: Proceedings of the 2018 IEEE Conference on Computer Vision and Pattern Recognition (CVPR), pp. 528–537. IEEE, Salt Lake City (2018)

22. Kim, K., Hong, S., Roh, B.: PVANET: deep but lightweight neural networks for real-time object detection. arXiv preprint arXiv:1608.08021 (2016)

23. Huang, J., Rathod, V., Sun, C.: Speed/accuracy trade-offs for modern convolutional object detectors. In: Proceedings of the 2017 IEEE Conference on Computer Vision and Pattern Recognition (CVPR), pp. 3296–3297. IEEE, Honolulu (2017)

24. Cai, Z., Fan, Q., Feris, R.S., Vasconcelos, N.: A unified multi-scale deep convolutional neural network for fast object detection. In: Leibe, B., Matas, J., Sebe, N., Welling, M. (eds.) ECCV 2016. LNCS, vol. 9908, pp. 354–370. Springer, Cham (2016). https://doi.org/10.1007/978-3-319-46493-0_22

25. Kong, T., Yao, A., Chen, Y.: HyperNet: towards accurate region proposal generation and joint object detection. In: Proceedings of the 2016 IEEE Conference on Computer Vision and Pattern Recognition (CVPR), pp. 845–853. IEEE, Las Vegas (2016)

26. Long, J., Shelhamer, E., Darrell, T.: Fully convolutional networks for semantic segmentation. IEEE Trans. Pattern Anal. Mach. Intell. 39(4), 640–651 (2014)

27. Li, Z., Zhou, F.: FSSD: feature fusion single shot multibox detector. arXiv preprint arXiv: 1712. 00960 (2017)

28. Lin, T., Dollár, P., Girshick, R.: Feature pyramid networks for object detection. arXiv preprint arXiv: 1612.03144 (2016)

29. Dai, J., Li, Y., He, K.: R-FCN: object detection via region-based fully convolutional networks. In: NIPS'16 Proceedings of the 30th International Conference on Neural Information Processing Systems (NIPS), pp. 379–387. ACM, Barcelona (2016)

Semi-direct Tracking and Mapping
with RGB-D Camera

Ke Liu$^{(\boxtimes)}$, Xiaolin Gu, Min Yang, Yi Zhang, and Shun Guan

Beijing Sun Wise Space Technology Ltd., Beijing, China
liuke@sunwisespace.com

Abstract. In this paper we present a novel semi-direct tracking and mapping approach for RGB-D cameras, which inherits the advantages of both direct and feature-based methods, and achieves high accuracy and robustness. The proposed method comprises three threads: tracking, local mapping and loop closing. In the tracking thread, the input RGB-D frames are tracked with a direct method and refined by minimizing geometric error. Since RGB-D cameras can obtain depth maps directly, we take both appearance and depth information into account for feature extraction and matching, that improves the tracking accuracy of the approach. The local mapping is performed to process new keyframes and refine the local map for improving the local consistency of SLAM. The loop closing detects and corrects loops, so that the consistent SLAM map can be obtained. Experiments on two benchmark datasets show that our approach performs well in scenes with low-texture and large moving objects, and obtains results with high accuracy.

Keywords: RGB-D SLAM · Semi-direct method · Tracking · Mapping

1 Introduction

Visual odometry (VO) and simultaneous localization and mapping (SLAM) play an important role in many robotic technologies, such as virtual/augmented reality and service robots. In particular, RGB-D sensors which provide both color and depth images directly have become a popular choice for dense reconstruction of unknown indoor environments [1].

Traditional VO and SLAM algorithms relied on feature extraction and matching to estimate structure and motion [2]. Feature descriptors such as SIFT [3] or SURF [4] have a high degree of invariance to illumination and scale changes, and they can be matched over wide baselines. Such properties are favorable for tracking large inter-frame motions and recognizing revisited places. In contrast to feature-based methods, direct methods are capable of leveraging raw photometric information from a chosen set of pixels in the image [5]. This removes the need for costly per-frame feature extraction and matching. Also, they are shown to be relatively more robust in low-texture scenes. Direct methods have their own merits in several aspects, but they also have some limitations.

© Springer Nature Switzerland AG 2019
H. Yu et al. (Eds.): ICIRA 2019, LNAI 11744, pp. 461–472, 2019.
https://doi.org/10.1007/978-3-030-27541-9_38

For example, direct methods seem to lack robustness against moving objects, since pixels from small baselines may lead to many error correspondences and result in poor motion estimations.

In this paper, we propose a novel semi-direct approach for RGB-D SLAM that inherits both the robustness of direct VO and the map-reusing capability of feature-based method. In the tracking thread, a direct method is used to track the camera pose firstly and a feature-based method is performed to refine the pose. Most feature-based methods only take the appearance information into account for feature extraction and matching. However, they suffer from the absence of depth information. We combine the appearance and depth information together to extract and match feature points, and improve the accuracy of tracking. In the local mapping thread, the keyframe-based map is partly updated according to the most recently tracking results. We implement a local BA (bundle adjustment) to optimize both local keyframes and map points. Moreover, we employ a loop closing thread to detect and close loops. Once a loop closure is detected, the global optimization is performed to reduce global drift and obtain a consistent map. Compared with state-of-the-art works, our method achieves higher accuracy and robustness for low-texture and large moving objects.

2   Related Work

2.1   Feature-Based Methods

Feature-based methods recover camera pose by matching features and performing geometric BA that minimizes the reprojection error. In [6], the RGB-D SLAM is explored to estimate the pose of Kinect and reconstruct the indoor environment. It uses the SIFT features for pose estimation and loop detection. PTAM [7] is one of the most representative systems of this type, and it was first proposed to split tracking and mapping into two parallel threads. ORB-SLAM2 [8] uses ORB features [9] to perform tracking, mapping, re-localization and loop detection, which is arguably the best-performing feature-based system.

2.2   Direct Methods

Direct methods estimate structure and motion by minimizing the photometric error between corresponding pixels in images. RGB-D SLAM [10] registers two consecutive RGB-D frames directly upon each other by minimizing the photometric error. It estimates the camera motion using non-linear minimization in combination with a coarse-to-fine scheme. DVO [11] minimizes both the photometric and the depth error over all pixels to estimate the pose of camera. Furthermore, it uses an entropy-based similarity measure for keyframe selection and loop closure detection.

2.3   Semi-direct Methods

Semi-direct methods estimate camera poses using both direct and feature-based methods. In [12] and [13], different semi-direct approaches were proposed for stereo odometry. Both methods use feature-based tracking to obtain a motion prior, and then perform direct method to refine the camera pose. In [14], an approach was proposed for RGB-D camera that adopts direct method for tracking and keyframes are refined by minimizing both geometric and depth error. SVO [15] performs direct sparse image alignment to estimate the initial guess of the camera pose and feature correspondences. Afterwards, it performs geometric BA to refine the pose and structure. Although this system is highly efficient, it is only a visual odometry without back-end optimization and loop detection.

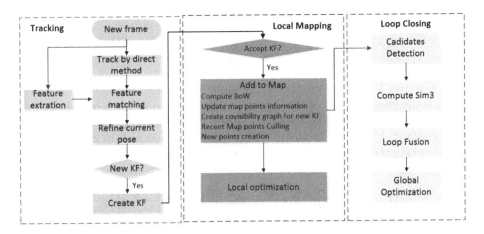

Fig. 1. The framework of the proposed method. RGB-D frames are tracked by direct method firstly, and then refined by minimizing the reprojection error. When new keyframe is created, it is inserted to the global map and a local optimization is performed to optimize the local map. Meanwhile, the loop is detected with a BoW (Bag of Word) method and closed by a pose graph optimization.

3   Semi-direct Tracking and Mapping

The overview of the proposed semi-direct tracking and mapping method is shown in Fig. 1, which contains three main threads: tracking, local mapping and loop closing.

- In the tracking thread, the pose of new RGB-D frame is estimated by minimizing the photometric residuals firstly, and then refined by the feature-based method. Moreover, tracking thread decides if a new keyframe is generated.
- The local mapping processes new keyframes and inserts them to the global map. Then a local BA is performed to achieve an optimal reconstruction in the surroundings of the camera pose.

– The loop closing searches for loops with every new keyframe. If a loop is detected, a pose graph optimization over similarity constraints is taken to close the loop. Afterwards, a full BA optimizes all keyframes and feature points in the map for global consistency.

3.1   Tracking

Track Based on Direct Method. Once a new frame is obtained from the RGB-D camera, we first use direct method to estimate the initial pose. When a point $\mathbf{k}$ in a reference frame I_j is observed in current frame I_i, the photometric error is defined as the weighted SSD over the 8-point neighborhood pixels $\mathcal{N}_\mathbf{k}$ as proposed in [16],

$$E_{ij}^{\mathbf{k}} := \sum_{\mathbf{k} \in \mathcal{N}_\mathbf{k}} \omega_\mathbf{k} \left\| I_i \left[\mathbf{k}' \right] - b_i - \frac{t_i e^{a_i}}{t_j e^{a_j}} \left(I_j \left[\mathbf{k} \right] - b_j \right) \right\|_\gamma, \tag{1}$$

$$\mathbf{k}' = \mathbf{\Pi}_c \left(\mathbf{T}_{iw}^{-1} \mathbf{T}_{jw} \mathbf{\Pi}_c^{-1} \left(\mathbf{k}, d_\mathbf{k} \right) \right), \tag{2}$$

where t, a and b are exposure time and affine brightness function parameters, and $d_\mathbf{k}$ is the inverse depth of $\mathbf{k}$ in the reference frame I_j, which is obtained from RGB-D camera directly. The weight $\omega_\mathbf{k}$ down-weights high-gradient pixels with some constant. $\mathbf{k}'$ stands for the projected point position of $\mathbf{k}$ in current frame I_i. The total energy function to be minimized is given by the full photometric error plus a prior pulling the affine brightness parameters to zero,

$$E_{photo} := \sum_{i \in \mathcal{F}} \sum_{\mathbf{k} \in \mathcal{K}_i} \sum_{j \in obs(\mathbf{k})} E_{ij}^{\mathbf{k}} + \sum_{i \in \mathcal{F}} \left(\lambda_a a_i^2 + \lambda_b b_i^2 \right), \tag{3}$$

where i runs over all frames in the window $\mathcal{F}$, $\mathbf{k}$ overall points $\mathcal{K}_i$ in frame i, and j over all frames $obs(\mathbf{k})$ in which the point $\mathbf{k}$ is visible. When exposure times are known, we set λ_a and λ_b to some constant values. Otherwise, we set $\lambda_a = \lambda_b = 0$. The optimization is performed using an iteratively reweighted Gauss-Newton algorithm in a coarse-to-fine scheme. The update equation is given by

$$\delta\xi = - \left(\mathbf{J}^\top \mathbf{W} \mathbf{J} \right)^{-1} \mathbf{J} \mathbf{W} \mathbf{r}, \tag{4}$$

$$\xi^{new} \leftarrow \delta\xi \oplus \xi, \tag{5}$$

where $\mathbf{r}$ is the stacked vector of residuals, $\mathbf{J}$ is its Jacobian and $\mathbf{W}$ is the diagonal weight matrix. The state variable ξ is the Lie Algebraic representation of camera pose.

Refine Based on Feature-Based Method. Given the initial pose provided by direct method, we refine it by using motion only geometric BA with respect to the local feature map.

While estimating pose by direct method, we extract feature points of current frame in another thread. In this paper, we combine both appearance and depth information for feature extraction and matching. A new feature point has two different descriptors, one is ORB feature descriptor [9] and the other is described by depth information. We employ the template of ORB feature descriptor to calculate depth descriptor, but use depth value instead of gray value. Hamming distance is a weighted combination of two descriptors between feature points with matched,

$$D_{\mathbf{p}} = \omega_1 D_f + \omega_2 D_d, \tag{6}$$

where D_f is the Hamming distance for ORB feature descriptor, and D_d is computed for depth. ω_1 and ω_2 denote the weight of the distances, which are set to 0.5 in this paper.

We therefore do not use the motion model in tracking and instead rely on brute force matching between local map points and feature points in current frame [17]. To insure the accuracy of tracking, a large number of feature points, around 1000, are detected in each image. With so many feature points, some might have similar appearance although they correspond to different map points in the 3D environment. By using the depth information to compare patches surrounding the feature point, our algorithm is able to filter out wrong matches that are only visually similar.

In order to reduce the interference of moving objects, we select the map points whose matching error is less than the threshold as the effective map points, and optimize the camera pose by minimizing the reprojection error of them,

$$E_{reproj} = \sum_{i \in \mathcal{F}_{local}} \sum_{\mathbf{p} \in \mathcal{P}_i} \sum_{j \in obs(\mathbf{p})} \left\| \frac{\mathbf{p}_i - \mathbf{\Pi}_c\left(\mathbf{T}_{iw}\mathbf{x}_w\right)}{\sigma_{\mathbf{p}_i}^2} \right\|, \tag{7}$$

where i runs over all local keyframes in $\mathcal{F}_{local}$, $\mathbf{p}$ over effective map points $\mathcal{P}_i$, and j over all frames $obs(\mathbf{p})$ in which the map point $\mathbf{p}$ is visible. $\mathbf{p}_i \in \mathbb{R}^2$ is the match to $\mathbf{p}$ in frame i, $\sigma_{\mathbf{p}_i}^2$ is the variance of the feature location in frame i, and $\mathbf{x}_w$ is the 3D world coordinate of $\mathbf{p}$.

Posture Estimation and Relocation. Direct methods are more robust in low-texture environment, where feature-based methods sometimes will track fail. In order to improve the tracking accuracy, we use a heuristic strategy to determine whether to optimize the pose. If the number of feature points is small and the confidence of the direct method is higher than the threshold value, the initial posture will be output directly.

When the direct method fails, we generate initial pose based on motion model, and use the feature-based method to optimize pose directly. The photometric error of current frame is recalculated after pose optimization. If the error is small enough, the pose will be output.

Once the tracking is lost, a relocalization procedure should be done to recover tracking system from failure. We search for candidate keyframes and match map points based on BoW model [18], then a coarse motion is estimated with RANSAC [8] algorithm based on correspondences between current frame and candidates. After successful relocation, the direct window will be re-initialized with the latest image frames and depth maps.

3.2   Local Mapping

New keyframes are processed by the local mapping in several steps:

- **BoW Computation.** The BoW vector of new keyframe is computed and registered to a keyframe database for triangulation, loop closure detection and relocalization.
- **Update the Covisibility Graph.** We update the covisibility graph by adding a new node for current keyframe and updating the edges resulting from the shared map points with other keyframes.
- **New Map Points Creation.** We estimate the world coordinate $\mathbf{x}_w$ of the new map point $\mathbf{p}$ with the inverse project function,

$$\mathbf{x}_w = \mathbf{T}_{iw}^{-1}\mathbf{\Pi}_c^{-1}\left(\mathbf{p}_i - d_{\mathbf{p}_i}\right), \tag{8}$$

where $\mathbf{p}_i$ is the pixels coordinate of map point $\mathbf{p}$, and $d_{\mathbf{p}_i}$ is the depth value obtained by RGB-D camera. For map points without valid depth information, we find their correspondences by epipolar search in nearby keyframes and obtain their 3D positions by triangulation.
- **Local Bundle Adjustment.** The local BA optimizes the currently processed keyframe, all the keyframes connected to it in the covisibility graph, and all the map points seen by those keyframes. All other keyframes that see those points but are not connected to the currently processed keyframe are included in the optimization but remain fixed.

3.3   Global Optimization

In the loop closing thread, the place recognition module based on BoW detects large loops by querying the keyframe database. Once a loop is detected, the map points and keyframes on each side of the loop are aligned and fused.

Pose graph optimization is performed over the essential graph minimizing,

$$E_{graph} = \sum_{(i,j)\in l_{edge}} \left\| \log_{Sim(3)}\left(S_{ij,0}S_{jw}S_{iw}^{-1}\right) \right\|_2^2, \tag{9}$$

where l_{edge} denotes the set of edges in the essential graph, and $S_{ij,0}$ is the fixed similarity transformation between the frame i and j just prior to the pose graph optimization. If the edge is created from a loop closure, this transformation is instead computed using the method of Horn [19]. Finally, a full BA is performed afterwards.

After loop fusion, the cumulative error of the feature-based method can be eliminated, but the window in direct method is not updated. In this paper, the sliding window is re-initialized by image frames and depth maps obtained after loop fusion to reduce the cumulative error in the direct method [20].

Table 1. RMSE of absolute trajectory error (m) for four different competing methods on ICL dataset. The smallest values are highlighted in bold.

Dataset	Our method				ORB-SLAM2			
	Direct+ORB		Direct+ORB+depth		ORB		ORB+depth	
	VO	w/ loop	VO	w/ loop	VO	w/ loop	VO	w/ loop
room_traj1	0.020	0.020	0.013	**0.013**	0.095	0.095	0.030	0.030
room_traj2	0.018	0.018	0.015	0.015	0.019	0.019	0.014	**0.014**
traj2_frei_png	0.012	0.012	0.007	**0.007**	0.011	0.011	0.010	0.010
room_traj3	0.018	0.011	0.013	**0.010**	0.016	0.010	0.012	0.010
room_traj3n	0.016	0.010	0.014	**0.010**	0.017	0.011	0.014	0.010
traj3_frei_png	0.022	0.016	0.017	**0.013**	0.082	0.067	0.037	0.016
traj3n_frei_png	0.018	0.014	0.015	**0.011**	0.094	0.065	0.042	0.014

4   Evaluation

We evaluate the proposed approach on two widely used RGB-D benchmark datasets: ICL [21] and TUM [22], since they both provide synchronized ground-true poses which can be adopted to evaluate the tracking accuracy. All results were obtained in real-time on a standard desktop PC running 64-bit Ubuntu 16.04 Linux with an Intel Core i5-8400 2.8GHz CPU.

4.1   Experiment on ICL Dataset

In the first set of experiments, we evaluate the benefit of semi-direct method for tracking. Table 1 indicates the RMSE (root mean square error) of absolute trajectory error for the four different competing methods: the direct method for estimating initial pose plus the feature-based method which only uses ORB descriptor (Direct+ORB); the direct method and feature-based method that combines ORB and depth descriptor (Direct+ORB+depth); ORB-SLAM2 [8] only used ORB descriptor (ORB); and ORB-SLAM2 combined both descriptors (ORB+depth). Each method shows two results, one with loop closing and the other without.

Our algorithm uses the direct method to estimate initial pose, while ORB-SLAM2 estimates the pose by minimizing the reprojection error of map points in last frame. Due to the cumulative error of direct methods is less than feature-based methods [16], our approach achieves better accuracy in most sequences, such as sequence room_traj1 and sequence traj2_frei_png.

Due to the ability of filtering out wrong matches of map points that are only visually similar by using the depth information, the methods combined ORB and depth descriptors for tracking show higher accuracy than only using ORB descriptor, especially in sequences room_traj1 and traj3_frei_png.

In the last four sequences, the methods with loop closing achieve better accuracy than those without, as loop closing reduces the global drift in tracking.

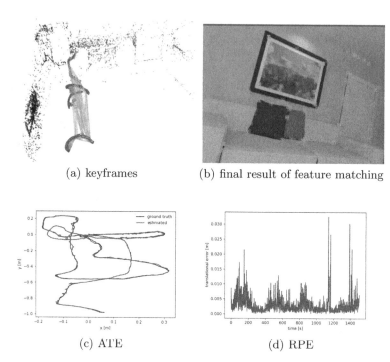

(a) keyframes   (b) final result of feature matching

(c) ATE   (d) RPE

Fig. 2. The results of sequence *room_traj0*. (a) All keyframes in the sequence, where keyframes are shown in blue, and the keyframe connections in green. (b) The result of feature matching for one frame. (c) The two-dimensional plot of estimated trajectory compared with ground truth trajectory. (d) The relative pose error plot indicates a small drift of our approach. (Color figure online)

Other rows got the same RMSE with or without loop fusion since no loop is detected in these sequences.

The results of the proposed method in sequence *room_traj0* are shown in Fig. 2. All keyframes selected by our method are shown in (a), where the keyframes is blue, and the keyframe connections is green. An example of feature matching result is shown in (b), and matched feature points are evenly distributed in the scene. The ground-truth and estimated trajectories are shown in (c), and they are almost identical. We plot the relative pose error (RPE) with respect to time in (d). Most translation errors are below 1.5 cm, which indicates the small drift of our algorithm.

4.2 Experiment on TUM Dataset

TUM dataset has 39 sequences which are captured in two different indoor environments. It contains ground-truth trajectory from motion capture system and provides tools for trajectory accuracy evaluation. Results of our system are provided in Table 2. In addition, we compare our method to three state-of-the-art

Table 2. RMSE of absolute trajectory error (m) for our algorithm in comparison to three state-of-art methods. The smallest values are highlighted in bold.

Dataset	RGB-D SLAM [7]	DVO [18]	ORB-SLAM2 [8]	Ours
fr1/xyz	0.014	0.011	0.010	**0.009**
fr1/rpy	0.026	**0.020**	0.026	0.020
fr1/desk	0.023	0.021	0.016	**0.016**
fr1/desk2	0.043	0.046	**0.028**	0.031
fr1/room	0.084	**0.053**	0.112	0.092
fr1/plant	0.091	0.028	0.021	**0.017**
fr2/coke	-	-	0.368	**0.044**
fr2/flower	-	-	0.590	**0.036**
fr3/str_text_near	0.017	-	0.015	**0.011**
fr3/walk_halfsph	-	-	0.331	**0.038**
fr3/long	0.032	0.035	0.023	**0.010**
fr3/cabint	-	-	0.080	**0.023**

approaches: RGB-D SLAM [10], direct visual odometer (DVO) [11], and ORB-SLAM2. The table lists RMSE of the absolute trajectory error for different methods, where our approach achieves the best accuracy. It should be noted that our approach is robust for large moving objects and even works well in sequences with

(a) map points selection

(b) final results of feature matching

Fig. 3. Map points selection on *fr2/coke*. (a) Effective map points are red, and the removed map points are black. (b) The final results for feature matching.

low-texture, such as sequences *fr2/coke* and *fr3/cabinet*. In sequence *fr1/desk2*, where the camera moves fast, the estimation of the pose performs a small drift. It is resulted from that direct method is sensitive to the large baseline motion of the camera. In the case of inaccurate initial pose, the pose optimization based on feature-based method can only reduce the error, and reach the optimum difficulty.

The results of sequences *fr2/coke* and *fr2/flower* indicate that our system remains high accuracy and robustness in situations with moving objects while ORB-SLAM2 drifts a lot in these sequences. Figure 3 shows the result of map points selection in sequence *fr2/coke*. The effective map points are red, the removed points are black. The final matching results are shown in Fig. 3(b), where most of the map points on moving object are removed by our method.

In addition, we test the performance of our method in the sequences of texture and structure changes. Figure 4 shows the results of *fr3* sequences. The first column indicates the scenario of each sequence. Sequence *fr3/structure_notexture_far* only contains structure information, with low-texture, as shown in Fig. 4(a). Sequence *fr3/nostruct_texture_near*

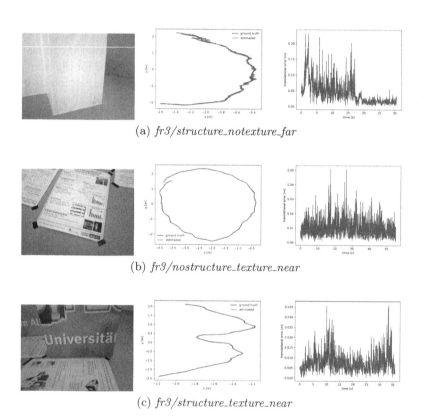

(a) *fr3/structure_notexture_far*

(b) *fr3/nostructure_texture_near*

(c) *fr3/structure_texture_near*

Fig. 4. Some results of our algorithm on *fr3* sequences. Scenario for each sequence (1st column), trajectory comparisons (2nd column), and relative pose errors (3rd column).

shown in (b) contains texture information without structure. And sequence *fr3/structure_texture_near* have both structure and texture information shown in (c). The second column shows the ground-truth and estimated trajectories, and they are almost identical. The third column displays the translational drift for every sequence, which indicates the small drift of our approach, since our method works well in the three different scenes, and remains high accuracy and robustness for sequences with low-texture.

5 Conclusions

In this paper, we presented a novel SLAM approach for RGB-D cameras by combining direct and feature-based methods. Our method uses the direct method to estimate the initial pose of the camera, and the feature-based method is performed to refine the pose. The system remains robust in challenging conditions with low-texture, and large moving objects. The evaluation results show small drift and high accuracy on trajectory thanks to the novel feature extraction and matching strategy, which take both appearance and depth information into account. As a next step, we plan to fuse IMU data to provide the initial rotation matrix for the direct method and further improve the tracking accuracy of the algorithm.

References

1. Zhang, G., Yao, E., Lin, Z., Xu, H.: Fast binocular SLAM algorithm combining the direct method and the feature-based method. Robot **39**(6), 879–888 (2017). (in Chinese)
2. Davison, A.J., Reid, I.D., Molton, N.D., Stasse, O.: MonoSLAM: real-time single camera SLAM. IEEE Trans. Pattern Anal. Mach. Intell. **6**, 1052–1067 (2007)
3. Jamieson, K., Balakrishnan, H., Tay, Y.C.: Sift: a MAC protocol for event-driven wireless sensor networks. In: Römer, K., Karl, H., Mattern, F. (eds.) EWSN 2006. LNCS, vol. 3868, pp. 260–275. Springer, Heidelberg (2006). https://doi.org/10.1007/11669463_20
4. Bay, H., Ess, A., Tuytelaars, T., Van Gool, L.: Speeded-up robust features (SURF). Comput. Vis. Image Underst. **110**(3), 346–359 (2008)
5. Engel, J., Schöps, T., Cremers, D.: LSD-SLAM: large-scale direct monocular SLAM. In: Fleet, D., Pajdla, T., Schiele, B., Tuytelaars, T. (eds.) ECCV 2014. LNCS, vol. 8690, pp. 834–849. Springer, Cham (2014). https://doi.org/10.1007/978-3-319-10605-2_54
6. Henry, P., Krainin, M., Herbst, E., Ren, X., Fox, D.: RGB-D mapping: using kinect-style depth cameras for dense 3D modeling of indoor environments. Int. J. Robot. Res. **31**(5), 647–663 (2012)
7. Klein, G., Murray, D.: Parallel tracking and mapping for small AR workspaces. In: Proceedings of the 2007 6th IEEE and ACM International Symposium on Mixed and Augmented Reality, pp. 1–10. IEEE Computer Society (2007)
8. Mur-Artal, R., Tardós, J.D.: "ORB-SLAM2": an open-source SLAM system for monocular, stereo, and RGB-D cameras. IEEE Trans. Robot. **33**(5), 1255–1262 (2017)

9. Rublee, E., Rabaud, V., Konolige, K., Bradski, G.R.: ORB: an efficient alternative to SIFT or SURF. In: ICCV, vol. 11, p. 2. Citeseer (2011)

10. Kerl, C., Sturm, J., Cremers, D.: Robust odometry estimation for RGB-D cameras, pp. 3748–3754 (2013)

11. Kerl, C., Sturm, J., Cremers, D.: Dense visual SLAM for RGB-D cameras, pp. 2100–2106 (2013)

12. Krombach, N., Droeschel, D., Behnke, S.: Combining feature-based and direct methods for semi-dense real-time stereo visual odometry. In: Chen, W., Hosoda, K., Menegatti, E., Shimizu, M., Wang, H. (eds.) IAS 2016. AISC, vol. 531, pp. 855–868. Springer, Cham (2017). https://doi.org/10.1007/978-3-319-48036-7_62

13. Kim, P., Lee, H., Kim, H.J.: Autonomous flight with robust visual odometry under dynamic lighting conditions. Auton. Robots **43**, 1605–1622 (2018)

14. Bu, S., Zhao, Y., Wan, G., Li, K., Cheng, G., Liu, Z.: Semi-direct tracking and mapping with RGB-D camera for MAV. Multimed. Tools Appl. **76**(3), 4445–4469 (2017)

15. Forster, C., Zhang, Z., Gassner, M., Werlberger, M., Scaramuzza, D.: SVO: semidirect visual odometry for monocular and multicamera systems. IEEE Trans. Robot. **33**(2), 249–265 (2017)

16. Engel, J., Koltun, V., Cremers, D.: Direct sparse odometry. IEEE Trans. Pattern Anal. Mach. Intell. **40**(3), 611–625 (2018)

17. Sheikh, R., OBwald, S., Bennewitz, M.: A combined RGB and depth descriptor for slam with humanoids. In: 2018 IEEE/RSJ International Conference on Intelligent Robots and Systems (IROS), pp. 1718–1724. IEEE (2018)

18. Gálvez-López, D., Tardos, J.D.: Bags of binary words for fast place recognition in image sequences. IEEE Trans. Robot. **28**(5), 1188–1197 (2012)

19. Horn, B.K.: Closed-form solution of absolute orientation using unit quaternions. JOSA A **4**(4), 629–642 (1987)

20. Gao, X., Wang, R., Demmel, N., Cremers, D.: "LDSO": direct sparse odometry with loop closure. In: 2018 IEEE/RSJ International Conference on Intelligent Robots and Systems (IROS), pp. 2198–2204. IEEE (2018)

21. Handa, A., Whelan, T., McDonald, J., Davison, A.J.: A benchmark for RGB-D visual odometry, 3D reconstruction and SLAM. In: 2014 IEEE International Conference on Robotics and Automation (ICRA), pp. 1524–1531. IEEE (2014)

22. Sturm, J., Engelhard, N., Endres, F., Burgard, W., Cremers, D.: A benchmark for the evaluation of RGB-D SLAM systems. In: 2012 IEEE/RSJ International Conference on Intelligent Robots and Systems, pp. 573–580. IEEE (2012)

Two-Person Interaction Recognition Based on Video Sparse Representation and Improved Spatio-Temporal Feature

Cao Jiangtao[1], Wang Peiyao[1], Chen Shuqi[1], and Ji Xiaofei[2(✉)]

[1] Liaoning Shihua University, Fushun, Liaoning, China
[2] Shenyang Aerospace University, Shenyang, Liaoning, China
Jixiaofei7804@126.com

Abstract. In order to solve the problems of two-person interaction recognition, a novel human interaction recognition method was proposed. Firstly, a distance extreme value algorithm based on HOG feature description was proposed to extract the key frames of the video. That is the sparse representation of the action video in temporal dimension. Secondly, the algorithm based on active curve is used to obtain the sparse representation of the key frames of the video. That is the sparse representation of the video in spatial dimension. Thirdly, STIPs were selected to be spatio-temporal feature. The STIPs of the key frames are extracted based on the sparse representation of the videos as well. Finally, two algorithms are used to identify the interaction behavior, include the BOW model combing with the nearest neighbor classifier and the improved SRC algorithm. Experimental results show that the improved SRC algorithm has a better recognition rate for the sparse representation in videos.

Keywords: Spatio-temporal feature · Sparse representation ·
Compressive Sensing (CS) · Active curve · Two-person interaction recognition

1 Introduction

Nowadays, the great need of society in the aspect of the human-computer interaction, intelligent monitoring and video retrieval leads to great scientific value and socioe-conomic benefits in the video study of human interaction recognition. The selection of interactive features and the effect of its expression ability on identify is very vital [1]. Different from the single behavior, due to the two-person interaction has higher ran-domness, diversity, and is vulnerable to the influence of noise, such as occlusions, illumination and the scene [2, 3], the selection of the features of the movement depends on spatio-temporal information, such as history, location, etc. The spatio-temporal feature can carry the rich information that the video image distributes in time and space at the same time, thus it is widely used in the field of behavior recognition.

The algorithm that extracts the spatio-temporal features from the whole video sequence mostly depends on the precision of moving targets detection and segmen-tation technology [4–6], leading to higher extracted feature dimension, poor expression ability, and low degree of differentiation. In order to solve this problem, a new way of

© Springer Nature Switzerland AG 2019
H. Yu et al. (Eds.): ICIRA 2019, LNAI 11744, pp. 473–488, 2019.
https://doi.org/10.1007/978-3-030-27541-9_39

thinking has been tried to be introduced, which can first eliminates a large number of redundant information in the interactive video, and then extracts a few key information with good separability, that is, the sparse representation of action video [7]. Extracting spatio-temporal features from video with sparse representation can accurately and simply find the most representative useful information, avoid massive useless feature extracting, and realize simplifies the computational complexity.

The sparse representation of motion video can be conducted in time and space dimensions respectively. In the field of action recognition, in order to reduce the amount of raw data, it is usual to extract the effective Key frames [8] or Key pose doublet [9] from the whole video. The key frame sequences can briefly and accurately describe the content of video sequences, and cannot lose the key information of the video. So the key frame sequence of video data can be used on sparse representation on the time dimension.

Key frames are able to comprehensively cover the key information of the video in the time dimension, but in each key frame, there are still a lot of redundant information. So image sparse representation can be introduced to conduct sparse representation of the key frame, aim to realize sparse representation of motion video in the spatial dimension. At present, the method of constructing image spatial sparse features can be divided into two categories, the method of mathematical modeling and the method of training learning. Mathematical modeling method is to obtain the Bandlet base of the edges of the image geometry, and then obtain the Curvelet base of the target contour [10] and other different shapes of basis functions in the image, combining and constructing the method of image sparse representation. The sparse representation model obtained through this method is relatively simple, but the sparse of the signal is poorer. Learning method is to study a set of suitable for certain types of signals through the training sample images. A common method is K-SVD learning algorithm put forward by Aharon [11]. The method obtains the ultimate ideal of sparse feature by alternating current sparse representation and between atoms to update process, but this method has a large amount of calculation and is lack of flexibility to express complex human behavior. Literature [12] put forward a kind of Active Basis Model that is used for the detection and sparse representation of the object. Active Basis Method is a modeling method to use the training sample to study out a variable template for testing and expressing target. In literature [13], active basis model is used to analysis behavior of the pedestrian, of which training efficiency and detection efficiency are improved greatly, but in view of the non-rigid human movement, the expression of active basis model is difficult to achieve its ideal effect. To solve this problem, Hu et al. [14] further optimize the algorithm on the basis of Active basis model, and put forward an algorithm of sparse representation based on Active Curve Model. The method uses simple geometry variable template for image sparse representation. At the same time, with the aid of multi-scale Gabor filter algorithm can guarantee the accurate and full sparse representation of the key information in the target image. The quality of the sparse representation of the motion video on the spatial dimension directly affect whether the video sequence image analysis and recognition result is good or not. Therefore, active curve model algorithm is tried to be introduced to two-person interaction identification field, using the algorithm to realize the space sparse representation of video key frames.

Extracting spatio-temporal interest points from the motion video after a sparse representation can greatly improve the speed, accuracy and presentation skills of the features. However, video representation obtained from combining the spatio-temporal sparse representation model with the spatio-temporal feature need to adopt a kind of classifier which faces the sparse representation and can identify two-person interactive action efficiently and accurately. Compressive Sensing (CS) [15] theory is a new information obtaining theory. The Sparse Representation-based Classification (SRC) has been widely used in face recognition, texture recognition [16], etc. Compressive sensing theory based on sparse coding broke the limitation of precise choice of the number of features. The compressive sensing theory can represent the features of a prospect area with features in less dimension according to the characteristics of the target. These sparse features include enough information to represent and store the key features possessed by the image itself, getting ideal effect of the classification. But this kind of algorithm regards the training samples as a whole, ignoring the category attribute between the samples, and it is difficult to obtain the ideal dimensionality reduction effect for the two-person interactive behavior video under the complex scene. In order to make the SRC algorithm more suitable for two-person interactive identification, the construction method of over-complete dictionary is needed to be improved. The over-complete dictionary is formed based on the spatio-temporal features of adjacent frame in this improved algorithm, that can increase the amount of information that the dictionary represent for the two-person interaction.

Aimed at the existing problem of the two-person interaction recognition method based on the spatio-temporal features, an interactive representation and recognition method is put forward, which is combining the spatio-temporal features under the video spatio-temporal sparse representation with the improved SRC algorithm. Algorithm overall block diagram is shown in Fig. 1.

Algorithm process is as follows:

(1) A distance extreme algorithm based on HOG feature description is put forward to extract video key frames, and then realize the sparse representation in the temporal dimension of the video.

(2) An algorithm based on activity curve is quoted to obtain the sparse representation of the video key frames of the two-person interaction, and then realize the sparse representation in the spatial dimension of the video.

(3) Extracting STIP features based on the spatio-temporal sparse representation of the video, and then describing the features. STIP feature is chosen as the spatio-temporal features and extract STIP of the video key frames on the basis of image sparse representation. Combined with BOW algorithm, result 1 is the recognition result that obtained from the nearest neighbor classifier.

(4) Improving the SRC algorithm to recognize the two-person interaction, obtain the result 2. Improved SRC algorithm face for sparse features, that can be more suitable for the algorithm which combines the features of STIP with sparse representation model.

By comparing the results of the frame-frame nearest neighbor classifier and the improved SRC algorithm, it is further proved that the proposed algorithm is effective in this paper.

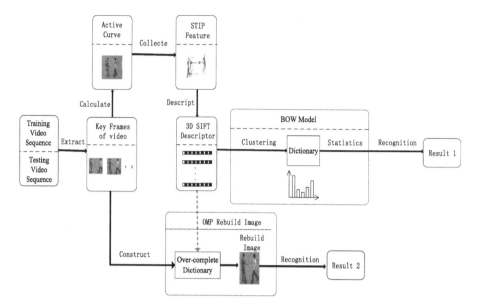

Fig. 1. The whole diagram of algorithm

2 The Spatio-Temporal Sparse Representation of Interactive Video

2.1 Video Temporal Sparse Representation Based on Key Frames

Selection of key frame sequence can realize the sparse representation of video on the temporal dimension. For the whole period of sequence images, changes are very small and not significant between one frame to another. Under the influence of some inevitable noise, it is very difficult to accurately obtain moving foreground area without sequence images of target detection. If an algorithm without need of moving target detection is wanted to locate the interest area of video sequence, changes are required to be significant enough between one frame to another, in order to make every effort to adopt less a few frames to represent the entire length of video image coherently. Extracting effective video key frames can solve the problem above and effectively reduce the amount of calculation of the later operation. Lv et al. [8] proposed a key frame extraction method based on maximum or minimum energy of the movement. But key frames obtained through this algorithm are relatively concentrated and have a large amount of calculation. Therefore, a distance extreme algorithm based on HOG feature description is put forward to extract the video key frames. The algorithm can effectively shorten the response time of spatio-temporal feature extraction. The algorithm implementation steps are as follow:

Step 1: All the frames in the video are represented by HOG. Every frame image is divided into p × p block, each block divided into fans in q directions on the basis of the circle center, and 360/q degrees in each direction. Conduct statistics on every sector of the gradient amplitude, and ultimately use $p \times p \times q$ dimension vector to represent the image.

Step 2: To cover the whole video of M frames, a matrix formed of $M \times p \times p \times q$ dimensions, HOG features of whole video cluster K class using K-means clustering algorithm and get K clustering center of $1 \times p \times p \times q$ dimensions.

Step 3: According to the HOG descriptor value of each frame image in video, and each cluster center value, find the euclidean distance between the two above.

Step 4: The distance difference is mapped to a coordinate plane. Extract the extreme value point of difference curve, containing information extraction of the position of peaks and troughs, find out K frames that are most familiar with the clustering center. Choose it as key frames to represent the whole video.

Key frame selection process of two-person interaction video is shown in Fig. 2.

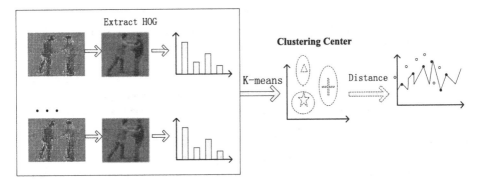

Fig. 2. Method of key frames selection from videos

2.2 Video Spatial Sparse Representation Based on Active Curve Model

The algorithm based on the activity curve model is different from other sparse representation algorithms, such as edge detector [17], scale invariant feature [18], and so on. The use of the activity curve model to sparse representation of the image than other descriptors can cover a wider range of useful information integration, and can use less information to describe the key frame space key information. It does not depend on the preprocessing process of the image, nor does it need to block the image. In order to further test the reliability of the sparse representation of the video, the algorithm can be traced back to verify the feasibility of the algorithm results.

Interactive video in time and space sparse representation of the effect are shown in Fig. 3. Each interactive behavior video is ultimately sparsely represented by an activity curve on the sequence of key frames.

The sparse representation of the interactive video is carried out by the active curve algorithm. The concrete steps are as follows:

Step 1: Gabor filter. A Gabor filter is generated at different scales for the key frame sequence image, and multi-scale Gabor wavelet elements are obtained.

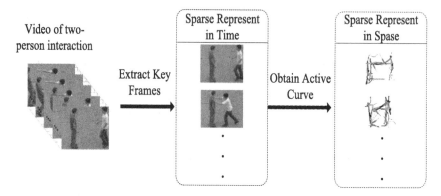

Fig. 3. The diagram of spatio-temporal sparse representation

Step 2: Get the variable template. Sum-Max Maps method (the specific algorithm see [14], not repeat here) to determine the video segment of the active curve variable template.

Step 3: Determine the active angle. The variable template is used to construct each key frame image in the interactive video, forming a number of complicated curves. In contrast to other key frames, the intersection angle formed by the template with a large curvature change at the intersection of the curve is defined as the activity angle. As shown in Fig. 4(b).

Step 4: Determine the active curve. The tag finds all the variable templates that make up each active corner and defines it as an active curve. As shown in Fig. 4(c).

Step 5: Retrospective correction. The result of the obtained activity curve is checked. Keep the calibration activity curve.

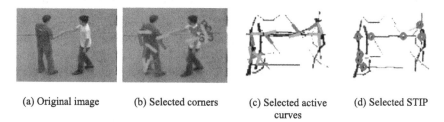

(a) Original image   (b) Selected corners   (c) Selected active   (d) Selected STIP
                                                              curves

Fig. 4. The diagram of spatio-temporal sparse representation

3   Extraction and Representation of Improve STIP Feature

Active curve can express the trajectory of the moving target. Through the retrospective link, each active basis and node information on each active curve can be obtained, and the points between the nodes, endpoints and the two endpoints of each active basis that are saved as STIPs, as shown in Fig. 4(d). The STIP obtained by this algorithm can accurately carry the key information in the interactive action video.

However, STIP extracted by this algorithm only cover the basic position, gray and other information, so STIP is lack of discriminant interactive action recognition. The 3D-SIFT descriptor is used to describe STIP. The 3D-SIFT descriptor is clustered by using the K-means clustering method. In the training samples, the STIP features described by 3D-SIFT are clustered, and the clustering centers are defined as visual words. All the visual words are combined to form a visual dictionary. For each video of the key frame image using "sliding window method", that is, every two images to create a video block, the statistics of each video block on the key points, and its projection to the visual dictionary, and ultimately generate statistical statistics Graphic form. Through this algorithm, we increase the amount of information expressed by interactive behavior of word bag model, so that the characteristics of similar behavioral action are more obvious. Lay the foundation for subsequent identification processing. The operation is shown in Fig. 5.

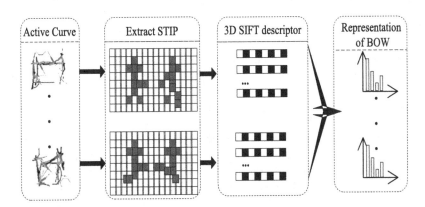

Fig. 5. The diagram of BOW model algorithm

4   Recognition Algorithm

4.1   Nearest Neighbor Classifier

The nearest neighbor classifier has the advantages of simple principle, fast classification and so on. In this paper, we use the frame-frame nearest neighbor classifier to simulate the proposed algorithm. The principle of the nearest neighbor of the frame is described in [20], and is not repeated here. It should be noted that, in order to increase the reliability of the simulation results, the experiment selected frame-frame nearest neighbor classifier combined with a cross validation method to test the database experiment. The specific practice is to use a cross-verification method to select the training samples and test samples for each experiment, that is, the same type of video each time select a video as a test sample, the rest of the video as a training sample, using the frame-frame nearest neighbor classifier Out of the first classification result.

And the next experiment will choose another video as a test sample, the rest as a training sample, followed by the cycle until each video have done a test sample so far. Finally, all the classification results obtained by the loop are substituted for the mean value, which is the final recognition result.

4.2 Improved SRC Recognition Algorithm

The theory of compression sensing is a new theory of information acquisition by Donoho et al. [15]. Its basic idea is to obtain the discrete samples of the signal by random sampling under the condition of far less than the Nyquist sampling rate by developing the sparse characteristic of the signal, and then perfect the reconstructed signal by the nonlinear reconstruction algorithm.

The classification method of sparse reconstruction based on compression sensing theory (SRC algorithm) has been widely used in face recognition, texture recognition and biometrics. In the field of identification, sparse coding based on the compression sensing theory to break the precise selection of the number of features of this limitation. It can characterize the foreground interest area with less dimensionality according to the characteristics of the target, and these sparse features cover enough information to represent and store the key features possessed by the image itself.

In this paper, the SRC algorithm is applied to the system of two-person interaction action recognition for the first time, and its algorithm is improved. Through some kind of orthogonal transformation, the two-person interactive behavior sequence image with sparse To observe, with the smallest possible observations instead of the original sequence image. Finally, by solving the reconstruction algorithm of the linear equation, the estimated value of the two-person interaction action is obtained accurately, and then the classification result is obtained. In the process of implementing the reconstruction algorithm, we need to solve a number of linear equations, because the number of unknowns in the actual problem is larger than the number of equations, resulting in an infinite number of solutions. If the training sample is sparseness, the L1 norm mini-mization algorithm can be used to solve the problem of the problem in the equation. But the computational complexity of the algorithm is higher. Therefore, it is important to select the reconstruction algorithm that is suitable for two-person interaction behavior recognition.

(1) Reconstruction algorithm

Common reconstruction algorithms are many, including Matching Pursuit (MP), Orthogonal Matching Pursuit (OMP) [21] and Stagewise Orthogonal Matching Pursuit (StOMP), etc. MP algorithm has a simple, easy to achieve the advantages of the shortcomings of the convergence of the number of times required. The OMP algorithm optimizes the vulnerability of the MP algorithm. It chooses all the atoms to be orthogonalized, avoids the selection of the repetition of atoms with nonorthogonality, and ensures the optimality of the iterative results, thus effectively reducing the iterative iteration frequency. The StOMP algorithm is an improved algorithm based on the OMP algorithm, which can select multiple atoms for each iteration. However, due to the large amount of interactive video data, such a large number of parallel computing is likely to cause the computer beyond the computing power of the situation, and improve the operation effect is not significant. So, we choose the ideal result and run efficient OMP algorithm. The effect of OMP reconstruction at different sparsities is shown in Fig. 6.

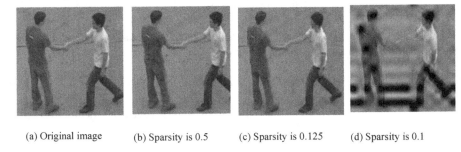

(a) Original image   (b) Sparsity is 0.5   (c) Sparsity is 0.125   (d) Sparsity is 0.1

Fig. 6. Effect of OMP reconstruction with different sparsity

The basic process of reconstructing the algorithm is as follows:

Step 1: Extract the complete atomic library from the image and find the atoms that best match the observed signal (or the participating component);

Step 2: Project the signal in the space formed by these orthogonal atoms;

Step 3: Get the signal in each of the atomic component and participation components;

Step 4: The finite iteration calculation The residual component decreases rapidly and eventually converges to the sparse solution.

(2) Improved SRC algorithm implementation

In this paper, we use the spatio-temporal feature of adjacent frames to form a complete dictionary. This improved algorithm can increase the amount of information expressed by the dictionary for interactive behavior. Based on the improved SRC two-person interactive action recognition algorithm specific steps are as follows:

Step 1: Build a complete dictionary. The algorithm of the STIP feature synthesis of each frame image in each frame of the training sample is constructed with the complete dictionary D and divided into T sub-training matrix according to the class: $D = [D1, D2, \ldots, DT]$.

Step 2: Sparse modeling of training samples. The linear projection of the reconstructed training samples is obtained by modeling. The equation is

$$y = D_j z_j, \, j = 1, 2, \ldots, t_j \qquad (3)$$

Where z_j is the original signal of the training sample and y is the sparse observation signal. The equation can be understood as the fact that the linear projection of the original signal z_j is y and z_j is reconstructed by y under the action of $D_{j.}$ But in reality, the equation is often a poor equation, that is, the number of unknown equations is greater than the number of equations.

Step 3: Use OMP algorithm to reconstruct the image. Using the OMP algorithm with greedy thought to solve the equation, we get $z_1, z_2, \ldots, z_T$.

Step 4: Solve the residuals. The recognition coefficient z_j for each class corresponds to the test sample for the residual, that is,

$$e_j = \left\| y - D_j z_j \right\|_2, \ j = 1, 2, \ldots, T \tag{4}$$

Step 5: Identify the classification. The smallest vector residual corresponding to the vector y_j belongs to the category of test data y.

$$Identity(y) = arg\,min(e_j) \tag{5}$$

It should be noted that here also use the use of a cross-validation method to verify the results of the experiment.

5 The Simulation Experiment

5.1 Database Introduction

Selecting the international general UT-Interaction database as test data, the test is based on video sparse representation and the effectiveness and superiority of the two-person interaction identification algorithm of the improved spatio-temporal features. The database has been widely used in two-person interaction identification field. The database contains six kinds of the continuous human interaction action videos, which are shake hands, hug, kick, pointing, boxing and pushing, as shown in Fig. 7. Each type of action contains 10 action videos. The entire database consists that 15 individuals in real monitoring scenarios (including dynamic background, chaotic scene, camera shake, different dress and other noise effect) complete all the two-person interaction actions.

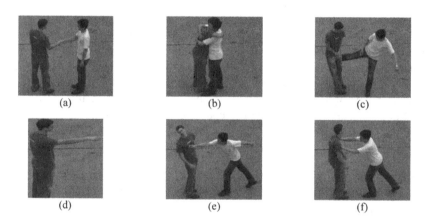

Fig. 7. Exemplar Frames from UT-Interaction Dataset, they should be listed as: (a) Handshake; (b) Hug; (c) Kick; (d) Point; (e) Punch; (f) Push.

5.2   Setting of Parameter

5.2.1   The Determination of Key Frames

For each section of the video sequences, selecting the ideal number of key frames and making the system response to achieve the best effect is a important problem. If the number of key frames is less, the amount of the information of the action itself that features carry is less, which will have great influence on the final recognition results; If more, the number of key frames can increase the algorithm complexity but have little contribution to the final recognition results. Aimed at the size of each period of the video in database, this paper will lock the key frames number K to 3 to 30. In the Fig. 8 according to comparing the recognition rate of two recognition algorithm under different number of key frames, when the number of key frames of the video sequence is 21, the best recognition effect with the least number of video frames. Therefore, the number of the key frames in the test K = 21. Figure 9 is the extraction results of "handshake" action.

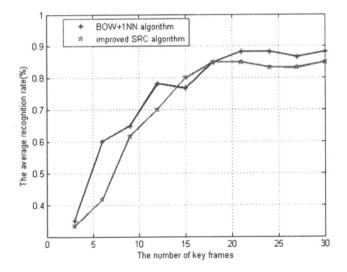

Fig. 8. The average recognition rates of different key frames number

According to the analysis of the results and experience of the previous experiment, in the process of using HOG representation on the whole period of video images, every image is first divided into small average pieces of 4 × 4, (i.e. p = 4). Then each small piece is divided into 12 fans for q = 12 direction based on the center of the circle center, 30° in each direction. Finally statistics on each sector gradient amplitude, 192 dimensional vector is used to represent each frame of video images. Such representation can simply, efficiently and comprehensively reflect the prospect of dynamic changes of each frame image compared with the other frames in the video, and effectively find the whole period of video key frames.

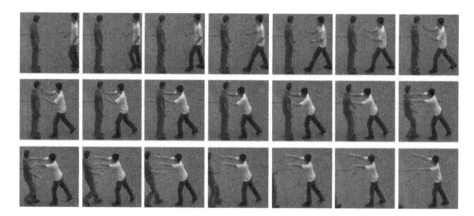

Fig. 9. Selection result of push key frames

5.2.2 The Determination of Sparse Degree

In the algorithm based on improved SRC, the sparse degree values of OMP reconstruction algorithm will affect the image reconstruction effects. After compression, there are certain differences between reconstructive image and the original image. In order to measure the difference, measuring Peak Signal to Noise Ratio (PSNR) of the image is usually adopted. PSNR is the mean square error between original image and processed image relative to $(2^n - 1)^2$ for value (n is the number of bits per sample), the unit is the dB. The greater the PSNR value is, the less the distortion is and the more ideal the effect of the reconstructive image. Figure 10 shows the corresponding PSNR value and error value of different sparse degree of a key frame image in the handshake action. According to the comprehensive analysis of Fig. 10, more ideal image reconstruction effect is get and lower computational complexity is achieved while 0.5 is selected as sparse degree.

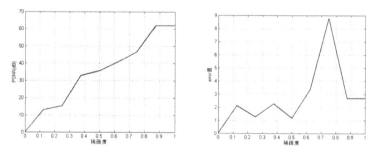

Fig. 10. Left(a): The value of PSNR with different sparsity. Right(b): The value of error with different sparsity.

5.3   Effectiveness Test Algorithm

In order to prove the validity of the algorithm, identify experiments are conducted on UT-Interaction database. 60 sections of video image in total containing six kinds of action are selected to conduct experiment. Two identification algorithms are used for identification experiment of the improved spatio-temporal features of sparse representation of the video. Experiment 1 firstly distance using HOG feature description extremal algorithm to extract key frames of video; Secondly, the spatio-temporal interest points based on activity curve model are extracted from key frames. Thirdly, BOW model is used to describe the spatio-temporal features; Finally, frame-frame nearest algorithm is used to identify. With the best parameters, the recognition rate of 6 kinds of two-person interaction can reach 85%. Identification and confusion matrix is shown in Fig. 11(a). Experiment 2 firstly use the distance extremal algorithm of HOG feature description to extract key frames of video, which is as same as Experiment 1; Secondly the improved SRC algorithm is used for video identification, including using the OMP reconstruction algorithm to achieve image reconstruction on the key frames. It is important to notice that an over-complete dictionary is make up by 3D-SIFT description of the STIP in the image before or after the key frames. With the best parameters, the recognition rate of 6 kinds of two-person interaction can reach 88.33%. Identification the confusion matrix is shown in Fig. 11(b).

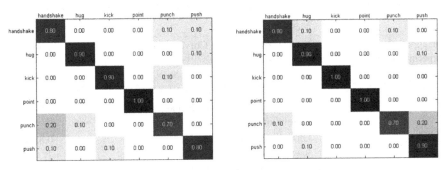

Fig. 11.   Left(a): The Confusion Matrix of the BOW combined with 1NN Method. Right(b): The Confusion Matrix of the improved SRC Method.

5.4   The Experiment Results Compared with Other Literature

In this paper, the two-person interaction recognition algorithm based on improved spatio-temporal feature sparse representation is compared with the other algorithms based on UT-Interaction database to illustrate the effectiveness of the proposed algorithm. The experimental results are shown in Table 1. The recognition rate in the use of the improved SRC recognition algorithm is significantly higher than the nearest neighbor classifier recognition algorithm combined with BOW model. The experimental results proved the effectiveness of the improved SRC recognition algorithm proposed in this paper. Although the recognition rate that this paper put forward is slightly lower than the method of literature [6] (the method of using a variety of features fusion STIPs), the algorithm of literature [6] need extracting STIP, Motion Context (MC), and other features and construction of STIP Occurrence Sequences on the basis of it, the complexity of which for feature extraction is higher. And it use the random forests of GA training method and the spatio-temporal matching method to realize two-person interaction identification, which needs a lot of training time. However, this paper use the recognition rate which uses the improved sparse representation spatio-temporal interest points as the feature on the video key frames. Compared with the literature [6] algorithm computational complexity is reduced greatly. In addition, the average recognition rate of the algorithm in this paper have more accuracy than the literature [26] and literature [15] recognition. It prove the validity of the video-key-frame-extraction algorithm in this paper. And there is no need of silhouette or other moving target detection before extracting features, which greatly simplifies the algorithm complexity, and improve the efficiency of the response. Finally, the algorithm identification accuracy in this paper is greatly higher than the two-person interaction recognition method in the literature [7, 8] both using the STIP features and the global and local feature representation identification method in the literature [1]. The experiment proved that priority of that SRC recognition method combining video sparse representation based on activity curve model with improved spatio-temporal features is applied in the two-person interaction recognition system.

Table 1. Font sizes of headings. Table captions should always be positioned *above* the tables.

Literature	Method	Accuracy
Our approach (Experiment 2)	Key Frame + Active Curve + STIP + Improved SRC	0.883
Our approach (Experiment 1)	Key Frame + Active Curve + STIP + BOW + 1NN	0.85
[6]	STIP + GA search based random forest + S-T correlation	0.917
[1]	Global template + local 3D feature + discriminative mode	0.85
[15]	Key pose doublet	0.85
[26]	HOG + BOW + 1NN	0.833
[7]	STIP + BP + SVM	0.833
[8]	STIP + Implicit Shape Model	0.733

6   Conclusion

Aimed at the problem that the spatio-temporal feature dimension in the two-person interaction recognition algorithm is too high and the express ability is not strong, our innovation is to put forward a kind of recognition algorithm based on the spatio-temporal sparse representation interactive video. The sparse representation of the whole period of video on the time dimension is a process of video key frame extraction based on a distance extremal algorithm of the HOG feature description. This will realize that hundreds of moving are represented coherently by a few frames of images. The sparse representation of the whole period of video on the spatial dimension makes use of advantage that the activity curve has a strong ability of the sparse representation of the target and put forward a kind of two-person interaction identification space sparse representation algorithm based on activity curve. Based on the spatio-temporal sparse representation of the video, STIPs are extracted and described by 3D-SIFT. Combined with the word bag algorithm, the recognition results are obtained from the nearest neighbor classifier. In addition, an improved SRC algorithm is used to identify the two-person interaction. Improved SRC algorithm for sparse features can adapt to the algorithm combining spatio-temporal interest points with sparse representation model. The experimental results show that the algorithm based on key frames and active curve model not only conducts spatio-temporal sparse representation for two-person interaction, but also has stronger robustness. Besides, the improved SRC algorithm can achieve ideal two-person interaction identification. The algorithm enriches the application of the sparse representation of the spatio-temporal features in the field of two-person interaction identification, with strong scientific research value. It combines with the improved SRC recognition algorithm to get ideal effect. Its disadvantages is that activity curve model algorithm in some degree has higher computational complexity, higher requirement of the simulation hardware equipment. With the popularity of cloud server, the problem will be solved step by step.

Acknowledgements. This work is supported by the Program for Science Research Local Project of Education Department of Liaoning province (No. L201708) and Liaoning Science Public Welfare Research Fund Project (No. 2016002006)

References

1. Kong, Y., Liang, W., Dong, Z., Jia, Y.: Recognizing human interaction from videos by a discriminative model. Inst. Eng. Technol. Comput. Vis. **4**(8), 77–286 (2014)
2. Sivarathinabala, M., Abirami, S.: Human interaction recognition using improved spatio-temporal features. In: Nagar, A., Mohapatra, D.P., Chaki, N. (eds.) Proceedings of 3rd International Conference on Advanced Computing, Networking and Informatics. SIST, vol. 43, pp. 191–199. Springer, New Delhi (2016). https://doi.org/10.1007/978-81-322-2538-6_20
3. Huynh-The, T., Le, B.V., Lee, S., et al.: Interactive activity recognition using pose-based spatio-temporal relation features and four-level pachinko allocation model. Inf. Sci. **369**, 317–333 (2016)
4. Meng L., Qing L., Yang P., Miao J., Chen X.: Activity recognition based on semantic spatial relation. In: Proceedings of 21st International Conference on Pattern Recognition, Tsukuba, Japan, pp. 609–612 (2012)
5. Felzenszwalb, P., McAllester, D., Ramanan, D.: A discriminatively trained, multiscale, deformable part model. In: 2008 IEEE Conference on Computer Vision and Pattern Recognition, CVPR 2008, pp. 1–8. IEEE (2008)
6. Sahbi, H., Audibert, J.Y., Rabarisoa, J., et al.: Context-dependent kernel design for object matching and recognition. In: 2008 IEEE Conference on Computer Vision and Pattern Recognition, CVPR 2008, pp. 1–8. IEEE (2008)

7. Wang, S.K., Xu, L., Xu, X.: Pedestrian detection based on active basis. In: Applied Mechanics and Materials, vol. 263, pp. 2635–2638. Trans Tech Publications (2012)
8. Lv, F., Nevatia, R.: Single view human action recognition using key pose matching and viterbi path searching. In: 2007 IEEE Conference on Computer Vision and Pattern Recognition, CVPR 2007, pp. 1–8. IEEE (2007)
9. Mukherjee, S., Biswas, S.K., Mukherjee, D.P.: Recognizing interaction between human performers using key pose doublet. In: Proceedings of the 19th ACM International Conference on Multimedia, pp. 1329–1332. ACM (2011)
10. Peyré, G.: Best basis compressed sensing. In: Sgallari, F., Murli, A., Paragios, N. (eds.) SSVM 2007. LNCS, vol. 4485, pp. 80–91. Springer, Heidelberg (2007). https://doi.org/10.1007/978-3-540-72823-8_8
11. Aharon, M., Elad, M., Bruckstein, A.M.: The K-SVD: an algorithm for designing over complete dictionaries for sparse representation. IEEE Trans. Signal Process. **54**(11), 4311–4322 (2006)
12. Wu, Y.N., Si, Z., Gong, H., et al.: Learning active basis model for object detection and recognition. Int. J. Comput. Vis. **90**(2), 198–235 (2010)
13. Wang, S., Xu, L., Liu, X., et al.: A pedestrian detection method based on active basis model. Res. Notes Inf. Sci. **12**, 15 (2013)
14. Hu, W., Wu. Y.N., Zhu, S.C.: Image representation by active curves. In: 2011 IEEE International Conference on Computer Vision (ICCV), pp. 1808–1815. IEEE (2011)
15. Donoho, D.L.: Compressed sensing. IEEE Trans. Inf. Theory **52**(4), 1289–1306 (2006)
16. Liu, L., Fieguth, P., Kuang, G.: Compressed sensing for robust texture classification. In: Kimmel, R., Klette, R., Sugimoto, A. (eds.) ACCV 2010. LNCS, vol. 6492, pp. 383–396. Springer, Heidelberg (2011). https://doi.org/10.1007/978-3-642-19315-6_30
17. Canny, J.: A computational approach to edge detection. IEEE Trans. Pattern Anal. Mach. Intell. **6**, 679–698 (1986)
18. Lowe, D.G.: Object recognition from local scale-invariant features. In: The Proceedings of the Seventh IEEE International Conference on Computer Vision, 1999, vol. 2, pp. 1150–1157. IEEE (1999)
19. Scovanner, P., Ali, S., Shah, M.A.: 3-dimensional sift descriptor and its application to action recognition. In: Proceedings of the 15th International Conference on Multimedia, pp. 357–360. ACM (2007)
20. Ji, X., Wang, C., Zuo, X., et al.: Multiple feature voting based human interaction recognition. Int. J. Signal Process. Image Process. Pattern Recogn. **9**(1), 323–334 (2016)
21. Haupt, J., Nowak, R.: Compressive sampling for signal detection. In: 2007 IEEE International Conference on Acoustics, Speech and Signal Processing, ICASSP 2007, vol. 3, pp. III-1509–III-1512. IEEE (2007)

Human Interaction Recognition Based on the Co-occurring Visual Matrix Sequence

Xiaofei Ji[✉], Linlin Qin, and Xinmeng Zuo

Shenyang Aerospace University, Shenyang, Liaoning, China
Jixiaofei7804@126.com

Abstract. The human interaction recognition methods based on motion co-occurrence have been an efficient solution for its reasonable expression and simple operation. However this kind of methods has relatively low recognition accuracy. An innovative and effective way based on the co-occurring visual matrix sequence was proposed to improve the accuracy in this paper, which sufficiently utilized the superiority of co-occurring visual matrix and probability graph model. In the individual segmentation framework, ROI was firstly extracted by frame difference and the distance analysis between two interacting persons, and segmented into two separate interacting persons with prior knowledge, such as color and body outline. Then the k-means algorithm was utilized to build the bag of visual words (BOVW) with HOG feature from all the training videos, and each frame in a video was described by co-occurring visual matrix with BOVW, and the video was represented by the co-occurring visual matrix sequence. Finally, HMM method was utilized to model and recognize the human interactions. Experimental results on the UT-Interaction dataset show that the method achieved better recognition performance with simple implementation.

Keywords: Interaction recognition · HOG ·
Co-occurring visual matrix sequence · Hidden markov model

1 Introduction

The research on human interaction recognition has broad application foreground [1] in the field of smart surveillance system, video retrieval, smart homes and virtual reality. So it has great practical value and realistic significance and is receiving increasing attention in the domain of computer vision. Recently, more and more researchers have paid their attention to this research direction.

Generally wo frameworks are utilized for achieving human interaction recognition. **Interaction is recognized as a general action.** This kind of method [2–4] usually treats people involved in the interaction as a single entity and does not extract the motion of each person from the video, and needs not segment the feature of individual in the interaction. However, the better performance of this kind of method always needs comprehensive motion features and matching method. **Interaction is recognized based on individual segmentation.** Human interaction is generally combined by multiple elementary actions chronologically, this kind of framework considers that the

© Springer Nature Switzerland AG 2019
H. Yu et al. (Eds.): ICIRA 2019, LNAI 11744, pp. 489–501, 2019.
https://doi.org/10.1007/978-3-030-27541-9_40

interaction between individuals are composed of a set of temporally ordered elementary actions performed by the different persons involved in the interaction, which obtains abundant interactive information. So this kind of method is more suitable for the human interaction recognition, and it has been received wide attention by many researchers. This framework mainly includes three methods as follows:

(1) **Interaction recognition based on semantic description:** This kind of method focuses on semantic representation of single body posture, atomic action or general action. Ryoo *et al.* improved context-free grammar by utilizing well-define grammar rules and obtained successful human interaction recognition [5]. Kong *et al.* proposed a novel approach by using interactive phrases to describe motion relationships between interacting people, and utilized a discriminative model to encode interactive phrases based on the latent SVM formulation [6]. The method obtains better recognition accuracy, however the process with pre-defined production rule is relatively complex.

(2) **Interaction recognition based on probability graph model:** This kind of method usually utilizes probability graph model to achieve hierarchical modeling and recognition for individual actions and interactive actions. Brendle *et al.* proposed spatio-temporal graphs based on multi-scale video segmentation to capture hierarchical and spatio-temporal relationships from interactive actions [7]. Dong *et al.* proposed a hierarchical random field model which incorporates both large-scale global feature based HOF and local body part features at different levels to recognize human interactions [8, 9]. The method which regards complex interactive actions as the cascade system of the action of each person and local body part can better model complicated interactions, but usually relies on accurate motion detection of several body part regions.

(3) **Interaction recognition based on motion co-occurrence:** This kind of method considers that the interaction template is introduced to describe pairs of elementary actions performed by the different persons, and then uses template matching for recognition. Yuan *et al.* represented the individual motion in interactions by using consistent spatial structure and motion components, then human interaction can be recognized by capturing their spatial and temporal relationship [10]. Slimani *et al.* proposed a co-occurrence of visual words method for human interaction recognition [11]. The method extracts 3D-SIFT [12] feature and represents the interaction between persons by calculating the number of times that visual words occur simultaneously for each person involved in the interaction. The implementation of this method is very simple. However, high computational complexity of feature extraction, weak feature representation and the inappropriate classifier, which result in the low recognition accuracy of the kind of method.

In view of advantages of interaction recognition methods based on motion co-occurrence and probability graph model, this paper incorporates two kinds of the approaches to solve the problem of low recognition accuracy. Therefore, a novel human interaction recognition method based on the co-occurring visual matrix sequence is proposed in this paper. The method considers the following three aspects to improve the accuracy of human interaction. Firstly, in the process of the choice of low-level feature, the sub-regional HOG feature [13] is utilized to realize a lower computational complexity, which has both advantages of local features and context positional relationship of cells. Secondly, in the step of feature representation based on videos, the co-occurring visual matrix is built in every frame, then the co-occurring visual matrix sequence is obtained to represent a whole video rather than only a single co-occurring visual matrix which some researcher proposed [11]. The method adds the inner information implied in videos and enhances the discriminability of various interactions. Finally, in the process of the choice of classifier, HMMs [14] is introduced to model and recognize human interactions considering the advantages of perfectly modeling dynamic process of probability graph model. The algorithm proposed in this paper is tested on standard database of human interaction and greatly increases the accuracy rate and improves the efficiency of computation.

2 Framework of Our Method

The overall approach is sketched in Fig. 1, which has the following modules:

(1) Input test video: The input information of the algorithm is the test video or serial images.
(2) Segment individual: Prior to feature extraction, two separate individuals need to be obtained by Video Preprocessing.
(3) Extract HOG feature: The step is the key step of feature description. Through the HOG algorithm, we can get the low features of interaction.
(4) Describe the Co-occurring Visual Matrix Sequence. This step is a Co-occurring description of interaction behavior based on HOG feature, which determined the recognition performance of the algorithm.
(5) Classify by HMM. After get the Co-occurring Visual Matrix Sequence, We can category the interaction behavior by HMM.

Acquire final result: According to the classification results obtained and Class labels, we can get the final identification results.

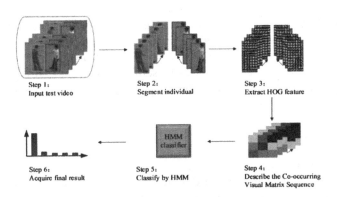

Fig. 1. The framework of proposed approach.

3   Feature Extraction and Representation

3.1   Video Preprocessing

In order to improve the accuracy and validity of recognition, video preprocessing is an indispensable step before the feature extraction and description of video. ROI of 2-D space and 1-D time is respectively extracted by frame difference and the distance analysis between two interacting persons, and algorithm implementation is as follows:

Step 1: 2-D space preprocessing. Frame difference is utilized to obtain the interest foreground boundary contours. And then the minimum boundary rectangle for ROI position is detected, which can reduce the redundant information in videos.

Step 2: 1-D time preprocessing. Considering that some interactions may be of great similarity at initial stage and separate phases, and the feature description has a weak distinguish ability, such as "Punch" and "Kick". Hence, the primary interactive video clip is obtained by comparing the body-centered distance T (Synthesize the different interactions) between two interactive persons. The method is shown as follows.

$$\alpha = (\frac{1}{m_1} \sum_{i=1}^{m_1} x_i, \frac{1}{m_1} \sum_{i=1}^{m_1} y_i)$$
$$\beta = (\frac{1}{n_1} \sum_{j=1}^{n_1} x_j, \frac{1}{n_1} \sum_{j=1}^{n_1} y_j) \tag{1}$$

$$L = \|\alpha - \beta\| - T \begin{cases} \geq 0, \ keep \\ < 0, \ remove \end{cases} \tag{2}$$

Where, α, β is the body center coordinate of two interactive persons respectively, m_1 and n_1 are the number of pixels of the two persons involved. (x_i, y_i) and (x_j, y_j) represent the pixel coordinate. Threshold T is a positive integer, and L is identifier that remove the frame when $L < 0$ and otherwise keep it. And the final ROI fragments are acquired.

To achieve the recognition framework based on individual segmentation, two separate interacting persons is segmented with prior knowledge, such as color and body outline. The inaccurate segmentation used for training will largely affect the recognition accuracy, so manually adjustment of each person in the video is utilized. However, in order to maintain objectivity in the recognition process, testing videos are segmented by completely automatic extraction.

3.2   Feature Extraction

In order to perform recognition quickly, it is indispensable to represent a video with a kind of simple and discriminative feature. It has been proved that sub-regional HOG descriptors significantly outperform existing feature sets for human detection in previous research. The HOG feature reflects the edge gradient information of human motion, and need not to complex edge detection process. This method can overcome the disturbance changes due to illumination, scale, wearing and background, even in complex background environment still has strong stability. The HOG representation is formed by calculating the gradient histogram in local areas under the main idea that the local target appearance and shape can be described by the density distribution of light intensity gradient or edge direction in an image. The extraction process of HOG feature is as follows:

Step 1: Extract the gradient magnitude and gradient direction in videos.

$$\begin{cases} G_x = f(x+1,y) - f(x-1,y) \\ G_y = f(x,y+1) - f(x,y-1) \end{cases} \tag{3}$$

Where, G_x is the horizontal gradient of the pixel (x,y), and G_y is the vertical gradient. The gradient magnitude $G(x,y)$ and the gradient direction $\varphi(x,y)$ are shown at Eqs. 4 and 5.

$$G(x,y) = \sqrt{G_x(x,y)^2 + G_y(x,y)^2} \tag{4}$$

$$\varphi(x,y) = ac\,\tan(\frac{G_y(x,y)}{G_x(x,y)}) \tag{5}$$

Step 2: The whole frame is divided into $c \times r$ cells, and histogram of oriented gradient of each pixel is statistics in each cell, the number of gradient direction is q (where $q = 12$), then all histograms of all cell unites are combined to generate the final descriptor, which HOG feature vector dimension is $c \times r \times q$, as shown in Fig. 2.

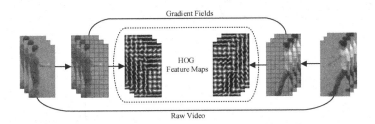

Fig. 2. The graphical representation of HOG descriptor generation

3.3 The Co-occurring Visual Matrix Sequence Representation

When the texture of images needs to be described, gray-level co-occurrence matrix [15] (GLCM) is generally effective tool and its core thought is frequency statistics by analyzing the gray-level correlations between neighbor pixels. Due to co-occurring relations mostly occur in local regions of different interactive actions in the framework based on individual segmentation, and traditional BOW model can represent videos as unordered visual words set, which is simple and efficient. Furthermore regional HOG feature can represent details and distribution feature of videos well. Hence, this paper intends to utilize the idea of GLCM and combine the superiority of HOG and BOW to construct a new co-occurring visual matrix sequence and represent the spatial correlation of visual words. The process of description method is achieved as shown in Fig. 3 and the algorithm steps are followed.

Step 1: Extract HOG feature vectors of the left executor and the right executor respectively in frames, and obtain feature vector dataset *Set* in training videos. And then utilize K-means clustering method to create a visual dictionary $W = \{w_1, w_2, \cdots, w_n\}$ with dataset *Set*, where n is the number of visual words.

Step 2: The HOG feature vector in frame blocks is projected to the visual dictionary by using similarity measure function. The most similar visual word is achieved and marked in an appropriate place. Finally a whole video of left executor and right executor is marked by repetitive operation.

Step 3: The frequency of co-occurrence of visual words is modeled by building a $n \times n$ co-occurring visual matrix in frames of video. For example, the frequency of the visual word w_i of left executor and w_j of right executor co-occurring at the same time in video is k, then mark k on row w_i column w_j in the visual co-occurring matrix. Finally, the integral visual matrix representation vc is achieved for describing one frame, and then the co-occurring visual matrix sequence $VC = \{vc_1, vc_2, \cdots, vc_{num}\}$ is obtained from time dimension T to describe the interactive information, where num is the number of temporal points in the dimension T, and so do the testing videos.

Step 4: In order to improve the robustness to the relative position of the persons, the co-occurrence matrix is modified by letting $vc = vc_i + vc_i^T$, where $vc \in VC$. And then keep the upper triangular part of the matrix for representing the interaction.

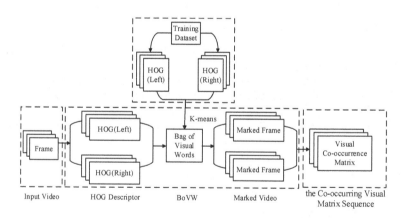

Fig. 3. The framework of the proposed approach

4 HMM Training and Recognition

Considering HMMs are good at modelling the dynamic process of interactions. HMM is chosen to train for each action class in this paper. The first order HMM is taken for building the action model, that is, the conditional probability distribution of the state at a certain time of the process depends only upon the previous state.

4.1 Description of HMM

An HMM is denoted as $\lambda = \{A, B, \pi\}$, and in doubly embedded stochastic process. The parameters π and A describe the Markov chain and B describes the relation between state and observation symbol respectively. The detail of the parameters is presented below and classical graph model of HMM is shown in Fig. 4.

(1) A: State transition matrix $A = (a_{ij})_{N \times N}$, where $(a_{ij}) = p(q_{t+1} = s_j | q_t = s_i)$, $1 \leq i, j \leq N, a_{ij}$ is the probability of reaching state at time t + 1 from state at time t.
(2) B: Observation symbol probability distribution $B = \{b_i(o_t)\}$, where $b_i(o_t) = p(o_t | s_i)$, $b_i(o_t)$ is the probability of generating observation symbol from state at time t.
(3) π: The initial state distribution $\pi = \{\pi_1, \pi_2, \ldots, \pi_N\}$. Where π_i is the probability of initial state.

The probability of generating observation symbol from each state can be computed by Gaussian probability-density function Eq. (6)

$$b_i(o_t) = b_{(u_i, \sum_i)}(o_t) = \frac{1}{\sqrt{2\pi}^d \sqrt{|\Sigma_i|}} e^{-\frac{1}{2}(o_t - u_i)^T \Sigma_i^{-1}(o_t - u_i)} \qquad (6)$$

Where $u_i, \sum_i$ is respectively the mean and covariance matrix of observations classified in cluster i; d is the dimension of observation symbol o_t; $(o_t - u_i)^T$ is the transpose of matrix $(o_t - u_i)$; Σ_i^{-1} is the inverse of matrix Σ_i.

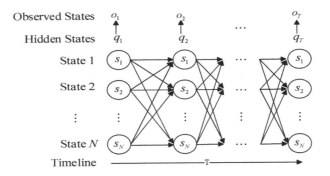

Fig. 4. The classical graph model of HMM

4.2   Training and Recognition Problem

In this paper Baum-Welch algorithm [14] is used to train the co-occurring visual matrix sequence based interaction HMM, however it is depended on the choice of initial parameter. If the initial improper parameter is chosen, it can lead procedure to the locally maximized. Thus, we take the result of K-means algorithm as initial input of the Baum-Welch algorithm. K-means algorithm employs the distance between data and means to update the parameter. The equation of distance is shown as follows:

$$d_i(o_t) = \sqrt{(o_t - u_i)^T (o_t - u_i)} \tag{7}$$

Where Eq. (7) is the distance between observation o_t and the mean u_i in cluster i. The detail process of K-means algorithm is outlined in the following:

(1) **Initialization:** Supposing $U^{(K-start)} = \{u_1^{(K-start)}, u_2^{(K-start)}, \ldots, u_N^{(K-start)}\}$ is the initial parameter of K-means. In this paper $U^{(K-start)}$ is chosen as the feature vectors of N equal interval frames in one training action class.
(2) **Induction:** We compute the distance $d_i(o_t)$ between each observation o_t and each u_i, where $t = 1, 2, \ldots, T$, $i = 1, 2, \ldots, N$. According to the principle of minimum distance, we will get the new N classes of observation by assigning the o_t for the clusters corresponding to the minimum distance. And then each new mean value $u_i^{(K-new)}$ is calculated by the mean Eq. (8)

$$u_i^{(K-new)} = \frac{1}{N_i} \sum_{xi=1}^{N_i} o_{xi} \tag{8}$$

Where o_{xi} is the observation and belongs to cluster i. N_i is the number of observation in cluster i.
(3) **Termination:** There is no change between each mean $u_i^{(K-new)}$.

The clustering centers calculated by K-means algorithm are regarded as the initial parameters of each corresponding action HMM. Multiple training sequences are used to train each action HMM for recognizing by Baum-Welch algorithm. In the training stage, in order to solve the problem of value close to 0 caused by cumulative production and avoid the underflow, we will introduce the scale factor method [14] to inhibit the above problem.

For the recognition problem, supposing that $\lambda^{(1)}, \lambda^{(2)}, \ldots, \lambda^{(H)}$ are the training HMMs of given action1, action2, ..., action H and $O = \{o_1, o_2, \ldots, o_T\}$ is the query (test) observation sequence. We compute the likelihood which is shown in the following between the test sequence and each given trained action HMM using forward-backward algorithm [14]: $p(O|\lambda^{(1)})$, $p(O|\lambda^{(2)})$, ..., $p(O|\lambda^{(H)})$. And the action corresponding to the maximum likelihood is chosen as the best recognition action:

$$test\_number = \arg\max_{1 \le h \le H}(p(O|\lambda^{(h)})) \tag{9}$$

5   Algorithm Verification and Results Analysis

5.1   Dataset Introduction

To test the effectiveness of our approach, the UT-interaction set 1 benchmark dataset [16] was chosen, which contains 6 classes of human interactive behaviors performed by 15 peoples: Handshake, Hug, Kick, Point, Punch and Push. Each class contains 10 video sequences. It is noteworthy that we have omitted the "Point" class because it can be considered as a human action and not an interaction. Some challenging factors in this dataset include moving background, cluttered scenes, camera jitters/zooms and different clothes. The segmented UT-interaction sequences were used for evaluating the recognition accuracy and speed of our method in the experiments. As presented in Fig. 5.

Handshake   Hug   Kick   Punch   Push

Fig. 5.   The examples of UT-interaction dataset

5.2   Experimental Setup and Result Analysis

To assess the performance of the proposed algorithm, Leave-one-out cross validation method is used on the UT-interaction dataset for three times. Before the test, the parameters of experiment need to be chose and determined. First, the choice of the scale parameter of input videos should be decided. Owing to the length-width ratio of a single human sequence of images after preprocessing is mostly between 4:1 (such as handshake and hug) and 4:3 (such as punch and push), so the choice of 2:1 is better to ensure that input videos is consistent. Then, the choice of region partition of HOG parameter is considered. Grids size of 12 * 6 is relatively suitable for obtaining rich information in the co-occurring visual matrix sequence with low computational complexity. In addition, in creating the co-occurring visual matrix sequence, the number of visual words needs to be chosen. Considering that both the matrix in the co-occurring visual matrix sequence are not of excessive sparsity, and mutual information can be fully described, the choice of 20 visual words is better than the other by experiments.

The experiment 1: Low-level feature test. We find that research [11] use 3D-SIFT feature as low-level feature and obtain the 40.63% recognition rate. We know that extraction speed of 3D-SIFT is very slow, so HOG is used instead of 3D-SIFT to embody its effectiveness in this test. And an interactive video is mapped to a visual occurring matrix and nearest neighbor classifier is utilized to complete the interaction recognition. The recognition rate is 64% as shown in Table 1. In addition, Table 2 also shows the recognition results from research [11] for experimental comparative study and analysis.

Table 1. The recognition results (%) of the experiment 1

Action class	Handshake	Hug	Kick	Punch	Push	Average
Result	90	90	30	60	50	64

Table 2. The recognition results (%) of the article 11

Action class	Handshake	Hug	Kick	Punch	Push	Average
Result	50	75	14	33	33	40.63

From Tables 1 and 2 we can see that the experiment 1 improved the research [11] in recognition rate with relatively computational complexity.

The Experiment 2: Feature Representation Test. According to HOG feature, the proposed algorithm based on the co-occurring visual matrix sequence is utilized to describe the interactive videos and nearest neighbor classifier is chosen for interaction recognition. The experiment aims to verify the validity of core algorithm in this paper. The average recognition result and other interactions result is shown in Table 3.

Table 3. The recognition results (%) of the experiment 2

Action class	Handshake	Hug	Kick	Punch	Push	Average
Result	100	100	40	50	60	70

The experiment adopts the co-occurring visual matrix sequence instead of the co-occurring matrix to represent the interaction video on the basis of the experiment 1. The recognition rate of 70% fully shows the success of the innovative algorithm compared with the experiment 1.

The Experiment 3: The Performance Of Classifier Test. Based on the experiment 2, nearest neighbor classifier is replaced by HMMs for testing its capability of modeling the dynamic process. HMMs needs to choose the number of hidden nodes, we firstly select the hidden state numbers from 3 to 6 for training the HMMs and recognizing the interaction. The experimental results show that we can get the best recognition result when the number is chosen as 4. Even though keeping on improving the state number, there is little effect on recognition accuracy. So we adapt 4 hidden states for recognizing in this experiment. The final recognition results are shown in Table 4 and the confusion matrix is shown in Fig. 6 accordingly.

Table 4. The recognition results (%) of the experiment 3

Action class	Handshake	Hug	Kick	Punch	Push	Average
Result	100	100	90	70	40	80

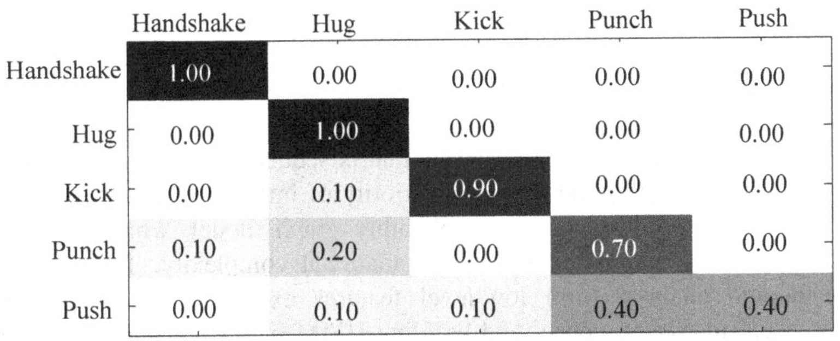

	Handshake	Hug	Kick	Punch	Push
Handshake	1.00	0.00	0.00	0.00	0.00
Hug	0.00	1.00	0.00	0.00	0.00
Kick	0.00	0.10	0.90	0.00	0.00
Punch	0.10	0.20	0.00	0.70	0.00
Push	0.00	0.10	0.10	0.40	0.40

Fig. 6. The confusion matrix of the proposed method

The final average recognition rate reaches 80%, which is the best result using our proposed algorithm, and outperforms the previous two experiments. It fully shows that combining feature description base on the co-occurring visual matrix sequence and HMMs is quite significant. Although the results of "Punch" and "Push" need further improvement, the action classes ("Handshake", "Hug" and "Kick") have a better performance without much confusion. From analysis we can find there are some similarities between "Punch" class and "Push" class, this is why they are confused.

The comparisons of performance between the proposed method and the recent related works based on UT-Interaction dataset are shown in Table 5. From Table 5 we can see that the [3, 8, 9] based on the general action are all superior to the proposed method in recognition results. However, those research all utilized the multi-feature fusion method, in which HOF (Histogram of Optical Flow) feature is extracted from the original videos to achieve the recognition tasks. As we all know that the computational complexity of HOF of extraction is very high. In conclusion, the proposed method is an effective and stable method of resolving human interaction problem based on motion co-occurrence.

Table 5. Comparison with related work in recent years

Literature	Method	Accuracy
Slimani *et al.* [11]	3D-SIFT + Co-occurrence matrix	40.63
Yuan *et al.* [10]	Co-components + Motion descriptor	78.20
Brendle *et al.* [7]	Spatiotemporal graphs with multiscale video segments	78.92
Our approach	**HOG + co-occurring visual matrix sequence + HMM**	**80.00**
Dong *et al.* [9]	HOF + Multi-class AdaBoost	85.00
Dong [8]	HOF + local body part features + hierarchical random field	86.67
Peng [3]	DT shape + HOG + HOF + MBH	94.50

6   Conclusion

This paper proposed the co-occurring visual matrix sequence representation for human interaction recognition by utilizing the superiority of interaction recognition methods based on motion co-occurrence and probability graph model, which improves the recognition accuracy and reduces the computational complexity. The paper makes experiments and analysis from low-level features extraction, generating the co-occurring visual matrix sequence, and building HMM interaction model. The experimental results verify that the method is able to recognize complex interactive activities preferably real-time. However, the precision of recognition needs to be further enhanced. Therefore, analyzing and modeling in different interaction stages will be considered in a follow-up study for improving the recognition accuracy rate.

Acknowledgements. This work is supported by the Program for Science Research Local Project of Education Department of Liaoning province (No. L201708) and Scientific Research Youth Project of Education Department of Liaoning Province, China (No. L201745).

References

1. Li, N., Cheng, X., Guo, H., Wu, Z.: A hybrid method for human interaction recognition using spatio-temporal interest points. In: Proceedings of 22nd International Conference on Pattern Recognition. Stockholm, Sweden, pp. 2513–2518 (2014)
2. Zhang, B., Rota, P., Conci, N., et al.: Human interaction recognition in the wild: analyzing trajectory clustering from multiple-instance-learning perspective. In: Proceedings of IEEE International Conference on Multimedia and Expo, Torino, Italy, pp. 1–6 (2015)
3. Peng, X., Peng, Q., Qiao, Y.: Exploring dense trajectory feature and encoding methods for human interaction recognition. In: Proceedings of Conference on Internet Multimedia Computing and Service, Huangshan, China, pp. 23–27 (2013)
4. Gaur, U., Zhu, Y., Song, B., Roy-Chowdhury, A.: A "string of feature graphs" model for recognition of complex activities in natural videos. In: Proceedings of IEEE Conference on Computer Vision, Barcelona, Spain, pp. 2595–2602 (2011)
5. Ryoo, M.S., Aggarwal, J.K.: Recognition of composite human activities through context-free grammar based representation. In: Proceedings of IEEE Computer Society Conference on Computer Vision and Pattern Recognition, NY, USA, pp. 1709–1719 (2006)

6. Kong, Y., Jia, Y., Fu, Y.: Interactive phrases: semantic descriptions for human interaction recognition. IEEE Trans. Pattern Anal. Mach. Intell. **36**(9), 1775–1788 (2014)
7. Brendle, W., Todorovic, S.: Learning spatiotemporal graphs of human activities. In: Proceedings of IEEE Conference on Computer Vision, Barcelona, Spain, pp. 778–785 (2011)
8. Dong, Z., Kong, Y., Liu, C., Li, H., Jia, Y.: Recognizing human interaction by multiple features. In: Proceedings of 1st Asian Conference Pattern Recognition, Beijing, China, pp. 77–81 (2011)
9. Kong, Y., Liang, W., Dong, Z., Jia, Y.: Recognising human interaction from videos by a discriminative model. Inst. Eng. Technol. Comput. Vis. **8**(4), 277–286 (2014)
10. Yuan, F., Prinet, V., Yuan, J.: Middle-level representation for human activities recognition: the role of spatio-temporal relationships. In: Proceedings of 11th European Conference on Computer Vision, Heraklion, Greece, pp. 168–180 (2010)
11. Slimani, K., Benezeth, Y., Souami, F.: Human interaction recognition based on the co-occurrence of visual words. In: Proceedings of IEEE Conference on Computer Vision and Pattern Recognition Workshops, Columbus, Ohio, USA, pp. 461–466 (2014)
12. Scovanner, P., Ali, S., Shah, M.: A 3-dimensional sift descriptor and its application to action recognition. In: Proceedings of ACM International Multimedia Conference and Exhibition, Augsburg, Bavaria, Germany, pp. 357–360 (2007)
13. Weizman, L., Goldberger, J.: Urban-area segmentation using visual words. Proc. IEEE Geosci. Remote. Sens. Lett. **6**(3), 388–392 (2009)
14. Rabiner, L.R.: Tutorial on hidden Markov models and selected applications in speech recognition. Proc. IEEE **77**(2), 257–286 (1989)
15. Yu, L., et al.: Recognition of fracture image based on gray level co-occurrence matrix. Comput. Simul. **27**(4), 224–227 (2010)
16. Ryoo, M., Aggarwal, J.: Spatio-temporal relationship match: video structure comparison for recognition of complex human activities. In: Proceedings of the IEEE International Conference on Computer Vision. Kyoto, pp. 1593–1600 (2009)

A Stereo Matching Method Combining Feature and Area Information for Power Line Inspection

Jing Wang[1], Dongsheng Zhang[1($\boxtimes$)], Xinghan Sun[1],
and Xinrong Zhang[2]

[1] Department of Mechanical Engineering, Xi'an Jiaotong University,
Xi'an 710049, Shaanxi, China
{wjysk680308,zds,star3211}@xjtu.edu.cn
[2] Key Laboratory of Road Construction Technology and Equipment of MOE,
Chang'an University, Xi'an 710064, Shaanxi, China
zxrong@chd.edu.cn

Abstract. Since the stereo vision has the advantages of providing autonomous navigation information for unmanned aerial vehicle (UAV) without environmental constraints. In this paper, the UAV is combined with stereo vision to perform the power line inspection. With the stereo vision system the line segments are reconstructed to obtain the orientation information, which provides reference for the attitude adjustment of the UAV. During the line construction, in order to make the line inspection more natural and reasonable, an efficient stereo line matching method which combines feature matching and block matching is proposed with artificial screening. Firstly, the image returned by the on-board binocular camera is used to click on the specific line to eliminate interference in the clutter background. The region of interest is filtered in the Hough space of the left image, and the Iterative Closest Point algorithm is used to filter the matching area in the right image. Secondly, The SAD matching cost function is used to merely recover the disparity map of the region of interest for the stereo frames after line screening. The reconstruction of a particular line is performed by least squares. To the performance of the proposed approach, the cyclic experiments on the ground are carried out. Based on the results, the proposed method improves the angle measurement accuracy of line segments. The orientation information can be utilized to provide reference for the attitude adjustment of the UAV.

Keywords: Power line inspection · Stereo matching · Line construction

1 Introduction

Regular inspection of power lines is to ensure the normal operation of the transmission line. Using the technology of unmanned aerial vehicle (UAV) to replace the traditional method of power system maintenance is of great significance to the safe of the power grid. Traditional solutions for global guidance of UAVs use the available accuracy of Global Positioning System (GPS) [1], which are limited to the condition of signal

© Springer Nature Switzerland AG 2019
H. Yu et al. (Eds.): ICIRA 2019, LNAI 11744, pp. 502–514, 2019.
https://doi.org/10.1007/978-3-030-27541-9_41

receiving and are unable to estimate the orientation of power lines. Since the stereo vision has the advantages of providing autonomous navigation information for UAV without environmental constraints [2–4]. In this paper, the UAV is combined with stereo vision to perform the inspection of the transmission lines.

The key feature of this project which arises directly from its main goal, is the fact that the UAV uses the overhead power line as a permanent visual guidance for its trajectory [5]. To achieve the goal, the extraction of line segments from both stereo images with a clutter background is essential. With the stereo vision system the line segments are reconstructed to obtain the orientation information, which provides reference for the attitude adjustment of the UAV. As a result, the power line will be in sight and continuously followed.

One of the most difficult problems in stereo vision is correspondence [6]. Once corresponding points in the pair of images are identified, their disparity values can be calculated and used to recover the depth using triangulation. Stereo correspondence algorithms can be rough divided into feature based and area based methods [7]. The former uses characteristics in the images like edges or corners to solve the correspondence problem in each stereo frame. The displacement between those features is used to build the disparity map and its density is directly related to the number of found features. The latter matches blocks of pixels to find correspondences in the images. Area based methods usually aggregate the sum of absolute differences (SAD) [8] or squared differences (SSD) over a window, which assumes brightness constancy for corresponding pixels.

The number of feature based approaches using linear features has increased dramatically during the last decade. In [9], the authors propose to perform an earlier verification on the gradient magnitude and orientation of the line in the right image before computing the SAD. However, the power line images belong to repetitive and poorly textured environment. In this case, the same gradient magnitude and orientation between lines will deteriorate the accuracy and robustness of correspondence. In [10] the Iterative Closest Multiple Lines (ICML) approach is proposed to estimate the camera pose at the same time as the line matching inside an iterative non-linear optimization, which tend to fall into local minimum, making a failure detection step required. In [11] Iterative Closest Point (ICP) algorithm is adapted to the domain of lines. But point sequences are not a very compact representation for intensity edges such as straight lines. This leads to significantly higher computation times than for most feature point based methods.

On the one hand, area based methods compute the cost function for each pixel along the epipolar line, which is time consuming and low accuracy. On the other hand, feature based methods can not be adapted to the environment with repetitive textures such as transmission lines and tend to fall into local minimum. In this paper, we propose to combine the feature based and area based method in a simple and efficient manner. According to the process of power line inspection, the image returned by the on-board binocular camera is utilized to click on the specific line to eliminate interference from towers and trees in the clutter background. The region of interest extraction with artificial screening makes the line inspection more natural and reasonable. The proposed approach is carried out in two main steps. Firstly, the region of interest is filtered in the Hough space of the left image, and the Iterative Closest Point algorithm is utilized to filter the matching area in the right image. Secondly, the SAD matching cost function is used to merely recover the disparity map of the region of interest for the left and right image after line screening, which can improve the accuracy of orientation. Ultimately loop experiments were designed to verify the accuracy of the approach.

2 Region of Interest Extraction

In this section the region of interest is extracted in each stereo frame. The specific line is filtered in the Hough space of the left image, and the Iterative Closest Point algorithm is used to filter the matching area in the right image.

Firstly the entire image is processed to determine the position of the lines in the left and right image. The point of interest (x_0, y_0) is generated when the mouse clicks in the left image. Edges are detected with a Canny detector in the left and right image of a stereo frame (Figs. 1, 2, 3 and 4).

Let L_l and L_r be the corresponding lines in the left and right images, represented by

Fig. 1. The left image

Fig. 2. The right image

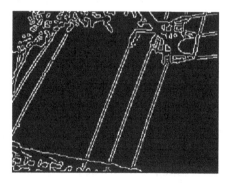

Fig. 3. Edge detection of the left image

Fig. 4. Edge detection of the right image

$$L_l : \rho_l = x_l \cos \theta_l + y_l \sin \theta_l,$$
$$L_r : \rho_r = x_r \cos \theta_r + y_r \sin \theta_r, \tag{1}$$

Where ρ_l and ρ_r denote the normal distances from the lines to the origins, and θ_l and θ_r are the edge gradient directions which are perpendicular to the line orientations. After the points on L_l and L_r vote on the accumulators, peaks will be formed at (ρ_l, θ_l) in the left Hough space, and at (ρ_r, θ_r) in the right Hough space, each representing a line.

The point of interest (x_0, y_0) is converted into a sinusoid in the Hough space. If the sinusoid passes any peak in the Hough space, the line in the image space corresponding to the peak is extracted as the target line, and the screening of the specific line in the left image is completed.

In the right image, the image of lines is in a repetitive, low textured environment, depending on the proximity parallelism of the overhead lines. In order to avoid the influence of textures with the same gradient magnitude and orientation during stereo matching, the corresponding line in the right image should be filtered for interest. As depicted in Figs. 5 and 6, for a particular θ there may exist more than one contending line in both left and right images. Accordingly, more than one peak is located for the same θ in both left and right Hough spaces.

Because of the epipolar constraint, each pair of matching points on the corresponding lines in the left and right images are considered to have an identical coordinate, i.e., $y_l = y_r$. According to the epipolar of the input cursor point and the lines in

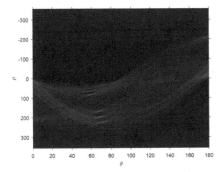

Fig. 5. The left Hough space

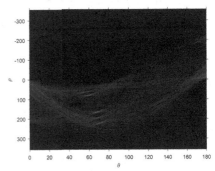

Fig. 6. The right Hough space

the left and right images, multiple intersection points can be determined. Iterative Closest Point algorithm is adopted to determine the matching relationship between the intersection point set in the left image and the one in the right image (Figs 7, 8 and 9).

The point set in the left image is defined as X, and the point set in the right image is defined as P. The center of mass μ_x of the point set X and the center of mass μ_p for the point set P are given by

Fig. 7. The point set in the left and right image

$$\mu x = \frac{1}{N}\sum_{i=1}^{N} p_i \qquad \mu p = \frac{1}{N}\sum_{i=1}^{N} x_i \tag{2}$$

The cross-covariance matrix $\sum_{px}$ of the sets X and P is given by

$$\sum_{px} = \frac{1}{N}\sum_{i=1}^{N}[(x_i - \mu_x)(p_i - \mu_p)^T] = \frac{1}{N}\sum_{i=1}^{N}(x_i p_i^T) - \mu_x \mu_p^T \tag{3}$$

The anti-symmetric matrix $A_{ij} = \left(\sum_{px} - \sum_{px}^T\right)_{ij}$ is used to form the column vector $\Delta = [A_{23}\ A_{31}\ A_{12}]^T$, which is used to form the symmetric 4×4 matrix Q

$$Q = \begin{pmatrix} tr(\sum_{px}) & \Delta^T \\ \Delta & \sum_{px} + \sum_{px}^T - tr(\sum_{px})I_3 \end{pmatrix} \tag{4}$$

where I_3 is the 3×3 identity matrix. The unit eigenvector $q_R = [q_0\ q_1\ q_2\ q_3]^T$, the maximum eigenvalue of Q, is selected as the optimal rotation. The optimal translation vector is given by

$$q_T = \mu_x - R(q_R)\mu_p \tag{5}$$

The objective function to be minimized is

$$f(q) = \frac{1}{N}\sum_{i=1}^{N}||x_i - R(\vec{q}_R)p_i - q_T||^2 \tag{6}$$

$$R = \begin{pmatrix} q_0^2 + q_1^2 - q_2^2 - q_3^2 & 2(q_1 q_2 - q_0 q_3) & 2(q_1 q_3 + q_0 q_2) \\ 2(q_1 q_2 + q_0 q_3) & q_0^2 + q_2^2 - q_1^2 - q_3^2 & 2(q_2 q_3 - q_0 q_1) \\ 2(q_1 q_3 - q_0 q_2) & 2(q_2 q_3 + q_0 q_1) & q_0^2 + q_3^2 - q_1^2 - q_2^2 \end{pmatrix} \tag{7}$$

The optimal match is achieved by iteration until the objective function is at a minimum. The specific line to be tracked is screened in a image coordinate system for the following line reconstruction.

3 Line Reconstruction

After extracting a pair of matching lines in the
left

Fig. 8. ROI extraction in the left image   **Fig. 9.** ROI extraction in the right image

and
right
image, it is necessary to perform stereo matching and three-dimensional reconstruction of the sample points on the line. The spatial fit of the sample points is based on the spatial position of the sample points. Stereo correspondence methods rely on matching costs for computing the similarity of point locations. The algorithm is based on the Sum of Absolute Differences (SAD) and computes the disparity map using 320×240 input images with a maximum disparity of 80 pixels.

A matching strategy from left to right is used in this section. Let $L_1 = (p', p'')$ be a line detected in the left image described by its endpoints $p' = (u', v')$ and $p' = (u'', v'')$. Extract fifty equidistant sample points $\mathbf{p}_j, j = 1, 2 \ldots, 20$ from L_1 and compute the corresponding points in the right image. In the left image, the area with the window size of 5*5 is selected centering on the sample point. Search with the SAD window along the epipolar in the right image. The matching cost function is given by

$$\text{SAD}(i,j,d) = \sum_{h=-\frac{w-1}{2}}^{h=\frac{w-1}{2}} \sum_{h=-\frac{w-1}{2}}^{h=\frac{w-1}{2}} |P_L(i+h, j+k) - P_R(i+h, j+k-d)| \qquad (8)$$

where d called disparity is the distance that the window on the right image moves on the epipolar, $P_L(i,j)$ represents the gray value of the datum point in the left image, and $P_R(i,j)$ represents the gray value of the point to be matched in the right image.

Calculate the SAD value for different disparity. The point corresponding to the minimum value of SAD is the best corresponding point in the right image.

After obtaining the disparity map, the three-dimensional information of the sampling points can be recovered according to the triangulation principle of stereo vision. The reprojection matrix which projects the 2D coordinate information into 3D coordinate is calculated based on the internal and external parameters obtained by the camera calibration.

Since the images after ROI extraction have a high precision of the stereo matching of the sample points, the work of outlier rejection can be omitted. Therefore, the sample points are directly used to fit the spatial line in the camera coordinate using least squares. First, the arithmetic mean of all sample point coordinates ($mean_x$, $mean_y$, $mean_z$) are calculated, which are used to obtain the covariance matrix. The singular transformation is performed on the covariance matrix of the three-dimensional information of all sample points. And the direction vector $\mathbf{L} = (L_x, L_y, L_z)$ of the selected line is the singular vector V corresponding to the largest singular value. The spatial parameter equation of the line is given by

$$\begin{cases} x = mean_x + L_x t \\ y = mean_y + L_y t \qquad (-200 \le t \le 200) \\ z = mean_z + L_z t \end{cases} \qquad (9)$$

The angle information of the straight line in the pitch direction and the yaw direction can be obtained. As depicted in Fig. 10, the angle of pitch is the angle between the direction of the line and the horizontal plane, where $\vec{n}$ is the normal vector of horizontal plane. The angle of yaw is the one between the projection of the line on the horizontal plane and the y axis of the camera coordinate system.

$$\text{pitch} = \cos^{-1} \frac{|\vec{n} \cdot \vec{L}|}{|\vec{n}| \cdot |\vec{L}|} \qquad \text{yaw} = \tan^{-1} \frac{L_y}{L_x} \qquad (10)$$

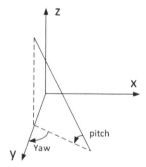

Fig. 10. The angle information

4 Experiments

In this section we present experiments for angle measurement of outdoor environment because of the difficulty of obtaining the precise location in the real scene. A cyclic verification is designed to analyze the angle measurement error. We compare our approach to the area based method using in global images.

The experimental device includes a 3D module USB drive-free color camera, a common tripod and a tripod with the cloud platform of pitch and yaw directions. The ordinary tripod is fixed with the No. 2 pole as the target position reference. The tripod with the cloud platform is used to fix the No. 1 pole for angle adjustment. The angular difference of the pitch and yaw directions is obtained by recovering the position and orientation information of the two poles. Then the difference is adjusted by the cloud platform of the No. 1 tube. As a result, the angle difference between the adjusted poles in both directions is calculated using our algorithm (Figs. 11, 12, 13, 14, 15, 16, 17 and 18).

Fig. 11. The experimental device

The measurement accuracy of the pitch and the yaw direction between the two lines in space is determined by the following cyclic verification. Firstly, the pitch angle of line 1 is initialized with respect to line 2, and then the region of interest in the left and right images is filtered to complete stereo matching and 3D reconstruction. Least squares is performed on the reconstructed sample points to obtain the spatial equation of the matching line before the pitch direction adjustment. The spatial equations of two lines is given by

$$
\begin{cases}
x_1 = -42.3349 - 0.0281t \\
y_1 = 5.6548 + 0.8624t \\
z_1 = 761.7487 + 0.5054t
\end{cases}
\qquad
\begin{cases}
x_2 = 225.8568 + 0.0027t \\
y_2 = -24.1281 + 0.9999t \\
z_2 = 1096.3 + 0.0129t
\end{cases}
\tag{11}
$$

Table 1. Comparison of the pitch difference of SAD and the proposed approach

	Pitch(SAD)	Pitch(Proposed Approach)
1	30.0168	30.3689
2	1.4215	0.7409
Difference	28.5953	29.628

The pitch angle of the cloud platform of the fixed No. 1 pole is adjusted according to the calculated difference between the two lines given in Table 1. Then the algorithm is used to process the adjusted line to obtain the space equation of the lines.

$$\begin{cases} x_1 = -43.0276 + 0.0012t \\ y_1 = 4.2837 - 0.9996t \\ z_1 = 1012.5 - 0.027t \end{cases} \qquad \begin{cases} x_2 = 235.8046 + 0.0012t \\ y_2 = -12.6187 - t \\ z_2 = 1089.3 - 0.0058t \end{cases} \qquad (12)$$

Table 2. Comparison of the pitch measurement error of SAD and the proposed approach

	Pitch(SAD)	Pitch(Proposed Approach)
1	0.0036	5.1307
2	7.8872	0
Absolute Error	7.8836	5.1307
Relative Error	26.28%	17.1%

The pitch measurement results are given in Table 2. Our approach led to massive improvement after the region of interest extraction. The relative error of pitch direction is reduced from 26.28% to 17.1%.

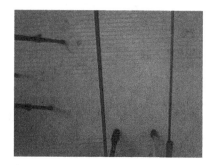

Fig. 12. Left image before pitch adjustment

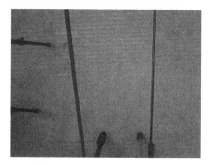

Fig. 13. Right image before pitch adjustment

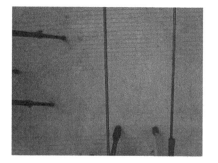

Fig. 14. Pitch adjustment +30° in the left image

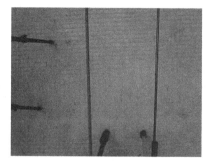

Fig. 15. Pitch adjustment +30° in the right image

Fig. 16. Pitch direction initialization   **Fig. 17.** Pitch adjustment +30°

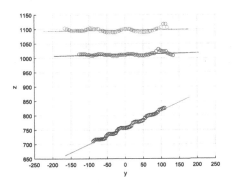

Fig. 18. Fitting line in the y-z plane projection

The yaw angle of line 1 is initialized with respect to line 2, and then the regions of interest in the left and right images are filtered for stereo matching and 3D reconstruction. Least squares is performed on the reconstructed sample points to obtain the spatial equation of the matching line before the yaw direction adjustment. The spatial equations of two lines is given by

$$\begin{cases} x_1 = 77.7875 + 0.3147t \\ y_1 = 5.9267 - 0.9487t \\ z_1 = 1091.3 - 0.0296t \end{cases} \qquad \begin{cases} x_2 = 245.9661 - 0.0085t \\ y_2 = -10.0919 + 0.9992t \\ z_2 = 1096.5 - 0.0380t \end{cases} \qquad (13)$$

Table 3. Comparison of the yaw difference of SAD and the proposed approach

	Yaw(SAD)	Yaw(Proposed Approach)
1	71.5660	71.6493
2	84.2225	89.5114
difference	12.6565	17.8621

The yaw angle of the cloud platform of the fixed No. 1 pole is adjusted according to the calculated difference between the two lines given in Table 3. Then the algorithm is used to process the adjusted line to obtain the space equation of the lines

$$\begin{cases} x_1 = -43.0276 + 0.0012t \\ y_1 = 4.2837 - 0.9996t \\ z_1 = 1012.5 - 0.027t \end{cases} \qquad \begin{cases} x_2 = 235.8046 + 0.0012t \\ y_2 = -12.6187 - t \\ z_2 = 1089.3 - 0.0058t \end{cases} \qquad (14)$$

Table 4. Comparison of the yaw measurement error of SAD and the proposed approach

	Yaw(SAD)	Yaw(Proposed approach)
1	89.9998	89.9342
2	88.2815	89.9284
Absolute error	1.7183	0.0058
Relative error	13.57%	0.0322%

The yaw measurement results are given in Table 4. As expected, our approach led to massive improvement after the region of interest extraction. The relative error of yaw direction is reduced from 13.57% to 0.0322% (Figs. 19, 20, 21, 22, 23, 24 and 25).

Fig. 19. Left image before yaw adjustment

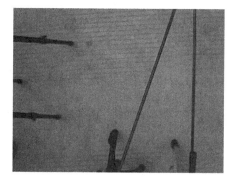

Fig. 20. Right image before yaw adjustment

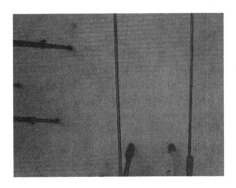

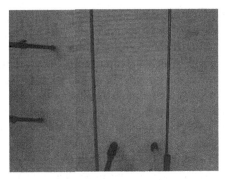

Fig. 21. Yaw adjustment −18° in the left image

Fig. 22. Yaw adjustment −18° in the right image

Fig. 23. Yaw direction initialization

Fig. 24. Yaw adjustment −18°

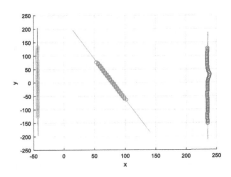

Fig. 25. Fitting line in the x-y plane projection

5   Conclusion

Traditional solutions for global guidance of UAVs use the available accuracy of GPS systems, which are limited to the condition of signal receiving and are unable to estimate the orientation of power lines. Since the stereo vision has the advantages of providing autonomous navigation information for UAV without environmental constraints. In this paper, the UAV is combined with stereo vision to perform the inspection of the transmission lines. With the stereo vision system the line segments are reconstructed to obtain the orientation information, which provides reference for the attitude adjustment of the UAV. In order to make up for the deficiency of the existing methods used alone, an efficient stereo line matching method which combines feature matching and block matching is proposed. To the performance of the proposed approach, the cyclic experiments on the ground are carried out. Based on the results, the proposed method improves the angle measurement accuracy of line segments. The orientation information can be utilized to provide reference for the attitude adjustment of the UAV.

Acknowledgments. This project was supported by Shaanxi Science and Technology Coordinated Innovation Project (Grant Nos. 2016KTZDGY-02-03).

References

1. Woodley, B., Jones II, H., LeMaster, E., Frew, E.: Carrier phase GPS and computer vision for control of an autonomous helicopter. ION GPS-96, Kansas City, Missouri, September 1996
2. Gomez-Ojeda, R., Gonzalez-Jimenez, J.: Robust stereo visual odometry through a probabilistic combination of points and line segments. IEEE International Conference on Robotics & Automation. IEEE (2016)
3. A stereo vision system for UAV guidance. In: 2009 IEEE/RSJ International Conference on Intelligent Robots and Systems. IEEE (2009)
4. Stefanik, K.V., Gassaway, J.C., Kochersberger, K., et al.: UAV-Based stereo vision for rapid aerial terrain mapping. GIScience & Remote Sens. **48**(1), 24–49 (2011)
5. Campoy, P., Garcia, P.J., Barrientos, A., et al.: An Stereoscopic Vision System Guiding an Autonomous Helicopter for Overhead Power Cable Inspection (2001)
6. Marr, D., Poggio, T.: Cooperative computation of stereo disparity. Science **194**, 283–287 (1976)
7. Ambrosch, K., Kubinger, W., Humenberger, M., et al.: Hardware implementation of an SAD based stereo vision algorithm. In: 2007 IEEE Conference on Computer Vision and Pattern Recognition. IEEE (2007)
8. Banks, J., Bennamoun, M., Corke, P.: Non-parametric techniques for fast and robust stereo matching. In: Proceedings of IEEE Conference on Speech and Image Technologies for Computing and Telecommunications (1997)
9. Koletschka, T., Puig, L., Daniilidis, K.: MEVO: multi-environment stereo visual odometry. In: IEEE/RSJ International Conference on Intelligent Robots and Systems, 14–18 September 2014
10. Witt, J., Weltin, U.: Robust stereo visual odometry using iterative closest multiple lines. In: IEEE/RSJ International Conference on Intelligent Robots and Systems, November 2013
11. Besl, P.J., Mckay, N.D.: A method for registration of 3-D shapes. IEEE Trans. Pattern Anal. Mach. Intell. **14**(2), 239–256 (2002)

Image Stitching Based on Improved SURF Algorithm

Jinxian Qi[1], Gongfa Li[1,2(✉)], Zhaojie Ju[3], Disi Chen[3],
Du Jiang[1,2,3,4,5,6], Bo Tao[4,5], Guozhang Jiang[6], and Ying Sun[4,5]

[1] Key Laboratory of Metallurgical Equipment and Control Technology
of Ministry of Education, Wuhan University of Science and Technology,
Wuhan 430081, China
ligongfa@wust.edu.cn
[2] Precision Manufacturing Research Institute,
Wuhan University of Science and Technology, Wuhan 430081, China
[3] School of Computing, University of Portsmouth, Portsmouth PO1 3HE, UK
[4] Research Center of Biologic Manipulator and Intelligent Measurement and
Control, Wuhan University of Science and Technology, Wuhan 430081, China
[5] Hubei Key Laboratory of Mechanical Transmission and Manufacturing
Engineering, Wuhan University of Science and Technology,
Wuhan 430081, China
[6] 3D Printing and Intelligent Manufacturing Engineering Institute,
Wuhan University of Science and Technology, Wuhan, China

Abstract. In order to solve the problem of uneven distribution of picture features and stitching of images, an improved SURF feature extraction method is proposed. Image feature extraction and image registration are the core of image stitching, which is directly related to stitching quality. In this paper, a comprehensive and in-depth study of feature-based image registration is carried out, and an improved algorithm is proposed. Firstly, the Heisen detection operator in the SURF algorithm is introduced to realize feature detection, and the features are extracted as much as possible. Secondly, the characteristics are described by BRIEF operator in the ORB algorithm to realize the invariance of the rotation change. Then, the European pull distance is used to complete the similarity calculation, and the KNN algorithm is used to realize the feature rough matching. Finally, the distance threshold is used to remove the matching pair with larger distance, and then the RANSAC algorithm is used to complete the purification. Experiments show that the proposed algorithm has good real-time performance, strong robustness and high accuracy.

Keywords: Image stitching · SURF algorithm · RANSAC

1 Introduction

Image stitching mainly includes two modules: image registration technology and image fusion technology. Image registration is the basis of image fusion, and image fusion is an important branch and research hotspot of image processing. Image fusion technology extracts and synthesizes information from two or more source images to obtain

© Springer Nature Switzerland AG 2019
H. Yu et al. (Eds.): ICIRA 2019, LNAI 11744, pp. 515–527, 2019.
https://doi.org/10.1007/978-3-030-27541-9_42

a more accurate, comprehensive and reliable description of a region or target, and then captures similar regions in the image for stitching and fusion processing. Complete panoramic image to meet the collection and understanding of image omnidirectional information and target detection, recognition and tracking. In response to this characteristic, image mosaic fusion technology has been widely used in urban transportation, airport scenes, military exercises and medical images. The technology has a basic architecture, and its main contents include image preprocessing, image stitching processing, image stitching evaluation and panoramic image results. The image stitching fusion module is the core technology, so the image fusion algorithm is directly related to the quality. The quality of the fusion after the entire image is stitched.

At present, the more commonly used image fusion algorithms are linear weighted fusion algorithms, such as the direct averaging method, but the pixel values of the overlapping regions are not simply superimposed but are first weighted and then superimposed and averaged, by selecting appropriate weights, the overlapping area can be smoothly smoothed during processing, and the splicing ghost is effectively avoided [1]. Therefore, the method is simple and fast, but is easily interfered by the transition bandwidth, which causes the smoothness of the spliced image and the problem of ghosting, resulting in poor stability of the algorithm. The multi-band fusion algorithm proposed in is based on the idea of decomposing images in different frequencies, using different transition band widths for weighted interpolation processing and then performing fusion processing, although the image quality after stitching and fusion is good [2, 3]. However, pictures with unevenly distributed features cannot be stitched together efficiently, and the algorithm has a large workload and a long calculation time, so the real-time performance is poor.

2 Related Work

For the fast extraction and matching algorithm of image features, many effective image feature extraction and matching algorithms have been proposed by scholars at home and abroad. The representative methods are Harris corner and SIFT feature points [4].

The image registration algorithm based on eigenvalue usually needs the following steps:

- Feature extraction is the most important and difficult step of eigenvalue-based registration algorithm. Feature extraction has a strong impact on the results. There are a lot of information that can be used to represent similarity in images, so there are various processing methods. Common image features include corners, high curvature points, straight lines, contours, closed areas, moment invariants, center of gravity, etc.
- Feature matching, comparing the features extracted from the image to be registered.
- Image registration is achieved by transforming the matched eigenvalues into corresponding images.

In 2006, Bay et al. improved the SIFT algorithm and proposed the SURF (Speeded Up Robust Features) algorithm [5]. The stitching speed was significantly improved. In 2011, Ruble et al. proposed the ORB (Oriented fast and Rotated BRIEF) algorithm based on the algorithm of Brief (Binary Robust Independent Elementary Features) [6]. The stitching speed is further improved than SURF, and the noise resistance is good. transsexual. In 2004, an algorithm was proposed to automatically implement robust splicing [7]. The algorithm uses Harris to perform feature detection. Although the calculation speed is general, the image mosaic robustness is improved. In 2007, SIFT-based seamless splicing was proposed, which is robust to illumination changes and has scale invariance [8]. In 2010, the SIFT algorithm was used to splicing the remote sensing image of the drone, and good experimental results were obtained [9]. After the ORB algorithm was proposed, domestic research was also quickly integrated, and the image stitching method based on the ORB algorithm was continuously innovated and widely used [10, 11]. In 2016, a method to improve the combination of ORB and symmetric matching was proposed [12]. In 2017, an improved algorithm for ORB feature image stitching was proposed [13].

3 Feature Extraction Algorithms Based on Optimized SURF and RANSAC

3.1 The Experimental Steps in This Paper

According to the registration process, this paper introduces the algorithm, and verifies the practicability of the algorithm by comparing the experiments in each link. In the process of image feature extraction, after the research and analysis of SURF and ORB algorithms, this paper introduces Heisen detection operator in SURF to feature detection, and BRIEF operator in ORB algorithm is selected for feature description (Fig. 1).

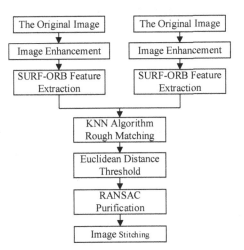

Fig. 1. The block diagram of the algorithm in this paper.

In the process of feature matching, after the research and analysis of and KNN (K-Nearest Neighbors) algorithm, this paper proposes to use Hamming distance to complete the similarity calculation of descriptors, using BF algorithm. The algorithm realizes rough matching of image features. In view of the mismatch of rough matching, an improved RANSAC algorithm is proposed to achieve accurate registration.

3.2   Feature Extraction Algorithm Based on SURF-ORB Algorithm

As an upgraded version of SIFT algorithm, SURF algorithm not only has the characteristics of high accuracy and robustness of SIFT algorithm, but also significantly improves its speed.

Feature Detection Based on SURF. The SIFT algorithm uses the DoG (Difference of Gaussian) operator for feature detection, and the SURF algorithm uses the Heisson detection operator to approximate the DoG operator, and the algorithm speed is improved by the integral graph [14].

Integral Map. The integral map of $p(x, y)$ in image I is the sum of all pixels from P to the origin of the image.

$$I_{\Sigma}(x, y) = \sum_{x' \leq x, y' \leq y} I(x', y') \tag{1}$$

Among then, $I_{\Sigma}(x, y)$ is the integral map and $I(x', y')$ is the original image.

After calculating the integrated image, the sum of any rectangular partial pixels in the original image can be calculated by three additions. Calculate the sum of the pixels in the original image, just add 3 additions according to Eq. (2).

$$\sum = A - B - C + D \tag{2}$$

Among then, $\sum$ is the sum of the rectangular partial pixels, and A, B, C, and D are the pixel values of the four corners of the rectangular portion, respectively.

Therefore, the size of the filter has no effect on the calculation of the integral map. The use of a large-sized filter in the SURF algorithm can significantly increase the speed of the algorithm.

Constructing Scale Space. The SURF algorithm uses the Hessian matrix for feature detection, and uses the matrix determinant to calculate the extreme value as the image feature [15]. This image feature has a patchy structure called a speckle feature. Given an image $I(x, y)$, the Hessian matrix with scale σ is:

$$H(x, \sigma) = \begin{bmatrix} L_{xx}(x, \sigma) & L_{xy}(x, \sigma) \\ L_{xy}(x, \sigma) & L_{yy}(x, \sigma) \end{bmatrix} \tag{3}$$

Among then, Lxx, Lxy, Lyy is the filtered second derivative.

Theoretically, the Gaussian function is the most ideal function for analyzing the scale space, but in practical applications, the Gaussian function needs to be interrupted and then discretized. In fact, the standard filter effect is sometimes not ideal. The SIFT algorithm uses the DoG operator to approximate the LoG (Laplacian of Gaussian) operator to achieve better results [16]. Therefore, in order to find the extreme point, the SURF algorithm approximates the Hessian matrix, using square matrix filtering as a template to simulate Gaussian filtering.

The SURF algorithm groups the scale spaces when constructing the scale space, and the same group represents the response graph of the convolution of an image with different size square matrix filter templates magnified by the arithmetic progression. Figure 2 shows the pyramid of the constructed scale space. There are 3 groups of 4 layers. The 1st layer of the 1st group is a 9 × 9 square matrix filter. After that, the size of the first layer of the square matrix filter in each group is in the upper scale space.

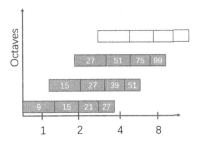

Fig. 2. SURF algorithm scale space.

Finding Extreme Points. After constructing the scale space, the Hessian matrix is then used to calculate the extreme points. The result of convolving the image with the template is denoted by Dxx, Dxy, Dyy, respectively, to replace the Lxx, Lxy, Lyy to obtain a simplified version of the Hessian matrix determinant:

$$\det(H_{approx}) = D_{xx}D_{yy} - (0.9D_{xy})^2 \tag{4}$$

By increasing the size of the square matrix filter template, the value of the approximate Hessian matrix determinant of the pixel at each scale can be obtained. This value is compared with the values of other pixels in the three-dimensional region of the pixel. If a pixel is an extreme value in its own scale and 26 pixels in its upper and lower scales, then the pixel is a feature point.

Looking for the Main Direction. The SURF algorithm defines the main direction for the feature points, making the algorithm invariant to the rotation. The SURF algorithm uses Harr wavelet to calculate the gradients in both horizontal and vertical directions. The response template is (Fig. 3):

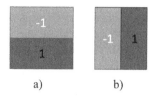

a)   b)

Fig. 3. Harr wavelet response template. (a) is X-direction template and (b) Y-direction template.

Feature Description Based on BRIEF of ORB. The feature points are used as the center of the square region with a side length of 20σ, which is divided into 16 small squares of the same size, and the small square is divided into 25 smaller areas. The sampling of each small area is shown in the Fig. 4.

Thus, the entire square area together form a 64-dimensional feature vector. As an expression of the feature, it embodies the basic information of the feature point, and can perform feature matching instead of the image pixel.

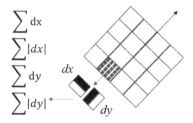

Fig. 4. SURF feature vector.

The ORB algorithm feature description is implemented by the BRIEF descriptor, and the descriptor obtained by the BRIEF is a binary string for easy operation. Take the pixel block P of $S \times S$ size and define the binary test as:

$$\tau(p; x, y) = \begin{cases} 1 & p(x) < p(y) \\ 0 & \text{otherwise} \end{cases} \tag{5}$$

Where p_x is the gray value of pixel block P on x. The gray point centroid method is used to calculate the main direction of the feature point, and a feature descriptor of the n-dimensional binary string is generated. The transformed feature descriptor is:

$$g_n(p, \theta) = f_n(p) | (x_i, y_i) \in S_\theta \tag{6}$$

3.3   Feature Matching and Purification

Image Feature Matching Based on KNN. The two images will enter the feature matching link after the feature extraction is completed. Fast and accurate matching helps to obtain better transformation matrices and improve image stitching efficiency and quality. The image feature matching completes the search and matching process by calculating the similarity degree of the feature descriptors by a certain measurement method. The similarity calculation is done by using the Euclidean distance and the Hamming distance. The Euclidean distance can be used simultaneously for the case where the feature descriptor is a binary string and a feature vector. Commonly used matching algorithms include KNN algorithm and BF algorithm. In order to ensure the matching accuracy, this paper uses KNN algorithm to achieve image feature matching.

The KNN algorithm calculates the degree of similarity based on the Euclidean distance. The selection of K value is directly related to the effect of the algorithm. The selection of K value is too small, and the calculation of the algorithm becomes more complicated and cannot achieve the effect of approximate expression. If the K value is selected too large, the point with less correlation is also taken into account. Affect the accuracy of the match, so the value of K is critical.

Image Matching Purification Based on RANSAC. RANSAC (Random Sample Consensus) is an abbreviation of the random sampling consensus algorithm. It is essentially a process of searching through continuous iterations and finding model parameters that can contain more interior points. The algorithm retains the "inner point" in the sample (that is, it can satisfy the model constraint within the error range) by setting a certain threshold, and eliminates the "outer point" or "noise point" (the model constraint cannot be satisfied at a given threshold). The algorithm first selects a small number of sub-point sets that are consistent with the original feature points in the feature points, uses the sub-point set to obtain the transformation matrix, and then detects the original feature point set according to the obtained transformation matrix, so that the error range can be obtained. And you can satisfy all the points of the model constraint and record it as an interior point. This process is continuously carried out. When the number of points obtained is large enough and the number does not change substantially, the transformation matrix obtained at this time is used as the final transformation matrix, and the outer points are eliminated, and all the obtained inner points are retained (Fig. 5).

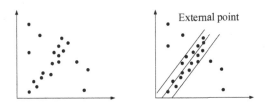

Fig. 5. Straight line fit.

Let q be the probability of the inner point in the feature point. At least n pairs of points are needed. p is the probability that the randomly selected feature point is the inner point. The iteration number is calculated as shown in Eq. (7):

$$C = \frac{\log(1-p)}{\log(1-q^n)} \tag{7}$$

RANSAC uses a univariate matrix as a transformation model, as shown in Eq. (7).

$$\begin{bmatrix} x_2 \\ y_2 \\ 1 \end{bmatrix} = \begin{bmatrix} m_0 & m_1 & m_2 \\ m_3 & m_4 & m_5 \\ m_6 & m_7 & 1 \end{bmatrix} \begin{bmatrix} x_1 \\ y_1 \\ 1 \end{bmatrix} \tag{8}$$

The implementation steps of RANSAC algorithm can be expressed as follows:

(1) Four pairs of matching points are randomly selected from the matching point pairs, and the transformation matrix H is obtained according to the relationship between the pairs of points.
(2) Set a threshold, calculate the distance between each point in the original feature set and the corresponding point according to the transformation matrix H obtained in step 1. If the distance obtained is smaller than the given threshold, keep it and record the correct matching points.
(3) Repeat the steps mentioned above. The iteration stops when the correct matching points are large enough and there is no change at all. In this case, the collocation point is the maximum internal point allowed in the threshold range, and the transformation matrix obtained is the transformation matrix of the original feature point set.

4   Analysis of Experimental Results

4.1   Data Acquisition and Platform Construction

In the experiment, indoor and outdoor images were collected by color CCD camera as shown in Fig. 6, in which group A was outdoor and group B was indoor.

Picture Mosaic Experiments. As shown in Fig. 7, the feature point map extracted for the SURF algorithm is improved. In order to better display the effect, the color picture is grayed out. It can be seen that the number of feature points extracted by the algorithm is more and the distribution is more uniform. When feature extraction, the number of feature points, dimensions, time and average number of feature points extracted per second are shown in Table 1.

a) Left Graph of Group A   b) Right Graph of Group A

c) Left Graph of Group B   d) Right Graph of Group B

Fig. 6. They are divided into two groups, A and B, showing outdoor and indoor maps respectively.

Table 1. Comparison of feature extraction effects

Group	Algorithm	Number of feature points	Time/s
A	SURF	480/367	0.6250
	O-SURF	565/482	0.6563
B	SURF	485/432	0.7031
	O-SURF	607/556	0.6719

a) Left Graph of Group A   b) Right Graph of Group A

c) Left Graph of Group B   d) Right Graph of Group B

Fig. 7. Improved SURF feature extraction

As shown in Fig. 8, for the image of feature matching effect after the purification of RANSAC algorithm, it can be seen from the graph that the matching effect after the purification of feature matching is significantly improved compared with that before purification. The connection lines between each feature are horizontally distributed, and there is no crossover. This also shows that the RANSAC algorithm can effectively improve the matching accuracy.

a) Feature matching effect of group A

b) Feature matching effect of group B

Fig. 8. Feature point matching effect based on RANSAC purification.

As shown in Fig. 9, it is the effect diagram of the final stitching. The picture can be seamlessly docked without significant distortion. According to the splicing effect of the A outdoor and the B indoor, a good splicing can be achieved in some areas without features. This shows that the algorithm has strong generalization ability. For images with uneven feature distribution, a good stitching function can also be achieved.

a) Group A outdoor stitching effect diagram

b) Group B indoor stitching effect diagram

Fig. 9. Resulting picture after stitching.

5   Conclusion

Image and video stitching technology has become a research hotspot in the field of digital image processing. The stitching technology can broaden the field of view and reduce redundancy while ensuring image resolution. In this paper, the splicing core technology is studied for the problem of uneven distribution of features.

The Heisson detection operator in the SURF algorithm is introduced in feature detection, and the feature description selects BRIEF operator in the ORB algorithm. In the feature matching process, through the research and analysis of KNN algorithm, this paper proposes to use the Euler distance to complete the descriptor similarity calculation, and use the KNN algorithm to perform image feature rough matching. And for the rough matching, there may be mismatches, and the improved RANSAC algorithm is proposed to complete the purification. Before the RANSAC algorithm, the matching of the Euclidean distance greater than a certain threshold is removed, the search range is reduced, the calculation amount is reduced, and the efficiency and accuracy of the feature matching are ensured.

Acknowledgements. This work was supported by Grants of National Natural Science Foundation of China (Grant Nos. 51575407, 51505349, 51575338, 51575412, 61733011), the Grants of National Defense Pre-Research Foundation of Wuhan University of Science and Technology (GF201705) and Open Fund of the Key Laboratory for Metallurgical Equipment and Control of Ministry of Education in Wuhan University of Science and Technology (2018B07).

References

1. Adwan, S., Alsaleh, I., Majed, R.: A new approach for image stitching technique using dynamic time warping (DTW) algorithm towards scoliosis x-ray diagnosis. Measurement **84**, 32–46 (2016)
2. Suk, J.H., Lyuh, C.G., Yoon, S., Roh, T.M.: Fixed homography–based real-time SW/HW image stitching engine for motor vehicles. ETRI J. **37**(6), 1143–1153 (2015)
3. Li, G.F., Jiang, D., Zhou, Y.L., Jiang, G.Z., Kong, J.Y., Gunasekaran, M.: Human lesion detection method based on image information and brain signal. IEEE Access **7**, 11533–11542 (2019)
4. An, J., Koo, H.I., Cho, N.I.: Unified framework for automatic image stitching and rectification. J. Electron. Imaging **24**(3), 033007 (2015)
5. Bang, S., Kim, H., Kim, H.: Uav-based automatic generation of high-resolution panorama at a construction site with a focus on preprocessing for image stitching. Autom. Constr. **84**, 70–80 (2017)
6. Holmes, G., Hale, M., Mcalindon, M.E., Anderson, S.: PTH-185 mapping the gastric mucosal surface: image mosaicking for capsule endoscopy. Gut **64**(Suppl. 1), A490.1–A49491 (2015)
7. Sun, Y., et al.: Gesture recognition based on Kinect and sEMG signal fusion. Mob. Netw. Appl. **23**(4), 797–805 (2018)
8. Sjodahl, M., Oreb, B.F.: Stitching interferometric measurement data for inspection of large optical components. Opt. Eng. **41**(2), 403–408 (2015)
9. Johnson, B.G.: Recommendations for a system to photograph core segments and create stitched images of complete cores. J. Paleolimnol. **53**(4), 437–444 (2015)
10. Cheng, W.T., Sun, Y., Li, G.F., Jiang, G.Z., Liu, H.H.: Jointly network: a network based on CNN and RBM for gesture recognition. Neural Comput. Appl. **31**(Suppl. 1), 309–323 (2018)
11. Lee, C.O., Lee, J.H., Woo, H., Yun, S.: Block decomposition methods for total variation by primal—dual stitching. J. Sci. Comput. **68**(1), 273–302 (2016)
12. Berriman, G.B., Good, J.C.: The application of the montage image mosaic engine to the visualization of astronomical images. Publ. Astron. Soc. Pac. **129**(975), 058006 (2017)
13. Chen, D.S., et al.: An interactive image segmentation method in hand gesture recognition. Sensors **17**(2), 253 (2017)
14. Frankl, A., Seghers, V., Stal, C., Maeyer, P.D., Petrie, G., Nyssen, J.: Using image-based modelling (Sfm-MVS) to produce a 1935 ortho-mosaic of the ethiopian highlands. Int. J. Digit. Earth **8**(5), 421–430 (2015)
15. Vargiu, L., Rodrigueztomé, P., Sperber, G.O., Cadeddu, M., Grandi, N., Blikstad, V.: Classification and characterization of human endogenous retroviruses; mosaic forms are common. Retrovirology **13**(1), 7 (2016)
16. Mort, R.L.: Quantitative analysis of patch patterns in mosaic tissues with clonaltools software. J. Anat. **215**(6), 698–704 (2015)

Neural Network Based Electronics Segmentation

Senwei Ma, Xiaoyuan Fan, Lei Wang$^{(\boxtimes)}$, Jun Cheng, and Chengjun Xu

Guangdong Provincial Key Laboratory of Robotics and Intelligent System,
Shenzhen Institutes of Advanced Technology,
Chinese Academy of Sciences, Shenzhen, China
{xy.fan1,lei.wang1}@siat.ac.cn

Abstract. In traditional automated assembly lines, operations of the robotic arm settings always rely on programming, which is unconvenient and time consuming. To solve this problem, computer vision is an alternative choice, and popular in robotics recently. With the great breakthrough of deep learning in the field of computer vision, image processing methods based on deep neural network (DNN) have been applied in various industry scenes. This paper explores the application of DNN-based image segmentation technology in factory assembly lines. We have developed one electronics' image datasets for experiments. And deep convolution neural networks (CNN) based on region proposal have been used to detect, segment objects, and generate masks for corresponding electronics. Experimental results show that the proposed framework has high recognition accuracy and strong robustness, which will be helpful when applied in robotic arm settings in automated assembly lines.

Keywords: Deep neural network · Detection of electronics object ·
Image mask · Robotic

1 Introduction

Nowadays, pipelines using robot arms to install electronics still depend on programming heavily, with low functional integration and compatibility. In recent years, with the improvement of algorithms, continuous increase of computation power and large scale dataset, the technologies of deep learning have developed rapidly. The raise of deep learning provides a new possible solution for the traditional automatic detection of electronics.

Classification, detection and segmentation of objects in images are three major tasks in the field of computer vision. The traditional object detection method is based on the region selection strategy of sliding window, which has poor robustness of manually designed features on target diversity. Defects, covering and shadows will have a huge impact on detection results. In contrast,

---

S. Ma and X. Fan—Equal contributions.

H. Yu et al. (Eds.): ICIRA 2019, LNAI 11744, pp. 528–540, 2019.
https://doi.org/10.1007/978-3-030-27541-9_43

proposal area based neural network provides a better solution. By using the image texture, edge and color information in advance to find latent objects, neural network can use less selection windows while keeping higher recall rate, which greatly reduces the complexity of the follow-up operation and produces higher quality windows. Semantic segmentation [1,8–11] is a further task. In addition to detecting where the object is located, each pixel should be classified to the target category. On this basis, instance segmentation [6,7] is to further separate each object of the target category and mark it with different masks.

This paper simulates the scene of electronics identification and presents one electronics' image datasets which contains images of ten kinds of electronics. We design a convolution neural network (CNN) to classify and detect the location of the electronics, then output an instance segmentation for each object. We use a quantitative indicator to measure the quality of segmentation and conclude whether this proposal based neural network is practical in this task.

Our contributions can be summarized as follows:

- We present one electronics' image datasets, which contains two subsets. The datasets includes images of ten kinds of electronic components, as well as labels and bounding boxes on each instance object.
- We have designed a proposal based neural network for recognition and segmentation the objects in the dataset, which will be helpful for the industrial scene to solve the automatic assembly problem.

2 Related Work

Traditional Object Detection. Traditional object detection methods are always based on the edge detection with simple convolution filters such as Sobel [16] or Canny [17].

Hand-Engineered Features. Scale-invariant feature transform (SIFT) [19] and Histogram of oriented gradients (HOG) [20] have been designed, and corresponding features are calculated densely on overall image pyramids. These HOG and SIFT pyramids have been applied in many works for object classification, object detection, human pose estimation, and so on.

Neural Network for Object Detection. With the development of deep neural network, some object detectors, such as like OverFeat [21] and R-CNN [10] have shown great improvement compared with hand-engineered features. OverFeat [21] adopted a strategy by applying a ConvNet [13] as a sliding window detector on an image pyramid. R-CNN [10] applied a region proposal-based method [11]. Recently, more accurate detectors like Fast [22] and Faster R-CNN [2] use features map computed from a single scale, due to the fact that it provides a great trade-off between detection accuracy and speed. However, multi-scale detection still performs better in detection task, especially for small objects with low resolution. You only look once (YOLO) [18] is another method for instance segmentation. In the framework of YOLO, it does not need to get the proposal of the area first, but just process the whole image.

Instance Segmentation. One-stage instance segmentation method [23] generates position-sensitive maps assembled into masks with position-sensitive pooling. Mask-RCNN [3] is a representative two-stage method for instance segmentation that first generates proposals and then classifies and segments those proposals in the second stage. We should notice that the accuracy of one-stage method is far behind that of two-stage method.

3   Electronics Dataset

3.1   Overview

In order to test the efficiency of deep neural network in the scene of assembly line, we first establish a dataset, named ECAL-10 (Electronics Components of Automatic Assembly Line, including 10 classes).

The dataset includes ten classes of components, including Dynatron, Mos tube, XO, Toroid Coil, Trimmer Potentiometer, Relay, Radiator, Buzzer, ISP interface and DC socket.

The ECAL-10 contains two subsets. In the first subset, data is collected from the Internet, named ECAL-10-I. In the second subset, one fixed distance camera is used to collect unified image data of the electronics, named ECAL-10-II.

ECAL-10-I consists of 1000 images, divided into 800 samples for training and 200 for test. Each training sample contains 1 to 5 targets. ECAL-10-II contains 1167 images, divided into 900 samples for training and 267 for test. Each training sample contains 3 to 8 targets.

Due to the diversity of Internet data sources, the samples in the ECAL-10-I always have complex background, and the electronics components are always occluded. The sizes of electronics are not uniform, and the images' initial resolutions are different. So ECAL-10-I is suitable to detect the effectiveness and robustness of the neural network in an unstable environment.

ECAL-10-II is used to simulate the real application scene of the pipeline of fixed operation distance and unified background. The dataset is used to detect the efficiency of the neural network in a stable environment.

Table 1. Overview of ECAL-10 dataset

Dataset	Training set	Testing set	Number of 2D box	Bit	Size	Background
ECALEASL-10-I	800	200	3000+	24	640 × 400	Complex
ECALEASL-10-II	900	267	6800+	24	640 × 400	Simple

The average object numbers in images of ECAL-10-II is more than that of ECAL-10-I, while the background in ECAL-10-II is clearer than that in ECAL-10-I.

In order to keep the consistency of the input image size of the network, the original images have been uniformly cropped to the size of 640 × 400. The dataset's information is summarized in Table 1.

3.2 Establishment of Dataset

Once the samples have been obtained, the collected image data are precisely annotated with 2D labeling method. Due to the demand of instance segmentation, electronics need to be labeled on different layers.

After the annotation, the image file will be exported. The output .json files are packaged to include the original image, mask image, layer information file and the annotation result image.

The Open Computer Vision library in Matlab and C++ was used for processing of the masks, and the images of mask were converted into 8-bit depth map for subsequent training and testing.

We also use data augmentation to improve the generalization ability and robustness of the network. The specific operation of data augmentation is to apply specular reflection, up-down inversion and specular reflection plus down-down inversion to the images of all training sets.

4 Framework

4.1 Overview

Currently, there are three major approaches to deal with the problem of instance segmentation, instance-first method, segmentation-first method and synchronous method.

Compare of the three approaches, the first has the highest segmentation accuracy. Therefore, we choose the first to build the neural network. In order to improve the speed, we will compare the networks of different sizes to ensure the accuracy and improve the speed as much as possible.

The structure of the network is shown in Fig. 1.

4.2 Backbone

The main function of backbone network is to extract multilevel electronics features and build feature pyramid to generate regions of interest for subsequent region proposal networks.

To avoid the problem of gradient explosion or disappearance, we choose a residual network [14,15] as backbone. Compared with the ordinary network, the residual network adds a skip connection structure between layers, so that the input of each layer can be directly mapped to the network of the next layer through an identity mapping. By using the skip connection, the neural network can highlight the tiny change and perform better than the network without it. Thus, the features of electronics can be better extracted and high-quality electronics feature maps can be constructed. We should realize that in the scene of automatic assembly line, it is essential to get high precision result of object detection due to the high precision requirements in industrial production.

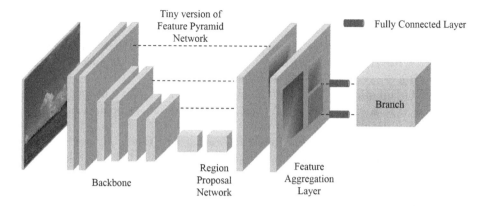

Fig. 1. Overview of the network: The network is a typical two-stage structure. In the first stage, the network outputs some possible area of electronics, then in the second stage, the network gives a confidence map for every proposal and predicts classes, bounding boxes and masks for the high score object.

4.3   Tiny Version of Feature Pyramid Network

In the neural network, the image will be continuously convoluted and pooled [12], so that the image dimension will be reduced, and some small objects mapped to the feature image will be reduced to pixels, which will be unable to be captured by the following network. Therefore, it is necessary to use various scales of images for training and testing.

Traditional image processing methods scale the image into multiple different proportions, and extract the feature graph of each proportion image separately for prediction. These methods can get better prediction results, but have a high cost in time and space. In the convolution neural network, there exist multilevel feature graphs, and the scales of feature graphs of different layers are different. The feature pyramid network [4] is based on this objective fact.

However, the traditional feature pyramid network still has a considerable number of network parameters when outputting the feature maps on the side. In order to accelerate training, we reduce the number of feature channels output in each stage by using 1×1 convolution on the basis of guaranteeing the generated feature quality. At the same time, due to the particularity of the pipeline scene, we have some prior knowledge of the detecting objects, so the number of pyramid layers can be reduced to a minimum level that the smallest electronics can be detected as before. Specifically, we detach the last down sampling procedure and keep only four stages of feature maps. The details can be seen in Fig. 2. We call this fined feature pyramid network as tiny version one. We should clarify that the tiny here means less parameters and less channels.

By constructing this network, the semantic information of high-level features is combined with the high resolution of low-level features to improve the feature expression ability of the network while the training and testing speed are guaranteed. In the scene of automatic assembly line, high quality of detection and identification of electronics targets can be better realized.

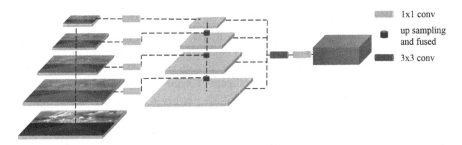

Fig. 2. The structure of the tiny version of Feature Pyramid Network: We remove the pooling operation of the feature 5 in the original feature pyramid network and add 1 × 1 convolution to all feature maps which can decrease the channels of the features, thus decreasing the parameters of the network.

4.4 Region Proposal Network

A region proposal network is a class-independent region candidate generation network. In the multi-scale feature graph generated by feature pyramid network, a 3 × 3 convolution is designed as a sliding window in each layer of feature graph and two 1 × 1 convolution are used for binary classification and bounding box regression respectively. Binary classification (foreground and background) is defined based on the anchor box. Anchor points are defined as regions with different proportional pixels on feature maps of different scales, and there are multiple aspect ratios on each anchor point.

After the initial region candidate boxes generated, we sorts the confidence score of each candidate region in the classification network and only keeps the boxes with high score.

4.5 Feature Aggregation Layer

The role of the feature aggregation layer is to generate fixed size feature map for subsequent training.

Specifically, the feature aggregation layer consists of two steps. Firstly, we directly transform the coordinates of proposals from original graph to feature map. Secondly, the feature map will be divided into small regions of fixed size. Bi-linear interpolation is performed at the center point of each region, and its result represents the value of this small region.

After traversing all the region candidate boxes, we will obtain a lot of fixed size feature maps, which will be served as the input of the next layer.

4.6 Classification, Detection and Segmentation Branch

The branch is composed of several small fully connected layers, and its main function is to realize electronics classification, detection and instance segmentation for input convolution feature graph.

Specifically, we use softmax function to generate a probability map after calculation of each fixed sized feature map in the fully connected layers. We use this probability map to determine which class the electronics component belongs to. We should notice that this judgement is different from that in region proposal network because this branch predict a certain class of the object, not just the foreground and background. Then we also apply a bounding box regression method to get an exact result of the box location.

Finally, a parallel fully connected layer is added after the fixed size feature map for the target mask generation. Each candidate region is segmented pixel by pixel by the network branch to generate k-dimensional segmentation results, and the prediction class is finally selected as the final segmentation.

4.7   Loss Function

The first part of the loss function is the loss of the region proposal network, and the second part is the loss of the whole network.

The loss function of the region candidate network is as follows:

$$L_{rpn} = \frac{1}{N_{cls}} \sum_i L_{cls}(p_i, p_i^*) + \lambda \frac{1}{N_{reg}} \sum_i p_i^* L_{reg}(t_i, t_i^*) \tag{1}$$

where p_i is the probability that the anchor is the target, p_i^* is the ground truth probability, $t_i = \{t_x, t_y, t_w, t_h\}$ represents the coordinates parameters of the predicted bounding box, is the coordinates of the ground truth.

L_{cls} represents the category prediction loss:

$$L_{cls}(p_i, p_i^*) = -log[p_i^* p_i + (1 - p_i^*)(1 - p_i)] \tag{2}$$

L_{box} represents the bounding box regression loss:

$$L_{reg}(t_i, t_i^*) = smooth_{L1}(t_i - t_i^*) \tag{3}$$

$$smooth_{L1}(x) = \begin{cases} 0.5x^2 & f|x| < 1 \\ |x| - 0.5 & otherwise \end{cases} \tag{4}$$

The overall loss function of the network is as follows:

$$L = L_{cls} + L_{reg} + L_{mask} \tag{5}$$

L_{mask} represents the mask predicted loss:

$$L_{mask} = \frac{1}{N} \sum_i [y ln(p_i) + (1 - y) ln(1 - p_i)] \tag{6}$$

where y is the truth label, p_i is the probability of pixels.

Each time the loss is calculated, only the mask loss with the highest classification probability is considered.

5   Details of Training and Testing

5.1   Configuration and Training

The network training environment is Ubuntu 16.04.3.

Before training, we used the migration learning method and the pre-trained weight on the COCO dataset [5] as initial parameters. In the training stage, the region proposal network is trained separately first, and then the whole network is trained.

5.2   Metric

We first give some basic concepts of measurement.

Intersection-over-Union (IoU) is used in target detection. It is the overlapping rate of the generated candidate box and the original mark box, namely the ratio of their intersection and union. When they overlap completely, the ratio is 1. We calculate the mean IoU of all the detected objects and use it to decide the quality of the mask the network produces.

After selecting a suitable threshold, then for a certain class of electronics c, if the intersection ratio between the detection result and the real result is larger than the threshold, we judge the detection result as True Positive. The detection accuracy (P) of the class c electronics in the ith picture can be calculated. Then the average accuracy (AP) of such electronics on K pictures can also be calculated. Finally, a metric is used to uniformly measure the performance of the entire model, and the average value of all classes' AP is defined as the mean average precision (mAP).

5.3   Testing Results and Analysis

ECAL-10-I is a basic version of the dataset, and we only focus on the mAP metric, the results of which have been listed in Table 2. There is a large noise in the samples. The test results show that the network can still achieve more than 90% detection and recognition accuracy when the picture elements are complex and the electronics are of different sizes, indicating that the network has strong robustness for the learning of samples and can still play a role under unstable conditions. For a specific pipeline production environment, the detection, recognition and segmentation tasks of each specific target are programmed separately, which is inefficient and does not have the conditions for wide promotion. Compared with traditional methods, the deep neural network method has stronger ductility and adaptability, and can recognize and segment objects in one framework.

ECAL-10-II is a simulated version of the real scene. The sample background is uniform and the object size of the same category has no significant difference. The test results (up to 99.4%) in Table 3 show that the network has a very high detection and segmentation accuracy on the electronics under the simulated pipeline background. The extremely high values (0.99+) of mIoU indicates that the masks produced by the mask branch are all in high quality. It is obvious that to reduce the parameters by applying the tiny version of feature pyramid network will not heavily decrease the performance of the network. This indicates that the neural network method has the potential to meet the accuracy requirements of industrial production. The test results shown in Appendix indicate that the network can correctly identify and segment the dense objects that are crowded and occluded.

Multi-objects detection is a difficult task for traditional methods, not to say the instance segmentation. They require a lot of prior designed features and designed templates to match the objects in the sample, so we only gives a ceiling of the traditional method and obviously it is far behind the neural network based method.

At last, we should point out that under the conditions of industrial production, it is feasible to obtain a large amount of data for training, which means it is feasible to improve the test performance of the network with more data. Consequently, the results presented in this paper are still far from reaching their upper limits, and the main value of the results is to find out whether the proposal based neural network can substitute the traditional method in automatic assembly line.

Table 2. The experiment results of ECAL-10-I

Backbone+Features+Batch size	mAP
Resnet50+FPN+8	0.9004
Resnet50+FPN+16	0.9105
Resnet50+TFPN+16	0.9088

Table 3. The experiment results of ECAL-10-II

Backbone+Features+Batch size	mIoU	mAP
Resnet50+FPN+8	0.99+	0.9940
Resnet50+FPN+16	0.99+	0.9956
Resnet50+TFPN+16	0.99+	0.9952
Resnet101+FPN+8	0.99+	0.9952
Resnet101+FPN+16	0.99+	0.9965
Resnet101+TFPN+16	0.99+	0.9960
Traditional method (HOG/SIFT)	<0.8000	<0.8000

In the simulation condition, the method based on deep neural network meets the two important standards of industrial production, stability and high precision. In the application scenario of automatic detection and segmentation of electronics in the assembly line, it is feasible to use the method based on deep neural network to replace the traditional method of robotic programming.

6   Conclusions

This paper only tested the effectiveness of the network on the dataset of two simulated scenes. Further, it is necessary to establish a large scale of ECAL for more classes of electronics. The electronics data will be collected from the assembly line, and used to train the network.

In practice, the robot arm not only needs to detect and segment the target electronics, but also determines the grasping center of the electronics. In the future work, we will add a layer after the mask branch structure of the network to locate and mark the grabbing center of electronics.

Acknowledgement. This work was supported in part by the National Key R&D Program of China (2018YFB1308000), in part by the National Natural Science Foundation of China (61772508 and U1713213); in part by Shenzhen Technology Project (JCYJ201704 13152535587, JCYJ20170307164023599, and JSGG20170823091924128); in part by CAS Key Technology Talent Program, Guangdong Technology Program (2016 B010108010, 2016B010125003, and 2017B010110007); and in part by Shenzhen Engineering Laboratory for 3D Content Generating Technologies ([2017] 476).

Appendix

In this part, we will show some testing results.

In the last two rows of images, we choose the test samples with complex object distribution, which can better illustrate the effectiveness of the neural network in this task. We should notice that even though the objects are crowded and some are occluded by another, the neural network can still detect and segment them with high accuracy (Fig. 3).

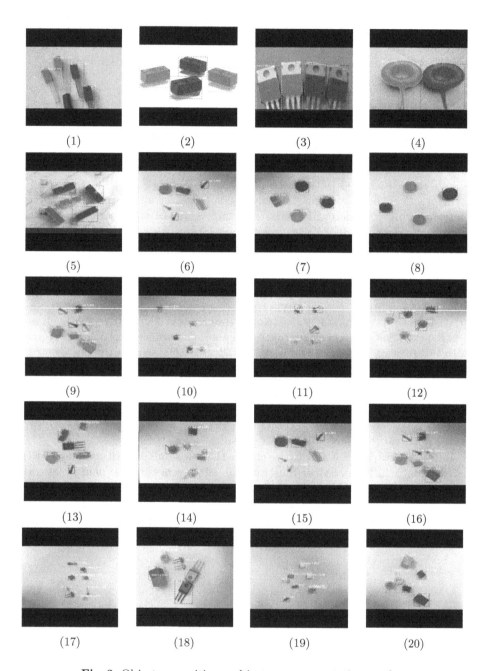

Fig. 3. Object recognition and instance segmentation results

References

1. Long, J., Shelhamer, E., Darrell, T.: Fully convolutional networks for semantic segmentation. IEEE Trans. Pattern Anal. Mach. Intell. **39**(4), 640–651 (2014)
2. Ren, S., He, K., Girshick, R., et al.: Faster R-CNN: towards real-time object detection with region proposal networks. IEEE Trans. Pattern Anal. Mach. Intell. **39**(6), 1137–1149 (2015)
3. He, K., Gkioxari, G., Dollár, P., Girshick, R.: Mask R-CNN. In: 2017 IEEE International Conference on Computer Vision (ICCV), Venice, pp. 2980–2988 (2017)
4. Lin, T.Y., Dollár, P., Girshick, R., et al.: Feature pyramid networks for object detection. In: IEEE Conference on Computer Vision and Pattern Recognition (CVPR), Honolulu, HI, pp. 936–944 (2017)
5. Lin, T.-Y., et al.: Microsoft COCO: common objects in context. In: Fleet, D., Pajdla, T., Schiele, B., Tuytelaars, T. (eds.) ECCV 2014. LNCS, vol. 8693, pp. 740–755. Springer, Cham (2014). https://doi.org/10.1007/978-3-319-10602-1_48
6. Arnab, A., Torr, P.H.S.: Pixelwise instance segmentation with a dynamically instantiated network. In: 2017 IEEE Conference on Computer Vision and Pattern Recognition (CVPR), Honolulu, HI, pp. 879–888 (2017)
7. Bai, M, Urtasun, R.: Deep watershed transform for instance segmentation. In: IEEE Conference on Computer Vision and Pattern Recognition (CVPR), pp. 2858–2866 (2017)
8. Cordts, M., Omran, M., Ramos, S., et al.: The cityscapes dataset for semantic urban scene understanding. In: 2016 IEEE Conference on Computer Vision and Pattern Recognition (CVPR), Las Vegas, NV, pp. 3213–3223 (2016)
9. Gidaris, S., Komodakis, N.: Object detection via a multi-region and semantic segmentation-aware CNN model. In: IEEE International Conference on Computer Vision (ICCV), pp. 1134–1142 (2015)
10. Girshick, R., Donahue, J., Darrelland, T., et al.: Rich feature hierarchies for object detection and semantic segmentation. In: IEEE Conference on Computer Vision and Pattern Recognition (CVPR). IEEE (2014)
11. Uijlings, J.R.R., van de Sand, K.E.A., et al.: Selective search for object recognition. Int. J. Comput. Vis. **104**(2), 154–171 (2013)
12. He, K., Zhang, X., Ren, S., et al.: Spatial pyramid pooling in deep convolutional networks for visual recognition. IEEE Trans. Pattern Anal. Mach. Intell. **37**(9), 1904–1916 (2015)
13. Krizhevsky, A., Sutskever, I., Hinton, G.: ImageNet classification with deep convolutional neural networks. In: Advances in Neural Information Processing Systems, vol. 25(2) (2012)
14. He, K., Zhang, X., Ren, S., et al.: Deep residual learning for image recognition. In: Proceedings of the IEEE conference on Computer Vision and Pattern Recognition, pp. 770–778 (2016)
15. Szegedy, C., Ioffe, S., Vanhoucke, V.: Inception-v4, inception-ResNet and the impact of residual connections on learning (2016)
16. Kittler, J.: On the accuracy of the Sobel edge detector. Image Vis. Comput. **1**(1), 37–42 (1983)
17. Canny, J.: A computational approach to edge detection. IEEE Trans. Pattern Anal. Mach. Intell. **8**(6), 679–698 (1986)
18. Redmon, J., Farhadi, A.: YOLO9000: better, faster, stronger. In: IEEE Conference on Computer Vision and Pattern Recognition (CVPR), pp. 6517–6525 (2017)

19. Lowe, D.G.: Distinctive image features from scale-invariant keypoints. Int. J. Comput. Vis. **60**(2), 91–110 (2004)
20. Dalal, N., Triggs, B.: Histograms of oriented gradients for human detection. In: 2005 IEEE Computer Society Conference on Computer Vision and Pattern Recognition (CVPR 2005), San Diego, CA, USA, vol. 1, pp. 886–893 (2005)
21. Sermanet, P., Eigen, D., Zhang, X., et al.: OverFeat: integrated recognition, localization and detection using convolutional networks. In: The International Conference on Learning Representations (ICLR) (2014)
22. Girshick, R.: Fast R-CNN. In: 2015 IEEE International Conference on Computer Vision (ICCV), Santiago, pp. 1440–1448 (2015)
23. Dai, J., He, K., Li, Y., Ren, S., Sun, J.: Instance-sensitive fully convolutional networks. In: Leibe, B., Matas, J., Sebe, N., Welling, M. (eds.) ECCV 2016. LNCS, vol. 9910, pp. 534–549. Springer, Cham (2016). https://doi.org/10.1007/978-3-319-46466-4_32

Visual-Based Crack Detection and Skeleton Extraction of Cement Surface

Du Jiang[1(⊠)], Gongfa Li[1,2,3], Ying Sun[4], Jianyi Kong[1], Bo Tao[2],
Dalin Zhou[5], Disi Chen[5], and Zhaojie Ju[5]

[1] Key Laboratory of Metallurgical Equipment and Control Technology, Ministry
of Education, Wuhan University of Science and Technology,
Wuhan 430081, China
1439078161@qq.com, ligongfa@wust.edu.cn,
15697188659@wo.com.cn
[2] Institute of Precision Manufacturing,
Wuhan University of Science and Technology, Wuhan 430081, China
taoboq@wust.edu.cn
[3] Research Center for Biomimetic Robot and Intelligent Measurement
and Control, Wuhan University of Science and Technology,
Wuhan 430081, China
[4] Hubei Key Laboratory of Mechanical Transmission and Manufacturing
Engineering, Wuhan University of Science and Technology,
Wuhan 430081, China
sunying65@wust.edu.cn
[5] School of Computing, University of Portsmouth, Portsmouth PO1 3HE, UK
{Dalin.zhou, zhaojie.ju}@port.ac.uk,
chendisi@foxmail.com

Abstract. In order to realize the design of vision-based cement crack repair robot, it is necessary to accurately recognize and extract features of cracks. In this paper, three kinds of typical crack are selected to study, which are fine crack, reticulated crack and dark crack. Firstly, image filtering and image enhancement are used to pre-process the collected image to reduce the influence of noise on detection and enhance the contrast between image background and crack area. Then, the multi-scale morphological operation is applied to extract the fracture edge features effectively. The experimental results show that the proposed edge regions are obviously different from the background regions. Furthermore, by calculating and selecting the area of the largest connected area, the noise can be eliminated to the greatest extent. Finally, the traditional skeleton extraction algorithm is improved to eliminate the number of burrs in the traditional skeleton algorithm. By remapping the cracks images to color images, it can be found that the crack recognition and skeleton extraction meet the requirements, which can provide corresponding technical support for the navigation design of the crack repair robot.

Keywords: Crack recognition · Multi-scale morphology · Skeletonization

© Springer Nature Switzerland AG 2019
H. Yu et al. (Eds.): ICIRA 2019, LNAI 11744, pp. 541–552, 2019.
https://doi.org/10.1007/978-3-030-27541-9_44

1 Introduction

With the national investment in infrastructure, China's urban underground pipeline network has been greatly developed and upgraded. With the increasing complexity of urban underground space and pavement construction, the maintenance and management of underground pipeline network has become more and more important. At present, the underground pipelines are mainly maintained through manual work when there is some problems such as burst, leak and so on, which greatly the increase the upkeep. Generally, if the sewage pipeline can be treated in time before the problem is complicated, it can effectively reduce the loss. Because of the special environment of underground sewage pipeline, it is difficult to detect and repair it in time. With the development of robotics technology, it brings new methods and solutions to solve this problem. Currently, there are mature products on the market to capture video of the environment of pipeline, which saves the cost of manpower and equipment needed for pipeline detection, however, their level of automation needs to be further replaced. With the development of computer hardware and digital image processing technology, vision-based target location and detection technology have made great progress. Because of its accurate recognition and location, it provides a safe and efficient navigation means for the pipeline crack detection and repair robot based on digital image.

Visually, the enhancement and location of crack image on cement surface belongs to linear target detection while it has some unique characteristics, such as low contrast, intermittent, bifurcation and background noise. There are many research results on crack detection, such as threshold segmentation, edge detection, wavelet transform and so on [1]. Yoo et al. [2] used neural network to detect cracks, which improved the accuracy of crack detection. Shu et al. [3] provided an improved contour algorithm for crack detection. Petrik et al. [4] applied fuzzy idea to recognize crack. However, due to the poor shooting environment in the pipeline, the quality of the collected images will be poor, leading to the inability of the automatic detection algorithm. Therefore, it is necessary to add some image pre-processing before crack recognition to improve the quality of the images and reduce the interference of background noise. Image pre-processing is generally used as a pre-processing based on visual recognition whose main purpose is to highlight the features of the detected object and the region of interest, eliminate and reduce the interference of noise, such as image enhancement, image de-noising and edge feature extraction. Generally, the crack image will be disturbed by the environment. At the same time, because of the uncertainty of the crack and the uncertainty of the environment, it is difficult for the collected image to meet the requirements of detection. As a result, it is often necessary to add image preprocessing before realizing vision-based target recognition and detection.

The main purpose of our research is to study the crack detection on cement surface. Based on this, the information characteristics of crack skeleton need to be extracted, to provide the corresponding reference for the trajectory generation of automatic repair robot. In this paper, multi-scale morphological calculation and skeleton algorithm are mainly used to identify and extract the skeleton of multiple cracks. The proposed method further improves the accuracy of crack detection, and the experimental results show that it is helpful to the design of pipeline crack repair robot. Three typical fracture images are selected for study, as shown in Fig. 1.

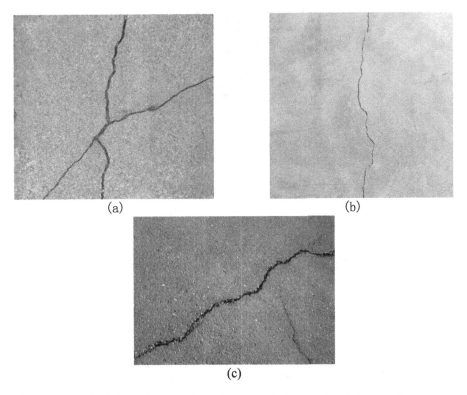

(a)

(b)

(c)

Fig. 1. Original image. (a): mesh crack, (b): fine crack, (c) dark crack

2 Image Preprocessing

2.1 Image Filtering

In order to improve the image quality and increase the accuracy of target detection and judgment, it is necessary to filter and de-noise the image by means of image processing [5]. In which, the commonly used filtering methods are Gauss filtering, mean filtering and median filtering. Because crack images often contain a large amount of particle noise, the median filtering method is used [6]. Median filtering is a kind of non-linear filtering method, which is simple and efficient. It can effectively remove impulse noise and protect edge information. Therefore, this paper uses median filter and square template to eliminate most of the noise in the original image and highlight the information of crack edge, which is conducive to the subsequent extraction of crack features. The effect of middle finger filtering is displayed on Fig. 2.

Fig. 2. Median filtering effect

2.2   Image Enhancement

Pipeline image acquisition environment is generally complex, and it is easy to affect the quality of the image. The collected image may have a whole dark or low contrast image just like Fig. 3(c), which will lead to difficulties in subsequent crack detection and feature extraction so it is necessary to use image enhancement technology to ameliorate the corresponding situation to a certain extent [7, 8].

Histogram, as a statistical tool, can display the specific information of contrast to a certain extent. The gray histogram of the image shows the frequency of different gray levels in the gray level type of the image. Histogram equalization mainly uses gray histogram to adjust the image contrast, so as to enhance the image. With transformation, the histogram of the original image is transformed from a small gray scale to a uniform distribution in a larger gray scale, so as to enhance the overall contrast of the image.

Crack image area usually belongs to the gray-scale region with darker color, and the background area is brighter. However, due to the influence of environment, it is difficult to form obvious differences between the background area and the fracture area. Thus, histogram equalization can effectively enhance the contrast of images and highlight the difference between background and cracks. As can be seen from Fig. 3, the fracture area is obviously enhanced.

Fig. 3. Image enhancement effect

3   Extraction of Cement Crack Contour Based on Multi-scale Morphology

3.1   Principles of Multiscale Morphology

Mathematical morphological image processing is based on set theory [9, 10]. Morphological transformation of images is essentially a set-oriented processing process. Morphological operations can be used to represent the shape of objects, whose shape determines the shape information of objects matched by it. Therefore, the morphological operation of the image is to calculate the structural elements in the image and get the processing result matrix. The basic morphological operations of mathematical morphological image processing are corrosion and expansion. Their combination can be called opening and closing operations. Its basic principles are as follows:

Expand:

$$A \oplus B = \max_{(i,j)}[A(x-i,y-j)+B(i,j)] \tag{1}$$

Corrosion:

$$A \ominus B = \min_{(i,j)}[A(x+i,y+j)-B(i,j)] \tag{2}$$

Two combinations of expansion and corrosion operations can be obtained:
Opening operation:

$$A \circ B = (A \ominus B) \oplus B \tag{3}$$

Closing operation:

$$A \bullet B = (A \oplus B) \ominus B \tag{4}$$

In the above formulas, $A(x,y)$ represents the input image, and $B(x,y)$ represents structural elements. $\ominus$ and $\oplus$ represent Corrosion operation and expansion operation in morphology respectively.

Multiscale morphology is achieved by selecting the type and scale of structural elements, such as processing different images or dealing with different structural elements, which requires the selection of appropriate scale. Generally, with the increase of the scale of structural elements, the amount of computation will increase correspondingly, and even the geometric properties of images will be affected correspondingly, which will affect the final processing results. Selecting appropriate small-scale structural elements can improve the operation efficiency to a certain extent. Therefore, the edge detection of crack image is carried out by structural elements of different scales, and then the detected edge information is integrated by weighted fusion, so as to reduce the influence of noise in the image.

According to the concepts of mathematical morphology, the definition of multi-scale iterative filters is as follows:

$$\psi(A) = (A \circ B_1 \bullet B_2) \bullet B_2 \circ B_2 \tag{5}$$

Multiscale structural elements are defined as:

$$nB = B \oplus B \oplus \cdots \oplus B \tag{6}$$

Among them, n is a scale parameter.
Multi-scale edge detection algorithm:

$$G_i^n = (A \circ nB_i) \oplus nB_i - (A \bullet nB_i) \ominus nB_i \tag{7}$$

Multi-scale edge fusion algorithm:

$$GA^n = \sum_{i=1}^{K} u_i G_i^n \tag{8}$$

In which, u_i is weighting coefficients for fusion of multi-scale edge detection images.

The set of positions where the values around the pixels change sharply is generally referred to as the image edge, which is one of the basic features of the image. Image edges generally exist between objects, background and regions, so edge extraction is one of the key steps in image segmentation. The image edges include the following kinds: step edge and roof edge. The gray value of the pixels around the step edge is obviously different, showing a step shape; the pixel value around the roof edge will have a peak value, showing the roof style.

3.2   Result Analysis and Processing

Through multi-scale edge extraction of three kinds of images, the results are as follows, shown on the Fig. 4. By the way, the crack features of three types of crack images are effectively extracted, and the noise is effectively smoothed. From the analysis of the generated three-dimensional pseudo-color image (Fig. 5), it can be found that there are obvious differences between the crack edge area and the background area, which provides a sufficient basis for the subsequent crack skeleton extraction.

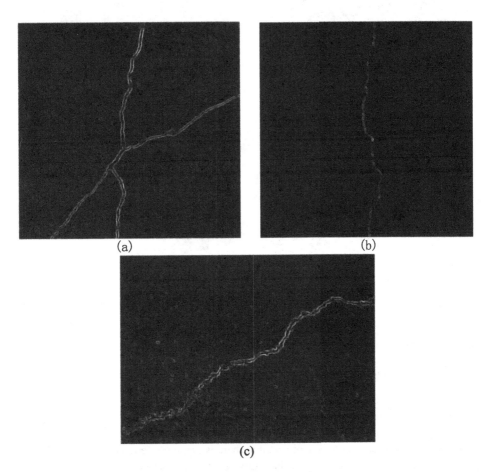

(a)   (b)

(c)

Fig. 4. Edge contour extraction.

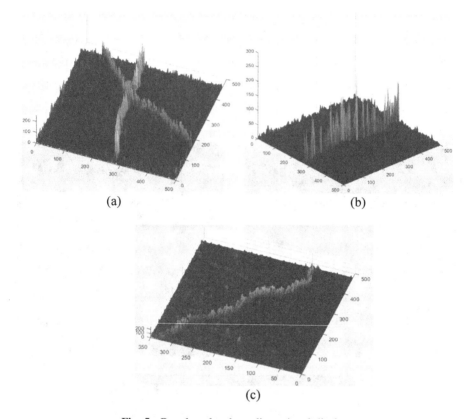

(a)   (b)

(c)

Fig. 5. Pseudo-color three-dimensional display.

4 Skeleton Extraction of Cement Cracks

4.1 Adaptive Threshold Image Binarization

The binarization of an image usually uses a threshold to segment the target area from the background. The pixels within the threshold are marked as 1, while the others belonging to the background are marked as 0. Through the observation of the results of multi-scale edge extraction, we can find that there is a great difference in the gray value between the fracture target and the background area. Therefore, in order to segment fracture target and background to a greater extent, it is necessary to select appropriate threshold. There are two main methods for calculating thresholds: global thresholds and adaptive thresholds.

(1) Global threshold: The threshold is determined based on the histogram or gray spatial distribution of the image.
(2) Adaptive threshold: Based on the gray level change of the image pixel itself and its domain, threshold segmentation is carried out, and then the binary segmentation of gray image is realized.

The quality of crack image will change because of the change of shooting environment. Therefore, it is necessary to select a suitable threshold calculation method to achieve effective comparison between the edge area of crack and the background. This paper chooses an adaptive threshold calculation method. Figure 6 shows the binarization result of mesh crack with adaptive threshold.

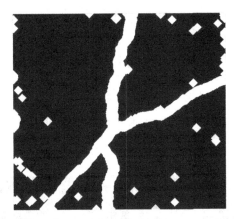

Fig. 6. The effect of adaptive image binarization

4.2 Maximally Connected Region Segmentation

After binary segmentation, it can be found that there are still many noise points in the image. In order to further eliminate the noise in the background and highlight the crack area, it is necessary to expand the edge of the crack to form a larger connected area. Then, the connected area with the largest area is selected to eliminate the small noise points effectively (Fig. 7).

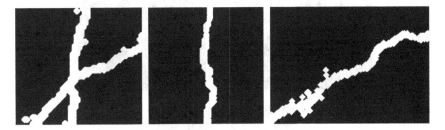

Fig. 7. The effect of maximally connected region segmentation

4.3 Skeleton Extraction

In traditional skeleton extraction algorithms, the image is refined step by step by step through iterative etching operation, and skeleton extraction is finally realized [11, 12].

But this will lead to a lot of burrs in the process of skeleton extraction, as shown in the Fig. 8. The existence of burrs interferes greatly with the trajectory generation of the robot. Therefore, it is necessary to deal with these burrs further. In this paper, a simple skeleton extraction algorithm is proposed. The skeleton extraction is realized by calculating the mean value of the crack area.

The flow chart of the algorithm is as follows:

(1) Judging the direction of cracks in the image area by row/column projection.
(2) Traversing the image with row/column benchmark to find the index value marked as 1.
(3) By averaging the index value, the image is taken as the skeleton point of the base row/column.
(4) The skeleton is formed by recording these skeleton points.

The experimental structure shows that this method can effectively remove skeleton burrs. However, there are still some shortcomings, such as the inaccurate judgment of

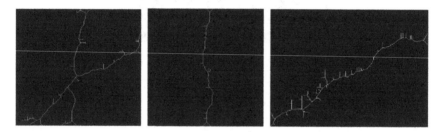

Fig. 8. Skeleton obtained by traditional skeleton algorithm.

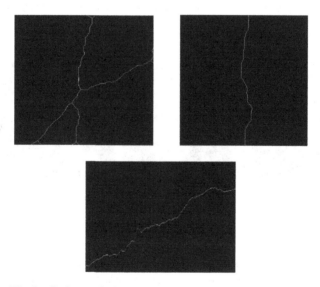

Fig. 9. Skeleton obtained by the improved skeleton algorithm.

traversal by rows and columns when extracting mesh cracks, which leads to the inaccurate average index value, especially the index value of mesh endpoints. By projecting the skeleton information of the crack onto the color image (Fig. 10), it can be found that the method adopted in this paper can basically realize the marking of the crack on the cement surface (Fig. 9).

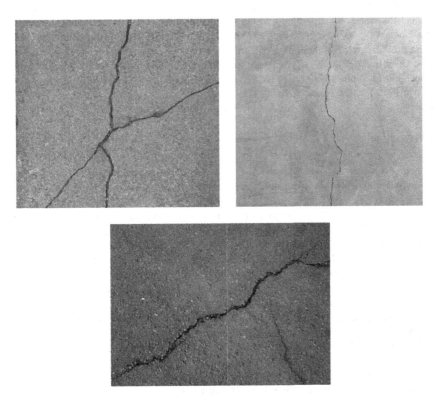

Fig. 10. Crack mark.

5 Conclusion

With the development of image processing technology and robotic technology, the requirement of robotic technology for the maintenance of underground sewage pipeline is becoming higher and higher. In this paper, visual-based detection of cement cracks is studied. The main research objects are mesh cracks, fine cracks and dark cracks. Through the comprehensive application of image processing technology, the effective extraction of fracture features is realized. The multi-scale edge feature extraction adopted in this paper can effectively realize the feature extraction of fracture edge. By calculating the area of the maximum connected area, the further de-noising of the fracture image is realized, which is especially suitable for the de-noising of the fracture image. Aiming at the problem that there are many burrs in traditional skeleton algorithm, this paper proposes a new skeleton algorithm and effectively eliminates most of the burrs, which provides corresponding technical support for the subsequent design of crack repair robot. The crack identification method adopted in this paper can basically meet the requirements, but there are still some shortcomings in the identification of reticulated cracks and skeleton extraction, which need further experimental research.

Acknowledgment. This work was supported by grants of National Natural Science Foundation of China This work was supported by grants of National Natural Science Foundation of China (Grant Nos. 51575407, 515505349, 51575338, 51575412, 61733011), the Grants of National Defense Pre-Research Foundation of Wuhan University of Science and Technology (GF201705) and the Open Fund of the Key Laboratory for Metallurgical Equipment and Control of Ministry of Education in Wuhan University of Science and Technology (2018B07) and the DREAM project of EU FP7-ICT (grant no. 611391).

References

1. Chen, F.C., Jahanshahi, M.R.: NB-CNN: deep learning-based crack detection using convolutional neural network and Naïve Bayes data fusion. IEEE Trans. Ind. Electron. **65**(5), 4392–4400 (2018)
2. Yoo, H.-S., Kim, Y.-S.: Development of a crack recognition algorithm from non-routed pavement images using artificial neural network and binary logistic regression. KSCE J. Civ. Eng. **20**(4), 1151–1162 (2016)
3. Shu, Z., Guo, Y.: Algorithm on contourlet domain in detection of road cracks for pavement images. J. Algorithms Comput. Technol. **7**(1), 15–26 (2013)
4. Petrik, M.: Climber-Inspired fuzzy logic approach to crack localization using image analysis. J. Adv. Concr. Technol. **13**(2), 103–111 (2015)
5. Jiang, D., Zheng, Z., Li, G., et al.: Gesture recognition based on binocular vision. Cluster Comput. (2018). https://doi.org/10.1007/s10586-018-1844-5
6. Li, G., Wu, H., Jiang, G., et al.: Dynamic gesture recognition in the Internet of Things. IEEE Access **7**, 23713–23724 (2019)
7. Nam, Y., Choi, D.Y., Song, B.C.: Power—constrained contrast enhancement algorithm using muhiscale retinex for OLED display. IIEEE Trans. Mage Process. **23**(8), 3308–3320 (2014)
8. Li, G., Jiang, D., Zhou, Y., et al.: Human lesion detection method based on image information and brain signal. IEEE Access **7**, 11533–11542 (2019)
9. Silverberg, J., Yin, P.: Morphology of embryonic epidermis: an empirical multiscale biophysics approach. Biophys. J. **114**(3), 205a (2018)
10. Li, H., Song, D., Liu, Y., et al.: Automatic pavement crack detection by multi-scale image fusion. IEEE Trans. Intell. Transp. Syst. **20**(6), 2025–2036 (2018)
11. Fei, Y., Wang, K.C.P., Zhang, A., et al.: Pixel-level cracking detection on 3D Asphalt pavement images through deep-learning-based CrackNet-V. IEEE Trans. Intell. Transp. Syst. **PP**(99), 1–12 (2019)
12. Jiang, D., Li, G., Sun, Y., et al.: Gesture recognition based on skeletonization algorithm and CNN with ASL database. Multimedia Tools Appl. (2018). https://doi.org/10.1007/s11042-018-6748-0

Visual Servoing Control Based on Reconstructed 3D Features

Degang Xu[1(✉)], Lei Zhou[1], Yifan Lei[1], and Tiantian Shen[2]

[1] School of Automation, Central South University,
Changsha 410083, People's Republic of China
`dgxu@csu.edu.cn`
[2] Department of Electronic Information Engineering, College of Polytechnic,
Hunan Normal University, Changsha 410082, People's Republic of China
`tiantianshen@gmail.com`

Abstract. Image-based visual servoing (IBVS) is an automatic control technique which uses image information to control the camera moving to a desired location. To solve the problems of unsmooth trajectories and slow convergence rate caused by classical IBVS during the servo process, a visual servoing method based on reconstructed three-dimensional features is proposed. First, the camera pose was estimated, to obtain the depth information of the target by solving the Perspective-Four-Point (P4P) problem. Then, the new three-dimensional features for visual servoing is constructed. Finally, the visual servoing model is established based on classical IBVS control structure in terms of cuboid. Simulation results show that the proposes method has higher convergence speed and smoother convergence trajectories compared with the classical IBVS method.

Keywords: Visual servoing · IBVS · Three-dimensional features · Perspective-Four-Point problem · Pose estimation

1 Introduction

Visual servoing is an automatic control technique which uses visual information to control the motion of a robot and has been attracting the attention of researchers from the robotics and automation society for decades [1]. Classical visual servoing include image-based visual servoing (IBVS) and position-based visual servoing (PBVS) [2]. For a static target, The desired position of the eye-in-hand system is fixed, both IBVS and PBVS can achieve better control effects [3]. IBVS uses image features as a control input, the method is robust to image noise and camera calibration errors. PBVS estimates the pose information of the camera from the image information as a control input, the method can obtain a better servo path and is exceedingly sensitive to image noise.

In order to better satisfy constraints that arise in visual servoing, there appeared many advance approaches: Malis et al. [4] proposed a 2 1/2-D visual

© Springer Nature Switzerland AG 2019
H. Yu et al. (Eds.): ICIRA 2019, LNAI 11744, pp. 553–564, 2019.
https://doi.org/10.1007/978-3-030-27541-9_45

servoing method to combine the advantage of the IBVS and PBVS. Chaumette [5–7] proposed an image Jacobian matrix derivation method based on Green's theorem is proposed to apply image moments to visual servo control. Liu et al. [8] presented an adaptive visual servoing method based on the depth-independent image Jacobian matrix using common image features, in which the depths are estimated online for the features. Xu et al. [9] used point, line and contour area as visual features, and combines the least squares depth estimation to realize the position and posture control of the robot. Shen et al. [10–13] proposed new moment based features from elliptical projections of circles or spheres and solve for constraints like persistent visibility of circles or spheres, occlusion avoidance among spheres and etc. The above methods all uses two-dimensional image informations to for visual servoing. Compared with the two-dimensional image, the three-dimensional features can better represent the relative pose relationship between the target and the robot, and has better servo tracking performance [14]. Therefore, this paper combines camera pose estimation to reconstruct 3D information based on the premise of known the target model, and establish the mapping relationship between the three-dimensional features and the camera motion speed, which is achieving a visual servoing control based on the three-dimensional geometric features in terms of cuboid. The effectiveness of the method is demonstrated through some simulation examples.

The paper is organized as follows. Section 2 introduces the notation and background. Section 3 proposes new feature errors are applied to visual servoing for achieving convergence to the desired location. Lastly, Sect. 4 concludes with some final remarks.

2   Preliminaries

2.1   Notations

Let $\mathbf{K}$ denote the camera's intrinsic parameters, $\mathcal{R}$ denote the real number set, $\mathbf{e}_n$ the n-th column of $n \times n$ identity matrix, $\mathbf{0}_n$ the $n \times 1$ null vector, $[\mathbf{v}]_\times$ the skew-symmetric matrix of $\mathbf{v} \in \mathcal{R}^3$, f the approximated camera focal length, $\zeta_x \times \zeta_y$ the image size, $\mathbf{R} \in \mathcal{R}^{3\times3}$ the camera rotation matrix and $\mathbf{t} = [x, y, z]^\top$ the camera translation. The rotation matrix of the camera is represented by cayley notation that $\mathbf{R} = e^{[\mathbf{r}]_\times}$ with $\mathbf{r} = [r_1, r_2, r_3]^\top$ [15].

2.2   Camera Pose Estimation

The Perspective-n-Point (PnP) problem is originated from camera's frame [16]. Pose estimation is determine the position and orientation of the camera with relatived to a scene object from n correspondent points. Assuming that the position of four 3D points P_i in the workspace is known and the spatial coordinate of these points in the image space are (u_i, v_i), the imaging point coordinate of these points in the normalized plane of the camera are (x_{1c_i}, y_{1c_i}). Note that the coordinates of these 3D points in the reference coordinate are (x_i, y_i, z_i) and the coordinate of these points in the camera's frame are (x_{ci}, y_{ci}, z_{ci}). These 3D points have the relation between the camera's frame and the reference coordinate:

$$\begin{cases} x_{ci} = n_x x_i + o_x y_i + a_x z_i + p_x \\ y_{ci} = n_y x_i + o_y y_i + a_y z_i + p_y \\ z_{ci} = n_z x_i + o_z y_i + a_z z_i + p_z \end{cases} \tag{1}$$

where $\mathbf{M}_c$ is external parameters of the camera relative to the reference coordinate. $\mathbf{n} = [n_x, n_y, n_z]^\top$ is the direction vector of $\mathbf{M}_c$ on the X-axis, $\mathbf{o} = [o_x, o_y, o_z]^\top$ is the direction vector of $\mathbf{M}_c$ on the Y-axis, $\mathbf{a} = [a_x, a_y, a_z]^\top$ is the direction vector of $\mathbf{M}_c$ on the Z-axis, $\mathbf{p} = [p_x, p_y, p_z]^\top$ is the position vector of $\mathbf{M}_c$.

There is the following relation between the normalized image plane and the camera's frame [17]:

$$\begin{bmatrix} u_i \\ v_i \end{bmatrix} = \mathbf{K} \begin{bmatrix} x_{1c_i} \\ y_{1c_i} \\ 1 \end{bmatrix} = \mathbf{K} \begin{bmatrix} x_{c_i}/z_{c_i} \\ y_{c_i}/z_{c_i} \\ 1 \end{bmatrix} \tag{2}$$

Substituting the above formula into (1):

$$\begin{cases} x_i n_x + y_i o_x - x_{1c_i} x_i n_z - x_{1c_i} y_i o_z + p_x - x_{1c_i} p_z = 0 \\ y_i n_y + y_i o_y - y_{1c_i} x_i n_z - y_{1c_i} y_i o_z + p_y - y_{1c_i} p_z = 0 \end{cases} \tag{3}$$

For the four known 3D points, four sets of equations shown above can be obtained, which can be rewritten into a simplified form:

$$\mathbf{G}_1 \mathbf{H}_1 + \mathbf{G}_2 \mathbf{H}_2 = 0 \tag{4}$$

$$\mathbf{G}_1 = \begin{bmatrix} x_1 & 0 & -x_{1c_1} x_1 \\ 0 & x_1 & -y_{1c_1} x_1 \\ \vdots & \vdots & \vdots \\ x_4 & 0 & -x_{1c_4} x_4 \\ 0 & x_4 & -y_{1c_4} x_4 \end{bmatrix} \tag{5}$$

$$\mathbf{G}_2 = \begin{bmatrix} y_1 & 0 & -x_{1c_1} y_1 & 1 & 0 & -x_{1c_1} \\ 0 & y_1 & -y_{1c_1} y_1 & 1 & 0 & -y_{1c_1} \\ \vdots & \vdots & \vdots & \vdots & \vdots & \vdots \\ y_4 & 0 & -x_{1c_4} y_4 & 1 & 0 & -x_{1c_4} \\ 0 & y_4 & -y_{1c_4} y_4 & 1 & 0 & -y_{1c_4} \end{bmatrix} \tag{6}$$

$$\begin{cases} \mathbf{H}_1 = [n_x, n_y, n_z]^\top \\ \mathbf{H}_2 = [o_x, o_y, o_z, p_x, p_y, p_z]^\top \end{cases} \tag{7}$$

where $\mathbf{H}_1$ is a unit vector and $\|\mathbf{H}_1\| = 1$, it is a constraint for solving (4). Therefore, the following index function is constructed to convert the solution problem of the (4) into an optimization problem:

$$G_R = \|\mathbf{G}_1 \mathbf{H}_1 + \mathbf{G}_2 \mathbf{H}_2\|^2 + \lambda(1 - \|\mathbf{H}_1\|^2) \tag{8}$$

The objective of the optimization problem is to ensure that the index function $\mathbf{G}_R$ is minimum for any real number λ. So we can construct the following equation:

$$
\begin{cases}
\mathbf{BH}_1 = \lambda \mathbf{H}_1 \\
\mathbf{H}_2 = -(\mathbf{G}_2{}^\top \mathbf{G}_2)^{-1}\mathbf{G}_2{}^\top \mathbf{G}_1 \mathbf{H}_1 \\
\mathbf{B} = \mathbf{G}_1{}^\top \mathbf{G}_1 - \mathbf{G}_1{}^\top \mathbf{G}_2(\mathbf{G}_2{}^\top \mathbf{G}_2)^{-1}\mathbf{G}_2{}^\top \mathbf{G}_1
\end{cases}
\tag{9}
$$

In the above formula, $\mathbf{H}_1$ is the eigenvector corresponding to the minimum eigenvalue of $\mathbf{B}$, so $\mathbf{H}_1$ and $\mathbf{H}_2$ can be solved by the (9). The external parameters of the camera relative to the reference coordinate:

$$
\mathbf{M}_c = \begin{bmatrix} \mathbf{n} \ \mathbf{o} \ \mathbf{a} \ \mathbf{p} \\ 0 \ 0 \ 0 \ 1 \end{bmatrix}
\tag{10}
$$

where $\mathbf{a} = \mathbf{n} \times \mathbf{o}$ can be obtained from the rotation matrix property. The positional relationship between the point P_i in the reference coordinate and the camera's frame:

$$
\begin{bmatrix} x_{ci} \\ y_{ci} \\ z_{ci} \\ 1 \end{bmatrix} = \mathbf{M}_c \begin{bmatrix} x_i \\ y_i \\ z_i \\ 1 \end{bmatrix}
\tag{11}
$$

Problem. By solving the PnP problem for camera pose estimation, the depth information of feature points can be calculated. Thus, it provides a basis for obtaining three-dimensional features of the target. How to combine camera pose estimation to describe the three-dimensional features of the object and how to research the visual servoing control based on three-dimensional features are our major concern.

3   Visual Servoing Control for Cuboid Object

3.1   Visual Servoing Based on Four Endpoints

We estimate camera displacement via a virtual visual servoing (VVS) method [18] that moves a virtual camera from one place to another with instant camera velocities computed from selected features:

$$
\mathbf{T} = -\lambda_1 \hat{\mathbf{L}}^+ (\mathbf{s}(t) - \mathbf{s}^*)
\tag{12}
$$

where $\mathbf{T} = [v_x, v_y, v_z, \omega_x, \omega_y, \omega_z]^\top$ describes camera velocities in translation and rotation at time t, which decrease along with the falling trend of $\|\mathbf{s}(t) - \mathbf{s}^*\|$. $\mathbf{s}(t)$ holds current feature values at time t and $\mathbf{s}^*$ the desired feature values. λ_1 is a positive gain that controls the servo progress. $\hat{\mathbf{L}}^+$ is the pseudo-inverse of the estimated image Jacobian related to the selected features. Feature construction will affect the servo performance. The feature set that achieves, in average, the least converge error will be adopted in a path-planning VS based task [11].

The coordinate of a point P_i on the normalized imaging plane is given (13) in when the camera moves [19]:

$$
\begin{bmatrix} \dot{x}_{1c_i} \\ \dot{y}_{1c_i} \end{bmatrix} = \begin{bmatrix} -1/z_{c_i} & 0 \\ 0 & -1/z_{c_i} \\ x_{1c_i}/z_{c_i} & y_{1c_i}/z_{c_i} \\ x_{1c_i}y_{1c_i} & 1+y_{1c_i}^2 \\ -(1+x_{1c_i}^2) & -x_{1c_i}y_{1c_i} \\ y_{1c_i} & -x_{1c_i} \end{bmatrix}^{\mathsf{T}} \mathbf{T} = \mathbf{L}_{P_i}\mathbf{T} \tag{13}
$$

where $\mathbf{L}_{P_i}$ is the image Jacobian matrix for the point P_i. The camera should be calibrated in advance and the calculation of x_{1c_i} and y_{1c_i} from the point's image coordinates. In addition, the point's depth z_{c_i} in the camera's frame must be estimated in order to compute the image Jacobian matrix.

Calculating the image Jacobian matrix as described above requires depth information of target. In recent years, many scholars have proposed many methods for estimating the depth value. The depth estimation methods are applied to robot visual servoing control can be roughly divided into two categories: One is the use of computer vision technology to estimate depth information from successive camera positions, the other type is online estimation using robot motion state and optical flow information. This article uses the second method, decompose the (13), we have

$$
\begin{bmatrix} \dot{x}_{1c_i} \\ \dot{y}_{1c_i} \end{bmatrix} = \begin{bmatrix} -\frac{1}{z_{c_i}}\mathbf{L}_{cv} & \mathbf{L}_{c\omega} \end{bmatrix} \mathbf{T} \tag{14}
$$

$$
\mathbf{L}_{cv} = \begin{bmatrix} -1 & 0 \\ 0 & -1 \\ x_{1c_i} & y_{1c_i} \end{bmatrix}^{\mathsf{T}} \tag{15}
$$

$$
\mathbf{L}_{c\omega} = \begin{bmatrix} x_{1c_i}y_{1c_i} & 1+y_{1c_i}^2 \\ -(1+x_{1c_i}^2) & -x_{1c_i}y_{1c_i} \\ y_{1c_i} & -x_{1c_i} \end{bmatrix}^{\mathsf{T}} \tag{16}
$$

Thus, the depth of point P_i can be estimated with its coordinate on the normalized imaging plane and the camera's motion velocity. From (14), we have

$$
\frac{1}{z_{c_i}}\mathbf{L}_{cv}\begin{bmatrix} v_x \\ v_y \\ v_z \end{bmatrix} = \begin{bmatrix} \dot{x}_{1c_i} \\ \dot{y}_{1c_i} \end{bmatrix} - \mathbf{L}_{c\omega}\begin{bmatrix} \omega_x \\ \omega_y \\ \omega_z \end{bmatrix} \tag{17}
$$

In summary, the linear equation of online depth estimation by optical flow method:

$$
\begin{cases} z_{c_i} = \dfrac{1}{2}\dfrac{x_{1c_i}v_z - v_x}{\dot{x}_{1c_i} - x_{1c_i}y_{1c_i}\omega_x + (1+x_{1c_i}^2)\omega_y - y_{1c_i}\omega_z} \\ \qquad +\dfrac{1}{2}\dfrac{y_{1c_i}v_z - v_y}{\dot{y}_{1c_i} + x_{1c_i}y_{1c_i}\omega_y - (1+y_{1c_i}^2)\omega_x + x_{1c_i}\omega_z} \end{cases} \tag{18}
$$

The projection of a cuboid in the normalized plane of the image shown in Fig. 1a. If we take the four vertices on the surface of the cuboid as the features applied to the visual servoing, Useful features of a cuboid used in VS are:

$$\mathbf{s}_{cub}(t) = [x_{1c_1}, y_{1c_1}, x_{1c_2}, y_{1c_2}, x_{1c_3}, y_{1c_4}, x_{1c_4}, y_{1c_4}]^\top \qquad (19)$$

Approximations and concatenation of their Jacobian matrices are brought in (12) to generate instant camera velocities. Assigned with a certain time interval, camera moves iteration by iteration until feature errors $\|\mathbf{s}(t) - \mathbf{s}^*\|$ is smaller than a given threshold, Take scenery in Fig. 1b with a cuboid as an example, F^*, F° is the desired and initial position of the camera.

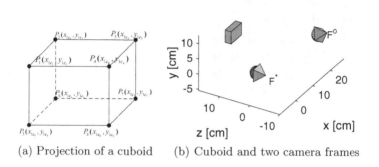

(a) Projection of a cuboid   (b) Cuboid and two camera frames

Fig. 1. Scenario

If we extract features in (19) for a cuboid in the above two views and group them into totally eight feature errors, and bring them into the computation of (12) with approximated image Jacobian matrices and depth estimation in (13), (18). The controller (12) adjustment factor including the sampling cycle time t, $\lambda_1 t$, was set to 0.2, which directs the camera's motion path show in Fig. 2a. As we can see, the selection of the four endpoints to construct the features of the visual servoing control will cause the singularity of the Jacobian matrix in the servo process, so that the control errors cannot be stably reduced. The camera isn't directs to the desired location by feature information. At the same time, Fig. 2d–e show the pose changes during camera movement.

3.2   Visual Servoing Based on Four Endpoints and Centroid Point

Considering that using the four feature points of the plane for visual servoing control may cause the singularity of the Jacobian matrix, the servo control task will eventually fail. Therefore, on the basis of the endpoints, the centroid point (x_{1c_o}, y_{1c_o}) on the surface of the cuboid is added to form the feature vector:

$$\mathbf{s}_{cub}(t) = \begin{matrix} [x_{1c_1}, y_{1c_1}, x_{1c_2}, y_{1c_2}, x_{1c_3}, \\ y_{1c_4}, x_{1c_4}, y_{1c_4}, x_{1c_o}, y_{1c_o}]^\top \end{matrix} \qquad (20)$$

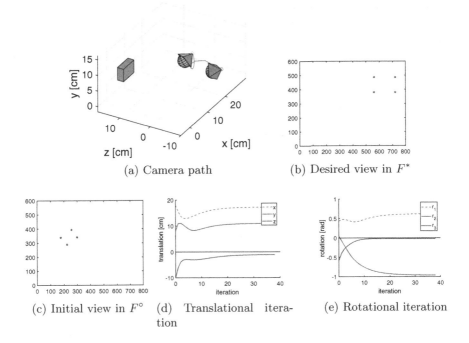

(a) Camera path   (b) Desired view in F^*

(c) Initial view in F° (d) Translational itera-   (e) Rotational iteration
                                      tion

Fig. 2. Virtual visual servoing based on four endpoints.

we extract features in (20) for a cuboid and group them into totally ten feature errors, and bring them into the computation of (12) with approximated image Jacobian matrices and depth estimation in (13). The controller adjustment factor $\lambda_1 t$ was set to 0.2, the camera successfully directs to the desired location by image features. The associated image trajectories show in Fig. 3d. Figure 3e–f show the pose changes during camera movement.

Although the selected features in (19) for the cuboid converge finally to their desired values, also convergence in workspace to F^*, the camera's motion path is S-shaped. The translation and rotation velocity of the camera are not uniform, The camera moves unevenly between translation and rotation. The camera's position errors along the y-axis and the rotation errors r_3 both showed large overshoot.

3.3 Visual Servoing Based on Reconstructed 3D Features

Considering the disadvantages of using traditional 2D image information for visual servoing in the above experiments, we propose to use the three-dimensional features of the cuboid applied to visual servoing, that is the point $P_i(i = 1, 2, ..., 8)$ shown in Fig. 1a, to constitute new feature errors using the

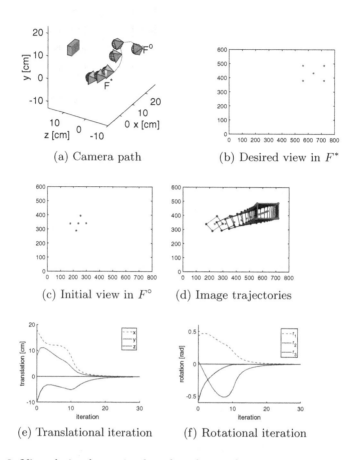

(a) Camera path   (b) Desired view in F^*

(c) Initial view in F° (d) Image trajectories

(e) Translational iteration   (f) Rotational iteration

Fig. 3. Virtual visual servoing based on four endpoints and centroid point.

coordinates of these points in the normalized plane and the depth information of these points:

$$\mathbf{s}_{cub}(t) = [x_{1c_1}z_{c_1}, y_{1c_1}z_{c_1}, z_{c_1}, ..., x_{1c_8}z_{c_8}, y_{1c_8}z_{c_8}, z_{c_8}]^\top. \tag{21}$$

where $x_{1c_i}, y_{1c_i}, z_{c_i} (i = 1, 2, ..., 8)$ are the coordinates of the points P_i projection to the normalized plane and the associated depth information. Therefore, we can define the three-dimensional feature errors:

$$\mathbf{e}_{cub}(t) = \mathbf{s}_{sub}(t) - \mathbf{s}^* \tag{22}$$

where $[x_{1c_i}z_{c_i}, y_{1c_i}z_{c_i}, z_{c_i}]$ can be calculated by (11). The external parameters $\mathbf{M}_c$ can be calculated by submitting the pixel coordinate of the points P_1, P_2, P_3 and P_4 to Sect. 2.2.

The coordinate of P_i in the camera frame is $(x_{c_i}, y_{c_i}, z_{c_i})$. The relationship between the coordinate of P_i and the moving camera frame is [2]:

$$\dot{z}_{c_i} = x_{c_i}\omega_y - y_{c_i}\omega_x - v_z \tag{23}$$

Combining (13) and (23), the relationship between the three-dimensional features and camera motion can be expressed as,

$$\dot{s}_{cub}(t) = \begin{bmatrix} -1 & 0 & 0 & 0 & -z_{c_1} & y_{1c_1}z_{c_1} \\ 0 & -1 & 0 & z_{c_1} & 0 & -x_{1c_1}z_{c_1} \\ 0 & 0 & -1 & -y_{1c_1} & x_{1c_1}z_{c_1} & 0 \\ \vdots & \vdots & \vdots & \vdots & \vdots & \vdots \\ -1 & 0 & 0 & 0 & -z_{c_8} & y_{1c_8}z_{c_8} \\ 0 & -1 & 0 & z_{c_8} & 0 & -x_{1c_8}z_{c_8} \\ 0 & 0 & -1 & -y_{1c_8} & x_{1c_8}z_{c_8} & 0 \end{bmatrix} \mathbf{T} \tag{24}$$

(24) can be rewritten into a simplified form:

$$\dot{s}_{cub}(t) = \mathbf{L}_{s_{cub}(t)}\mathbf{T} \tag{25}$$

where $\mathbf{L}_{s_{cub}}$ is the estimated image Jacobian related to the three-dimensional features.

Therefore, visual servoing controller based on reconstruction of three-dimensional features can be designed as:

$$\mathbf{T} = -\lambda_2 \mathbf{L}^+_{s_{cub}} \mathbf{e}_{cub}(t) \tag{26}$$

where λ_2 is a positive gain that control the servo progress. $\mathbf{L}^+_{s_{cub}}$ is the pseudo-inverse of the image Jacobian matrix $\mathbf{L}_{s_{cub}(t)}$.

Synthetic scenes are generated using MATLAB. Combining the pose estimation method based on P4P problem to calculation the external parameters of the camera, the three-dimensional features of the cuboid was reconstructed, and bring them into the computation of (26) with approximated image Jacobian matrices in (24), the controller (26) finally directs the camera to the desired location shown in Fig. 4.

Same as the classical IBVS, the visual servoing controller (26) gain setting too small, which will cause the system to converge too slowly, and too large setting will cause the system to be unstable. In experiments, The controller (26) adjustment factor including the sampling cycle time t, $\lambda_2 t$, also was set to 0.2. The adjustments finished once the errors were smaller than the thresholds. The camera's pose and the three-dimensional features in each step were recorded as experimental data. The experimental results show that the camera motion rate changes uniformly without terrible shake, and the workspace servo path is superior, which realizes the global convergence of the visual servoing control system, and verifies the effectiveness of the method.

The servo tasks of Fig. 3 are same as Fig. 4. From the comparison results we can obtain that Fig. 3 uses IBVS method based on 2D image information to

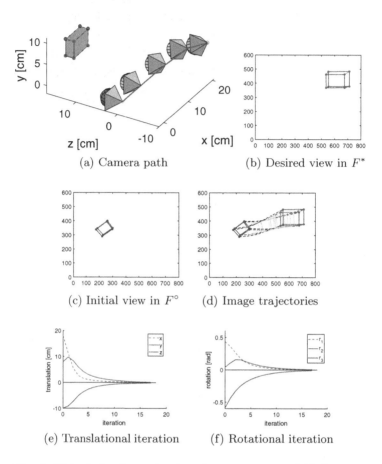

(a) Camera path   (b) Desired view in F^*

(c) Initial view in F° (d) Image trajectories

(e) Translational iteration   (f) Rotational iteration

Fig. 4. Virtual visual servoing based on reconstructed 3D features.

directly use the image features as the control variable and ignore the process of spatial pose estimation of the target. Although the image features can finally converge to the desired state, the camera motion trajectories in the workspace has a distortion and the motion rate changes unevenly in the actual servo process, which will affect the stability of the system. This paper defines three-dimensional visual servoing features based on the camera coordinate system and the normalized image plane, which can describe the relative pose relation between the camera and the target more accurately, so that the control results maintain good in both the image space and the workspace, the validity and advancement of the method are verified.

4   Conclusions

This paper proposes three-dimensional reconstruction features applied to VS with cuboid, which is based on camera pose estimation and normalized plane image information. Simulation results show that the proposes method has higher convergence speed and smoother convergence trajectories compared with the classical IBVS method. In the future, experiments with real object will be conducted to further validate and improve the proposed method.

Acknowledgements. This work is supported by the National Key Research and Development Program of China under Grant 2018YFB1309000 and by the National Natural Science Foundation of China under Grant 61803152.

References

1. Weiss, L.E., Sanderson, A.C., Neuman, C.P.: Dynamic sensor-based control of robots with visual feedback. IEEE J. Robot. Autom. **3**(5), 404–417 (1987)
2. Chaumette, F., Hutchinson, S., Corke, P.: Visual servoing. In: Khatib, O., Siciliano, B. (eds.) Handbook of Robotics, 2nd edn, pp. 841–866. Springer, Cham (2016). https://doi.org/10.1007/978-3-319-32552-1_34
3. Chaumette, F.: Potential problems of stability and convergence in image-based and position-based visual servoing. In: Kriegman, D., Hager, G., Morse, A.S. (eds.) The Confluence of Vision and Control. LNCIS, vol. 237, pp. 66–78. Springer, London (1998). https://doi.org/10.1007/BFb0109663
4. Malis, E., Chaumette, F., Boudet, S.: 2 1/2 D visual servoing. IEEE Trans. Robot. Autom. **15**(2), 238–250 (1999)
5. Chaumette, F.: Image moments: a general and useful set of features for visual servoing. IEEE Trans. Robot. Autom. **20**(4), 713–723 (2004)
6. Malis, E., Chaumette, F.: 2 1/2 D visual servoing with respect to unknown objects through a new estimation scheme of camera displacement. Int. J. Comput. Vis. **37**(1), 79–97 (2000)
7. Tahri, O., Chaumette, F.: Point-based and region-based image moments for visual servoing of planar objects. IEEE Trans. Robot. **21**(6), 1116–1127 (2005)
8. Liu, Y.-H., Wang, H., Chen, W., Zhou, D.: Adaptive visual servoing using common image features with unknown geometric parameters. Automatica **49**(8), 2453–2460 (2013)
9. De, X., Jinyan, L., Wang, P., Zhang, Z., Liang, Z.: Partially decoupled image-based visual servoing using different sensitive features. IEEE Trans. Syst. Man Cybern. Syst. **47**(8), 2233–2243 (2017)
10. Shen, T., Chesi, G.: Visual servoing path-planning with spheres. In: 9th International Conference on Informatics in Control, Automation and Robotics, Italy, Rome, pp. 22–30 (2012)
11. Shen, T., Chesi, G.: Following a straight line in visual servoing with elliptical projections. In: 13th International Conference on Informatics in Control, Automation and Robotics, Lisbon, Portugal, pp. 47–56 (2016)
12. Shen, T., Chesi, G.: Visual servoing path-planning with elliptical projections. In: Andrade-Cetto, J., Felipe, J., Ferrier, J.-L. (eds.) Informatics in Control Automation and Robotics. Springer, Cham (2018). https://doi.org/10.1007/978-3-319-55011-4_2

13. Shen, T., Yang, J., Cai, Y., Li, D., Chesi, G.: Visual servoing with cylinders: reaching the desired location following a straight line. In: 2017 36th Chinese Control Conference (CCC), pp. 11183–11188. IEEE (2017)

14. Zhang, G., Jixiang, D., Wang, T.: Study on model-based visual servoing with reconstructed 2D features. J. Syst. Simul. **28**(6), 1255–1260 (2016)

15. Shen, T., Chesi, G.: Visual servoing path-planning for cameras obeying the unified model. Adv. Robot. **26**(8–9), 843–860 (2012)

16. Gao, X.-S., Hou, X.-R., Tang, J., Cheng, H.-F.: Complete solution classification for the perspective-three-point problem. IEEE Trans. Pattern Anal. Mach. Intell. **25**(8), 930–943 (2003)

17. Chaumette, F., Hutchinson, S.: Visual servo control, Part I: basic approaches. IEEE Robot. Autom. Mag. **13**(4), 82–90 (2006)

18. Tahri, O., Mezouar, Y., Chaumette, F., Araujo, H.: Visual servoing and pose estimation with cameras obeying the unified model. In: Chesi, G., Hashimotos, K. (eds.) Visual Servoing via Advanced Numerical Methods. Lecture Notes in Control and Information Sciences, vol. 401, pp. 231–252. Springer, Verlag (2010). https://doi.org/10.1007/978-1-84996-089-2_13

19. Chaumette, F.: De la perception à l'action: l'asservissement visuel; de l'action à la perception: la vision active. Habilitation à diriger les recherches, Université de Rennes 1, January 1998

Landmark Based Eye Ratio Estimation for Driver Fatigue Detection

Ramiro Galindo[1(✉)], Wilbert G. Aguilar[1,2,3(✉)], and Rolando P. Reyes Ch.[1(✉)]

[1] CICTE, Universidad de las Fuerzas Armadas ESPE, Sangolquí, Ecuador
{ragalindo1, wgaguilar, rpreyes1}@espe.edu.ec
[2] FIS, Escuela Politécnica Nacional, Quito, Ecuador
[3] GREC, Universitat Politècnica de Catalunya, Barcelona, Spain

Abstract. In this paper, we present an algorithm for drowsiness detection in drivers of several vehicles based on eye-shape. We use a combination of HOG Linear SVM to locate the face in real-time video, and feature point detection on face region for delimiting the ocular area. The feature point detector use 68-point facial landmark, but we constrain landmarks to the ocular area. We calculate the ocular aspect ratio (EAR), in order to detect driver eye closure, i.e., to detect drowsiness. Results show high sensitivity of the algorithm in the tests performed on a vehicle with a webcam and a warning alert, nevertheless, there is affected by the illumination.

Keywords: Fatigue detection · Facial landmark · HOG · SVM

1 Introduction

Drivers and operators of several transportation vehicles, including aerial vehicles [1, 2], must be professionally prepared to have a quick and efficient reaction on the roads. Completing a long trip could take a large amount of time, in which the driver is expected to remain attentive at all times. However, after a long period of driving fatigue symptoms develop quickly until succumbing to drowsiness, which causes the driver to fall asleep causing serious accidents. In fact, one of the major factors in traffic accident causation is the effects of fatigue on drivers, but the contribution of fatigue to accidents is often underestimated in official reporting [3].

Statistics show that in a 24-h period about 38% of truck drivers exceed 14 h of driving, and 51% exceed 14 h of driving plus other non-driving work [4]. In one of several working days many of these drivers experience less than 4 h of sleep, causing a favorable scenario for the appearance of symptoms of fatigue. Driving in a state of fatigue causes the driver to lose attention and the quick and adequate response to an unexpected or dangerous situation [5], and lack of concentration, as well as poorer decision-making and worsened mood [6].

The affiliations of the Universitat Politècnica de Catalunya and Escuela Politécnica Nacional are exclusively of the corresponding author Dr. Wilbert G. Aguilar. The payment of the paper registration was funded exclusively by Universidad de las Fuerzas Armadas ESPE.

© Springer Nature Switzerland AG 2019
H. Yu et al. (Eds.): ICIRA 2019, LNAI 11744, pp. 565–576, 2019.
https://doi.org/10.1007/978-3-030-27541-9_46

In the field of professional drivers fatigue [7] various studies have been carried out on truck drivers [4, 8, 9], aircraft pilots [10, 11], car drivers [8, 10], taxi drivers [6] and bus drivers [9]. And as a method to recognize fatigue and somnolence, neurophysiological measurements have been used, such as electroencephalography: EEG, electrooculography: EOG and heart rate: HR [10]. Psychological measures have also been used, such as mood [6], accumulated sleep [4, 6, 8] and stress [7].

In the field of software and signal analysis, systems capable of detecting fatigue of drivers have been developed through heart rate monitoring and grip pressure on the steering wheel [12], other systems include electroencephalography-based monitoring (EEG) and electrooculography (EOG) in driving simulators [13]. On the other hand, in the field of computer vision [14–17], specifically for perception [18–21], has been used the recognition and monitoring of the eyes [22, 23], pupils and mouth [24, 25] in videos of drivers [26], road detection [27], path planning [28], object detection [29], and in real time [11, 30, 31].

Our proposal for detection of fatigue in drivers is detect and monitoring the shape of the eye. To do this we first detect the people face [32] in the video of a HD camera that will be right in front of the driver. This is done using HOG [33, 34] linear SVM [35], which detects the movement vectors of the face, by placing it in a visible area on the PC screen. Then we build a face landmark using a trained algorithm based on the 68-point facial landmark detector. Our intention is delimiting the eye area and build an eye-landmark, through which we will calculate the ocular aspect ratio (EAR). So, we can know if the eyes are open or closed. The second state being the characteristic for the detection of drowsiness in the drivers.

2 Related Works

Two important algorithms for face detection and object detection in general have been developed: Haar-like features [36] and HOG [37] by Dalal and Tiggs. Both algorithms have been used in many applications and have generated more than 40 new approaches [38]. Several methods for face detection include feature extraction algorithms: HAAR [36], HOG [37], HOG-LBP [39], working with machine learning based on SVMs [39] [40] or Adaboost [41]. Other methods, a bit more robust and accurate, use deep learning [42, 43].

On the other hand, for detection of key points of interest [44–46] and the development of a landmark along the shape of the face, a very important algorithm has been developed: The facial landmark detector [47] by Kazemi and Sullivan. Other methods of shape detection include the diffuse spatial clustering c-means (s-FCM) [26], edge recognition [23] and LDA [24]. Also, more robust methods have been developed based on deep learning [48] and constrained neural fields [49].

For detection of faces and people, different datasets have been created, such as ETH [50], focused on detection of locomotion patterns, and MIT-CBCL [51] based on edge detection. Within the algorithm to develop the facial landmark there are three main pre-trained facial landmark detectors, based on different datasets created by several research groups. The most common is the shape predictor with 68 key points trained on 300-W dataset [52–54]. There is also the shape predictor with 194 key points trained on HELEN dataset [55], and the most recent, with 5 key points trained on FRGC [52, 54].

The combination between HOG Linear SVM facial detection and facial landmark detector has been widely used for facial recognition [56], 3D facial scans [57], estimation of posture [58]. Other authors have delimited the detection of certain areas of the face, for example the ocular zone, for Eye blink detection [59], face alignment [60] and drowsiness detection in car drivers [61].

3   Our Approach

3.1   Face Detection

Our approach is the use of HOG [37] for detection of faces in real time. We decided to use this method because, although there is slower, it provides greater accuracy with less falses positives than Haar cascades. We combined this method with machine learning based on SVM, through which we can train the tracking of the moving face and classify it with a high accurate.

For the training we used the CBCL [6] face data base, from where we obtained the positive samples (P, that we want to detect) and the negative samples (N, that we do not want to detect). From both we extracted the HOG descriptors. Then, we trained at SVM on the positive and negative samples. Finally, we applied the hard-negative mining technique to record the false-positives and sort them according to their classification probability, and then re-train the classifier using them as negative samples (Fig. 1).

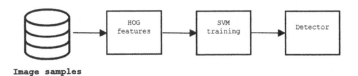

Fig. 1. HOG features with SVM.

A very important factor is obtaining the face bounding box (the (x, y)-coordinates of the face in the image). Based on it we will realize the facial landmark. We applied the technique of the sliding window in all the test images, extracting the HOG descriptors and applying the classifier in each case. The process must iterate until a sufficiently large probability is detected, and then record the bounding box.

3.2   Facial Landmarks Detection

Facial landmarks are used to localize and represent salient regions of the face, such as eyes, eyebrows, nose, mouth and jawline. In this context, our goal was detected important facial structures on the face using shape prediction methods.

The facial landmark detector is an implementation of [47] by Kazemi and Sullivan. This method starts by using a training set of labeled facial landmarks on an image and the probability on distance between pairs of input pixels. We used the original pre-trained facial landmark detector with 68 (x, y)-coordinates. The indexes of the 68 coordinates can be visualized on the image below (Fig. 2).

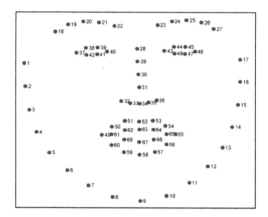

Fig. 2. Visualizing the 68 facial landmark coordinates from the iBUG 300-W dataset.

These annotations are part of the iBUG 300-W data set [52–54], which the facial landmark predictor was trained on.

Eye Aspect Ratio (EAR). To detect the drowsiness, we analyzed the driver eyes using a metric called the eye aspect ratio (EAR) introduced by Soukupová and Čech [59]. This method was fast, efficient, and easy to implement.

We extracted the ocular structure of the facial landmark. Each eye is represented by 6 (x, y)-coordinates starting at the left-hand corner of the eye and then working clockwise around the remainder of the region (Fig. 3: Top-left).

The EAR is a relationship between the width and the height of these coordinates, and is calculated by the following equation:

$$EAR = (|p2 - p6| + |p3 + p5|)/(2|p1 - p4|) \tag{1}$$

Where p1, ..., p6 are 2D facial landmark locations.

The EAR is approximately constant while the eye is open, but it will rapidly fall to zero when the eye is closed. Through this information we could know if the driver has been closing his eyes for a considerable time, a clear sign of drowsiness. To make this clear, consider the following figure:

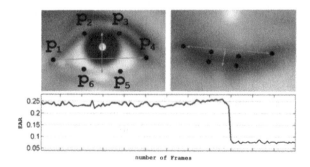

Fig. 3. Top-left: A visualization of eye landmarks when then the eye is open. Top-right: Eye landmarks when the eye is closed. Bottom: The eye aspect ratio EAR in Eq. (1) plotted for several frames of a video sequence.

I applied a threshold to know if a closed or open eye is considered. The threshold will be a value between 65–70%.

$$TH = 0.65 * (EAR_{max} - EAR_{min}) + EAR_{min} \qquad (2)$$

The calibration was based on the two eyes. The average is made between the threshold values found individually. This is because the program has problems detecting the blinking of a single eye.

Finally, we implemented a timer to avoid activating events through involuntary flashes. While the eye is not closed for a certain time, no action will be triggered.

3.3   Drowsiness Detection Algorithm

First, we detected the face of the driver through HOG Linear SVM and got the face bounding box. Then we detected the facial landmarks using the original pre-trained detector with 68 (x, y)-coordinates. We delimited the ocular zone of the facial structure formed, i.e., we obtained the eyes landmark. Finally, we calculated the EAR and performed the respective calibration for each frame of the video.

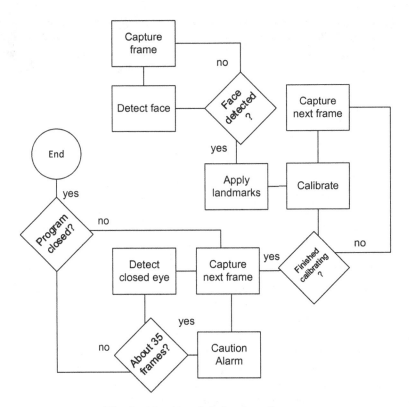

Fig. 4. Algorithm Solution flow diagram.

To detect drowsiness, we set a threshold of 0.3 for the EAR value. If this metric exceeds or stays at the value of 0.3 it means that the driver is awake. If the metric is smaller, and stays that way for more than one second (approximately 40 frames of consecutive video) it means that the driver has symptoms of drowsiness and is falling asleep at the wheel. If the second case occurs, an alarm is triggered that alerts the driver to be alert.

This is presented graphically in Fig. 4.

4   Results and Discussion

To test the operation of our algorithm we did several tests on a car. We placed a high-resolution webcam on the upper part of a car dash connected to a standard computer. We made sure the camera clearly focused on the driver face (Fig. 5).

Fig. 5. Left: Mounting camera to our car dash for drowsiness detection. Right: Using a PC to run the actual drowsiness detection algorithm.

We used a PC because there is the best device to perform tests and thus evaluate the performance of our algorithm. But for a real application a microcontroller will be used that is compatible with the algorithm and can execute it without difficulty.

Then, once the test devices were ready, we ran the algorithm and went out to drive normally. The eyes landmarks are detected and developed normally, and the EAR is calculated continuously in real time (Fig. 6 Left). When the person pretended to fall asleep, the value of the EAR decreased to a value less than 0.3 for a little more than a second, after which the warning alarm that woke person up and alerted him was activated (Fig. 6 Right).

The parameters considered for the evaluation of a good performance of the algorithm were the EAR and the number of false positives.

In Fig. 3 it can be clearly seen that the EAR for normal conditions is equal to or greater than 0.3, which is within the usual value. On the other hand, the EAR drops to a value less than 0.3 when the driver narrows his eyes. In this case the value of the ratio was 0.16. This also depends on the geometry of the eye.

In the experiment participated 10 drivers. Five tests were performed for each driver. The number of true positives and false negatives were counted in 3 situations. The data found are shown below.

Fig. 6. Left: Detection of a driver eyes with normal gestures. Right: Detection of a drowsy driver.

Table 1. Counting of true positives (TP) and false negatives (FN).

Car driver	Situation					
	Sunny day		Cloudy day		Night	
	TP	FN	TP	FN	TP	FN
Driver 1	5	0	5	0	3	2
Driver 2	5	0	5	0	4	1
Driver 3	5	0	5	0	4	1
Driver 4	5	0	5	0	3	2
Driver 5	5	0	5	0	4	1
Driver 6	4	1	5	0	4	1
Driver 7	5	0	5	0	4	1
Driver 8	5	0	5	0	3	2
Driver 9	5	0	4	1	4	1
Driver 10	4	1	5	0	4	1

When the driver looks down the algorithm recognizes that as a sign of drowsiness. Something similar happens when very abrupt changes in brightness are made, like when the driver is against light.

From the data in Table 1 we can calculate the sensitivity of the system:

$$Sensitivity = True\,positives/(True\,positives + False\,negatives) \qquad (3)$$

We obtain the table below (Table 2):

Table 2. Sensitivity of the System.

Situation	Sensitivity
Sunny day	0.96
Cloudy day	0.98
Night	0.74

It is an acceptable value of sensitivity, although it could be increased by filters and an algorithm with a more sophisticated structure.

The best situation for our algorithm is a cloudy day, because it presents a sensitivity of 98%. The recognition of the ocular zone was carried out effectively, and landmark being visible in the contours of the eyes of the person detected. The method was very stable and robust because the detection ran without errors for a long period of time and is not sensitive to sudden movements. The method worked so well that it even detect the shape of the eyes through lenses. The number of frames allowed before the alarm was activated was adequate. There is not so short that it detects a flicker as a sign of drowsiness and nor so long that the driver falls asleep long enough to produce an accident. The same can be said for the ratio of the eyes (EAR): the value 0.3 was the most appropriate, i.e., the better threshold between activity and drowsiness.

5 Conclusions and Future Works

Our system uses a predictor file and detection algorithm for the detection of face landmarks, focusing on the eyes which is the main area that shows a symptom of fatigue in a driver. By means of a timer we set a time to determine that the EAR has been reduced to zero, therefore it is determined that the driver has fallen asleep and will emit an alarm. At first, we used the Haar algorithm but due to the fact that many false positives came out and it was not robust, we decided to lean towards landmarks that through a mathematical relationship manages to establish an EAR that decides whether the driver is awake or asleep. Improve the algorithm to be immune to the lack of illumination or inaccuracy that occurs when turning the head or extending and contracting the neck. The detection of the eye contour by the "Landmark detection" method was effective in terms of robustness and precision. This was evidenced in the continuous recognition of the eyes of the person detected, even with changes in luminosity and sudden movements. Getting to detect even when the person is in profile. A good feature of the algorithm is that it performs continuous recognition and detection for long periods of time. This was due to the while cycle programmed for this purpose, which only breaks if the program is completely closed. A very suitable application is the detection of drowsy drivers, since it would be possible to prevent accidents due to drivers who are sleeping while driving. This represents a high social impact, since it would prevent many accidents and save more than one life. The final objective is to apply the algorithm in a real situation. For that objective we pretend to install or simulate a situation where the driver starts to feel fatigated and through the algorithm, the car starts to stop.

References

1. Orbea, D., Moposita, J., Aguilar, W.G., Paredes, M., León, G., Jara-Olmedo, A.: Math model of UAV multi rotor prototype with fixed wing aerodynamic structure for a flight simulator. In: De Paolis, L.T., Bourdot, P., Mongelli, A. (eds.) AVR 2017. LNCS, vol. 10324, pp. 199–211. Springer, Cham (2017). https://doi.org/10.1007/978-3-319-60922-5_15

2. Orbea, D., Moposita, J., Aguilar, W.G., Paredes, M., Reyes, R.P., Montoya, L.: Vertical take off and landing with fixed rotor. In: Chilean Conference on Electrical, Electronics Engineering, Information and Communication Technologies (CHILECON), Pucón, Chile (2017)

3. Brown, L.D.: Driver fatigue. Hum. Factors **36**, 238–314 (1994)

4. Arnold, P.K., Hartley, L.R., Corry, A., Hochstadt, D., Penna, F., Feyer, A.M.: Hours of work, and perceptions of fatigue among truck drivers. Accid Anal and Prev. **29**(4), 471–477 (1997)

5. Wang, T., Shi, P.: Yawning detection for determining driver drowsiness. In: IEEE 1768 (2015)

6. Dalziel, J.R., Job, R.F.S.: Motor vehicles accidents, fatigue and optimism bias in taxi drivers. Accid. Anal. Prev. **29**(4), 489–494 (1997)

7. Taylor, A.H., Dorm, L.: Stress, fatigue, health, and risk of road traffic accidents among professional drivers: the contribution of physical inactivity. Annu. Rev. Public Health **27**, 371–391 (2006)

8. Summala, H., Mikkola, T.: Fatal accidents among car and truck drivers: effects of fatigue, age, and alcohol consumption. Hum. Factors **36**(2), 315–326 (1994)

9. Milosevic, S.: Driver's fatigue studies. Ergonomics **40**(3), 381–389

10. Borghini, G., Astolfi, L., Vecchiato, G., Mattia, D., Babiloni, F.: Measuring neurophysiological signals in aircraft pilots and car drivers for the assessment of mental workload, fatigue and drowsiness. Neurosci. Biobehav. Rev. **44**, 58–75 (2014)

11. McKinley, R.A., McIntire, L.K., Schmidt, R., Repperger, D.W., Cadwell, J.A.: Evaluation of eye metrics as a detector of fatigue. Hum. Factors **53**(4), 403–414 (2011)

12. Rogado, E., García, J.L., Barea, R., Bergasa, L.M., López, E.: Driver fatigue detection system. In: IEEE International Conference on Robotics and Biomimetics (2008)

13. Bouchner, P., Pieknic, R., Novotný, S., Pekný, J., Hajný, M., Borzová, C.: Fatigue of car drivers – detection and classification based on the experiments on car simulators. In: 6th WSEAS International Conference on Simulation, Modelling and Optimization (2006)

14. Aguilar, W.G., Angulo, C.: Real-time model-based video stabilization for microaerial vehicles. Neural Process. Lett. **43**(2), 459–477 (2016)

15. Aguilar, W.G., et al.: Real-time detection and simulation of abnormal crowd behavior. In: De Paolis, L.T., Bourdot, P., Mongelli, A. (eds.) AVR 2017. LNCS, vol. 10325, pp. 420–428. Springer, Cham (2017). https://doi.org/10.1007/978-3-319-60928-7_36

16. Aguilar, W.G., Angulo, C.: Real-time video stabilization without phantom movements for micro aerial vehicles. EURASIP Journal on Image and Video Processing **1**, 1–13 (2014)

17. Aguilar, W.G., et al.: Statistical abnormal crowd behavior detection and simulation for real-time applications. In: Huang, Y., Wu, H., Liu, H., Yin, Z. (eds.) ICIRA 2017. LNCS (LNAI), vol. 10463, pp. 671–682. Springer, Cham (2017). https://doi.org/10.1007/978-3-319-65292-4_58

18. Basantes, J., et al.: Capture and processing of geospatial data with laser scanner system for 3D modeling and virtual reality of Amazonian Caves. In: IEEE Ecuador Technical Chapters Meeting (ETCM), Samborondón, Ecuador (2018)

19. Aguilar, W.G., Rodríguez, G.A., Álvarez, L., Sandoval, S., Quisaguano, F., Limaico, A.: On-Board visual SLAM on a UGV using a RGB-D camera. In: Huang, Y., Wu, H., Liu, H., Yin, Z. (eds.) ICIRA 2017. LNCS (LNAI), vol. 10464, pp. 298–308. Springer, Cham (2017). https://doi.org/10.1007/978-3-319-65298-6_28

20. Aguilar, W.G., Rodríguez, G.A., Álvarez, L., Sandoval, S., Quisaguano, F., Limaico, A.: Real-time 3D modeling with a RGB-D camera and on-board processing. In: De Paolis, L.T., Bourdot, P., Mongelli, A. (eds.) AVR 2017. LNCS, vol. 10325, pp. 410–419. Springer, Cham (2017). https://doi.org/10.1007/978-3-319-60928-7_35

21. Aguilar, W.G., Rodríguez, G.A., Álvarez, L., Sandoval, S., Quisaguano, F., Limaico, A.: Visual SLAM with a RGB-D camera on a Quadrotor UAV using on-board processing. In: Rojas, I., Joya, G., Catala, A. (eds.) IWANN 2017. LNCS, vol. 10306, pp. 596–606. Springer, Cham (2017). https://doi.org/10.1007/978-3-319-59147-6_51

22. Aguilar, W.G., Estrella, J.I., López, W., Abad, V.: Driver fatigue detection based on real-time eye gaze pattern analysis. In: Huang, Y., Wu, H., Liu, H., Yin, Z. (eds.) ICIRA 2017. LNCS (LNAI), vol. 10463, pp. 683–694. Springer, Cham (2017). https://doi.org/10.1007/978-3-319-65292-4_59

23. Devi, M.S., Bajaj, P.R.: Driver fatigue detection based on eye tracking. In: IEEE First International Conference on Emerging Trends in Engineering and Technology (2008)

24. Fan, X., Yin, B.-C., Sun, Y.-F.: Yawning detection for monitoring driver fatigue. In: IEEE International Conference on Machine Learning and Cybernetics (2007)

25. Saradadevi, M., Bajaj, P.: Driver fatigue detection using mouth and yawning analysis. Int. J. Comput. Sci. Network Secur. 8(6), 183–188 (2008)

26. Azim, T., Jaffar, M.A., Mirza, A.M.: Fully automated real time fatigue detection of drivers through fuzzy expert systems. Appl. Soft Comput. 18, 25–38 (2014)

27. Galarza, J., Pérez, E., Serrano, E., Tapia, A., Aguilar, W.G.: Pose estimation based on monocular visual odometry and lane detection for intelligent vehicles. In: De Paolis, L.T., Bourdot, P. (eds.) AVR 2018. LNCS, vol. 10851, pp. 562–566. Springer, Cham (2018). https://doi.org/10.1007/978-3-319-95282-6_40

28. Aguilar, W.G., Morales, S.: 3D environment mapping using the Kinect V2 and path planning based on RRT algorithms. Electronics 5(4), 70 (2016)

29. Aguilar, W.G., Casaliglla, V.P., Pólit, J.L.: Obstacle avoidance based-visual navigation for micro aerial vehicles. Electronics 6(1), 10 (2017)

30. Dong, W., Wu, X.: Fatigue detection based on the distance of eyelid. In: IEEE International Workshop on VLSI Design and Video Technology (2005)

31. Horng, W.-B., Chen, C.-Y., Chang, Y., Fan, C.-H.: Driver fatigue detection based on eye tracking and dynamic template matching. In: IEEE International Conference on Networking, Sensing and Control (2004)

32. Andrea, C.C., Byron, J.Q., Jorge, P.I., Inti, T.C.H., Aguilar, W.G.: Geolocation and counting of people with aerial thermal imaging for rescue purposes. In: De Paolis, L.T., Bourdot, P. (eds.) AVR 2018. LNCS, vol. 10850, pp. 171–182. Springer, Cham (2018). https://doi.org/10.1007/978-3-319-95270-3_12

33. Aguilar, W.G., et al.: Pedestrian detection for UAVs using cascade classifiers and saliency maps. In: Rojas, I., Joya, G., Catala, A. (eds.) IWANN 2017. LNCS, vol. 10306, pp. 563–574. Springer, Cham (2017). https://doi.org/10.1007/978-3-319-59147-6_48

34. Aguilar, W.G., Luna, M., Moya, J., Abad, V., Parra, H., Ruiz, H.: Pedestrian detection for UAVs using cascade classifiers with meanshift. In: IEEE 11th International Conference on Semantic Computing (ICSC), San Diego (2017)

35. Aguilar, W.G., Cobeña, B., Rodriguez, G., Salcedo, V.S., Collaguazo, B.: SVM and RGB-D sensor based gesture recognition for UAV control. In: De Paolis, L.T., Bourdot, P. (eds.) AVR 2018. LNCS, vol. 10851, pp. 713–719. Springer, Cham (2018). https://doi.org/10.1007/978-3-319-95282-6_50

36. Viola, P., Jones, M.: Rapid object detection using a boosted cascade of simple features. In: Conference on Computer Vision and Pattern Recognition, pp. 1–9 (2001)

37. Dalal, N., Triggs, W.: Histograms of oriented gradients for human detection. In: 2005 IEEE Computer Society Conference on Computer Vision and Pattern Recognition. CVPR05, vol. 1, no. 3, pp. 886–893 (2004)

38. Benenson, R., Omran, M., Hosang, J., Schiele, B.: Ten years of pedestrian detection, what have we learned? In: Agapito, L., Bronstein, Michael M., Rother, C. (eds.) ECCV 2014. LNCS, vol. 8926, pp. 613–627. Springer, Cham (2015). https://doi.org/10.1007/978-3-319-16181-5_47

39. Wang, X., Han, T.X., Yan, S.: An HOG-LBP human detector with partial occlusion handling. In: IEEE 12th International Conference on Computer Vision (2009)

40. Osuna, E., Freud, R., Girosit, F.: Training support vector machines: an application to face detection. In: IEEE Computer Society Conference on Computer Vision and Pattern Recognition (1997)

41. Viola, P., Jones, M.J.: Robust real-time face detection. Int. J. Comput. Vision 57(2), 137–154 (2004)

42. Rosebrock, A.: Face detection with OpenCV and deep learning, pyimagesearch (2018). https://www.pyimagesearch.com/2018/02/26/face-detection-with-opencv-and-deep-learning/ . Accessed 01 2019

43. Aguilar, W.G., Quisaguano, F.J., Rodríguez, G.A., Alvarez, L.G., Limaico, A., Sandoval, D. S.: Convolutional neuronal networks based monocular object detection and depth perception for micro UAVs. In: Peng, Y., Yu, K., Lu, J., Jiang, X. (eds.) IScIDE 2018. LNCS, vol. 11266, pp. 401–410. Springer, Cham (2018). https://doi.org/10.1007/978-3-030-02698-1_35

44. Amaguaña, F., Collaguazo, B., Tituaña, J., Aguilar, W.G.: Simulation system based on augmented reality for optimization of training tactics on military operations. In: De Paolis, L. T., Bourdot, P. (eds.) AVR 2018. LNCS, vol. 10850, pp. 394–403. Springer, Cham (2018). https://doi.org/10.1007/978-3-319-95270-3_33

45. Aguilar, W.G., Salcedo, V.S., Sandoval, D.S., Cobeña, B.: Developing of a video-based model for UAV autonomous navigation. In: Barone, D.A.C., Teles, E.O., Brackmann, C. P. (eds.) LAWCN 2017. CCIS, vol. 720, pp. 94–105. Springer, Cham (2017). https://doi.org/10.1007/978-3-319-71011-2_8

46. Salcedo, V.S., Aguilar, W.G., Cobeña, B., Pardo, J.A., Proaño, Z.: On-board target virtualization using image features for UAV autonomous tracking. In: Boudriga, N., Alouini, M.-S., Rekhis, S., Sabir, E., Pollin, S. (eds.) UNet 2018. LNCS, vol. 11277, pp. 384–391. Springer, Cham (2018). https://doi.org/10.1007/978-3-030-02849-7_34

47. Kazemi, V., Sullivan, J.: One millisecond face alignment with an ensemble of regression trees. In: IEEE Conference on Computer Vision and Pattern Recognition (2014)

48. Zhang, Z., Luo, P., Loy, C.C., Tang, X.: Facial landmark detection by deep multi-task learning. In: Fleet, D., Pajdla, T., Schiele, B., Tuytelaars, T. (eds.) ECCV 2014. LNCS, vol. 8694, pp. 94–108. Springer, Cham (2014). https://doi.org/10.1007/978-3-319-10599-4_7

49. Baltrusaitis, T., Robinson, P., Morency, L.P.: Constrained local neural fields for robust facial landmark detection in the wild. In: IEEE International Conference on Computer Vision, pp. 354–361 (2013)

50. Ess, A., Leibe, B., Schindler, K., Gool, L.V.: Robust multiperson tracking from a mobile platform. IEEE Trans. Pattern Anal. Mach. Intell. 31(10), 1831–1846 (2009)

51. MIT: Face Data: CBCL face database No. 1. MIT (2000)

52. Sagonas, C., Antonakos, E., Tzimiropoulos, G., Zafeiriou, S., Pantic, M.: 300 faces In-the-wild challenge: database and results. In: Image and Vision Computing (IMAVIS), Special Issue on Facial Landmark Localisation "In-The-Wild" (2016)
53. Sagonas, C., Tzimiropoulos, G., Zafeiriou, S., Pantic, M.: 300 faces in-the-wild challenge: the first facial landmark localization Challenge. In: IEEE International Conference on Computer Vision (ICCV-W), 300 Faces in-the-Wild Challenge (300-W) (2013)
54. Sagonas, C., Tzimiropoulos, G., Zafeiriou, S., Pantic, M.: A semi-automatic methodology for facial landmark annotation. In: IEEE International Conference on Computer Vision and Pattern Recognition (CVPR-W), 5th Workshop on Analysis and Modeling of Faces and Gestures (AMFG 2013) 2013
55. Le, V., Brandt, J., Lin, Z., Bourdev, L., Huang, Thomas S.: Interactive facial feature localization. In: Fitzgibbon, A., Lazebnik, S., Perona, P., Sato, Y., Schmid, C. (eds.) ECCV 2012. LNCS, vol. 7574, pp. 679–692. Springer, Heidelberg (2012). https://doi.org/10.1007/978-3-642-33712-3_49
56. Segundo, M.P., Silva, L., Pereira, O.R., Queirolo, C.C.: Automatic face segmentation and facial landmark detection in range images. IEEE Trans. Syst. Man, Cybernet. Part B (Cybernetics) **40**(5), 1319–1330 (2010)
57. Perakis, P., Passalis, G., Theoharis, T., Kakadiaris, L.A.: 3D facial landmark detection under large yaw and expression variations. IEEE Trans. Pattern Anal. Mach. Intell. **35**(7), 1552–1564 (2013)
58. Zhu, X., Ramanan, D.: Face detection, pose estimation, and landmark localization in the wild. In: IEEE Conference on Computer Vision and Pattern Recognition (2012)
59. Soukupová, T., Cech, J.: Real-time eye blink detection using facial landmark. In: 21st Computer Vision Winter Workshop (2016)
60. Rosebrock, A.: "Face alignment with OpenCV and Python," pyimagesearch (2017). https://www.pyimagesearch.com/2017/05/22/face-alignment-with-opencv-and-python/. Accessed 01 2019
61. Rosebrock, A.: Drowsiness detection with OpenCV. pyimagesearch (2017). https://www.pyimagesearch.com/2017/05/08/drowsiness-detection-opencv/. Accessed 01 2019

Automatic Analysis of Calibration Board Image Orientation for Online Hand-Eye Calibration

Shan Du, Jianhua Zhang, and Xiaoling Lv[(✉)]

College of Mechanical Engineering, Hebei University of Technology,
Tianjin 300000, China
lxl000418@163.com

Abstract. Visual robot hand-eye calibration is the most basic step in robots researching, and the accuracy of hand-eye calibration has a great impact on the working process. In order to perform hand-eye calibration accurately, it is necessary to collect a large amount of robot position data and calibration plate image data effectively. Different data will bring different calibration results. Collecting reasonable data will improve the accuracy of calibration results. This paper proposes an analytical method for the orientation of the calibration board, which can achieve the automatic adjustment of the shooting position of the robot arm. The method combines the image ratio analysis with the block image histogram to complete the calibration board orientation analysis. The image ratio analysis first blocks the image, then binarizes the sub-image, and obtains the proportional parameter of the desired pixel in the sub-image. The block image histogram uses the second-order Gaussian function to fit the histogram to obtain the peak, peak position and half-width information, and obtains the orientation information of the calibration board by solving the peak position and the area of the peak. Experiments show, this method can accurately determine the orientation of the calibration board, then improve the data acquisition efficiency of the calibration board and hand-eye calibration accuracy.

Keywords: Image ratio analysis · Block image histogram · Orientation analysis

1 Introduction

With the popularity of visual robots, the requirements for accuracy and automation are getting higher and higher. Especially in the development of the electronics industry, which poses new challenges for visual robots [1]. The problem of an eye-in-hand system is how to estimate the rotation and translation of the robot's end effector or gripper relative to the camera mounted on it [2]. In many practical situations, it is necessary to perform multiple hand-eye transformation calculations in the life cycle of the system [3]. So excessive manual intervention is required. Especially when shooting calibration board images, a large number of pictures with different positions and different angles are required.

© Springer Nature Switzerland AG 2019
H. Yu et al. (Eds.): ICIRA 2019, LNAI 11744, pp. 577–589, 2019.
https://doi.org/10.1007/978-3-030-27541-9_47

In order to obtain the calibration data conveniently for eye-to-hand system. Author Agile proposed [4] proposed a hand-eye calibration method for automatically generating the calibration posture. It is combined with the K-means clustering algorithm to screen the posture of the robot arm which is beneficial to improve the accuracy of the result. Literature [5] proposed a method for planning the motion space planning of the board. The calibration board is restricted from moving within the field of view of the camera, during the process of capturing the data of the calibration board by the camera, to ensure that the collected calibration board data is valid. However, this method is not suitable for systems where the camera is attached to the end of the robot arm (eye-in-hand) system.

For the eye-in-hand system, Shi et al. [6] proposed a method of motion selection to improve the accuracy of robotic online hand-eye calibration. Zhang et al. [7] proposed an adaptive motion selection method. The number of calibrations of the robot's online hand-eye is improved, and the robustness of the hand-eye calibration is improved, but the invalidation of the image of the calibration board is not considered. In the process of online calibration, it is convenient and accurate to collect image data of calibration board, which is of great significance to improve the accuracy and speed of calibration.

This paper presents a method for automatic screening and orientation analysis of the calibration board. The method combines the image ratio analysis with the block image histogram to complete the calibration board orientation analysis. Based on the currently captured image, an effective calibration board image is screened based on the image segmentation. The orientation of the calibration board is analyzed by image ratio analysis and histogram data processing when the image is invalid. Then guiding the robot arm for the next shot to ensure a fast and efficient acquisition of the calibration board image. The experimental results show that the method of this paper effectively improves the shooting speed of the calibration board.

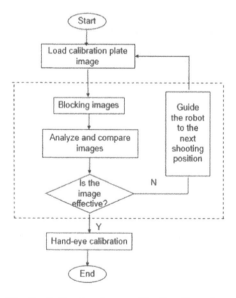

Fig. 1. Online hand eye calibration flow chart

During the online hand-eye calibration process, when an invalid image is acquired, the robot system needs to react quickly, analyze the orientation information of the image, and provide guidance for the next motion [8]. The online hand-eye calibration flow chart is shown in Fig. 1. The main work of this paper is the content in the dotted line box.

2 Calibration Board Image Classification and Segmentation

2.1 Image Orientation Classification

According to the orientation information of the plane, Fig. 2(a), we divide the state of the calibration board image into 9 kinds. That is, the center position and eight directions: top, bottom, left, right, and upper left, upper right, lower left, and lower right as shown in Fig. 2(b). Only Fig. (5) is a valid calibration board image. Other images are considered as invalid calibration board images. The main task of this paper is to analyze and determine the orientation of the invalid calibration board image after screening.

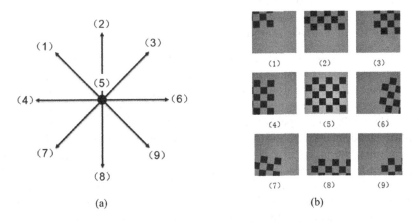

(a)   (b)

Fig. 2. Calibration board image

2.2 Image Segmentation

In order to obtain the position information of the calibration board. We divided the image into 9 pieces and arrange them in 3*3 [9]. sub-images are connected to each other [10]. For example, an image of M × N, M and N respectively represent the number of pixels per column and each row, the size of the sub-image is M/3, N/3, and those 9 sub-images are numbered:

$$I_i \ (i = 1, 2 \cdots 9)$$

Where i denotes the i-th sub-image. For example, the block processing is performed on (4) in Fig. 2(ii), and the obtained image after 3×3 uniform block is as shown in Fig. 3.

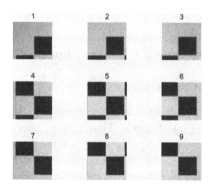

Fig. 3. Image segmentation

3   Calibration Board Orientation Analysis

3.1   Image Ratio Analysis Method

The checkerboard calibration board image is in black and white. Black and white pixel values are not absolutely equal to 0 and 255 due to factors such as illumination and shadow. Image binarization using Otsu segmentation algorithm. The effect diagram is shown in Fig. 4(a), and the black and white effects of the image display are more obvious. Combining the block of the image, binarize the nine sub-images of each calibration board image, as shown in Fig. 4(b). For the black background image, the proportion of white pixels in each sub-image is obtained; for the white background image, the proportion of black pixels in each sub-image is obtained and recorded to the position corresponding to the nine-square grid, as shown in Table 1. When the sub-images are all the calibration board images, the ratio is close to 0.5, and the sub-image does not contain the calibration board image, the ratio is 0, or close to 0.

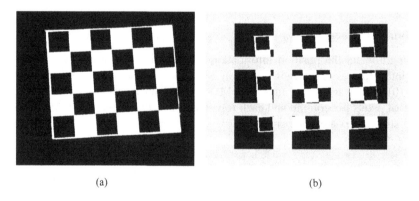

(a)   (b)

Fig. 4. Binarization and block image

Table 1. Image ratio data table.

Label of sub-image	I_1	I_2	I_3	I_4	I_5	I_6	I_7	I_8	I_9
Proportion of black pixels	0.1642	0.3763	0.2606	0.2778	0.5080	0.3844	0.0498	0.2927	0.1647

3.2   Block Image Histogram Method

Block Image Histogram and Gaussian Fitting. The histogram of monochrome image is the image representation of the frequency of each gray value in the image. [11, 12]. Its mathematical expression is:

$$n(k) = card\{(x,y)|r_j \leq f(x,y) < r_{j+1}\}$$
$$P_{(r_k)} = n_k / n$$

Where n is the total number of pixels in the image, $P(r_k)$ is the probability of the kth gray level (r_k).

Since the checkerboard calibration board has only two colors of black and white, the histogram of the checkerboard image is bimodality. Figure 5 is a valid histogram of the acquired calibration board image (the horizontal axis represents the corresponding gray level r_k and the vertical axis represents the value of the corresponding $P(r_k)$).

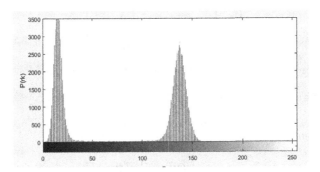

Fig. 5. Calibration board image histogram

The histogram distribution of the image is a Gaussian distribution or an approximate Gaussian distribution. The principle of Gaussian fitting is to describe the law of data according to the data change with the expression y = f(x) [13]. Gaussian function expression:

$$f(x) = a_1 * \exp\left(-\left(\frac{x - b1}{c1}\right)^2\right) \tag{1}$$

a1,b1,c1 is the pending parameter.

For easy solution, take the logarithm of (1):

$$\ln(f(x)) = \ln a_1 - \frac{(x - b_1)^2}{c_1} = \left(\ln a_1 - \frac{b_1^2}{c_1}\right) + \frac{2xb_1}{c_1} - \frac{x^2}{c_1} \tag{2}$$

Let:

$$Z_i = \ln(f(X))$$

$$B_0 = \left(\ln a_1 - \frac{b_1^2}{c_1}\right)$$

$$B_1 = \frac{2xb_1}{c_1}$$

$$B_2 = -\frac{x^2}{c_1}$$

Use matrix to represent formula (2):

$$\begin{bmatrix} Z_1 \\ Z_2 \\ \vdots \\ Z_n \end{bmatrix} = \begin{bmatrix} 1 & x_1 & x_1^2 \\ 1 & x_2 & x_2^2 \\ \vdots & \vdots & \vdots \\ 1 & x_n & x_n^2 \end{bmatrix} \begin{bmatrix} B_0 \\ B_1 \\ B_2 \end{bmatrix}$$

Recorded as:

$$Z = XB$$

Solving parameters by least squares principle [14]:

$$B = (X^T X)^{-1} X^T Z$$

Then can find the value of a_1, b_1, c_1. Where a_1 is the peak value, b_1 is the peak position, and c_1 is the half width information.

Combine the image block, then output 9 sub-image histograms of each calibration board image, and perform the second-order Gaussian curve fitting to extract the parameters of the histogram. The fitting function is:

$$f(x) = a_1 * \exp\left(-\left(\frac{x - b1}{c1}\right)^2\right) + a_2 * \exp\left(-\left(\frac{x - b2}{c2}\right)^2\right) \tag{3}$$

The obtained a_1 and a_2 are the two peaks of the curve, and b_1 and b_2 are the peak positions, c_1, c_2 are half width. Such as Fig. 6, where $a1 = 2862, b1 = 16.29$, $c1 = 6.011, a2 = 2017, b2 = 134.7, c2 = 9.904$.

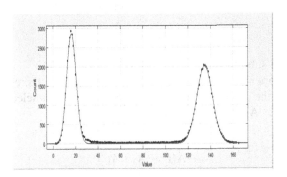

Fig. 6. Gaussian fitting

Calibration Board Orientation. Since each image is divided into 9 sub-images, the 9 sub-images have the same shooting environment. The image orientation is determined based on the values of a_1, a_2, b_1, b_2, c_1, and c_2 of the nine sub-images. What should be determined firstly is whether the sub-image has double peaks. Considering that the second-order Gaussian curve fits the single-peak data, the two parameters of a_1, a_2, b_1, b_2, c_1, and c_2 are still obtained, but the peak position of the fitting (that is, the value of b) is significantly different. Therefore, the method of setting the threshold is adopted, and the judgment is completed by comparing with the threshold. Find the difference between b_1 and b_2

$$D(i) = |b_1 - b_2| \tag{4}$$

Find the average of 9 sub-images

$$D = \frac{1}{9} \sum_{i=1}^{9} D(i) \tag{5}$$

When $D(i) > D$, the image (i) satisfies the bimodal characteristic and is regarded as the portion containing the calibration board image;

When $D(i) < D$, the image (i) does not satisfy the bimodal feature and is regarded as a portion that does not contain the calibration board image.

D is a threshold for judging whether the bimodal characteristic is satisfied. The threshold for each image is unique, and is only used to determine 9 sub-images of the image, and has the characteristics of strong adaptability and high accuracy. After the comparison, the sub-image i satisfying the bimodal condition is obtained, and according to the block, each i value corresponds to one position, whereby the orientation of the calibration board can be determined.

Further utilizing the peak area to determine the magnitude of the offset. In order to simplify the calculation process, the area of the triangle is used instead of the peak area. Since the value of c in the Gaussian fitting is half width, the area is expressed as:

$$A_1(i) = a_1 * c_1$$

$$A_2(i) = a_2 * c_2$$

i represents the i-th sub-image.

Since only the orientation of the image needs to be judged, there is no requirement for the accuracy of the pixel, so the highest bit of each value is selected. Among them $A_1(1) = 17203.482$, $A_2(1) = 19976.368$.

Let:

$$A(i) = A_2 / A_1 \tag{6}$$

When A(i) = 1, the sub-images i are all the calibration board images;

when A(i) = 1/3, half of the sub-images i are the calibration board images.

Corresponding to the block information, the size of the calibration board offset can be determined.

4 Experiment Results

4.1 Simulation Experiments

The simulation experiment is used to test the accuracy of the orientation analysis of the calibration board after the invalid image is acquired. We set up three simulation environments: no light source, low intensity light source and high intensity light source, and carried out simulation experiments on black background and white background.

The orientation information of the image can be obtained, by Simulate 300 images with MATLAB. Let's take the example of 9 orientations on a black background. We can see that the block effect of 9 directions is shown in Fig. 7. The image ratio method is shown in Table 2. The first 3*3 matrix in the table, only the data of I_1 is not zero. It corresponds to the position of the orientation (1), so the calibration board is in the topper left corner. The block image histogram is shown in Fig. 8. We only give images of orientation (1) and orientation (4), Fig. 8 (A), Only the sub-image I_1 has a bimodal feature. It corresponds to the position of the orientation (1), so the calibration board is on the topper left corner. Figure 8 (B), the sub-image I_1、I_2、I_4、I_5、I_7、I_8 has a bimodal feature. It corresponds to the position of the orientation (4), so the calibration board is on the left of the image. The simulation results show that the method has certain reference value.

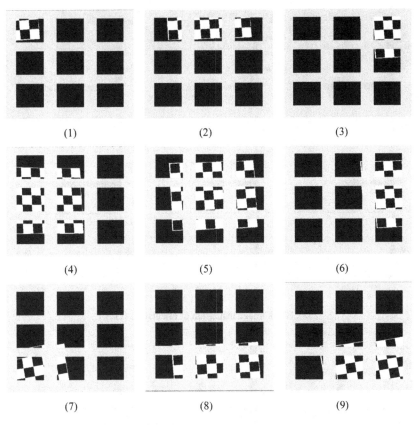

Fig. 7. Blocking result

Table 2. Proportion of white pixels in each sub-image.

Sub-image	I_1	I_2	I_3	I_4	I_5	I_6	I_7	I_8	I_9
Orientation (1)	0.42	0	0	0	0	0	0	0	0
Orientation (2)	0.26	0.50	0.27	0	0	0	0	0	0
Orientation (3)	0	0.01	0.55	0	0	0.17	0	0	0
Orientation (4)	0.27	0.24	0	0.53	0.45	0	0.29	0.34	0
Orientation (5)	0.16	0.38	0.26	0.28	0.51	0.38	0.05	0.29	0.16
Orientation (6)	0	0.03	0.36	0	0.01	0.55	0	0	0.17
Orientation (7)	0	0	0	0.02	0.04	0	0.53	0.22	0
Orientation (8)	0	0	0	0.01	0.05	0.07	0.18	0.55	0.46
Orientation (9)	0	0	0	0.01	0.07	0.21	0.02	0.52	0.52

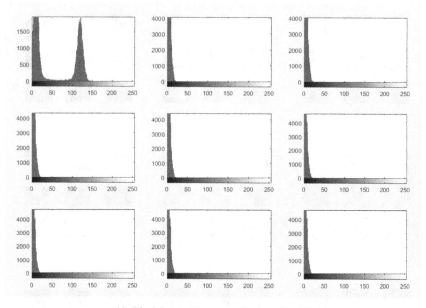

(a). Block image histogram of orientation (1)

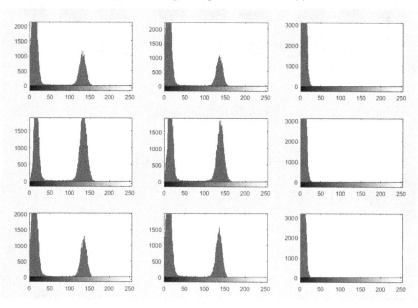

(b). Block image histogram of orientation (4)

Fig. 8. Block image histogram

4.2   Real Experiments

Experiment Apparatus. In the real experiment, the Hikvision CA series CCD camera and the MF series lens were used. The camera was fixed at the last joint of a 6-DOF UR robot, as shown in Fig. 9.

Fig. 9. Experimental equipment

Method Combination. The image ratio analysis method has the advantages of being simple and fast. The block image histogram method is more intuitive, and it is easy to judge the proportion of the image occupied by the calibration board. After analysis, combining the two methods to determine the orientation of the calibration board will get the best results. For the image analysis of the calibration board of Fig. 2 (4), the binarized image of the image ratio method is shown in the Fig. 10, and the results are shown in Table 3. When the sub-images are all the calibration board images, the ratio is close to 0.5, and the sub-image does not contain the calibration board image, the ratio is 0, or close to 0. The block image histogram method is shown in the Fig. 11, and the results are shown in Table 4. The ratio is 1 when all sub-images are calibration board images. Combine the two methods by adding data. When the sub-images are all the calibration board images, the value is 1.5, which is used as a standard to judge the orientation of the calibration board.

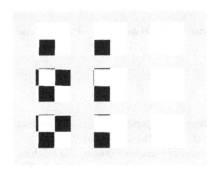

Fig. 10. Image ratio method

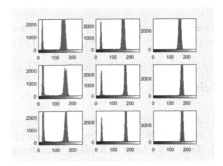

Fig. 11. The block image histogram method

Table 3. Black pixel ratio data table.

Label of sub-image	I_1	I_2	I_3	I_4	I_5	I_6	I_7	I_8	I_9
Proportion of black pixels	0.2120	0.2060	0	0.4695	0.2271	0	0.4690	0.2203	0

Table 4. Area ratio (A) data sheet.

Label of sub-image	I_1	I_2	I_3	I_4	I_5	I_6	I_7	I_8	I_9
Proportion of black pixels	1/3	1/3	*	1	1/3	*	1	1/3	*

* Represents a sub-image of a non-bimodal feature.

When shooting the calibration board image, the image analysis, after the image acquisition fails, can analyze the orientation of the calibration board in time, and guide the robot arm to find the correct shooting position. After several experiments, the two methods were combined to analyze the orientation. When one of the methods has an error, the deviation of the result will not be large due to the influence of the other method. The results are more reliable and more efficient than the single orientation analysis method.

5 Conclusion

We propose a method for automatic screening and orientation analysis of calibration boards. This method combines image pixel ratio and block image histogram methods. On the one hand, by image binarization, the pixel ratio is solved to obtain the direction of the calibration board. On the other hand, the characteristics of the calibration board are found by the image gray histogram. Then, a Gaussian fit is used to obtain the parameters, and the threshold and area are solved to obtain the direction information of the calibration board. In this way, the efficiency and accuracy of data acquisition of the calibration board are improved, thereby improving the accuracy of hand-eye calibration. Through experimental verification, this method can quickly and accurately capture the effective calibration board image.

Acknowledgements. This work was financially supported by the National Key Research and Development Plan Program (2017YFB1303701).

References

1. Zhang, J., Dong, Y., Wangning, H.U., et al.: Hardware and algorithm design of industrial robot for 3C products manufacturing. Mach. Des. Res. **231**, 2912–2924 (2017)
2. Tsai, R.Y., Lenz, R.K.: Real time versatile robotics hand/eye calibration using 3D machine vision. In: 1988 IEEE International Conference on Robotics and Automation, pp. 554–561, IEEE (1988)
3. Antonello, M., et al.: A fully automatic hand-eye calibration system. In: European Conference on Mobile Robots IEEE (2017)

4. Agile, L., Qixin, C.: Hand-eye calibration method for automatic generation of calibration gesture. Mach. Des. Manuf. **15**(S2), 164–167 (2018)
5. Cheng, Y.: Hand-eye calibration and object localization for industrial robotic applications. Zhejiang University (2016)
6. Shi, F., Wang, J., Liu, Y.: An approach to improve online hand-eye calibration. In: Marques, J.S., Pérez de la Blanca, N., Pina, P. (eds.) IbPRIA 2005. LNCS, vol. 3522, pp. 647–655. Springer, Heidelberg (2005). https://doi.org/10.1007/11492429_78
7. Zhang, J., Shi, F., Liu, Y.: An adaptive selection of motion for online hand-eye calibration. J. Shanghai Jiaotong Univ. **40**(7), 1089–1093 (2006)
8. Bishop, B.E., Spong, M.W.: Adaptive calibration and control of 2D monocular visual servo systems. Control Eng. Pract. **7**(3), 423–430 (1999)
9. Liu, P., Zhuang, M., Guo, H., et al.: Adding spatial distribution clue to aggregated vector in image retrieval. EURASIP J. Image Video Process. **2018**(1), 9 (2018)
10. Shaila, S.G., Vadivel, A.: Block encoding of color histogram for content based image retrieval applications. Procedia Technol. **6**(4), 526–533 (2012)
11. Wan, L., Zhang, T., You, H.J.: Multi-sensor remote sensing image change detection based on sorted histograms. Int. J. Remote Sens. **39**(11), 3753–3775 (2018)
12. Liu, P., et al.: Fusion of color histogram and LBP-based features for texture image retrieval and classification. Inf. Sci. **390**, 95–111 (2017)
13. Liu, J.S., et al.: Optical fiber positioning based on four-quadrant detector with Gaussian fitting method. Res. Astron. Astrophys. **17**(7), 75 (2017)
14. Markovsky, I., Van Huffel, S.: Overview of total least-squares methods. Signal Process. **87**(10), 2283–2302 (2007)

Image Deblurring Based on Fuzzy Kernel Estimation in HSV Color Space

Aidi Zhao, Jianhua Zhang, Xiaoling Lv$^{(\boxtimes)}$, and Minglu Zhang

School of Mechanical Engineering, Hebei University of Technology,
Tianjin, China
lxl000418@163.com

Abstract. Image deblurring is intended to restore the clear images from the damaged images. The main factor of the image deblurring is to precisely estimate the fuzzy kernel in the unknown blurring process. For color images, the fuzzy kernel is estimated by converting them into the gray domain with the most existing effective image deblurring approaches. In fact, the influence of the fuzzy kernel function on each channel in the HSV color space is different. In this paper, a more accurate image deblurring algorithm is proposed. In HSV color space, the Radon transform based on the spectral edge detection is used to estimate the fuzzy kernel. For the fuzzy kernel obtained from the different channels independently, the deblurring restoration based on Richardson-Lucy guided filter is carried out in each channel. The Simulation results demonstrate that the proposed method is effective.

Keywords: HSV color space · Spectral edge detection ·
Fuzzy kernel estimation · Linear motion blurring

1 Introduction

With the further application of the scientific and technological innovation, the development of 3C electronic industry requires to accelerate the speed of production. The application of machine vision technology in electronic industry is imperative. However, due to the influence of the speed change of the conveyor belt or the underexposure of the camera, the motion blurring which would hinder the following detection and identification is produced on the images, so the image deblurring is necessary.

There are lots of related researches at home and abroad in view of the image motion deblurring. The classical Wiener filter [1] assumes that the noise is a random process and the minimum variance is calculated to recover the images, and the commonly used Richardson-Lucy deconvolution [2] assumes that the pixels of the natural image obey Poisson distribution and is solved by their iteration. But the serious ringing effect produces with this method. In [3], a method based on partial differential equation (PDE) is used to restore the fuzzy images, and the ringing effect was weakened by combining the anti-reflection boundary conditions and the step of re-blurring. In [4], the derivative sparseness of natural images is used as a constraint to reduce the ringing effect in the deconvolution process. Some original methods [5–9] were proposed. In view of the estimation of fuzzy kernel of the linear motion, the spectrum graph by many

© Springer Nature Switzerland AG 2019
H. Yu et al. (Eds.): ICIRA 2019, LNAI 11744, pp. 590–603, 2019.
https://doi.org/10.1007/978-3-030-27541-9_48

scholars is used to obtain the fuzzy parameters. The methods of obtaining the fuzzy angle are the radon transform [10], Hough transform [11], etc. Jia [12] improves the process of getting fuzzy angle by the Radon algorithm. The Canny edge detection is carried out to reduce the influence of the center bright line of the spectrum map on the process of calculating the fuzzy angle. For the noisy images, Jiang [13] adds Z function to the radon algorithm formula in order to enhance the features, and the double threshold method is used to enhance the stability of the algorithm. However, the current image restoration methods have a good effect in the gray domain, but they will be weaken in various degrees in the color images. Therefore, In this paper, we studied the method of motion deblurring the three channels of HSV color space instead of the gray or RGB color space and then the Radon transform based on the spectral edge detection was used to estimate their fuzzy kernel. For the fuzzy kernel obtained from different channels, the deblurring restoration based on Richardson-Lucy guided filter is carried out in each channel. Finally the final restored images are obtained.

2   Fuzzy Kernel Estimation in the HSV Color Space

2.1   Analysis of Spectrum Characteristics of Motion Blurring

When the camera is exposed, the motorial object produces a smear on the CCD, and the direction and distance of the motion determine the parameters of the fuzzy kernel (PSF). For the digital images, an image can be regarded as a two-dimensional discrete function $f(x, y)$. The spatial coordinate of the image is a finite value (x, y). The process of forming the motion blurring images can be regarded as a convolution process of a natural clear image and a fuzzy kernel function (PSF). And if the noise exists, the effect of the noise interference shall be taken into account, and it is generally assumed that the noise is additive. The blurring process of the images can be described as:

$$g(x,y) = h(x,y) \otimes f(x,y) + n(x,y) \tag{1}$$

Where $g(x, y)$ corresponds to the fuzzy image; $h(x, y)$ to the fuzzy kernel function, and $n(x, y)$ is the additive noise; $\otimes$ denotes the convolution operation. Based on the convolution theorem, the frequency domain expression of Eq. (1) is as follows:

$$G(u,v) = F(u,v)H(u,v) + N(u,v) \tag{2}$$

The process of the uniform motion blurring can be regarded as the process of the integral of a scene $f(x, y)$ to be acquired during the exposure time. Let's assume the component motion of the image during this exposure time in the direction of x direction and the y direction are $x_0(t)$ and $y_0(t)$ respectively, and $n(x, y)$ is the additive noise. Hence, the actual acquired blurring images can be expressed as:

$$g(x,y) = \int_0^T f(x - x_0(t), y - y_0(t))dt + n(x,y) \tag{3}$$

Let's assume that $n(x, y)$ is small firstly, and the Fourier transform is taken on the Eq. (3) to obtain:

$$G(u, v) = \int_{-\infty}^{\infty} \int_{-\infty}^{\infty} [\int_0^T f(x - x_0(t), y - y_0(t)) dt] e^{-2j\pi(ux + vy)} dxdy$$

$$\Rightarrow G(u, v) = F(u, v) \int_0^T e^{-2j\pi(ux_0(t) + vy_0(t))} dt \tag{4}$$

$$\Rightarrow H(u, v) = \int_0^T e^{-2j\pi(ux_0(t) + vy_0(t))} dt \tag{5}$$

Assume the x direction moves m pixels and the y direction moves n pixels. Namely:

$$x_0(t) = mt/T, y_0(t) = nt/T$$

$$\Rightarrow |H(u, v)| = \left| \frac{T}{\pi(um + vn)} \sin(\pi(um + vn)) \right| \tag{6}$$

The Eq. (7) is discretized:

$$|H(u, v)| = \left| \frac{T}{\pi(\frac{um}{N} + \frac{vn}{M})} \sin(\pi(\frac{um}{N} + \frac{vn}{M})) \right| \tag{7}$$

From Eq. (7), we can see that the spectrum of fuzzy kernel is a $\sin c(x)$ function, and the maximum value of $H(u, v)$ is equal to T when $\frac{um}{N} + \frac{vn}{M} = 0$, and $H(u, v)$ is equal to 0 when $\frac{um}{N} + \frac{vn}{M}$ is a non-zero integer. Therefore, when the noise is inexistent or very small, the center of the spectrum image G is two bands, and there are parallel dark fringes with equal spacing on both sides, and the inclination of the dark stripes (denoted as β) is the inclination of the straight line $\frac{um}{N} + \frac{vn}{M} = 0$, that is, $\tan \beta = -\frac{M}{N} \cdot \frac{a}{b}$. Let's α represents the inclination of the motion blurred direction, then $\tan \alpha = \frac{b}{a}$. Then the relationship between the motion blurred direction α, the size of the image $M \times N$ and the inclination of the parallel dark fringes of the spectrum β can be obtained:

$$\tan \alpha = \frac{M}{N} \tan(\beta - \frac{\pi}{2}) \tag{8}$$

After the fuzzy direction angle α is obtained, the image is rotated α to make it parallel to the X axis. Then the differential autocorrelation method is used to estimate the fuzzy length, and the distance between the minimum values is the fuzzy kernel length. As shown in Fig. 5 (a3), the distance between the two minimum peaks is 4 pixels, so the corresponding PSF has a fuzzy kernel length of 4.

Therefore, the fuzzy kernel function PSF is determined by identifying the spacing and direction of the dark stripes.

2.2 Fuzzy Kernel Estimation in the HSV Color Space

At present, the existing methods are used to estimate the fuzzy kernel of the images in the gray domain. In fact, the effect of the fuzzy kernel function on the component map of each channel in the color images is different. In [14], the fuzzy kernel is estimated in each component of RGB color space, it is easy to observe that the fuzzy kernel is alike, and the difference between their shape and value is small.

HSV color space is a subjective color model. H, S, V refer to hue, color saturation and luminance value respectively. The effects of the blurring images in their hue, saturation and brightness are different to a great extent. Such as, the blurring length $L = 35$ and the blurring angle $\alpha = 45°$ were added to an image, as shown in Fig. 1. After the color image was transformed into HSV color space, the three components H, S and V were separated and analyzed by the spectrum analysis, as shown in Fig. 2. It is clear to observe that the effects of the motion blurring on the three components are different: the spectrum direction of the three components is little different, while the H and S component are less affected by the same fuzzy length (the fuzzy length $L = 4$) and the V component is greatly influenced by the fuzzy length (the fuzzy length $L = 30$). Therefore, the image restoration on three components is very meaningful respectively.

a
b

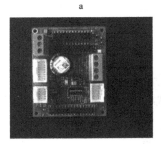
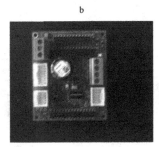

Fig. 1. (a) A clear image with 2048×2448. (b) The blurring image with the blurring length $L = 35$ and the blurring angle $\alpha = 45°$.

2.3 Fuzzy Direction Estimation Based on Spectrum Edge Detection and Radon Transform

As far as the images is concerned, the Radon transform reflects the projection property of the image in different directions. For the spectrum images G, its Radon transform is as follows:

$$R(G)(\rho, \theta) = \int_{-\infty}^{\infty} G(\rho \cos \theta - t \sin \theta, \rho \sin \theta + t \cos \theta)dt \qquad (9)$$

It can be seen that the Radon transform of spectrum map G is a linear integral along the distance ρ from the origin and the angle θ between it and the Y axis. Since there is a group of parallel fringes in the motion blurring spectrum map, the integral value in that direction is bound to be the largest. Therefore, the fuzzy angle can be determined by the Radon transform.

Edge detection aims at extracting the abrupt boundary lines between the target and the background on grayscale or texture features. There are obvious bright and dark stripes in the spectrum images, and the edge lines obtained from edge detection should be parallel to the direction of stripes and can weaken the high gray value of the bright cross, thereby reducing the interference of the bright cross. Therefore, the Canny operator with better detection performance is selected for the detection. Because the three channels processing method is the same, only one channel effect diagram is displayed here. As shown in Fig. 3(a), the outline of the parallel dark lines are highlighted. Although the bright cross is still faintly visible, the interference has become very weak compared with the strengthened parallel boundary.

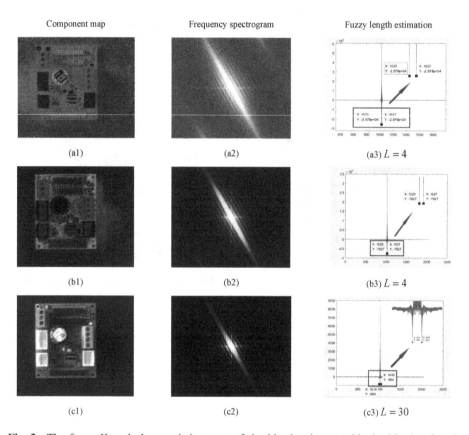

Fig. 2. The fuzzy Kernel characteristic curve of the blurring image with the blurring length $L = 35$ and the blurring angle $\alpha = 45°$. The three rows correspond to analysis at H, S, and V component map of HSV color space, respectively. The first column is component map of HSV color map; the second column is their frequency spectrogram map, and the third column is their fuzzy length estimation.

 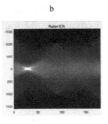

a   b

Fig. 3. (a) Canny edge detection for S component; (b) Radon transformation for Fig. (a)

The binary spectrum of the Canny edge detection image is transformed using the Radon transform by $0° - 180°$, as shown in Fig. 3(b). The angle $\theta = 34°$ corresponded to the maximum value of the transformation is found, which is the angle between the direction of the dark fringes of the spectrum and the Y axis. Therefore, the inclination of the dark fringes is $\beta = \theta + \frac{\pi}{2} = 124°$. The size of the image is 2048×2448, and the Eq. (8) is used to calculate the direction angle of the motion blurring $\alpha = 29.44°$.

3 Deblurring Method Based on Richardson-Lucy Guided Filter [15]

The Richardson-Lucy algorithm assumes that the imaging follows the distribution:

$$I(i) = \sum P(i|j)O(j) \tag{9}$$

Where I corresponds to a fuzzy image, O represents the original image and $P(i|j)$ to a point spread function. The combined probability distribution of the observed count value $D(i)$ and the expected count value $I(i)$ is:

$$\ln \Pi = \sum_i D(i) \ln I(i) - I(i) - \ln D(i) \tag{10}$$

By substituting Eq. (10) into Eq. (9), an iterative formula can be obtained and the following results can be obtained:

$$O_{new(j)} = O(j) \frac{\sum_i P(i|j)D(i)}{\sum_i P(i|j)I(i)} \tag{11}$$

The Richardson-Lucy algorithm uses the maximum likelihood method to estimate, and the execution speed is faster. However, because the noise estimation of the original image is not accurate, obvious ringing effect is produced on the restored image. Therefore, the gradient synchronization characteristics of guided filter are used to suppress it.

Guided filtering assumes that there is a linear relationship between the input image and the guided image in the local range. Let's p responds to the input image, q is the output image, and I represents the guided image, then in the window ω_k with a center k, there are:

$$q_i = a_k I_i + b_k, \forall i \in \omega_k \tag{12}$$

In order to determine the coefficients, it can be converted into optimal problems:

$$E(a_k, b_k) = \sum_{i \in \omega_k} ((a_k I_i + b_k - P_i)^2 + \varepsilon a_k^2) \tag{13}$$

Where P_i is the image to be processed, in order to prevent the parameter a_k too large, the parameter ε can be solved by linear regression, that is,

$$a_k = \frac{\frac{1}{|\omega|} \sum_{i \in \omega_k} I_i P_i - \mu_k \overline{p_k}}{\sigma_k^2 + \varepsilon} \tag{14}$$

$$b_k = \overline{p_k} - a_k \mu_k \tag{15}$$

Where $\overline{p_k}$ is the mean value of P in the window ω_k, and σ_k^2 represents the variance of I in the window ω_k. Since pixels are covered by multiple windows, the average value of a_k and b_k for all possible windows is taken at the end.

Let's I represents the fuzzy image, κ which sets up the size of PSF responds to the size of sliding windows and the smoothing strength is set to 0.16. τ is the weight of the guide image in the deblurred image and can be expressed as

$$\tau = \text{sgn}(|\nabla_{axis} I|) + \xi \tag{16}$$

Where $\nabla_{axis} I$ is the gradient of the image in the direction of motion, and ξ is a small number in order to make symbol function be non-zero.

After the channels H, S and V are deblurred by the above-mentioned methods, merge the three channels into RGB space, and the final deblurred color image can be obtained.

4   Experiments

In this paper, three color images were simulated, as shown as in Fig. 4. The "fspecial" command in the Matlab toolbox was used to set the motion blurring in Fig. 4. The fuzzy angle α is $0°$, $25°$ and $45°$ and the fuzzy length L is 25 or 35, as shown in Fig. 5.

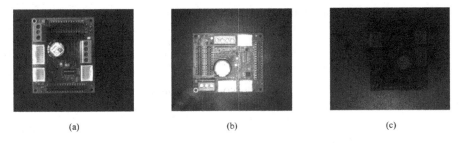

(a)   (b)   (c)

Fig. 4. Three color images used to experiment. (a) A normal exposure image; (b) A multi-exposure image; (c) A low illumination image

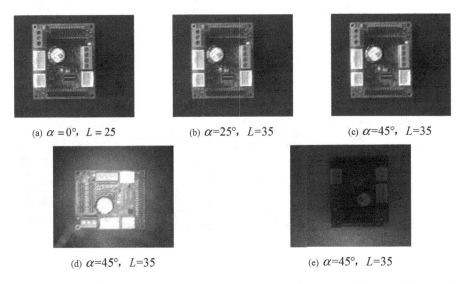

(a) $\alpha = 0°$, $L = 25$ (b) $\alpha = 25°$, $L = 35$ (c) $\alpha = 45°$, $L = 35$

(d) $\alpha = 45°$, $L = 35$ (e) $\alpha = 45°$, $L = 35$

Fig. 5. Images adding motion blurring. (a)–(c) the normal exposure images with $\alpha = 0°$, $L = 25$, $\alpha = 25°$, $L = 35$ and $\alpha = 45°$, $L = 35$ respectively; (d) the multi-exposure image with $\alpha = 45°$, $L = 35$; (e) the low illumination image with $\alpha = 45°$, $L = 35$

In this paper, subjective visual comparison, mean square error (MSE) and the peak signal to noise ratio (PSNR) were used to evaluate the quality of the image restoration. The mean square error (MSE) is defined as:

$$MSE = \frac{1}{MN} \sum_{m=1}^{M} \sum_{n=1}^{N} \left| \tilde{f}(m,n) - f(m,n) \right|^2 \tag{18}$$

Where $\tilde{f}(m,n)$ is the restored image and $f(m,n)$ represents the clear image. The smaller the MSE, the better the image quality.

The peak signal to noise ratio (PSNR) is defined as:

$$PSNR = 10 \lg \frac{255^2}{MSN} (dB) \qquad (19)$$

The result in the HSV color space was compared with the traditional Wiener filter, constrained least square filter and Richardson-Lucy restoration.

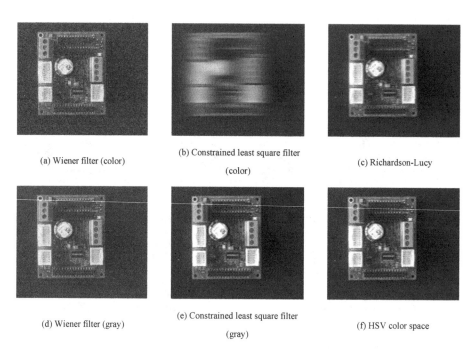

(a) Wiener filter (color)

(b) Constrained least square filter
(color)

(c) Richardson-Lucy

(d) Wiener filter (gray)

(e) Constrained least square filter
(gray)

(f) HSV color space

Fig. 6. Comparisons of the normal exposure fuzzy images with $\alpha = 0°$, $L = 25$ deblurring visual effects

The results were measured in a PC with a 2.2 GHz Inter 8750H CPU by Matlab 2016a. In this paper, the effects of image restoration are illustrated, as shown in Figs. 6, 7, 8 and 9. Because the objective data of the restoration effects can reflect more intuitively than their subjective vision, the details of the MSE and PSNR data for all simulation restoration images are listed in Tables 1 and 2.

We can easily observe that Wiener filter in the color images can roughly restore clear images, but the ringing effect is obvious and lots of noise emerge on the image that will seriously affect the subsequent detection and identification, while the effect in gray-scale restoration images is better. In gray-scale most of the details are restored and a bit of noise is generated that will weakly affect the subsequent detection and iden-tification. Constrained least square filtering is invalid in color images, while it is better in gray images. We can easily observe that the results of Wiener filter in gray images are worse than that of the Constrained least square filtering. Mass stripes produce on the background of Wiener filter in gray images. And Richardson-Lucy-guided restoration algorithm in HSV color space is better than Richardson-Lucy algorithm, and the results of Richardson-Lucy algorithm in color images are worse than that of the Constrained least square filtering in gray images.

For the multi-exposure color images, we can easily observe that Wiener filter can restore clear images, and its effect is little better than that in the normal exposure images and in the low illumination images, but the ringing effect is still obvious and lots of noise emerge on the images, while the effects in gray-scale images are better. In gray-scale, most of the details are restored and a bit of noise is generated. Constrained least square filtering is still invalid in color images, while it is better in gray images. And we can observe that the results in the low illumination images are better than that in the multi-exposure images. And Richardson-Lucy-guided restoration algorithm in HSV color space is better than Richardson-Lucy algorithm, and the results of Richardson-Lucy algorithm in color images are worse than that of the Constrained least square filtering in gray images. In the multi-exposure images, the proposed method produces black dots in the high-brightness area, and the trifling contrast change produces in the edge which little affect the detail of images. The details of the MSE and PSNR data for all simulation restoration images are listed in Tables 1 and 2.

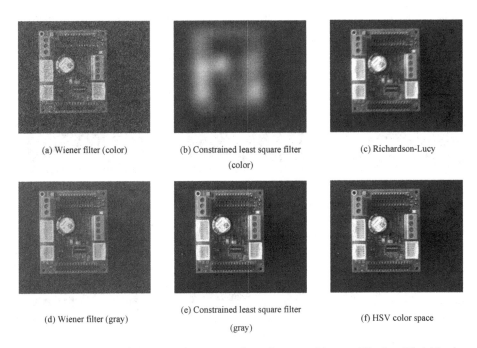

(a) Wiener filter (color)   (b) Constrained least square filter (color)   (c) Richardson-Lucy

(d) Wiener filter (gray)   (e) Constrained least square filter (gray)   (f) HSV color space

Fig. 7. Comparisons of the normal exposure fuzzy images with $\alpha = 45°$, $L = 35$ deblurring visual effects

The effects of deblurring in HSV color space are better than that of the traditional Richardson-Lucy algorithm by comparing their PSNR and MSE. Especially when the

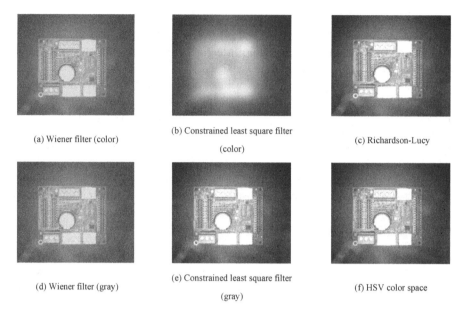

Fig. 8. Comparisons of the multi-exposure fuzzy images with $\alpha = 45°$, $L = 35$ deblurring visual effects

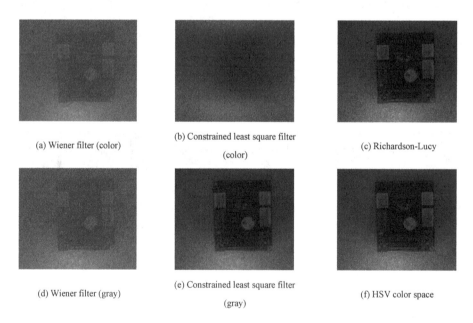

Fig. 9. Comparisons of the low illumination fuzzy images with $\alpha = 45°$, $L = 35$ deblurring visual effects

Table 1. Comparisons of MSE values of image restoration under different conditions of motion blurring

Algorithm	The normal exposure fuzzy images with $\alpha = 0°$ $L = 25$	The normal exposure fuzzy images with $\alpha = 25°$ $L = 35$	The normal exposure fuzzy images with $\alpha = 45°$ $L = 35$	The multi-exposure fuzzy images with $\alpha = 45°$ $L = 35$	The low illumination fuzzy images with $\alpha = 45°$ $L = 35$
Wiener filter (color)	110.61	112.49	114.55	107.72	95.74
Wiener filter (gray)	79.78	81.36	83.32	89.17	87.72
Constrained least square filter (color)	344.41	368.54	378.35	485.05	535.49
Constrained least square filter (gray)	35.90	36.89	38.76	33.61	30.16
Richardson-Lucy algorithm	40.49	42.56	43.53	49.42	38.83
HSV color space	32.67	33.34	32.33	36.16	29.98

Table 2. Comparisons of PSNR values of Image Restoration under different conditions of motion blurring (dB)

Algorithm	The normal exposure fuzzy images with $\alpha = 0°$ $L = 25$	The normal exposure fuzzy images with $\alpha = 25°$ $L = 35$	The normal exposure fuzzy images with $\alpha = 45°$ $L = 35$	The multi-exposure fuzzy images with $\alpha = 45°$ $L = 35$	The low illumination fuzzy images with $\alpha = 45°$ $L = 35$
Wiener filter (color)	27.6929	27.6197	27.5409	27.8078	28.3199
Wiener filter (gray)	29.1119	29.0267	28.9233	28.6286	28.6998
Constrained least square filter (color)	22.7600	22.4660	22.3519	21.2729	2.8433
Constrained least square filter (gray)	32.5799	32.4617	32.2470	32.8661	33.3365
Richardson-Lucy algorithm	32.0573	31.8408	31.7429	31.1918	32.2391
HSV color space	32.9893	32.9011	33.0347	32.5485	33.3625

fuzzy angle and the fuzzy length are large ($\alpha = 45°$, $L = 35$), the PSNR value of the proposed method increases by 1.3567 dB compared to the Richardson-Lucy algorithm. The recovery results of the proposed method are similar to the Constrained least square filtering in gray images. The PSNR value of the proposed method decreases by 0.3176 dB compared to the Constrained least square filtering in gray multi-exposure images, while the PSNR values of the proposed method are higher than the Constrained least square filtering in other motion blurring conditions.

5 Conclusions

In this paper, we observed that the effects of the motion blurring on the three components of HSV color space are different, therefore we studied the method of motion deblurring the three channels of HSV color space. The Radon transform based on the spectral edge detection was used to estimate the fuzzy kernel in the three components of HSV color space. For the fuzzy kernel obtained from different channels, the deblurring restoration based on Richardson-Lucy guided filter is carried out in each channel. We used our proposed method to experiment on three kinds of color images that are normal exposure, multi-exposure and low illumination images. Though the subjective vision and the objective data of the MSE and PSNR data, the effects of our proposed method is superior than that of the traditional Richardson-Lucy algorithm and the image restoration effect is clearer than that of the current method which only considers the fuzzy kernel estimation in the gray domain. The PSNR value of the proposed method decreases by 0.3176 dB compared to the Constrained least square filtering in gray multi-exposure images, and increases 0.7877 dB in normal images and 0.0260 dB in low illumination images. Therefore, our method is effective in all cases. So the images have preprocessed by the proposed method will be propitious to the subsequent detection and identification.

Acknowledgments. This work was financially supported by the National Key Research and Development Plan Program (2017YFB1303701).

References

1. Wiener, N.: Extrapolation, Interpolation, and Smoothing of Stationary Time Series. MIT Press, Cambridge (1949)
2. Richardson, W.H.: Bayesian-based iterative method of image restoration. J. Astron. **79**, 745 (1974)
3. Donatelli, M., Estatico, C., Martinelli, A.: Improved image deblurring with anti-reflective boundary conditions and re-blurring. Inverse Prob. **22**(6), 2035 (2006)
4. Levin, A., Fergus, R., Durand, R., et al.: Image and depth from a conventional camera with a coded aperture. ACM Trans. Graph. **26**(3), 70 (2007)
5. Yan, H.: Research on motion deblurring reduction method of high dynamic image. Dalian University of Technology, Dalian (2018)
6. Zhao, Y.: Research on Motion Image deblurring technique. Xi'an University of Electronic Science and Technology, Xi'an (2014)

7. Bao, Z.: Research on the blind deblurring technique of moving image. Hangzhou Electronic Science and Technology University, Hangzhou (2017)
8. Yao, H., Jiang, J., Qi, M., Wang, C.: Laplacian and bilaterally filtered image de-blurring algorithm. Sens. Microsyst. **36**(01), 139–142 (2017)
9. Lu, J., Yang, H., Shen, L., Zou, Y.: Ultrasound image restoration based on a learned dictionary and a higher-order MRF. Comput. Math. Appl. **77**(4), 991–1009 (2019)
10. Liao, Y., Cai, Z., He, X.: A blind deconvolution algorithm for fast motion fuzzy image. Opt. Precision Eng., **21**(10) (2013)
11. Ge, Y.: Research on the blind restoration algorithm of motion-blurred image. In: Advanced Information Management, Communicates, Electronic and Automation Control Conference (IMCEC), pp. 394–397 (2016)
12. Jia, C., Cui, L.: Direction estimation of motion blurred image based on spectral edge detection and Radon transform. J. Graph. **37**(3), 434–438 (2016)
13. Jiang, J., Huang, J., Zhang, G.: An accelerated motion blurred star restoration based on single image. IEEE Sens. J. **17**(5), 1306–1315 (2017)
14. Xu, X., Liu, H., Li, Y., et al.: Image de-blurring based on fuzzy kernel estimation in RGB channel. J. Chongqing Univ. Posts Telecommun.: Nat. Sci. Ed. **30**(2), 216–221 (2018)
15. Zhu, F., Jin, P.: Industrial detection-oriented image fast de-blurring method for linear motion. J. Harbin Univ. Technol. **50**(09), 129–135 (2018)

Infrared and Visible Image Fusion: A Region-Based Deep Learning Method

Chunyu Xie[1] and Xinde Li[1,2(✉)]

[1] Key Laboratory of Measurement and Control of CSE, School of Automation,
Southeast University, Nanjing, China
{cyxie,xindeli}@seu.edu.cn
[2] School of Cyber Science and Engineering, Southeast University, Nanjing, China

Abstract. Infrared and visible image fusion is playing an important role in robot perception. The key of fusion is to extract useful information from source image by appropriate methods. In this paper, we propose a deep learning method for infrared and visible image fusion based on region segmentation. Firstly, the source infrared image is segmented into foreground part and background part, then we build an infrared and visible image fusion network on the basis of neural style transfer algorithm. We propose foreground loss and background loss to control the fusion of the two parts respectively. And finally the fused image is reconstructed by combining the two parts together. The experimental results show that compared with other state-of-art methods, our method retains both saliency information of target and detail texture information of background.

Keywords: Infrared image · Visible image · Image fusion · Region segmentation · Deep learning

1 Introduction

The purpose of infrared and visible image fusion is combining the images obtained by infrared and visible sensors to generate robust and informative images for further processing. Infrared images can distinguish targets from their backgrounds based on the radiation difference while visible images can provide texture details with high spatial resolution and definition in a manner consistent with the human visual system [1]. The target of infrared and visible image fusion is to combine thermal radiation information in infrared image with detailed texture information in visible image. In recent years, research on fusion algorithms has been developing rapidly. However, an appropriate image information extraction method is key to ensuring good fusion performance of infrared and visible images.

The existing fusion algorithms are divided into seven categories including multi-scale transform [2], sparse representation [3], neural network [4], subspace [5], and saliency based [6] methods, hybrid models [7], and other methods [8].

© Springer Nature Switzerland AG 2019
H. Yu et al. (Eds.): ICIRA 2019, LNAI 11744, pp. 604–615, 2019.
https://doi.org/10.1007/978-3-030-27541-9_49

The main steps of these methods are decompose source images into several levels, fuse corresponding layers with particular rules, and reconstruct the target images. Many fusion methods are based on pixel-level image fusion. These methods can not effectively extract the target area we interested in and heavily depend on predefined transforms and corresponding levels for decomposition and reconstruction. However, in several practical applications, our attention is focused on the objects of images at the region level [1]. Hence, region-level information should be considered during image fusion [9]. Consequently, region-based fusion rules have been widely used in infrared and visible image fusion [10]. Many region-based fusion methods have been proposed for infrared and visible image fusion, such as feature region extraction [11], regional uniformity [12], regional energy [10], and multi-judgment fusion rule [13]. Some representative methods are based on the salient region [13]. These method aims to identify regions that are more salient than other areas. This model has been used to extract visually salient regions of images, which can be used to obtain saliency maps of multi-scale sub-images [1]. Zhang et al. adopted the super-pixel-based saliency method to extract salient target regions; then, the fused coefficient could be obtained by the extracted target region using a morphological method [14]. There are two disadvantages in these methods. (1) These methods adopt the same fusion rules for target and background areas. (2) These methods can not extract the region of target accurately. Therefore, in order to solve these existing problems, it is necessary to propose better methods.

In this paper, we propose a region-based fusion method to solve these problems. The source infrared image is segmented into foreground part and background part by semantic segmentation. We propose a deep learning fusion method and propose foreground loss and background loss to control the fusion of different regions respectively. The fused image is reconstructed by combining the foreground part and the background part. The rest of this paper is structured as follows. In Sect. 2, the background of this research will be introduced. In Sect. 3, the methods we proposed is introduced in detail. The performance of our method and experimental results on public data sets are shown in Sect. 4. Finally, we draw a conclusion of our proposed method in Sect. 5.

2   Background

Semantic segmentation, also called scene labeling, refers to the process of assigning a semantic label to each pixel of an image [15]. With the development of deep learning, research in semantic segmentation has been significantly improved. Semantic segmentation based on deep learning can accurately classify each pixel and have already achieved well performance on very complex RGB image data sets. Compared with RGB images, infrared images are usually gray-scale images, the difference between target area and background area is more obvious. Therefore, we believe that semantic segmentation will also achieve good results on infrared images. Gatys et al. [16] proposed a deep learning method in creating artistic imagery by separating and recombining image content and style.

This process of using Convolutional Neural Networks (CNNs) to render a content image in different styles is referred to as Neural Style Transfer (NST) [17]. They extract deep features at different layers from images by using CNNs. Content loss and style loss are defined to control the fusion of content and texture. Different from traditional methods, they use deep features to reconstruct images.

Inspired by their work, we segment the source infrared image into sub-regions and fuse them with visible image separately. We propose foreground loss and background loss to control the fusion of the two different regions based on the works of Gatys et al [16]. The details of our method will be presented in the next section.

3 Method

In this section, our proposed method is presented in four parts. To solve the problems raised in section II, we propose an infrared and visible image fusion method based on deep learning. The infrared image is segmented into foreground and background parts by semantic segmentation. The two parts are fused separately by using deep learning network based on NST. The framework of our proposed method is shown in Fig. 1.

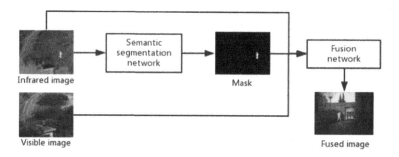

Fig. 1. The framework of our method

3.1 Segmentation of Foreground and Background

In this paper, we define the target area as foreground which is usually the region of interest in an infrared image, and the other areas as background. The purpose of foreground fusion is preserving the saliency information of target in infrared image while reserving the texture information of visible image as much as possible. The purpose of background fusion is preserving the features of infrared image while retaining the texture details of visible image. In order to achieve better fusion performance, we divide the source images into foreground and background, and fused with different strategies and parameters for each part. For the input image I, it can be represented as a combination of foreground and background parts as follow:

$$I = I_f + I_b \tag{1}$$

I_f is the foreground part, and I_b is the background part. To divide the image, we use a semantic segmentation network to segment an infrared image into foreground part and background part, and train it on TNO and INO datasets.

3.2 Fusion of Foreground and Background

Fusion of Foreground. In an infrared image, foreground is usually the salient area. Hence, we take foreground part of the source infrared image as the basis of the fused image, so that the salient information of the target will be preserved. We extract texture and detail features from foreground part of the source visible image. In order to extract the optimal detail features, we use CNNs to extract the deep features of the image. We define the foreground loss to control the fusion of foreground. In Gatyss work, the content loss of the I-th layer is defined as:

$$L_c^l = \frac{1}{2N_l D_l} \sum_{ij} (F_l[O] - F_l[I])_{ij}^2 \tag{2}$$

The style loss of the l-th layer is defined as:

$$L_s^l = \frac{1}{2N_l^2} \sum_{ij} (G_l[O] - G_l[S])_{ij}^2 \tag{3}$$

I is the input image, O is the output image and S is the reference style image. N_l is the number of filters in the l-th layer. D_l is the size of vectorized feature map of each filter in the l-th layer. $F_{f,l}[\cdot]$ is the feature matrix with (i, j) indicating its index. $G_{f,l}[\cdot] = F_{f,l}[\cdot]F_{f,l}[\cdot]^T$ is the Gram matrix which is defined as the inner product between the vectorized feature maps. Inspired by Gats'work, we use content loss to constrain the basic content information and style loss which is defined as texture loss in this paper to constrain the details and texture information of the fused image. For the input infrared image I, the input visible image V and the output fused image O, the foreground loss function of the fusion network is defined as:

$$L_f = \sum_{l=1}^{L} \alpha_f^l L_{f,c}^l + \sum_{l=1}^{L} \beta_f^l L_{f,s}^l \tag{4}$$

The network contains L layers, $L_{f,c}^l$ and $L_{f,s}^l$ indicate the content loss and texture loss of the foreground fusion in the l-th layer. The content loss and texture loss of foreground fusion are controlled by α_f^l and β_f^l. The content loss and texture loss are defined as follow. The content loss of l-th layer is:

$$L_{f,c}^l = \frac{1}{2N_l D_l} \sum_{ij} (F_{f,l}[O] - F_{f,l}[I])_{ij}^2 \tag{5}$$

and the texture loss of the l-th layer is:

$$L_{f,s}^l = \frac{1}{2N_l^2} \sum_{ij} (G_{f,l}[O] - G_{f,l}[V])_{ij}^2 \tag{6}$$

and:

$$F_{f,l}[O] = F_l[O]M_{f,l}[I] \tag{7}$$

$$F_{f,l}[I] = F_l[I]M_{f,l}[I] \tag{8}$$

$$F_{f,l}[V] = F_l[V]M_{f,l}[I] \tag{9}$$

$M_{f,l}[I]$ denotes the foreground segmentation mask. To adapt each layer, the mask is down sampled to $M_{f,l}[I]$. In our test data, infrared and visible images have been strictly registered and there is $M_{f,l}[I] = M_{f,l}[V]$. All the $M_{f,l}[V]$ items have been replaced by $M_{f,l}[I]$ in formulas above.

Fusion of Background. Deferent from foreground, we pay more attention to detail textures in background. Hence, we take background part of the source visible image as the basis of the fused image, so that the detail information of visible image will be preserved. We extract textures from the source infrared image. For background part, we define the background loss to control the fusion. The loss function is defined as:

$$L_b = \sum_{l=1}^{L} \alpha_b^l L_{b,c}^l + \sum_{l=1}^{L} \beta_b^l L_{b,s}^l \tag{10}$$

$L_{b,c}^l$ and $L_{b,s}^l$ indicate the content loss and texture loss of the background fusion in the l-th layer. The weights of content loss and texture loss of background fusion are α_b^l and β_b^l. The content loss and texture loss are defined as follow. The content loss of the l-th layer is:

$$L_{b,c}^l = \frac{1}{2N_l D_l} \sum_{ij} (F_{b,l}[O] - F_{b,l}[V])_{ij}^2 \tag{11}$$

and the texture loss of the l-th layer is:

$$L_{b,s}^l = \frac{1}{2N_l^2} \sum_{ij} (G_{b,l}[O] - G_{b,l}[I])_{ij}^2 \tag{12}$$

and:

$$F_{b,l}[O] = F_l[O]M_{b,l}[I] \tag{13}$$

$$F_{b,l}[I] = F_l[I]M_{b,l}[I] \tag{14}$$

$$F_{b,l}[V] = F_l[V]M_{b,l}[I] \tag{15}$$

Similar to the foreground fusion, $M_{b,l}[I] = M_{b,l}[V]$, and all the $M_{b,l}[V]$ items have been replaced by $M_{b,l}[I]$ in formulas above.

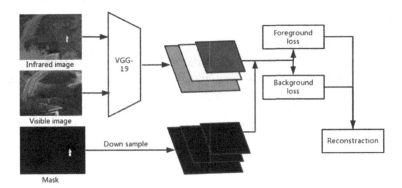

Fig. 2. The procedure of fusion

3.3 Reconstruction

We reconstruct the fused image by combining the fused foreground part and background part. The total loss function of the fusion network is formulated by combining the foreground loss and the background loss together. We add L_{tv} term to suppress the noise generated in the fusion process. The total loss of the fusion network is:

$$
\begin{aligned}
L_{total} &= L_f + L_b + L_{tv} \\
&= \sum_{l=1}^{L} (\alpha_f^l L_{f,c}^l + \alpha_b^l L_{b,c}^l) + \sum_{l=1}^{L} (\beta_f^l L_{f,s}^l + \beta_b^l L_{b,s}^l) + L_{tv}
\end{aligned}
\tag{16}
$$

3.4 Implementation Details

In this part, the implementation details of our method will be described. We adopt a state-of-art semantic segmentation network SegNet [18] on the segmentation of infrared images, and generate masks for further processing. We use it to segment the image into two categories, and the network is trained on 1000 images from the TNO and INO data sets. To generate the mask, we only segment the infrared image since the infrared and visible image pairs have been registered, and it is not difficult mapping the segmentation mask to the visible image. In our fusion network, as shown in Fig. 2, a pre-trained VGG-19 network is employed as the feature extractor. For foreground fusion, we choose layer $conv2\_2$ to extract the content feature, and layer $conv1\_1$, $conv2\_1$ to extract the texture feature. For background fusion, we choose layer $conv4\_2$ to extract the content feature, and layer $conv3\_1$, $conv4\_1$, $conv5\_1$ to extract the texture feature. The mask is down sampled to correspond feature maps of different layers.

4 Results and Comparison

In this section, the performance of our method will be evaluated by experiments on common data sets and compared with other methods.

4.1   Results

We select 1000 pairs of infrared and visible images from TNO and INO data sets, format them into 360 by 480 small images and input into SegNet [18]. We trained a well performed semantic segmentation network and use it to segment the input infrared images. To test the performance of our method, we select 20 pairs of infrared and visible images from TNO data set for experiment. Several segmentation results are shown in Fig. 3. After segmentation, the mask, infrared and visible images are put into the fusion network. The fusion result is shown in Fig. 4.

Fig. 3. The results of semantic segmentation on TNO dataset. The input infrared images are shown in first row, the output masks are shown in second row.

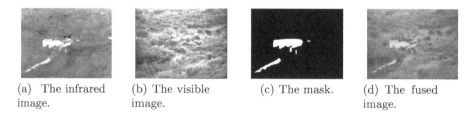

(a) The infrared image.   (b) The visible image.   (c) The mask.   (d) The fused image.

Fig. 4. The fusion result of our method.

4.2   Comparison

In the experiment, we select several state-of-art methods of infrared image and visible image fusion for comparison. These methods including curvelet transform (CVT) [19], dual-tree complex wavelet transform (DTCWT) [20], weighted least square optimization-based method (WLS) [7], gradient transfer fusion (GTF) [21], and a generative adversarial network for infrared and visible image fusion (FusionGAN) [22]. The experiment is carried out on a 3.4 GHz Intel(R) Core(TM) CPU with 8 GB RAM.

Subjective Evaluation. Five pairs of infrared and visible images are selected for subjective evaluation. As shown in the Fig. 5, the first two lines show the original infrared images and the visible images and the last row shows the results of our method while the other rows correspond to the five methods for comparison. All the methods have fused the features of infrared image and visible image successfully. The fusion results of CVT and DTCWT contain rich detail features, but the targets are not obvious. Compared with CVT and DTCWT, WLS has stronger target saliency, but some infrared features are lost in the background.

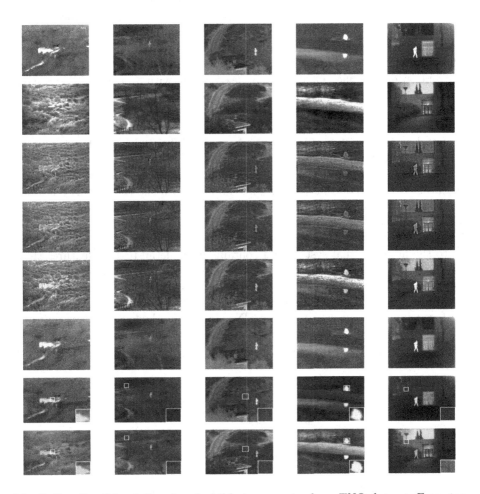

Fig. 5. Results of five infrared and visible image pairs from TNO dataset. From top to bottom: infrared images, visible images, results of CVT, DTCWT, WLS, GTF, FusionGAN and our method. Some detail parts are zoomed in and put at the bottom right corner for clear comparison.

GTF and FusionGAN have achieved a good balance between target saliency and detail texture, however there are still not enough detail features in the background. Compared with the five methods, our method retains the saliency of target while contains rich detail features in the background, and achieve a better balance between infrared features and visible features.

Objective Evaluation. Since there is no unified evaluation metric for infrared and visible image fusion, multiple metrics are used to make the evaluation more persuasive. Five metrics are chosen to evaluate the performance of different methods, these are: entropy (EN) [23], average gradient (AG) [24], Spatial frequency (SF) [25], structural similarity index measure (SSIM) [26], root mean squared error (RMSE). The EN metric measures the amount of information contained in a fused image. The larger the EN, the more information is contained in the fused image. The AG metric quantifies the gradient information of the fused image and represents its detail and texture. The larger the AG, the more gradient information the fused image contains. The SF metric measures the gradient distribution of an image effectively. A fused image with a large SF is sensitive to human perception and has rich edges and textures. The SSIM metric is proposed to model image loss and distortion. The larger the SSIM, the better the fusion algorithm performs. The RMSE metric denotes the dissimilarity between the fused and infrared/visible images. A small RMSE indicates that the fused image has a small amount of error and distortion.

As shown in Fig. 6 and Tab. 1, the results of the six methods are very close. Our method achieved good performance and perform the best in EN, AG and SSIM metrics. Compared with the other five methods, our method fused more information and kept high structure similarity with the source image. Except WLS, results of our method is more sensitive to human visual perception according to the human visual system and contains more detail texture features than the other four methods. Results on RMSE shows that our method has less dissimilarity between the fused and source images than CVT, DTCWT and WLS, but there are still some defects compared with GTF and FusionGAN. Since the fused image is reconstructed by CNN in our method, the fusion network will produce some distortion which causes the imperfect performance on RMSE metric.

Table 1. The average performance of six methods in the five metrics: EN, AG, SF, SSIM and RMSE

Fusion	Fusion metrics				
Methods	EN	AG	SF	SSIM	RMSE
CVT	6.4266	2.6068	8.9001	1.0164	0.0215
DTCWT	6.4031	2.5302	8.8383	1.0136	0.0215
WLS	6.6249	3.0508	**10.0276**	1.0521	0.0213
GTF	6.4154	3.2080	8.4923	0.9324	0.0156
FusionGAN	6.3641	2.4327	6.0529	0.8698	**0.0088**
Ours	**6.8021**	**3.4563**	9.2064	**1.0549**	0.0180

[a]The best values for each column have been roughened.

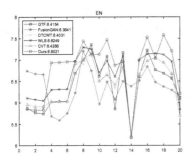

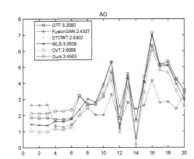

(a) The results of six methods on EN metric.

(b) The results of six methods on AG metric.

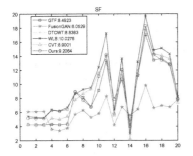

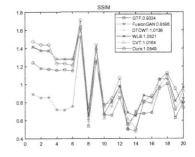

(c) The results of six methods on SF metric.

(d) The results of six methods on SSIM metric.

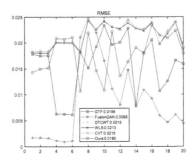

(e) The results of six methods on RMSE metric.

Fig. 6. Quantitative comparisons of the five metrics: EN, AG, SF, SSIM and RMSE, on twenty image pairs from the TNO dataset, the average scores are shown in each sub image.

5 Conclusion

In this paper, we propose a region-based deep learning method for infrared and visible image fusion. Firstly, the infrared image is segmented into foreground and background parts by semantic segmentation. Then, different loss functions are proposed to fuse foreground and background parts. The fused image is reconstructed by combining the two parts together. We evaluate our method subjectively and objectively. The experimental results show that our method retains the saliency of the target while contains rich infrared feature information and detailed visible information. Our method can also be used for infrared image and RGB image fusion, and will provide a basis for target detection, recognition and other tasks. In the experiment, we notice that our method will produce some distortion to fused image. In the future, we will focus on solving this problem.

Acknowledgment. This work was supported in part by the National Natural Science Foundation of China under Grant 61573097 and 91748106, in part by Key Laboratory of Integrated Automation of Process Industry (PAL-N201704), the Advanced Research Project of the 13th Five-Year Plan (31511040301), the Fundamental Research Funds for the Central Universities (3208008401), the Qing Lan Project and Six Major Top-talent Plan, and in part by the Priority Academic Program Development of Jiangsu Higher Education Institutions. The authors thank the reviewers and editors for giving valuable comments, which are very helpful for improving this manuscript.

References

1. Ma, J., Yong, M., Chang, L.: Infrared and visible image fusion methods and applications: a survey. Inf. Fusion **45**, S1566253517307972 (2019)
2. Li, S., Yang, B., Hu, J.: Performance comparison of different multi-resolution transforms for image fusion. Inf. Fusion **12**(2), 74–84 (2011)
3. Wang, J., Peng, J., Feng, X., He, G., Fan, J.: Fusion method for infrared and visible images by using non-negative sparse representation. Infrared Phys. Technol. **67**, 477–489 (2014)
4. Xiang, T., Li, Y., Gao, R.: A fusion algorithm for infrared and visible images based on adaptive dual-channel unit-linking PCNN in NSCT domain. Infrared Phys. Technol. **69**, 53–61 (2015)
5. Bavirisetti, D.P., Bavirisetti, D.P.: Multi-sensor image fusion based on fourth order partial differential equations. In: International Conference on Information Fusion (2017)
6. Xiaoye, Z., Yong, M., Fan, F., Ying, Z., Jun, H.: Infrared and visible imagefusion via saliency analysis and local edge-preserving multi-scaledecomposition. J. Opt. Soc. Am. A **34**(8), 1400–1410 (2017)
7. Ma, J., Zhou, Z., Bo, W., Hua, Z.: Infrared and visible image fusion based on visual saliency map and weighted least square optimization. Infrared Phys. Technol. **82**, 8–17 (2017)
8. Zhao, J., Cui, G., Gong, X., Yue, Z., Tao, S., Wang, D.: Fusion of visible and infrared images using global entropy and gradient constrained regularization. Infrared Phys. Technol. **81**, 201–209 (2017)
9. Piella, G.: A region-based multiresolution image fusion algorithm. In: International Conference on Information Fusion (2002)
10. Kong, W.: Technique for gray-scale visual light and infrared image fusion based on non-subsampled shearlet transform. Infrared Phys. Technol. **63**(11), 110–118 (2014)

11. Xiangzhi, B., Fugen, Z., Bindang, X.: Fusion of infrared and visual images through region extraction by using multi scale center-surround top-hat transform. Opt. Express **19**(9), 8444–57 (2011)

12. Adu, J., Gan, J., Yan, W., Jian, H.: Image fusion based on nonsubsampled contourlet transform for infrared and visible light image. Infrared Phys. Technol. **61**(5), 94–100 (2013)

13. Chen, Y., Xiong, J., Liu, H.L., Fan, Q.: Fusion method of infrared and visible images based on neighborhood characteristic and regionalization in NSCT domain. Opt. - Int. J. Light Electron Opt. **125**(17), 4980–4984 (2014)

14. Zhang, B., Lu, X., Pei, H., Zhao, Y.: A fusion algorithm for infrared and visible images based on saliency analysis and non-subsampled shearlet transform. Infrared Phys. Technol. **73**, 286–297 (2015)

15. Yu, H., Yang, Z., Lei, T., Wang, Y., Wei, S., Sun, M., Tang, Y.: Methods and datasets on semantic segmentation: a review. Neurocomputing **304**, S0925231218304077 (2018)

16. Gatys, L.A., Ecker, A.S., Bethge, M.: Image style transfer using convolutional neural networks. In: Computer Vision & Pattern Recognition (2016)

17. Y. Jing, Y. Yang, Z. Feng, J. Ye, M. Song, Y. Jing, Y. Yang, Z. Feng, J. Ye, and M. Song, "Neural style transfer: A review," 2017

18. Badrinarayanan, V., Kendall, A., Cipolla, R.: Segnet: A deep convolutional encoder-decoder architecture for image segmentation (2015)

19. Nencini, F., Garzelli, A., Baronti, S., Alparone, L.: Remote sensing image fusion using the curvelet transform. Inf. Fusion **8**, 143–156 (2007)

20. Lewis, J.J., OCallaghan, R.J., Nikolov, S.G., Bull, D.R., Canagarajah, C.N.: Pixel- and region-based image fusion with complex wavelets. Inf. Fusion **8**(2), 119–130 (2007)

21. Ma, J., Chen, C., Li, C., Huang, J.: Infrared and visible image fusion via gradient transfer and total variation minimization. Inf. Fusion **31**, 100–109 (2016)

22. Jiayi, M., Wei, Y., Pengwei, L., Chang, L., Junjun, J.: Fusiongan: a generative adversarial network for infrared and visible image fusion. Inf. Fusion **48**, 11–26 (2019)

23. Roberts, W.J., Van, J.A.A., Ahmed, F.: Assessment of image fusion procedures using entropy, image quality, and multispectral classification. J. Appl. Remote Sens. **2**(1), 1–28 (2008)

24. Cui, G., Feng, H., Xu, Z., Qi, L., Chen, Y.: Detail preserved fusion of visible and infrared images using regional saliency extraction and multi-scale image decomposition. Opt. Commun. **341**(341), 199–209 (2015)

25. Eskicioglu, A.M., Fisher, P.S.: Image quality measures and their performance. IEEE Trans. Commun. **43**(12), 2959–2965 (1995)

26. Wang, Z., Bovik, A.C., Sheikh, H.R., Simoncelli, E.P.: Image quality assessment: from error visibility to structural similarity. IEEE Trans. Image Process. **13**(4), 600–612 (2004)

A Coarse Registration Algorithm Between 3D Point Cloud and CAD Model of Non-cooperative Object for Space Manipulator

Qimeng Tan[✉], Delun Li, Congcong Bao, Ming Chen,
and Yun Zhang

Beijing Key Laboratory of Intelligent Space Robotic Systems Technology
and Applications, Beijing Institute of Spacecraft System Engineering,
Beijing 100094, China
tanqimeng@foxmail.com

Abstract. Data registration between 3D point cloud and CAD model of non-cooperative object has been considered as one of key technologies for estimating spatial position and orientation of target spacecraft. The registration result will directly affect the success or failure of on-orbit capture mission for space manipulator. Usually, 3D CAD model needs to discretize into point cloud of model which can be applied to match the corresponding 3D measuring point clouds. In this article, a coarse registration algorithm of curvature features based on distance constraint consistency is proposed to solve data registration between 3D point cloud and CAD model of non-cooperative object. According to the principle of invariant curvature of rigid transformation, a set of curvature feature points which satisfies the consistency of distance constraint can be selected to calculate rotation matrix and translation vector between both sets of point clouds. Experimental results have shown that the proposed registration algorithm can achieve higher registration accuracy to provide reliable initial values of transformation parameters for subsequent fine registration work.

Keywords: Space manipulator · Non-cooperative object ·
Registration between measuring point cloud and CAD model ·
Invariant curvature of rigid transformation · Consistency of distance constraint ·
Coarse registration algorithm

1 Introduction

In 1986, the concept of On-Orbit Servicing (OOS) [1] is firstly proposed with combination of NASA, the United States TRW Corporation, Lockheed Missile and Space Corporation, which mainly refers to complete a series of spatial operations e.g. extending working life of spacecraft, enhancing the working abilities by the cooperation of astronauts, robots or both. At present, space manipulator can be applied not only for on-orbit maintenance of spacecraft, but also for orbital debris shielding. In general, there are two types target spacecraft: cooperative goals and non-cooperative targets. The former refers to the attachment or installation of artificial visual markers with few

© Springer Nature Switzerland AG 2019
H. Yu et al. (Eds.): ICIRA 2019, LNAI 11744, pp. 616–626, 2019.
https://doi.org/10.1007/978-3-030-27541-9_50

known patterns on the surface of the spacecraft, which can provide effective cooperation information for space targets. Both NASA OE and the Japanese ETS-VII apply few cooperative markers on-orbit service considered as two success cases. In contrast, the non-cooperative target is impossible to provide effective space pose information of spacecraft without any known markers in advance, which will face huge challenges to the on-orbit service technology inevitably. Currently, 3D pose of non-cooperative targets can be calculated from dense 3D point cloud by binocular or multi-vision cameras, which can be used to match its CAD model in order to compute 3D pose of the non-cooperative spacecraft. Therefore, the registration of space non-cooperative target model has become a key technology to accurately estimate the position and attitude of the target spacecraft, and its registration accuracy will directly affect the success or failure of the final space manipulator in-orbit acquisition of non-cooperative targets.

To solve the problem data registration between the measuring point cloud and the CAD model, the design coordinate system of CAD model is firstly considered as a reference coordinate system, CAD model expressed by NURBS surface then should be sampled uniformly to extract a discrete point cloud with the similar quantity of 3D measuring point cloud [2] for data registration. Essentially, data registration mainly adjusts the spatial position and posture of various 3D data sets (e.g., point clouds, models, etc.) through Euclidean coordinate transformation, so that different data sets can not only be unified to the same reference coordinate system ensuring minimizing the difference between overlapping regions of different 3D data sets. The process of data registration [3] can mainly divided into two stages: coarse registration and fine registration. In the former, the approximate solution of the rotation and translation matrix can be directly calculated by the coordinates of both sets of point cloud as the initial value without introducing any initial information. Subsequently, the optimal solution of rotation and translation matrix can be computed by several iterations minimizing the error function in the latter.

There are few common coarse registration algorithms [4] such as known markers, principal curvatures, traversal searching method based on random consistency and algebraic surface model. In the method of known markers, several markers with a known pattern can be set to establish their relationship between both point cloud by invariance of their positions and every unique encoder information to calculate a set of approximate solution. In the method of principal curvature, the question of data registration can be solved by introducing principal curvature to describe the distribution form of both point clouds. Also called as three-point alignment method, the traversal searching method based on random consistency mainly calculates the corresponding rotation and translation matrix based on three pairs of reference points with fixed relative positions in both sets of point cloud. The third method has an advantage of few disturbance of gross error but only suitable for a small amount points. According to the principle of least square, the method of algebraic surface model [5] needs to fitting point cloud into an algebraic surface model composed of different implicit polynomial functions, which can be processed to compute reliable transform parameters by minimizing the distance between the two groups of point cloud. Although the last method needs less calculating time and no corresponding relation between two certain points, the overlap between both point clouds should be no less 85%.

In accordance with the advantages and disadvantages of every above method, an algorithm for coarse registration of curvature features based on distance constraint consistency is proposed for the registration problem between spatial and non-cooperative target point cloud and CAD model. According to the invariance of rigid body transformation of curvature, the set of curvature feature points satisfying the principle of distance constraint consistency is selected as the reference, so that the initial parameters of the rotation matrix and translation vector between the two sets of point clouds can be solved.

2   Curvature Invariance of Rigid Transformation

2.1   Definition

Usually, if there are both orthogonal and conjugate directions at any point P (not an umbilical point) on the 3D free surface, then the above directions should be defined as both main directions of point P on the surface [6]. The normal curvatures of both main directions can be expressed as k_1 and k_2 respectively. Corresponding to the maximum and minimum of all normal curvatures at point P on the surface, the product, average and absolute sum of both principal curvatures should be defined as Gaussian curvature K_{gas}, average curvature K_{avg} and absolute curvature K_{abs} separately.

2.2   Curvature Estimation of Point Cloud

Both 3D measuring point cloud and CAD model discretized into few point clouds of non-cooperative object belong to discrete point sets. To estimate curvature of each point, few measuring points need to be fitting a continuous and differentiable surface within a certain area in order to obtain the first and second basic representations and forms of the local surface [7].

Suppose that some a local surface in the point cloud can be shown as $Q = Q(u, v)$, whose the first basic form can be described as

$$I = (dQ)^2 = Edu^2 + 2Fdudv + Gdv^2 \tag{1}$$

Where, the coefficients are E, F, G the first basic quantities of the 3D surface, and they are constant values at each measurement point.

Then define the unit normal vector of the surface at a certain measurement point, whose mathematical formula is expressed as follows:

$$\vec{n} = \frac{Q_u \times Q_v}{\|Q_u \times Q_v\|} \tag{2}$$

According to Eq. (2), the normal vector explains the function of u, v whose differential equation shown as $d\vec{n} = n_u du + n_v dv$, which represents a tangent vector at the certain point on the surface. Here the second basic formula can be written as

$$II = -dQ \cdot d\bar{n} = -(Q_u du + Q_v dv) \cdot (n_u du + n_v dv) = -Q_u \cdot n_u du^2$$
$$- (Q_u \cdot n_v + Q_v \cdot n_u) du dv - Q_v \cdot n_v dv^2 = L du^2 + 2M du dv + N dv^2 \tag{3}$$

Then the second basic coefficients can be described as L, M, N, whose explains the function relationship of few parameters u, v.

In combination with the surface curvature definition given earlier, Gaussian curvature and mean curvature can be formulated as

$$K_{gas} = \frac{LN - M^2}{EG - F^2}, \quad K_{avg} = \frac{LG - 2FM + NE}{2 \cdot (EG - F^2)} \tag{4}$$

Where, both formulas of main principal curvatures at the certain point on the surface show as follows:

$$k_1 = K_{avg} + \sqrt{K_{avg}^2 - K_{gas}}, \quad k_2 = K_{avg} - \sqrt{K_{avg}^2 - K_{gas}} \tag{5}$$

2.3 Formulation to Curvature Invariance of Rigid Transformation

The curvature is only related to the surface geometry of the surface itself, and is not affected by the parameter representation of the surface and the positional attitude of the space. The rigid body transformation mainly involves the change of the position and orientation of the surface in Euclidean space. Therefore, the curvature has the invariance of rigid body transformation, namely the invariance of rotation and translation. From the perspective of differential geometry, it can be explained that the curvature at each discrete point on the surface and the curvature distribution trend on the entire surface do not change with the change of the direction, position and attitude angle of the surface.

A detailed proof of the rigid body transformation invariance of the curvature of the surface is as follows: Assume that there is a spatial surface $\Gamma : Q(u, v)$ in the Euclidean space, and after a set of rigid body transformation motion, transform into another spatial surface $\tilde{\Gamma} : \tilde{Q}(u, v)$. Among them, the set of rigid body transformation only involves one rotation matrix R and one translation vector T. Then the relationship between the two surfaces can be expressed as follows:

$$\tilde{Q}(u, v) = R \cdot Q(u, v) + T \tag{6}$$

Two basic forms (I and II) of the spatial surface $\Gamma : Q(u, v)$ have been given above, and their respective first and second basic quantities E, G, F, L, M, N, the unit normal vector $\bar{n}$, and the Gaussian curvature K_{gas}, K_{avg} mean curvature are calculated. Here, it is assumed that two basic forms of another spatial surface $\tilde{\Gamma} : \tilde{Q}(u, v)$ can be denoted as $(\tilde{I}, \tilde{II})$, and their respective first and second basic quantities are respectively written as $\tilde{E}, \tilde{G}, \tilde{F}, \tilde{L}, \tilde{M}, \tilde{N}$, and the unit normal vector can be expressed as $\tilde{\bar{n}}$, whose Gaussian curvature and the average curvature is recorded as $\tilde{K}_{gas}$ and $\tilde{K}_{avg}$. Therefore, it is proved that the curvature of the curved surface $\Gamma : Q(u, v)$ has a rigid body transformation invariance equivalent to that the curved surface $\Gamma : Q(u, v)$ and the other curved surface $\tilde{\Gamma} : \tilde{Q}(u, v)$ have equal surface curvatures, such as Gaussian curvature and average curvature.

First, calculate the first-order partial derivative of the parameter u, v for another spatial surface $\tilde{\Gamma} : \tilde{Q}(u, v)$,

$$
\begin{aligned}
\tilde{Q}_u &= \frac{\partial \tilde{Q}}{\partial u} = \frac{\partial}{\partial u}[R \cdot Q(u, v) + T] = R \cdot \frac{\partial Q}{\partial u} = R \cdot Q_u \\
\tilde{Q}_v &= \frac{\partial \tilde{Q}}{\partial v} = \frac{\partial}{\partial v}[R \cdot Q(u, v) + T] = R \cdot \frac{\partial Q}{\partial v} = R \cdot Q_v
\end{aligned}
\tag{7}
$$

Then the second derivative of the surface $\tilde{\Gamma} : \tilde{Q}(u, v)$ with respect to the parameter u, v can be calculated.

$$
\begin{aligned}
\tilde{Q}_{uu} &= \frac{\partial \tilde{Q}_u}{\partial u} = \frac{\partial}{\partial u}(R \cdot Q_u) = R \cdot \frac{\partial Q_u}{\partial u} = R \cdot Q_{uu} \\
\tilde{Q}_{uv} &= \frac{\partial \tilde{Q}_u}{\partial v} = \frac{\partial}{\partial v}(R \cdot Q_u) = R \cdot \frac{\partial Q_u}{\partial v} = R \cdot Q_{uv} \\
\tilde{Q}_{vv} &= \frac{\partial \tilde{Q}_v}{\partial v} = \frac{\partial}{\partial v}(R \cdot Q_v) = R \cdot \frac{\partial Q_v}{\partial v} = R \cdot Q_{vv}
\end{aligned}
\tag{8}
$$

Secondly, the first basic form of the surface can be obtained by following the formula (1):

$$
\tilde{I} = \tilde{E} du^2 + 2\tilde{F} du dv + \tilde{G} dv^2
\tag{9}
$$

Then, the following mathematical relationship can be derived between the first type of basic quantity $\tilde{E}, \tilde{G}, \tilde{F}$ of the curved surface $\tilde{\Gamma} : \tilde{Q}(u, v)$ represented by the Eq. (9) and the first type of basic coefficient parameter E, G, F corresponding to the curved surface $\Gamma : Q(u, v)$.

$$
\begin{aligned}
\tilde{Q}_{uu} &= \frac{\partial \tilde{Q}_u}{\partial u} = \frac{\partial}{\partial u}(R \cdot Q_u) = R \cdot \frac{\partial Q_u}{\partial u} = R \cdot Q_{uu} \\
\tilde{Q}_{uv} &= \frac{\partial \tilde{Q}_u}{\partial v} = \frac{\partial}{\partial v}(R \cdot Q_u) = R \cdot \frac{\partial Q_u}{\partial v} = R \cdot Q_{uv} \\
\tilde{Q}_{vv} &= \frac{\partial \tilde{Q}_v}{\partial v} = \frac{\partial}{\partial v}(R \cdot Q_v) = R \cdot \frac{\partial Q_v}{\partial v} = R \cdot Q_{vv}
\end{aligned}
\tag{10}
$$

Here, it is worth noting that the rotation matrix $R = \{r_{ij}, i = 1, 2, 3, j = 1, 2, 3\}$ in the rigid body transformation is an orthogonal matrix of dimension 3×3, and $|R| = 1$, for each of the elements, the following properties exist:

$$
\sum_{j=1}^{3} r_{pj} \cdot r_{qj} = \begin{cases} 1, & p = q \\ 0, & p \neq q \end{cases}
\tag{11}
$$

Therefore, the product of the rotation matrix and its transposed array is equal to one-unit matrix of 3×3.

Since the first type of basic coefficient parameters of the surface and the surface are exactly equal, the first basic representation of the two surfaces should also be consistent, scilicet

$$\tilde{I} = \tilde{E}du^2 + 2\tilde{F}dudv + \tilde{G}dv^2 = Edu^2 + 2Fdudv + Gdv^2 = I \tag{12}$$

Next, we need to establish the relationship between the unit normal vectors $\vec{n}$ and $\tilde{\vec{n}}$ of the above two surfaces and the relationship between:

$$\tilde{\vec{n}} = \frac{Q_u \times Q_v}{\|Q_u \times Q_v\|} = \frac{(R \cdot Q_u) \times (R \cdot Q_v)}{\sqrt{\tilde{E}\tilde{G} - F^2}} = \frac{R \cdot (Q_u \times Q_v)}{\sqrt{EG - F^2}} = R \cdot \vec{n} \tag{13}$$

According to the second basic form formula, the second basic form of the surface can be expressed as:

$$\tilde{L} = \tilde{Q}_{uu} \cdot \tilde{\vec{n}} = (R \cdot Q_{uu}) \cdot (R \cdot \vec{n}) = Q_{uu} \cdot (R \cdot R^T) \cdot \vec{n} = Q_{uu} \cdot \vec{n} = L$$

$$\tilde{M} = \tilde{Q}_{uv} \cdot \tilde{\vec{n}} = (R \cdot Q_{uv}) \cdot (R \cdot \vec{n}) = Q_{uv} \cdot (R \cdot R^T) \cdot \vec{n} = Q_{uv} \cdot \vec{n} = M \tag{14}$$

$$\tilde{N} = \tilde{Q}_{vv} \cdot \tilde{\vec{n}} = (R \cdot Q_{vv}) \cdot (R \cdot \vec{n}) = Q_{vv} \cdot (R \cdot R^T) \cdot \vec{n} = Q_{vv} \cdot \vec{n} = N$$

Based on the above analysis, the second type of basic coefficients of the surface $\Gamma : Q(u, v)$ and the surface $\tilde{\Gamma} : \tilde{Q}(u, v)$ are also completely equal, which means that the two surfaces have the same second type of basic form representation equation, namely:

$$\tilde{II} = \tilde{L}du^2 + \tilde{M}dudv + \tilde{N}dv^2 = Ldu^2 + Mdudv + Ndv^2 = II \tag{15}$$

Then the Gaussian curvature and the average curvature of the surface $\tilde{\Gamma} : \tilde{Q}(u, v)$ can be calculated separately.

$$\tilde{K}_{gas} = \frac{\tilde{L}\tilde{N} - \tilde{M}^2}{\tilde{E}\tilde{G} - \tilde{F}^2} = \frac{LN - M^2}{EG - F^2} = K_{gas}, \quad \tilde{K}_{avg} = \frac{\tilde{L}\tilde{G} - 2\tilde{M}\tilde{F} + \tilde{N}\tilde{E}}{2(\tilde{E}\tilde{G} - \tilde{F}^2)} = \frac{LG - 2MF + NE}{2(EG - F^2)} = K_{avg} \tag{16}$$

In summary, it is proved by theory that both the curved surface $\Gamma : Q(u, v)$ and the other curved surface $\tilde{\Gamma} : \tilde{Q}(u, v)$ have exactly the same Gaussian curvature and average curvature. Moreover, their basic representations of the first and second types are also identical, which fully proves the proposition in this section, the curvature of the surface $\Gamma : Q(u, v)$, has rigid body transformation invariance.

3 Consistency of Distance Constraint

According to the previous analysis, the curvature has rigid body transformation invariance, and the curvature feature is used as the basis for feature point selection. However, relying solely on curvature, high registration accuracy cannot be obtained. To this end, it is necessary to introduce the principle of distance constraint consistency to assist in finding curvature feature points.

In theory, the rigid body transformation in Euclidean space mainly involves the rotation matrix and the translation vector, the shape and size of the objects participating in the transformation have not changed. According to the invariance of the Euclidean transformation, in the transformation process, not only the angle between any two intersecting lines in the Euclidean space is constant, but also the Euclidean distance between any two points on the two lines is constant.

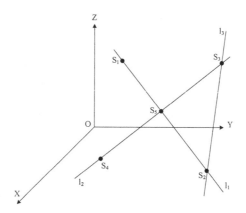

Fig. 1. Schematic diagram of Euclidean transformation invariance

As shown in Fig. 1, it is assumed that in the Euclidean space coordinate system $O - XYZ$, l_1, l_2 are two spatial straight lines intersect each other at a point S_5, and the other spatial line l_3 intersects the straight line l_1, l_2 at the point S_2, S_3. The points S_2, S_3 are all on a straight line l_1, and the points S_3, S_4 are all on a straight line l_2, and the points S_2, S_3 are on a straight line l_3. The five points in the figure are the set of curvature feature points that need to be selected. Obviously, these five points S_1, S_2, S_3, S_4, S_5 are coplanar but not collinear. Now define the distance constraint relationship between the above points:

$$d_1 = \frac{\overline{S_1 S_5}}{\overline{S_1 S_2}}, \quad d_2 = \frac{\overline{S_3 S_5}}{\overline{S_3 S_4}} \tag{17}$$

where $\overline{S_i S_j}$ $(i, j = 1, 2, \cdots, 5)$ represents the Euclidean distance between two points. The principle of distance constraint consistency means that the distance constraint represented in the above formula should have the same proportional relationship between the measurement point cloud and the discrete model point cloud, that is, maintain consistency.

4 Coarse Registration Algorithm

As one of inherent attributes of the surface, curvature reflects all different local shape of the surface, whose invariance of rigid body transformation has been formulated. Therefore, curvature has obvious advantages in data registration of point cloud. Traditional method of principal curvature compute transformation parameters by only one correspondences of principal curvature between both sets of point cloud. However, the traditional method has high calculating efficiency and simple principle, computational error is inevitable and obvious in practice because of depending on only one pair of principal curvature totally. In order to further improve the coarse registration accuracy between two sets, a coarse registration algorithm based on distance constraint consistency for spatial non-cooperative target model curvature is proposed. The specific process can be summarized as follows:

Table 1. Distribution of curvature characteristics on the surface of CAD model

Area distribution	Gaussian curvature	Average curvature
Convex distribution	$K_{gas} \geq 0$	$K_{avg} < 0$
Concave distribution	$K_{gas} \geq 0$	$K_{avg} > 0$
Saddle distribution	$K_{gas} < 0$	K_{avg} is an arbitrary value
Plane distribution	$K_{gas} = 0$	$K_{avg} = 0$

In the first step, according to the distribution of the curvature characteristics of CAD model described in Table 1, the surface of the CAD model is divided into n sub-regions, each sub-region represents only one convex or concave distribution, and then the discrete model point cloud can be divided into corresponding sub-point cloud sets. Every sub-point cloud need to be sorted in descending order according to Gaussian curvature and mean curvature at each discrete point, and the first three discrete points are selected to represent the curvature characteristics of the sub-point set. Corresponding to every the sub-point cloud set, three discrete feature points constitute a discrete point curvature feature sequence, which can be expressed as $M = \{m_i, i = 1, 2, \cdots, 3n\}$.

In the second step, in the above-mentioned discrete point curvature feature sequence M, first, the point with the largest curvature is selected as the point S_1, and all the three points included in the set of the sub-point cloud to which the point belongs are excluded from the sequence; With the point S_1 as the starting point, the Euclidean distance between each point and S_1 is calculated separately in the remaining feature sequences, and the feature point corresponding to the maximum value of the interval can be recorded as S_2, and at the same time, the three points included in the set of sub-point clouds to which the point S_2 belongs are removed from the sequence, so that the representation of the spatial line l_1 can be shown as

$$\overline{S_1 S_2} = max\left(\overline{S_1 m_i}\right) \tag{28}$$

Then, starting from the point S_2, the Euclidean distance from S_2 is greater than a certain distance constraint *dis_threshold* (which can be set according to the actual surface shape), and the clip between the straight line and the straight line l_1 is selected among the remaining feature sequences. The feature point with the largest angle can be written as point S_3, and all the three points included in the set of sub-point clouds to which point S_3 belongs are also removed from the sequence, so that the line determined by point S_2 and point S_3 can be recorded as a spatial straight line l_3.

$$\begin{cases} \overline{S_2 S_3} = dis\_threshold \\ \quad max[\theta(l_1, l_3)] \end{cases} \tag{39}$$

Next, using the point S_3 as a starting point, the solution in the remaining sequence is the largest distance from the point S_3, and the angle between the line formed by the point and the point S_3 and the line l_3 is greater than or equal to a certain angle threshold *ang_threshold* (usually not less than $10°$), then the point can be determined as point S_4, so that the equation for obtaining the line l_2 is expressed as:

$$\begin{cases} \overline{S_3 S_4} = max\left(\overline{S_3 m_i}\right) \\ \theta(l_2, l_3) \geq ang\_threshold \end{cases} \tag{20}$$

Finally, the linear equations are established by the simultaneous space lines l_1, l_2. The solution of the system can be used as the point S_5, and the five curvature feature points sequentially selected above constitute the model curvature feature point set, so that the group features can be calculated. The distance of the points constrains the relationship of d_1, d_2.

In the third step, the measurement point cloud data is also divided into n different sub-point cloud regions by calculating the curvature value at each measurement point in the measurement point cloud, and each sub-region represents only one convex surface distribution or concave surface distribution pattern. In order to accurately obtain the set of curvature feature points satisfying the distance constraint consistency, according to the descending order of curvature, eight feature points are selected in each sub-point cloud region to form a measurement point curvature feature sequence.

In the fourth step, according to the selecting method introduced in the second step, five characteristic points are sequentially determined from the series of curvature points of the measurement points to form a set of measured curvature feature points corresponding to the set of curvature points of the model based on the principle of distance constraint consistency.

In the fifth step, the above five pairs of feature points satisfying the consistency of distance constraint are used as the reference set to compute the rotation matrix and shift vector between two groups of point clouds shown as quaternion based on curvature invariance of rigid body transformation after establishing the correspondence between the measuring point cloud and the discrete CAD model point cloud.

5 Experiments

In the experiment, the face region of Venus avatar was selected to simulate the spatial non-cooperative target free surface to be registered. On the one hand, the face region of Venus was captured by ATOS I 3D scanner to obtain a set of 9772 points. On the other hand, the CAD model of the known Venus avatar is uniformly discretized to generate a set of discrete model point clouds with the same quantity of the measurement point cloud including 10,000 points. Subsequently, two sets between the measuring point cloud and the generated discrete model point cloud are respectively introduced into the proposed coarse registration algorithm to calculate transformation parameters by applying both evaluating methods of coordinate error and root mean square error as shown in Table 2. Finally, an improved ICP algorithm [10] is applied to finish data registration between two sets of point clouds through several iterative calculations. Figure 2 illustrates the original point clouds, the results after coarse and fine registration between the measurement point cloud and the discrete CAD model point cloud data in details.

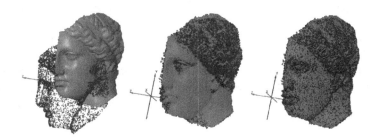

Fig. 2. Measure the registration result between point cloud data and CAD design model. From left to right, the original position renderings, coarse registration renderings, fine registration renderings

According to Table 2, both evaluating results have shown that parameter errors calculated by the proposed coarse registration are slightly lower than that of the fine registration with little difference. For example, the error of root mean square of the coarse registration is 2.055 mm, and the error of root mean square obtained by fine registration is reduced to 1.920 mm. This indicates that 5 pairs of curvature feature points satisfying the Euclidean space constraint consistency have been selected as the reference set to acquire better registration accuracy according to the proposed method during the registration process of measuring point cloud and discrete CAD model point cloud. The registration result can provide accurate and reliable initial value for next fine registration algorithm.

Table 2. Data registration evaluation results between measurement point cloud and CAD simulation model (Unit: mm)

| Registration step | Coordinate value error method | | | | | | | | | Root mean square Error method |
| | X axis | | | Y axis | | | Z axis | | | |
	Average error	Standard deviation	Maximum absolute error	Average error	Standard deviation	Maximum absolute error	Average error	Standard deviation	Maximum absolute error	RMS
Coarse registration	0.354	1.329	7.939	0.066	0.962	7.639	0.190	1.238	7.797	2.055
Fine registration	0.287	1.255	7.755	−0.087	0.871	7.262	0.090	1.163	7.539	1.920

6 Conclusion

During the on-orbit service of the space manipulator, data registration between the non-cooperative target measuring point cloud and 3D CAD model has become one of key technologies for estimating 3D pose of target spacecraft will directly restrict the success or failure of the space manipulator on-orbit servicing task. A coarse registration algorithm for curvature features of spatial non-cooperative target models based on distance constraint consistency is proposed in this paper to solve the problem of poor accuracy of coarse registration. Firstly, the principle of curvature invariance of rigid body transformation has been formulated and generalized. Secondly, a set of curvature feature points which satisfy the requirement of distance constraint consistency is selected as the reference set to calculate transformation parameters between the measuring point cloud and the discrete CAD model accurately. Finally, the experimental results have shown that the proposed algorithm can provide few initial values of rotation matrix and translation vector with higher accuracy for subsequent fine registration.

References

1. NASA. Satellite Servicing. A NASA report to Congress. NASA Office of Space Flight, Washington DC (1988)
2. Piegl, L., Tiller, W.: The NURBS Book, 2nd edn. Tsinghua University Press, Beijing (1996)
3. Tucker, T.M., Kurfess, T.R.: Point cloud to CAD model registration methods in manufacturing inspection. J. Comput. Inf. Sci. Eng. **6**, 418–421 (2016)
4. Salvi, J., Matabosch, C., Fofi, D., Forest, J.: A review of recent range image registration methods with accuracy evaluation. J. Image Vis. Comput. **25**, 578–596 (2007)
5. Tarel, J., Civi, H., Cooper, D.: Pose estimation of free-form 3D objects without point matching using algebraic surface models. In: Proceedings of IEEE Workshop on Model-Based 3D, USA, pp. 13–21 (1998)
6. Wu, J., Liu, W., Wang, T., Wang, H.: Estimating curvatures for point-sampled surfaces. J. Instrum. **27**(12), 1557–1562 (2006)
7. Xu, J., Liu, W., Sun, Y.: Algorithm for free-form surface matching based on curvatures. J. Comput. Aided Des. Graph. **19**(2), 193–197 (2017)

Robot Mechanism and Design

Dexterity-Based Dimension Optimization of Muti-DOF Robotic Manipulator

Yang Jing, Hu Ming$^{(\boxtimes)}$, Jin Lingyan, and Zhao Deming

Faculty of Mechanical Engineering and Automation,
Zhejiang Sci-Tech University, Hangzhou 310018, China
huming@zstu.edu.cn

Abstract. In order to improve the dexterity of the manipulator in the global space, a kinematic model of the manipulator is established based on the D-H method. The Jacobian matrix of the manipulator is obtained. Based on the Jacobian matrix, the mean and the volatility of condition number index of the multi-DOF manipulator in the global space are established. The influence of rod parameters on the condition number index in the global space are analyzed by simulation. Through the variation of the mean condition number and the volatility index in the range of the design variable, the weighted coefficient of the two indicators are determined, and the comprehensive optimization indexes are established. Based on the comprehensive optimization index, the rod length parameters are optimized. The results show that the optimized dexterity indexes of the manipulator is improved.

Keywords: Manipulator · Jacobian matrix · Dexterity · Global space · Condition number

1 Introduction

The series manipulator is a common manipulator used in modern industry. It can meet a variety of operational tasks. The flexibility of the manipulator is very important for the kinematics performance of manipulator [1].

Dimensional optimization of manipulator based on the dexterity index has been extensively investgated. Shi et al. [2] optimized the size of the manipulator based on the mean and volatility index of condition number of the manipulator in the global space. Tian et al. [3] presented that the dimensional parameters of the manipulator was optimized based on its workspace index. Ding et al. [4] established workspace and energy consumption index of manipulator to optimize dimensional parameters. Sun et al. [5] established their comprehensive performance indexes based on speed performance, force bearing performance and motion performance. Xiao et al. [6] regarded energy consumption as the index to optimize the dimensional parameters of the manipulator. Chen et al. [7] analyzed the kinematics performance of redundant parallel mechanism and optimized the size of parallel mechanism. Dong et al. [8] Studied the kinematic performance of redundantly actuated 4-UPS&UP parallel manipulator. Yang et al. [9] studied the kinematic model of a novel parallel perfusion robot, and the dimensional parameters were optimized.

© Springer Nature Switzerland AG 2019
H. Yu et al. (Eds.): ICIRA 2019, LNAI 11744, pp. 629–636, 2019.
https://doi.org/10.1007/978-3-030-27541-9_51

In this paper, for the optimization of the motion performance of the multi-DOF manipulator, the rod length parameters of the manipulator are optimized by establishing a weighted comprehensive index of the mean and the volatility of condition number in the global space.

2 Multi-DOF Manipulator Jacobian Matrix

2.1 Kinematics Analysis

The D-H kinematics coordinate system is established by analyzing the structure of the multi-DOF manipulator, as shown in Fig. 1, where J_i is the rotation axis of the joint. There are three rod length parameters of the mechanical arm, which are defined as L_1, L_2 and L_3 respectively. The D-H parameters of the multi-DOF manipulator are depicted in Table 1, the coordinate transformation matrix between adjacent joints can be obtained between adjacent coordinate systems (Eq. 1). The position and posture of the end-effector of the manipulator in its own basic coordinate system can be obtained through the transformation between coordinate systems.

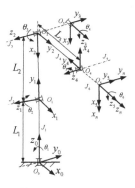

Fig. 1. The kinematic coordinate system of multi-DOF manipulator

Table 1. D-H parameters of the multi-degree of freedom manipulator

Joint i	$\theta_i(°)$	d_i(mm)	a_i(mm)	$\alpha_i(°)$
1	$\theta_1(0)$	L_1	0	90
2	$\theta_2(-90)$	0	$-L_2$	0
3	$\theta_3(0)$	0	0	-90
4	$\theta_4(180)$	L_3	0	-90
5	$\theta_5(180)$	0	0	-90
6	$\theta_6(0)$	0	0	0

$$i-1 T_i = \begin{bmatrix} c\theta_i & -s\theta_i \cdot c\alpha_i & s\theta_i \cdot s\alpha_i & a_i \cdot c\theta_i \\ s\theta_i & c\theta_i \cdot c\alpha_i & -c\theta_i \cdot s\alpha_i & a_i \cdot s\theta_i \\ 0 & s\alpha_i & c\alpha_i & d_i \\ 0 & 0 & 0 & 1 \end{bmatrix} \tag{1}$$

In the transformation matrix, where s, c, θ_i denote the sin, the cos, and the joint angle of the i-th joint respectively.

2.2 Jacobian Matrix Solution

Through the positive kinematics model of the manipulator, the Jacobian matrix at the end can be obtained, and its solution method for each joint is shown in Eq. 2.

$$\mathbf{J}_i = \begin{bmatrix} (\mathbf{p} \times \mathbf{n})_z & (\mathbf{p} \times \mathbf{o})_z & (\mathbf{p} \times \mathbf{a})_z & \mathbf{n}_z & \mathbf{o}_z & \mathbf{a}_z \end{bmatrix} \tag{2}$$

Where p is the position vector of the transformation matrix from the end coordinate system to the base coordinate system, n, o and a are the column vectors in the attitude transformation matrix, and i_z is the z-direction component of the vector. The complete Jacobian matrix obtained is shown as follows:

$$\mathbf{J} = \begin{bmatrix} \mathbf{J}_1 & \mathbf{J}_2 & \mathbf{J}_3 & \mathbf{J}_4 & \mathbf{J}_5 & \mathbf{J}_6 \end{bmatrix}$$

$$\mathbf{J}_1 = \begin{bmatrix} -(c\theta_4 s\theta_6 + c\theta_5 c\theta_6 s\theta_4)(L_2 s\theta_2 - L_3 c\theta_2 c\theta_3 + L_3 s\theta_2 s\theta_3) \\ -(c\theta_4 c\theta_6 - c\theta_5 s\theta_4 s\theta_6)(L_2 s\theta_2 - L_3 c\theta_2 c\theta_3 + L_3 s\theta_2 s\theta_3) \\ s\theta_4 s\theta_5 (L_2 s\theta_2 - L_3 c\theta_2 c\theta_3 + L_3 s\theta_2 s\theta_3) \\ c\theta_6(s\theta_5(c\theta_2 s\theta_3 + c\theta_3 s\theta_2) - K_{J1}^1 \\ c\theta_6 s\theta_4(c\theta_2 c\theta_3 - s\theta_2 s\theta_3) - K_{J1}^2 \\ c\theta_5(c\theta_2 s\theta_3 + c\theta_3 s\theta_2) + c\theta_4 s\theta_5(c\theta_2 c\theta_3 - s\theta_2 s\theta_3) \end{bmatrix}$$

$$K_{J1}^1 = c\theta_4 c\theta_5(c\theta_2 c\theta_3 - s\theta_2 s\theta_3)) + s\theta_4 s\theta_6(c\theta_2 c\theta_3 - s\theta_2 s\theta_3)$$

$$K_{J1}^2 = s\theta_6(s\theta_5(c\theta_2 s\theta_3 + c\theta_3 s\theta_2) - c\theta_4 c\theta_5(c\theta_2 c\theta_3 - s\theta_2 s\theta_3))$$

$$\mathbf{J}_2 = \begin{bmatrix} L_3 s\theta_4 s\theta_6 - L_3 c\theta_4 c\theta_5 c\theta_6 + K_{J2}^1 \\ L_3 c\theta_6 s\theta_4 + L_3 c\theta_4 c\theta_5 s\theta_6 + K_{J2}^2 \\ L_3 c\theta_4 s\theta_5 - L_2 c\theta_3 c\theta_5 + L_2 c\theta_4 s\theta_3 s\theta_5 \\ -c\theta_4 s\theta_6 - c\theta_5 c\theta_6 s\theta_4 \\ c\theta_5 s\theta_4 s\theta_6 - c\theta_4 c\theta_6 \\ s\theta_4 s\theta_5 \end{bmatrix}$$

$$K_{J2}^1 = - L_2 c\theta_3 c\theta_6 s\theta_5 + L_2 s\theta_3 s\theta_4 s\theta_6 - L_2 c\theta_4 c\theta_5 c\theta_6 s\theta_3$$

$$K_{J2}^2 = L_2 c\theta_6 s\theta_3 s\theta_4 + L2 c\theta_3 s\theta_5 s\theta_6 + L_2 c\theta_4 c\theta_5 s\theta_3 s\theta_6$$

$$\mathbf{J}_3 = \begin{bmatrix} L_3 s\theta_4 s\theta_6 - L_3 c\theta_4 c\theta_5 c\theta_6 \\ L_3 c\theta_6 s\theta_4 + L_3 c\theta_4 c\theta_5 s\theta_6 \\ L_3 c\theta_4 s\theta_5 \\ -c\theta_4 s\theta_6 - c\theta_5 c\theta_6 s\theta_4 \\ c\theta_5 s\theta_4 s\theta_6 - c\theta_4 c\theta_6 \\ s\theta_4 s\theta_5 \end{bmatrix} \quad \mathbf{J}_4 = \begin{bmatrix} 0 \\ 0 \\ 0 \\ -c\theta_6 s\theta_5 \\ -s\theta_5 s\theta_6 \\ c\theta_5 \end{bmatrix} \quad \mathbf{J}_5 = \begin{bmatrix} 0 \\ 0 \\ 0 \\ -s\theta_6 \\ -c\theta_6 \\ 0 \end{bmatrix} \quad \mathbf{J}_5 = \begin{bmatrix} 0 \\ 0 \\ 0 \\ 0 \\ 0 \\ 1 \end{bmatrix} \quad (3)$$

$$\text{each corner range:} \begin{cases} \theta_1 \in [-\pi/2, \pi/2] \text{ rad} \\ \theta_2 \in [-2\pi/3, 2/3\pi] \text{ rad} \\ \theta_3 \in [-\pi/3, \pi/2] \text{ rad} \\ \theta_4 \in [-\pi/2, \pi/2] \text{ rad} \\ \theta_5 \in [-2\pi/3, 2/3\pi] \text{ rad} \\ \theta_6 \in [-2\pi/3, 2\pi/3] \text{ rad} \end{cases}$$

3 Dexterity Analysis of the Manipulator

3.1 Dexterity Index Establishment

The dexterity index of the manipulator has many indicators. The condition number is an important index to describe the kinematic performance of the manipulator. It reflects the relationship between the amount of end motion and the active joint, and is also widely used in the optimization of the manipulator. The condition number is related to the singular value of the Jacobian matrix. Its definition is as shown in Eq. 4. $\sigma_{\min}(\mathbf{J})$ is the minimum singular value of the Jacobian matrix and $\sigma_{\max}(\mathbf{J})$ is the maximum singular value of the Jacobian matrix. The condition number reflects the accuracy of the inversion of the Jacobian matrix, that is The relationship between the amount of change in each joint angle and the amount of change in the fixed point at the end. The closer the theoretical is to 1, the better the uniformity of motion of each joint, the higher the dexterity of the manipulator.

$$K_J = \frac{\sigma_{\max}(\mathbf{J})}{\sigma_{\min}(\mathbf{J})} \quad (4)$$

However, there is a disadvantage in the condition number index, and it can only be aimed at a fixed position. that is, the condition number can only be used for a certain fixed pose, and the number of conditions under different pose conditions also differs. The index does not reflect the kinematic performance in the global workspace. Aiming at above problems, the mean of condition number index is adopted. The definition is shown in Eq. 5, which is the average value of K_J in the global workspace.

$$\eta = \frac{\int\limits_{S} K_J \cdot d_s}{d_s} \tag{5}$$

Where, K_J is the condition number in a single position, and s is the global work-space of the manipulator.

Since the average condition number η reflects the dexterity of the various directions of the manipulator in the global workspace, it does not reflect the volatility in the whole space. Therefore, the volatility of the condition number in the global space is also a kind of dexterity for manipulator. The important indicator is defined as Eq. 6, which is the variance of the condition number in the global space.

$$\sigma = \sqrt{\frac{\int\limits_{S} (K_J - \eta)d_s}{d_s}} \tag{6}$$

Considering that two dexterity indicators are very important for the manipulator, the two indicators are weighted as a comprehensive dexterity indicator reflecting the kinematic performance in global workspace of the manipulator, where k_1 and k_2 are the weighted coefficients.

$$\zeta = k_1\eta + k_2\sigma \tag{7}$$

3.2 Dexterity Index Establishment

The dimensional parameters of the manipulator are three rod length parameters (L_1, L_2, L_3). Firstly, the influence of the three rod length parameters on the average condition number and the volatility condition number is analyzed. The result is shown in Fig. 2. Keep the other rod lengths constant when analyzing the influence of a rod length. The results show that the parameter L_1 has no influence on the dexterity index, so the optimization of the parameters of the L_2 and L_3 is only considered when optimizing the dimensional of the manipulator.

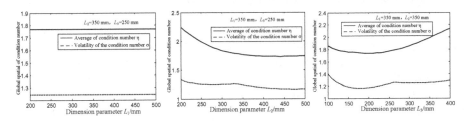

Fig. 2. Influence of dimension parameters on optimization indexes of condition number

The parameters L_2 and L_3 are regarded as variables to analyze the dexterity index changes within the global workspace, and the analysis results are shown in Fig. 3. The results shown that the variation range of the average condition number is [1.2, 1.8], and the variation range of the volatility condition number is [1.7, 2.8]. Considering the variation range of two dexterity indexes, the weighted coefficient is set as $k_1 = 0.4$ and $k_2 = 0.6$ (Fig. 4).

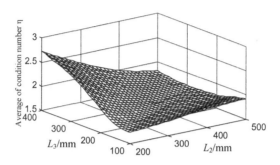

Fig. 3. Influence of optimization variables on the average of condition number

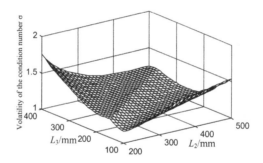

Fig. 4. Influence of optimization variables on the volatility of condition number

4 Dimensional Optimization of Manipulator

According to the limitation of the actual installation size, the variables is limited to $200 \leq L_2 \leq 500$ mm and $100 \leq L_3 \leq 400$ mm. By writing M file, the rod length corresponding to the minimum value of the comprehensive index is obtained as the optimal length of the rod. The optimal rod length is $L_2 = 200$ mm, $L_3 = 110$ mm, and the corresponding average of condition number η is 1.73, the volatility of the condition number σ is 1.16, and the comprehensive dexterity index ζ is 1.39. The average of the global spatial condition number η under the initial size condition is 1.77, the volatility of the condition number σ is 1.24, and the comprehensive dexterity index ζ is 1.45. After optimization, the indicators are improved (Fig. 5).

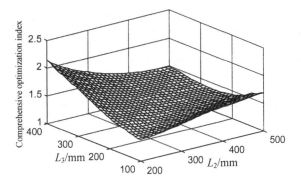

Fig. 5. Influence of optimization variables on comprehensive indexes

5   Conclusions

Based on the kinematics model of the manipulator, the Jacobian matrix was calculated. The average and volatility of the condition number indexes were established. By analyzing the influence of the length parameter on the indicator, weighting factor was determined and the comprehensive optimization indicator was established. Based on the comprehensive optimization index, the dimension parameters were optimized, and the optimal dimensional parameters were obtained. The results show that the dexterity index of the manipulator is improved after optimization.

Acknowledgements. The authors gratefully acknowledge the financial supports for this research from National key research and development plan project (2018YFB1308100), the National Natural Science Foundation of China (Nos. 51805488; 51375458). This work is supported by Science Foundation of Zhejiang Sci-Tech University (ZSTU) under Grant No. 19022104-Y.

References

1. Wang, X.L., Zhao, D.J., Zhang, B., et al.: Kinematics analysis and optimization design of noval 4-DOF parallel mechanism. J. Northeast. Univ. (Nat. Sci.) **39**(04), 532–537 (2018)
2. Shi, Z., Luo, Y., Chen, H., et al.: On global performance indices of robotic mechanisms. Robot **27**(5), 420–422 (2005)
3. Tian, H.B., Ma, H.W., Wei, J.: Workspace and structural parameters analysis for manipulator of serial robot. Trans. Chin. Soc. Agric. Mach. **4**, 196–201 (2013)
4. Ding, Y., Wang, X.: Optimization method of serial manipulator structure. J. Zhejiang Univ. Eng. Sci. **44**(12), 2360–2364 (2010)
5. Sun, W., Li, G.: Multiobjective optimization for the forging manipulator based on the comprehensive manipulation performance indices. J. Mech. Eng. **50**(17), 52–60 (2014)
6. Xiao, Y.F., Wang, X.L., Zhang, F.H., et al.: A global-parameter optimal design method for serial manipulators. China Mech. Eng. **25**(16), 2235–2239 (2014)

7. Chen, X.L., Jiang, D.Y., Chen, L.L., et al.: Kinematics performance analysis and optimal design of redundant actuation parallel mechanism. Trans. Chin. Soc. Agric. Mach. **47**(06), 340–347 (2016)
8. Dong, C., Liu, H., Huang, T.: Kinematic performance analysis of redundantly actuated 4-UPS&UP parallel manipulator. J. Mech. Eng. **50**(17), 52–60 (2014)
9. Yang, H., Fang, H., Li, D., et al.: Kinematics analysis and multi-objective optimization of a novel parallel perfusion robot. J. Beijing Univ. Aeronaut. Astronaut. **44**(03), 568–575 (2018)

Design and Experimental Analysis of a Planar Compliant Parallel Manipulator

Congcong Du[1], Genliang Chen[2(✉)], Zhuang Zhang[1], Liqing Tang[1], and Hao Wang[2]

[1] Shanghai Jiao Tong University, 800 Dongchuan Road, Shanghai, China
{DuCongcong,leungchan,z.zhang,tangliqing,wanghao}@sjtu.edu.cn
[2] State Key Laboratory of Mechanical System and Vibration, Shanghai, China

Abstract. This paper presents a new type of flexible planar parallel manipulator, which driven by three motors. Compared to the conventional robot, this robot realizes planar degrees of freedom through the elastic rod deformation. Based on this principle, the prototype was designed and produced, and its workspace was analyzed by motion capture experiments. The repeating position accuracy is 0.0771 mm. With high-precision and high-load characteristics, this robot can protect the workpiece when the load exceeds its threshold. It can accomplish difficult tasks for rigid robots, such as inserting shafts into holes or grabbing fragile items, as shown in the demo.

Keywords: Flexible parallel robot · Compliant manipulator

1 Introduction

Owing to the safety it brings to the Human-Robot Interaction [3] and the protection it brings to the system when misalignment happens [17], compliance in pick-and-place manipulation is now grabbing more attention with the increasing demands of automation. There are mainly two ways to obtain compliance [1]. One of them is to manipulate robots with stiff joints and arms. This kind of compliance is referred to as active compliance and can be realized by means of control [9,12,14]. In this case, the controller has to introduce soft touch of all time to keep the manipulator compliant [6], which means the manipulator will thoroughly lose its compliance in the presence of malfunctions from sensors or controllers. Moreover, the manipulator will not perform well when facing shocks because of the limited bandwidth of the controller [15]; injuries are more likely to be caused when using rigid structures [16]. Thus, in order to avoid incidental hard collision, flexible structures can be integrated into manipulators; it is how another kind of compliance, passive compliance, is attained. Due to its inherent flexible structure, passive compliance provides more sensitive and reliable protection that is irrelevant to control algorithm [13]. The most common methods to obtain passive compliance are designing compliant joints or end-of-arm tools

© Springer Nature Switzerland AG 2019
H. Yu et al. (Eds.): ICIRA 2019, LNAI 11744, pp. 637–647, 2019.
https://doi.org/10.1007/978-3-030-27541-9_52

[5, 7, 10, 18]. However, integrating compliant elements into rigid structures only, the range of compliance is easily restricted by the size of the compliant elements. Then, the passive compliance is correspondingly diminished. Hence, for a better performance, structures with larger scales of compliance are needed.

To alleviate the above shortcomings, soft robots, which aim to accomplish tasks in unstructured environments [8] with their thoroughly compliant structures, have been extensively researched in recent years. Soft robotics refers to robots utilizing materials and actuation methods that are soft, flexible and compliant [11]; it has already become one of the most popular topics in robotics [2]. However, among these designs, most of them have the problems of positioning accuracy and load-carrying capacity while performing compliantly in manipulation tasks. The positioning errors and low load-carrying capacity mainly come from the softness of their intrinsic structures, so that the problems are inevitable in a sense. Thus, in order to overcome such weaknesses and, at the same time, keep compliant, a feasible solution is to use flexible materials with higher Young's modulus, which means using elastic structures instead of soft ones.

In order to improve performance, parallel continuum manipulators that are combination of a conventional continuum robot and a parallel robot was proposed. Given the advantages of parallel complaint manipulators, in this paper, a novel planar three degrees of freedom flexible parallel manipulator, as well as its experimental analysis is reported. The manipulator, mainly designed for pick-and-place manipulation, is composed of two parallelogram linkages; one consists of rigid links, the other consists of flexible ones. Connecting with the elastic links that are capable of producing large deformation, the end effector of the manipulator can generate wide-range motions and is compliant in both the vertical and the horizontal directions. At the same time, the load-carrying capacity and positioning accuracy are improved by its parallel structure. Based on the approach to large deflection problems using principal axes decomposition of compliance matrices [4], the kinematics and the compliance of the flexible manipulator are analyzed. The main merit of the proposed manipulator is its intrinsic passive compliance and the boundaries of the generated force, which offers reliable passive compliance when positioning errors or collisions happen during pick-and-place tasks.

2   Mechanism Design and Prototyping

This section mainly introduces the mechanism design of a planar-degree-of-freedom flexible parallel manipulator and the corresponding prototype. The three parallel linear actuators are used to drive the parallelogram connecting-rods, aiming to achieve high-precision motion and excellent force flexibility. In addition, the design of parallelogram links with different stiffness level avoids the motion-coupling of the parallel mechanism. The single-degree-freedom motion guiding of the elongated elastic plate is realized by the constraint of the pulley block, while the contact friction of the moving weight is reduced.

2.1   Architecture of the Flexible Planar Parallel Manipulator

As shown in Fig. 1, the robot is mainly divided into two parts: the drive mechanism and the rigid-flex link. The rigid-flexible link is composed of two sets of parallel four-bar linkages with different stiffness levels, which are called the outer ring parallelogram rod and the inner ring parallelogram rod respectively, referred to as outer rod and inner rod. The long sides of the parallelogram mechanism is made up of elastic metal sheets, and the upper and lower short sides are rigid body rods. The long side of the inner rod passes through the sliding pair, which is set on short side of the outer rod, and the sliding pair contains four plastic-coated pulleys. These linear actuators are fixed on the frame, and the short side of the inner rod is used as the mounting interface for the manipulator output.

Since the drive sections are arranged in a parallel mechanism, the two sets of four-bar linkage structures are geometrically symmetrical. At the same time, during the deformation of the elastic rod, the ratio of the long side and the short side of the parallelogram remains constant, via the precise motor control. Thus, during the movement, the short side of the inner rods (i.e., the manipulator output) keeps a purely horizontal state. As shown in Fig. 1, when the linear actuator motors of the outer rods run at a constant speed, the rigid-short side position of the outer rod is deflected. However, due to the linear sliding pair and the geometrical symmetry, the short rod of the inner rods still outputs a simple translational motion pattern, which is parallel to the Y-axis direction. The movement of the inner rod linear actuator controls the displacement of the end effector in the X-axis direction, as shown in Fig. 1. Because the rigidity of the inner elastic rod is only 1/64 of the stiffness of the outer rod, the movement of the inner ring four rods cannot influence the position and posture of the outer rods. In short, the motion of the inner and outer rods are decoupled from each other to some extent.

In summary, by driving three motors independently, the end of the compliant manipulator has three degrees of freedom. It is controlled by outer and inner rods.

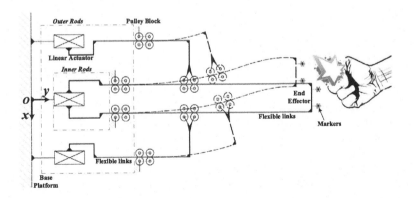

Fig. 1. 2D simplified diagram of the parallel manipulator

2.2   Prototyping

As shown in Fig. 2, the prototype is compact and is mainly divided into three layers. The lowest layer is the basic frame, built from easy-to-obtain industrial aluminum profiles. A cover plate is mounted on the frame and is produced by low-cost resin 3D printing. The middle layer is composed of three parallel linear actuators and is fixedly connected with the cover plate. The linear module is driven by DC servo Maxon motors with ball screws (diameter: 16 mm, pitch: 5 mm). Thereby the mechanical device guarantees better motion accuracy and rigidity. The top layer is outer and inner rod mechanism. The upper end short rod of the parallelogram is fixedly connected to the slider of the linear module. The elastic rod is used as the long side of the parallelogram, one end of the rod is fixed to the upper short rod, and the other end is fixed to the lower short rod.

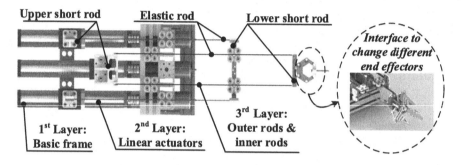

Fig. 2. 3D rendered model

Among them, the thickness of the two elastic rods are: 0.5 mm and 2 mm, made of 65 Mn spring steel. This material is easy to machine and has stable mechanical properties. The elastic rod is stagnate back under repeated bending conditions, and metal fatigue is less likely to occur. The long side of the inner four rod passes through the sliding pair on the outer rod, which is composed of four sets of pulleys (rolling bearings). The gap between the pulleys is equal to the thickness of the elastic plate to be constrained. Taking into account the position error of the pulley caused by machining and parts assembly, M2 screws are used to adjust the clearance between the pulleys, ensuring the reliable sliding constraints. Thus, the elastic rod has only one simple movement in the sliding pair, and there is no jumping. The introduction of the guide wheel not only makes the necessary geometric constraints on the elastic rod, but also transforms the linear sliding into the rolling of the pulley bearing, which significantly reduces the friction between the elastic rod and the bottom plate, during the whole movement.

The flexibility of the robot mainly utilizes the width direction of the elastic plate. When the end of the manipulator is subjected to the load in the X and Y directions, the elastic piece can be flexibly deformed correspondingly to avoid local stress concentration caused by hard collision. The end effector of the mechanism achieves good compliance finally. Of course, in the actual case, the elastic rod is a constraint in the cantilever beam form. And inevitably, there is a force load in the thickness direction. In order to reduce the rod deformation caused by the force in the thickness direction, or even lose stability, the nylon sliding needle row (product model: FF2010) is arranged under the non-deformed area of the outer and inner rods. Thus, by the above measures, the rigidity of the manipulator in the thickness direction is enhanced. The needles are made of high-frequency hardened bearing steel (material mark: CGR15), with high hardness. Compared with plastic material, material wear loss is not easy to occur, when the spring steel sheet slides on the needle roller row.

The control system consists of a Windows PC running 64-bit TwinCat3, elmo G-MOLWHI10/100 drivers and RE40 Maxon motors. The drivers and PC are connected via industrial gigabit cable and the communication period is 2 ms, to ensure communication reliability and control synchronization.

3   Experimental Analysis

Based on the previous research work, for the superelastic link mechanism, the kinematics of the elastic mechanism can be well analyzed by the principal axes decomposition of compliance matrices [4]. Drive the motors to make the equivalent passive joints of the discretized segments produce kinematic amount, and let the amount of motion meet the static equilibrium configuration.

Therefore, the forward kinematics model of the planar degree-of-freedom elastic parallel mechanism is established, which will be useful in the trajectory planning of the end effector. The rigid rotating joint is improved to a kind of flexible rotating hinge, eliminating joint clearance and realizing a fully flexible platform in a true sense. Compared with the soft-rigid mechanism, the new mechanism has a greater improvement in motion accuracy, flexibility and safety.

As described in the second section, the connecting rod of the planar mechanism is a long thin-walled superelastic sheet. The movement state of the end effector is controlled by the combination of sheets' deformation. Therefore, mechanism movement can be simplified to a pure two-dimensional plane deformation, as torsional deformation of the sheets is ignored. The linear actuators on the frame drive the linear motion of the inner rod, which is the motion freedom of in one direction. The other two linear actuators on two sides drive the outer rod independently, to control the differential displacement momentum.

3.1   Setup

To analyze the open loop control accuracy of the compliant mechanism, we used six Optitrack cameras (prime 41/17W series) to construct a motion capture system, measuring the position and attitude of the end effector. The maximum frame number of the camera is 250 FPS. In the cubic space of 15 m, the capture accuracy is 0.1 mm, tracing the movement of the 850 nm infrared Markers. After setting up the measurement hardware, environment needs to be calibrated. The corner point of the operate platform is selected to establish the world coordinate system. The overall reprojection mean 3D error is 0.270 mm finally. After that, two new coordinate systems on the fixed platform and the moving platform, T1 and T2 will be made respectively. As shown in Fig. 3, three markers are placed on the device frame to establish the fixed coordinate while two markers are set on the end effector as the moving coordinate.

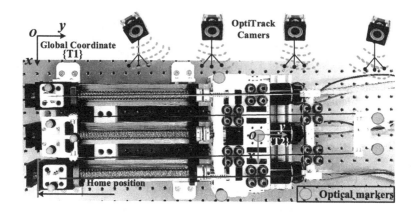

Fig. 3. Measurement environment based on Optitrack system

3.2   Reachable Workspace

The actual marker data is measured in the world coordinate system. Via transforming matrix, the motion data of the end effector which is captured in global coordinate system {T1} is converted into the fixed frame coordinate system {T2}. Thus the motion trajectory of the end effector can be expressed more intuitively.

In order to characterize the motion space of the planar mechanism, we set the same length of motion range on the three actuators. The end of the screw which is close to the Maxon motor is set as home position point, shown in Fig. 3. The three coordinate axes are equally divided into 15 position points, and the three sets of points are sufficiently arranged and combined to generate 3725 different motion data scatter points. The motion data is then input to three servo motors, and the end of the planar mechanism traverses all possible spatial position points. By measuring the point cloud data of the markers on the moving platform and converting the data to the fixed frame coordinate system {T2}, the motion space of the mechanism can be obtained.

At the same time, Fig. 4 describes the motion data of the end moving platform in the direction perpendicular to the plane. The maximum displacement in Z axis direction is 1.0 mm and increases along the Y-axis, as the base frame of the manipulator is slightly tilted. Through experimental measurements, it was confirmed that the moving platform has planar degrees of freedom. The maximum distance of the working space in the X direction is 280 mm, and 160 mm in the Y direction.

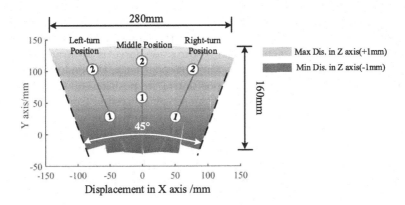

Fig. 4. Reachable workspace

3.3   Repeatability

The left side of the three linear actuators shown in Fig. 3 is defined as the home position point. At the same time, the shape of the inner rods and the outer rods are all standard rectangles. We select 6 desired positions in the workspace, and each position is measured 10 times. Then, we calculate the deviation of end effector of these six positions, as depicted in Table 1. The average standard deviation of end effector movement is 0.1240 mm, 0.0720 mm, 0.0352 mm in horizontal, vertical and width direction.

Table 1. Repeatability standard deviation of end effector

Three directions displacement	Horizontal	Vertical	Width
Middle Pos. 1 [mm]	0.0584	0.0294	0.0782
Middle Pos. 2 [mm]	0.0492	0.0295	0.0185
Left-turn Pos. 1 [mm]	0.3885	0.0308	0.0502
Left-turn Pos. 2 [mm]	0.1051	0.0577	0.0360
Right-turn Pos. 1 [mm]	0.1139	0.1230	0.0244
Right-turn Pos. 2 [mm]	0.0292	0.1618	0.0041

In the repeated positioning accuracy experiment, the main error may come from the 25 arcmin return clearance of the motor reducer. And there also exists tiny clearance between the two pulleys due to the bending load.

3.4   Force Compliance Experiment

In order to express the force compliance characteristics more intuitively, we conducted several mechanical testing and further analysis of the planar complaint mechanism. As shown in Fig. 5, a contact block is connected at the end effector of the mechanism. In order to eliminate the interference caused by friction, a rolling-flexible bearing bovine is mounted on the contact block. This can ensure the force sensor measurement of the Y direction force is accurate. The force measurement process is divided into three steps: firstly, the end effector of the mechanism moves to several different positions (two positions on the left and two positions on the right). Secondly, the force sensor is fixed in front of the contact block. The sensor is attached to the 6060 aluminum profile, which combined to the optical table. The four-bar mechanism drives the inner rod, allowing the contact block to collide with the front force sensor actively. Lastly, the inner rod performs the same displacement increment $\Delta L = 2.5\,\text{mm}$ each time, which is from 2.5 mm to 12.5 mm, respectively. The force sensor model is ATI Mini45 (F/T Sensor), resolution is 0.025 N.

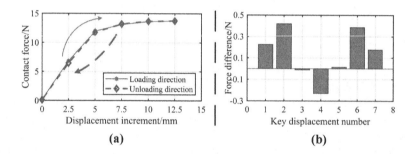

(a)   (b)

Fig. 5. Mechanical properties

For the rigid body robot, when the end hits the object, the contact force increases with the displacement until the weaker side is crushed. It can be seen from the Fig. 5 that the relationship between force and displacement is the shape of the hillside. The specific performance is that the contact force rises as the end effector displacement increases. However, when the displacement reaches a certain level, the contact force will be stable after reaching the peak which realizes the protection of the operating object. This indicates the output of the external force of the end moving platform and has a force threshold. As shown in Fig. 5, after the displacement hits 7.5 mm, the force will remain at around 13 N. At the same time, the curves of loading and releasing forces are coincident, the energy loss is tiny. When the end effector is in the left-right symmetrical position, the force measurement error under the same displacement is less than 0.5 N, indicating the force control has higher precision.

4   Application

The planar compliant parallel manipulator has high precision and high safety. The elastic links will deform when subjected to an unexpected load, to protect the workpiece and itself. As a new compliant planar mechanism, it can be applied in medical, logistics, manufacturing fields and so on.

The first example shown in Fig. 6(A) is a process of inserting a shaft into four holes of the plastic bone one by one. When the shaft and the target hole have a small position or angular deviation, the parallel compliant mechanism can still complete the assembly task perfectly, avoiding the hard contact and damage to the workpiece. As shown in Fig. 6(B), a flexible gripper is attached to the end effector, aiming to grab irregular-shaped fragile items. This flow chart demonstrates the action of grabbing a spiral-shaped glass LED bulb and placing it in the charging socket. When encountering an obstacle, this kind of manipulator can passively deform, evade, and complete the target task eventually.

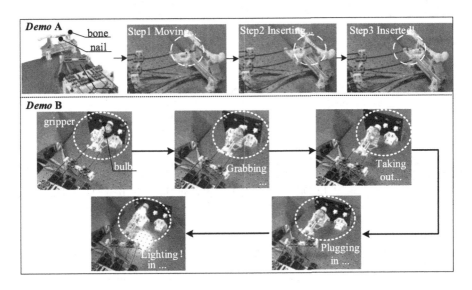

Fig. 6. Process of application examples

5   Conclusion

In this paper, a new type of flexible parallel robot is proposed, which is driven by three linear actuators redundantly. The end effector has planar degrees of freedom. The flexibility of the manipulator is achieved by bending the elastic sheets. Compared to the conventional mechanism using the mutual rotation of the rigid joints, this new type of mechanism realizes the output of planar degrees of freedom by the elastic rod deformation. Based on this concept, the prototype was designed and produced, and its workspace (length: 280 mm, width: 160 mm) was confirmed by optical motion capture experiments. At the same time, the repeating position accuracy of the mechanism were tested, the average errors were 0.0771 mm. Through the experimental and theoretical calculations above, the parallel compliant mechanism inherits the high-precision and high-load characteristics of the parallel mechanism, and can protect the workpiece when the load exceeds the threshold. It can accomplish difficult tasks for industrial robots, such as inserting shafts into holes and grabbing fragile items. At the end of the article, two possible application demos are proposed perfectly.

Acknowledgment. This work was jointly supported by the Natural Science Foundation of China under Grant 51875334.

References

1. Albu-Schaffer, A., et al.: Soft robotics. IEEE Robot. Autom. Mag. **15**(3), 20–30 (2008)
2. Bao, G., et al.: Soft robotics: academic insights and perspectives through bibliometric analysis. Soft Robot. **5**(3), 229–241 (2018)
3. Bicchi, A., Tonietti, G.: Fast and "soft-arm" tactics [robot arm design]. IEEE Robot. Autom. Mag. **11**(2), 22–33 (2004)
4. Chen, G., Zhang, Z., Wang, H.: A general approach to the large deflection problems of spatial flexible rods using principal axes decomposition of compliance matrices. J. Mech. Robot. **10**(3), 031012 (2018)
5. Choi, J., Hong, S., Lee, W., Kang, S., Kim, M.: A robot joint with variable stiffness using leaf springs. IEEE Trans. Robot. **27**(2), 229–238 (2011)
6. Goris, K., Saldien, J., Vanderborght, B., Lefeber, D.: How to achieve the huggable behavior of the social robot probo? A reflection on the actuators. Mechatronics **21**(3), 490–500 (2011)
7. Hong, M.B., Choi, Y.J.: Design method of planar three-degrees-of-freedom serial compliance device with desired compliance characteristics. Proc. Inst. Mech. Eng. Part C J. Mech. Eng. Sci. **226**(9), 2331–2344 (2012)
8. Hughes, J., Culha, U., Giardina, F., Guenther, F., Rosendo, A., Iida, F.: Soft manipulators and grippers: a review. Front. Robot. AI **3**, 69 (2016)
9. Khan, S.G., Herrmann, G., Pipe, T., Melhuish, C., Spiers, A.: Safe adaptive compliance control of a humanoid robotic arm with anti-windup compensation and posture control. Int. J. Soc. Robot. **2**(3), 305–319 (2010)
10. Kuo, P.H., Deshpande, A.D.: A novel joint design for robotic hands with humanlike nonlinear compliance. J. Mech. Robot. **8**(2), 021004 (2016)
11. Laschi, C., Cianchetti, M.: Soft robotics: new perspectives for robot bodyware and control. Front. Bioeng. Biotechnol. **2**, 3 (2014)
12. Mehdi, H., Boubaker, O.: New robust tracking control for safe constrained robots under unknown impedance environment. In: Herrmann, G., Studley, M., Pearson, M., Conn, A., Melhuish, C., Witkowski, M., Kim, J.-H., Vadakkepat, P. (eds.) TAROS 2012. LNCS (LNAI), vol. 7429, pp. 313–323. Springer, Heidelberg (2012). https://doi.org/10.1007/978-3-642-32527-4_28
13. Park, J.J., Song, J.B.: A nonlinear stiffness safe joint mechanism design for human robot interaction. J. Mech. Des. **132**(6), 061005 (2010)

14. Shetty, B.R., Ang, M.H.: Active compliance control of a puma 560 robot. In: 1996 IEEE International Conference on Robotics and Automation, 1996. Proceedings, vol. 4, pp. 3720–3725. IEEE (1996)

15. Van Ham, R., Sugar, T.G., Vanderborght, B., Hollander, K.W., Lefeber, D.: Compliant actuator designs. IEEE Robot. Autom. Mag. **16**(3), 81–94 (2009)

16. Wang, W., Loh, R.N., Gu, E.Y.: Passive compliance versus active compliance in robot-based automated assembly systems. Ind. Robot. Int. J. **25**(1), 48–57 (1998)

17. Whitney, D.E.: Quasi-static assembly of compliantly supported rigid parts. J. Dyn. Syst. Meas. Control **104**(1), 65–77 (1982)

18. Zhao, Y., Yu, J., Wang, H., Chen, G., Lai, X.: Design of an electromagnetic prismatic joint with variable stiffness. Ind. Robot. Int. J. **44**(2), 222–230 (2017)

Safety and Waterproof Design
of Multi-functional Assisted Bath Robot

Yuan Fu, He Zhimin, and Chen Diansheng[⊠]

School of Mechanical Engineering and Automation, Beihang University,
Beijing, China
chends@163.com

Abstract. For the elderly who stay in bed for a long time, the bath has many benefits such as keeping the skin clean and hygienic, promoting the blood circulation of the epidermis, and the multifunctional assisted bath robot can well assist the nursing staff for daily cleaning for the elderly. Based on a versatile bathing robot, this paper aims at designing safety aids devices for bath safety during bathing. In view of the condition that the multi-functional bathing robot has direct contact with the bathing water, the waterproof system was designed from the aspects of waterproof structure and material selection. Finally, the integrated prototype of the multi-functional bathing robot was tested to verify the reliability, safety and comfort of its features.

Keywords: Assisted bath robot · Safety aid · Waterproof design

1 Introduction

With the rapid development of the economy, the continuous improvement of people's living standards and the vigorous development of the healthcare industry, the aging of the population has become a major social problem in China [1, 2]. Due to birth control reasons, China's population is aging faster than most countries in the world, thus has entered the ranks of an aging population in advance. China is not only the country with the most aging population in the world, but also one of the fastest aging countries by report. China's elderly population over 60 years old was 241 million, accounting for 17.3% of the total population up to 2017. It is predicted that by 2025, the total number of elderly people in China will reach 284 million, accounting as high as 19.3% [3–5] of all.

The degree of population aging in China, however, is obviously not consistent with the current economic and social development. Countries with a high degree of population aging in the world are often developed countries with better medical and social security systems, and our country has ushered in an aging society with insufficient economic development, which brings unprecedented pressure to medical and social welfare, leading to particularly prominent problems [6, 7]. In the long run, the use of assisted and service robots for the elderly and the disable will be an important

This research was supported by the National Key R&D Program of China (2017YFB1304102).

H. Yu et al. (Eds.): ICIRA 2019, LNAI 11744, pp. 648–659, 2019.
https://doi.org/10.1007/978-3-030-27541-9_53

development direction for elderly care therefor can help the old who are in bed for a long period of time to better adapt to their daily lives, and to a large extent compensate their weakened body functions [8, 9].

Helping the old to take a bath is one of the most difficult care items in the daily care [10–12]. As the serious declining of physical fitness, balance and flexibility and the relatively slippery environment in the bathroom, the elderly are prone to slipping and fainting during the bathing process. Often, one or more caregivers are required to assist in the bathing work, which is quite burdensome for nursing staff. Therefore, it is a very practical study to develop an auxiliary bathing device to solve the difficulties of bathing. According to the needs of the elderly bathing, companies and research institutions at home and abroad have carried out plenty of related research. The company Arjohuntleigh of the United States designed and produced an electric sanitary chair which relies on the motor to change the height and inclination of the seat back, thus brings convenience for the nursing staff to clean the elderly. However, this sanitary chair is extremely expensive and has no design of Auxiliary organization [13] for safety concern. A multi-function electric bath chair from domestic Taicang Kanghui Technology Development Co. Ltd. can adjust the angle by electric push rod using back plate and can be docked with the toilet to facilitate the elderly to go to the toilet. This device satisfies the basic needs of the old in the bathing process with unclear logic of the control system and the simplex human-computer interaction mode as a consequence has potential safety hazards [14, 15]. In view of the problems in the above products, this paper aims to design a safety aid mechanism for bathing based on a multi-functional bathing robot. The waterproof system is designed from the aspects of waterproof structure and material selection considering that the robot will mostly have direct contact with water. Finally, we develop and integrate the prototype of the multi-functional assisted bath robot, and carried out experimental tests to verify the reliability, safety and comfort.

2   Mechanical Introduction

As shown in Fig. 1, the multifunctional assisted bathing robot is composed of six parts.

(1) A back posture adjusting mechanism, which is driven by a backplane motor and the torque amplified by the angle adjuster to drive two parallel four-bar mechanisms, can adjust the entire seat back and the seat plate angle to change the sitting posture and lying posture.

(2) The seat lifting mechanism, including the electric push rod connecting mechanism and the lifting parallel four-bar mechanism, the two are connected by the supporting cross bar. The execution end of the four-bar mechanism is the seat plate, connecting to the back plate mechanism with a shaft linkage.

(3) The armrest linkage mechanism, driven by two motors and changing the motor rotation into a linear motion with a gear rack system, can rotate the armrest through the back posture adjustment mechanism and separate the armrest from the backing plate when the linkage pin is recovered.

(4) Chassis movement mechanism. The chassis of the assisting bath robot is an I-shaped round tube steel frame structure, which is the supporting member of the whole robot. The front end adopts two universal wheels, and the rear uses two directional wheels for convenient movement and steering.

(5) The pedal protection mechanism is symmetrically distributed on both sides of the front end of the seat, and can be unfolded and stowed by a rotating mechanism, and can be stepped on by the person on the seat when deployed, and at the same time, prevents falling.

(6) Brake mechanism. Brake system of rear wheel directional wheel realizes braking through a set of crank linkage mechanism. The versatile bathing robot has three main modes of operation: seat lift, backboard armrest incline with the backboard pitch.

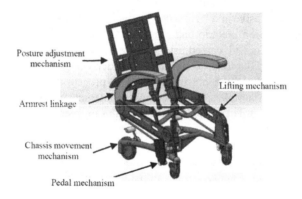

Fig. 1. Mechanical structure

A. Seat lift mode

When the nursing staff uses the lifting function of the assisting robot, the electric push rod drives the parallel four-bar mechanism to raise or lower the whole seat, which is convenient for the nursing staff to perform service in the standing state. Since the installation of the electric push rod is not in the vertical direction, during the lifting process of the push rod, the back plate and the seat plate are rotated at a certain angle.

B. Backboard pitch mode

When the nursing staff uses the tilting function of the assisting robot, the backplane motor will rotate the backboard back and forth by forward and reverse rotation, thereby adjusting the posture of the elderly during the bathing process. It is convenient for the nursing staff to clean the back hips and other parts.

C. Backboard armrest incline with the backboard pitch

When the nursing staff uses the backboard armrest incline with the backboard pitch function, the armrest linkage mechanism will eject the linkage pin and connect with the hole corresponding to the armrest, so that the backboard rotates the armrest together during the rotation process. It's convenient for the old to grasp to assist nursing staff to undress the pants and clean the relevant parts of the elderly.

In practical application, the nursing staff first lowers the assisting bath robot to the lowest position, and then lifts the old man into the assisting bath robot and pushes it to the bathroom. Then the height is raised by using the lifting function, and the back angle is constantly adjusted during the nursing process. After the bath is completed, the bathing robot will be pushed out of the bathroom and lowered to the lowest position so that the old can get off.

3 Control System Introduction

Figure 2 shows the main modules of the multi-functional bath chair control system: artificial input module, position detection module, main control module, servo-driven module, executable module, user notification module (Power supply module is omitted).

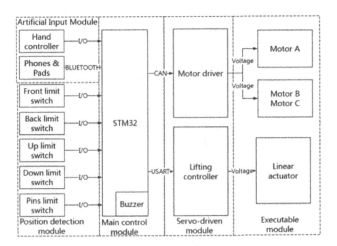

Fig. 2. Control system

A. Artificial input module

This module provides basic buttons and user interfaces for users to control the robot, including hand controller with entity buttons and control software which can be installed on mobile devices such as mobile phones and tablets.

B. Position detection module

This module contains three groups of micro switch to limit the height of the bath chair, the angel between backrest plate and support plate and the position of pins. It is also used to check the initial position of the robot when started.

C. Main control module

This module, based on STM32 microprocessor, is responsible for communicate with artificial input module, position detection module and servo-driven module.

D. Servo-driven module

This module serves to drive all the motors and electrical push rods of the system, using USART port and CAN bus port to communicate with control system.

E. Executable module

This module is for connection between the motors and the corresponding mechanisms, transforming the rotation of the motors to the linear movement of the mechanisms.

F. User notification module

This module is composed of the buzzer module which is integrated on the main control module, giving voice prompts to nursing staff when the system booting or responding to user actions.

4 Design of Safety Assistance Mechanism

According to the overall framework and function of the multi-functional bathing robot, the safety auxiliary mechanism of the assisting bath robot is designed, which mainly includes two parts: the seat handle of the assisting bath robot and the protective pedal. The seat handle is installed on the inner side of the left and right handrails, and the protective pedal is welded on the bottom mechanism of the assisting robot, connecting with the support arm of the seat, and the installation position is shown in Fig. 3.

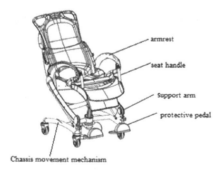

Fig. 3. Safety guard installation location

4.1 The Design of the Seat Handle

When the nursing staff scrubs the back of the old man, the old man leans forward and easily slides out of the bath chair. In order to prevent the above accidents, the design of the seat handle is carried out. The seat handle is mainly composed of a handle body and a handle base. The main body is mounted on the base of the handle by the support bolt and can be rotated around the connection screw. Meanwhile, the inner side of the joint of the handle body is machined with a 270° curved groove whose opening directions are respectively open to the other end of the main body, making the left and right symmetrical forms. The left arc groove opening direction of the main body of the handle is as shown in Fig. 4(a). The handle base is machined with a handle slide key, as shown in Fig. 4(b). The position corresponds to the arc groove, and when installed, the handle slide key is embedded in the arc groove.

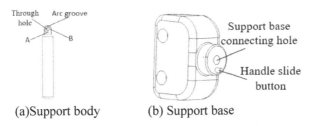

(a)Support body   (b) Support base

Fig. 4. Composition of support arm

When the handle slider is located at the A end of the arc groove, the main body of the handle is in a natural sagging state, and the old man can conveniently enter and exit the seat of the bathtub. When the handle slider is located at the B end of the arc groove, the main body of the handle is in the unfolding working state. Due to the action of gravity, the main body of the handle is in a stable balance and will not change its' state due to the force of the external disturbance. The old man can hold the main body of the handle to protect himself from falling out of the seat and being injured.

4.2   Protective Foot Pedal Design

The design of the protective foot pedal structure is mainly due to two considerations:

(1) Starting from safety and user experience: In order to avoid a floating state of feet when the old man is sitting on the assisting bath robot, which causes the old man to feel unreliable and insecure. At the same time, the front end of the pedal is processed with a semi-open protective cover, which prevents the old man's feet from colliding sitting on the assisting robot when the assisting robot passes through the narrow passage.

(2) Starting from ergonomics and biophysiology: Avoid the weight of the human body is mainly carried by the thighs and buttocks when the old man's feet are suspended. If the compression time of thighs and buttocks is long, it is easy to cause local limb paralysis and hemorrhoids caused by poor blood circulation which highly reduce the use of comfort.

In summary, the main purpose of the protective pedal is to improve the safety and comfort of the bathing robot by carrying the foot part of the elderly. Its main structural components are rotating frame, rotary joints, pedals, limit components, etc. In addition, since the foot pedal device is integrally mounted on the main bearing seat in the chassis moving mechanism, the main bearing seat needs to be structurally adjusted on the basis of the previous design, and the mounting boss of the foot pedal is added, and the structure thereof is also part of the pedal structure design. The design of the pedal is shown in Fig. 5.

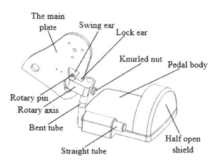

Fig. 5. Composition of protective foot pedal

The working principle is roughly as follows: the rotating frame can be rotated about the axis of the pin hole around the main bearing frame and the rotary axis is rotated around the axis in the range of 180°. That is, the axis plane of the rotating frame and the main bearing seat are parallel to each other in the front and back directions at two extreme positions. In addition, the limit component is to define the posture state when the axis plane of the rotating frame is parallel to the plane of the main bearing seat side. The pedal is rotated by the straight tube axis below the rotating frame, and the rotary motion is performed within the range of 90° around the shaft, that is, the upper (lower) plane of the pedal is nearly parallel or perpendicular to the axis plane of the rotating frame. Based on this, when the pedal is not working, the pedal can be rotated and folded, so that the upper (lower) plane is nearly parallel to the axis plane of the rotating frame, and then the rotating frame is rotated around the main bearing seat, along the side of the main bearing seat. When the pedals need to work, the rotating frame is first rotated to the working position by the reverse operation sequence. As the rotation process, the limit pin automatically enters the limiting hole to fix the posture, and then the pedal is rotated to the limit position for use.

The main innovations and advantages of this design are:

(1) Structurally: non-fixed installation avoids interference with other functional structures, and can be close folded to the bath chair, making the structure more compact, reducing space occupation and avoiding damage.

(2) Functionally: Improve the comfort and safety in sitting position and solve possible physiological problems that may be caused thus greatly enhance the user experience.

5   Waterproof Design

Because most of the use environment of the multi-functional bathing robot is in the bathroom, the safety waterproof design is an essential indicator of its reliability. For the special case of its use, we mainly implement waterproof designs from the aspects of external waterproofing and internal sealing.

5.1   Waterproof Parts

The multi-function bathing robot has the functions of movement, lifting and posture adjustment, so some of its motion pairs and drive components are exposed to the outside. These motion pairs and drive components are required to meet the requirements of waterproofing. Among them, the electric push rod driven by the lifting mechanism belonging to the purchased parts is proposed to use the LIN31 LA31 electric push rod, as shown in Fig. 6. The push rod is considered to be self-contained with upper and lower limit functions, which is more reliable than the self-designed push rod; and the thrust and self-locking force are large, no other mechanical locking is required; and the self-contained waterproof property does not require excessive consideration. The rotating pair of the lifting and lowering mechanism is partially exposed to the outside, and choosing self-lubricating rod end joint bearing can improve the smoothness of the movement while achieving the waterproof effect.

Fig. 6. LA31 waterproof electric push rod

5.2   Mold Sealing Waterproof

Many components of the multi-function bathing robot are made of plastic parts, which makes the whole seat more light and comfortable. For example, back plates, seat plates, leg plates, thigh plates, etc., most of these components are molded from thermoplastic materials. In particular, the back plate is an notable part of the attitude adjustment mechanism, and also afford accommodation for control system of the entire bathing robot, including a central controller, a central control lock, a drive motor, a worm, a battery, etc., so the overall mold can effectively improve its waterproof performance, as shown in Fig. 7.

The seat plate, considering the requirements for assembly and strength, is embedded with a stainless steel seat plate for cooperation with the turbine, the main lifting arm and the armrest, as shown in Fig. 8. The plastic material selected is polyethylene (PE), which is a thermoplastic resin obtained by polymerizing ethylene. It has good chemical stability, is resistant to most acid and alkali corrosion, has low water absorption (good water resistance), and has excellent electrical insulation.

Fig. 7. Backplane shell schematic

Fig. 8. The seat plane   **Fig. 9.** The waterproof cover

In addition, the outer cover of the main lifting arm is made of ABS resin. As shown in Fig. 9, it is also a thermoplastic engineering plastic, but the processing technology is digital engraving. It also has good waterproofness and is compatible with the bathing robot.

6   Prototype Development and Experimental Testing

In order to verify the correctness and rationality of the safety auxiliary mechanism and waterproof system design of the multi-functional bathing robot, we integrated the mechanical system and electronic control system to produce a multi-functional bathing robot prototype shown in Fig. 10.

The experimental test is divided into three parts: the lift function index test, the backboard pitch function index test and the load test.

6.1   The Lift Function Index Test

When performing the test of the lifting function of the assisting bath robot, the main evaluation index is the lifting movement stroke. The test method adopted is as follows: in the case of no-load, select a point on the seat plate as the test reference point, and

Fig. 10. The multi-functional bathing robot

select the floor level as the test reference plane, and measure the seat plate at the lowest position and the highest position with the ground reference respectively. The difference obtained is the desired lifting stroke value shown as Table 1.

It can be seen from the test results that in the test of the lifting stroke, the error of the stroke measurement value is about 409.3 mm, and the error fluctuation is 0.1%. Minor errors caused by component fit errors and corresponding mechanical deviations, load deformations, and offsets are also within the tolerances allowed by the system.

Table 1. The lifting stroke

Number	Lowest position (mm)	Highest Position (mm)	Stroke (mm)
1	490.2	899.5	409.3
2	490.4	899.6	409.2
3	490.2	899.55	409.35
4	490.1	899.4	409.3
5	490.2	899.5	409.3

6.2   The Backboard Pitch Test

When performing the test of the backplane pitch function of the assisting bath robot, the main evaluation index is the pitch angle of the backboard rotation. The specific test method adopted is as follows: in the case of no-load, a certain two-point connection on the backplane is selected as the measurement reference line, and the angle between the reference line and the ground reference are respectively measured when the backboard plate is at the two extreme positions of the pitching motion. The difference between these two angles are the range of motion angle of the backplane. The test results are shown in Table 2.

Table 2. The backboard pitch test

Number	Initial angle (deg)	Last angle (deg)	Deflection (deg)
1	80.30	47.90	32.40
2	80.15	47.80	32.35
3	80.08	48.23	31.85
4	80.42	48.06	32.36
5	80.33	47.98	32.35

It can be seen from the test results that the initial position angle measurement value of the back plate is about 80°, the ultimate position angle measurement value is about 48°, and the pitch motion angle change measurement value is about 32° with the fluctuation under 1.5%, within the tolerance allowed by the system. Therefore, the backplane pitch index of the bathing robot meets the requirements: the backplane movement angle is 48°–80° (50°–80° required).

6.3   The Load Test

The load-bearing capacity of the multi-functional bathing robot determines the applicable population and is a key indicator. When carrying out the load performance test, the main evaluation index is the bearing capacity of the electric push rod. The specific test method used is: load test with 25 kg standard weight and 10 kg sandbag respectively, wherein the sandbag stack can better simulate the pressure state of the bath chair when the robot is practically used. In order to ensure safety, the initial test weight of the load test is set to 75 kg, step by step, the maximum test weight is 110 kg, and the number of safe load times is set to 15 times. The continuous action of completing the target action within the specified number of times is regarded as passing the weight test. The test results are shown in Table 3.

Table 3. The load test

Number	Weight (kg)	Times
1	75	15
2	85	15
3	95	15
4	100	15
5	110	15

It can be seen from the test results that the assisting bath robot can achieve the normal lifting of the specified number of times under the load of 110 kg, so it can be considered that its maximum carrying capacity must be greater than 100 kg.

7   Conclusions

Based on a multi-functional bathing robot, this paper designs safety aids for bath safety in bathing. In view of the actual use of the multi-functional bathing robot, the waterproof system design was carried out from the aspects of waterproof structure and material selection. Finally, the prototype of the multifunctional bathing robot was developed and tested to verify the reliability, safety and comfort.

References

1. Cheng, Z.Q., Ma, J.Q.: The evolution of China's population aging and its countermeasures. Acad. Exch. **12**, 101–109 (2018)
2. Liu, J.M.: Research on the Design of Lifting Bathing Aids. Tianjin University of Science and Technology, Tianjin (2015)
3. Li, L.F.: Design and Simulation Study of Personal Health Care Machine Bathing Mechanism. Henan University of Science and Technology, Henan (2014)
4. Xu, J.: Research on the Control System of Intelligent Aids Bathing Appliance for the Disabled. Huazhong University of Science and Technology, Wuhan (2013)
5. Yang, Z.X.: Design and Development of Bathing Aids for Disabled Elderly Families. Dalian Jiaotong University, Dalian (2017)
6. Bezerra, K., Machado, J.M., Silva, B., Carvalho, V., Soares, F., Matos, D.: Mechatronic system for assistance on bath of bedridden elderly people. In: 2015 IEEE 4th Portuguese Meeting on Bioengineering (ENBENG), Porto, pp. 1–4 (2015)
7. Chen, Z.S.: Construction of China's disabled aids service system. Chin. J. Rehabil. Theor. Exp. **17**(6), 83–85 (2017)
8. Yang, S., Chen, D., Que, J., Wang, M.: Design and analysis of a multifunctional electric bath chair. In: 2017 IEEE International Conference on Real-time Computing and Robotics (RCAR), Okinawa, pp. 223–228 (2017)
9. Li, H.Z.: Modeling and Simulation of Personal Health Care Robots. Henan University of Science and Technology, Henan (2014)
10. Luo, Y.M.: Suitable old appliances and modern nursing rehabilitation. Stand. Sci. **05**, 59–62 (2018)
11. Wang, J.P.: Research on the Design of Household Baths. Southwest Jiaotong University, Shanghai (2017)
12. Zheng, W.: Research on the Design of Bathing Aids Based on Extended Finite Element Method. Tianjin University of Science and Technology, Tianjin (2017)
13. Ji, L.: Design and Research of Multi-posture Elderly Chair. Zhejiang University of Technology, Hangzhou (2014)
14. Li, X.L.: Innovative Design of Aged Bath Products. Beijing Institute of Technology, Beijing (2015)
15. Lei, L., Guan, T.M., Xuan, L.: Design and simulation of horizontal bathing car based on ergonomics. J. Dalian Jiaotong Univ. **2**, 57–60 (2016). K. Elissa, Title of paper if known, unpublished

Dynamics Analysis of 3-CPaR&R₁R₂ Hybrid Mechanism with Joint Clearance

Junchen Liu[1,2], Minghao Zhai[1,2], Baoxing Wang[1,2], Miao Lin[1,2], Wei Li[3], and Yi Cao[1,2(✉)]

[1] School of Mechanical Engineering, Jiangnan University,
Wuxi 214122, Jiangsu, China
caoyi@jiangnan.edu.cn
[2] Jiangsu Key Laboratory of Advanced Food Manufacturing Equipment
and Technology, Wuxi 214122, Jiangsu, China
[3] Suzhou Vocational Institute of Industrial Technology, Suzhou 215000,
Jiangsu, China

Abstract. In order to study the effect of joint clearance on the dynamic characteristics and chaos phenomena of the hybrid mechanism, 3-CPaR&R₁R₂ hybrid mechanism is taken as an example. The clearance of revolute joint is taken into consideration and the normal and tangential contact force between the joint components are calculated based on the Flores contact model and the modified Coulomb friction model. Moreover, the dynamic model of the hybrid mechanism with joint clearance is established based on the Lagrange equation. Finally, the influence of different driving velocity and clearance value on dynamic characteristics and chaos phenomena is analyzed in detail through numerical examples. In addition, the relationship between the stability of the mechanism and the collision of joint components is investigated at the same time. The results show that, chaos phenomena can be alleviated and dynamic characteristics can be improved by increasing driving velocity and reducing the clearance value; Mechanism stability is related to the impact phenomenon between joint elements.

Keywords: Hybrid mechanism · Joint clearance · Dynamics · Chaos

1 Introduction

The hybrid mechanism has become a central issue of current institutional studies because it has the advantages both of serial mechanism and parallel mechanism, such as large working space, high rigidity and large carrying capacity [1–4]. So, the hybrid mechanism is widely used in many fields, such as industrial robots, additive manufacturing, and surgical robots [5, 6]. However, the joint clearance inevitably caused by dimensional tolerances, assembly errors, and material defects in the manufacturing process affect the dynamic behaviors and accuracy of the hybrid mechanism seriously [7].

Domestic and foreign scholars have conducted a lot of effort on the mechanism with joint clearance, including dynamic modeling [8], chaos identification and analysis [9], dynamic behaviors analysis [10], etc. Erkaya et al. [11, 12] used the way of

© Springer Nature Switzerland AG 2019
H. Yu et al. (Eds.): ICIRA 2019, LNAI 11744, pp. 660–672, 2019.
https://doi.org/10.1007/978-3-030-27541-9_54

numerical calculations and experimental analysis to compare the influence of joint clearance on the dynamics of mechanism under rigidity and partly compliant condition. Bai et al. [13, 14] used a hybrid contact model to study the contact force and wear of a planar four-bar mechanism containing a revolute joint with clearance, and used quantitative analysis to study its dynamic behaviors under different physical parameters. Xu et al. [15, 16] researched a planar multi-body systems which contain deep groove ball bearings and the dynamic behaviors of a 2-DoF mechanism both with joint clearance. Varedi [17] lightened the collision and improves the dynamics of the mechanism by optimizing of the mass distribution of the components. Flores et al. [18, 19] researched the dynamic performance of the crank-slider mechanism with clearance by numerical calculation and experimental analysis, and verified the correctness of the contact model. Zhao et al. [20] compared the influence of joint clearance on mechanism dynamics and wear under dry friction and lubrication conditions. Zhu, et al. [21] used the normal distribution model to analyze the influence of multiple cylindrical clearances on the dynamic behaviors of 3-CPaRR parallel mechanism based on the Flores contact model. Generally, it is clearly observed that current research on the dynamics of multi-body systems with joint clearance is mainly focused on parallel mechanisms and series mechanisms, while the research on the dynamics of hybrid mechanism with joint clearance is still in the exploration.

Chaos is one of the important features of nonlinear dynamic systems. Olyaei, et al. [22] successfully transformed the mechanism with joint clearance from chaotic to periodic motion by delayed feedback control strategy, which improved the dynamic behaviors of the system and enhanced the stability of the mechanism. Chen, et al. [23, 24] carried out an elastic dynamics modeling of a complex planar mechanism and a 4-UPS-UPU parallel mechanism both with joint clearance, and make a lot of efforts on the research of chaos phenomena and dynamic behaviors of the mechanism.

On the basis of previous studies, this paper takes the 3-CPaR&R_1R_2 hybrid mechanism with joint clearance as an example and establishes the kinematic model of the revolute joint clearance. The normal and tangential contact force between the joint components is calculated by the Flores contact model and the modified Coulomb friction model respectively. Finally, the dynamic model of the hybrid mechanism with joint clearance is established by the Lagrange equation method. The equation is numerically solved by the variable time-step fourth-order Runge-Kutta method. Besides, the chaos phenomenon in the dynamics of the 5-DoF hybrid mechanism is identified, and the effects of different physical parameters on the chaos, collision phenomenon and generalized driving force of the mechanism are analyzed in detail.

2   The Structure Description of 3-CPaR&R_1R_2 Hybrid Mechanism

3-CPaR&R_1R_2 hybrid mechanism is shown in Fig. 1, which consist of a parallel module and a series module. The parallel module is a 3-DoF decoupling parallel mechanism consisting of a moving platform and three identical CPaR (cylindrical joint C, parallelogram hinge Pa, revolute joint R) branches, which is connected by pins to provide the mechanism with freedom of movement in the X, Y, and Z directions.

The series module is composed of two revolute joint R_1 and R_2, which respectively rotate around the Y axis and the X axis and perpendicular to each other.

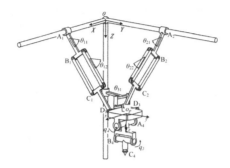

Fig. 1. The coordinate system of the hybrid mechanism

The global coordinate system O-XYZ and the local coordinate system op-xyz are respectively set at the fixed platform and the moving platform, the point op is located at the geometric center of the moving platform. The lengths of links A_iB_i, B_iC_i and C_iD_i are respectively defined as l_{i1}, l_{i2}, l_{i3} ($i = 1, 2, 3$), and the length, width and height of the moving platform are defined as l_x, l_y, l_z respectively. The series module is connected to the underneath of moving platform, and the lengths of the rod A_4B_4 and B_4C_4 are defined as l_{41} and l_{42} respectively. In the parallel module, q_1, q_2, q_3 represent the movement of cylindrical joint of each branch in the X, Y, Z direction. The passive angles formed by link A_1B_1, B_1C_1, A_2B_2, B_2C_2 and the plane XOY are denoted as θ_{11}, θ_{12}, θ_{21}, θ_{22} respectively and the passive angles formed by link A_3B_3, B_3C_3 and the plane YOZ are respectively denoted as θ_{31} and θ_{32}, the angles of the revolute joint rotating around the X axis and Y axis in the series module are q_4, q_5 respectively. Assume that there is a clearance at D_3 revolute joint.

Although the 3-CPaR&R_1R_2 hybrid mechanism contains a lot of cylindrical joint and revolute joints, only the D_3 rotating joint is considered in this paper, the specific reasons are as follows: ① The movement of each components of the A_3D_3 branch is less affected by gravity, which is favorable for the analysis of collision and chaos; ② Based on the structural characteristics of the hybrid mechanism, the revolute joint is more common and more general than the cylindrical joint in the mechanism; ③ Taking only one revolute clearance joint into consideration can simplify the kinematic model of the clearance joint and the dynamics model of the system.

3   Kinematics Analysis of 3-CPaR&R1R2 Hybrid Mechanism with Joint Clearance

It is worth noting that a revolute joint with planar clearance introduce two extra DoFs which are defined as x, y respectively, they represent the relative displacement between the center of shaft and bearing in the X and Y direction of global coordinate system.

Generalized coordinates of the hybrid mechanism are selected as follows: q_1, q_2, q_3, q_4, q_5, x, y.

Based on the above analysis, the constrains between the passive angles and the parameters of the ideal hybrid mechanism without clearance are as follows:

$$l_{11}c\theta_{11} + l_{12}c\theta_{12} + l_{13}c\theta_{11} + l_y/2 = l_{31}s\theta_{310} + l_{32}s\theta_{320} + l_{33}s\theta_{310}$$
$$l_{21}c\theta_{21} + l_{22}c\theta_{22} + l_{23}c\theta_{21} = l_{31}c\theta_{310} + l_{32}c\theta_{320} + l_{33}c\theta_{310} + l_x/2 \qquad (1)$$
$$l_{21}s\theta_{21} + l_{22}s\theta_{22} + l_{23}s\theta_{21} + l_z/2 = l_{11}s\theta_{11} + l_{12}s\theta_{12} + l_{13}s\theta_{11}$$

Where θ_{310} and θ_{320} are the passive angles formed by the A_3B_3, B_3C_3 and the plane YOZ in the hybrid mechanism without joint clearance, $c\theta_{11} = \cos\theta_{11}$, $s\theta_{11} = \sin\theta_{11}$.

For the hybrid mechanism with joint clearance at the revolute joint D_3, the closed-chain equation is as follows:

$$l_{11}c\theta_{11} + l_{12}c\theta_{12} + l_{13}c\theta_{11} + l_y/2 = l_{31}s\theta_{31} + l_{32}s\theta_{32} + l_{33}s\theta_{31} + y$$
$$l_{21}c\theta_{21} + l_{22}c\theta_{22} + l_{23}c\theta_{21} = l_{31}c\theta_{31} + l_{32}c\theta_{32} + l_{33}c\theta_{31} + l_x/2 + x \qquad (2)$$
$$l_{21}s\theta_{21} + l_{22}s\theta_{22} + l_{23}s\theta_{23} + l_z/2 = l_{11}s\theta_{11} + l_{12}s\theta_{12} + l_{13}s\theta_{11}$$

Let the passive angles of the branches in the hybrid mechanism with clearance are composed of the disturbing angles caused by the clearance and passive angles of the ideal hybrid mechanism without clearance:

$$\begin{cases} \theta_{31} = \theta_{310} + \Delta\theta_{31} \\ \theta_{32} = \theta_{320} + \Delta\theta_{32} \end{cases} \qquad (3)$$

Substitution of Eq. (3) in Eq. (2) and simultaneous Eq. (1) yields:

$$\begin{cases} \Delta\theta_{31} = a_1 x + b_1 y \\ \Delta\theta_{32} = a_2 x + b_2 y \end{cases} \qquad (4)$$

$$\text{where} \quad \begin{cases} a_1 = -\cos\theta_{320}/(l_{31} + l_{33})\sin(\theta_{310} - \theta_{320}) \\ a_2 = -\cos\theta_{310}/l_{32}\sin(\theta_{310} - \theta_{320}) \\ b_1 = \sin\theta_{320}/(l_{31} + l_{33})\sin(\theta_{310} - \theta_{320}) \\ b_2 = \sin\theta_{310}/l_{32}\sin(\theta_{310} - \theta_{320}) \end{cases} \qquad (5)$$

4 Contact Force Analysis of Revolute Joint with Clearance

The revolute joint with clearance is shown in Fig. 2, where O_i and O_j are the center points of the bearing and the shaft respectively, and r_i^o and r_j^o are the position vectors of them in the global coordinate system, thus the eccentricity vector between the joint components is:

$$e = r_j^O - r_i^O \tag{6}$$

Therefore, the value of eccentricity between the bearing and the shaft is $e = \sqrt{e^T e}$.

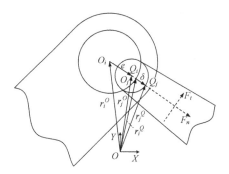

Fig. 2. The model of revolute joint with clearance

The unit vector n normal to the surface of the collision point can be derived based on Eq. (6):

$$n = e/e \tag{7}$$

Therefore, the penetration depth between the joint components when the shaft collides with the bearing is calculated as:

$$\delta = e - c \tag{8}$$

Where: $c = R_i - R_j$, R_i and R_j are the radius of the bearing and the shaft respectively.

Let points Q_i and Q_j represent the contact points of the bearing and the shaft respectively. The corresponding position vectors r_i^Q and r_j^Q of them in the global coordinate system can be expressed as:

$$r_k^Q = r_k^O + R_k n (k = i, j) \tag{9}$$

Equation (9) is differentiated with respect to time t, and the velocity vector of the contact point is obtained as:

$$\dot{r}_k^Q = \dot{r}_k^O + R_k \dot{n} (k = i, j) \tag{10}$$

According to the position and velocity vector of the contact point in the global coordinate system, the relative v between the components of the revolute joint with clearance can be obtained as follows:

$$\begin{cases} v_n = \left[\left(\dot{r}_i^Q - \dot{r}_j^Q\right)^T n\right] n \\ v_t = \left(\dot{r}_i^Q - \dot{r}_j^Q\right) - v_n \end{cases} \tag{11}$$

The revolute clearance joint will inevitably generate contact force, which affect the stability of the mechanism. Therefore, it is necessary to choose appropriate contact model to analyze the contact force caused by the clearance. At present, the Flores contact model is widely used in the dynamic contact force analysis, the structure of Flores contact model is relatively simple and its numerical solution is relatively stable [26]. In addition, the Flores contact force model is not restricted to the choice of the recovery coefficient. Based on the above research, the Flores contact model is used to calculate the normal contact force in this paper [25]:

$$F_n = K\delta^n \left[1 + \frac{8(1 - c_r)}{5c_r} \frac{\dot{\delta}}{\dot{\delta}^{(-)}}\right] \tag{12}$$

Where, δ, $\dot{\delta}$, $\dot{\delta}^{(-)}$ represent contact deformation quantity, relative contact velocity and initial contact speed, C_r is recovery coefficient, n is a non-linear index and set to 1.5 for the metal surface. K is the generalized contact stiffness coefficient which is expressed as follows:

$$K = \frac{4}{3\pi(\sigma_i + \sigma_j)} \left(\frac{R_i R_j}{R_i - R_j}\right)^{\frac{1}{2}} \tag{13}$$

$$\sigma_{(k=i,j)} = \frac{1 - v_k^2}{\pi E_k} \tag{14}$$

Where v_k, E_k, and R_k are the Poisson ratio, the elastic modulus, and the radius of the joint components; the subscripts i and j represent the bearing and the shaft respectively.

The tangential contact force used in the calculation is based on the modified Coulomb friction model, which is expressed as follows:

$$F_t = \begin{cases} 0 & v_t < v_0 \\ -\mu_d \frac{v_t - v_0}{v_1 - v_0} F_n \mathbf{v_t} & v_0 \leq v_t \leq v_1 \\ -\mu_d F_n \mathbf{v_t} & v_t > v_1 \end{cases} \tag{15}$$

In which u_d is a friction coefficient, v_t is a tangential velocity. v_0 and v_1 are the given tolerances for velocity.

Based on Eqs. (12) and (15), the contact force of the shaft to the bearing can be expressed as:

$$F = F_n n + F_t t = \left(f_x f_y \right)^T \tag{16}$$

Where the tangential vector t is obtained by rotating the normal vector n anti-clockwise by 90°, and f_x and f_y are the contact force between the shaft and the bearing in the X direction and the Y direction respectively in the global coordinate system. The contact force F is located at the revolute joint, in order to establish a dynamic model of the hybrid mechanism with joint clearance, the contact force between the components of revolute clearance joint is converted to corresponding generalized contact force Q_i by the transformation matrix R which based on the kinematic constraint characteristics of the hybrid mechanism:

$$Q_i = RF = \left(f_{q_1} \ f_{q_2} \ f_{q_3} \ f_{q_4} \ f_{q_5} \right) \tag{17}$$

5 Dynamic Model of 3-CPaR&R1R2 Hybrid Mechanism with Joint Clearance

In order to study the influence of joint clearance on the dynamic characteristics and chaos phenomena of the hybrid mechanism, this paper established the dynamics model of the hybrid mechanism with clearance based on the Lagrange's equation. The centroid coordinates of link l_{ij} (i, j = 1, 2, 3) and l_{41}, l_{42} in the hybrid mechanism with clearance are denoted as (x_{ijc}, y_{ijc}, z_{ijc}) respectively in the global coordinate system and the velocities of them are respectively denoted as $v_{ji} = \left(\dot{x}_{jic} \ \dot{y}_{jic} \ \dot{z}_{jic} \right)^T$. The symbols of inertia around the center of mass is denoted as J_{ij} respectively. The mass of the moving platform is m_0, and its velocity relative to the global coordinate system is defined as $v_0 = \left(\dot{q}_1 \ \dot{q}_2 \ \dot{q}_3 \right)^T$, The angular velocities of the series module rotating around the X axis and the Y axis are $\dot{q}_4$ and $\dot{q}_5$ respectively. Defining the planar XOY as the gravity zero potential energy planar and g as gravity acceleration, the kinetic energy T and potential energy V of the mechanical system are expressed respectively as follows:

$$T = \frac{1}{2} \sum_{i=1}^{3} \sum_{j=1}^{3} [m_{ij}(\dot{x}_{ijc}^2 + \dot{y}_{ijc}^2 + \dot{z}_{ijc}^2)] + \frac{1}{2} \sum_{i=1}^{2} [m_{4j}(\dot{x}_{4jc}^2 + \dot{y}_{4jc}^2 + \dot{z}_{4jc}^2)]$$
$$+ \frac{1}{2} m_0 v_p^T v_p + \frac{1}{2} \sum_{i=1}^{3} \sum_{j=1}^{3} J_{ij} \dot{\theta}_{ij}^2 + \frac{1}{2} \left[J_{41} \dot{\phi}_X^2 + J_{42} \dot{\phi}_Y^2 \right] \tag{18}$$

$$V = \sum_{i=1}^{4} \sum_{j=1}^{3} m_{ij} g Z_{ijc} + m_p g Z_p \tag{19}$$

Substituting the centroid coordinates and velocity of each link into Eq. (18), so:

$$T = \frac{1}{2}(\hat{H}_{11}\dot{q}_1^2 + \hat{H}_{22}\dot{q}_2^2 + \hat{H}_{33}\dot{q}_3^2) + \hat{H}_{12}\dot{q}_1\dot{q}_2 + \hat{H}_{13}\dot{q}_1\dot{q}_3 + \hat{H}_{23}\dot{q}_2\dot{q}_3 + \hat{G}_1\dot{q}_4^2 \qquad (20)$$
$$+ \hat{G}_2\dot{q}_5^2 + \hat{G}_3\dot{q}_1\dot{q}_5 + \hat{G}_4\dot{q}_2\dot{q}_4 + \hat{G}_5\dot{q}_2\dot{q}_5 + \hat{G}_6\dot{q}_3\dot{q}_4 + \hat{G}_7\dot{q}_3\dot{q}_5$$

It is worth noting that the parameter $\hat{H}_{11}$, $\hat{H}_{22}$, $\hat{H}_{33}$, $\hat{H}_{12}$, $\hat{H}_{13}$, $\hat{H}_{23}$, $\hat{G}_1$, $\hat{G}_2$, $\hat{G}_3$, $\hat{G}_4$, $\hat{G}_5$, $\hat{G}_6$, $\hat{G}_7$ are the equivalent mass function of the hybrid mechanism with clearance.

Substituting Eqs. (19) and (20) into Lagrange's equation of non-holonomic systems:

$$\frac{d}{dt}\left(\frac{\partial T}{\partial \dot{q}_i}\right) - \frac{\partial T}{\partial q_i} + \frac{\partial V}{\partial q_i} = F_i + Q_i \ (i = 1, 2\ldots5, x, y) \qquad (21)$$

In Eq. (21), Q_i is the generalized restraining reaction force provided by non-holonomic constraints

6   Numerical Analysis

In order to study the effects of joint clearance on the dynamic characteristics and chaos phenomena of the hybrid mechanism through numerical example. Table 1 shows the structural parameters of the 3-CPaR&R_1R_2 hybrid mechanism ($i = 1, 2, 3$), Table 2 shows the dynamic simulation parameters of the hybrid mechanism with clearance.

Table 1. Structural parameters of hybrid mechanism

Parameter	Value	Parameter	Value
Link l_{i1}/mm	150	m_{41}/K$_g$	1.913
Link l_{i2}/mm	230	m_{42}/K$_g$	1.022
Link l_{i3}/mm	140	m_0/K$_g$	6.701
Link l_{41}/mm	190	J_{i1}/K$_g$·m^2	0.00282
Link l_{42}/mm	105	J_{i2}/K$_g$·m^2	0.00568
m_{i1}/K$_g$	0.607	J_{i3}/K$_g$·m^2	0.00125
m_{i2}/K$_g$	1.372	J_{41}/K$_g$·m^2	0.00354
m_{i3}/K$_g$	0.406	J_{42}/K$_g$·m^2	0.00056

Table 2. Dynamics simulation parameters of hybrid mechanism with joint clearance

Parameter	Value	Parameter	Value
Radius R_j/mm	10	Young modulus E_i, E_j/Gpa	200
Clearance c/mm	0.05, 0.25	Recovery coefficient C_r	0.8
Integral step size	0.0001	Friction coefficient u_d	0.01
Integral step deviation	0.00001	Poisson ratio v_i, v_j	0.3

Set the system movement rule with time as follows: $q_1 = 0.354\text{-}0.001\sin wt$, $q_2 = 0.409\text{-}0.005\cos wt$, $q_3 = 0.415\text{-}0.005\cos wt$, $q_4 = 0.1\sin wt$, $q_5 = 0.2\sin wt$.

Driving velocity and clearance value are important factors affecting the dynamic behaviors of the mechanism and chaotic phenomena [24]. In this paper, Numerical simulation is carried out under three driving velocities ($w = 8\pi$, 16π, 32π) and two clearance values ($c = 0.05$ mm, 0.25 mm) to compare and analyze the effects of different driving velocities and clearance values on the dynamic characteristics of the hybrid mechanism.

Firstly, based on the parameters listed in Tables 1 and 2, Eq. (21) is calculated under the clearance value $c = 0.25$ mm and the driving velocity $w = 8\pi, 16\pi$, 32π by variable time-step fourth-order Runge-Kutta method. Figure 3 shows the Contact force variation law of hybrid mechanism under different driving velocities. Figure 4 shows the trajectory of the center of the shaft with clearance relative to bearing, and Fig. 5 shows the generalized driving force of the mechanism at different driving velocities. To simplify calculation, only the generalized driving force at the cylindrical joint A_1 is calculated. Figure 6 shows the Poincare map of the hybrid mechanism and the discrete points of the Poincare map can describe the motion characteristics of the system. The discrete points with regional distribution and hierarchical structure indicate that the system is in chaotic motion state, and a few discrete points and closed curves indicate the system in periodic motion and quasi-periodic motion respectively.

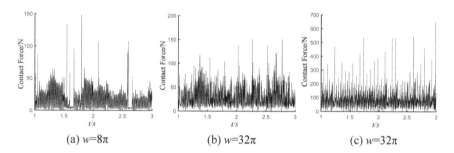

Fig. 3. Contact forces of 3-CPaR&R_1R_2 hybrid mechanism with different driving velocities

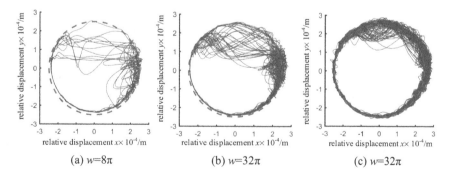

Fig. 4. Shaft center trajectory of the clearance joint with different driving velocities

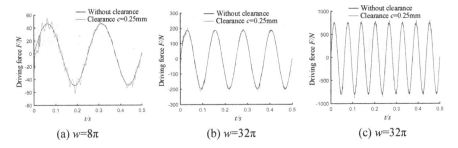

Fig. 5. The driving forces of 3-CPaR&R_1R_2 hybrid mechanism with different driving velocities

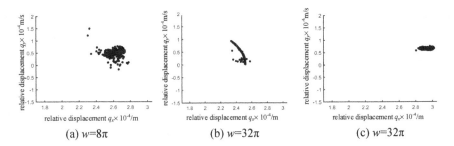

Fig. 6. Poincare mapping of 3-CPaR&R_1R_2 hybrid mechanism with different driving velocities

It can be seen from Figs. 3 and 4 that with the increase of driving velocity, the contact force and its peak value increase, which indicates that the increase of the driving velocity make the collision and the penetration depth between the shaft and the increase, It can be seen from the Fig. 6 that the mapping points are distributed regionally and there is no correlation between adjacent mapping points, so it can be judged that the hybrid mechanism is in a chaotic motion at this time. However, as the driving velocity increases, the distribution range of the Poincare mapping point decreases and shrinks towards the point-like shape, indicating that the chaos phenomenon in the system is alleviated. The driving force in Fig. 5 also shows this characteristic. When the driving velocity increases, the generalized driving force curve becomes smooth and stable. Further analysis of the shaft center trajectory of Fig. 4 shows that when the system driving velocity is gradually increased, the penetration depth between the joint components and the contact force increases, but the proportion of continuous contact phase between shaft and bearing increases and separation between them is reduced in the operating cycle, so that the impact phenomenon in the mechanism is alleviated, and the stability of the system is improved. This is consistent with the characteristics of Figs. 3, 5, and 6, which indicates that increasing the driving velocity is beneficial to improve the dynamic characteristics of the mechanism for a given clearance value, and also indicates that the stability of the system depends on the specific collision form between the clearance joint components. Besides, the alleviation of the impact between the joint components are essential to improve the stability of the mechanism with clearance.

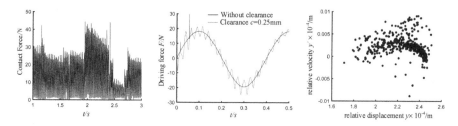

Fig. 7. The dynamic characteristics of 3-CPaR&R$_1$R$_2$ hybrid Mechanism when $c = 0.25$ mm

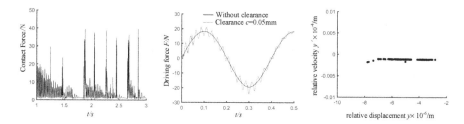

Fig. 8. The dynamic characteristics of 3-CPaR&R$_1$R$_2$ hybrid Mechanism when $c = 0.05$ mm

Secondly, let the driving velocity be $w = 5\pi$ and take clearance value of $c = 0.25$ mm and 0.05 mm into calculation in turn referring to the above simulation method, the corresponding contact force, driving force and Poincare map are respectively shown in Figs. 7 and 8

It can be clearly observed by analyzing Figs. 7 and 8 that, the peak value of the contact force and the fluctuates amplitude of the generalized driving force decreases when the clearance value is reduced, the mapping point of the Poincare shrinks from the regional distribution to the liner distribution. Besides, the chaos phenomenon of the hybrid mechanism is significantly alleviated, indicating that a larger clearance value is unfavorable to the dynamic characteristics of the mechanism.

7 Conclusion and Future Works

Based on the Flores contact model and the modified Coulomb friction model, a 3-CPaR&R$_1$R$_2$ hybrid mechanism dynamic with clearance was established by the Lagrange equation method. The variable time-step fourth-order Runge-Kutta is used in the calculation and the chaos phenomenon in the 3-CPaR&R$_1$R$_2$ hybrid mechanism with clearance is confirmed. Through the analysis of the dynamic behaviors of the 3-CPaR&R$_1$R$_2$ hybrid mechanism under three different driving velocities and two clearance values, the faster driving velocity and the smaller clearance value are beneficial to the stability of the mechanism and the alleviation of the chaos phenomenon of the hybrid mechanism with joint clearance. It is worth noting that, only the influence of the single revolute joint with clearance on the dynamic performance of the hybrid mechanism has been studied in this work, the influence of more clearance joint and the impact of clearance considering lubrication remains to be further studied.

Acknowledgements. This work reported here was supported by the National Natural Science Foundation of China (Grant No. 51375209), 111 Project (Grant No. B18027), the Six Talent Peaks Project in Jiangsu Province (Grant No. ZBZZ-012), and the Research and the Innovation Project for College Graduates of Jiangsu Province (Grant No. SJCX18-0630, KYCX18-1846).

References

1. Ottaviano, E., Rea, P., Castelli, G.: THROO: a tracked hybrid rover to overpass obstacles. Adv. Robot. **28**(10), 683–694 (2014)
2. Zhou, H., Qin, Y., Chen, H.: Structural synthesis of five-degree-of-freedom hybrid kinematics mechanism. J. Eng. Des. **27**(4–6), 390–412 (2016)
3. Cao, Y., Zhou, H., Qin, Y.L.: Type synthesis and type analysis of 3T2R hybrid mechanisms via G_F set. Int. J. Robot. Autom. **32**(4), 342–350 (2017)
4. Shi, X.H., Ren, L.X., Liao, Z.Y.: Design & analysis of the mechanical system for a spacial 4-DoF series-parallel hybrid lower limb rehabilitation robot. J. Mech. Eng. **53**(13), 48–54 (2017)
5. Cao, Y., Zhou, R., Qin, Y.L.: Structural synthesis of fully-isotropic five degree-of-freedom hybrid kinematic mechanisms. J. Mech. Eng. **54**(05), 29–37 (2018)
6. Gherman, B., Pisla, D., Vaida, C.: Development of inverse dynamic model for a surgical hybrid parallel robot with equivalent lumped masses. Robot. Comput.-Integr. Manuf. **28**(3), 402–415 (2012)
7. Chebbi, A.H., Affi, Z., Romdhane, L.: Prediction of the pose errors produced by joints clearance for a 3-UPU parallel robot. Mech. Mach. Theor. **44**(9), 1768–1783 (2009)
8. Zhao, G.L., Jiang, Y., Hao, J.G.: Computional method of rigid multibody system dynamics considering cylinder joint clearance. J. Vib. Shock **32**(17), 171–176 (2013)
9. Hou, Y.L., Wang, Y., Jin, G.N.: Chaos and impact phenomena of a RU-RPR decoupled parallel mechanism containing clearance. J. Vib. Shock **36**(01), 215–239 (2017)
10. Muvengei, O., Kihiu, J., Ikua, B.: Dynamic analysis of planar rigid-body mechanical systems with two-clearance revolute joints. Nonlinear Dyn. **73**, 259–273 (2013)
11. Erkaya, S., Doğan, S., Ulus, S.: Effects of joint clearance on the dynamics of a partly compliant mechanism: numerical and experimental studies. Mech. Mach. Theor. **88**, 125–140 (2015)
12. Erkaya, S., Doğan, S.: A comparative analysis of joint clearance effects on articulated and partly compliant mechanisms. Nonlinear Dyn. **81**(1–2), 323–341 (2015)
13. Bai, Z.F., Zhao, Y., Chen, J.: Dynamics analysis of planar mechanical system considering revolute clearance joint wear. Tribol. Int. **64**, 85–95 (2013)
14. Bai, Z.F., Zhao, Y.: Dynamics modeling and quantitative analysis of multibody systems including revolute clearance joint. Precis. Eng. **36**(4), 554–567 (2012)
15. Xu, L.X., Yang, Y.H., Li, Y.G.: Modeling and analysis of planar multibody systems containing deep groove ball bearing with clearance. Mech. Mach. Theor. **56**, 69–88 (2012)
16. Xu, L.X., Li, Y.G.: Investigation of joint clearance effects on the dynamic performance of a planar 2-DoF pick-and-place parallel manipulator. Robot. Comput.-Integr. Manuf. **30**(1), 62–73 (2014)
17. Varedi, S., Daniali, H., Dardel, M.: Optimal dynamic design of a planar slider-crank mechanism with a joint clearance. Mech. Mach. Theor. **86**, 191–200 (2015)

18. Flores, P., Koshy, C., Lankarani, H.: Numerical and experimental investigation on multibody systems with revolute clearance joints. Nonlinear Dyn. **65**(4), 383–398 (2011)
19. Flores, P.: A parametric study on the dynamic response of planar multibody systems with multiple clearance joints. Nonlinear Dyn. **61**(4), 633–653 (2010)
20. Zhao, B., Zhou, K., Xie, Y.B.: A new numerical method for planar multibody system with mixed lubricated revolute joint. Int. J. Mech. Sci. **113**, 105–119 (2016)
21. Zhu, J.Y., Wang, J., Ding, Z.: Kinematics and dynamics analysis of 3-CPaRR parallel mechanism with joint clearance. J. Vib. Shock **37**(18), 9–17 (2018)
22. Olyaei, A.A., Ghazavi, M.R.: Stabilizing slider-crank mechanism with clearance joints. Mech. Mach. Theor. **53**, 17–29 (2012)
23. Chen, X.L., Jiang, S., Deng, Y.: Dynamics analysis of 2-DoF complex planar mechanical system with joint clearance and flexible links. Nonlinear Dyn. **93**(1), 1–26 (2018)
24. Chen, X.L., Wu, L., Deng, Y.: Dynamic response analysis and chaos identification of 4-UPS-UPU flexible spatial parallel mechanism. Nonlinear Dyn. **87**(4), 2311–2324 (2017)
25. Flores, P., Machado, M., Silva, M.T.: On the continuous contact force models for soft materials in multibody dynamics. Multibody Syst. Dyn. **25**(3), 357–375 (2011)

Underactuated Robot Passability Analysis and Optimization

Lingyu Sun, Xiaoya Liu[(⊠)], and Zhilong Li

College of Mechanical Engineering, Hebei University of Technology,
No. 1 Dingzigu Road, Hongqiao District, Tianjin 300000, China
18202669185@163.com

Abstract. In order to improve the performance of robots in complex terrain, a crawler underactuated robot is proposed, which is mainly composed of car body module and track module. The link mechanism of the track module has a degree of freedom and is an underactuated mechanism. This paper introduces the obstacle course of the crawler module across the steps, establishes a mathematical model, analyzes its passability, optimizes the rod length parameters of the linkage mechanism, and performs simulation motion analysis on the optimized linkage mechanism. Experiments on the passability of the prototype verified the rationality of the design and structural parameters of the robot.

Keywords: Passability · Track module · Linkage mechanism · Optimization

1 Introduction

In unstructured terrain such as dangerous disasters and earthquakes, mobile robots are required to have good passability and terrain adaptability and operability [1]. Research on underactuated robots, including wheeled robots: Micro5 robots [2], guide-bar linkage walking obstacle-obstacle robots [3], triangular linkage detonation robots [4], etc.; can be divided into three types of crawler robots: Single track double track, double track double track and multi-section double track. The single-section double track includes crawler robot [5], Packbot robot [6] and VSTR robot [7, 8]; double-section double track including China Mining University's passive swing arm crawler robot [9] and Korea Science and Technology Research Institute development track Passive adaptive robot [10], double-section double track including North China Institute of Science and Technology design flexible crawler mobile robot [11]; and Chinese Academy of Sciences designed wheel composite robot [12], forward and reverse quadrilateral suspension mechanism lunar rover [13], etc.

In this paper, a crawler underactuated robot is proposed. In order to improve the passability of the robot, it can be better adapted to the complex terrain environment, analyze the structural design and passability of the robot, and optimize and simulate it. Verification and experimentation on prototype passability verified the rationality of robot's pass performance and structural parameter design.

Hebei Province Applied Basic Research Program Key Basic Research Project (NO. 17961820D)

H. Yu et al. (Eds.): ICIRA 2019, LNAI 11744, pp. 673–683, 2019.
https://doi.org/10.1007/978-3-030-27541-9_55

2 Robot Structure Analysis

The crawler underactuated crawler module structure is mainly composed of three parts: a link mechanism, a crawler belt and a pulley. The linkage mechanism adopts a six-bar linkage design. According to the stability characteristics of the triangle, since a regular quadrilateral mechanism is a parallel mechanism, it is easy to deform and the direction and size of the deformation are easy to grasp, but it has an unstable performance [14] for the obstacle-obscuring performance, and it is evolved into a five-bar linkage mechanism. It has the characteristics of large deformation and instability. It adopts two quadrilateral splicing linkage mechanism, which evolves into a six-bar linkage mechanism. The mechanism is easy to deform, and the two quadrilaterals are mutually constrained, which overcomes the instability during the obstacle crossing process. The six-bar linkage mechanism facilitates deformation and obstacles.

As shown in Fig. 1, $A_6A_3A_4$ is a fixed frame, A_1A_2, A_2A_3, A_4A_5, A_1A_5 and A_1A_6 links are a front link, a lower link, a rear link, an upper link, and an auxiliary link, respectively, and the links are connected by a rotating pair. Together, the other pulleys rotate around the wheel center. The degree of freedom of the structure is:

$$F = 3 * n - 2 * p_1 = 3 * 5 - 2 * 7 = 1 \tag{1}$$

The deformation of the mechanism is that there is no original member, and the number of the original moving parts of the mechanism is less than the degree of freedom, so it is an underactuated mechanism. According to the law of minimum resistance, it can be concluded that the link mechanism moves in the direction with the least resistance.

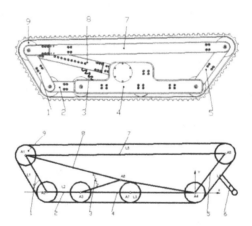

1- front link; 2-low link; 3-spring; 4-fixing frame; 5--back link; 6-tail wheel; 7-up link; 8-auxiliary link;9--pulleys

Fig. 1. Structure diagram of the linkage mechanism

3   The Theoretical Analysis of the Passability of Robots

3.1   Passivity Analysis of Robots

The passability of a robot refers to the ability of the robot to pass certain road conditions [15]. Specifically, in a complex terrain environment (steps, climbs, gullies, etc.), the center of mass of the robot can cross the critical boundary line of the obstacle so that it does not rollover and recline, without obstacles being blocked, and has good passability. This paper mainly analyzes the topographical features of the steps, and uses the structural schematic diagram of the mechanism to pass the performance analysis during the obstacle crossing process.

Tracked underactuated robots perform tasks in an unstructured environment. The unstructured environment is diverse, including rugged, rugged, stepped, and graded 3D terrain environments, and therefore has a high level of robotic throughput. The underactuated mechanism can adapt to the terrain. When an obstacle is encountered, the deformation occurs under the action of an external force, so that the coordinate position of the center of mass of the robot changes, and the obstacle can be successfully climbed over the boundary line of the obstacle.

3.2   Passage Through the Steps

When the crawler underactuated robot crosses the step, the angle between the track and the ground is called the elevation angle, and the elevation angle will gradually increase. Under the premise that the flipping does not occur, the center of mass of the robot crosses the boundary line of the obstacle. Achieving a successful obstacle [16]. The whole process is divided into five phases:

a. The pulley of the front connecting rod of the crawler module comes into contact with the edge of the step. Under the action of the driving force, the robot moves slowly and uniformly, so that the front connecting rod and the lower connecting rod are deformed by force, and the robot moves up slowly, the crawler belt contact with the boundary line of the step.

b. Under the action of the obstacle, the link mechanism is deformed by force, and the centroid of the front quadrilateral $A_1A_2A_3A_6$ is $G_1(k_1 \quad h_1)$ As shown in Fig. 2, just as the center of mass G_1 reaches the horizontal line with the step, it has a certain critical condition of obstacle-obstacle ability. The elevation angle of the robot is θ, the height of the step is H, and the radius of the pulley is R. According to the coordinate transformation method:

$$^A P = {}^A_B R\, {}^B P + {}^A_B O \qquad (2)$$

The functions that can be built are:

$$H(k_1, h_1, \theta) = R + k_1\sin\theta + h_1\cos\theta \qquad (3)$$

In the case of ensuring that the robot comes into contact with the steps, θ The range of values is $(0 \quad 0.5\pi)$, the coordinates of the front quadrilateral G_1 are variables, functions $H(k_1, h_1, \theta)$ The derivation of k_1 and h_1 can be concluded as follows:

$$\frac{\partial H}{\partial k_1} = \sin\theta \succ 0 \tag{4}$$

$$\frac{\partial H}{\partial h_1} = \cos\theta \succ 0 \tag{5}$$

Equations (4) and (5) result in that the centroid G_1 is biased forward and upward, which is beneficial to improve the passability and height of the robot.

$H(k_1, h_1, \theta)$ Find the first and second partial derivatives for θ:

$$\frac{\partial H}{\partial \theta} = k_1 \cos\theta + h_1 \sin\theta$$
$$\frac{\partial^2 H}{\partial \theta^2} = -k_1 \sin\theta + h_1 \cos\theta \tag{6}$$

θ in $\left(0, \frac{\pi}{3}\right)$ Value van $\frac{\partial H}{\partial \theta} > 0$, $H(k_1, h_1, \theta)$ About the function of θ, when $\theta = \frac{\pi}{3}$ When, is:

$$H_{\max} = R + \frac{\sqrt{3}}{2}k_1 + \frac{1}{2}h_1 \tag{7}$$

When the step is higher than $H_{\max}$ The robot cannot cross the steps.

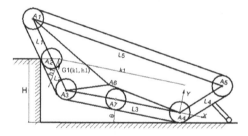

Fig. 2. Schematic diagram of the second stage of robot obstacle crossing

c. Under the action of the driving force, the track module moves slowly upwards, the elevation angle θ It is also constantly growing. As shown in Fig. 3, the link structure is almost restored to its original state. The tail wheel has a supporting effect, which is more conducive to stable obstacles and prevents the robot from rolling over.

d. When the gravity line of the robot just passes directly above the boundary line of the step, the boundary condition of the obstacle is reached. As shown in Fig. 4, the elevation angle is known as θ. The height of the step is H, the radius of the pulley

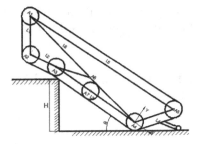

Fig. 3. Schematic diagram of the third stage of robot obstacle crossing

is R, and the maximum height of the support of the tail wheel is a. The function that can be obtained is:

$$H(k, h, \theta) = R + a + (k - h \tan \theta) \sin \theta - \frac{R}{\cos \theta} \tag{8}$$

The lower center of gravity of the robot is more conducive to obstacles. $H(k, h, \theta)$ make a first and second derivative for θ:

$$\frac{\partial H}{\partial \theta} = k \cos \theta - h \sin \theta - \frac{(h + R) \sin \theta}{\cos^2 \theta}$$
$$\frac{\partial^2 H}{\partial \theta^2} = -k \sin \theta - h \cos \theta - (h + R) \frac{\sin^2 \theta + \cos \theta}{\cos^3 \theta} \tag{9}$$

Take $\theta \in (0, 2\pi)$, $\frac{\partial^2 H}{\partial \theta^2} < 0$, H has a maximum value. When $\theta_{max} = \arcsin \frac{h}{\sqrt{k^2 + h^2}} \in (0, \frac{\pi}{2})$, H is max H'_{max}. So the conclusion that can be drawn is:

(1) When the height of the step is less than H'_{max}, and the robot can smoothly cross the obstacle, it will not flip.
(2) When the height of the step is greater than H'_{max}. At the time, the robot will roll over or flip and cannot cross the obstacle.

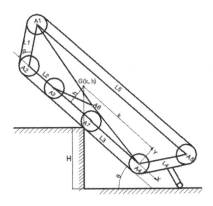

Fig. 4. Schematic diagram of the fourth stage of robot obstacle crossing

e. Under the action of gravity and driving force, the robot's center of mass is continuously lowered and successfully passed through the steps.

4 Structural Parameters Optimization and Simulation of Robot Track Module

The structural parameters of the under-actuated crawler module mainly include: the length and position of each link of the track support part; the diameter of the drive wheel and the driven wheel and the position of the wheel center; the installation position of the return spring, the stiffness coefficient and the amount of tensile change; The deformation of the rod during the obstacle crossing and the height of the obstacle. For the optimization of the structural parameters of the track module, it is beneficial to improve the performance and stability of the robot during the obstacle crossing process.

4.1 Optimization of Structural Parameters of the Track Module

As shown in Fig. 5, the wheel center A_4 is established as a coordinate origin, the X axis coincides with the A_3A_4 frame, and the Y axis is perpendicular to A_3A_4. The angle between A_1A_2 and the X axis is α, the angle between A_2A_3 and the X axis is β, and the angle between A_1A_5 and the X axis is γ. The angle between A_4A_5 and the X-axis is δ, and the lengths of the respective rods are respectively expressed as: $\left| A_1A_2 \right| = L_1$, $\left| A_2A_3 \right| = L_2$, $\left| A_3 \ A_4 \right| = L_3$, $\left| A_4 \ A_5 \right| = L_4$, $\left| A_5 \ A_6 \right| = L_5$ and $\left| A_1 \ A_6 \right| = L_6$.

Parameter design requirements for rod length optimization:

a. The track module is within a certain range, and the total length of the rod is small, which reduces the overall quality of the robot.
b. The link mechanism prevents the track from being derailed during the deformation process.
c. The deformation mechanism of the track module can achieve better obstacle performance under a certain range of sizes.

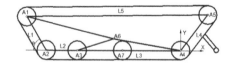

Fig. 5. Schematic diagram of the linkage mechanism

The coordinates of the wheel centers A_1, A_2, A_3, A_4, and A_5 are expressed as:

$$P_{A1} = \begin{pmatrix} L_3 + L_2\cos\beta + L_1\cos\alpha \\ L_2\sin\beta + L_1\sin\alpha \end{pmatrix}$$
$$= \begin{pmatrix} L_4\cos\gamma + L_5\cos\delta \\ L_4\sin\gamma + L_5\sin\delta \end{pmatrix} \tag{10}$$

$$P_{A2} = \begin{pmatrix} L_3 + L_2\cos\beta \\ L_2\sin\beta \end{pmatrix} \tag{11}$$

$$P_{A3} = \begin{pmatrix} L_3 \\ 0 \end{pmatrix} \tag{12}$$

$$P_{A4} = \begin{pmatrix} 0 \\ 0 \end{pmatrix} \tag{13}$$

$$P_{A5} = \begin{pmatrix} L_4\cos\gamma \\ L_4\sin\gamma \end{pmatrix} \tag{14}$$

According to the design requirement a of the parameter, the rod length relationship between the links is established, and the distances of A_1A_4 and A_1A_3 are expressed as:

$$
\begin{aligned}
L_{A1A4} &= \sqrt{(P_{A1} - P_{A4})^2} = L_1^2 + L_2^2 + L_3^2 \\
&\quad + 2L_1L_2\cos(\alpha - \beta) + 2L_1L_3\cos\alpha + 2L_2L_3\cos\beta \\
&= L_4^2 + L_5^2 + 2L_4L_5\cos(\gamma - \delta)
\end{aligned} \tag{15}
$$

$$L_{A1A3} = \sqrt{(P_{A3} - P_{A1})^2} = L_1^2 + L_2^2 + 2L_1L_2\cos(\alpha - \beta) \tag{16}$$

In order to achieve the obstacle performance of the robot, the height variation of the wheel center A_1 is optimized and used as an objective function. The design variables are:

$$X = \begin{bmatrix} L_1 & L_2 & L_4 & L_5 & \alpha & \gamma \end{bmatrix} \tag{17}$$

The objective function is the difference between the maximum deformation and the undeformed height of the linkage:

$$\Delta h(X) = \max_\beta(h(\beta\backslash X)) - \min_\beta(h(\beta\backslash X)) \tag{18}$$

According to the above analysis, the constraint conditions are self-constraints of independent variables, and the constraint equations without other independent variable functions can be transformed into unconstrained optimization problems by limiting the range of independent variables, and the objective function is optimized by coordinate rotation method. According to the optimization problem, select the initial value of the parameter of the linkage:

$$X_0 = \begin{bmatrix} 120 & 90 & 140 & 564 & 0 & \frac{\pi}{20} \end{bmatrix} \tag{19}$$

The optimization problem is transformed into a mathematical function problem, and expressed in the M file by Matlab. The running solution and simplification can be concluded as follows:

$$X = \begin{bmatrix} 116.2 & 93.8 & 135 & 550 & 0 & \frac{\pi}{15} \end{bmatrix} \tag{20}$$

According to the geometric constraint relationship between the links, $L_3 = 314.7$ mm, $L_6 = 271.03$ mm, and the radius of the pulley is 28 mm. The optimization result is the change of the height optimization of the wheel center A_1 in the process of the link mechanism being undeformed to the maximum deformation amount, as shown in Fig. 6.

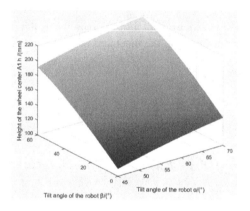

Fig. 6. Curve of the height h function of the wheel center A_1

4.2   Simulation Analysis of Linkage Mechanism

According to the passability analysis of the robot, when the center of gravity of the robot is biased forward or downward, the obstacle performance is better. In order to improve the obstacle-resistance performance, the mass distribution of the connecting rods L_1, L_2, L_5 and L_6 are designed, which does not affect the deformation of the link mechanism and ensures the quality of the robot is within a certain range. The inside remains unchanged, so that the center of gravity of the robot is biased forward and downward.

For the motion simulation of the optimized design of the linkage mechanism, the change of the centroid of each rod during the deformation process of the connecting rod. The Adams software was used to analyze the kinematics of the deformation of the linkage mechanism. The centroid, velocity and acceleration of each rod are analyzed. The performance of the rod is mainly related to the change of the centroid, that is, the key rods are analyzed. As shown in Fig. 7, it can be observed that the coordinate change of the centroid of the 1-front link is the largest, and the 5-upper link changes relatively slowly on the X and Y axes.

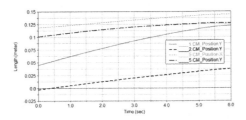

Fig. 7. The centroid coordinate change of the connecting rod

As shown in Fig. 8, the speed of the center of mass of the connecting rod changes. Among them, the speed of the 1-front link changes a lot, while the 4-post link changes slowly. As shown in Fig. 9, the acceleration of the centroid of the connecting rod is changed. The changes of the centroid acceleration of the 1-front link, 4-postlink and 6-assisted link are similar, the change is relatively large, and the 5-uplink The change is relatively slow.

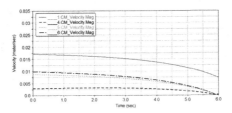

Fig. 8. Centroid speed change of the connecting rod

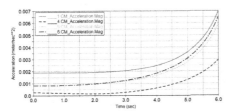

Fig. 9. Centroid acceleration change of the connecting rod

5   Prototype Experiment Analysis

After the theoretical analysis and the virtual simulation obtained the expected data, the obstacle-obstacle experiment was carried out according to the self-designed crawler underactuated robot. The length x width x height of the machine dyeing is 700 mm × 550 mm × 250 mm, and a detection module is designed on the body module to detect the external environment information. The boss was built outside, and the latter test was 10 mm higher than the previous test; the operating robot crossed the boss. As shown in Fig. 10, in ①, the robot touches the obstacle and the track is deformed; in ②, the robot continues to climb by the friction between the track and the boss; in ③, more than half of the body jumps onto the boss, and the tail wheel supports The ground supports the robot to continue climbing; in ④, the robot climbs the boss under the action of the center of mass. After repeated tests, the robot can pass over a 200 mm boss.

Fig. 10.   Robot boss experiment

6   Conclusion

(1) From the perspective of mechanism, the structure design of the linkage mechanism of the robot is analyzed, and the degree of freedom is 1, which is an underactuated mechanism.

(2) From the point of view of kinematics, with the contact force between the robot and the obstacle, the caterpillar module will be deformed, the position of its center of mass will change forward and upward, and the center of mass will cross the boundary of the step.

(3) According to the obstacle analysis mechanism of the robot, optimize the rod length parameters of the linkage mechanism and simulate the optimized linkage mechanism, and analyze the prototype experiment to verify the rationality of the structural design and improve the robot's passability performance. It can be concluded that the position of the center of mass of the robot and the maximum height of the wheel center A_1 provide a theoretical basis for the optimal obstacle-obstacle performance of the robot.

References

1. Xu, G., Tan, M.: The development status and trend of mobile robots. Robot Technol. Appl. (03), 7–14 (2001)
2. Kubota, T., Kuroda, Y., Kunii, Y., et al.: Small, light-weight rover "Micro5" for lunar exploration. Acta Astronaut. **52**(2), 447–453 (2003)
3. Wei, Y.: Design and research of coal mine underground detection and search and rescue robot mechanical system. China University of Mining and Technology (2014)
4. Yin, L.: Design and research of six-wheel rescue robot. Tianjin University of Technology (2016)
5. Liu, M., Wang, Y., Zhang, J., Zhang, H.: Optimization of the ability of crawler robots to overcome obstacles. Manuf. Autom. **40**(05), 24–27+76 (2018)
6. Yamauch, B.M.: Pack Bot: a wersatile platform for military robotics. In: Proceedings of SPIE on Unmanned Ground Vehicle Technology, vol. 5422, pp. 228–237 (2004)
7. Choi, K.H., Jeong, H.K., Hyunetal, K.H.: Obstacle negotiation for the rescue robot with variable ingle-tracked mechanism. In: Proceedings of the 2007 IEEE/ASME International Conference on Advanced Intelligent Mechatronics, Zurich, pp. 1–6. IEEE (2007)
8. Lim, S.K., Park, D., Kwak, Y.K., et al.: Variable geometry single-tracked mechanism for a rescue robot. In: Proceedings of the 2005 IEEE International Workshop on Safety, Security and Rescue Robotics, pp. 111–115. IEEE, Kobe (2005)
9. Fang, H., Ge, S., Li, Y.: Analysis of the obstacle performance of four crawler robots with passive swing arm. J. China Univ. Min. Technol. **39**(05), 682–686 (2010)
10. Deng, L., Xie, G.: Research on the obstacle performance of tandem crawler robots. J. Henan Inst. Technol. (Nat. Sci. Ed.) **32**(01), 56–61 (2013)
11. Luo, J., Bu, Z.: Analysis of obstacles in crawler rescue robots with flexible structures. J. North China Inst. Sci. Technol. **15**(01), 55–61 (2018)
12. Li, Z., Ma, S., Li, B., Wang, M., Wang, Y.: Development of a mobile robot with adaptive ability wheel-to-roll composite deformation. J. Mech. Eng. **47**(05), 1–10 (2011)
13. Chen, B.: Research and Dynamics Simulation of Lunar Rover Suspension. Jilin University (2006)
14. Ebrahimzadeh, A.A., Khazaee, I., Fasihfar, A.: Numerical investigation of dimensions and arrangement of obstacle on the performance of PEM fuel cell. Heliyon **4**(11), e00974 (2018)
15. Xue, Y., Zhang, J., Zhang, L.: Design and obstacle analysis of automatic adaptation mechanism for pipeline robots. Manuf. Autom. **40**(06), 23–26 (2018)
16. Wang, C., Wang, D., Chen, Y., Liu, Z., Xiang, C.: Analysis and simulation of the obstacle performance of six-wheeled all-terrain mobile robots. Manuf. Autom. **38**(12), 72–77 (2016)

A Novel Hedgehog-Inspired Pin-Array Robot Hand with Multiple Magnetic Pins for Adaptive Grasping

Hang Yuan and Wenzeng Zhang[(⊠)]

Department of Mechanical Engineering, Tsinghua University,
Beijing 100084, China
wenzeng@tsinghua.edu.cn

Abstract. Advanced service robots and flexible production lines demand more universal grippers than conventional ones. In response to the deficiencies of Omnigripper proposed by previous scholars, this paper proposes a novel hedgehog-inspired robot hand (HIPA Hand) with multiple magnetic pins for general self-adaptive grasping. The HIPA hand utilizes electromagnets as the main driving part and the motor as another driving part. HIPA hand can grasp the object of different sizes and shapes. The theoretical analysis and simulation experimental results show that this device has a special advantage of quick grasping and big grasping force compared with the traditional pin-array grippers.

Keywords: Robot hand · Universal gripper · Pin-array · Self-adaptive grasping

1 Introduction

The manipulator, which has a wide range of applications in many fields, is the most important actuator and the interaction link between the robot and the outside world.

To achieve grasping, industrial gripper is firstly proposed. For example, SCHUNK [1] makes the industrial gripper with two relative motion parts, which has the advantages of low cost and easy control, but the reliability of the industrial gripper is poor.

Some dexterous hand adopts the method of highly imitated human hand mechanism to realize the multi-direction grasping of the target object. The grasping stability is obviously improved, but each finger is equipped with multiple joints and sensors, resulting in high cost and complicated control system [2–4], such as Utah/MIT Dexterous Hand [5], Gifu Hand II [6], the Shadow Hand, Stanford/JPL Hand [7] and so on.

The bionic manipulator Octopus Gripper [8] recently launched by FESTO, has good adaptability, that is, it can grasp the object without knowing what shape and size the objects are before fetching. This automatic adaptation to the shape and size of an object allows the manipulator to grasp objects more widely.

For self-adaption, there are some grippers with pin-array has been proposed. This type of gripper can be traced back to the Omnigripper [9] proposed by British scholars in the 1980s, as shown in Fig. 1. The Omnigripper has two sets of pin-array, each pin-array consists of several slidable pins. When this gripper grasping object, the two sets

© Springer Nature Switzerland AG 2019
H. Yu et al. (Eds.): ICIRA 2019, LNAI 11744, pp. 684–695, 2019.
https://doi.org/10.1007/978-3-030-27541-9_56

of pin-array adapt to the shape of the object from the vertical direction. After adaption, the two sets of pin-array move together to form grasping force from two sides of the object. The Omnigripper has a good ability of self-adaption and large grasping force, but it has some shortcomings:

(i) Over-simple grasping method. When the device exerts a grasping force on the target object, the grasping force can only be along the direction where the two groups of pin-array together, and cannot achieve multi-direction grasping, thus the grasping effect is poor.

Fig. 1. Universal grasping device Omnigripper

(ii) For a long strip placed in a particular direction, the grip fails.
(iii) The complex structure and high energy consumption. The device has 2 groups of pin clusters, 2 supporting pieces, 1 set of linear guide, 2 sliders, drive, drive mechanism and so on. The structure is relatively complex, and it is of high energy consumption to make one group of heavy pins clusters with many long poles move together.
(iv) Poor reliability in long-term use. All the long pins and chutes are exposed in the working environment, and the dust is absorbed and concentrated in the long pins and chutes, which greatly affects the sliding effect of the long pins in the base and even causes failure.

In order to solve the shortcomings of Omnigripper, scholars from Tsinghua University in China proposed some pin-array grippers [10–13]. These pin-array grippers can achieve good adaptive crawling.

While most of these pin-array grippers are driving by motors or negative pressure, which has the shortcoming of slow grasping. In order to achieve faster grabbing, this paper proposes a new type of pin-array gripper driven by an electromagnet.

2 Hedgehog-Inspired Pin-Array Robot Hand

The device uses the combination of motor, electromagnet, oscillating pin, sliding tube and so on to realize the spatial discrete adaptive grasping function, as shown in Fig. 2. The device has the following advantages:

  (i) It has sensitive movement and adjustable grip force.

 (ii) It can adapt itself to the shape and size of the object in both horizontal and vertical directions, and it has large grasping force, high reliability, simple structure, and low cost.

(iii) The sliding tube has the ability of radial swing and wide grasping range.

(iv) It is able to grab multiple objects at the same time, and it is of simple structure and low energy consumption.

Fig. 2. Design of hedgehog-inspired pin-array robot hand

2.1   Composition Principle

The component structure of the device is as shown in Fig. 3, including the base, hemispheric parts, motors, magnetic driving pins, and other components. According to the structural function, it can be divided into two major parts: the executive part and the control part, which will be discussed in Sects. 2.2 and 2.3.

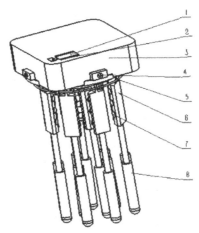

1- Motor, 2-Reel, 3-Base, 4-Bolt, 5-Elastic cord, 6-Oscillating pin,
7- Electromagnet, 8-Slide bar.

Fig. 3.   Schematic of the hedgehog-inspired pin-array robot hand structure

2.2   Executive Part

The magnetic drive pin is the actuating mechanism of the Hedgehog Imitation Magnetic Drive Pin Ball Adaptive Robot Hand Device. The electromagnet is its main driving element, and the power supply makes it attract (repel) each other, thus making the magnetic drive pin gather (disperse) in the radial direction. In addition, the motor power source and elastic cord are combined to make up for the insufficient attraction of electromagnet.

Magnetic drive pin consists of an electromagnet, oscillating pin, rubber head, and sliding tube, as is shown in Fig. 4(a). Among them, the oscillating pin is hinged on the base, as is shown in Fig. 4(b), and it can swing in the radial direction. Meanwhile, the sliding tube can slide along the axis of the guide bar under the action of the reset spring, so that it can adapt to the shape and size of the object both horizontally and vertically. In order to reduce the friction of the sliding tube along the direction of the oscillating pin, the guide rod adopts a relatively smooth PTFE rod, which saves the bearing and reduces the volume of cluster-hand.

The execution of the auxiliary drive part mainly consists of the motor and elastic cord, as is shown in Figs. 3 and 4(b). The motor is connected with an elastic cord by winding wheel, with the elastic cord playing the role of tightening slide tube, which makes the outer slide tube gather towards the center, so as to achieve the purpose of

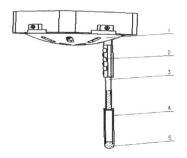
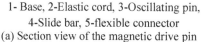

1- Base, 2-Elastic cord, 3-Oscillating pin,
4-Slide bar, 5-flexible connector
(a) Section view of the magnetic drive pin   (b) Base design blueprint

Fig. 4. Internal structure design drawings

auxiliary grasping objects. In addition, the elasticity of the elastic cord can also play the role of holding the grasping force.

The magnetic drive pin of the device is divided into two laps of internal lap and external lap, and the magnetic drive pin at both laps are of polyhedron structure and separate design, so as to ensure the electromagnet between the bars are two facing two in the initial state of the device, so that when objects are clamped, it can achieve the maximum grasping force. In order to obtain greater electromagnetic attraction force, three columns of electromagnets are arranged for each magnetic drive pin, the specific layout form is as shown in Fig. 5a and b.

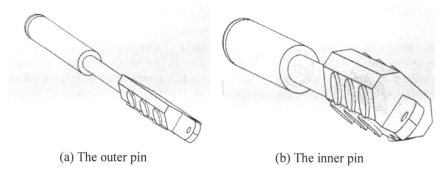

(a) The outer pin   (b) The inner pin

Fig. 5. The pin of hedgehog-inspired pin-array robot hand

2.3 Control Part

The control system adopts the Arduino controller. For the control of the electromagnet, the volume of the output voltage is adjusted through the Arduino PWM output pin to achieve the purpose of the current regulation, so as to realize the control of the gravity of the electromagnet or change the direction of current to achieve rapid dispersion of magnetic drive pins.

When the grasping force provided by the electromagnet is insufficient to pick up the object, the motor assistance is launched to realize the control of the elastic pin to the magnetic drive pin by controlling its circle number. Among them, the current adjustment is controlled by a potentiometer, and the grasping force can be adjusted at any time. The circuit connection and working flow diagram of the device are as shown in Fig. 6.

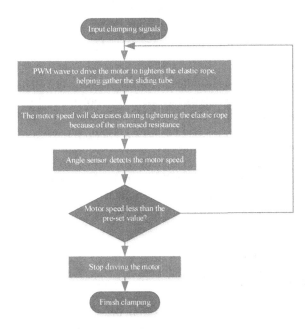

Fig. 6. Logical flow diagram for grasping

2.4 Working Principle

When an object is grasped, with the electromagnet force, the robot arm vertically gets close to the object and compresses it. If the rubber head touches the object or supporting surface in the vertical direction, the sliding tube slides upward relative to the oscillating pin under the compression of the object. Due to the reactive force of the object, the sliding tube produces varying degrees of sliding, then it wraps the objects. For objects of different shapes and sizes, the device has good adaptability, as shown in Fig. 7.

When the device touches an object, the electromagnet is energized, and the magnetic drive pin gathers to the center under the action of radial suction, so that the sliding tube can stick to the object and move the mechanical arm, so as to realize the grasping of the object.

Fig. 7. Grasping various objects

If the radial suction force is insufficient for the magnetic drive pin in the process of grasping objects, the motor will start and drive the spring rope to tighten. The tightening force of the spring string is coupled with the electromagnet suction force to make the sliding tube clamp the objects and have the grasping process go on consecutively.

When an object is released, the device places objects to the bearing surface vertically under the drive of the robot arm, then the electromagnet is cut off from power. At the same time, the motor stops working. The suction force of the electromagnet and the tightening force of the spring rope disappear, thus the sliding tube is in the free state and the object is released.

3 Theoretical Analysis

3.1 Model Design Analysis

The main driving force of the device comes from the electromagnet. The calculation is complicated because there are many influencing factors for the acting force between two electric solenoids. Now, for the convenience of calculation and force analysis, the electromagnet of the device is assumed to be of enfilade deployment. Meanwhile, each electric solenoid generates a magnetic field and produces an influence on other solenoids when calculating the force analysis, so the superposition effect of the magnetic field is neglected for the convenience of calculation. That is, the force analysis of two electromagnets is to calculate the force analysis of two electric cylindrical solenoids.

By referring to literature, Newton's third law is applicable among electricity cylindrical solenoids, and electromagnetic forces only own component in the axis direction. By the electromagnetic field theory, the field energy for the two coaxial electric cylindrical solenoid system is:

$$W = I_1 I_2 M \tag{1}$$

I_1, I_2 are respectively the current of the two electric cylindrical solenoids. M is the mutual inductance of two electric cylindrical solenoids, The force calculation of the upper component along the axis in the external magnetic field of the current-carrying system is based on the principle of virtual work:

$$F = I_1 I_2 \frac{\partial M}{\partial h} \tag{2}$$

The sizes of the magnets of the device are the same, the current of each magnet is the same. By a study of the data, it is found that when the radius of the two coaxial electric cylindrical solenoids is the same, the electromagnetic force F decreases with the increase of the distance. Within a certain range, the electromagnetic force F decreases rapidly with the increase of the distance h. When it is beyond the scope, the decreasing speed of electromagnetic force F slows down with the increase of the distance h; when the distance approaches infinity, the acting force F tends to be zero. The place where h is equal to zero is considered to be a physical singularity because the center of two coaxial solenoids whose radius are the same is impossible to overlap.

3.2 Grasping Force Analysis

Only the gravitational action between adjacent electromagnets is considered here. The external force on the magnetic drive pin is as shown in Fig. 8.

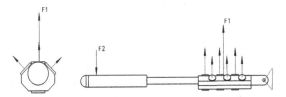

Fig. 8. Force analysis diagram of an oscillating pin.

For the rotation angle of the component of the oscillating pin is small, ignoring the impact of the oscillating angle of the component of the oscillating pin on the force, the force F_1 of the electromagnet on the oscillating pin and the force F_2 of an object on the oscillating pin are both perpendicular to the oscillating pin. In the vertical state, the distance between two adjacent magnetic drive pins in the 3d model is measured and denoted as d, $\frac{F}{\mu I_1 I_2}$ can be obtained. By referring to the data, the magnetic conductivity of the electromagnetic iron core μ was selected, the power voltage U was selected, the voltage was adjusted by potentiometer, and the values of I_1, I_2, and F were obtained. Since the magnetic drive pin is uniformly distributed with 9 electromagnets, it can be obtained that $F_1 = 9F$, where F_1 is the synthetic force of three columns of electromagnets on a single magnetic drive pin. In order to obtain the grasping force F_2, it is set that F_2 works at Point B at the end of the oscillating pipe. Then the entire oscillating pipe assembly is considered as a whole, with the moment balance, it can be obtained that:

$$F_2 \times l_{OB} = F_1 \times l_{OA} \tag{3}$$

In it, l_{OA} and l_{OB} are respectively the point at which the electromagnet acts on the oscillating pin and the distance of the object from the point of action of the oscillating pipe to the hinged point O, thus the size of extrusion pressure of a pin on the device on the object is:

$$F_2 = \frac{F_1 \times l_{OA}}{l_{OB}} \tag{4}$$

In the formula, l_{OA} and l_{OB} are respectively, the arm of the force of F_1 and F_2.

The static friction coefficient μ is also included. Since the inner layer is equipped with 4 magnetic drive pins, the gravity of the weight that can be clamped is:

$$G = 4\mu F_2 \tag{5}$$

F_1 is an electromagnetic force varying with distance. In this device, in order to obtain a large grasping force, measures such as selecting electromagnets with greater magnetic induction intensity, increasing the current passing through electromagnets, increasing the number of electromagnets, increasing l_{OA} and decreasing l_{OB} can be adopted.

In this device, the electromagnetic force generated between adjacent electric solenoids is used to provide the inward contraction force so as to produce grasping force, so the distance between magnetic drive pins and the swinging angle of the magnetic drive pin are the important factors that affect the size of grasping force.

4 Experiment

4.1 Experiment Design

With the three dimensional models, the angle and distance of objects grabbed with different dimensions are simulated, as shown in Fig. 9. The size and shape of the different object are as shown in Table 1. According to the formula for calculating electromagnetic force given above, the maximum weight of the object of this shape and size is obtained theoretically, which provides guidance and reference for practical application.

4.2 Experimental Data Processing

Through grasping simulation of objects of different sizes, we get the maximum grasping force under different conditions through theoretical calculation. In addition, mathematical analysis tools were used to fit the experimental data and the surface diagram shown in Fig. 10 was obtained. In Fig. 10, the horizontal coordinate of the

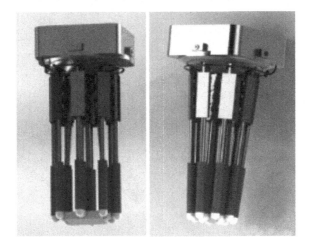

Fig. 9. The experiment of the robot hand grasping objects.

Table 1. Objects of different sizes in the experiment

Width length	10 mm	20 mm	30 mm	40 mm	50 mm	60 mm
10 mm	Ball	Cuboid	Cuboid	Cuboid	Cuboid	Cuboid
20 mm		Ball	Cuboid	Cuboid	Cuboid	Cuboid
30 mm			Ball	Cuboid	Cuboid	Cuboid
40 mm				Ball	Cuboid	Cuboid
50 mm					Ball	Cuboid
60 mm						Ball

surface graph is the horizontal dimension of the clamped object, the vertical coordinate is the longitudinal dimension of the clamped object, and the vertical coordinate is the maximum grasping force of the magnetic drive pin on the object of this size.

The three-dimensional simulation grasping experiment of HIPA Hand is as seen in Fig. 10. By adding the ideal physical model in the three-dimensional model, the shrinkage or opening degree of the magnetic drive pin in the real object grasping process is demonstrated, which is used to provide the swinging angle and relative distance of magnetic drive pin of a specific size. The maximum grasping force can be obtained by applying the corresponding calculation formula.

Through the simulation experiment analysis, we can get the conclusions that the device has the advantages of large grasping force, stable grasping, and strong self-adaptability. But there are still some shortcomings, such as the small grasping force of the overlarge object and the great influence of grasping posture. For improving the deficiency existing at present, we will reduce the distance between magnetic pole displacement in the design of the device in the subsequent versions, and design more laps magnetic pin displacement and more electromagnets. And this will give full play to the advantages of the hedgehog imitation magnetic drive pinball adaptive robot hand device.

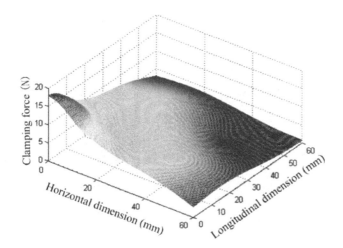

Fig. 10. Relationship between the maximum grasping force and the size of the target object.

5   Conclusion

This paper proposes a novel hedgehog-inspired robot hand (HIPA Hand) with multiple magnetic pins for general self-adaptive grasping. The HIPA hand utilizes electromagnets as the main driving part and the motor as another driving part. HIPA hand can grasp the object of different sizes and shapes. The theoretical analysis and simulation experimental result show that the HIPA hand has the advantage of the quick grasping speed and big grasping force compared with the traditional pin-array grippers.

In future work, we will focus on the development of prototypes and the improvement of experimental performance.

Acknowledgment. This research was supported by National Nature Science Foundation of China (No. 51575302) and Beijing Science Foundation (J170005) and National Key R&D Program of China (No. 2017YFE0113200).

References

1. MPG: The Most Proven Premium Small Components Gripper in the World. https://de.schunk.com/de_en/gripping-systems/series/mpg/. Accessed 20 Apr 2019
2. Liu, H., Wang, T., Fan, W., et al.: Study on the structure and control of a dexterous hand. In: International Conference on Control Automation Robotics & Vision (ICARCV), Singapore, pp. 1589–1593 (2010)
3. Mattar, E.: Dexterous robotics hands: ANN based artificial muscles control. In: International Conference on Computer Modelling and Simulation, Cambridge, pp. 224–229 (2011)
4. Hua, W., Xiaodiao, H., Jin, H.: Finger tracking control of underwater dexterous hand based on fuzzy CMAC. In: Chinese Control Conference, Hunan, China, pp. 121–124 (2007)
5. Jacobsen, S.C., Iversen, E.K., Knutti, D.F., et al.: Design of the Utah/MIT dextrous hand. IEEE Trans. Robot. **3**, 1520–1532 (1986)

6. Kawasaki, H., Komatsu, T., Uchiyama, K.: Dexterous anthropomorphic robot hand with distributed tactile sensor: gifu hand II. IEEE/ASME Trans. Mechatron. **7**(3), 296–303 (2002)
7. Loucks, C.S.: Modeling and control of the stanford/JPL hand. In: International Conference on Robotics and Automation, pp. 573–578 (1987)
8. Festo Company: Octopus Gripper. http://v.youku.com/v_show/id_XOTMwMTI2NDU2. html?from=s1.8-1-1.2. 3 April 2019
9. Scott, P.B.: The 'Omnigripper': a form of robot universal gripper. Robotica **3**(3), 153–158 (1985)
10. Mo, A., Zhang, W.: A universal robot gripper based on concentric arrays of rotating pins. Sci. Chin. **62**, 050214:1–050214:3 (2019)
11. Mo, A., Zhang, W.: Pin array hand: a universal robot gripper with pins of ellipse contour. In: IEEE International Conference on Robotics & Biomimetics (ROBIO), Macau, China, 5–8 December, pp. 2075–2080 (2017)
12. Fu, H., Yang, H., Song, W., Zhang, W.: A novel cluster-tube self-adaptive robot hand. Robot. Biomim. **4**, 25 (2017)
13. Fu, H., Zhang, W.: The development of a soft robot hand with pin-array structure. Appl. Sci. **9**(5), 1011 (2019)

Kinematic Analysis of a Flexible Planar 2-DOF Parallel Manipulator

Jiaqi Zhu[1], Bin Li[1(✉)], Haozhi Mu[1], and Qi Li[2]

[1] Tianjin Key Laboratory for Advanced Mechatronic System Design
and Intelligent Control, School of Mechanical Engineering,
Tianjin University of Technology, Tianjin, China
cnrobot@163.com
[2] Tianjin Key Laboratory of Aerospace Intelligent Equipment Technology,
Tianjin Institute of Aerospace Mechanical and Electrical Equipment,
Tianjin, China

Abstract. In this paper, a 2-DOF (degrees of freedom) translational parallel mechanism with the structure of timing belt transmission is studied. This article mainly focuses on the kinematic analysis. Firstly, the structural characteristics of the mechanism are described. Secondly, the kinematic analysis for the mechanism is carried out and the mathematical model is established. Thirdly, the analysis of the experimental data and simulation result prove the feasibility of the mechanical system simulation with RecurDyn. Finally, some conclusions are given.

Keywords: Parallel · Kinematic performance · RecurDyn · Timing belt

1 Introduction

1.1 A Subsection Sample

In the industrial field, robots usually do not need a full six degrees of freedom to complete the task. Therefore, lower-mobility translational parallel mechanism (TPMs) in industrial production has a wide range of applications. In packaging and sorting operations, robots are only required to perform high-speed grip in one plane. For example, battery sorting, bottled or bagged food and pharmaceutical packing operations. At present, the picking work for the plane is mainly done by the cross-slide.

The existing 2-DOF positioning platform (cross-slipway) mostly uses the motor-screw structure, among which the ball screw is the most commonly used. The structure of ball screw is the most common, traditional form of driving and an ideal structure for turning rotary motion into linear motion. However, many problems have also been exposed in the use of the ball screw structure. First of all, the limited load of the screw, it is difficult to meet the modern equipment on the movement process of high-speed, high acceleration requirements. Secondly, because the disturbance of the screw itself has a great influence on the motion precision of the servo system, the ball screw is difficult to use in the large stroke equipment. In addition, there are problems such as high processing costs, large noise, high environmental requirements, and no self-lock.

© Springer Nature Switzerland AG 2019
H. Yu et al. (Eds.): ICIRA 2019, LNAI 11744, pp. 696–706, 2019.
https://doi.org/10.1007/978-3-030-27541-9_57

In the production process, in order to improve production efficiency and save production time, the frequency of pick-and-place applications need to reach hundreds of times per minute. Accordingly, the pickup device industry is developing toward high speed and flexibility. In this paper, the flexible 2-DOF mechanism adopts the synchronous belt drive system. The timing belt itself has good ductility and damping characteristics. The timing belt is generally made of heat-resistant synthetic rubber and glass fiber cord with high tensile modulus, its noise of vibration is small and the fatigue life is high. It is a combination of belt drive, chain drive and gear drive. It has the advantages of simple structure, stable transmission, high efficiency and energy saving, low noise and no lubrication. It is especially suitable for the occasion of high speed and large stroke.

2 Structural Characteristics

As shown in Fig. 1, the CAD model of the mechanism is established in RecurDyn software, which is mainly composed of frame, slider, movable bar, timing belt, synchronous pulleys, rollers. The slider can slide in the X direction on the guide of frame, and the movable bar can slide in the Y direction on the guide of slider. The winding method of the synchronous belt is shown as the Fig. 1, one of the bands of the timing belt of the lower end is fixedly contacted with the timing pulley 1, and the synchronous pulley 1 is fixed with timing belt. The combination motion of the two linear motion units can be realized by driving the two synchronous pulleys A and B with different directions and sizes. The plane movement of the two linear degrees of motion in the XY axis can be generated, complete sorting and picking up operation.

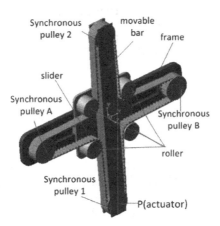

Fig. 1. CAD model of the manipulator

3 Kinematic Analysis of Mechanisms

3.1 Position Analysis

As shown in Fig. 2, the center point of A and B is the coordinate origin O, the direction of the slider rail is the X coordinate axis, the direction is from A to B, and the coordinate system O-XY is established. The length of the belt between the two points A and B is L_H, the length of the belt between the two points C and P is L_V. So the coordinates of point A is $A(-\frac{1}{2}L_H, 0)$, point B is $B(\frac{1}{2}L_H, 0)$. The distance from point A to the center of the slider is L_1, the distance from point B to the center of the slider is L_3. The distance from the center of the timing pulley 2 to the center of the slider is L_2. The distance from the timing pulley 1 to the center of the slider is L_4. The total length of the sync band is L_B. There are:

$$L_1 + L_3 = L_H$$
$$L_2 + L_4 = L_V \qquad\qquad (1)$$
$$2L_H + 2L_V = L_B$$

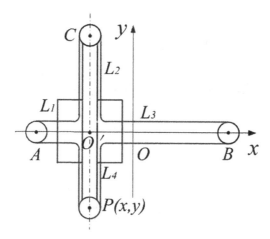

Fig. 2. Diagram of the mechanism

The process of calculating L_1 and L_4 by the coordinates of point P in the working space is the inverse solution of the mechanism. On the other hand, the kinematic positive solution of the mechanism is getting the coordinates of the output point P by the input L_1 and L_4.

1. Positive solution of position

   give input L_1, L_4 at a certain moment, solve the coordinates of the point P. by the Eq. (1):

$$P\begin{cases} x = -\frac{1}{2}L_H + L_1 \\ y = -L_4 \end{cases} \tag{2}$$

2. Position inverse solution

   It is known that the point P(x, y) at a certain position, and the input L_1, L_4 are obtained by the Eq. (1):

$$\begin{cases} L_1 = X + \frac{1}{2}L_H \\ L_4 = -y \end{cases} \tag{3}$$

3.2 Velocity Analysis

Two synchronous pulleys A and B (the radius of both pulleys are r) rotate respectively at the angular speeds of ω_A and ω_B, angular acceleration θ_A and θ_B. Set a point P on the movable bar, its location is P′ after t time. After t time, the movement distance of slider in the X direction is Δx, the movement distance of moveable bar in the Y direction is Δy. So the moving speed of the slider is $v_y = \Delta x/t$, the moving speed of the movable bar in the Y direction is $v_y = \Delta y/t$, and the included angle between v_x and v_y is θ. According to the speed of the pulleys A and B, the movement of moveable bar can be divided into two categories, each class has two different situations.

(1) When the direction of rotation of pulleys A and B is the same, the fixed end of the movable bar and the synchronous belt are shown in Fig. 3a and b. When the direction of rotation is the same, the timing belt will cause the slider to slide in the same direction along the rails on the rack. When the two rotational speeds are different ($v_A \neq v_B$), in addition to the horizontal movement of the slider, a synchronous traction rod is used to achieve the upper and lower movement of the slide block on the slide guide rail. At this point, the coupling motion of the moving rod in the two directions of X and Y is realized.

   For Fig. 3a, when $v_A \neq v_B$, in t time, for the left synchronization of the movable bar, $\Delta x - \Delta y = v_A t$; for the right side of the synchronization $\Delta x + \Delta y = v_B t$. Simultaneous:

$$\begin{cases} \Delta x - \Delta y = v_A t \\ \Delta x + \Delta y = v_B t \end{cases} \tag{4}$$

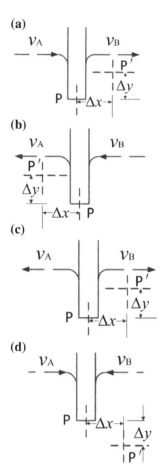

Fig. 3. (a) and (b) Both A and B turn anticlockwise clockwise. (c) A wheel clockwise rotation, B wheel counterclockwise rotation. (d) A wheel counterclockwise rotation, B wheel clockwise rotation

So,

$$\begin{cases} v_x = \frac{\Delta x}{t} = \frac{1}{2}(v_A + v_B) \\ v_y = \frac{\Delta y}{t} = \frac{1}{2}(v_B - v_A) \end{cases} \tag{5}$$

Similarly, for Fig. 3b, when $v_A \neq v_B$, there is

$$\begin{cases} -\Delta x + \Delta y = v_A t \\ -\Delta x - \Delta y = v_B t \end{cases} \tag{6}$$

So,

$$\begin{cases} v_x = \frac{\Delta x}{t} = -\frac{1}{2}(v_A + v_B) \\ v_y = \frac{\Delta y}{t} = -\frac{1}{2}(v_B - v_A) \end{cases} \tag{7}$$

In summary, when rounds of the A and B are the same, the moving speed of the slider in the X direction and the moving speed of the rod in the Y direction are

$$\begin{cases} v_x = \frac{\Delta x}{t} = \pm\frac{1}{2}(v_A + v_B) \\ v_y = \frac{\Delta y}{t} = \pm\frac{1}{2}(v_B - v_A) \end{cases} \tag{8}$$

(When the A and B wheels turn counterclockwise, take " + "; when the A and B wheels rotate clockwise, take "-", and $\tan\theta = \frac{v_y}{v_x} = \frac{v_B - v_A}{v_B + v_A} = \frac{\omega_B - \omega_A}{\omega_B + \omega_A}$)

When A and B turn opposite, as shown in Fig. 3c and d, the fixed ends of the movable bar and the synchronous belt are shown. At the same speed of the two wheels, the timing belt will be implicated that the movable bar slides along the slider rail in the Y direction. When the two rotational speeds are different ($v_A \neq v_B$), in addition to the movement of the movable bar in the Y direction, the synchronous belt pulls the slide block to realize the X direction movement on the rack guide rail. At this point, the coupling motion of the moving rod in the two directions of X and Y is realized.

For Fig. 3c, when $v_A \neq v_B$, in t time, for the left synchronization of the moving lever, $-\Delta x + \Delta y = v_A t$; for the right side of the synchronization $\Delta x + \Delta y = v_B t$. Simultaneous:

$$\begin{cases} -\Delta x + \Delta y = v_A t \\ \Delta x + \Delta y = v_B t \end{cases} \tag{9}$$

So,

$$\begin{cases} v_x = \frac{\Delta x}{t} = \frac{1}{2}(v_B - v_A) \\ v_y = \frac{\Delta y}{t} = \frac{1}{2}(v_B + v_A) \end{cases} \tag{10}$$

Similarly, for Fig. 3d, when $v_A \neq v_B$, there is

$$\begin{cases} \Delta x - \Delta y = v_A t \\ -\Delta x - \Delta y = v_B t \end{cases} \tag{11}$$

So,

$$\begin{cases} v_x = \frac{\Delta x}{t} = -\frac{1}{2}(v_B - v_A) \\ v_y = \frac{\Delta y}{t} = -\frac{1}{2}(v_B + v_A) \end{cases} \tag{12}$$

In summary, when the A and B rounds are the same, the speed of the slider in the X direction and the speed of the rod in the Y direction are:

$$\begin{cases} v_x = \frac{\Delta x}{t} = \pm\frac{1}{2}(v_B - v_A) \\ v_y = \frac{\Delta y}{t} = \pm\frac{1}{2}(v_B + v_A) \end{cases} \tag{13}$$

(When the B wheel rotates counterclockwise, take " + "; when the B wheel rotates clockwise, take "-"", and $\tan\theta = \frac{v_y}{v_x} = \frac{v_B + v_A}{v_B - v_A} = \frac{\omega_B + \omega_A}{\omega_B - \omega_A}$)

To sum up, the speed at any point on the movable bar can be obtained:

$$\begin{aligned} v &= \sqrt{v_x^2 + v_y^2} \\ &= \frac{1}{2}\sqrt{(v_A + v_B)^2 + (v_A - v_B)^2} \\ &= \frac{1}{2}\sqrt{2v_A^2 + 2v_B^2} \\ &= \frac{\sqrt{2}}{2}\sqrt{\omega_A^2 r^2 + \omega_B^2 r^2} \\ &= \frac{\sqrt{2}}{2}r\sqrt{\omega_A^2 + \omega_B^2} \end{aligned} \tag{14}$$

3.3   Acceleration Analysis

When the steering of the A and B wheels is the same, derived by the Eq. (8)

$$\begin{cases} a_x = \pm\frac{r}{2}(\varphi_A + \varphi_B) \\ a_y = \pm\frac{r}{2}(\varphi_B - \varphi_A) \end{cases} \tag{15}$$

$$\begin{aligned} a &= \sqrt{a_x^2 + a_y^2} \\ &= \frac{r}{2}\sqrt{(\varphi_A + \varphi_B)^2 + (\varphi_A - \varphi_B)^2} \\ &= \frac{\sqrt{2}}{2}r\sqrt{\varphi_A^2 + \varphi_B^2} \end{aligned} \tag{16}$$

$(\tan\theta = \frac{a_y}{a_x} == \frac{\varphi_B - \varphi_A}{\varphi_B + \varphi_A})$

When A and B turn opposite, the acceleration is derived by formula (13):

$$\begin{cases} a_x = \pm\frac{r}{2}(\varphi_B - \varphi_A) \\ a_y = \pm\frac{r}{2}(\varphi_B + \varphi_A) \end{cases} \tag{17}$$

$$a = \sqrt{a_x^2 + a_y^2}$$

$$= \frac{r}{2}\sqrt{(\varphi_A - \varphi_B)^2 + (\varphi_A + \varphi_B)^2} \tag{18}$$

$$= \frac{\sqrt{2}}{2}r\sqrt{\varphi_A^2 + \varphi_B^2}$$

$$(\tan\theta = \frac{a_y}{a_x} == \frac{\varphi_B + \varphi_A}{\varphi_B - \varphi_A})$$

To sum up, by Eqs. (16) and (18), the acceleration of the moving point is:

$$a = \frac{\sqrt{2}}{2}r\sqrt{\varphi_A^2 + \varphi_B^2} \tag{19}$$

4   Kinematic Analysis of Mechanisms

In this paper, wheel A and B choose trapezoidal synchronous belt wheel with the same parameters uniform motion. Set $\omega_A = 2.5$ rad/s, $\omega_B = 1.5$ rad/s speed synchronous belt wheel drive clockwise and counterclockwise rotation, radius r is 100 mm, the other parameters of synchronous pulleys are shown in the following table Tables 1 and 2:

Table 1. Parameters of synchronous belt pulley.

The number of teeth	20
Teeth half-angle (A)	20°
Tooth height (Hr)	10.29 mm
Addendum thickness (Bg)	11.61 mm
Tip radius (R1)	2.69 mm
Tooth fillet radius (R2)	2.82 mm
Outside diameter (Do)	199.08 mm
Pulley width	91.3 mm

Table 2. Synchronous belt parameters.

The number of teeth	20
Pitch (Pb)	31.75 mm
Tooth profile angle (A)	20°
Tooth height (Ht)	9.53 mm
Tooth length (S)	19.05 mm
Tooth fillet radius (Rr)	2.29 mm
Tip radius (Ra)	1.52 mm
Norminal height (Hs)	15.7 mm
Bandwidth (W)	76.2 mm

Substitution Eq. (10):

$$v_x = \frac{v_B - v_A}{2} = -50 \, \text{mm/s}$$

$$v_y = \frac{v_B + v_A}{2} = 200 \, \text{mm/s}$$

The dynamic characteristics of related parameters are obtained in RecurDyn. Then the theoretical results are compared with the simulation results in MATLAB, and the following results are obtained.

The displacement of the movable bar in the direction of X and Y is compared with the simulation data. As shown in Figs. 3 and 4, the displacement size is basically linear with time. The X direction basically agrees with each other, slightly fluctuates, because in the X direction, between the moving rod and the slide block is the rigid connection, the error is smaller. In order to verify the correctness of the model, the reason for the Y shift to the displacement may be that the tension of the synchronous belt is not enough, and the synchronous belt drive itself also has some errors, resulting in a certain fluctuation of the displacement.

X, Y pneumatic rod speed to the theoretical values and simulation data were compared as shown in Fig. 5a and b, according to the calculation results, the dynamic speed in X, Y direction of the rod should be a constant value, but in the beginning

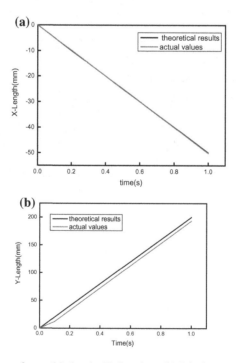

Fig. 4. (a) Displacement of movable bar in X direction. (b) Displacement of movable bar in Y direction

stages of velocity fluctuations are relatively large, moving rod at X speed to begin to increase from 0 then, gradually after 0.2 s reached a steady speed, the fluctuation of around −50 mm/s; Y to the speed in the 0.1 s after the last stable in 200 mm/s. This shows that at the beginning of the movement, is not with the wheel while the movement speed of belt transmission is a lag time.

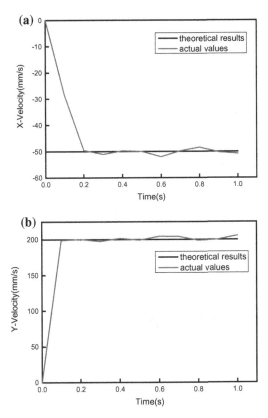

Fig. 5. (a) Displacement of movable bar in X direction. (b) Velocity of movable bar in Y direction

The curve of acceleration is shown as Figs. 6a and b, instantaneous acceleration of rod is changing, this is due to material of the belt, resulting in the shrinking belt and pulley contact process and elongation caused by belt tension in constant motion, thus cause the change with the instantaneous velocity and instantaneous acceleration effect the speed of the movable bar. The fluctuation of acceleration results in the change of dynamic tension in belt transmission. The dynamic tension in high speed and the transmission distance is small, less affected, but for high speed transmission belt and the transmission distance is larger, along with the spread of these dynamic tension superimposed on each other, makes dynamic tension value is far greater than the static tension, thus becoming the velocity and acceleration of wave elements.

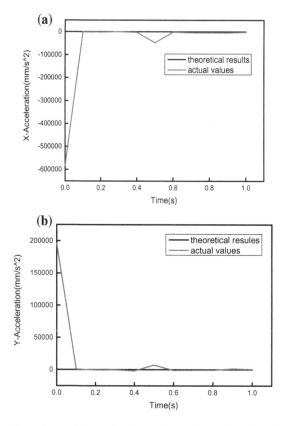

Fig. 6. (a) Acceleration of movable bar in X direction. (b) Acceleration of movable bar in Y direction

5   Conclusions

In this paper, a mathematical model of a flexible planar two degree of freedom mechanism is established. The kinematic characteristics of the mechanism are studied. The equations of position and inverse solutions, as well as the velocity and acceleration equations are derived. The synchronous belt is discretized by RecurDyn software, and the CAD model is established. The simulation and contrast analysis provide a reference for the actual movement of the mechanism. The experimental results show that the mechanism has good motion accuracy and sufficient speed. It can be used in sorting, picking, packing and other operations. Besides, the main advantages of the mechanism are that the structure is light and novel, and it can realize high speed movement. It is easy to be used as a module independently. It can also be connected with a single degree of freedom feeding mechanism into 3-DOF translational hybrid manipulator. The rest of the mechanism's performance remains to be researched.

Double-Source Fluid Bending and Side-Swing Compound Multi-joint Finger

Weiping Kong and Wenzeng Zhang$^{(\boxtimes)}$

Department of Mechanical Engineering, Tsinghua University, Beijing 100084, China
wenzeng@tsinghua.edu.cn

Abstract. The middle joint of the finger in traditional multi-finger hand has no ability of bending and side swing motion. To solve this problem, this paper proposes a double-fluid drive method: the double-fluid drive realizes the multi-joint coupling bending, coupling side swing and bending and side swing motion of the finger. A double-fluid bending and side-swing multi-joint robot finger (DFBS finger) was developed. The DFBS finger consists of two independent fluid routes that run through all joints and are driven by double fluids, three phalanx and three joint springs. The force change assembly is mainly composed of a spring and a balloon. The spring and the balloon are coordinated to make the fingers stably grasp. The double fluid bending and side swing multi-joint finger can be forwardly bent for forward adaptive grasping, lateral adaptive grasping to the side, and grasping in different direction from left to right. The theoretical analysis and experimental results show that the DFBS fingers can realize the envelope grasping for different shapes and sizes.

Keywords: Robot hand · Multi-joint finger · Double-source fluid driving · Self-adaptive grasping · Bending and side-swing compound

1 Introduction

In the past few decades, the field of robotic grasping and smart operation has received more and more attention. Over the years, robots have begun to interact with their surroundings and assist humans in performing dexterous tasks. Because human hands are considered to be the most dexterous end effectors in nature, there are numerous anthropomorphic hands in the field of research and industrial production. For example, the Stanford/JPL dexterous hand [1] was designed and analyzed by J. Salisbury et al., which drives three 3-DOF fingers from 12 DC motors, each of which can be independently stretched by an actuator. Designed by Kawasaki H. et al., the Gifu II hand [2] has 5 fingers. All joints are driven by servo motors and can manipulate objects like human hands. The Utah/MIT dexterous hand [3] is designed by S. Jacobsen et al., it has four 4 degree of freedom fingers, 32 independent tendons and 32 pneumatic cylinders [4], which can be used as a highly flexible tool to study the dexterity of the machine. A dexterous hand can do almost all the movements and gestures of a human hand. In fact, a dexterous hand requires an actuator to drive almost every degree of freedom,

© Springer Nature Switzerland AG 2019
H. Yu et al. (Eds.): ICIRA 2019, LNAI 11744, pp. 707–714, 2019.
https://doi.org/10.1007/978-3-030-27541-9_58

which makes the hand dependent on control high, and the manufacturing and use costs are high.

In contrast, underactuated hands use less motor to drive more degrees of freedom, while underactuated hands have a very surprising feature: self-adaptation during grip, making it easy to control. Many studies on underactuated hands: L. Birglen et al. [5–7] designed a variety of underactuated grippers and analyzed them. A. Dollar et al. [8, 9] presented an SDM robust robot gripper that uses an actuator to drive eight degrees of freedoms; L. Tan, et al. [10] designed a fluid-based implemented hydraulically actuated multi-finger hand, it has 14 degrees of freedom that can be bent when the pump applies hydraulic pressure. Liang Dazhao et al. proposed a parallel self-adaptive robotic hand, PASA hand [11]. Underactuated robot hands do not have complex sensors, algorithms, and control systems. However, the shortcoming of the underactuated robot hands is that the dexterity at the time of grabbing is relatively weak, and it is impossible to adapt the object well.

In order to make up for the above hand shortages, some flexible robotic hands have received extensive attention and research. Excellent examples are Pneumatic software hand [12], PneuNet grippers [13], RBO Hand 2 [14], and OS hands. Inspired by the bionics research on the fishtail propulsion movement, Festo developed the fishtail hand [15]. The fishtail hand adopts a special hollow flexible structure to independently carry out the choice of parallel clamping and centripetal gripping. In addition, Festo cooperated with Beijing University of Aeronautics and Astronautics to imitate the tentacles of octopus and jointly developed an octopus tentacle [16], which was first exhibited at the Hannover Industrial Exhibition in 2017. However, these hands still cannot perform the functions of the in-hand operation.

Therefore, combining the characteristics of underactuated hand and flexible hand, a double-source fluid bending and side-swing compound multi-joint robot finger device is proposed. The double fluid bending and side swing multi-joint finger can be forwardly bent for forward adaptive grasping, lateral adaptive grasping to the side, and grasping in different direction from left to right. The device has many degrees of freedom, is smart to grasp, and can be manipulated in the hand, and can be widely used in industrial fields.

2 Design of DFBS Finger

The double-fluid bending and side-swing compound (DFBS) finger (Fig. 1) designed in this paper includes a base, the 1st phalanx, the 2nd phalanx, the end phalanx, the 1st joint spring, the 2nd joint spring, the 3rd joint spring, the 1st fluid source (actuator), the 2nd fluid source (actuator), a left fluid route and a right fluid route.

Wherein, the 1st joint spring is connected to the base and the 1st phalanx, the 2nd joint spring is connected to the 1st and 2nd phalanx, and the 3rd joint spring is connected to the 2nd phalanx and the end phalanx, the left fluid route and the right fluid route extend through all joints. The springs are embedded outside the fluid passages to support two adjacent upper and lower finger phalanges. The 3rd spring is arranged forming an equilateral triangle with the 1st joint spring and the 2nd joint spring.

The idea of design: The bending and side-swing compound motion at the joint of the finger is realized by two independent fluid routes driven by double fluid source

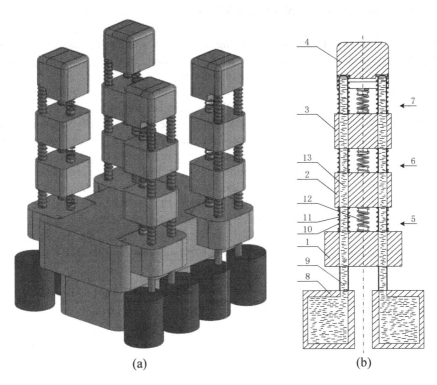

Fig. 1. Structure of the DFBS finger

(actuator). Left fluid route: including a left fluid source, a left hose, three balloons and three springs. Right fluid route is similar like the left fluid route.

1-base, 2, 3, 4-1st, 2nd, 3rd phalanx, 5, 6, 7-1st (proximal), 2nd (middle), 3rd (distal) joint, 8-fluid source (actuator), 9-fluid passage, 10-spring, 11-balloon, 12-spring.

The whole DFBS hand device consists of four DFBS fingers. The left and right sides of the fingers are axis-symmetrical. Two through holes are arranged on the base, the 1st phalanx, the 2nd phalanx and the 3rd phalanx. Two fluid passages run through the base, the 1st phalanx, the 2nd phalanx and the 3rd phalanx, and the liquid power of the left part and the right part are provided by the left fluid source and the right fluid source individually. The fluid source is filled with liquid, and a hydraulic pump is installed to provide upward hydraulic power.

The 1st (proximal), 2nd (middle) and 3rd (distal) joint are between the respective phalanges. Each joint is supported by three springs arranged in an equilateral triangle. Two of the springs are set on the periphery of the fluid passage, the third spring is set to support the other side of the joint.

3 Working Principle of DFBS Finger

The double-fluid bending and side-swing compound multi-joint finger has three grasping movement process categories: forward bending grasping, side-swing grasping, and bending and side-swing compound grasping.

The forward bending grasping is achieved by simultaneously elongating the equal length of the two fluid routes to achieve the forward bending of the finger.

The side-swinging grasping is achieved by the one fluid route not extending while the other side of the fluid route is elongated to realize the lateral gripping of the finger. The combined motion of the bending and side swing is achieved by the two fluid routes simultaneously elongating unequal lengths to achieve 180° grasping from left to right.

Let the left fluid route and the right fluid route have the original lengths L_1 and L_2. The amount of elongation of the left fluid route and the amount of elongation of the right fluid route are x_1 and x_2, respectively. When the grasping operation is performed, the first phalanx has a rotation angle of θ_1 with respect to the base; the second phalanx has a rotation angle of θ_2 with respect to the base; and the third phalanx rotates at an angle of θ_3 with respect to the base.

3.1 Forward Bending Grasping

When the finger is grasped forward, the left fluid drive mechanism elongation amount, the right fluid drive mechanism elongation amount x_1, x_2 are equal. The joint spring is subjected to a right component F_1 and a left component F_2 of the left fluid drive mechanism and the right fluid drive mechanism, and the two are equal, laterally balanced. The first joint spring, the second joint spring, the third joint spring are subjected to a forward component force f_1, f_2 of the left fluid drive mechanism and the right fluid drive mechanism, and the first joint spring, the second joint spring, and the third joint spring are bent forward, thus the finger realize forward grasping (Fig. 2).

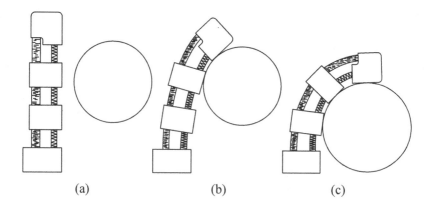

(a)   (b)   (c)

Fig. 2. Forward bending grasping process

3.2 Side-Swing Grasping

When the finger is grasping to the left: the left fluid drive mechanism elongation x_1 is equal to 0, the right fluid drive mechanism extension x_2 is large than 0, and the first joint spring, the second joint spring, and the third joint spring are subjected to the leftward force F_2 of the right fluid drive mechanism, the first joint spring, the second joint spring, and the third joint spring are bent to the left, and the finger is grasped to the left.

When the finger is grasping to the right: the right fluid drive mechanism is elongated as the quantity x_1 which is equal to 0, the left fluid drive mechanism elongation x_2 is equal large than 0, and the first joint spring, the second joint spring, and the third joint spring subjected to the rightward force F_1 of the left fluid drive mechanism. The first joint spring, the second joint spring and the third joint spring are bent to the right, and the fingers are grasped to the right (Fig. 3).

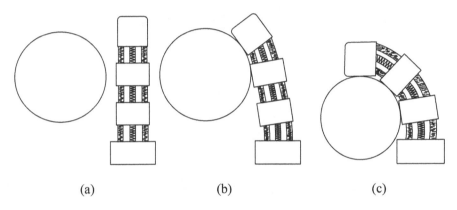

(a)   (b)   (c)

Fig. 3. Side-swing grasping process

3.3 Grasping from Left to Right Within 180°

When the finger is grasped within 180° from left to right, the left fluid drive mechanism elongation amount, the right fluid drive mechanism elongation amount x_1, x_2 are greater than 0, and the joint spring is subjected to the left fluid drive mechanism and the right fluid drive mechanism. The right component force F_1 and the left component force F_2 are equal, and the lateral force is balanced. The first joint spring, the second joint spring, and the third joint spring are forwarded by the left fluid drive mechanism and the right fluid drive mechanism with the component forces f_1, f_2. So the first joint spring, the second joint spring, and the third joint spring are bent forward, and the fingers are grasped forward.

4   Kinematic Analysis of DFBS Finger

All the rigid parts have very similar structure, so we can basically analyze the kinematics of one joint between two rigid parts.

Simplified connection diagram of the mechanism has been shown in Fig. 4, the two rigid parts connected with a flexible joint, and it's bending and torsion result in the change of the spatial location of second rigid part.

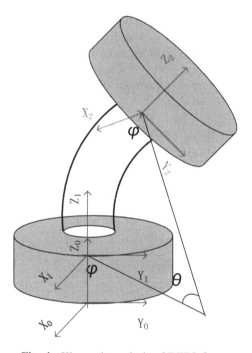

Fig. 4. Kinematic analysis of DFBS finger

Establish a base coordinate system $\{X_0, Y_0, Z_0\}$ and coordinate system $\{X_1, Y_1, Z_1\}$ on the bottom and top surfaces of the rigid body, and the height of the rigid body is h. Establish a coordinate system $\{X_2, Y_2, Z_2\}$ on the bottom of the second rigid body. Based on that, the angle of bending and the angle of deflection between the two rigid bodies can be represented by θ and φ.

The initial length of the flexible joint is L. Assume that during the bending of the soft body unit, the central axis of the flexible body joint is an arc of equal curvature and the length of the flexible joint keeps constant on the neutral axis. The spatial state between the two rigid bodies can be represented by the parameters θ and φ.

The position and orientation of the flexible joint's end relative to the base coordinate system can be represented by a homogeneous transformation matrix ${}^0_2T$ from the base coordinate system to the end coordinate system. According to the coordinate transformation relationship, the expression of ${}^0_2T$ is:

$$\frac{0}{2}T = \frac{0}{1}T\frac{1}{2}T \tag{1}$$

$\frac{0}{1}T$ is the homogeneous transformation matrix from the base coordinate system $\{X_0, Y_0, Z_0\}$ to the coordinate system $\{X_1, Y_1, Z_1\}$. $\frac{1}{2}T$ is the homogeneous transformation matrix from coordinate system $\{X_1, Y_1, Z_1\}$ to the coordinate system $\{X_2, Y_2, Z_2\}$. $\frac{0}{1}T$ is only relative to the dimension of the rigid part on the bottom, it can be represented as:

$$\frac{0}{1}T = \begin{bmatrix} 1 & 0 & 0 & 0 \\ 0 & 1 & 0 & 0 \\ 0 & 0 & 1 & h \\ 0 & 0 & 0 & 1 \end{bmatrix}$$

Drawing on the kinematics method proposed by Professor Walker, the expression of $\frac{1}{2}T$ can be obtained.

$$\frac{1}{2}T = rot(Z, \varphi)rot(Y, \frac{\theta}{2})trans(0, 0, L')rot(Y, \frac{\theta}{2})rot(Z, -\varphi)$$

L' is the chord length of the central axis of the flexible joint, also the linear distance between the two coordinate systems $\{X_1, Y_1, Z_1\}$ and $\{X_2, Y_2, Z_2\}$.

$$L' = \frac{2L}{\theta}\sin\frac{\theta}{2}$$

$$\frac{1}{2}T = \begin{bmatrix} 1 - c^2\varphi(1 - c\theta) & -s\varphi c\varphi(1 - c\theta) & c\varphi s\theta & \frac{L_0}{\theta}c\varphi(1 - c\theta) \\ -s\varphi c\varphi(1 - c\theta) & 1 - s^2\varphi(1 - c\theta) & s\varphi s\theta & \frac{L_0}{\theta}s\varphi(1 - c\theta) \\ -c\varphi s\theta & -s\varphi s\theta & c\theta & \frac{L_0}{\theta}s\theta \\ 0 & 0 & 0 & 1 \end{bmatrix}$$

$$\frac{0}{2}T = \frac{0}{1}T\frac{1}{2}T = \begin{bmatrix} 1 - c^2\varphi(1 - c\theta) & -s\varphi c\varphi(1 - c\theta) & c\varphi s\theta & \frac{L_0}{\theta}c\varphi(1 - c\theta) \\ -s\varphi c\varphi(1 - c\theta) & 1 - s^2\varphi(1 - c\theta) & s\varphi s\theta & \frac{L_0}{\theta}s\varphi(1 - c\theta) \\ -c\varphi s\theta & -s\varphi s\theta & c\theta & \frac{L_0}{\theta}s\theta + h \\ 0 & 0 & 0 & 1 \end{bmatrix}$$

5 Conclusion

This paper proposes a double-source fluid drive method: the double-source fluid drive realizes the multi-joint coupling bending, coupling side swing and bending and side swing compound motion of the finger. According to this, a double-source fluid bending and side-swing compound multi-joint robot finger (DFBS finger) was developed and it consists of two independent artificial fluid drive mechanisms that run through all joints and are driven by double source fluids, three finger segments and three joint springs. The force change assembly is mainly composed of a spring and an elastic rubber mold. The double source fluid bending and side swing composite multi-joint finger can be forwardly bent for forward adaptive grasping, lateral adaptive grasping to the side, and grasping in any direction of 180° from left to right. The theoretical analysis and experimental results show that the double-source fluid bending and the side-swing compound multi-joint fingers can realize the envelope grabbing for different shapes and sizes. Moreover, the grasping efficiency is high, the grasping force is sufficient and the stability is good.

References

1. Tuffield, P., Elias, H.: The Shadow robot mimics human actions. Ind. Robot Int. J. **30**(1), 55–60 (2003)
2. Kawasaki, H., Komatsu, T., Uchiyama, K., et al.: Dexterous anthropomorphic robot hand with distributed tactile sensor: Gifu hand II. In: IEEE International Conference on Systems, Man, and Cybernetics, Tokyo, Japan, October, pp. 782–787 (1999)
3. Liu, H., Meusel, P., Seitz, N.: The modular multisensory DLR-HIT-Hand. Mech. Mach. Theory **42**, 612–625 (2007)
4. Martin, T.B., Ambrose, R.O., Diftler, et al.: Tactile gloves for autonomous grasping with the NASA/DARPA Robonaut. In: IEEE International Conference on Robotics and Automation, New Orleans, LA, USA, May, pp. 1713–1718 (2004)
5. Dollar, M., Howe, R.D.: The SDM hand as a prosthetic terminal device: a feasibility study. In: IEEE International Conference on Rehabilitation Robotics, Noordwijk, Netherlands, June, pp. 978–983 (2007)
6. Chen, W., Xiong, C., Chen, W., et al.: Mechanical adaptability analysis of underactuated mechanisms. Robot. Comput. Integr. Manuf. **49**, 436–447 (2017)
7. Li, G., Zhang, C., Zhang, W., et al.: Coupled and self-adaptive under-actuated finger with a novel s-coupled and secondly self-adaptive mechanism. J. Mech. Robot. **6**, 1–10 (2014)
8. Birglen, L., Gosselin, C.M.: Kinetostatic analysis of underactuated fingers. IEEE Trans. Robot. Autom. **20**(2), 211–221 (2004)
9. Birglen, L., Gosselin, C.M.: Force analysis of connected differential mechanisms: application to grasping. Int. J. Robot. Res. **25**(10), 1033–1047 (2006)
10. Robotiq Inc., Saint-N: Gripper having a two degree of freedom underactuated mechanical finger for encompassing and pinch grasping. U.S. Pat. No. 8973958B2 (2012)
11. Liang, D., Zhang, W.: PASA-GB Hand: a novel parallel and self-adaptive robot hand with gear-belt mechanisms. J. Intell. Robot. Syst. **90**(1), 3–17 (2018)
12. Lessing, J., Knopf, R., Alcedo, K., et al.: Soft robotic grippers for cluttered grasping environments, high acceleration movements, food manipulation, and automated storage and retrieval systems: US, US20170203443A1 [P]
13. Ilievski, F., Mazzeo, A.D., Shepherd, R.F., et al.: Soft robotics for chemists. Angew. Chem. **123**(8), 1930–1935 (2011)
14. Deimel, R., Brock, O.: A novel type of compliant and underactuated robotic hand for dexterous grasping. Int. J. Robot. Res. **35**(1–3), 161–185 (2016)
15. Grzesiak, A., Becker, R., Verl, A.: The bionic handling assistant: a success story of additive manufacturing. Assembly Autom. **31**(4), 329–333 (2011)
16. OctopusGripper [EB/OL]. www.festo.com/bionics

Design and Simulation of a Miniature Jumping Gliding Robot on Water Surface

Jihong Yan[✉], Hongwei Yao, Kai Yang, Xin Zhang, and Jie Zhao

State Key Laboratory of Robotics and System, Harbin Institute of Technology,
Harbin 150001, Heilongjiang, China
jhyan@hit.edu.cn, 17S008075@stu.hit.edu.cn

Abstract. The water surface jumping robot is limited by the complexity of its movement, and has the problems of low efficiency, insufficient jump height, poor stability, and even easy to sink. Therefore, based on the maximization of effective energy, a new type of robot with water surface jumping and low altitude gliding is proposed. The force model of robot water surface jumping and gliding motion is established. The influences of take-off angles, spring stiffness and spring combination types on the robot performance are analyzed, and the robot gliding wings, jumping mechanism and support system are optimized. The performance of the designing mechanism was verified by robotic water surface jumping and gliding dynamics simulation with different parameters.

Keywords: Miniature robot · Water surface jumping · Gliding ·
Dynamics simulation

1 Introduction

In recent years, researchers are widely attracted by miniature robots because of the good concealed performance, maneuverability and environmental adaptability. The structure of miniature jumping robot was optimized by mimicking the jumping process of creature. Kovač et al. [1] designed a 7 g and 5 cm size robot which could jump over obstacles more than 27 times its own size. Jianguo Zhao et al. [2, 3] designed miniature robots that can self-right to leap over obstacles, and wheel on flat ground. many other jumping robots have been developed [4–6]. However, the jumping robot has a large impulse when it falls, which increases the difficulty of control. Water surface motion robot stands on the water surface by surface tension or buoyancy, and it relies on the swing of the driving legs to achieve high-speed sliding or jumping on water surface. Fei et al. [7] designed a 12.5 g miniature robot which can jump 9.5 cm in height on the water surface. Je-Sung Koh et al. [8] designed a robot with a mass of 68 mg which can jump efficiently and flexibility without puncturing the water. Similar robots have been recently developed [9, 10]. However, the water surface motion robot has weak anti-interference ability and load capacity. Gliding generally assists in jumping motion,

Research supported by Natural Science Foundation of China (NSFC, Grant 51775133) and National Defense Science and Technology Innovation Special Zone Project.

© Springer Nature Switzerland AG 2019
H. Yu et al. (Eds.): ICIRA 2019, LNAI 11744, pp. 715–725, 2019.
https://doi.org/10.1007/978-3-030-27541-9_59

which can reduce the impulse of the robot when it falls. It improves the stability of the robot during the gliding process, and increases the jumping distance. Woodward et al. [11] integrated the jumping and gliding motion of the robot into one component which can reduce the weight of the robot. Similar robots have been developed [12–14].

Based on the limitations of single motion mode of the robot, this paper proposes a miniature surface jumping gliding robot, which can adapt to the water and air. It has the ability to float on the water surface, continuous jumping, near-surface gliding and stable landing, the scale is small but the movement space is large. The robot consists of gliding wings, driving system, six-link jumping mechanism, and supporting mechanism. The driving system drives the six-link jumping mechanism to realize the motion of the robot. The gliding wings play a role in extending the stagnation time and balancing the robot. The support mechanism ensures stable floating and water-surface jumping of the robot under the condition that the mass is as small as possible.

In this paper, the force of the robot was analyzed firstly, and the force model including the gliding process, the energy storage process of the six-link jumping mechanism and the water surface jumping process was established. Then the structure of the robot gliding wings, the driving system, the jumping mechanism and the water surface supporting component was designed, and the related structure parameters were analyzed and optimized. Finally, the dynamic simulation of different jumping modes and take-off angles was analyzed to verify the jumping gliding motion of the robot.

2 Force Analysis of the Robot

2.1 Robot Water Surface Jumping Motion

(1) **Force Analysis of the Jumping Mechanism.** Considering the complexity of multi-link force [6], this paper adopts a six-link mechanism with good symmetry and stability. The parameters are shown in Fig. 1.

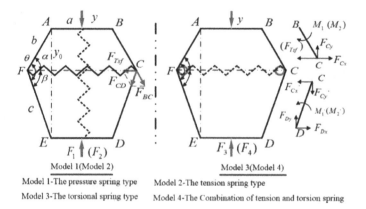

Fig. 1. Force analysis of four six-link jumping mechanisms

Assume that the springs modulus of elasticity is k_i, the stored energy is E_i, the force of the jump mechanism is F_i, the tension spring force is F_{Tsf}, the moment of torsion springs is M_i, the initial distance between AB and ED is y_0, the distance of relative motion is y, the total distance of motion is Δy, the distance between F point and C point is l. Then the relevant calculation is shown in Table 1.

Table 1. Four six-link jumping mechanism forces and energy storage expression

Spring types	Force	Stored energy
Model 1	$F_1 = k_1 y$	$E_1 = \frac{1}{2} k_1 \Delta y^2$
Model 2	$F_2 = 2k_2 \left(l - l_{y=0}\right) \frac{\sin \alpha}{\sin \theta} \sin \beta$	$E_2 = \frac{1}{2} k_2 \left(l_{y=\Delta y} - l_{y=0}\right)^2$
Model 3	$F_3 = \frac{2M_1 (b \sin \alpha + c \sin \beta)}{bc \sin \theta}$	$E_3 = k_3 \left(\theta_{y=0} - \theta_{y=\Delta y}\right)^2$
Model 4	$F_4 = \frac{2M_2(b \sin \alpha + c \sin \beta) + 2F_{Tsf} bc \sin \alpha \sin \beta}{bc \sin \theta}$	$E_4 = \frac{1}{2} k_4 \left(l_{y=\Delta y} - l_{y=0}\right)^2 + k_5 \left(\theta_{y=0} - \theta_{y=\Delta y}\right)^2$

(2) **Force Analysis of Robot Water Surface Jumping Motion.** The robot water surface jump process is shown in Fig. 2 and is divided into four steps. First the robot is stationary on the water surface and completes energy storage. In this case, the robot's force on the water surface is always its own gravity

$$F_f + F_r = (m_1 + m_2)g \tag{1}$$

Then the spring is released, the top and bottom masses are subjected to force analysis

$$\begin{cases} v_1 = \sum_{i=1}^{n} \frac{F_{sfi} - m_1 g}{m_1} \Delta t \\ h_{wj1} = \sum_{j=1}^{n} \left(\Delta t \sum_{i=1}^{j} \frac{F_{sfi} - m_1 g}{m_1} \Delta t\right) \end{cases} \tag{2}$$

$$\begin{cases} v_2 = \sum_{i=1}^{n} \frac{F_{sfi} + m_2 g - F_{fi} - F_{ri} - F_{di}}{m_2} \Delta t \\ h_{wj2} = \sum_{j=1}^{n} \left(\Delta t \sum_{i=1}^{j} \frac{F_{sfi} + m_2 g - F_{fi} - F_{ri} - F_{di}}{m_2} \Delta t\right) \end{cases} \tag{3}$$

Using the momentum theorem $v_{30} = \frac{m_1 v_1 - m_2 v_2}{m_1 + m_2}$

After the spring is completely released, the robot moves up to the water surface as a whole, and the whole robot is subjected to force analysis.

$$v_{40} = v_{30} - \sum_{i=1}^{n} \frac{(m_1 + m_2)g - F_{fi} - F_{ri}}{m_1 + m_2} \Delta t \tag{4}$$

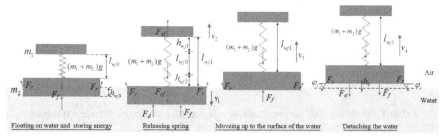

Illustration: h_{wj1} h_{wj2} indicate the movement displacement of the top and bottom masses when the spring is released, $h_{wj1} + h_{wj2} = \Delta y$, l_{wj0} l_{wj1} indicate the length of the spring after compression and the initial length of the spring, F_{sf} indicates the force of the six-link jumping mechanism, F_f F_r F_d indicate buoyancy, surface tension and hydrodynamic pressure, other parameters are shown in the figure above.

Fig. 2. Analysis of robot water surface jumping process

When the robot is out of the water surface, part of the water will be taken out due to the surface tension.

$$\begin{cases} v = v_{40} - \sum_{i=1}^{n} \frac{(m_1 + m_2)g + F_{fi} + F_{di} + F_{ri}}{m_1 + m_2} \Delta t \\ h_c = \sum_{j=1}^{n} \left(\Delta t \left(v_{40} - \sum_{i=1}^{j} \frac{(m_1 + m_2)g + F_{fi} + F_{di} + F_{ri}}{m_1 + m_2} \Delta t \right) \right) \end{cases} \quad (5)$$

Therefore, the efficiency of the robot jumping on the water surface can be obtained.

$$\eta = \left[\frac{(m_1 + m_2)v^2}{2} + (m_1 + m_2)gh_c \right] / E_{Total} \quad (6)$$

Which h_c is the height of the liquid level of the robot carrying, E_{Total} is the total energy stored by the six-link jumping mechanism.

2.2 Robot Gliding Motion

The gliding wings can make the robot jump more smoothly and increase the jumping distance. The robot jumping gliding motion can be divided into the ascending phase OA, the transition phase AG and the gliding phase GB. Figure 3 is a schematic diagram of the robot jumping gliding motion. According to the aerodynamics related theory, the air lift and resistance formula of the robot gliding.

$$L = \frac{1}{2} C_L \rho_{air} SV^2, D = \frac{1}{2} C_D \rho_{air} SV^2, C_D = C_{D0} + \delta C_L^2 \quad (7)$$

The horizontal distance formula of the robot jumping and gliding.

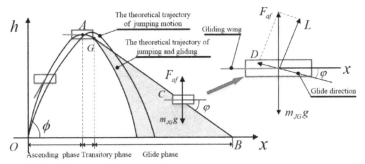

Illustration: m_{JG} ϕ φ indicate the total mass of the robot, the angle of take-off, and the angle of attack of the gliding motion, L D F_{af} indicate air lift, air resistance and resultant force.

Fig. 3. Schematic diagram of the robot jumping gliding motion

$$\begin{cases} x = \dfrac{V_0^2 \sin \phi \cos \phi}{g} + \dfrac{2V_{yG}V_0 \cos \phi}{3g} + \dfrac{V_0^3 \cos \phi \sin^2 \phi}{2gV_{yG}} \\ V_{yG} = 2\sqrt{\dfrac{m_{JG}g}{\rho_{air}S}}(4\delta^3 C_{D0})^{\frac{1}{4}} \end{cases} \tag{8}$$

Trajectory equations of robot jumping and gliding.

$$\begin{cases} h_1 = x \tan \phi - \dfrac{x^2 \tan \phi}{4Q}(x < x_1) \\ h_2 = Q \tan \phi + \dfrac{g^2}{12V_{yG} \cos^3 \phi}\left(\dfrac{m_{JG}}{2E_0}\right)^{\frac{3}{2}}(x - 2Q)^3 - \dfrac{\tan \phi}{4Q}(x - 2Q)^2(x_1 < x < x_1 + x_2) \\ h_3 = Q \tan \phi - \dfrac{4V_{yG}^2}{3g} - \dfrac{V_{yG}}{V_0 \cos \phi}\left(x - 2Q - \dfrac{2V_{yG}V_0 \cos \phi}{g}\right)(x_1 + x_2 < x < x_1 + x_2 + x_3) \end{cases} \tag{9}$$

$Q = \frac{E_0 \sin \phi \cos \phi}{m_{JG}g}$, $h_1 h_2 h_3 x_1 x_2 x_3$ is the vertical height and horizontal distance of the robot's three-stage motion, $E_0 V_0 V_{yG}$ indicate the robot's effective energy, initial velocity, and vertical velocity at point G. $\rho_{air}S$ indicate air density at standard atmospheric pressure, gliding wings area. $C_L C_D C_{D0} \delta$ indicate lift coefficient, drag coefficient, zero-lift drag coefficient, and lift-in resistance factor.

3   Robot Design

The overall structure of the robot mainly includes four parts: the gliding wings, the driving system, the six-link jumping mechanism and the water surface supporting component. The gliding wings realize the passive gliding motion of the robot near the water surface, and the six-link jumping mechanism is used as the energy storage component of the robot jumping motion. The water surface support system realizes stable floating and water surface jumping of the robot, and the driving system provides driving force and realizes the motion control of the robot (Fig. 4).

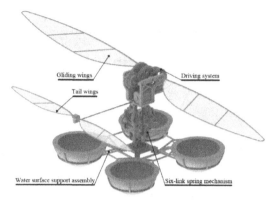

Fig. 4. Robot structural design

The robot is processed by high-precision 3D printing technology. The gliding wings are made of PET film. The bearings are installed at the rotating joints. The important parts use a lot of flanging and reinforcement to increase the strength. The reduction ratio of the gear reduction mechanism is 5320, and the final stage is the incomplete gear and the roller. The jumping mechanism is composed of a six-link, torsion springs, tension springs and guide rods. The front and rear sides are symmetrically arranged. The center of mass of the robot passes through the plane of the symmetry line, and the moving part of the guide rods are kept lubricated to reduce the frictional resistance. The output force of the driving system acts on the lower part of the six-link by the pull-up rope on the roller, to realize energy storage and release of the jumping mechanism. The water surface supporting component is composed of four evenly distributed support legs, support base and direction adjustment member. The support legs are made of high-density EPS foam board (ball), and the support base adopts truss structure, and is connected with the direction adjustment member through the positioning pin. In order to reduce the resistance of the robot when it leaves the water surface, the surface of the legs is treated with hydrophobic material (Fig. 5).

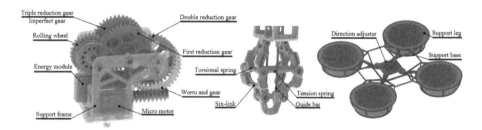

Fig. 5. Drive system, jump mechanism, support legs structure design

4   Robot Parameter Optimization

4.1   Gliding Wing and Take-Off Angle

Taking the maximum horizontal distance of the robot gliding as the optimization target, the Eq. (8) is the objective function, the parameters including the gliding wing's aspect ratio λ, area S and robot's take-off angle ϕ are optimized. The qualifications are as follows

$$\begin{cases} 10° \le \phi \le 80°, 4000\,\text{mm}^2 \le S \le 16000\,\text{mm}^2 \\ 2 \le \lambda \le 30, \ m_{JG0} = 24\,\text{g}, E_0 = 0.2\,\text{J} \end{cases} \tag{10}$$

m_{JG0} means that the robot quality is not included in the gliding wing, the optimization results are shown in Fig. 6.

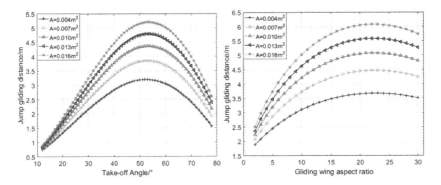

Fig. 6. Optimization analysis of gliding wing area, aspect ratio and take-off angle parameters

The gliding distance of the robot increases with the increase of the area of the gliding wing, and increases first and then decreases with the increase of the aspect ratio and the take-off angle. Limited by the overall size of the robot and the stiffness of the

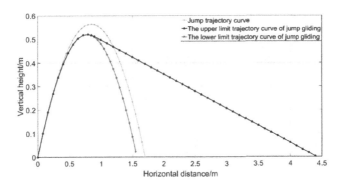

Fig. 7. Robot jumping gliding trajectory curves

gliding wings, the aspect ratio is 11, the area is 10000 square millimeter, the best take-off angle of the robot is 53^0. The Fig. 7 is the theoretical trajectory curve of robot jumping and gliding motion.

4.2 Six-Bar Jumping Mechanism

Taking the maximum effective energy of the six-link jumping mechanism as the optimization target, the parameters including the six-bar linkage geometry and spring stiffness are optimized. The qualifications are as follows

$$\begin{cases} 0.1\,\text{N/mm} \leq k_1/k_2/k_4 \leq 6\,\text{N/mm}, \ 1\,\text{N.mm}/(^0) \leq k_3/k_5 \leq 8\,\text{N.mm}/(^0) \\ m_1 \leq 15.5\,\text{g}, \ m_2 \leq 8.5\,\text{g}, \ 26\,\text{mm} \leq y_0 \leq 34\,\text{mm} \\ 12\,\text{mm} \leq b/c \leq 24\,\text{mm}, \ \Delta y = 16\,\text{mm}, F_{\max} \leq 55\,\text{N} \end{cases} \tag{11}$$

Then the spring stiffness, the six-link geometry (mm) and the total energy input $E_{Total}(J)$, the effective energy of the land jump $E_{Le}(J)$, and the effective energy of the water surface jump $E_{We}(J)$ in the four spring combinations are shown in Table 2.

Table 2. Six-link jumping mechanism parameter optimization results

Spring types	k_i	a	b	c	h	E_{Total}	E_{Le}	E_{We}
Mode 1	3.4	—	—	—	—	0.435	0.280	0.096
Mode 2	3.4	12	16	18	33	0.755	0.486	0.151
Mode 3	4.2	12	16	17	32	0.645	0.415	0.135
Mode 4	1.8	2.5	12	17	18 34	0.781	0.503	0.160

The force change of the four-mode for six-link jumping mechanism is shown in Fig. 8.

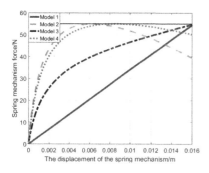

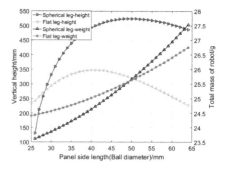

Fig. 8. The force of six-link jumping mechanism

Fig. 9. Optimization of robot support legs

4.3 Supporting Legs

Taking the maximum jumping height of the robot as the optimization target, the foam board (ball) side length (diameter) is used as the optimization parameter, and the robot water surface jumping force model is taken as the objective function, the qualifications are $25\,\text{mm} \leq L_f(D_f) \leq 65\,\text{mm}$. Then the optimization result is shown in Fig. 9.

When the size of the support legs changes, the weight of the robot and the drag of the water will change, which will affect the jump height of the robot. When the spherical support leg is out of the water surface, the drag resistance is negligible, and the diameter is 50 mm, the robot jump height is up to 525 mm. The flat support leg has a great influence on the drag resistance when it is out of the water surface, and the side length is 40 mm, the robot jump height is 350 mm at the maximum.

5 Robot Dynamics Simulation

In order to clarify the jumping performance of the robot, this section establishes the dynamic model of the robot by ADAMS dynamic analysis software. The supporting forces of the robot include hydrodynamic pressure, buoyancy and surface tension. When the vertical velocity of the robot increases to V_{yG} during the falling process, the robot will be subjected to a pneumatic resultant force opposite to the gravity, which will make the robot enter the gliding stage at the next moment. By changing the motion modes and take-off angles of the robot on the water surface, the jumping and gliding process of the robot on the water surface is analyzed. The simulation results are shown in Fig. 10.

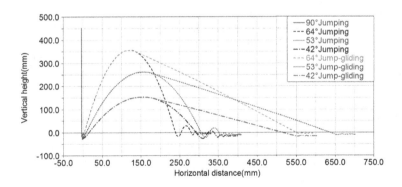

Fig. 10. Dynamic simulation of robot water surface jumping gliding

It can be seen from the figure that the vertical jump height of the robot is 452 mm. By comparing the two modes of water surface movement with different jump angles, the horizontal distance of the robot jumping gliding motion is obviously better than that of the jump motion, and reaches the maximum when the jump angle is about 53°, which is consistent with the theoretical optimization results. In addition, when the robot moves in jump mode, its falling impulse is large and its stability is poor. In contrast, in the jumping gliding mode, the falling impulse is smaller and the rebalancing time is shorter, the stability is obviously improved.

6 Conclusions

This paper designs a miniature water surface jumping gliding robot. A six-link energy storage mechanism was designed to maximize effective energy. The four stages of energy storage, release, overall movement of the robot to the surface of the water and disengage from the water surface are analyzed. Then optimized the parameters of the supporting structure and the gliding wing, and analyzed the influence of the angle of attack and the lift-drag ratio of the gliding process on the gliding trajectory. The results show that the combined of tension and torsion spring jumping mechanism has a maximum effective energy of 0.160 J. The effect of supporting sphere is significantly better than that of the supporting plate, and the robot has the largest horizontal distance when jumping angle is 53°. The gliding wing has an aspect ratio of 11, and the area is 10000 square millimeters. Finally, Simulation analysis based on ADAMS dynamics shows that the maximum height of the robot jump is 452 mm, and the horizontal distance of the jump-gliding motion is obviously better than the jump motion. When the take-off angle is 53°, it has the largest horizontal movement distance of 630 mm, which is close to the theoretical analysis. In the following research, we will make a robot prototype and carry out water surface jumping gliding experiments to verify the established model.

References

1. Mirko, K., Martin, F., Andre, G., et al.: A miniature 7g jumping robot. In: IEEE International Conference on Robotics and Automation (2008)
2. Jianguo, Z., Ning, X., Bingtuan, G., et al.: Development of a controllable and continuous jumping robot. In: IEEE International Conference on Robotics and Automation (2011)
3. Jianguo, Z., Tianyu, Z., et al.: MSU tailbot: controlling aerial maneuver of a miniature-tailed jumping robot. IEEE/ASME Trans. Mechatron. **20**, 2903–2914 (2015)
4. Tran, L.K.: Design, implementation and analysis of 3D printed grasshopper robot for jumping mechanism. J. Biomim. Biomater. Biomed. Eng. **28**, 1–13 (2016)
5. Gwang-Pil, J., Carlos, S.C., et al.: An integrated jumping-crawling robot using height-adjustable jumping module. In: IEEE International Conference on Robotics and Automation (2016)
6. Plecnik, M.M., Haldane, D.W., et al.: Design exploration and kinematic tuning of a power modulating jumping monopod. J. Mech. Robot. **9**(1), 011009 (2017)
7. Fei, J., Jianguo, Z., et al.: A miniature water surface jumping robot. IEEE Robot. Autom. Lett. **2**(3), 1272–1279 (2017)
8. Je-Sung, K., Eunjin, Y., Gwang-Pil, J., et al.: Jumping on water: surface tension-dominated jumping of water striders and robotic insects. Science **349**(6247), 517–521 (2015)
9. Xinbin, Z., Jie, Z.: Bio-inspired aquatic microrobot capable of walking on water surface like a water strider. ACS Appl. Mater. Interfaces. **3**, 2630–2636 (2011)

10. Jihong, Y., Tao, W., Xinbin, Z.: Structural design and dynamic analysis of biologically inspired water-jumping robot. In: IEEE International Conference on Information and Automation (ICIA) (2014)
11. Matthew, A.W., et al.: Design of a miniature integrated multi-modal jumping and gliding robot. In: International Conference on Intelligent Robots and Systems, pp. 25–30, September 2011
12. Vidyasagar, A., Jean-Christohphe, Z., et al.: Performance analysis of jump-gliding locomotion for miniature robotics. Bioinspiration Biomim. **10**(2), 025006 (2015)
13. Mirko, K., Wassim-H., Oriol, F., et al.: The EPFL jumpglider: a hybrid jumping and gliding robot with rigid or folding wings. In: IEEE International Conference on Robotics and Biomimetics, pp. 1503–1508 (2011)
14. Alexis, L.D., Morgan, T.P., et al.: Design principles for efficient, repeated jump-gliding. Bioinspiration Biomim. **9**(2), 025009 (2014)

Towards Intelligent Maintenance of Thermal Power Plants: A Novel Robot for Checking Water Wall Tube

Jun Yang[1], Hongwei Wang[1(✉)], Jian Zhang[2], and Xianming Zhou[2]

[1] Huadian Electric Power Research Institute Co. Ltd., Hangzhou, China
{jun-yang,hongwei-wang}@chder.com
[2] Zhejiang University of Technology, Hangzhou, China
1561912293@qq.com, 925797670@qq.com

Abstract. Intelligent operation and maintenance of thermal power plants enabled by advanced robotics and data analysis is an emerging field for reducing cost and increasing efficiency in their daily maintenance. In particular, the water wall is one of the vital units which are highly complex and work under very tough condition. Therefore, the intelligent operation of this kind of units faces great challenges. To move towards intelligent operation and maintenance for thermal power plants, this research puts forward a kind of intelligent inspection robot which possess unique superiority in terms of both system architecture and system application.

Specifically, to achieve increased safety and reliability and reduced cost in water wall inspection. An intelligent inspection robot was developed, which combines robot technology, non-destructive testing technology, machine vision technology and data analysis techniques. The developed inspection robot can climb on the water wall surface vertically as well as being able to move horizontally. In addition, the robot can also avoid obstacles through a combination of computer vision and ultrasonic technologies. In terms of tube inspection, the robot can obtain various parameters by means of ultrasonic testing and visual inspection. Data obtained can be sent to the central console for processing and analysis through wireless transmission. Testing work has been done in a power plant and the results obtained have shown that this kind of new intelligent inspection technologies have great potential in the intelligent operation and maintenance of thermal power plants.

Keywords: Intelligent operation and maintenance · Water wall · Inspection robot · Multi-points checking

1 Introduction

1.1 Background

In the thermal power generation industry, the capacity of units keeps growing and their complexity keeps increasing. As such, the equipment maintenance work is getting increasingly complicated and essential. Boiler Water Wall (BWW) is a collection of steel tube which have a working condition of very high temperature and pressure over a

© Springer Nature Switzerland AG 2019
H. Yu et al. (Eds.): ICIRA 2019, LNAI 11744, pp. 726–737, 2019.
https://doi.org/10.1007/978-3-030-27541-9_60

long period of time. In this case, there is a risk for brittle failure, degradation, cracking and endurance fracture. Some examples of BWW failure are showed in Fig. 1(a). It is thus necessary and important to do the periodic maintenance work.

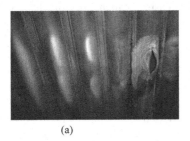 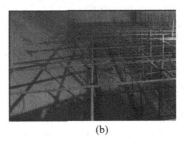

(a)   (b)

Fig. 1. BWW failure and scaffold built

In traditional methods, the inspection and cleaning work on BWW is mostly operated by manual labour which usually involves scaffolding at the first instance, as showed in the Fig. 1(b). And then,the operators use handhold gauge to inspect the tube one by one. The construction process within a boiler generally takes more than one week and costs over 100,000 USD to build.

However, due to the large number of water wall tubes and the great height of the work place, there exist certain problems to rely only on manual labour, including waste, inefficiency, diseconomy and long cycle. Furthermore, it has great risk for human beings to work in the higher and polluted working conditions. Moreover, the cleaning effect and the inspection results are often not satisfactory [1]. As a consequence, it generates enormous economic benefit to reduce scaffolding and eliminate unnecessary working time. In addition, the benefit in increasing health and safety in work has been increasingly valued in the past few years, which evidences the significance of doing work into automatic checking of BWWs.

It is highly difficult for the traditional machinery and equipment to be applied in complex working environments such as that in power plants boilers, due to their weakness in flexibility and data processing capability. It is thus quite urgent for power generation enterprises to develop inspection robots, which can adapt to varied and tough working environments and enable smart data collection, transmission and analysis [2].

1.2   Related Work

To develop a viable and economic solution for this intelligent inspection robot, there are some critical site conditions that need to be fully considered. First, it is the large area of BWWs. Generally, working boilers are about eighty metres tall and the over-haul period of a BWW is only a few days. This requires the inspection robot to be able to 'walk' along and across tubes as well as to inspect tube conditions with good efficacy and accuracy.

Second, due to the rough and uneven surface of a BWW, a solution is needed for keeping the robot staying on the BWW and climb on the BWW surface. Magnetic absorption is a common way of achieving this – however, the use of magnetic blocks unfortunately incurs additional weight for the robot. Moreover, the inner space of a boiler involves considerable amount of dusts and ashes, which, unfortunately, also pose great challenges to the checking process [3].

Intelligent inspection robots have studied for a long time by both academics and practioners, and there are already many influential and famous intelligent robot companies, such as ABB robotics from Sweden, GE from America, and KUKA Robot from Germany [4]. Their robot products have been widely used in equipment defect inspecting and health management. Additionally, there also exist great interests in academia in robots with novel and unique functions in climbing or inspecting. For instance, Kim developed a crawler-type robot equipped with vacuum chuck, to enhance the robot adsorption capacity [5], Inoue has developed a biomimetic multiped wall-climbing robot, it can imitate the spider to overstride the obstruction [6], and Ozgur developed a caterpillar track robot based on the bonding elastomer which can protect against impact and vibration [7].

Although the research of the intelligent robot has already been undertaken in a number of fields, it is still at a very early stage. First, there are only a few companies specializing in development of the intelligent inspection robot. Second, it is still a long way to balance the manufacturing cost and actual profits. Third, due to the strong environmental disturbance and the tight schedule in power plants, there are still many technical difficulties that need to be solved.

In this research, to address the challenge of a tight schedule, a new kind of robot is developed, which has the particular function of all-round walking on the BWW surface as well as multi-points checking in one position on tube. In this way, the detection efficiency can be nearly doubled, and, more importantly, the detection precision can also be ensured. It not only shortens the maintenance cycle and improves the maintenance efficiency, but also improves the quality of operations and ensures the safety of operations. In conclusion, the application of the robot can offer a solution to meet the urgent needs of power generation enterprises as an important part of a new generation of intelligent operation and maintenance systems.

2 Robot Design

2.1 Overall Design

The inspection robot needs to adsorb and move on the BWW surface in all position and direction while making spot checking all the way. The thickness data obtained by the ultrasonic thickness gauge and images filmed by the camera need be sent to the user through wireless communication in real time. In addition, the data collected also need be stored. Figure 2 illustrates the working process of the robot, which helps to identify the main functions of the robot.

In order to ensure a complete and stable inspecting process, a novel structure design has been created for the robot. Specifically, the robot body is composed by the straight-

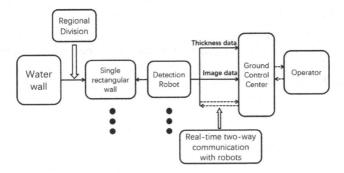

Fig. 2. The overall process of the robot

walking part, the sidesway-walking part, the magnetic adsorption part, the inspecting part and the images collection part.

In the straight-walking part, the robot is driven by four wheels with flanges-edges. Each wheel has a mounting flange which enables the robot to be attached to the BWW tubes. It also enables the robot to walk straight along the tube and prevents sideslips from happening. In the sidesway-walking part, the movement is enabled by two tracks. Specifically, these two tracks have the lifting function which can support the robot body away from the tube surface. In the magnetic adsorption part, the non-contact adsorption mechanism is applied and the magnet devices can be adjusted freely up and down. The adsorption force is adjusted by changing the distance between magnet and BWW. In the inspecting system, there is a four-direction moving probe, which achieves inspecting the four tubes one by one in a single time. In the images collection system, a holder is designed to hold a camera, which has two degrees of freedom. By moving the holder, the robot can file and collect the surrounding tubes conditions. The 3D model of the robot body is shown in Fig. 3.

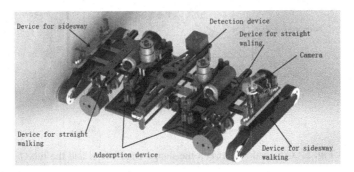

Fig. 3. The robot body structure

2.2   Walking System

2.2.1   Straight-Walking System

A straight-walking device is designed to enable the robot to walk forwards and backwards on the BWW surface. It has four driving wheel with flange-edges and two drive motors. Each drive motor will drive two coaxial wheels, and the belt-driven is applied between the drive motor and the axle. The structure of this subsystem is shown in Fig. 4.

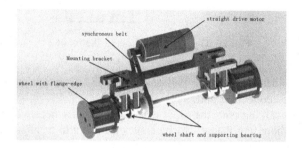

Fig. 4. Structure of the straight walking system

Wheels with the flange-rang are used to enable the robot to walk along the tube, which can also realize the function of fixation and navigation. Especially, a certain amount of space is remained (about 20% of the tube width) - this is reserved for the installation error, as shown in Fig. 5

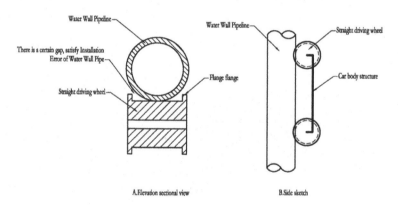

Fig. 5. Connection between the flange-edge wheel and the tube

2.2.2   The Sidesway-Walking System

In the sidesway-walking system, there are two sets of crawlers traveling device installed at the either end of the robot. This design enables the robot to realize sidesway-walking, as shown in Fig. 6(a).

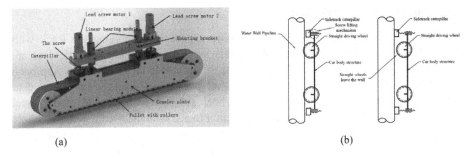

(a)   (b)

Fig. 6. The sidesway-walking devices

Since the crawler traveling mechanism is applied in the sidesway-walking system, there is a roller set beneath the crawler. The lifting function is of critical importance as it realizes the switch be between the straight-walking mode and the sidesway-walking mode. As showed in Fig. 6(b), when the two-motor screw synchronously rotate, the driving band will make the four wheels of the straight-walking devices to move away from the tube surface. And simultaneously, the crawler attachment will contact the tube surface to realize the sidesway-walking function. During the whole process, the robot body is guaranteed to be absorbed on the tube by appropriate magnetic force.

In this approach, the robot could make lateral movement, which is totally from other related academic research. So far, any other known robot might have good design in adsorbing or inspecting, but the robot body has to go along with each tube for up and down. It means that after inspecting one tube, the robot has to return to the operator for tube changing by manual work, and this will make a lot of extra work and take too much time. But in this research, it is the sidesway-walking function that could realize the function of moving to other tubes directly rather than back along the previous path. The process the robot movement locus has been showed in Fig. 7.

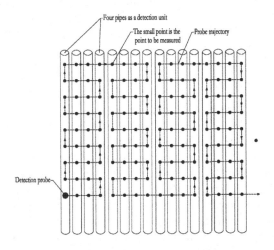

Fig. 7. Process of robot movement locus

2.3 The Magnetic Adsorption System

In other research, the most common adsorbing approach is applying the track with magnet blocks as introduce by Liu [8]. In this way, the robot adsorbing devices are directly contact with the tube surface. In contrast, the non-contact adsorbing approach is applied in this inspecting robot. The magnet part is designed as an independent device, rather than be a part of the moving wheel. As showed in the Fig. 8, the novel adsorbing device has ten specified size magnetic blocks, which are arranged as a whole plane. In particular, the blocks are with positive and negative in turns. This arrangement mode could produce a stronger adsorption capacity than an entire homopolar magnet block significantly.

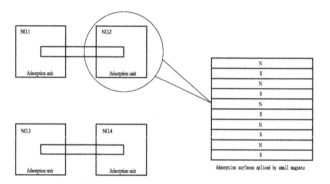

Fig. 8. The arranged magnets

In the whole robot, totally four adsorbing devices are designed to place around the robot symmetrically. The single adsorbing devices is showed in the Fig. 9. The model switch function is mainly implemented by the co-rotating from the upper motor and the lower lifting unit, which are driven by, the band and the screw humorous. Besides, the adsorbing strength can be changed by adjusting the distance between the surface and the magnet block. But during the model switch period, the adsorbing strength should better remain stable.

2.4 The Inspecting System

The inspecting device is the implementing mechanism, which is the core component in the whole inspection robot. It is installed in the middle position of the whole body. In this research, the ultrasonic inspection and measurement is applied. Furthermore, because the robot has played the role of carrying platform, more varieties of inspecting devices could be integrated based on the different inspecting requirements or working conditions. The Fig. 10 shows the structure of the inspecting device.

In this structure, the specially designed probe has two degree of freedom. During the test, it will firstly move to right above the tested tube and then descend to its surface. The flexible drive structure is applied in the driving device for effectively adsorbing the impact impulse when the probe comes into contact with the tube. And

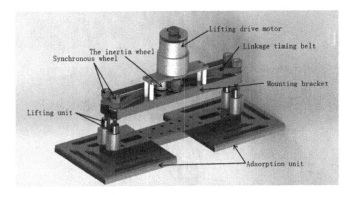

Fig. 9. The adsorption device

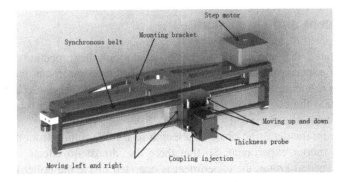

Fig. 10. The structure of the inspect system

also, this can improve the detection accuracy by coupling the probe with the BWWs surface. What's more important, as showed in the Fig. 7. Because the probe could move round with the belt, it means that when the robot stays fixed in one position, multiple tubes could be detected by just moving the probe. In this way, the inspecting efficiency has been raised.

2.5 The Images Collection System

The images collection device is installed in the front-end of the inspection robot. It can help the operators to make real-time judgement by filming the BWW surface condition. The filmed images or videos will be sent to the control terminal and stored in devices, using for the postmortem analysis. The images collection device is in consist of two parts, as showed in the Fig. 11, which respectively are the wide angle of the camera and the holder with two degree of freedom. The holder will be driven by two steering engines. The operator in the back-end can control the holder's direction for collecting surrounding tubes conditions.

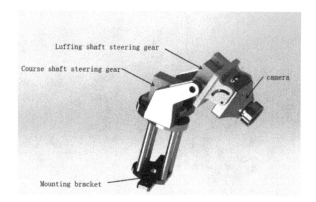

Fig. 11. The body structure of the images collection system

3   Experiment and Discussion

To verify the rationality and validity of the designed robot, the inspecting results for the two groups of experiment are showed and analysed. For comparison, the tube actual thickness data is measured by handhold gauge at first. And then the robot inspect is applied to obtain the contrasting data. to verify the feasibility of the robot., there are totally two groups of experiment.

In first group, the detection object is a length of BWW, cutting from the boiler and the test is an indoor experiment. So that there are almost no effects from the surroundings. In second group, the experiment is operated inside the boiler in one power plant. In industrial environment, the complicated field surrounding will bring lots of interference to recognize the characters exactly.

3.1   Laboratory Experiment

In group 1, by using the approach introduced earlier, the thickness data of 16 points among four tubes are showed in the Fig. 12(a). To begin with, the robot is applied to walk on the tube surface and a set of measuring data is obtained.

The data obtained by the robot and by the labour are respective showed in the Tables 1 and 2. In the table, all the data is measured in millimeters.

The statistical histogram is showed in the Fig. 13(a), and the error percentage is showed in the Fig. 13(b). Compared with the manual inspecting result, the max error percentage is four. It can be inferred that under ideal conditions, the robot has showed a good performance on thickness measurement.

3.2   Field Experiment

In group 2, similarly, the thickness data of 20 points among five tubes are showed in the Fig. 13(b). In this group, the experiment is operated in the field working environment during the plant overhaul period. After the same experiments approach and process as in group 1, the inspection result is showed in the Tables 3 and 4.

(a) Laboratory experiment   (b) Field experiment

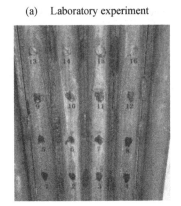 

Fig. 12. Inspecting points in group 1 and group 2

Table 1. Data comparison

Measurement	Sampling points								
	1	2	3	4	5	6	7	8	9
Robot	7.9	7.6	8.2	7.6	8.3	8.5	8.4	8.3	8.3
Manual	8.0	7.8	7.9	7.7	8.4	8.4	8.5	8.0	8.1

Table 2. Data comparison

Measurement	Sampling points						
	10	11	12	13	14	15	16
Robot	8.4	7.9	8.0	8.1	8.3	8.4	8.4
Manual	8.2	8.1	8.2	8.3	8.3	8.3	8.4

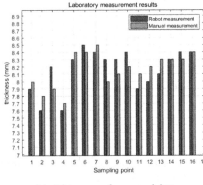

(a) Histogram of measured data   (b) Scatter diagram of errors

Fig. 13. The statistical result of the data

Table 3. Data comparison

Measurement	Sampling points									
	1	2	3	4	5	6	7	8	9	10
Robot	6.2	6.4	6.4	6.2	6.4	6.4	6.2	6.2	6.1	6.3
Manual	6.3	6.3	6.2	6.1	6.3	6.3	6.4	6.2	6.2	6.2

Table 4. Data comparison

Measurement	Sampling points									
	11	12	13	14	15	16	17	18	19	20
Robot	6.3	6.4	6.4	6.2	6.1	6.4	6.5	6.1	6.4	6.3
Manual	6.1	6.3	6.3	6.1	6.2	6.2	6.3	5.9	6.3	6.7

The statistical histogram is showed in the Fig. 14(a), and the error percentage is showed in the Fig. 14(b). Compared with the manual inspecting result, the max error percentage is getting bigger to six percentage, and also the data stabilization is getting a little worse. It seems that the most likely explanation is the unexpected sounding effect, which is deserved more further theoretical model and principal research. But in general, it can be inferred that even though in complex site situation, the robot still could take active functions for thickness measurement.

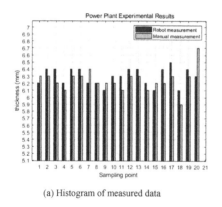

(a) Histogram of measured data

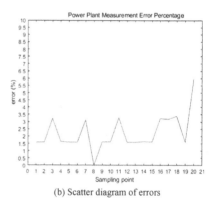

(b) Scatter diagram of errors

Fig. 14. The statistical result of the data

4   Conclusion and Future Work

In this research, a novel BWW inspection robot is designed and developed, which achieves the functionality of moving in both the horizontal and vertical directions and checking multiple points in a unit area. The design and development aim to solve real-world problems in power plants and provide a basis for a new generation of intelligent operation and maintenance of thermal power plants. Through incorporating a range of state-of-the-art technologies, the robot is developed to achieve good accuracy and efficiency with a reasonable cost. This robot has the great potential of finding major defects in BWWs so that major damage to plants can be prevented. Additionally, in terms of health and safety benefits, the robot is designed to be work autonomously so that human operators can be freed from the highly repetitive work in a tough environment.

Apart from the benefits mentioned above, the proposed solution also has great advantage in terms of both expansibility and expandability. First, the robot with all-around function has played the role of a carrying platform. For instance, if boiler inspection needs to address more tasks such as checking more parameters and improving precision, the robot has the flexibility of accommodating more inspection devices and integrate these into an integrated intelligent inspection system. Second, with the development of intelligent technologies, robotics can play an even more important role in the operation and maintenance of thermal power plants. The tough work like the descaling work in ash conveying pipe or the cleaning work in condenser can also potentially be solved by applying intelligent robots.

References

1. Li, X.: Talking about the maintenance scheme of water wall in pulverized coal boiler. Value Eng. **36**(27), 97–99 (2017)
2. Zhang, X.: Current situation and developing trends of industrial robot. Manuf. Technol. Equip. Mark. **10**(5), 33–36 (2014)
3. Li, J., Xing, Y., Yu, Z.: Design and study of water wall wear detection robot control system. Comput. Meas. Control **25**(10), 62–65 (2017)
4. Kou, C.: Autonomous Operation Control of Pipeline Climbing Detection Robot. Wuhan University (2018)
5. Kim, H., Kim, D., Yang, H.: Development of a wall climbing robot using a tracked wheel mechanism. J. Mech. Sci. Technol. **22**, 1490–1498 (2008)
6. Inoue, K, Tsurutani, T., Takubo, T.: Omni-directional gait of limb mechanism robot hanging from grid-like structure. In: Robots and Systems, pp. 1732–1737 (2006)
7. Unver, O., Sitti, M.: Tankbot: a palm size tank like climbing robot using soft elastomer adhesive treads. Int. J. Robot. Res. **29**(14), 1761–1777 (2010)
8. Liu, H., Li, J., Yu, Z.: Research on guiding andanti overturning device of wall-climbing robot for water cooled wall. Mach. Des. Res. **34**(06), 16–20+24 (2018)

Configuration Change and Mobility Analysis of a Novel Metamorphic Parallel Mechanism Constructed with (rA) Joint

Pu Jia[1,2], Duanling Li[1,2(✉)], and Jiazhou Li[1,2]

[1] Automation School, Beijing University of Posts and Telecommunications,
Beijing 100876, China
Jiapu1990@163.com, liduanling@163.com,
lijiazhou001@126.com
[2] Beijing Engineering Research Center of Intelligent Equipment,
Postal Scientific Research and Planning Academy, Beijing 100096, China

Abstract. This paper presents a unique feature of geometric and physical constraint of axes of the reconfigurable-axis (rA) joint and analyses the effectiveness in the constructed limb, resulting in variation of mobility configuration of metamorphic parallel mechanism. This change in mobility is completed by two cases illustrated by a $3(rA)PS$ metamorphic parallel mechanism having variable mobility from 3 to 6. The underlying principle of the metamorphosis of this rA joint is demonstrated by investigating the dependence of the corresponding screw system comprising of line vectors, leading to evolution of the rA joint from the two types of spherical joints to the three types of variable Hooke joints and the one revolute joint. This new type of metamorphic parallel mechanism has broad application prospects, especially in the field of 3d printing. According to the complexity of the shape of the workpiece, the degree of freedom corresponding to different topologies can be selected, which can reduce the costs and increase the adaptability to different working conditions.

Keywords: Reconfigurable axis · Metamorphic parallel mechanism · Constraint analysis · Screw system

1 Introduction

Metamorphic mechanisms derived from the metamorphosis concept in the sense of evolutionary design can change their structure and topology, and subsequent mobility changes depend on geometric constraints or physical constraints of joint variation [1]. For the study of metamorphic mechanisms, basic matrix operations [2] were introduced to describe changes in the mobility configuration during structural evolution. The characteristics and metamorphism of the metamorphic mechanism are proposed [3]. The built-in space module and metamorphic operation of the construction block are constructed with the physical constraint form introduced by the spatial motion pairing [4]. With the change of finite mobility, the motion of the bifurcation platform in the parallel mechanism [5] is revealed according to the geometric constraint analysis. Apply this principle to a parallel mechanism, Kong et al. [6] synthesized parallel

© Springer Nature Switzerland AG 2019
H. Yu et al. (Eds.): ICIRA 2019, LNAI 11744, pp. 738–749, 2019.
https://doi.org/10.1007/978-3-030-27541-9_61

mechanisms with multiple modes of operation. Kumar et al. [7] studied the parameters for developing a reconfigurable Stewart platform for contour generation applications. Gan et al. [8–11] proposed two types of metamorphic parallel mechanisms, which were developed using reconfigurable Hooke (rT) joints by integrating additional rotational degrees of freedom in the Hook joint and analyzing the mobility changes of the mechanism. Zhang et al. have proposed a metamorphic parallel mechanism [12, 13] which has the ability to achieve directional switching and mobility changes at the bifurcation. Similarly, a vA joint was also invented to have a metamorphic parallel mechanism with motion change between pure translation and pure rotation. Compare to those new developments, traditional parallel mechanisms that have specific mobility and cannot change it, resulting in limited workspace. The new metamorphic parallel mechanism has the potential to be developed as a multi-function machine [14], which reduces costs by changing the topology and allowing the tool to work in different motion modes. In addition, the metamorphic parallel mechanism can be applied to food packaging lines [15] and results in a unique production line that can switch to different multi-stage modes of operation during carton operation.

Metamorphic mechanisms [16] are a class of mechanisms that change the topological structure from one to another and consequently change the mobility of the mechanisms. Gnerally, this can be achieved by two approaches. One is to change the number of links by link coincidence and self-locking [17–19]. The other is to apply geometric constraint to joints. So, the two approaches are introduced in this paper.

Topological change [20] in a metamorphic mechanism presented a new way to change the DOF of a parallel mechanism. In this paper, in order to develop a new of parallel mechanisms with metamorphic properties, a 3DOF rA joint is proposed. With this (rA) joint, one of its revolute joints is used to modify the assembly of other joints; this changes the configuration of a parallel mechanism and qualifies it to be metamorphic.

This paper is arranged in the following structure. Section 2 presents the design of the generalized rA joint which embodies a typical kinematic chain with changeable mobility, and unravels the underlying principle of metamorphosis in this rA joint by investigating dependency of the corresponding line vectors. Section 3 introduces the working phases of the reconfigurable (rA)PS limb. Section 4 proposes a 3(rA)PS metamorphic parallel mechanism with the rA joint in the base that the mechanism changes its topological configuration to generate variants. Conclusions are made in Sect. 5.

2 The Design of the *rA* Metamorphic Joint

The rA joint mainly achieves the metamorphic characteristics by changing the axial position and direction, so it can also be called the Reconfigurable Axis. Figure 1 presents the design of the rA joint. This joint is denoted as rA joint, where r stands for the axis 2 along the groove and is used to change the orientation of revolute joint 2. A signifies the angel between three revolute joints can be variable. This symbol can also indicate that after bolting the joint 2, the rA joint contributes three rotational DOFs to the mechanism assembled with it.

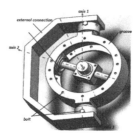

Fig. 1. The (rA) metamorphic joint

The new design inserts three extra rotational degrees of freedom between the resting ring and the connector. While axis 3 is perpendicular to the plane of groove, the direction of axis 2 can be changed within a groove in the ring which changes the relative angle between the axis 2 and axis 1 in contrast to a conventional design that the angle between the link and its corresponding rotational axis is constant. This rotational freedom is embedded in a groove that allows the connector to rotate. Thus axis 2 can rotate around axis 3 and can be fixed by bolting it to the groove which allows the revolute joint 2 to change its rotational axis with respect to the groove.

In addition to this, the joint 3 can also be fixed by the locking device on the back side, so that the rA joint lose a degree of freedom of rotation about the axis 3. Thus the orientation of one of the axes of the rA joint can be altered with respect to its fixed part either on a platform or a limb. Therefore, the configuration of the mechanism and its mobility are changed.

This new of metamorphic joint enables equivalent conversion between spherical joint, Hooke joint and rotation joint. As shown in Fig. 2, the new metamorphic joint transforms the connecting member of one of the rotation joints into a ring shape on the basis of the conventional Hook joint, and opens a track groove in the ring, so that the axis of the revolute joint 2 can be along the circular track. The groove is adjusted and can be fixed by bolt holes on both sides of the track groove; A vertical rotation is provided at the intersection of the two axes, which can be used not only for the positional adjustment of the horizontal axis, but also for the original Hooke joint to add a revolute joint equivalent to the spherical joint. As shown in Fig. 2, the rA joint have three different special configurations.

Configuration 1: The rA joint is a spherical joint, and the axis of the revolute joint 2 can be arbitrarily adjusted. When the three axes of the rA joint are perpendicular to each other, it is recorded as an rA-1, and the other state (axis 2 is not perpendicular to axis 1) is recorded as rA-2.

Configuration 2: When the axis of the revolute joint 2 in the groove is turned to a position coincident with the axis of the revolute joint 1 in the horizontal plane, the rA joint is equivalent to a Hook joint (The plane formed by the two axes of the Hooke joint is perpendicular to the horizontal plane.), which is recorded as the rA-3;The revolute joint 3 in the vertical direction is fixed, and the revolute joint 3 is currently only used to adjust the axial direction of the revolute joint 2 in the groove. At this time, the rA joint

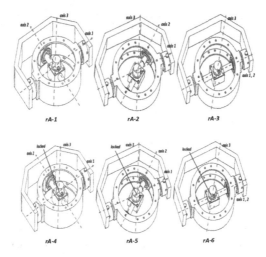

Fig. 2. The configurations of rA joint

is equivalent to the Hook joint, and the axis of the revolute joint 2 can be arbitrarily adjusted. When the axis of the revolute joint 1 and the revolute joint 2 are perpendicular to each other, the rA joint is recorded as rA-4 (The plane formed by the two axes of the Hooke joint is coplanar with the horizontal plane), and in other states, the Hooke joint is recorded as an rA-5 (Axis 2 is not perpendicular to axis 1).

Configuration 3: When the axis of the revolute joint 2 in the groove is turned to a position coincident with the axis of the revolute joint 1 in the horizontal plane. At the same time, the revolute joint 3 in the vertical direction is fixed, and the rA joint is equivalent to a revolute joint, which is denoted as rA-6.

3   Configuration Analysis of Metamorphic Limb

A variety of different s of parallel metamorphic mechanisms can be formed by different configuration of the metamorphic limbs, and the limbs of the various parallel metamorphic mechanisms can realize the conversion between different joints. As shown in Fig. 3, a new of parallel metamorphic mechanism $3(rA)PS$ consists of three limbs, the platform and the base, wherein each limb has a rA joint at the lower ends, and the middle is prismatic joint. The platform is connected with spherical joints at the upper end of the limb, and the base is connected with three rA metamorphic joints at the lower end of the limb. In addition, the three limbs are symmetrically connected with the platform and base.

According to the characteristics of the metamorphic joint, the three rA joints connected to the base in the parallel metamorphic mechanism can achieve any conversion between the six different joints in the above three configurations. Firstly, the transformation of the three metamorphic joints connected to the base is analyzed.

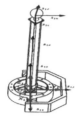

Fig. 3. (rA-1) PS limb

As shown in Fig. 3, the limb 1 is taken as the research object. At this time, the rA joint connected to the base is an initial state *rA-1* joint, and the local coordinate system O_1-$X_1Y_1Z_1$ is attached to the rA joint's center, wherein X_1 coincides with the axis of the joint 1, and Z_1 is vertically upward and perpendicular to the base.

The twist corresponding to each joint can be listed and the twist system of the limb as:

$$S_1 = \begin{cases} \$_{11} = [\ 1 \quad 0 \quad 0 \quad 0 \quad 0 \quad 0\ ]^T \\ \$_{12} = [\ 0 \quad \cos\alpha \quad \sin\alpha \quad 0 \quad 0 \quad 0\ ]^T \\ \$_{13} = [\ \sin\beta \quad -\sin\alpha\cos\beta \quad \cos\alpha\cos\beta \quad 0 \quad 0 \quad 0\ ]^T \\ \$_{14} = [\ 0 \quad 0 \quad 0 \quad \sin\beta \quad -\sin\alpha\cos\beta \quad \cos\alpha\cos\beta\ ]^T \\ \$_{15} = [\ 1 \quad 0 \quad 0 \quad 0 \quad l\cos\alpha\cos\beta \quad l\sin\alpha\cos\beta\ ]^T \\ \$_{16} = [\ 0 \quad \cos\alpha \quad \sin\alpha \quad -l\cos\beta \quad -l\sin\alpha\sin\beta \quad l\cos\alpha\sin\beta\ ]^T \\ \$_{17} = [\ \sin\beta \quad -\sin\alpha\cos\beta \quad coa\alpha\cos\beta \quad 0 \quad 0 \quad 0\ ]^T \end{cases} \quad (1)$$

The first three twists and the last three twists respectively are generated by the joints of the base rA joint and the spherical joint respectively, and the fourth twist is generated by the prismatic joint, α indicating the angle $\$_{12}$ with the Y_1 axis(or the combination of the axis 1 and the axis 2). The angle between the plane and the Y_1 axis) β indicates the angle $\$_{13}$ between the plane and the projection on the plane $O_1Y_1Z_1$,l indicating the distance between the centers of the upper spherical joint and base rA joints. In the twist notation $\$_{ij}$, the first subscript i denotes the limb number, the second subscript j denotes the joint number within the limb, and the leading super-script indicates the local frame.

It is clearly that twist $\$_{13}$ and $\$_{17}$ are the same. Therefore, the seven twists in Eq. (1) constitute a six-system, and the reciprocal screw system of Eq. (1) can be obtained. The constraints provided by the reciprocal screws determine motion of the moving platform and the degree of freedom of the parallel mechanism. The limb constraint system is given as:

$$S_1^r = [\ 0 \quad 0 \quad 0 \quad 0 \quad 0 \quad 0\ ]^T \quad (2)$$

This gives no constraint force acting along a line passing through the spherical joint center along a direction parallel to the fixed axis of the rA joint. Therefore, the limb *(rA-1) PS* in this configuration has no constraint on the platform.

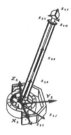

Fig. 4. (rA-2) PS limb

When the rA joint connected to the base in the limb is converted into the *rA-2* joint, as shown in Fig. 4, the twist system is obtained as follows:

$$S_1 = \begin{cases} \$_{11} = [\ 1\quad 0\quad 0\quad 0\quad 0\quad 0\ ]^T \\ \$_{12} = [\ \sin\gamma\quad \cos\alpha\cos\gamma\quad \sin\alpha\cos\gamma\quad 0\quad 0\quad 0\ ]^T \\ \$_{13} = [\ \sin\beta\quad -\sin\alpha\cos\beta\quad \cos\alpha\cos\beta\quad 0\quad 0\quad 0\ ]^T \\ \$_{14} = [\ 0\quad 0\quad 0\quad \sin\beta\quad -\sin\alpha\cos\beta\quad \cos\alpha\cos\beta\ ]^T \\ \$_{15} = [\ 1\quad 0\quad 0\quad 0\quad l\cos\alpha\cos\beta\quad l\sin\alpha\cos\beta\ ]^T \\ \$_{16} = [\ 0\quad \cos\alpha\quad \sin\alpha\quad -l\cos\beta\quad -l\sin\alpha\sin\beta\quad l\cos\alpha\sin\beta\ ]^T \\ \$_{17} = [\ \sin\beta\quad -\sin\alpha\cos\beta\quad coa\alpha\cos\beta\quad 0\quad 0\quad 0\ ]^T \end{cases} \quad (3)$$

The angle γ between $^1\$_{12}$ and its projection on the plane $O_1Y_1Z_1$ is expressed in Eq. (3). It can be clearly seen from Eq. (3) that the twist $\$_{13}$ is exactly same with $\$_{17}$. Therefore, the seven twists in Eq. (3) form a six-system, and the reciprocal screw system of Eq. (3) can be obtained according to solving the constraint provided by the limb to the platform, the reciprocal screw of the Eq. (3) is:

$$S_1^r = [\ 0\quad 0\quad 0\quad 0\quad 0\quad 0\ ]^T \quad (4)$$

Therefore, the limb *(rA-2) PS* has no constraint on the platform.

Fig. 5. (rA-3) PS limb

When the *rA* joint connected to the base in the limb is converted into the *rA-3*, as shown in Fig. 5, the twist system is obtained as follows:

$$
S_1 = \left\{
\begin{array}{l}
\$_{11} = [\ 1 \quad 0 \quad 0 \quad 0 \quad 0 \quad 0\ ]^T \\
\$_{12} = [\ 0 \quad -\sin\alpha \quad \cos\alpha \quad 0 \quad 0 \quad 0\ ]^T \\
\$_{13} = [\ 0 \quad 0 \quad 0 \quad 0 \quad -\sin\alpha \quad \cos\alpha\ ]^T \\
\$_{14} = [\ 1 \quad 0 \quad 0 \quad 0 \quad l\cos\alpha \quad l\sin\alpha\ ]^T \\
\$_{15} = [\ 0 \quad \cos\alpha \quad \sin\alpha \quad -l \quad 0 \quad 0\ ]^T \\
\$_{16} = [\ 0 \quad -\sin\alpha \quad \cos\alpha \quad 0 \quad 0 \quad 0\ ]^T
\end{array}
\right\} \tag{5}
$$

It can be clearly seen from Eq. (5) that the amount of twists is exactly the same. Therefore, the seven twists in Eq. (5) constitute a five-system. The reciprocal screws of Eq. (5) can be used to solve the constraint provided by the limb to platform. The reciprocal screw of the Eq. (5) is:

$$
S_1^r = [\ 0 \quad 0 \quad 0 \quad 0 \quad l\cos\alpha \quad l\sin\alpha\ ]^T \tag{6}
$$

This constrained twist indicates that the limb(*rA-3*) *PS* has a constraint force on the platform, the direction is consistent with the axis 1 of the lower end rA joint and passes through the center of the upper end rA joint.

When rA joint connected to the base in the limb is converted into the *rA-4* joint, the joint 3 in the direction of the axis 3 of the rA joint is fixed, and the limb *(rA-4) PS joint* can be obtained by referring to Eq. (1). The platform is unconstrained.

Similarly, when rA joint is converted to the *rA-5* joint, the limb *(rA-5) PS* is unconstrained to the platform. When rA joint is converted to the *rA-6* joint, the limb *(rA-6)* PS has a constraint force on the platform. The same limb *(rA-3) PS* is consistent with the constraints on the platform.

Therefore, for the limb *(rA)PS*, When the upper rA joint maintains the *rA-1*, it is equivalent to a spherical joint. When the lower rA joint is changed from the *rA-1* to the *rA-6*, the constraints imposed by the limb *(rA)PS* on the platform are:

$$
\begin{array}{l}
\$_1^r = [\ 0 \quad 0 \quad 0 \quad 0 \quad 0 \quad 0\ ]^T \\
\$_2^r = [\ 0 \quad 0 \quad 0 \quad 0 \quad 0 \quad 0\ ]^T \\
\$_3^r = [\ 1 \quad 0 \quad 0 \quad 0 \quad l\cos\alpha \quad l\sin\alpha\ ]^T \\
\$_4^r = [\ 0 \quad 0 \quad 0 \quad 0 \quad 0 \quad 0\ ]^T \\
\$_5^r = [\ 0 \quad 0 \quad 0 \quad 0 \quad 0 \quad 0\ ]^T \\
\$_6^r = [\ 1 \quad 0 \quad 0 \quad 0 \quad l\cos\alpha \quad l\sin\alpha\ ]^T
\end{array} \tag{7}
$$

From the above, constraints provided by the limb *(rA-4) PS*, the limb *(rA-5) PS*, and the limb *(rA-6)* PS on the platform are same as constraints provided by the limb SPS, the limb *(rA-2) PS,* and the limb *(rA-3) PS* on the platform The reason for this is that the direction of axis 3 in the rA joint is dependent to the axis 3 of the upper spherical joint. Therefore, the joint in the direction of the axis 3 in the rA joint has no effect on the motion of the limb.

4 Metamorphic Parallel Mechanism 3(rA)PS

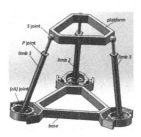

Fig. 6. Metamorphic parallel mechanism 3(rA)PS

According to the analysis of the metamorphic mechanism limb in the previous section, there are two metamorphic mechanism limbs that affect the degree of freedom of the metamorphic parallel mechanism 3*(rA)PS*. Here, the limb *(rA-4) PS* and the limb *(rA-6) PS* are selected as the object. The configuration of the mechanism will change as the rA joint at the lower end of the limb changes. Next, the metamorphism parallel mechanism as shown in Fig. 6 composed of the two kinds of variable metamorphic limbs will be analyzed.

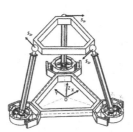

Fig. 7. Metamorphic parallel mechanism 3(rA-6) PS

As shown in Fig. 7, the rA joints at the end of the three limbs are all *rA-6*, and the 3 *(rA-6)* PS parallel mechanism is equivalent to a general *3RPS* parallel mechanism.

Establish the global coordinate system *O-XYZ*, the origin of the coordinate is located at the center of the equilateral triangle formed by the center line of the lower rA joint of the three limbs, the *X* axis is parallel to the line connecting the centers of the two joints, and the *Z* axis is perpendicular to the base of the parallel mechanism, as shown in Fig. 8.

The constrained system of the platform obtained by each limb in the local coordinate system O_1-$X_1Y_1Z_1$ is converted into the global coordinate system. For the parallel mechanism, the union of the constrained system of each limb under the same coordinate forms a platform constrained system. The constrained system can be used to obtain the motion of the parallel platform. The formula for the transformation of the constrained from the local coordinate system to the global coordinate system is:

$$S^r = T(^1S^r) \tag{8}$$

where

$$T = \begin{bmatrix} I & 0 \\ \hat{\omega} & I \end{bmatrix} \begin{bmatrix} ^O_{O_1}R & 0 \\ 0 & ^O_{O_1}R \end{bmatrix} \qquad \hat{\omega} = \begin{bmatrix} 0 & -\omega_3 & \omega_2 \\ \omega_3 & 0 & -\omega_1 \\ -\omega_2 & \omega_1 & 0 \end{bmatrix}$$

$^O_{O_1}R$ is the twist change of the local coordinate system in the global coordinate system. $\omega = [\omega_1 \quad \omega_2 \quad \omega_3]^T$ is the relative position of the origin of the local coordinate system with respect to the global coordinate system.

According to the conversion formula 8, the constrains of the three limbs to the platform is:

$$S^r = \begin{cases} \$^r_1 = [1 \quad 0 \quad 0 \quad 0 \quad l \cos \alpha \quad -b + l \sin \alpha]^T \\ \$^r_2 = [-\cos \frac{\pi}{3} \quad \sin \frac{\pi}{3} \quad 0 \quad -l \sin \frac{\pi}{3} \cos \alpha \quad -l \cos \frac{\pi}{3} \cos \alpha \quad -b + l \sin \alpha]^T \\ \$^r_3 = [-\cos \frac{\pi}{3} \quad -\sin \frac{\pi}{3} \quad 0 \quad l \sin \frac{\pi}{3} \cos \alpha \quad -l \cos \frac{\pi}{3} \cos \alpha \quad -b + l \sin \alpha]^T \end{cases} \tag{9}$$

In the above formula, b represents the distance from the origin of the local coordinate system to the origin of the global coordinate system, and its standard base can be expressed as:

$$S_f = \begin{cases} \$_1 = [-l \sin \alpha \quad 0 \quad 0 \quad 0 \quad 1 \quad 0]^T \\ \$_2 = [0 \quad l \sin \alpha \quad 0 \quad 1 \quad 0 \quad 0]^T \\ \$_3 = [0 \quad 0 \quad 1 \quad 0 \quad 0 \quad 0]^T \end{cases} \tag{10}$$

It can be seen that the parallel mechanism 3(rA-6) PS has a rotation about the Z axis and translation along the X axis and Y axis. It is finally determined that the mechanism has three degrees of freedom.

According to the modified degree of freedom calculation formula given in [8], it is verified whether the degree of freedom obtained by the previous analysis is correct.

$$M_N = d(n - g - 1) + \sum_{i=1}^{g} f_i + v - \xi \tag{11}$$

Where M_N is the degree of freedom of the mechanism; d is the order of the mechanism; g is the number of joints; f_i is the number of degrees of freedom of the i-th joint; v is the number of redundant constraints of the mechanism; ξ is the number of local degrees of freedom.

From the analysis of the metamorphic limb in Sect. 2, it can be seen that in the metamorphic parallel mechanism formed by the two kinds of metamorphic limb selected in this section, the number of redundant constraints is 0, and the number of local degrees of freedom is 0. In the metamorphic parallel mechanism $3(rA\text{-}6)$ PS, the order of the mechanism is 6, the number of links is 8, the number of moving joints is 9, and the sum of the degrees of freedom of each joint is obtained by Eq. (11). The degree of freedom of the metamorphic parallel mechanism in this configuration is:

$$M_N = 6 \times (8 - 9 - 1) + 15 + 0 - 0 = 3 \tag{12}$$

Since the twist in the direction of the axis 3 of the limb $(rA)PS$ is dependent to one axis of the spherical joint, it does not affect the degree of freedom of the limb and the metamorphic parallel mechanism. Therefore, the transformation between the limb $(rA\text{-}1)$ PS and the limb $(rA\text{-}4)$ PS, $(rA\text{-}2)$ PS and $(rA\text{-}5)$ PS, and $(rA\text{-}3)$ PS and $(rA\text{-}6)$ PS is an equivalent transformation, which is only changed in limb's configuration. In essence, there is no influence on the degree of freedom of the metamorphic parallel mechanism. Therefore, the transformation between the limb $(rA\text{-}1)$ PS and $(rA\text{-}4)$ PS, $(rA\text{-}2)$ PS and $(rA\text{-}5)$ PS, $(rA\text{-}3)$ PS and $(rA\text{-}6)$ PS is equivalent. This transformation essentially only affects the configuration of the metamorphic parallel mechanism which has no effect on the motion state and degree of freedom of the parallel mechanism.

The prototype of the parallel cell mechanism is shown in Fig. 8. The results of the previous section can be further verified by adjusting the rA joint at the lower end of the limb.

Fig. 8. Prototype of the metamorphic parallel mechanism

5   Conclusions

This paper presented a newly developed joint that is used to construct the metamorphic parallel mechanisms for mobility change. The key property of the rA joint is that one of the rotation axes can be altered freely with respect to the base or the limb even after the mechanisms are assembled and not only can it be used as a normal revolute joint, but it can also be used to adjust the direction of the another axis. while the traditional spherical joint does not have this ability. The rA joint designed in this paper can be transformed into six different configurations, which are equivalent to different spherical joint, Hooke joint and revolution joint. A parallel mechanism of different configurations can be obtained by adjusting the rA joints of the three limbs, and the degree of freedom of the parallel mechanism changes with the evolution of the configuration of the limbs. Two kinds of limbs with different degree of freedom are obtained by analyzing the six different configurations of the limb *(rA)PS*.

Acknowledgment. The work was supported by National Natural Science Foundation of China (Grant No. 51775052) and Beijing Key Laboratory of Space-ground Interconnection and Convergence.

References

1. Dai, J.S., Rees Jones, J.: Mobility in metamorphic mechanisms of foldable/erectable kinds. In: Proceedings 25th ASME Biennial Mechanisms and Robotics Conference, Atlanta, GA, September (1998)
2. Dai, J.S., Rees Jones, J.: Interrelationship between screw systems and corresponding reciprocal systems and applications. Mech. Mach. Theory **36**, 633–651 (2001)
3. Zhang, L., Wang, D., Dai, J.S.: Biological modeling and evolution based synthesis of metamorphic mechanisms. ASME J. Mech. Des. **130**, 072303 (2008)
4. Zhang, L., Dai, J.S.: Reconfiguration of spatial metamorphic mechanisms. ASME J. Mech. Rob. **1**(1), 011012 (2009)
5. Gogu, G.: Branching singularities in kinematotropic parallel mechanisms. In: Kecskeméthy, A., Müller, A. (eds.) Computational Kinematics. Springer, Berlin, Heidelberg (2009)
6. Kong, X., Gosselin, C.M., Richard, P.L.: Type synthesis of parallel mechanisms with multiple operation modes. Trans. ASME J. Mech. Des. **129**(7), 595–601 (2007)
7. Kumar, T.S., Nagarajan, T., Srinivasa, Y.G.: Characterization of reconfigurable stewart platform for contour generation. Rob. Comput.-Integr. Manuf. **24**(4–5), 721–731 (2009)
8. Gan, D.M., Dai, J.S., Dias, J., Seneviratne, L.D.: Reconfigurability and unified kinematics modeling of a 3rTPS metamorphic parallel mechanism with perpendicular constraint screws. Rob. Computer Integr. Manuf. **29**(4), 121–128 (2013)
9. Gan, D.M., Dai, J.S.: A reconfigurable Hooke joint, China Patent CN102152303A (2011)
10. Gan, D.M., Dai, J.S., Caldwell, D.G.: Constraint-based limb synthesis and mobility-change aimed mechanism construction, ASME. J. Mech. Des. **133**(5), 1–9 (2011)
11. Gan, D.M., Dai, J.S., Liao, Q.Z.: Mobility change in two types of metamorphic parallel mechanisms. Trans. ASME J. Mech. Rob. **1**, 041007 (2009)
12. Zhang, K.T., Dai, J.S., Fang, Y.F.: Geometric constraint and mobility variation of two 3SvPS v metamorphic parallel mechanisms. ASME J. Mech. Des. **135**(1), 11001 (2012)
13. Zhang, K.T., Dai, J.S., Fang, Y.F.: Topology and constraint analysis of phase change in the metamorphic chain and its evolved mechanism. Trans. ASME J. Mech. Des. **132**(12), 121001 (2010)
14. Gopalakrishnan, V., Fedewa, D., Mehrabi, M.G., Kota, S., Orlandea, N.: Parallel structures and their applications in reconfigurable machining systems. J. Manuf. Sci. Eng. **124**(2), 483–485 (2002)
15. Dai, J.S., Caldwell, D.G.: Origami-based robotic paper-and-board packaging for food industry. Trends Food Sci. Technol. **21**(3), 153–157 (2010)
16. Dai, J.S., Rees Jones, J.: Mobility in metamorphic mechanisms of foldable/erectable kinds. In: Proceedings 25th ASME Biennial Mechanisms and Robotics Conference, Atlanta, GA, September 1998

17. Leonesio, M., Bianchi, G., Manara, P.: A general approach for self-locking analysis in closed kinematic chains. In: Proceedings of the 12th World Congress in Mechanism and Machine Theory, Besancon, France, pp. 141–147, June 2007

18. Winder, B.G., Magleby, S.P., Howell, L.L.: Kinematic representations of pop-up paper mechanisms. ASME J. Mech. Rob. 1(2), 021009 (2009)

19. Dai, J.S., Zoppi, M., Kong, X.W.: Editorial preface. In: Dai, J.S., Zoppi, M., Kong, X.W. (eds.) Advances in Reconfigurable Mechanisms and Robots I, pp. v–viii. Springer, London (2012)

20. Dai, J.S., Rees Jones, J.: Matrix representation of topological changes in metamorphic mechanisms. ASME J. Mech. Des. 127(4), 610–619 (2005)

Author Index

Printed in the United States
By Bookmasters